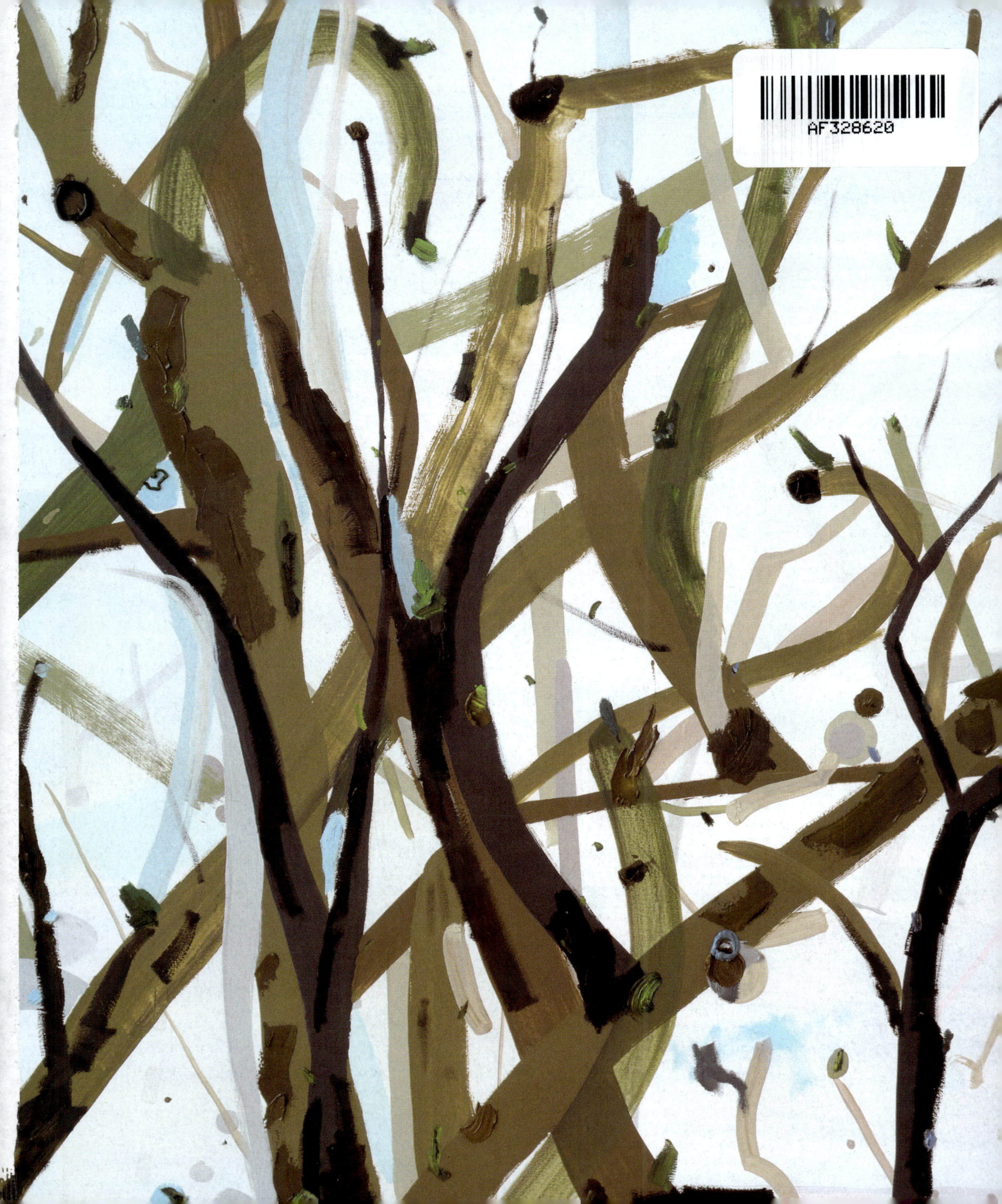
AF328620

DIE PARKETT-REIHE MIT GEGENWARTSKÜNSTLERN / THE PARKETT SERIES WITH CONTEMPORARY ARTISTS

Book Series with contemporary artists in English and German, published three times a year. Each volume is created in collaboration with artists, who contribute an original work specially made for the readers of Parkett. The works are reproduced in the regular edition and available in a limited and signed Special Edition.

Buchreihe mit Gegenwartskünstlern in deutscher und englischer Sprache, erscheint dreimal im Jahr. Jeder Band entsteht mit Künstlern oder Künstlerinnen, die eigens für die Leser von Parkett einen Originalbeitrag gestalten. Diese Werke sind in der gesamten Auflage abgebildet und zusätzlich in einer limitierten und signierten Vorzugsausgabe erhältlich.

PARKETT NR. 66 ENTSTEHT IN COLLABORATION MIT • ANGELA BULLOCH, DANIEL BUREN, PIERRE HUYGHE • WILL BE COLLABORATING ON PARKETT NO. 66

JAHRESABONNEMENT (DREI NUMMERN) / ANNUAL SUBSCRIPTION (THREE ISSUES) SFR. 116.– (SCHWEIZ), € 78 (BRD), € 82 (ÜBRIGES EUROPA), US$ 80 (USA AND CANADA ONLY)

ZWEI- UND DREIJAHRESABONNEMENTPREISE SIEHE GELBE BESTELLKARTE IM HEFT / FOR TWO & THREE YEAR RATES, PLEASE CONSULT YELLOW ORDER FORM.

Zürichsee Druckereien AG (Stäfa)   Satz, Litho, Druck/Copy, Printing, Color Separations

PARKETT-VERLAG AG, ZÜRICH, SEPTEMBER 2002   **PRINTED IN SWITZERLAND**   ISBN 3-907582-15-2   ISSN 0256-0917

HEFTRÜCKEN / SPINE 64–66: NIC HESS

Cover / Umschlag: JOHN CURRIN, HEARTLESS, 1997, oil on canvas / Öl auf Leinwand. (PHOTO: FRED SCRUTON)

Cover flap / Umschlagklappe: MICHAEL RAEDECKER, ONE, 2001, acrylic and thread on canvas / Acryl und Garn auf Leinwand.

Inside cover & flap / Innere Umschlagseite & Klappe: MICHAEL RAEDECKER, HAPPY, 2002, acrylic and thread on canvas / Acryl und Garn auf Leinwand.

Page 1 / Seite 1: LAURA OWENS, UNTITLED, 1999, acrylic and oil on canvas / Acryl und Öl auf Leinwand.

Back cover / Rückseite: LAURA OWENS, UNTITLED, 2001, oil and acrylic on canvas / Öl und Acryl auf Leinwand.

All images slightly cropped / Alle Bilder leicht beschnitten.

PARKETT Zürich New York Frankfurt

Bice Curiger Chefredaktorin/Editor-in-Chief; **Jacqueline Burckhardt** Redaktorin/Senior Editor; **Cay Sophie Rabinowitz** Redaktorin USA/Senior Editor US; **Suzanne Schmidt** Textredaktion und Produktion/Editing and Production; **Hanna Koller · Simone Eggstein · Trix Wetter** (beurlaubt/on temporary leave) Graphik/Design; **Catherine Schelbert** Englisches Lektorat/Editorial Assistant for English; **Claudia Meneghini Nevzadi** Korrektorat/Proof Reading

Beatrice Fässler Vorzugsausgaben, Inserate/Special Editions, Advertising; **Nicole Stotzer** Buchvertrieb, Administration/Distribution, Administration; **Mathias Arnold** Abonnemente/Subscriptions; **Ali Subotnick** Redaktion, Vorzugsausgaben und Marketing USA/Associate Editor, Editions and Marketing US; **Monika Condrea** Abonnemente USA/Subscriptions US; **Sarah Crowner** Praktikantin USA/Intern US; **Adrian Koerfer** Deutsche Verlagsvertretung/German Representative

Jacqueline Burckhardt – Bice Curiger – Dieter von Graffenried Herausgeber/Parkett Board; **Jacqueline Burckhardt – Bice Curiger – Dieter von Graffenried – Walter Keller – Peter Blum** Gründer/Founders

Dieter von Graffenried Verleger/Publisher

www.parkettart.com

PARKETT-VERLAG AG, QUELLENSTRASSE 27, CH-8031 ZURICH, TEL. 41-1-271 81 40, FAX 41-1-272 43 01
PARKETT, NEW YORK, 155 AV. OF THE AMERICAS, N.Y. 10013, PHONE (212) 673-2660, FAX (212) 271-0704

In ihren Bildern ist viel Raum. Nicht im Sinne jenes Illusionismus, der im Bild ein Fenster sieht, durch das wir schauen. Sondern ein atmender Raum, ein Feld der Freiheit ist's, was John Currin, Laura Owens, Michael Raedecker sich sorgsam mit jedem Pinselstrich erschaffen.

Ironischerweise erinnert ein solcher Satz an eine vergangene Kunstrichtung, in der die explosiven Gebärden walteten. Das Gegenteil ist hier der Fall. Die Bildwelten, die von den Collaboration-Künstlern dieses Bandes erschaffen werden, entstehen in langsamen Prozessen sorgfältiger Denk- und Handwerkspraxis.

Malerei schafft eine eigene Realität. Und doch ist sie von dieser Welt. Malerei setzt auf einzigartige Weise ein Entfaltungspotenzial frei – im Material selber sowie beim Betrachten im Emotionalen und im Intellekt. Man stellt sich den Prozess der Entstehung bei Currin, Owens und Raedecker als raffinierten geistigen Tanz vor, wo genussreich Möglichkeiten ausgekostet werden, denen nachgehangen und auf den Grund gegangen wird, um ihr wahres Gesicht zu erkennen. Und gleichzeitig lösen all diese Bewegungen Berührungen mit dem wirklichen Leben aus, in welchem irgendwo und irgendwann auch die Kunstgeschichte eine Rolle spielt.

Es ist eine Malerei der Stimmungskatalysatoren und diese selber sind ins Zentrum gerückt, damit sie mit befreiendem Abstand genauer betrachtet werden können. So sind in den Bildern von Michael Raedecker die Fäden, die Wollfusseln, die in Farbe versinken wie ein Pulloverärmel in der Mayonnaise, zugleich stark empathisch aufgeladene Zeichen, die ins Unbewusste, in die abgelagerten Niederungen unserer sensuellen Alltagserfahrungen zielen; Signale, die das Malen selber aus seinen traditionsverhafteten und lebensfernen Automatismen des Machens und des Wahrnehmens befreien wollen.

Es geht um eine Malerei, die ihrer eigenen heldenhaften Geschichte misstraut und deshalb befreiende Umwege sucht, die sie ausgerechnet in den Abgründen des «Gemüthaften» zu finden scheint. Laura Owens setzt auf exquisite kennerschaftliche Vorlagen und Praktiken, um anderes vorzutäuschen, wenn sie im gleichen Bild die ruhigen, weiten Farbflächen mit den konzeptuell raffiniert in Trompe-l'Œil-Manier gemalten, rustikalen Stoffmustern vermischt, die dicken pastosen oder aquarellhaft verfliessenden Striche neben Airbrush-Effekte setzt. Und John Currin wiederum hat sich einem zeitgenössischen «Rokoko» verschrieben, einer feinen Schwelgerei. Im Anvisieren desjenigen, was gewöhnlich als dubiose Ranken süsslicher Geschmacksempfindungen und -verwirrungen abqualifiziert wird und doch ein unausrottbares Dasein fristet, begibt sich Currin auf das Feld, wo keine falsche Scham herrscht. Nicht nur sind in dieser Malerei «Ähnlichkeiten mit lebenden Personen» unbeabsichtigt, sie sind unangebracht. Denn in diesem gemalten Kosmos geht es um Muster des Wiedererkennens, die mehr mit uns und unserer Psychologie zu tun haben als mit jener wildfremder Menschen.

Im INSERT dieser Ausgabe hat der Musiker Lou Reed mit den Mitteln der Kamera das Emotionspotenzial des Mediums im Prozess des Machens ausgelotet und eine Reihe erstaunlich einprägsamer Bilder geschaffen.

There is space in their pictures, not meaning the illusionism that sees the picture as a window through which we look. What John Currin, Laura Owens, and Michael Raedecker carefully conjure with every stroke of the brush is a space that breathes, a field of freedom.

Ironically, that statement recalls an artistic movement of the past in which explosive gesture prevailed. Here, the opposite is true. The imagery created by the collaboration artists in this volume is a product of slow processes involving considerable deliberation and exacting craftsmanship.

Painting creates a reality of its own. And yet it is also clearly of this world. Painting possesses unique potential not only in the act of developing its own materiality but also in the emotional and intellectual act of viewing. One imagines the process of creation in which Currin, Owens, and Raedecker engage as a sophisticated, mental dance, as voluptuous experimentation with a host of possibilities, explored in depth in order to discover their true nature. At the same time all of these movements entail contacts with real life, in which the history of art somehow and somewhere plays a role as well.

It is a painting of atmospheric catalysts, firmly placed center stage where they can be closely studied with liberating detachment. In Michael Raedecker's pictures, for example, thread and fluffs of wool sink into the paint like a sleeve in mayonnaise, but they also have a powerful empathetic thrust that targets the unconscious where the deepest layers of sensual, everyday experience have been deposited. Raedecker's signs and signals seek to emancipate painting from the automation of modes of production and perception that are ordinarily hampered by tradition and alienated from life.

This is painting that questions its own heroic history and therefore seeks liberating detours which paradoxically lead to the depths of "feeling." Exploiting exquisite sources and practices of great connoisseurship as a cover, so to speak, Laura Owens combines serene, expansive areas of color with ingeniously conceived, *trompe l'œil* renditions of rustic textiles, and places air-brush effects next to painting that runs the gamut from thick pastose application to lines that fade like watercolor washes—all on a single canvas. John Currin devotes himself to a delicately lush present-day rococo. Venturing into stylistic arenas that stubbornly persevere despite a widespread reputation for being of questionably convoluted and cloying taste, Currin moves into a realm where there is no false prudery. In his painting, "similarity with living persons" is not only unintended, it is inappropriate for his painted universe exhibits patterns of recognition that have more to do with us and our psychology than with that of perfect strangers.

In the INSERT, the musician Lou Reed has taken up the medium of photography to generate a rhythm that translates the emotional potential of sound into the visual potential of silence in a sequence of compelling images.

Bice Curiger

JEFF WALL
PHOTOGRAPHIERT
HERZOG &
DE MEURONS
WEINGUT DOMINUS

KURT W. FORSTER

In manchen Stummfilmen – etwa Griffiths *Birth of a Nation* – beginnen einzelne Episoden mit einem Lichtpunkt, der sich zum kreisrunden Feld mit schummrigem Rand erweitert, als öffnete sich einfach die Blende der Kamera. Dadurch entsteht für Augenblicke ein beinahe magischer Vorgang, der das Erwachen einer imaginären Welt suggeriert, einer Welt, die ihr Licht durch den dunklen Kinosaal in die Augäpfel hineinstrahlt. Distanz und Form verleihen ihm etwas Allumfassendes und nähern es dem Erdball selber an, der im Mantel seiner Atmosphäre das Dunkel des Alls durchläuft.

Als den kanadischen Photographen Jeff Wall die Anfrage erreichte, ein Gebäude der Architekten Herzog & de Meuron aufzunehmen, äusserte er zunächst Bedenken.[1] Wall pflegt keine Architekturaufnahmen zu machen – ein eigentliches Spezialgebiet der modernen Produktphotographie –, doch er wollte versuchen, ob ihm ein interessantes Bild dieses Baus gelingen könnte. Was ihm dabei ins Auge stach, war nicht so sehr das ungewöhnliche Gebäude mit seinen eindrücklichen Dimensionen und seiner Fassade aus Geröllbrocken, sondern «das perspektivische System, das den Weinberg mit dem geometrisch strengen Umriss des Gebäudes und der schnurgeraden Pflanzung der Reben verbindet».[2] Es war also grundsätzlich der Ort, den Wall ins Auge fasste und nach einigen Tagen des Pröbelns in verschiedenen Aufnahmen festhielt.

Zwei Umstände kamen ihm dabei zustatten: Er hatte seinen Besuch auf Dezember und Februar gelegt, als die blattlosen Reben dem Talboden des Napa Valley ein eher desolates Aussehen gaben, und er experimentierte mit verschiedenen Objektiven. Diese Umstände

KURT W. FORSTER, Professor an der Eidgenössischen Technischen Hochschule ETH in Zürich von 1992–1999, ist Initiator der Ausstellung «Herzog & de Meuron: Natural History». Sie wird im Oktober 2002 im Canadian Centre for Architecture CCA in Montreal eröffnet und geht später auf Tournee.

führten, beinahe durch Zufall, zu einem unerwarteten Resultat. Wall war beeindruckt von der Nässe und dem dunklen Erdreich und fasziniert von der starr reglementierten Bepflanzung des Weinguts.[3] Handelt es sich schon deshalb um eine Sicht *more geometrico*, so trug die Optik – das heisst die Wahl der Linsen in Bezug zum Format des Films – das ihre dazu bei, ein Rundbild statt einer flächendeckenden Aufnahme hervorzubringen. Wall erinnerte daran, dass «alle Linsen kreisförmige Bilder produzieren. Der Film ist aber rechteckig. Normalerweise ist die Kamera so ausgerüstet, dass sie ein Bild hervorbringt, das grösser als der verwendete Film ist, womit der kreisförmige Rand des Bildes verschwindet.»[4]

Die Aufnahme, die Wall schliesslich aus den mehrtägigen Versuchen auswählte, verfügt über genau die Eigenschaften, die das Bild in erster Linie als Produkt der Kamera ausgeben. Es rafft die parallelen Rebstockreihen, die sich durch die ganze Talsohle erstrecken, zusammen und suspendiert ihre rechtwinklige Geometrie in einem schwebenden Lichtkreis, der aus dem rechteckigen Rahmen des Photopapiers unmerklich über den oberen Rand hinauszugleiten scheint. Innerhalb dieses Dunstkreises verliert der Grund seine vormals betonte Schwere und das geometrische Netz der Reben seine Starrheit. Die diesige Winterzeit und der ferne Standpunkt des Photographen lassen das grosse Gebäude beinahe in seiner Umgebung verschwinden, denn es ist parallel zu den aufgereihten Rebstöcken ausgerichtet, die ihrerseits so ins Blickfeld treten, dass sich genau aus dem Kreismittelpunkt heraus eine senkrechte Linie bildet.

Der Talboden zieht eine abstrakte Horizontlinie, über der sich die baumbestandenen Hügel vor den blassen Winterhimmel legen. Der quer gestellte Riegel des Weinguts markiert lediglich dank seiner beiden Durchfahrten dunkle Stellen in der Tiefe des Gesichtsfeldes. In der Tat scheint der Blick aus einer Höhle zu dringen und sich in die Tiefe der Landschaft zu erstrecken. Das Bild lässt seine Gegenstände daher sowohl in übertriebener Distanz als auch in unwirklicher Nähe erscheinen. Nun stellt Distanz für die Photographie eine entscheidende Dimension und das kritische Mass ihrer Bildschärfe dar. Jeff Wall hat sogar die unterschiedlichen Bildgenres als Resultat der photographischen Distanz erklären wollen. Er findet die Bildgenres, vom Porträt bis zur Landschaft, wesentlich durch die Distanz bestimmt.[5] Indem er die optische Tatsache, dass Linsen runde Bilder liefern, mit der Distanz von den Objekten in einen ausdrücklichen Zusammenhang bringt, gibt er seiner Aufnahme des Weinguts einen doppelten Charakter: Einerseits bindet sein Bild alles an die Erde und ihre Geometrie, andererseits suspendiert es sie in einem schummrigen Kreis, der aus völliger Dunkelheit emporschwebt und sich nach oben in Helligkeit auflöst. Licht ist damit etwas, was allein dem Bild eignet, während alles jenseits seiner Sphäre in unergründlichem Dunkel verharrt. Der unscharfe Rand des kreisrunden Bildes lässt auch an den Blick durch ein Fernrohr denken.

Wenn ich gleich zu Beginn im Rundbild von Jeff Wall einen latent «globalen» Charakter vermutet und seiner Geometrie eine kennzeichnende Bedeutung zugeschrieben habe, so deshalb, weil Wall selber die photographische Linse als Auge auffasst und deshalb eine fundamentale Ähnlichkeit zwischen der Welt und unserem Sehorgan voraussetzt.[6] Als die Darstellung der bekannten Weltteile im Mittelalter in eine bestimmte Formel einging, entstand die Signatur des Erdkreises mit eingeschriebenem Buchstaben Tau, um die Kontinente Asien, Europa und Afrika zu unterscheiden. Dieses Schema taucht schon in einem Sallust-Manuskript (Vatikanische Bibliothek) des zwölften Jahrhunderts auf und fand mit dem Aufkommen von Druckwerken im fünfzehnten Jahrhundert weite Verbreitung. Die Tau-Form legt ihren Querbalken als künstlichen Horizont ungefähr durch die Mitte des Erdkreises,

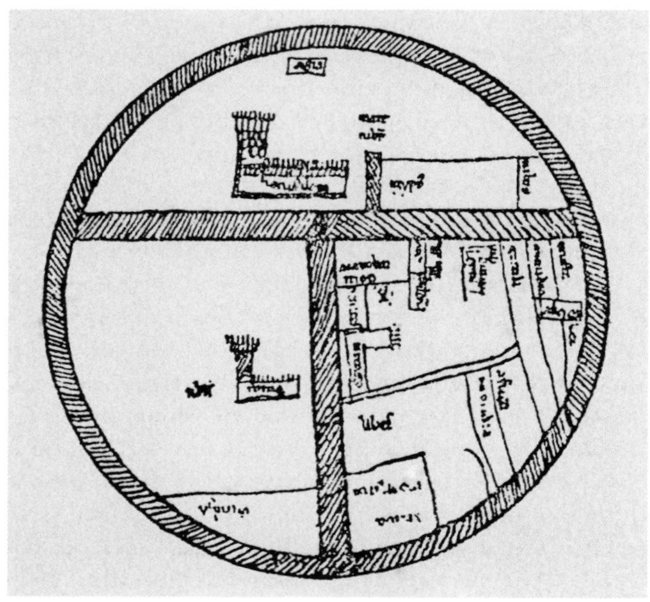

T-O-Weltkarte aus einem Manuskript von Sallust aus dem zwölften Jahrhundert, Vatikanische Bibliothek (oben); T-O-Weltkarte aus der gedruckten Ausgabe von Zacharias' «Orbis breviarium», Florenz 1493 (unten) / T-O map in a Sallust manuscript, twelfth century, Vatican Library (above); T-O map in the printed edition of Zacharias's "Orbis breviarium," Florence, 1493 (below).

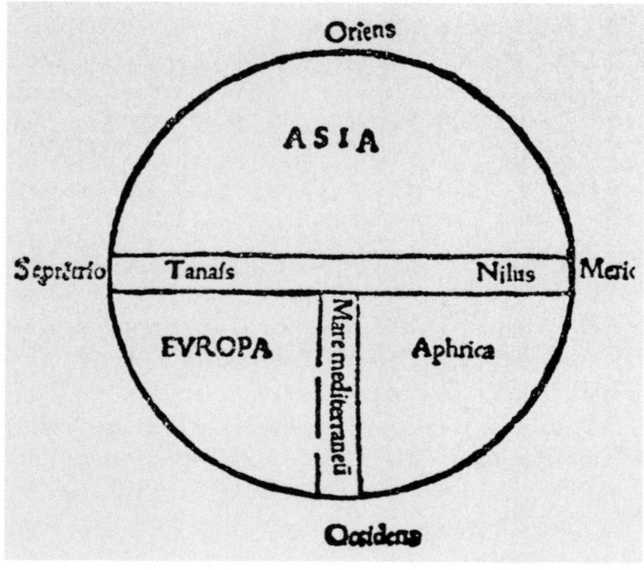

während ihr vertikaler Stamm die Weltteile Europa und Afrika trennt.[7] Als latente Figur
unterliegt das Tau auch Jeff Walls Photographie und lässt so eine vage Andeutung zum Hinweis auf seine «Welt-Sicht» werden. Tatsächlich teilt die Photographie ihre Scheibe in eine
obere und untere Hälfte und bestärkt den Horizont gleich doppelt – als abstrakte Linie und
als Hügelkontur – und spaltet linke und rechte Seite durch eine genau vertikale Flucht von
Rebstöcken. Der «Weltgehalt» der Aufnahme rührt also von präzisen Zusammenhängen mit
alten Schemata her und entspringt nicht einer grundlosen Spekulation. Dass auch andere
Aufnahmen von Jeff Wall eigentlich darauf abzielen, solche Welt-Zusammenhänge ins Bild
zu stellen, geht aus den umständlichen Vorkehrungen hervor, mit deren Hilfe er den raffenden Wind in der Art eines Hokusai-Holzschnittes oder den spannungsgeladenen Eindruck
einer bewachten Landesgrenze aufs photographische Bild gebannt hat. Die Aufnahme des
Weinguts Dominus besitzt einen solch bannenden Charakter, weil sie aus einer schwer kalkulierbaren Distanz in gleich bleibender Schärfe von den nahen Reben bis zu den fernen
Hügeln alles festhält, was die Landschaft um ein unauffällig gewordenes Gebäude ausmacht.

Der Bau von Herzog & de Meuron erscheint ebenfalls doppeldeutig, denn er liegt im Tal
wie die Spinne im Netz sitzt, aber das Rebgelände ist zugleich Voraussetzung für seinen rustikalen Charakter. Rustikal ist er, wie das Wort bereits andeutet, weil seine Fassaden aus dem
Material dieser Landschaft selber gebildet werden, zusammengehalten in eisernen Gitterkästen, die in luftige Höhe gestapelt sind. Wind, Licht und Schatten, Wärme und Kälte sind
seine wahren Elemente, genau wie Distanz, Kreisscheibe, Dunkel und Helligkeit das photographische Bild bestimmen. Man erzählte sich kurz nach dem Bau des Weinguts, dass die
Bruchsteinmassen, die einst mühsam aus den Rebfeldern entfernt worden waren, sich tagsüber erwärmen und aus den Hügeln Schlangen anzögen, die, nachdem sie sich zwischen die
Steinbrocken geringelt hatten, keinen Ausweg aus den Gitterkäfigen fänden und allmählich
in Verwesung übergingen. So hätte die Natur selber den Bau als ihr eigenes Produkt
(miss)verstanden und ihre Distanz zur Architektur (beinahe) annulliert.

1) Jeff Wall erklärt die Umstände dieses Auftrags in einem ausführlichen Interview, das Philip Ursprung am
11. Oktober 2000 mit ihm führte. Es erscheint in dem von Ursprung redigierten Katalog zur Ausstellung «Herzog & de Meuron: Natural History», Montreal 2002. (Die Ausstellung wird anschliessend in Pittsburgh, Rotterdam und Basel gezeigt werden.) Die Anfrage des Canadian Centre for Architecture an Jeff Wall entsprang dem
Wunsch, für die bevorstehende Ausstellung neben den zahlreichen Kunstwerken, die Herzog & de Meuron stets
angeregt haben, auch dem besonderen Interesse der Architekten an photographischen Darstellungen zu entsprechen. Alle weiteren Zitate von Jeff Wall stammen aus dem Interview mit Philip Ursprung.
2) "But [the circle] had a similar relation to the perspectival system of the vineyard, to the geometrical character of the straight lines in the building and in the layout of the vines." Vgl. Anm. 1.
3) "I thought it would be much more interesting to do the picture at the very bottom of the yearly cycle... when
the ground would be wet and everything would be very dark. With all the leaves gone, you could also see the
strictness of the layout of the vineyard, the rows, the regimentation of the wines."
4) "All lenses create circular images. Film is rectangular. Normally cameras are equipped with a lens that gives
you an image bigger than the film being used, so the circular edges of the image are not recorded."
5) "Genres in photography are determined to a great extent by very fundamental things like [distance]. Photographing some objects, like buildings, requires a certain kind of distance, ... I got interested in the idea of genre
because I felt it was an objective and inherent part of the nature of pictures themselves and of the picturemaking process."
6) Wall kam in seinem Interview mit Ursprung mehrmals auf diese Relation zu sprechen, etwa wenn er behauptet, "that resemblance [between pictures done in the Western perspectival way and the images we see when we
are not looking at pictures] is not really cultural, it is physical, caused by the nature of our organism, our eyes
and brain."
7) Es handelt sich um das Schema einer sogenannten T-O-Weltkarte, die in Zacharias' *Orbis breviarium*, Florenz,
1493, ihre klare Ausprägung fand.

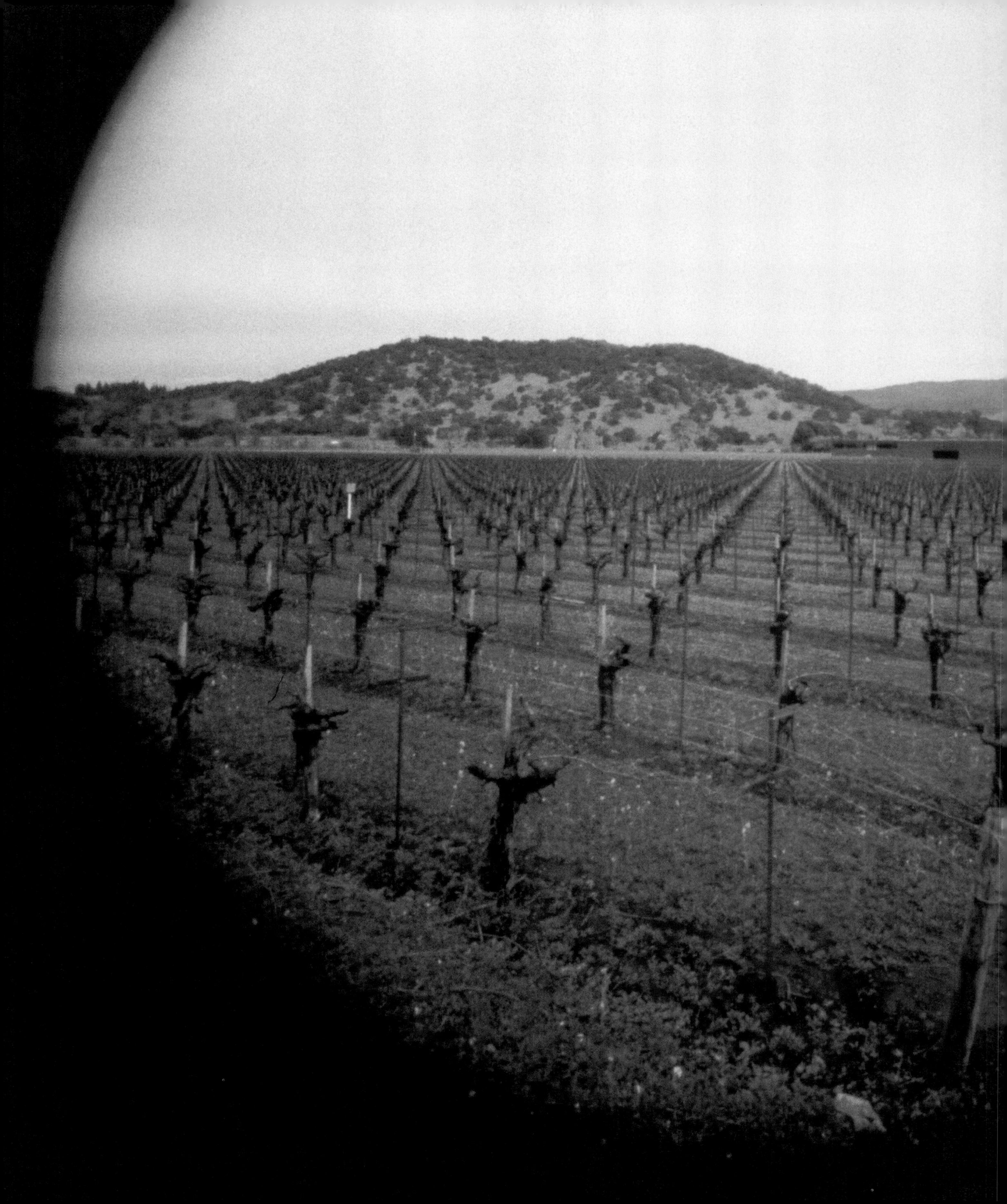

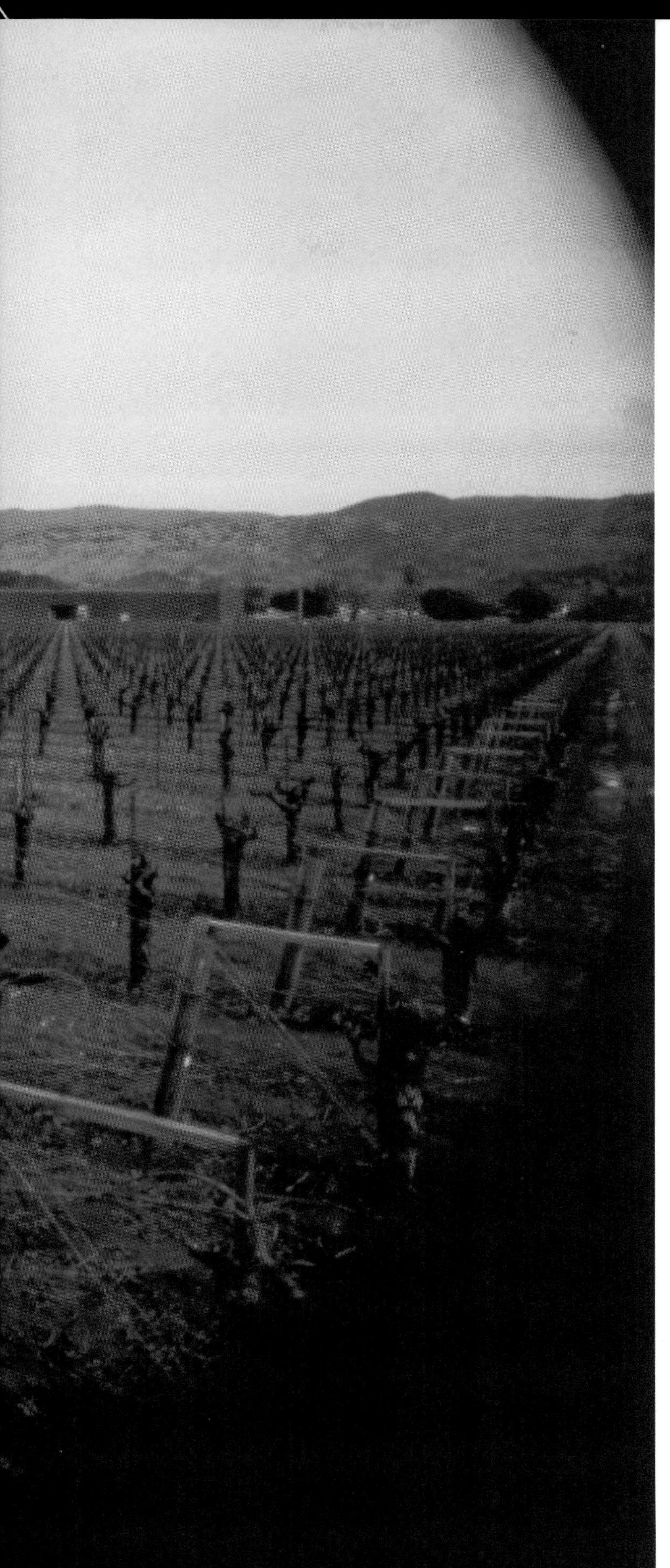

JEFF WALL, DOMINUS WINERY (1996–1998), YOUNTVILLE, NAPA
VALLEY, CALIFORNIA. ARCHITECTS: HERZOG & DE MEURON,
1999, gelatin silver print, 197,3 x 257 cm (image), edition of 3 /
WEINGUT DOMINUS. ARCHITEKTEN: HERZOG & DE MEURON.
(COLLECTION CENTRE CANADIEN D'ARCHITECTURE/CANADIAN CENTRE FOR
ARCHITECTURE, MONTRÉAL; AMERICAN FRIENDS OF THE CCA/GIFT OF SEA-
GRAM CHATEAU & ESTATE WINES COMPANY. COPYRIGHT BY JEFF WALL)

JEFF WALL
LOOKS AT THE DOMINUS WINERY BY
HERZOG & DE MEURON

KURT W. FORSTER

In certain silent films, like D. W. Griffith's *Birth of a Nation*, individual episodes open as a point of light that grows into a circle with a blurry perimeter like the expanding aperture of a camera. For an instant, this technique generates an almost magical sense of an imaginary world awakening, a world whose light dazzles the spectators in the darkness of the movie theatre. Distance and form combine to produce an all-embracing effect until the circle resembles the planet earth coursing through the darkness of the universe in an atmosphere of its own.

When the Canadian photographer Jeff Wall was asked to shoot a building by Swiss architects Herzog & de Meuron, he initially had misgivings about the proposal.[1] Wall does not usually take pictures of architecture—which is by now a specialized sort of product photography—but he was intrigued by the idea of trying to make an interesting picture of the building. The unusual structure with its impressive dimensions and the chunks of rock that form the facade did not strike him as much as the fact that the circle "had a similar relation to the perspectival system of the vineyard, to the geometrical character of the straight lines in the building and in the layout of the vines." So it was basically the physical location, rather than just the building, that attracted Wall's visual attention and was recorded in various shots after a few days of experimentation.

Two circumstances stood the artist in good stead: he went there in December and February when the leafless vines in Napa Valley look rather desolate; and he experimented with various lenses to gauge their effects. These circumstances led, almost by accident, to an un-

KURT W. FORSTER, professor at the Federal Institute of Technology (ETH) in Zurich from 1992–1999, initiated the exhibition "Herzog & de Meuron: Natural History." It will open at the Canadian Centre for Architecture CCA in Montreal (October 2002 – April 2003) and later go on tour.

expected result. Wall "thought it would be much more interesting to do the picture at the very bottom of the yearly cycle, when the ground would be wet and everything would be very dark. With all the leaves gone, you could also see the strictness of the layout of the vineyard, the rows, the regimentation of the wines." The strict geometric layout of the actual vineyards and Wall's choice of lens in relation to the format of his film thus played into the outcome: a round picture instead of the usual full-frame, squared image. Wall reminds us that "[a]ll lenses create circular images. Film is rectangular. Normally cameras are equipped with a lens that gives you an image bigger than the film being used, so the circular edges of the image are not recorded."

The shot Wall finally selected after several days' work possesses precisely those qualities that emphasize the fact that the picture is a photograph, the product of a camera. The parallel rows of vines that spread out across the entire floor of the valley are compressed, and their right-angled geometry is suspended in a hovering circle of light that seems to glide imperceptibly off the top of the rectangular frame of the photographic paper. Within this misty circle, the ground loses its previously accentuated heaviness, and the geometrical network of vines its rigidity. Due to the hazy winter atmosphere and the distant vantage point of the photographer, the large building almost fades into its surroundings, as it runs parallel to the rows of grapevines, which are in turn framed so that a vertical line runs from the exact center of the circle.

The floor of the valley forms an abstract horizon above which the tree-covered hills are seen against a pallid winter sky. The winery dwindles to a gray object in the distance, made more solitary by two dark driveways. The image actually gives the impression of having been shot from inside a cave and looking out into the depths of the landscape. The objects in the picture appear both exaggeratedly far away and unnaturally close up, reminding us that distance is a decisive factor in photography, one which defines the critical measure of its sharpness. Jeff Wall even suggests that "[g]enres in photography are determined to a great extent by very fundamental things like [distance]. Photographing some objects, like buildings, requires a certain kind of distance." He adds that he "got interested in the idea of genre because [he] felt it was an objective and inherent part of the nature of pictures themselves and of the picture-making process." The striking relationship between the optical fact that camera lenses deliver round images and the distance of camera from object invests Wall's picture of the Dominus Winery with two contradictory atmospheres: on one hand, everything in the photograph is bound to the earth and its geometry; on the other, the winery is suspended in an umbrous circle that surfaces out of complete darkness and dissolves as it emerges into lightness. Light is therefore primary in the image while all that lies outside its sphere is shrouded in unfathomable darkness. The blurred edge of the circular image also calls to mind the kind of view one sees through a telescope.

If I have forthwith presumed a latent "global" character in Jeff Wall's circular picture and ascribed a distinguishing significance to its geometry, it is because Wall himself considers the camera lens to be an eye and therefore assumes the existence of a fundamental similarity between the world and the organ of sight. In an interview with Philip Ursprung, Wall referred to this relationship several times, as when he claimed "that resemblance [between pictures constructed according to the conventions of Western perspective and the way that we see when we are not looking at pictures] is not really cultural, it is physical, caused by the nature of our organism, our eyes and brain." The medieval conception of the world's continental land masses was represented by a special formula: a circle with the letter Tau inscribed within it to distinguish the three continents of Asia, Europe, and Africa. This diagrammatic representation had already appeared in a Sallust manuscript, now in the Vatican Library, dating from the twelfth century which became more widely known in the fifteenth century with the introduction of the printing press. The top of the "T" in the Tau shape divides the circle (of the earth) into almost equal halves with Asia above and the vertical leg of the "T" separating the continents of Europe and Africa below.[2] The Tau, as a latent figure underlying Jeff Wall's photograph, thus transforms a vague hint into an indication of his "world-view." The disk of the photograph is indeed divided into an upper and a lower half, with the horizon doubly reinforced as an abstract line and as the outline of the hills, and the left and right sides divided by the strictly vertical vanishing line of the grapevines. The "world content" of the shot is thus derived from precise associations with very early diagrammatic representations and is not the product of random speculation. The fact that other shots by Jeff Wall also address such planetary associations is substantiated by the elaborate preparations undertaken in order to capture the gusty wind in the manner of a Hokusai woodcut or the electrically charged impression of a country's borders under guard. The spellbinding impact of Wall's rendition of the Dominus Winery lies in its depiction of everything that defines the landscape around a now inconspicuous building, from the nearby grapevines to the distant hills, all with a consistent sharpness of focus and from a distance that is difficult to assess.

The building by Herzog & de Meuron is lent an additional ambiguity because it sits in the valley like a spider in its web while the vineyards also function as the prerequisite for its rustic character. Rustic because, as the word itself indicates, its facades consist of material that comes from the immediate surroundings, held together in iron cages or gabions, stacked to airy heights. Wind, light, and shadow, heat and cold are its true elements, just as distance and the transition from dusk to brightness determine the photographed image. Shortly after the construction of the winery, the story circulated that the masses of rock that were laboriously removed from the vast vineyards warm up during the daytime, attracting snakes from the hills. They curl up in the cracks between the rocks and there—unable to find their way out of the cages again—they gradually rot and dry up. If so, it seems that nature has (mis)understood the building as its own product and thus (almost) eliminated its own distance from architecture.

(Translation: Catherine Schelbert)

1) Jeff Wall explains the circumstances of this commission in an interview conducted with Philip Ursprung on October 11, 2000, to be published in the forthcoming catalogue of the exhibition "Herzog & de Meuron: Natural History," Montreal, 2002. (The exhibition will later tour Pittsburgh, Rotterdam, and Basel.) The Canadian Centre for Architecture asked Jeff Wall to photograph the work of Herzog & de Meuron because, in addition to the numerous works of art which the architects have fostered, they also delight in discovering how photographers reinterpret their architecture. All of the following quotations are taken from the interview with Philip Ursprung.
2) The Tau shape goes back to the map of the world found in Zacharias' *Orbis breviarium*, Florence, 1493. See images on p. 8.

JOHN CURRIN

born 1962 in Boulder, Colorado, lives and works in New York /

geboren 1962 in Boulder, Colorado, lebt und arbeitet in New York.

LAURA OWENS

born 1970 in Euclid, Ohio, lives and works in Los Angeles /

geboren 1970 in Euclid, Ohio, lebt und arbeitet in Los Angeles.

MICHAEL RAEDECKER

born 1964 in Amsterdam, lives and works in London /

geboren 1964 in Amsterdam, lebt und arbeitet in London.

John Currin

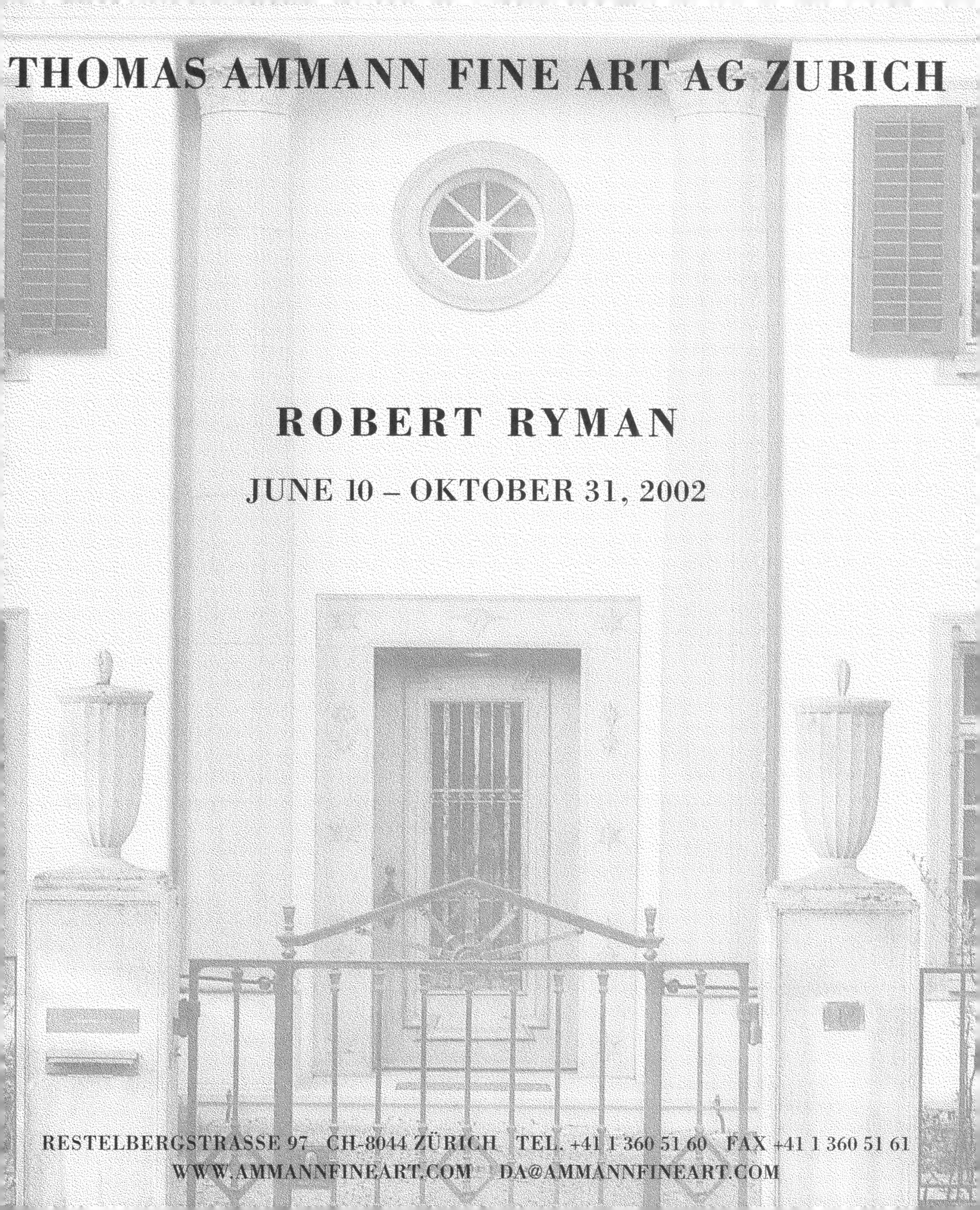

THOMAS AMMANN FINE ART AG ZURICH

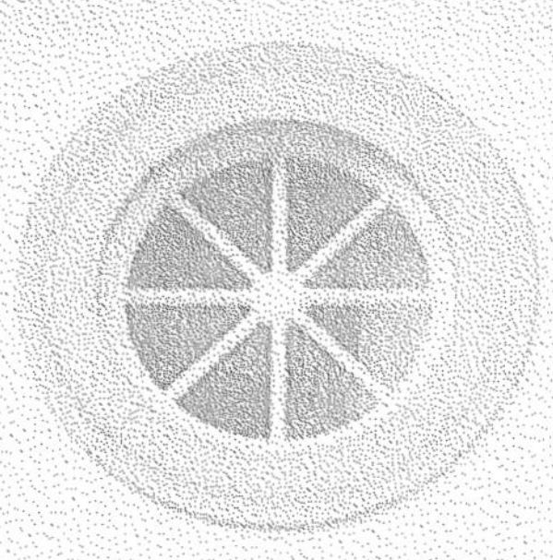

ROBERT RYMAN

JUNE 10 – OKTOBER 31, 2002

RESTELBERGSTRASSE 97   CH-8044 ZÜRICH   TEL. +41 1 360 51 60   FAX +41 1 360 51 61

WWW.AMMANNFINEART.COM   DA@AMMANNFINEART.COM

Alois **Lichtsteiner**

5. Oktober 2002 – 16. November 2002

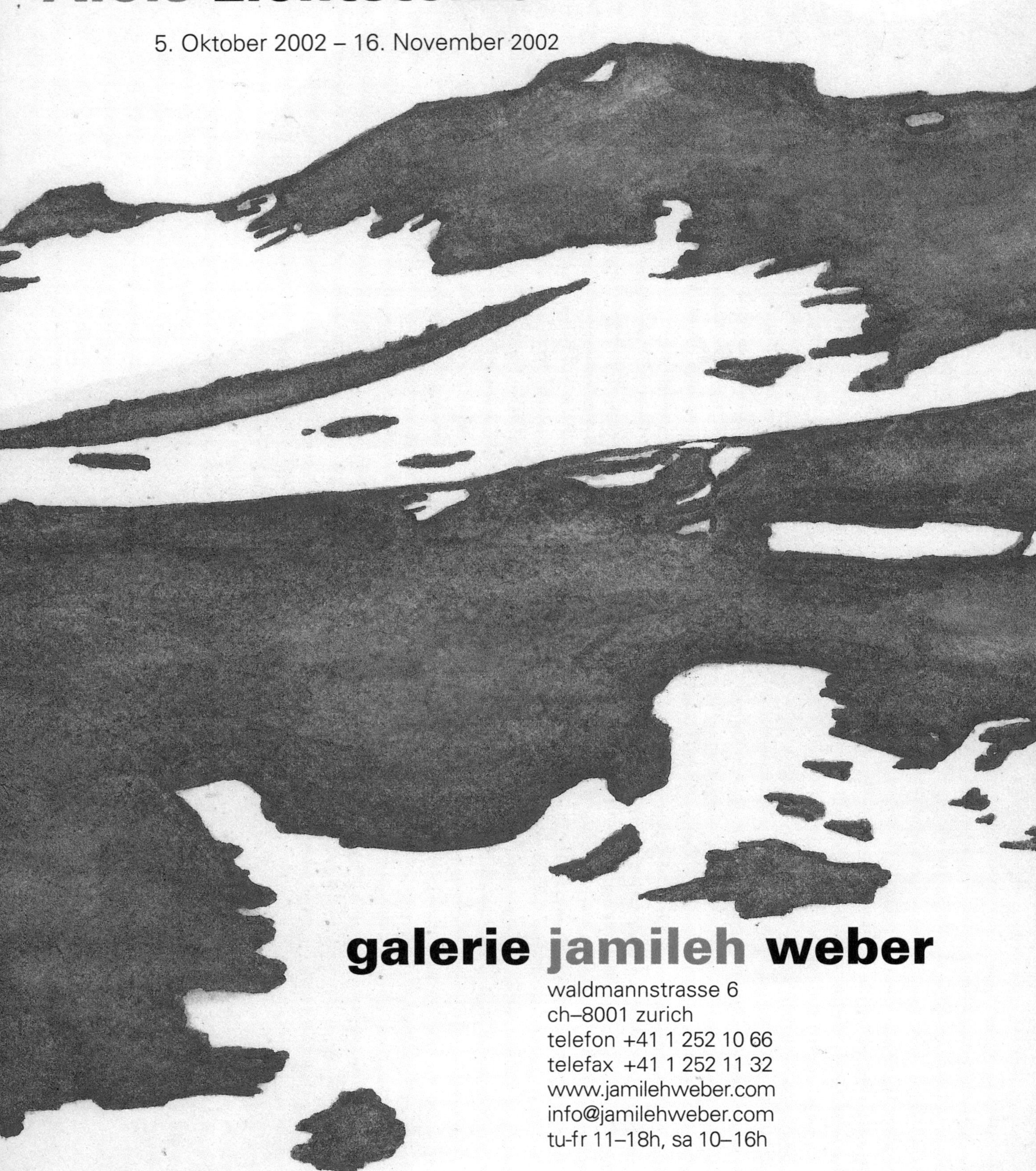

galerie jamileh weber

waldmannstrasse 6
ch–8001 zurich
telefon +41 1 252 10 66
telefax +41 1 252 11 32
www.jamilehweber.com
info@jamilehweber.com
tu-fr 11–18h, sa 10–16h

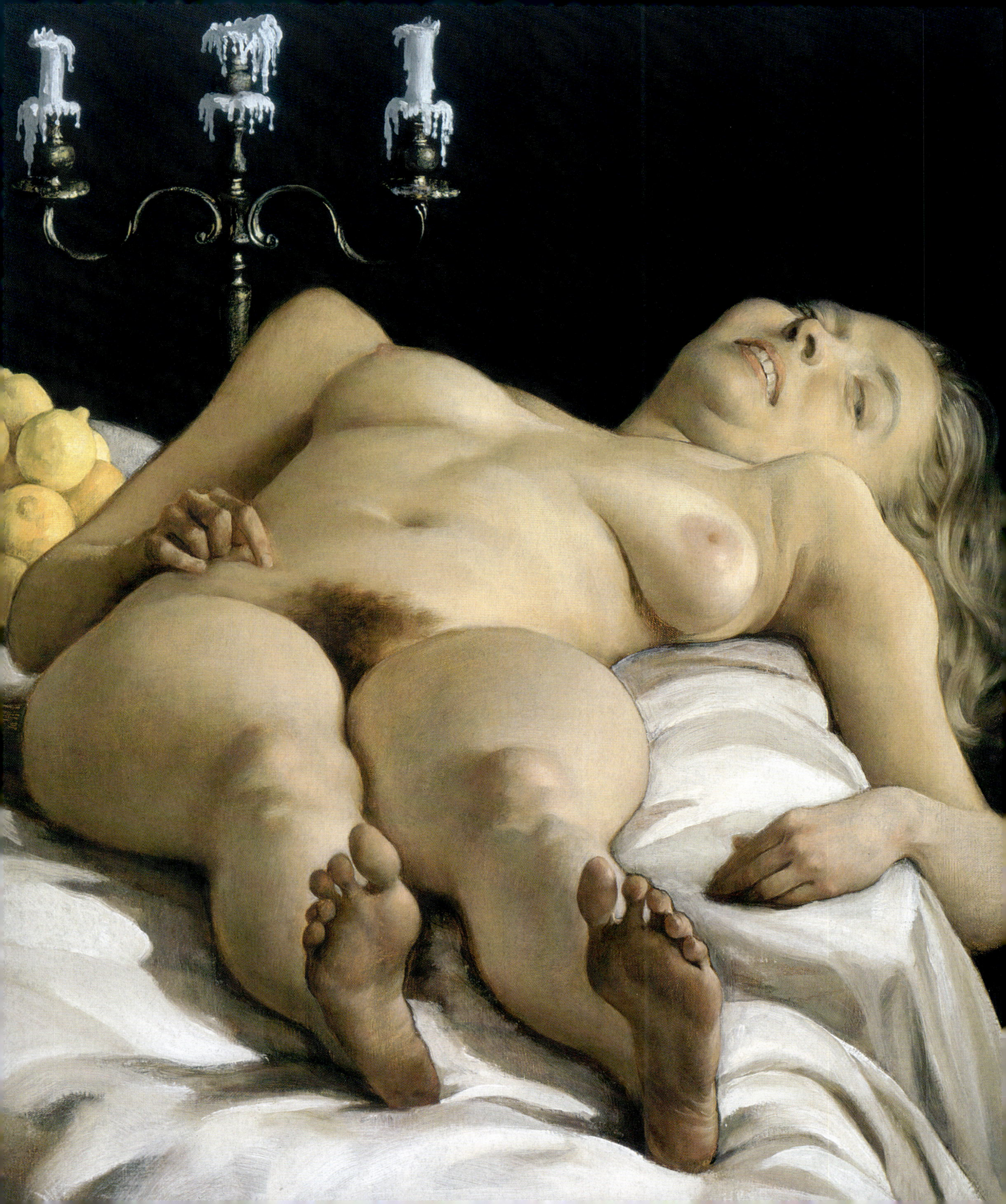

Currin's Nudes

KEITH SEWARD

People often comment how weird John Currin's nudes are without realizing how weird the nude is itself. You'd think it bizarre if, in the context of an art review, you were to read a description of Currin's penis. And yet when a painter paints a nude woman it seems perfectly natural. If you were to visit Currin's studio and the artist offered to show you his wife in a state of undress—the bride stripped bare by her husband, even—you'd think him a little strange. But if he only pulled out RACHEL WITH BUTTERFLIES (1999), a sweetly painted canvas depicting his wife as a faux-Flemish nude, you wouldn't give it a second thought. In psychology, to disrobe your wife or girlfriend before strangers is a perversion, and yet in art it's a figure study.

Evidently there is a blatant double standard with regard to display of the human body. You can go to a museum fully clothed and look at paintings of naked people, but you can't do the reverse, you can't go to a museum naked and look at paintings of clothed people. What is indecent exposure in society is merely a genre in art. This paradox was of course what made OLYMPIA so shocking in the nineteenth century. Prior to Manet, the nude had been an exercise in self-denial: a naked woman, but at the same time not really a naked woman—so they kidded themselves—because she was cloaked in the garb of mythology. The nude was not that girl from down the street, she was Venus. But Manet dropped this pretense. Olympia was not Venus, she was that girl from down the street—that streetwalker. And the artist, by implication, was suddenly a pimp, a displayer of female goods. Such a conceit was as shocking as the sight of a streaker in a museum, even though all Manet really did was bring out something already there: the nakedness of the nude.

As a genre, then, the nude is weird because it always contains this latent bit of indecent exposure, even perversion. Sometimes it's more obvious, as in

---

KEITH SEWARD is a writer and digital artist. His book, *Extraterrestrial Sex Fetish,* is available online at supervert.com.

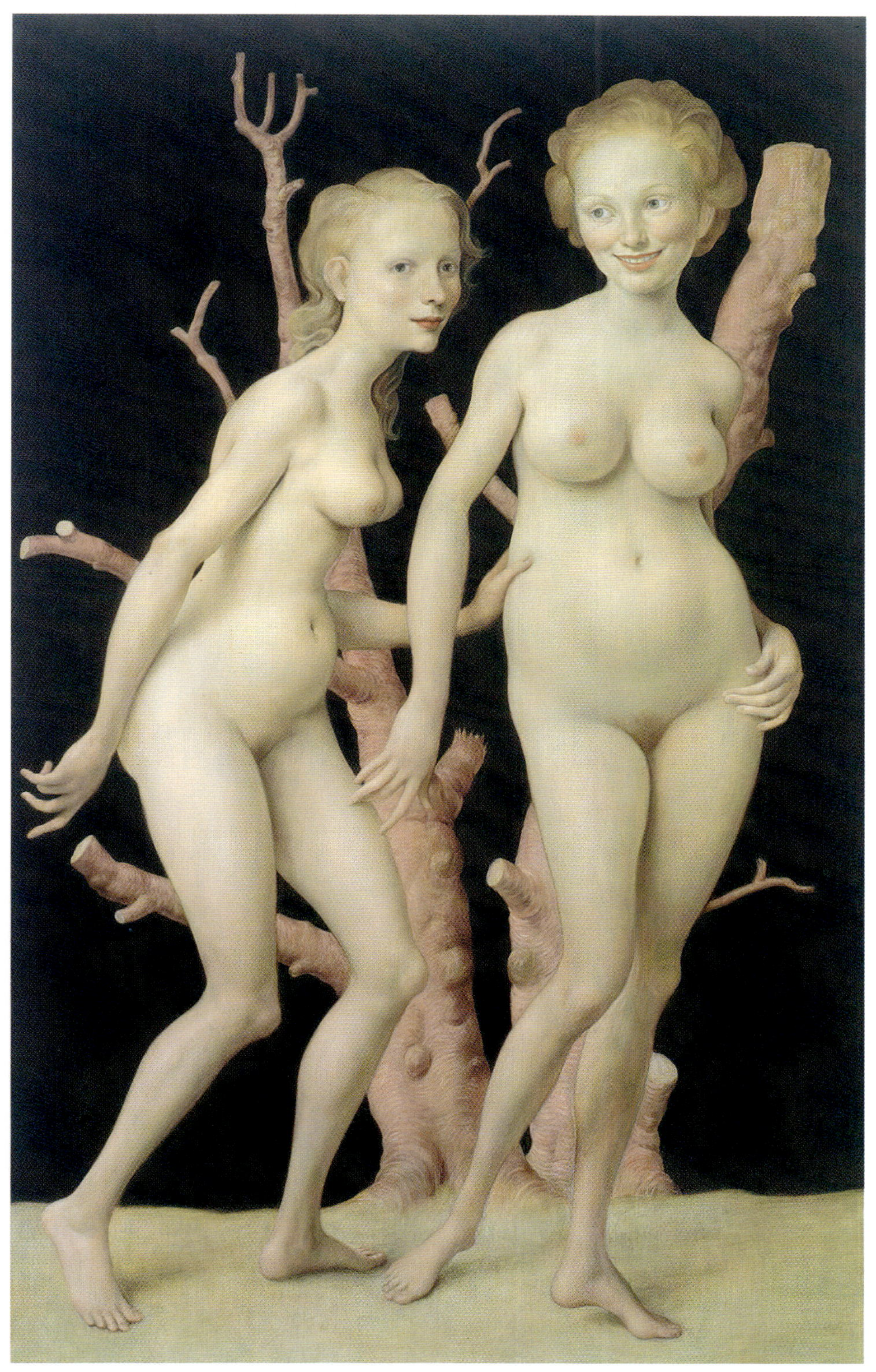

JOHN CURRIN, THE PINK TREE, 1999, oil on canvas, 78 x 48" / DER ROSA BAUM, Öl auf Leinwand, 198 x 122 cm. (PHOTO: FRED SCRUTON)

the borderline pedophilia of Balthus, other times less. "Cubism," Currin once noted in an interview, "was perverse when Picasso first did it. People justify it by talking about looking at an object from three sides and so on, but it always seemed to me much more about seeing the ass and the breast at the same time. That's basically what Picasso used it for, and even after he gave up Cubism, he still habitually drew the ass crack, the pussy and the breast on the front. The metaphor was not about time travel, it was about total sexual domination."[1] But if this is true, if the abstractions of Cubism could express a will toward sexual omnipotence, what do the strange nudes of Currin express?

THREE FRIENDS (1998) shows two naked women standing and a third at their feet. At first sight, you notice the figural distortions and the general old-master appearance of the painting, a variation on the traditional "three graces" theme. The painting is enigmatic—why are these three friends cavorting naked?—but not, as was the case with Manet, shocking. Why? Because the conceit of OLYMPIA was to re-situate the nude in contemporary reality. The girl was a prostitute, the painter a pimp, the viewer a john. With Currin, however, it's the exact opposite: The nude is put safely back into its art-historical tra-

dition. The painter is less a pimp than a museum guide. Of course OLYMPIA had its visual reference in Titian, and Currin's painting retains the exhibition-ism characteristic of the nude as such. But whereas Manet modernized Titian, Currin antiquates his three nude figures, projecting them into a tableau straight out of an art history textbook. It's what the sexual fantasy of a man aroused by the Louvre would look like—which is to say that sexuality recedes be-fore referentiality, as though Currin regains a bit of the repression characteristic of the old masters he admires. In other words, weird as it sounds to say, alongside Manet and Picasso, there's something al-most chaste about Currin's nudes. The drive is not for sexual but for stylistic omnipotence, and in con-sequence a cover is thrown over the nude again, not a mantle of mythology but a virtuosity of technique. It's not the subject who resembles Venus but the painter who resembles the Northern Renaissance.

"To whatever extent painting can be considered a moral act," Currin has said, "it necessarily goes in one of the worst possible directions... You can't make a painting without embracing your own desire as something good."[2] No doubt this is especially true of the nude, which—owing to the nature of the desires piqued by the sight of a naked body—thus becomes

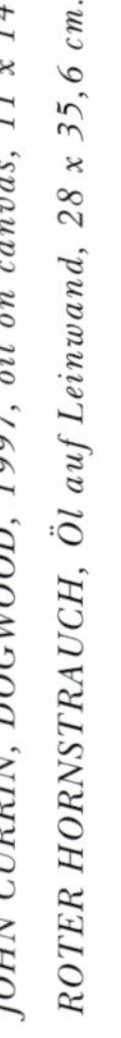

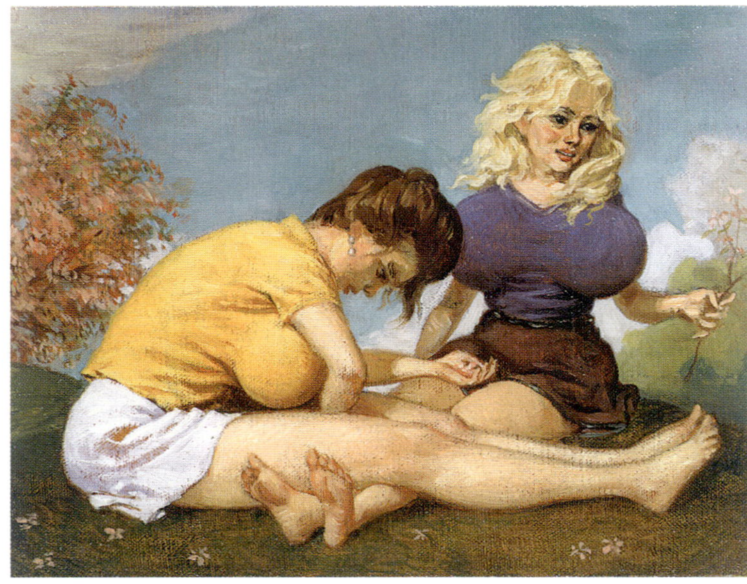

the *psychopathia sexualis* of painting, a compendium of lusts and urges, a public display of personal cravings. Conversely, if there is anything chaste about Currin's nudes, it is precisely because the artist is no longer able to embrace his own desire in this way, at least not unself-consciously. BEA ARTHUR NAKED (1991), for example, retains the intrinsic perversity of the nude insofar as it suggests a ruthless act of gerontophilia, stripping the clothes off an old lady and displaying her naked to strangers. And yet, if you look at the painting as a kind of bet the artist made with himself, an attempt to create a nude in which there was no longer a direct correspondence between sexual desire and visual representation—presuming, of course, that the artist does not harbor a secret fetish for the matronly television star—it becomes something else altogether: a moral nude.

Or is it just a joke on the concept of a moral nude? After all, how can chastity, repression, or morality be imputed to a painter who dedicated an entire show to depictions of grossly exaggerated breasts? Is it not an aggressively sexual drive that bloats the boobs in a painting such as DOGWOOD (1997)? Technically the work is not a nude, and yet the figures give the impression of being more naked with their clothes on than most nudes are without. In any event, big breasts here serve the same function as elongated arms, impossibly twisted legs, or other mannerisms of anatomy: they emphasize the artifice, the unreality, of the paintings. They're the hand of the artist displayed at the same time as the female body, like those porn videos where the cameraman films himself participating in the action. They are visual analogues of self-consciousness, not a desire for big breasts but a guy making fun of his desire for big breasts.

Without going so far as to psychoanalyze the artist, it is not difficult to see at least one cause of such self-consciousness—the artist is a man and as a man he naturally likes to paint female nudes. On the other hand, he is also a man of his time, and for this reason he cannot fail to acknowledge that women—in many cases powerful ones, such as dealers and magazine editors—will be the viewers of his paintings. Consequently, the situation confronting the artist is this: How do you paint female nudes palatable to women viewers? Would Picasso have sought

sexual omnipotence through Cubism if his dealer were not Mr. but Mrs. Kahnweiler? If you know in advance who constitutes your audience, how can it not influence the way you conceive your paintings? How can it not introduce self-consciousness? In a way, it's a generalization of the delicate situation that must occur when you decide to paint your wife naked. You still have to live with her afterward. What if she doesn't like it? Will she be able to separate her appreciation of your aesthetic goals from her own natural desire to be flatteringly portrayed? What do you opt for—artistic integrity? Domestic bliss? Can you have both? Or should you just avoid the whole mess and paint flowers?

Certainly none of this is psychologically explicit, and it would be a great error to imagine Currin scheming about how to get his latest nudie past his wife or dealer. Really it is less a matter of the artist's individual psyche than of the perverse paradoxes of the genre itself—for if it was Manet who demonstrated the nakedness of the nude, it is Currin who exhibits its psychopathology, the weirdness of doing in art what you can't always do in reality. No painting points up the discrepancy better than THE WIZARD (1994), in which a man wearing dark gloves lays his hands on a woman's ample breasts. Both figures close their eyes, as though to acknowledge something already dreamlike about the encounter. Why, though, is this man a wizard? Did he use magic to mesmerize the woman? To strip her naked? To enlarge her breasts? Even if he did, what does he gain? As a visualist, Currin was no doubt concerned with the contrast the black gloves formed against the white breasts, and yet these hand-coverings condemn the wizard to touch without feeling. THE WIZARD is both more and less than a man: more, because he's able to bring his fantasy to life; less, because without sight and touch he's weirdly incapable of enjoying it. And in that sense, the painting could serve as an allegory of the nude as such, since the same holds true of the artist: in the nude, he can realize, but not enjoy his fantasy.

1) John Currin: *Oeuvres 1989–1995*, ex. cat. (Limoges: F.R.A.C. Limousin, 1995), p. 38.
2) Ibid., p. 40.

JOHN CURRIN, FISHERMEN, 2002, oil on canvas, 50 x 41" /
FISCHER, Öl auf Leinwand, 127 x 104 cm. (PHOTO: OREN SLOR)

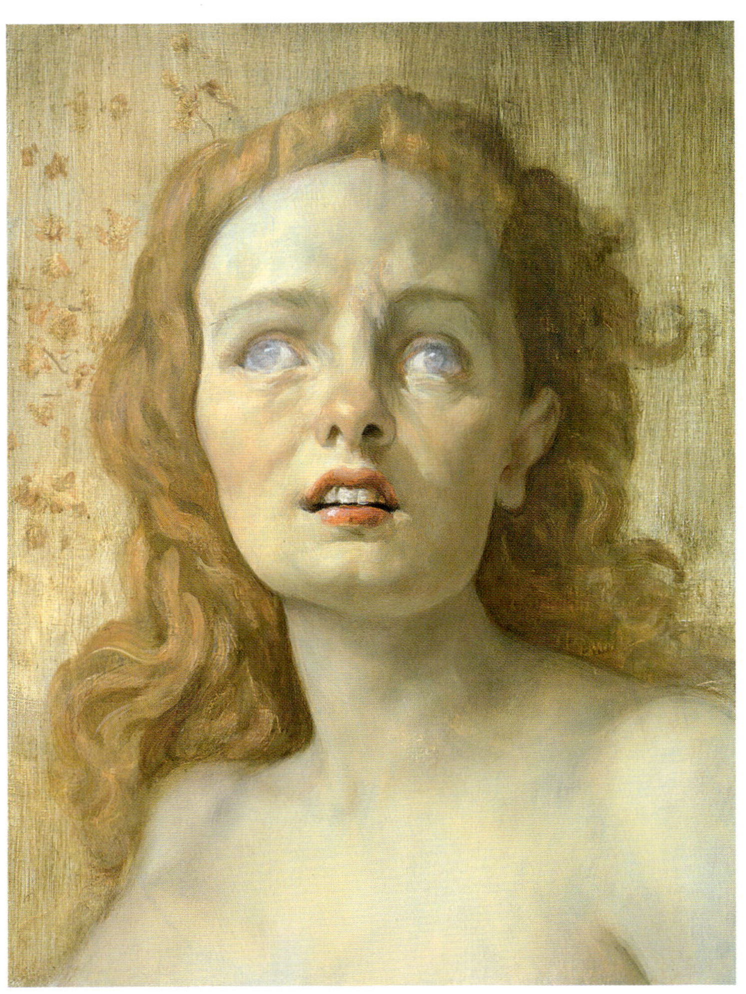

JOHN CURRIN, THE CLAIRVOYANT, 2001, oil on canvas, 22 x 16" /
DIE HELLSEHERIN, Öl auf Leinwand, 56 x 40,6 cm. (PHOTO: OREN SLOR)

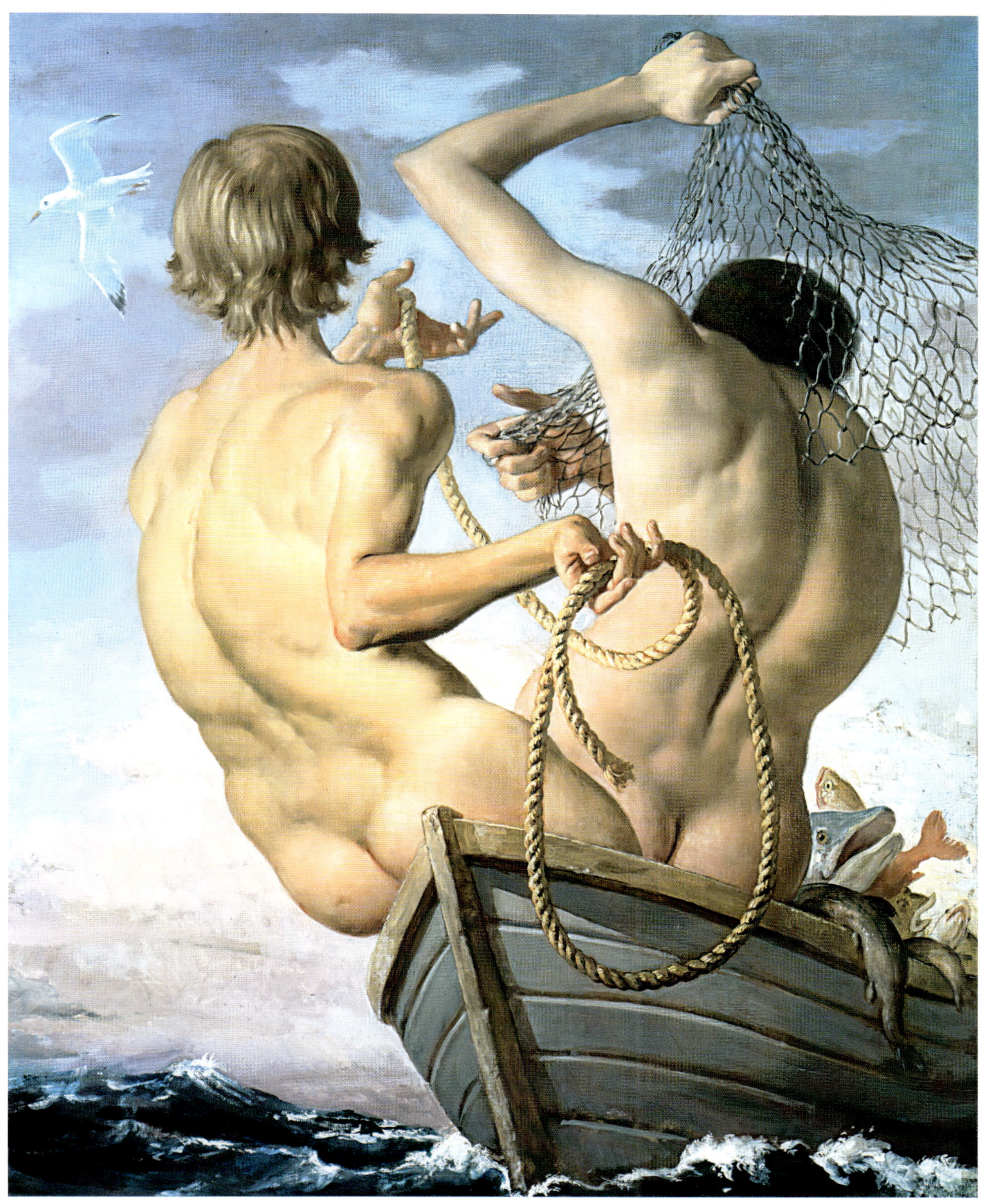

Currins Akte

KEITH SEWARD

Die Leute bemerken oft, wie seltsam John Currins Aktbilder seien, ohne sich darüber im Klaren zu sein, dass der Akt an sich etwas Seltsames ist. Bekäme man im kunstkritischen Kontext eine Beschreibung von Currins Penis zu lesen, fände man das bizarr. Malt ein Maler dagegen eine nackte Frau, kommt uns das ganz natürlich vor. Wenn Sie Currin in seinem Atelier aufsuchten und der Künstler würde Ihnen seine Frau nackt vorführen – oder gar als von ihrem Ehemann entkleidete Braut –, hielten Sie ihn für leicht verrückt. Zöge er dagegen nur RACHEL WITH BUTTERFLIES (Rachel mit Schmetterlingen, 1999) hervor, ein wunderbar gemaltes Bild, das seine Frau als pseudo-flämischen Akt zeigt, würden Sie nicht mit der Wimper zucken. In der Psychologie gilt es als Perversion, seine Frau oder Freundin vor Fremden zu entkleiden, aber in der Kunst ist das lediglich eine Aktstudie.

Offensichtlich sind die Spielregeln ambivalent, wenn es um die Zurschaustellung des menschlichen Körpers geht. Man kann vollständig bekleidet in ein Museum gehen und sich Gemälde von nackten Menschen anschauen, aber das Umgekehrte kann man nicht tun, man kann nicht nackt ins Museum gehen und sich Bilder von bekleideten Leuten ansehen. Was in der Gesellschaft als unanständig und exhibitionistisch gilt, ist in der Kunst lediglich ein Genre. Genau dieses Paradox machte Manets OLYMPIA für das neunzehnte Jahrhundert so schockierend. Vor Manet war der Akt eine Übung in Selbstverleugnung gewesen: eine nackte Frau, und doch nicht wirklich nackt – versuchte man sich weiszumachen –, da sie ja

KEITH SEWARD ist Schriftsteller und Computer-Künstler. Sein Buch *Extraterrestrial Sex Fetish* kann auf dem Internet unter supervert.com heruntergeladen werden.

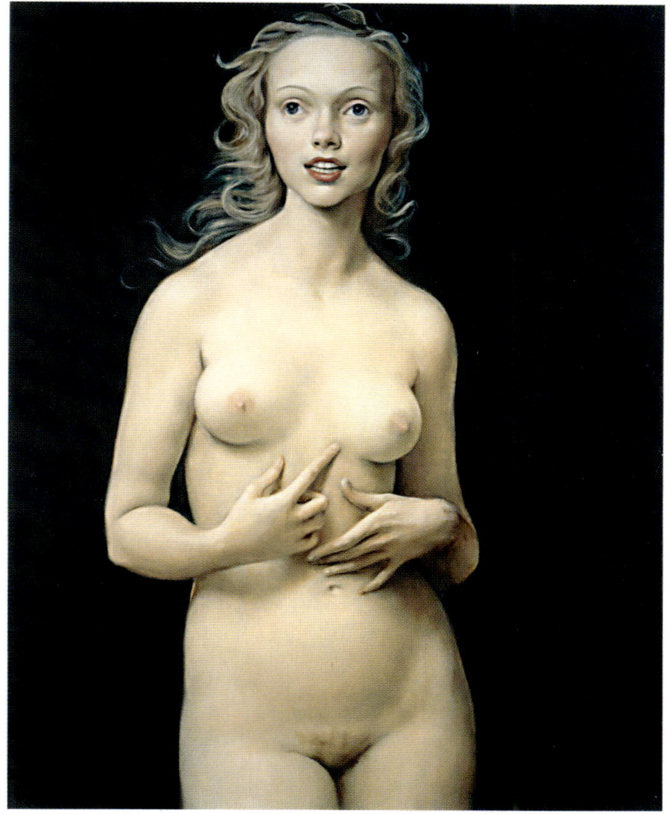

im Gewande der Mythologie daherkam. Der Akt war eben nicht irgendein Mädchen von der Strasse, sondern Venus. Manet gab diesen Vorwand auf. Olympia war nicht Venus, sie war ein Mädchen von der Strasse – eine Strassenhure. Und dadurch wurde der Künstler implizit plötzlich zum Zuhälter, zum Anbieter von Weiblichkeit als Ware. Diese Vorstellung wirkte genauso schockierend wie der Anblick eines Flitzers im Museum, obwohl Manet eigentlich nur sichtbar machte, was schon immer da war: die Nacktheit des Aktes.

Also ist der Akt als Genre seltsam, weil er immer diesen latenten Anteil schamloser Entblössung oder gar Perversion beinhaltet. Manchmal ist das augenfällig, etwa in den ans Pädophile grenzenden Bildern von Balthus, manchmal weniger. «Der Kubismus», bemerkte Currin einmal in einem Interview, «war pervers, als Picasso das zum ersten Mal machte. Die

Leute rechtfertigen ihn, indem sie sagen, es gehe darum, ein Objekt zugleich von drei Seiten zu sehen oder so, aber mir schien es immer sehr viel mehr darum zu gehen, Arsch und Titten gleichzeitig zu sehen. Dafür hat Picasso ihn im Grunde eingesetzt, und auch später, als er nicht mehr kubistisch malte, zeichnete er gewöhnlich Arschspalte, Möse und Brüste vorn. Bei dieser Metaphorik ging es nicht um Zeitexperimente, sondern um die totale sexuelle Dominanz.»[1] Aber wenn das zutrifft, wenn die Abstraktionen des Kubismus tatsächlich den Willen zur sexuellen Allmacht zum Ausdruck bringen, was sagen dann die merkwürdigen Akte von Currin aus?

THREE FRIENDS (Drei Freundinnen, 1998) zeigt zwei nackte stehende Frauen und eine dritte ihnen zu Füssen. Auf den ersten Blick fallen einem die Verzerrungen der Figuren auf und der allgemein altmeisterliche Eindruck, den das Bild vermittelt, das

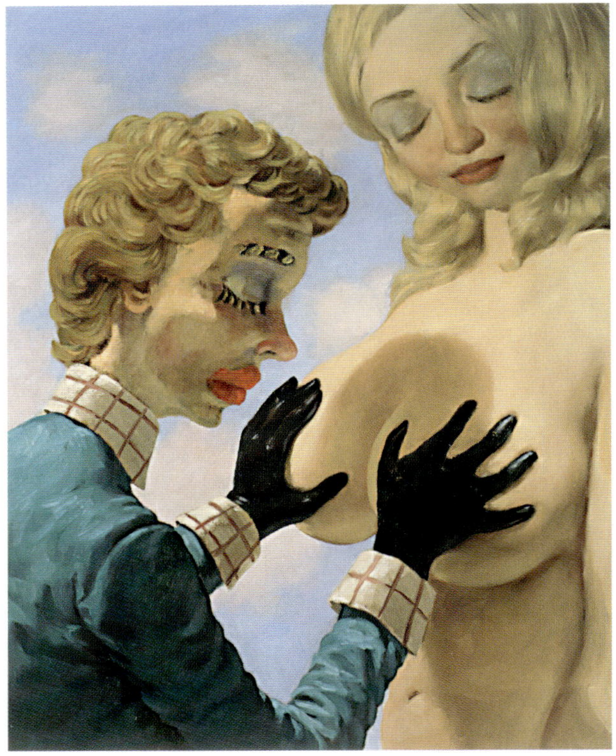

JOHN CURRIN, THE WIZARD, 1994, oil on canvas, 32 x 26" /
DER ZAUBERER, Öl auf Leinwand, 81,3 x 66 cm.
(PHOTO: FRED SCRUTON)

eine Variation auf das traditionelle Thema der drei Grazien darstellt. Das Bild ist zwar rätselhaft – warum hüpfen die drei Freundinnen wohl nackt herum? –, aber nicht schockierend wie bei Manet. Warum? Weil hinter OLYMPIA die Idee stand, den Akt in der zeitgenössischen Realität anzusiedeln. Das Mädchen war eine Hure, der Maler ein Zuhälter, der Zuschauer ein Freier. Bei Currin geschieht jedoch das genaue Gegenteil: Der Akt wird fein säuberlich in seine kunsthistorische Tradition zurückversetzt. Der Maler ist hier weniger Zuhälter als vielmehr ein Führer durch die Gemäldegalerie. Natürlich hatte OLYMPIA ihr Vorbild bei Tizian, und natürlich hat Currins Bild nach wie vor den exhibitionistischen Charakter, den jede Aktdarstellung hat. Aber während Manet Tizian modernisierte, antikisiert Currin seine drei Aktfiguren, indem er sie in ein Tableau der klassischen Kunstgeschichte projiziert. So sähe bestenfalls die sexuelle Phantasie eines Mannes aus, der sich im Louvre aufgeilt – das heisst, die Sexualität tritt hinter der Referenzialität zurück, als ob Currin etwas von der repressiven Qualität der von ihm bewunderten

alten Meister zurückgewänne. Mit anderen Worten, auch wenn es seltsam klingen mag: Neben Manet und Picasso haben Currins Akte beinahe etwas Züchtiges. Nicht sexuelle, sondern stilistische Allmacht ist hier angestrebt, was zur Folge hat, dass der Akt wieder verhüllt wird, und zwar nicht mehr mit dem Gewand der Mythologie, sondern mit dem der technischen Virtuosität. Das Sujet gleicht nicht der Venus, aber der Maler gemahnt an die Renaissance.

«Inwieweit auch immer die Malerei als moralischer Akt gelten mag», meinte Currin, «sie geht notgedrungen immer in eine verhängnisvolle Richtung… Man kann kein Bild malen ohne das eigene Begehren gutzuheissen.»[2] Ohne Zweifel gilt das insbesondere für den Akt, der – wegen der Art des Begehrens, das der Anblick eines nackten Leibes weckt – zu einer *Psychopathia sexualis* der Malerei wird, einem Kompendium der Lüste und Triebe, einer öffentlichen Zurschaustellung privater Sehnsüchte. Wenn Currins Akte dagegen etwas Züchtiges haben, so genau deshalb, weil der Künstler sein eigenes Begehren nicht länger in dieser Weise akzeptieren kann, oder zumindest nicht ohne Bewusstsein. BEA ARTHUR NAKED (Bea Arthur, nackt, 1991), zum Beispiel, weist nach wie vor die dem Akt inhärente Perversität auf, insofern als es ein unbarmherziger Ausdruck von Gerontophilie zu sein scheint, wenn eine alte Dame ihrer Kleider beraubt und fremden Leuten nackt zur Schau gestellt wird. Betrachtet man das Bild aber als eine Art Wette des Künstlers mit sich selbst, als Versuch, einen Akt zu schaffen, in dem sexuelles Begehren und visuelle Darstellung nicht mehr direkt miteinander korrespondieren – natürlich immer in der Annahme, dass der Künstler nicht heimlich eine

Schwäche für den matronenhaften Fernsehstar hegt –, so wird es zu etwas ganz anderem: ein moralisch integrer Akt.

Oder macht er sich vielleicht nur lustig über die Idee des moralisch integren Aktes? Denn wie kann man einem Künstler Keuschheit, Repression oder Moralität unterjubeln, der eine ganze Ausstellung mit Bildern übertrieben grosser Titten bestritten hat? Ist es nicht ein aggressiver Sexualtrieb, der die Titten in einem Bild wie DOGWOOD (Roter Hornstrauch, 1997) anschwellen lässt? Technisch betrachtet ist das kein Aktbild, aber die Figuren darin wirken samt ihren Kleidern nackter als die meisten Akte ohne Kleider. Wie dem auch sei, die grossen Brüste erfüllen dieselbe Funktion wie die überlangen Arme, unmöglich verdrehten Beine oder andere anatomische Manierismen: Sie unterstreichen das Artifizielle, Unwirkliche der Bilder. Sie stehen für die Hand des Künstlers, die zugleich mit dem Frauenkörper zur Schau gestellt wird, wie in jenen Pornovideos, in denen der Kameramann sich selbst als Teilnehmenden filmt. Es sind visuelle Analogien der Selbstreflexion; dahinter steht nicht das Begehren nach grossen Brüsten, sondern einer, der sich über seine Schwäche für grosse Brüste lustig macht.

Ohne so weit zu gehen und den Künstler analysieren zu wollen, ist doch ein Grund für diese Selbstreflexion unschwer erkennbar: Der Künstler ist ein Mann und malt als solcher natürlich gern weibliche Akte; auf der anderen Seite ist er aber auch ein Mann seiner Zeit und muss der Tatsache Rechnung tragen, dass Frauen – und in vielen Fällen sehr mächtige Frauen wie Kunsthändlerinnen und Redaktorinnen von Zeitschriften – sich seine Bilder anschauen werden. Demzufolge sieht die Lage des Künstlers so aus: Wie malt man weibliche Akte, die für weibliche Betrachter akzeptabel sind? Hätte Picasso die sexuelle Allmacht im Kubismus angestrebt, wenn sein Händler nicht Herr, sondern Frau Kahnweiler gewesen wäre? Wie sollte es keinen Einfluss auf die Bilder haben, wenn man sein Publikum im Voraus kennt? Wie sollte das nicht zur Selbstreflexion führen? In gewisser Weise ist es eine Verallgemeinerung der heiklen Situation, die entsteht, wenn man seine eigene Frau nackt malen will. Schliesslich muss man auch danach noch mit ihr leben können. Was, wenn ihr das Bild nicht gefällt? Wird sie in der Lage sein, ihre Beurteilung der ästhetischen Ziele ihres Mannes und ihren natürlichen Wunsch, vorteilhaft porträtiert zu werden, auseinander zu halten? Wofür soll man sich entscheiden? Für die künstlerische Integrität? Für den häuslichen Frieden? Kann man beides haben? Oder soll man das Ganze lieber vergessen und Blumen malen?

Natürlich ist nichts von alledem psychologisch aussagekräftig und es wäre hoffnungslos falsch, sich vorzustellen, wie Currin sein neustes Aktbildchen vor seiner Frau oder Galeristin zu verheimlichen sucht. Das Ganze ist in der Tat weniger eine Frage der individuellen Psyche des Künstlers als der perversen Paradoxitäten des Genres; denn wenn Manet die Nacktheit des Aktes aufgezeigt hat, so legt Currin das Psychopathologische der Aktmalerei offen, die Perversität, die darin liegt, in der Kunst das zu tun, was man in der Realität nicht immer tun kann. Kein Bild zeigt diese Diskrepanz deutlicher auf, als THE WIZARD (Der Zauberer, 1994): Ein Mann mit schwarzen Handschuhen legt seine Hände auf die grossen Brüste einer Frau. Beide haben die Augen geschlossen, als würden sie dem schon beinah Traumhaften der Begegnung Rechnung tragen. Warum aber ist dieser Mann ein Zauberer? Hat er Magie benützt, um die Frau zu verzaubern? Um sie auszuziehen? Um ihre Brüste zu vergrössern? Und wenn ja, was hat er damit gewonnen? Als visueller Mensch hat Currin zweifellos der Kontrast der schwarzen Handschuhe auf den weissen Brüsten interessiert, aber die behandschuhten Hände verdammen den Zauberer zu einer Berührung ohne Tasterlebnis. Der Zauberer ist zugleich mehr und weniger als ein Mann. Mehr, weil er seine Phantasien zum Leben erwecken kann; weniger, weil er ohne Gesichts- und Tastsinn auf seltsame Weise des Genusses beraubt bleibt. In diesem Sinn kann das Bild als Allegorie des Aktes an sich dienen, denn dasselbe gilt auch für den Künstler: Im Akt kann er zwar jede Phantasie realisieren, sie jedoch nicht geniessen.

(Übersetzung: Susanne Schmidt)

1) John Currin, *Œuvres 1989–1995*, Ausstellungskatalog, FRAC Limousin, Limoges 1995, S. 38. (Das Zitat wurde aus dem Englischen übersetzt.)
2) Ebenda, S. 40.

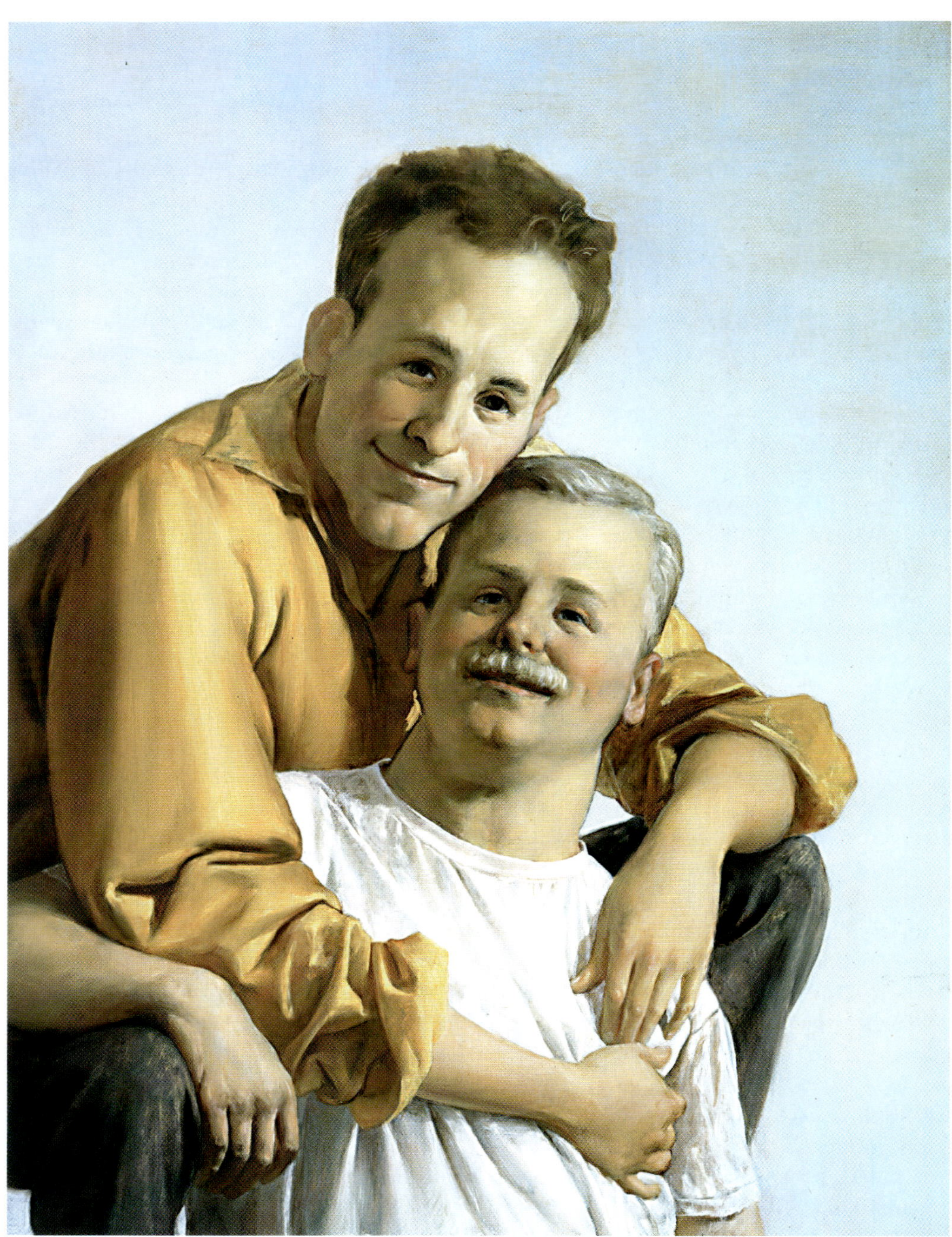

JOHN CURRIN, TWO GUYS, 2002, oil on canvas, 48 x 36" /
PAAR, Öl auf Leinwand, 122 x 91,4 cm. (PHOTO: OREN SLOR)

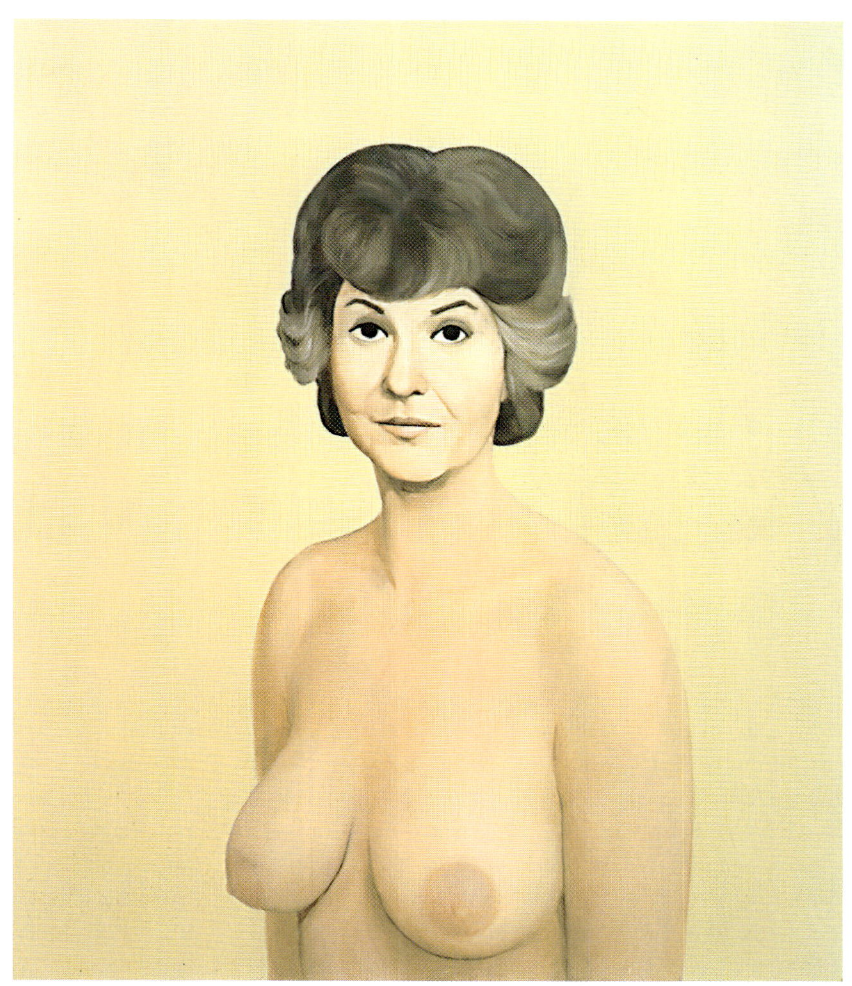

JOHN CURRIN, BEA ARTHUR NAKED, 1991, oil on canvas, 38 x 32" /
BEA ARTHUR, NACKT, Öl auf Leinwand, 96,5 x 81,3 cm. (PHOTO: PETER MUSCATO)

Which is what the Demon was counting on...
the Graces and nymphs, the smooth Madonnas, the tenderly strokable Venuses,
all supposedly finished forever; seem already to
be hovering on the future horizon of the possibilities of painting.

– Paul Valéry[1]

MARK VAN DE WALLE

Against Nature

John Currin is best known as a trafficker in perversity. Much of this reputation is attributable to the fact that he has long specialized in representations, equal parts luscious and louche, of variously unattainable objects of male desire. Some of his women are physically impossible, all Russ Meyer breasts and blond curls and legs that seem to stop just where the cleavage begins. Others are merely inappropriate, postmenopausal Park Avenue doyennes and Connecticut *hausfraus*, either dumpy or rail-thin and stretched to the point of snapping right there in front of you. And still others are just plain untouchable, a combination of art history and fashion model, poses like Botticelli angels and faces like catalog girls (or vice versa). Men show up, too, sometimes, but they are always notoriously lame: old or effeminate or wrong somehow, dressed in ridiculous cravats and polka-dotted shirts and with badly rendered skin. As though they were there specifically to not get the girl.

Early in his career, the simple fact that he was painting people was as weird (if not more weird) as anything else he might have been up to. For some time, figure painting had been a highly suspect activity. It belonged to the commercial realm, turning up in places like the covers of romance novels, where paintings of windswept Fabios and women with heaving bosoms inevitably appeared. Or it belonged to amateurs, people too far out of the stream of fashions in contemporary art to know any better, to know that history had left them behind. That he insisted on making them at all rendered Currin's paintings uncomfortable. There was always the creeping possibility—even the probability, given statements he kept on making to that effect—that he wasn't being ironic, that he really believed in what he was painting, clichés, impossibilities and all, and that all these women really were, one way or another, the objects of some kind of real desire. Later, after he had

MARK VAN DE WALLE has written on art and pop culture for a variety of magazines. He is currently at work on a book about trailer parks and other American nightmares.

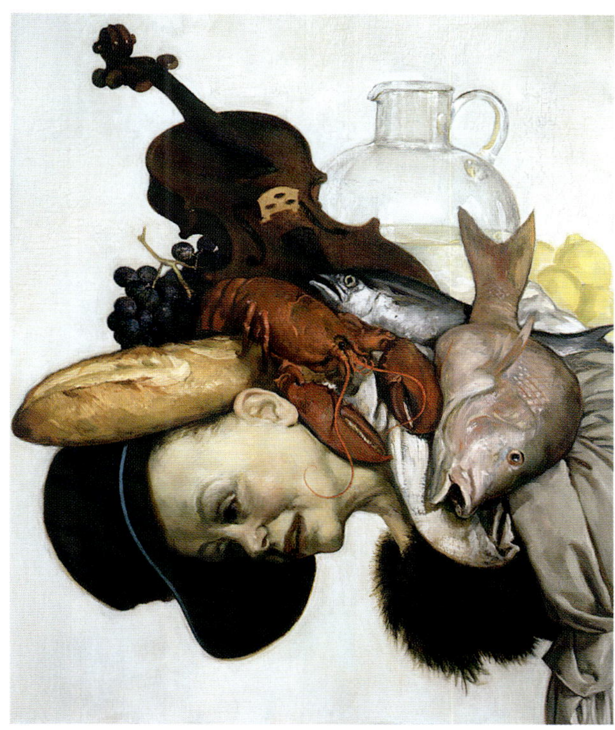

JOHN CURRIN, THE LOBSTER, 2001, oil on canvas, 40 x 32" /
DER HUMMER, Öl auf Leinwand, 101,6 x 81,3 cm.
(PHOTO: OREN SLOR)

helped to spearhead a revival of figure painting, this was the thing that gave the paintings their edge, that made them so hard to look away from. Being beautifully perverse, they were perversely beautiful.

Now though, Currin has abandoned his pin-up girls for something that looks suspiciously straight. The women are still there, and some of them still have impossible anatomies, but they're impossible like figures in a Cranach painting, with bulbous bellies and balloon breasts, golden hair floating against black backgrounds. Or they come with scare quotes hanging in the air around them: charcoal and pastel "sketches" and "life drawings" like pages from a spectacularly gifted art student's book, or an Old Master's study. There are "earthy" Courbet nudes and gardeners, where passages of lush and elegant brushwork alternate with palette-knifed insouciance. The woman in THE LOBSTER (2001) has what looks like a Chardin still life on her back. The light shimmers in a jug of water, caresses the lemon's skin, and the slime on the fish glistens just so. But it wears some-

thing like a cartoon smile; it's somehow not quite natural, like the woman herself.

To give you an idea of what his mindset is like, when I went to Currin's studio, he told me about a recent experience he'd had with a collector. The collector, it seemed, found the spirit of his work infectious, had decided to fly in the face of current fashion and get the painting framed; he wanted John to go with him to help pick out the frame. "So we went uptown," John said, "and into this shop. It was completely old-school, with a tiny, stooped European guy wearing a green eyeshade, running the place. He came out of the back and showed us a bunch of frames. Then, finally, he brought out one from the 1600s. It was totally lush—it was just huge and ornate and the carving was so elaborate. You could slide your finger in behind the leaves and it still had all the original gold on it. He brought out this velvet pillow and set up the painting inside the frame. And it was perfect. It was like it just locked the composition into place." Then he grinned and said "The frame

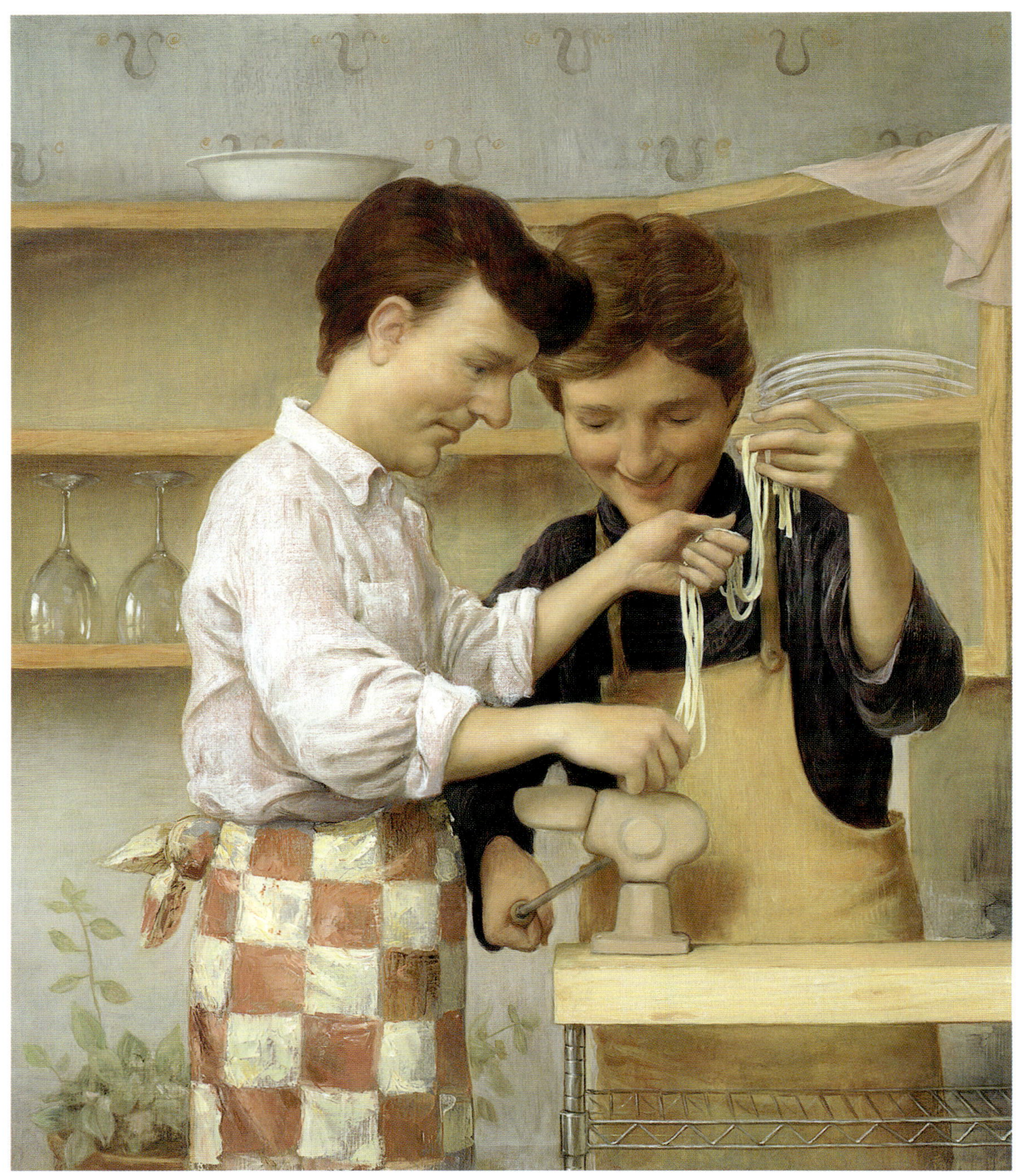

JOHN CURRIN, HOMEMADE PASTA, 1999, oil on canvas, 50 x 42" /
HAUSGEMACHTE NUDELN, Öl auf Leinwand, 127 x 106,7 cm. (PHOTO: FRED SCRUTON)

costs …," he named an astronomically high, five-figure sum. "If I had enough money, I'd put all my paintings in a frame like that," Currin said.

Don't be taken in. This isn't a retreat into irony. He's not after anything as safe as a simple rehearsal of art history. When you hear a story like that, you know what you're witnessing is an artist in the grip of a passion far stranger than any kind of kitsch love you could care to name: Currin has fallen for academic painting. He's found a fetish for technique, for style. And in a way, it's hard to imagine a less fashionable enthusiasm. High and low culture have been shacked up together for so long now that it's hard to think of what kind of junk you'd have to like for it to be shocking. But mannerism has been sneered at for ages; deciding to give yourself over to the pleasures of brushing round, peachy pink flesh and creating archly artificial poses is one of the few truly perverse gestures left. Diderot, as far back as the aftermath of the Salon of 1765, found that kind of impulse morally questionable when he saw it in Boucher's work (one of Currin's early heroes): *I don't know what to say about this man. Degradation of taste, color, composition, character … and drawing have kept pace with moral depravity… What can we expect this artist to throw onto the canvas? What he has in his imagination. And what can be in the imagination of a man who spends his life with prostitutes of the basest kind? There's too much…mannerism and affectation for an austere art.*[2]

Currin has always been one to turn to the basest materials for his lushest pleasures: he mines old magazines, ancient ephemera and other stuff that should, by all rights, already be trash for bits and pieces of inspiration. People have always talked about the debt Currin owes to Vargas, understandably taken in by all those billowy blondes. But Vargas was never actually much of an influence; he's both too good and not quite good enough, operating in an in-between state that doesn't go out far enough. He's mannered but not Mannerist. Instead, in a recent interview with Robert Rosenblum, Currin said that he got his real kicks from Frank Frazetta, the artist who did the covers for hundreds of fantasy and science fiction novels. Specializing in balloon-muscled barbarians (he did all the "good" covers for Robert E. Howard's Conan novels) and women with even more pneumatic physiques and chain-mail bikinis, Frazetta bent flesh and warped nature to suit his needs. All about lushly applied paint and hyped up sex, he was more of a mannerist than Vargas ever was. Catalogues of advertising stock photos are another favorite source. They are, more or less, the most debased form of photography in media. The catalogues come arranged according to subject matter and demographic, so you can shop for "men and women," "moving," "health," or, of course, "gay couples" according to what your pamphlet or too-low-budget-for-a-shoot-ad needs. The gay couple in HOMEMADE PASTA (1999) got their pose from a catalogue of stock photos, which may help account for why their presence is such a weird mix of the generic and the specific. In the studio, I saw an unfinished portrait of an effeminate man in a sheepskin coat—you could practically feel the powder-puff soft texture of the wool—and his fingers curled as though he had plastic instead of bones, as though he shared the anatomy of an Ingres odalisque, bred specifically for unnatural elegance and pleasures. He gets his pose and his clothes from a seventies Sears catalog, although no model there would ever be so swish.

Even though he gets his inspiration from various kinds of low life, none of his paintings come from real life, or from photographs: it's imagined, dreamed up. They inhabit a nature of their own—or rather Currin's own—making. Which is exactly the point. Currin, like the artists whose amorality Diderot decries, isn't interested in an "austere art." Quite the opposite, in fact, since austerity is anathema to pleasure. What you see in his work are "no longer actions unfolding in nature, they're carefully prepared and considered … acted out on the canvas."[3] The kind of painting that he's hooked on is painting against nature. It's not work that's supposed to be good for you, but work that's supposed to feel good. For him, if not for anyone else.

1) Paul Valéry, *Degas, Manet, Morisot*, transl. by David Paul (Princeton, New Jersey: Princeton University Press, Bollingen Series, 1989), p. 80.
2) Denis Diderot, *The Salon of 1765 and Notes on Painting* in *Diderot on Art*, vol. I, transl. by John Goodman (New Haven: Yale University Press, 1995), p. 22.
3) Ibid., p. 222.

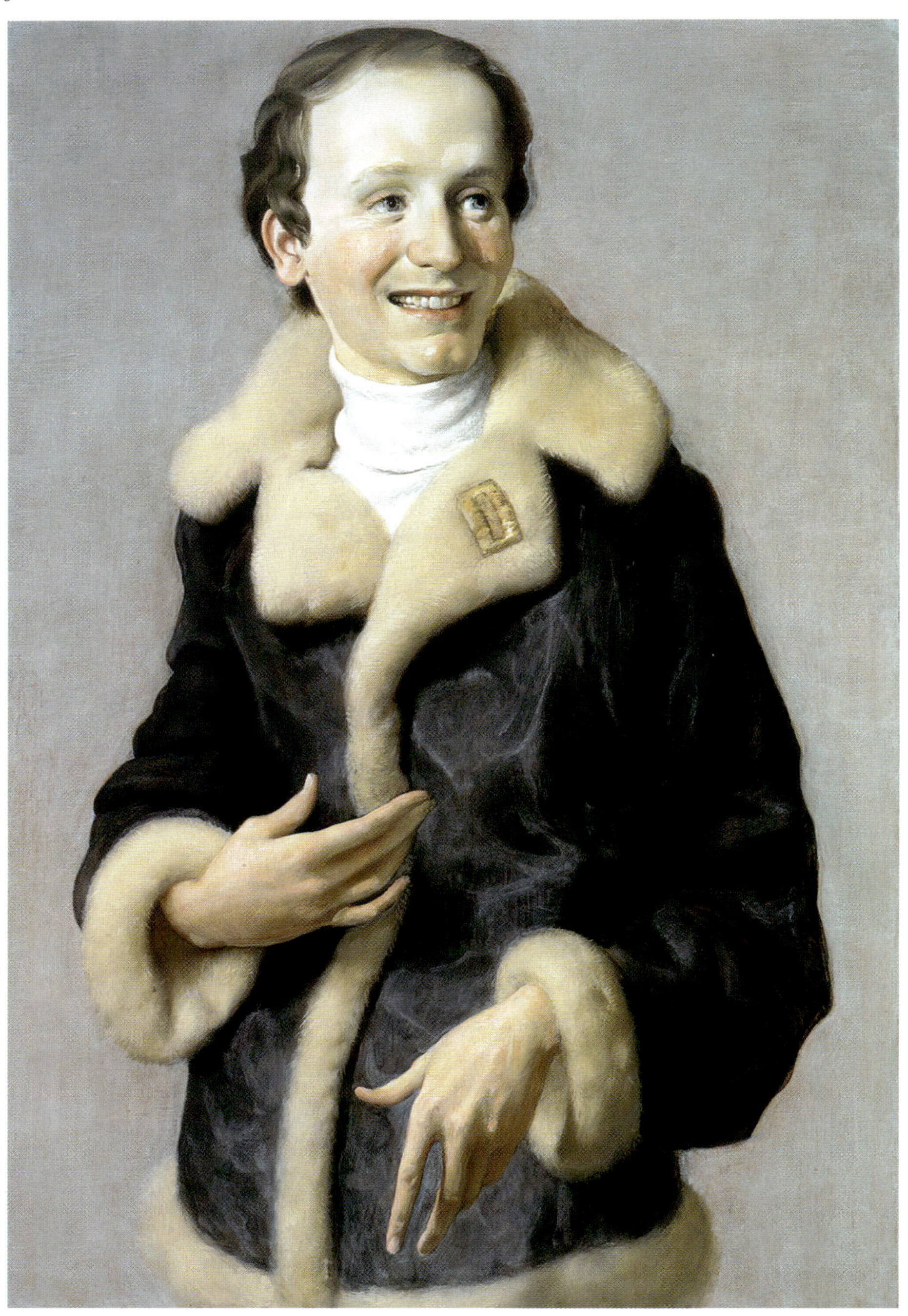

JOHN CURRIN, THE PRODUCER, 2002, oil on canvas, 48 x 32" /
DER PRODUZENT, Öl auf Leinwand, 122 x 81,3 cm. (PHOTO: OREN SLOR)

JOHN CURRIN, THE NEVER-ENDING STORY, 1994, oil on canvas, 38 x 30" /
DIE ENDLOSE GESCHICHTE, Öl auf Leinwand, 96,5 x 76,2 cm. (PHOTO: FRED SCRUTON)

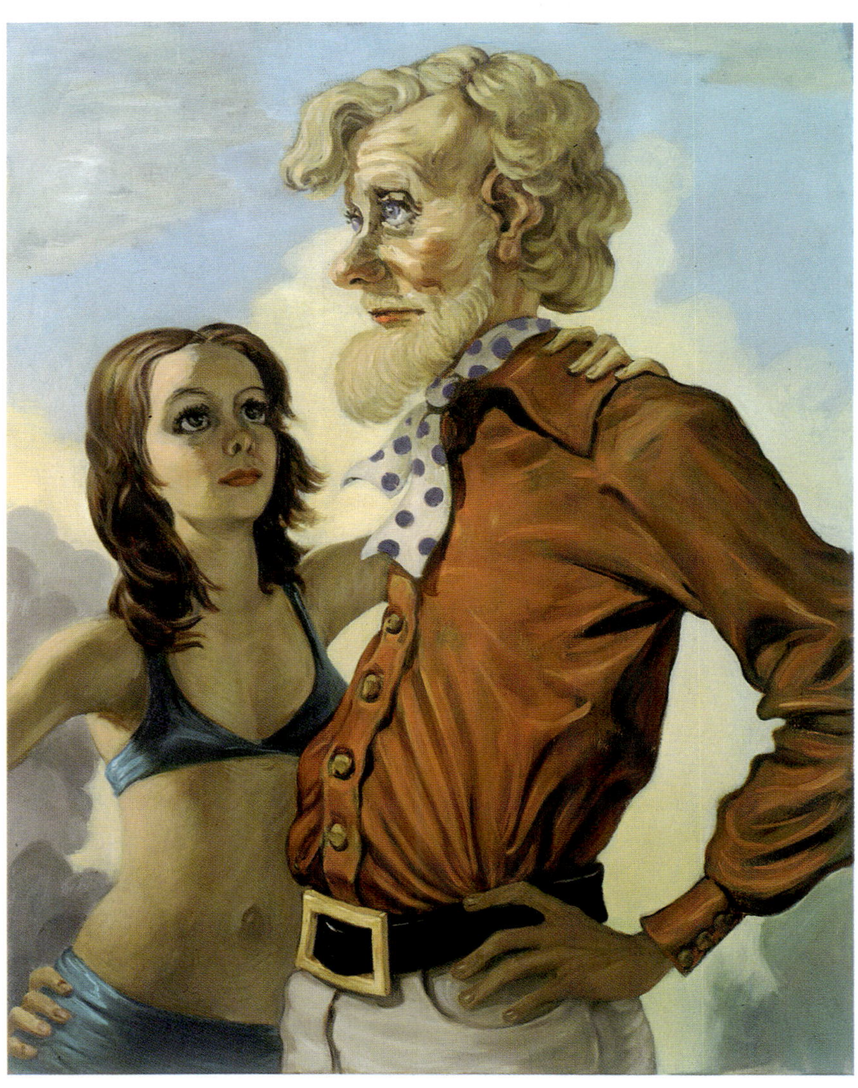

Und gerade damit hatte dieser Dämon gerechnet (…):
die Grazien und die Nymphen, die milden, in Mandelmilch gebadeten Madonnen,
die weich anzufühlenden Aphroditen, die man im Unendlichen glaubte,
scheinen bereits wieder am Horizont des in der Malerei Möglichen aufzutauchen.

– Paul Valéry[1]

MARK VAN DE WALLE

Gegen die Natur

Am bekanntesten ist John Currin als Anbieter von Perversitäten. Diesen Ruf verdankt er zum grossen Teil der Tatsache, dass er sich lange Zeit auf ebenso verlockend wie zweifelhaft wirkende Darstellungen diverser unerreichbarer Objekte männlicher Begierde spezialisiert hat. Einige seiner Frauen sind schiere körperliche Unmöglichkeiten, bestehend aus Russ-Meyer-Brüsten, blonden Locken und Beinen, die etwa dort aufhören, wo die Brüste beginnen. Andere sind einfach ungehörig, postklimakterische Park-Avenue-Fregatten und Hausfrauen aus Connecticut, entweder verfettet oder aber derart klapperdürr und in die Länge gezogen, dass sie auf der Stelle zusammenzuklappen drohen. Andere wiederum sind einfach unantastbar, eine Mischung aus Kunstgeschichte und Modepuppe in Posen von Bot-

MARK VAN DE WALLE hat in verschiedenen Zeitschriften über Kunst und Popkultur geschrieben. Zurzeit arbeitet er an einem Buch über Wohnwagenparks und andere amerikanische Alpträume.

ticelli-Engeln und mit Gesichtern von Models aus dem Katalog (oder umgekehrt). Auch Männer tauchen manchmal auf, aber immer nur als entsetzlich lahme Figuren: alt oder verweichlicht oder sonst irgendwie verquer, mit lächerlichen Krawatten, getupften Hemden und übel aussehender Haut. Als wären sie nur dazu da, das Mädchen nicht zu kriegen.

Am Anfang seiner Karriere war allein schon die Tatsache, dass er Menschen malte, mindestens so verstörend wie alles andere, was er sonst noch anstellen mochte (wenn nicht sogar noch verstörender). Die figürliche Malerei galt damals schon geraume Zeit als höchst suspekt. Sie gehörte ins Reich des Kommerzes und an Orte, wie auf Buchumschläge von Kitschromanen, auf denen unweigerlich vom Wind zerzauste Fabios und Frauen mit bebenden Brüsten abgebildet waren. Oder sie war die Sache von Dilettanten, die zu weit vom Zentrum des aktuellen Kunstgeschehens entfernt waren, um es besser zu wissen und sich darüber im Klaren zu sein, dass sie längst von der Geschichte überholt worden waren. Allein

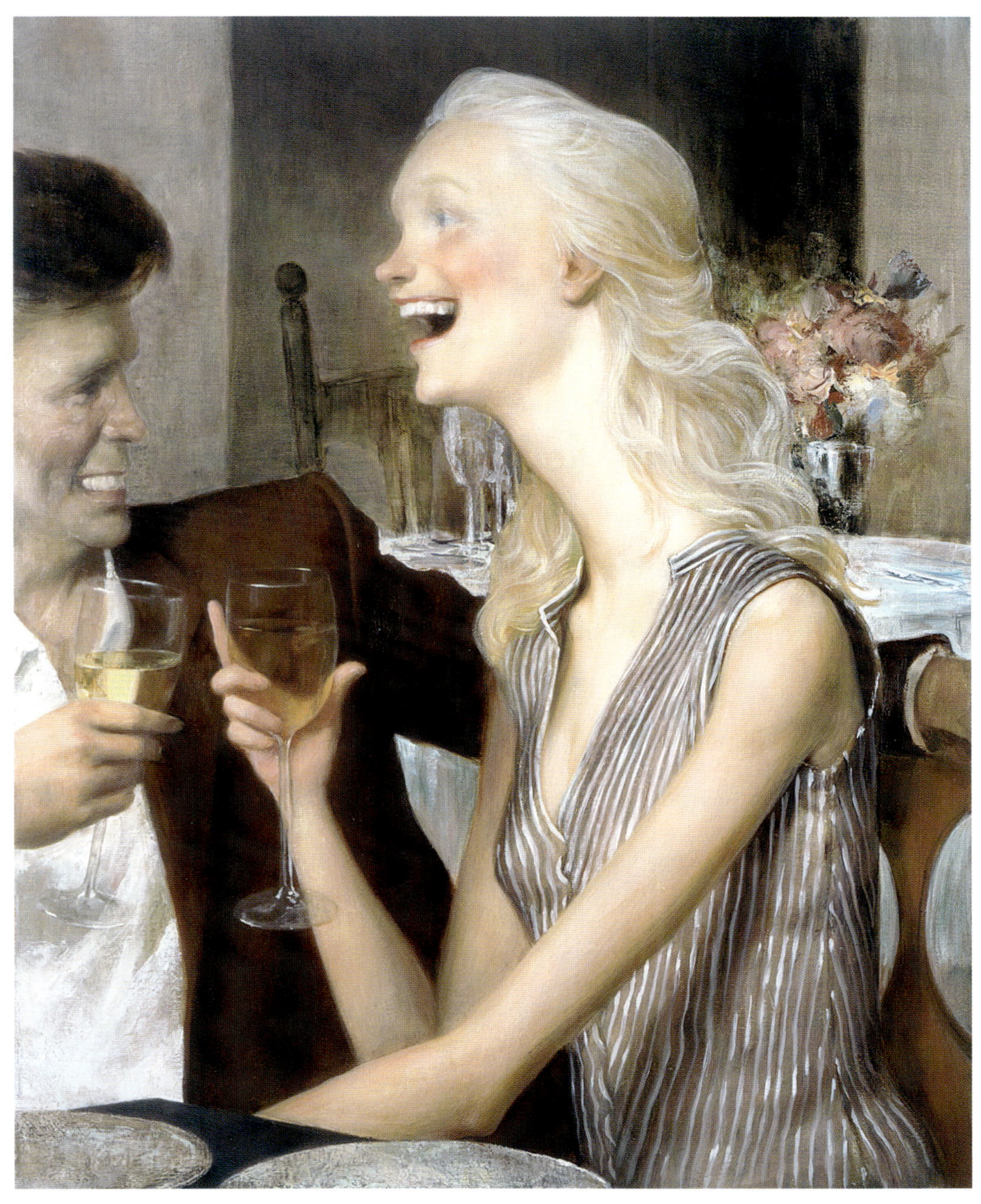

JOHN CURRIN, PARK CITY GRILL, 2000, oil on canvas, 38 x 30" /
Öl auf Leinwand, 96,5 x 76,2 cm. (PHOTO: ANDY KEATE)

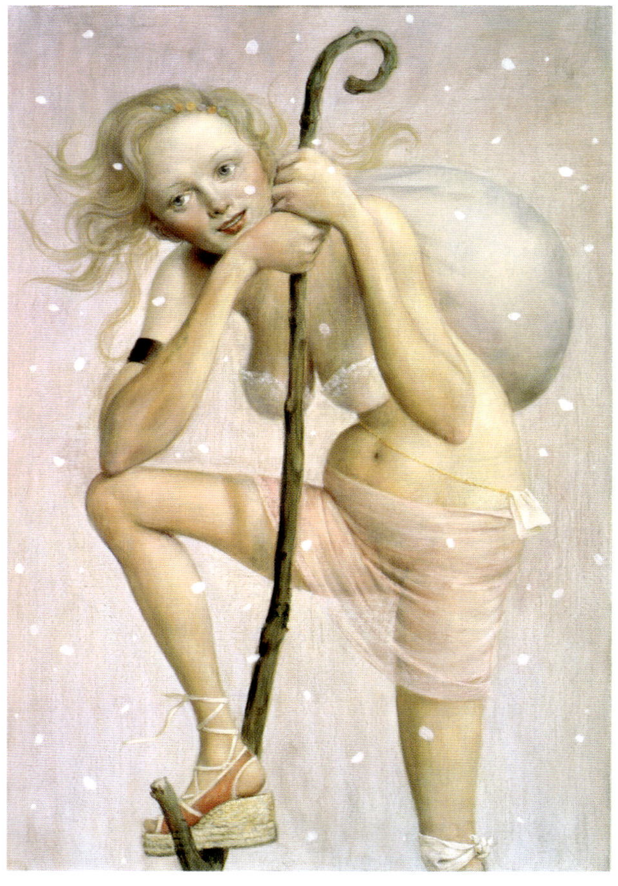

JOHN CURRIN, SNO-BO, 1999, oil on canvas, 48 x 32" /
SCHNEEGAMMLERIN, Öl auf Leinwand, 122 x 81,3 cm.
(PHOTO: FRED SCRUTON)

schon, dass Currin darauf bestand, diese Bilder zu malen, machte sie unbequem. Da lauerte immer die Möglichkeit – einigen wiederholt gemachten Äusserungen des Künstlers zufolge sogar die Wahrscheinlichkeit –, dass sie nicht ironisch gemeint waren; dass er wirklich an das glaubte, was er malte, einschliesslich aller Klischees und Unmöglichkeiten; und dass diese Frauen wirklich auf irgendeine Weise Objekte eines realen Begehrens waren. Später, nachdem er beim erneuten Aufleben der figürlichen Malerei massgeblich mitgewirkt hatte, war es genau dies, was seine Bilder ausmachte, was es einem so schwer machte, den Blick von ihnen zu lösen. Sie waren so schön pervers, dass sie auf perverse Weise schön waren.

Mittlerweile hat Currin jedoch seine Pin-up-Girls zugunsten von etwas aufgegeben, was geradezu verdächtig normal wirkt. Die Frauen sind zwar noch da, und manche haben noch immer eine unmögliche Anatomie, aber sie sind unmöglich wie in einem Gemälde von Cranach, mit gewölbten Bäuchen, Ballonbrüsten und golden sich kringelndem Haar vor schwarzen Hintergründen. Oder sie kommen in Begleitung Schreck einflössender Zitate daher, welche um sie herum in der Luft hängen: Kohle- und Pastell-«Skizzen» und «Studien nach dem Leben» wie Seiten aus dem Skizzenbuch eines hoch begabten Schülers oder Altmeisterstudien. Es gibt «erdige» Courbet-Akte und -Gärtner, in denen üppig elegante Pinselstriche mit sorglos hingespachtelten Stellen abwechseln. Die Frau in THE LOBSTER (Der Hummer, 2001) trägt auf dem Rücken etwas, was aussieht wie ein Stillleben von Chardin. Das Licht schimmert in einem Wasserkrug, liebkost die Schale einer Zitrone, und die feuchte Fischhaut glitzert nur so. Aber das Ganze hat etwas von einem Cartoon-

Lächeln; es wirkt wie die Frau selbst irgendwie nicht ganz natürlich.

Nur um eine Vorstellung davon zu vermitteln, wie dieser Künstler denkt: Als ich ihn in seinem Atelier aufsuchte, erzählte er mir ein Erlebnis, das er kürzlich mit einem Sammler hatte. Der Sammler liess sich, wie es scheint, vom Geist seines Werkes anstecken und hatte sich entschlossen sein Bild entgegen dem aktuellen Trend rahmen zu lassen; er wollte, dass John ihm bei der Wahl des Rahmens behilflich wäre. «Also gingen wir uptown in diesen Laden. Es war ein Geschäft nach alter Schule, geführt von einem winzigen, buckligen Europäer, der einen grünen Augenschirm trug. Er kam aus dem Hinterzimmer und zeigte uns einige Rahmen. Schliesslich brachte er einen aus der Zeit um sechzehnhundert. Er war die Üppigkeit selbst – riesig und mit raffinierten Schnitzereien verziert. Man konnte mit dem Finger hinter die Blattornamente fassen und die ganze Originalvergoldung war noch dran. Er zog sein Samtkissen hervor und steckte das Bild in den Rahmen. Perfekt. Es war, als würde die ganze Komposition dadurch erst ins rechte Licht gerückt. Dann grinste er und sagte ‹Der Rahmen kostet...›, er nannte eine astronomisch hohe fünfstellige Zahl. – Wenn ich genügend Geld hätte, würde ich all meine Bilder in solche Rahmen stecken.»

Aber lassen Sie sich nicht täuschen. Dies ist keine ironische List. Es geht Currin nicht um etwas so Narrensicheres wie eine einfache Rekapitulation der Kunstgeschichte. Wenn man eine solche Geschichte hört, weiss man, dass man einen Künstler in den Fängen einer Leidenschaft vor sich hat, die viel merkwürdiger ist als jede denkbare Art von Kitschverliebtheit. Er ist technik- und stilbesessen. Und eigentlich lässt sich kaum eine Begeisterung ausdenken, die weniger im Trend läge. Hohe und populäre Kultur gehen schon so lange Hand in Hand, dass es schwer fallen dürfte, überhaupt noch einen Schmonzes aufzutreiben, dessen Ernennung zum Objekt des Begehrens noch jemanden zu schockieren vermöchte.

Über den Manierismus jedoch rümpft man die Nase seit Jahrhunderten; die Entscheidung, sich den Freuden des Pinselns von üppigem, pfirsichrotem Fleisch hinzugeben und krude artifizielle Posen zu kreieren, ist eine der wenigen echt perversen Gebärden, die noch möglich sind. Diderot fand diesen Impuls schon vor langer Zeit – nach dem Salon von 1765 – moralisch anstössig, als er ihm bei Boucher – einem von Currins frühen Vorbildern – begegnete: *Ich weiss nicht, was ich über diesen Mann sagen soll. Der Verfall des Geschmacks, der Farbe, der Komposition, der Charaktere, des Ausdrucks und der Zeichnung folgte Schritt für Schritt der Verderbung der Sitten. Was kann dieser Künstler schon auf die Leinwand werfen? Nur das, was er in seiner Einbildungskraft vorfindet. Was aber kann ein Mann, der sein Leben mit den niedrigsten Prostituierten verbringt, in seiner Einbildungskraft vorfinden? (...) Da sind zu viele Larven, zu viel Manier, zu viel Geziertheit für ernste Kunst.*[2]

Currin war schon immer einer, der für seine üppigsten Freuden die billigsten Materialien heranzog: Er durchstöbert alte Zeitschriften, uralten Krimskrams und anderes Zeugs, das von Rechts wegen als Inspirationsquelle längst ausgedient hat und auf dem Abfall gelandet sein sollte. Die Leute haben immer davon geredet, was Currin Vargas verdanke, begreiflich, da sie sich von all den kurvenreichen Blondinen blenden liessen. Tatsächlich aber übte Vargas nie einen wirklich grossen Einfluss aus; er ist gleichzeitig zu gut und nicht ganz gut genug, weil er in einem Zwischenbereich arbeitet, der nicht weit genug reicht. Er ist maniriert, aber nicht manieristisch. In einem neueren Interview mit Robert Rosenblum meinte Currin jedoch, dass er seine grössten Kicks von Frank Frazetta bezogen habe, jenem Künstler, der die Buchumschläge für Hunderte von Fantasy- und Sciencefictionromanen gestaltet hat. Spezialisiert auf Barbaren mit Ballonmuskeln (er machte all die «guten» Umschläge für Robert E.Howards *Conan, der Barbar*, und dessen Fortsetzungen) und auf Frauen mit noch üppiger schwellenden Körpern und Kettenhemd-Bikinis formte Frazetta das Fleisch und verzerrte die Natur nach Bedarf. In Sachen üppigem Farbauftrag und übertriebenen Geschlechtsmerkmalen war er weit manieristischer, als es Vargas je war. Kataloge mit Werbephotographien sind eine weitere Lieblingsquelle Currins. Das ist mehr oder weniger die niedrigste Form von Photographie in den Medien. Solche Kataloge sind nach Themen und demographischen Kriterien geordnet. Man sucht darin

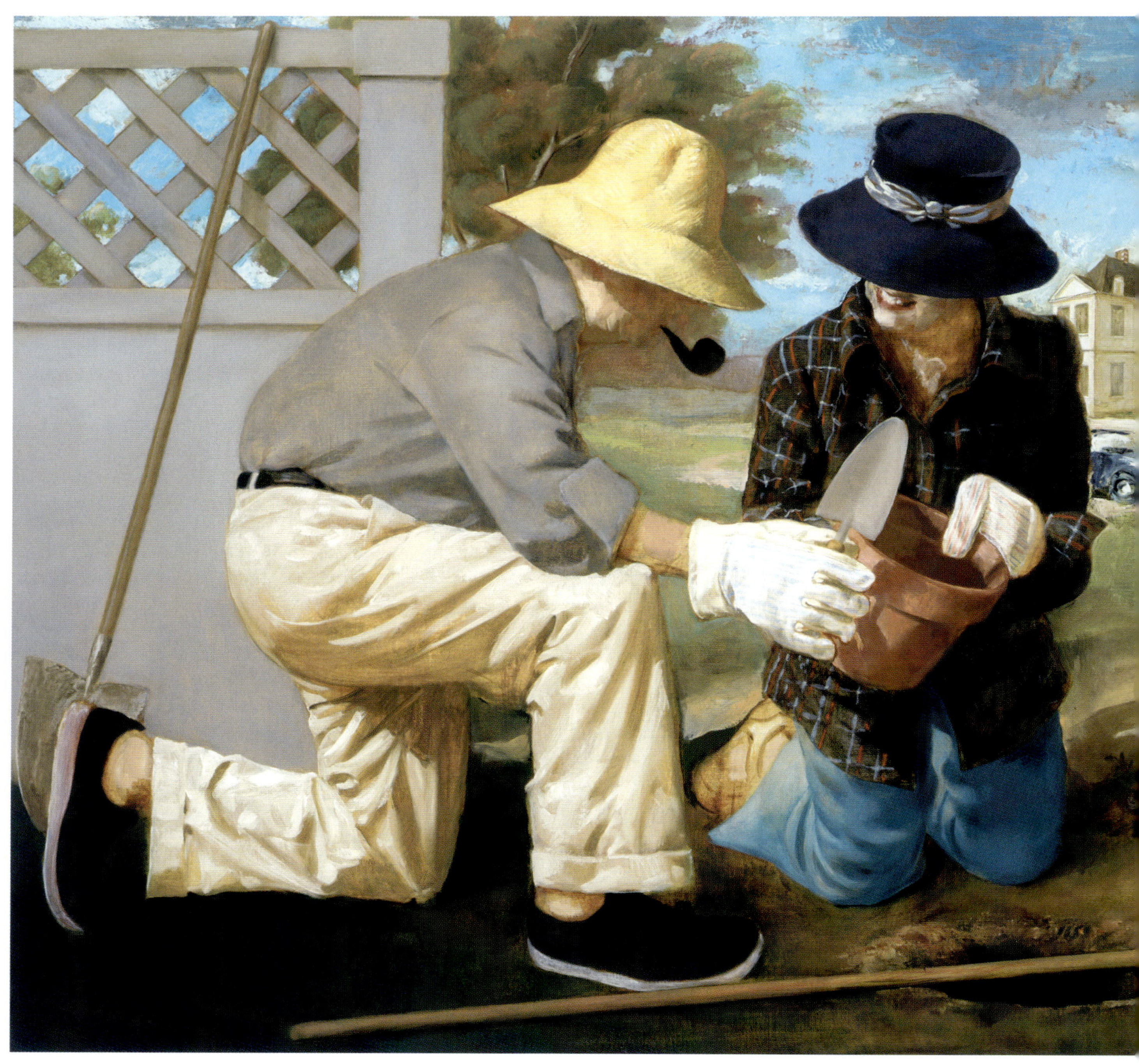

JOHN CURRIN, THE GARDENERS, 2001, oil on canvas, 52 x 75" / DIE GÄRTNER, Öl auf Leinwand, 132 x 190,5 cm. (PHOTO: OREN SLOR)

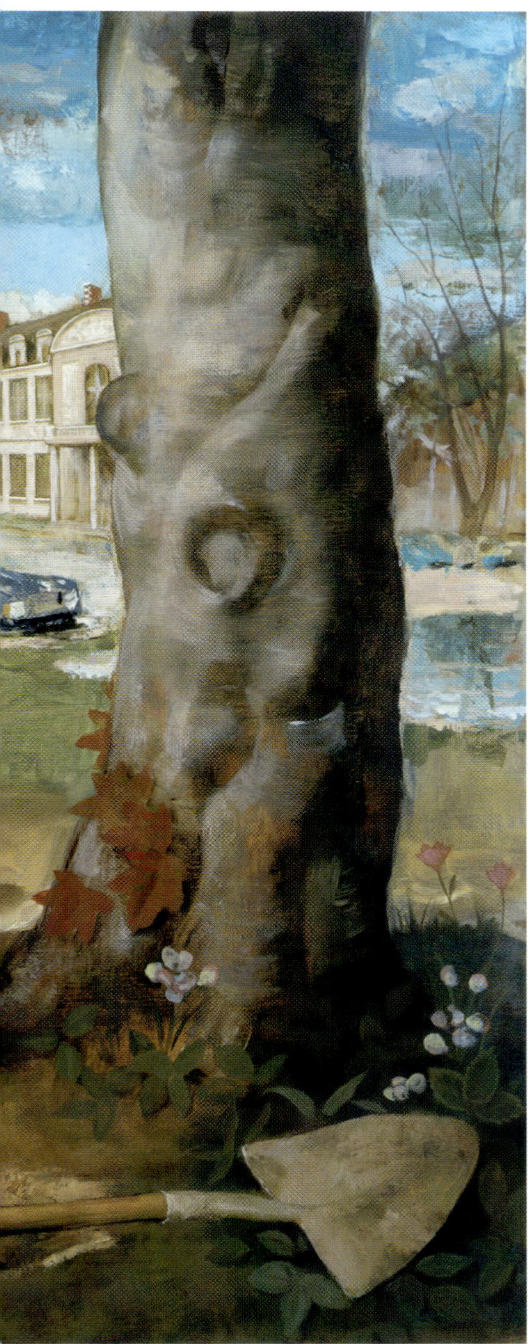

unter «Männer und Frauen», «Anrührendes», «Gesundheit», oder, natürlich, «Schwule Paare», je nachdem, was das geplante Pamphlet oder die Billiganzeige verlangt. Das schwule Paar in HOMEMADE PASTA (Hausgemachte Nudeln, 1999) verdankt seine Pose einem solchen Katalog pfannenfertiger Photos, was mit erklären mag, woher dieses seltsame Durcheinander von Allgemeinem und Besonderem kommt. In Currins Atelier sah ich ein unvollendetes Porträt eines weiblich wirkenden Mannes in einem Schaffellmantel – man konnte die puderquastenartige Weichheit der Wolle förmlich spüren –, seine Finger krümmten sich, als wäre das Skelett aus Gummi, als hätte er den Körper einer Odaliske von Ingres, die allein um einer widernatürlichen Eleganz und Lustbefriedigung willen entstanden ist. Seine Pose und seine Kleider stammen aus einem Sears-Katalog aus den 70er Jahren, obwohl darin natürlich keine derart halbseidenen Models zu finden sind.

Zwar lässt sich Currin von verschiedenen Halbweltsituationen inspirieren, aber keines seiner Bilder ist direkt dem wirklichen Leben oder einer Photographie entnommen: Es ist alles phantasiert, erträumt. Sie alle sind Teil einer eigenen, selbst erschaffenen – bzw. von Currin erschaffenen – Natur. Und das ist der springende Punkt. Wie die Künstler, deren Amoralität Diderot beklagt, ist Currin nicht an einer «ernsten Kunst» interessiert. Ganz im Gegenteil, ist doch das Ernste aller Lust abhold. Was man in seinen Bildern sieht, «ist nicht mehr eine Handlung, die sich in der Natur abspielt, sondern eine zurechtgemachte, abgezirkelte Handlung, die sich nur auf der Leinwand abspielt».[3] Die Malerei, um die es ihm geht, ist eine Malerei gegen die Natur. Es sind keine Bilder, die uns gut tun sollen, sondern Bilder, die sich gut anfühlen. Wenn nicht für jedermann, so doch für ihn selbst.

(Übersetzung: Wilma Parker)

1) Paul Valéry, «Tanz, Zeichnung und Degas», übers. v. Werner Zemp, in: Valéry, *Werke*, Frankfurter Ausgabe, Bd. 6, hg. v. Jürgen Schmidt-Radefeldt, Insel Verlag, Frankfurt am Main 1995, S. 337.
2) Denis Diderot, *Aus dem «Salon von 1765»*, in: Diderot, *Ästhetische Schriften*, Bd. I, hg. v. Friedrich Bassenge, Aufbau Verlag, Berlin und Weimar 1967, S. 527 und 528.
3) Denis Diderot, «Versuch über die Malerei», op. cit., S. 672.

John Currin

Viele bunte Bilder, darauf:

SIBYLLE BERG

Männer, die alt werden. Die fette Leiber haben, mehrere Kinne, die sich die Haare färben, oder die Haare, die sie noch haben, über die Glatze legen, die aus ihren Büros kommen oder vom Autoverkauf oder die arbeitslos sind, die nicht mehr ficken können, die vierzig sind und älter, die keine Frau gefunden haben, nie mehr eine haben werden, die, wenn sie eine Frau haben, die Frau nicht lieben, nie geliebt haben, die ausgebeulte Hosen tragen, oder Anzüge, die über dem Bauch spannen, die gelbe Füsse haben, die in Slippern stecken, die essen, viel essen und trinken, weil es dann für Sekunden verschwindet, das Gefühl, das sie nicht benennen können, weil sie doch Männer sind, die Angst haben, weil sie wissen, dass das Leben kein Wunder mehr für sie bereithält. Die betrogen wurden, aber worum, das könnten sie nicht sagen.

Da bin ich also umgefallen. Einfach so, wie man einen Fernseher ausschaltet. Am Rande der Strasse. Man schaltet ja gerne mal an Fernsehern herum. Auf dem Weg nach Hause wurden mir die Beine müde, waren so gelangweilt, die Beine, dass sie sich einfach ergaben. Bumm. Liegen. Liegen und warten. Nur nicht weinen jetzt.
Es schneit nicht.
Wie das ist. Das Weinen, ohne dass es wer sieht und bedauert.
Kein Reif.
Keinen gefunden, der mich liebt.
Das ist, was übrig bleibt.

Der Anfang ist schnell vorbei.

Der Anfang besteht aus Demütigung. Missbraucht, geschlagen, ignoriert, eingesperrt, zum Schweigen gebracht, überfüttert, unterfüttert, kalt oder zu heiss und keine Macht. Nicht über deinen Stuhlgang und deine Gefühle, gar nicht.

Du bist Kind und wartest. Wartest, und es tickt immer eine Uhr und immer ist Sonntag und immer sind sie dir fremd, die Personen, aus denen du entstanden, immer nicht du. Und sie mögen

---

SIBYLLE BERG ist Schriftstellerin und lebt in Zürich. Sie hat unter anderem die Romane *Amerika* (1999) und *Gold* (2000, beide Hoffmann und Campe, München) veröffentlicht.

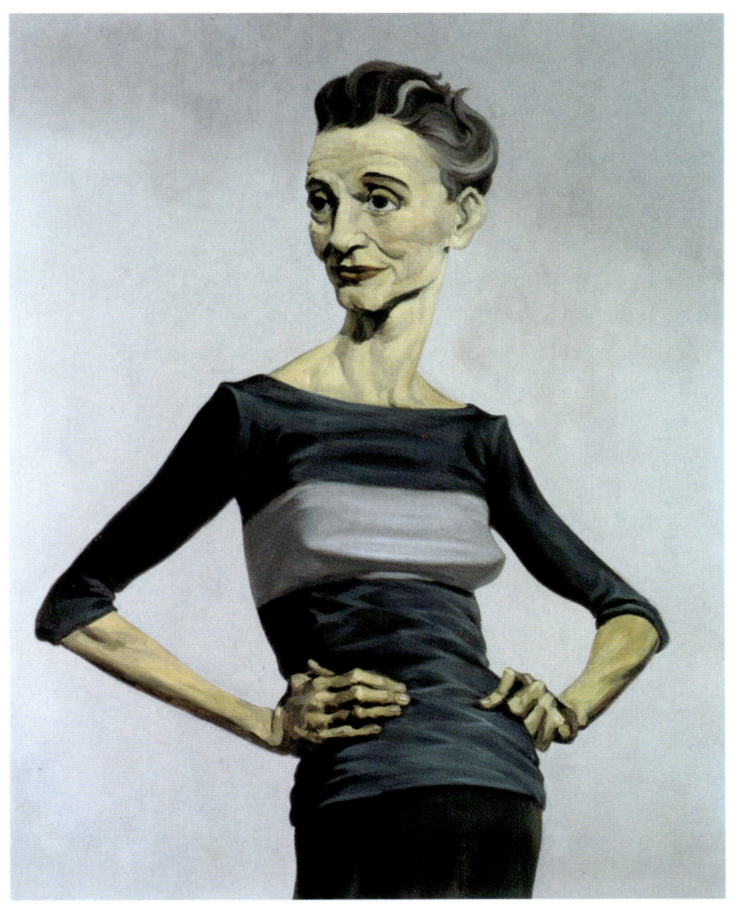

sich nicht, ihr Leben nicht, dich nicht. Glückliche Kindheit gibt es nicht, wie sollst du glücklich sein in Willenlosigkeit und dir fremd. Überall Dinge, vor denen du Angst hast, und noch nicht einmal das Wort dazu. Tiere und andere Kinder, die dich schlagen, dir auflauern, Schatten in der Nacht, Geräusche im Haus, die Gesichter deiner Eltern in unbeobachteten Momenten.

Und du stehst am Fenster und schaust auf Häuser und bist verzweifelt, weil du weisst, dass das, worauf du hoffst, in so einem Haus stattfinden wird und aus keinem kommt Lachen.

Danach –

Ein paar Jahre, in denen ich nicht auf den Tod gewartet habe. Waren die besten. Im Körper eines Menschen, mit dem Verstand eines Kindes.

Es ist kalt. Es schneit nicht. Ich bin dunkel.

Die Einsamkeit beginnt, wo wir anfangen. Eine Zeit lang torkeln wir doof durch die Welt, Kindheit ist das, da Hirn und Gefühl sich nicht recht verständigen. Die finden erst in der Pubertät wieder zusammen. In der Zeit, in der die meisten die erste Liebe erleben. Welche die romantischste ist, weil sie nur aus Illusion besteht. Die nichts will ausser Auflösung. Ein Mädchen, und ich wollte sie und wusste nicht, was ich mit ihr wollte, ausser nie mehr alleine sein. Stand an offenen Fenstern und draussen Frühling und an den Wänden *Kiss*-Poster und was ich über Liebe wusste ging so: Mit ihr auf einer Insel sein und sie ansehen, Tag und Nacht, und ihre Brust berühren. Tag und Nacht. So Traum wie damals, als ich noch nicht wusste, was Liebe ist, wird Liebe nie mehr, nie mehr würde ich so unendlich sein. Ahnte ich.

Es wird nicht dunkel. Am Rande der Strasse, und warum keiner hier läuft?

Der Rest ist schnell vergangen, ist schnell erzählt, ist niemals ein Wunder, ist Warten und Wiederholung, die du mitmachst, weil du glaubst, es käme noch etwas. Das, was einem versprochen wird, das käme noch, in den Jahren nach der Jugend. Doch sie machen falsche Versprechungen. Das ist das Spiel. Jeder verspricht jedem etwas, eingelöst wird nichts. Versprechen von ewiger Liebe, ewigem Leben, und so wird gelogen, von Spass in fernen Ländern mit schönen Frauen und Männern in bunten Badeanzügen mit Softdrinks und eleganten PKWs, und dass es sei, wie eine Party. Das Leben. Das sagen sie dir, zeigen es dir, und du wirst noch nicht einmal misstrauisch, wenn du beginnst auf Partys zu gehen und in der Ecke stehst, dir die Augen tränen, der Hals schmerzt, weil du so viel rauchst und trinkst aus Enttäuschung, dass Partys so etwas Langweiliges sind und keiner mit dir spricht und nichts. Und das Problem bei dem Leben nach der Jugend ist doch, dass du denkst, du wüsstest, wie sich alles anfühlen müsste, und danach suchst und es nie finden wirst, weil Ideen immer besser sind als Wahrheiten.

Du bist nicht mehr jung und noch nicht alt und das ist die längste Zeit, die du verbringst, und ohne es zu merken, sagen Menschen SIE zu DIR. Dann habe ich begonnen zu arbeiten. Habe gedacht, das würde ein Gefühl machen. Es ist immer ein Gefühl da gewesen. Es war wie Hunger und nicht wissen worauf.

Die Arbeit.

War jeden Morgen aufstehen. Viel zu früh, und immer zu kalt, der Wecker, der klingelte, der Kaffee am Küchentisch und weinen mögen und nicht wissen warum.

War nur Angst vor dem Zuspätkommen, vor dem Nichtgenügen, vor dem Gespräch mit dem Chef, dem Tragen falscher Trikotage, dem Sagen falscher Antworten, dem Ticken der Uhr und dem Warten auf den Sonntag, und das Nicht-wissen-was-Tun, und warten auf den Montag und nicht wissen warum, denn der Montag war Angst. War müdes Gehen zur vollen U-Bahn, war das Betreten eines Gebäudes, das falsch roch, und das Grüssen von Menschen, die nie nah waren, es war: entlassen werden, als ich zu alt war.

Ich, das steht mal fest, war mir nie ein Freund.

Ich habe keinen gefunden, der mich liebt. Die Liebe gab es nur in den Nächten, bevor ich mit dem Menschen war, den ich mir ausgesucht hatte. Der mich unglücklich machen sollte.

Lag ich in der Nacht, die vor der Liebe immer hell war, und habe gedacht: Wie ich ihn halten wollte, den Menschen, meinen Menschen, unter der Bettdecke mit kleinen Tieren spielen. Und singen wollte ich dem Menschen, bis er lacht, und lachen wollte ich mit ihm, bis wir aus dem Bett fielen, ihn wecken in der Nacht, wenn der erste Schnee fällt, und rauslaufen und dann ihn halten, bis ihm warm würde. Ich wollte alle Wege mit ihm gehen, die ich in meiner Einsamkeit gegangen bin, und die Wege wären neu. Ich wollte ihn füttern mit Kartoffelbrei und auf kalten Feldern laufen, nicht reden, weil das Gesicht gefroren, und heim ins Bett und unter der Bettdecke mit kleinen Tieren spielen. Ich wollte den Menschen in der Nacht an-

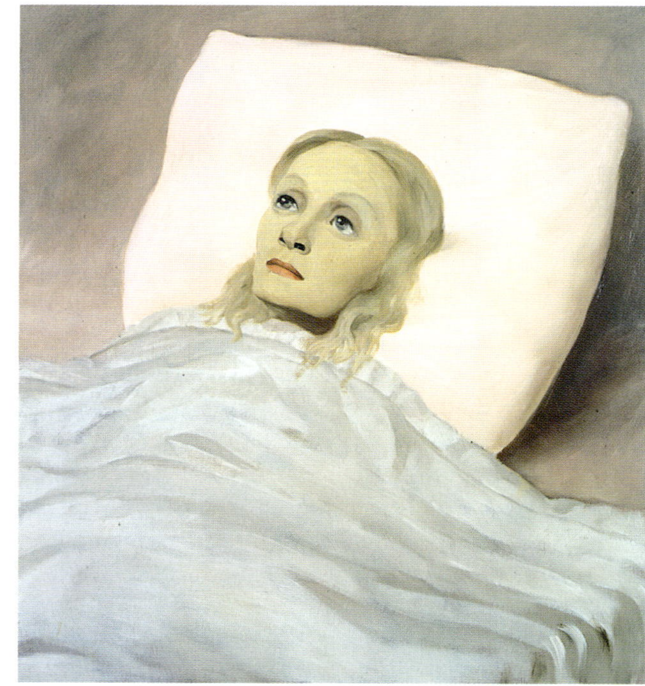

sehen, nie mehr schlafen, satt sein nur vom Betrachten seiner Arme, wollte ihm die Tränen essen, sagen: Du musst nicht mehr weinen, ich muss nicht mehr weinen, weil wir doch nicht mehr allein sind. Wollte Sandburgen bauen. Ihm aus Büchern lesen und die Fingerspitzen küssen, alle hundert nacheinander. Das dachte ich in den Nächten mit der Idee einer Person und war so aufgeregt, wie ein Geschenk erhalten, war es mir.
Und dann kam der Mensch, er war aus Fleisch und eigenen Gedanken und wurde meiner für eine Zeit, und nie fühlte es sich so an, wie in den Nächten, da ich träumte.
Er war nur Schweigen und Haut, die kalt war und mir fremd, und Gedanken, die ich nicht verstand, und Feindschaft von beiden, von mir und ihm, weil es sich für uns beide so anders anfühlte als die Idee. Und dann war das Schweigen zu gross, irgendwann, der Geruch zu schlecht, und dann ging ich oder der andere, es ist egal.
Es tat weh eine Zeit lang, so eine tote Idee ist schon nicht lustig, bis ich mich wieder ablenkte und von einem Menschen träumte, der mich retten würde. Hat nie einen gegeben.
Und kein Trost, in der Zeit nach der Liebe zu leben, allein sind wir alle und suchen nach wem nur, der uns liebt, und werden niemanden finden, keinen. Denn auf jeden, der sucht, kommt einer, der gesucht wird, und ich wollte ja auch keinen lieben, der mich wollte. Nie.
Bitte geh nicht, haben sie gesagt, die falschen Menschen und ich bin gegangen, habe gedacht, ich muss aber mal los, denn der richtige Mensch wartet da draussen auf mich. Niemand hat gewartet. Die Liebe sass in meiner Wohnung und ich habe die Tür geschlossen.
Weniger fand ich und jünger wurden sie nicht, ich schon, dachte ich und konnte mit ihrem alten Fleisch nicht umgehen, weil es mich an das erinnerte, was kommen musste.

Es wird nicht kalt. Am Rande der Strasse. Und in den Häusern gehen Lichter an. In den Häusern, hör nur: Sie schreien sich an, sie trinken und schlagen sich, schlagen die Kinder, ficken die Kinder, ficken sich, schlagen sich, sie schweigen und weinen, weil sie so traurig sind, weil sie scheitern, weil sie sehen, dass ihr schönes Leben nichts taugt, weil sie ahnen, dass es nicht besser wird, sondern schlechter und doch nicht wissen, was zu tun wäre. Und nie ist der Mensch, den sie haben, die Rettung, ist immer nur ein Mensch und nie der, den sie wirklich lieben könnten, aber ehrlich, einfach Pech gehabt, und geben ihm die Schuld, sie sagen: Ich hasse, wie du isst, wie du läufst, wie du riechst, und meinen sich damit, die Enttäuschung damit, wenn sie langsam begreifen.

Der Tag, als ich mich in einem Spiegel sah, als ich nicht mit mir in einem Spiegel rechnete. Einen unattraktiven Mann sah, mit Übergewicht und einem glänzenden Schädel, als mir klar wurde: Auf etwas Grosses zu warten ist Zeitverschwendung. Der Tag, als ich zu trinken begann und Würste mit in mein Bett nahm, einfach damit sie da waren, wenn ich erwachte, der Tag, als ich Krebs bekam und merkte, dass ich keine Freunde hatte, als mir klar wurde, dass ich ein Verlierer war, der Tag, als ich ahnte, dass nichts mehr folgen würde, als mir klar wurde, dass ich nicht wusste, wie ich die restliche Zeit mit was füllen sollte.

Schau, wie ich jetzt hier liege. Schau, wie ich keinen habe, der noch einmal mich berührt im Herzen, eingerollt in meine Arme, aber betrügen geht nicht, es sind meine Arme, die meine Beine halten.
Habe keine Angst, bin nicht traurig. Doch nach Hause schaffe ich es nicht mehr.
Zu müde.
Und nun, nun beginnt es zu schneien und ich habe keinen gefunden und dunkel wird es.

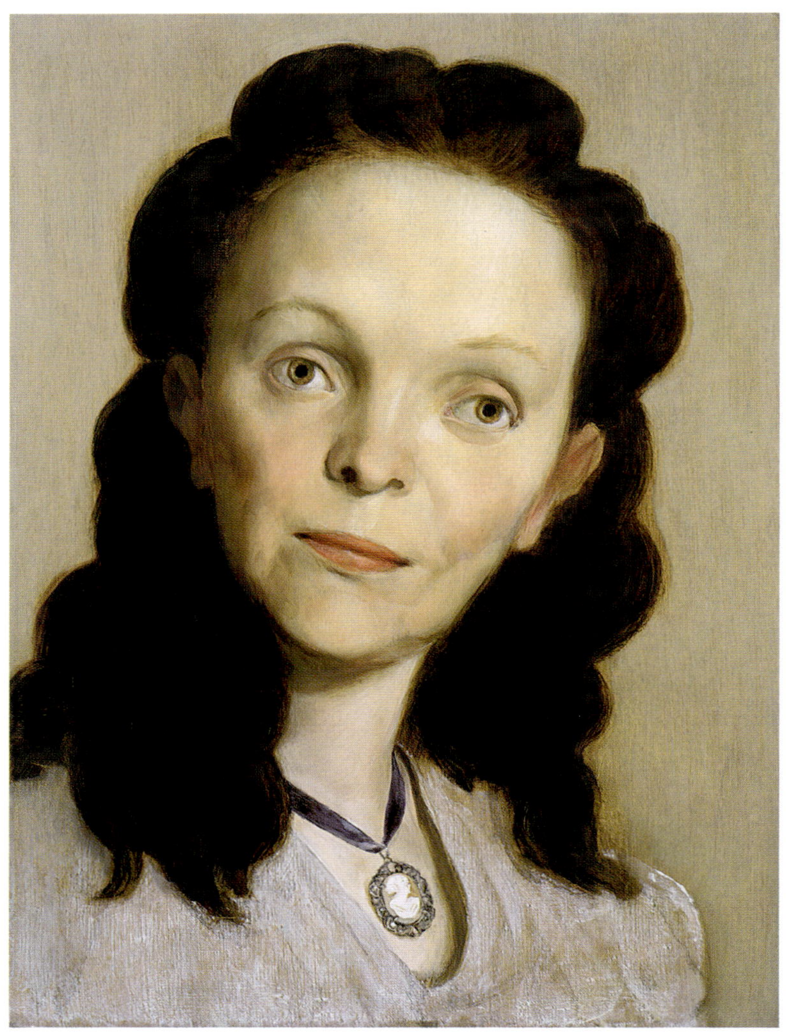

JOHN CURRIN, ANGELA, 2001, *oil on canvas, 22 x 16" /*
Öl auf Leinwand, 56 x 40,6 cm. (PHOTO: OREN SLOR)

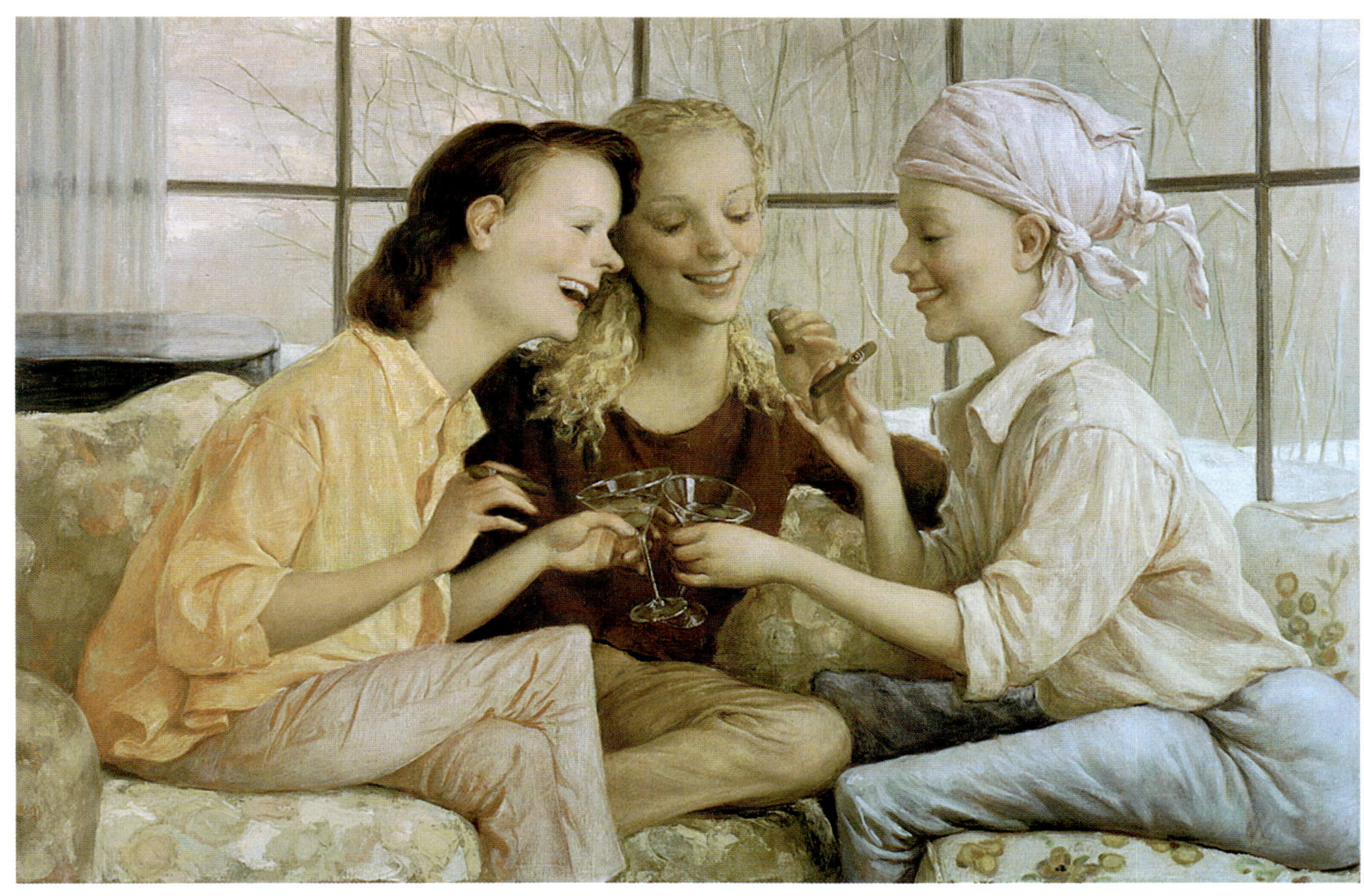

JOHN CURRIN, STAMFORD AFTER-BRUNCH, 2000,
oil on canvas, 40 x 60" / Öl auf Leinwand, 101,6 x 152,4 cm.
(PHOTO: FRED SCRUTON)

John Currin

Lots of colorful pictures, in them:

SIBYLLE BERG

Men who get older. Who have potbellies, double chins, who dye their hair or comb the few they have left over their bald heads, who come from their offices or from selling cars or are out of a job, who can't fuck anymore, who are 40 years old and older, who never had a woman and never will, who, when they do have a woman, don't love her, never did, who wear baggy pants, or suits that are too tight across their bellies, who have yellow feet, who wear slippers, who eat, who eat a lot and drink a lot, because then it disappears for a second, the feeling that they can't name because they are men who are afraid, because they know that life no longer has any miracles up its sleeve. Who were robbed, but they don't know of what.

So I fell down. Just like that, the way you turn off the TV set. At the edge of the street. People get a kick out of fiddling with the TV. My legs got tired on the way home, my legs so bored they just buckled. Thud. Lying there. Lying there and waiting. Just keep back the tears.
It's not snowing.
That's the way it goes. Crying and nobody notices or feels sorry.
No ring.
Didn't find anybody to love me.
That's it.

The beginning is over fast.

The beginning consists of humiliation. Abused, beaten, ignored, locked up, silenced, overfed, underfed, cold or too hot and no control. Not over your bowel movements, not over your feelings, nothing.

SIBYLLE BERG is a writer who lives in Zurich. Among her more recent works are the novels *Amerika* (1999) and *Gold* (2000), both Hoffmann & Campe, Munich.

You're a child and waiting. Waiting and the clock keeps ticking and it's always Sunday and they're always strangers to you, the people you came from, always never you. And they don't like themselves, don't like their lives, don't like you. There is no happy childhood, how are you supposed to be happy with no willpower and alienated. Things everywhere that scare you, and not even the word for them. Animals, and other children who hit you, who lie in wait for you, shadows at night, noises in the house, the faces of your parents in moments unobserved.

And you stand at the window and look at the buildings, and in despair because you know that what you were hoping for will happen in a building like that and no laughter's coming from any of them.

Afterwards—

A few years when I wasn't waiting for death. Were the best. In the body of a person with the mind of a child.

It's cold. It isn't snowing. I am dark.

Loneliness starts where we begin. For a while we totter stupidly through the world, that's childhood since brains and feelings aren't in sync. They don't join up again until adolescence. The time when most people first fall in love. The most romantic time because it's solid illusion. Wanting nothing except to melt. A girl, and I wanted her and didn't know what I wanted her for except never to be alone again. Stood at open windows and spring outside and *Kiss* posters on the walls and what I knew about love went like this: to be with her on an island and look at her day and night and touch her breasts. Day and night. Love will never be a dream like that again, before I knew what love was; never would I be so infinite again. I sensed it.

It's not getting dark. At the edge of the street, and how come nobody's walking here?

The rest is over quickly, quickly recounted, never a miracle, waiting and repetition that you go along with because you believe there's still something else. The things promised, in the years after youth. But they make false promises. That's the game. Everybody always making promises, everybody's always being promised, but promises unkept. Of eternal love, eternal life, and the lies circulating, about fun in distant countries with beautiful women and men in colorful bathing suits with soft drinks and elegant cars, and that life's a party. Life. That's what they tell you,

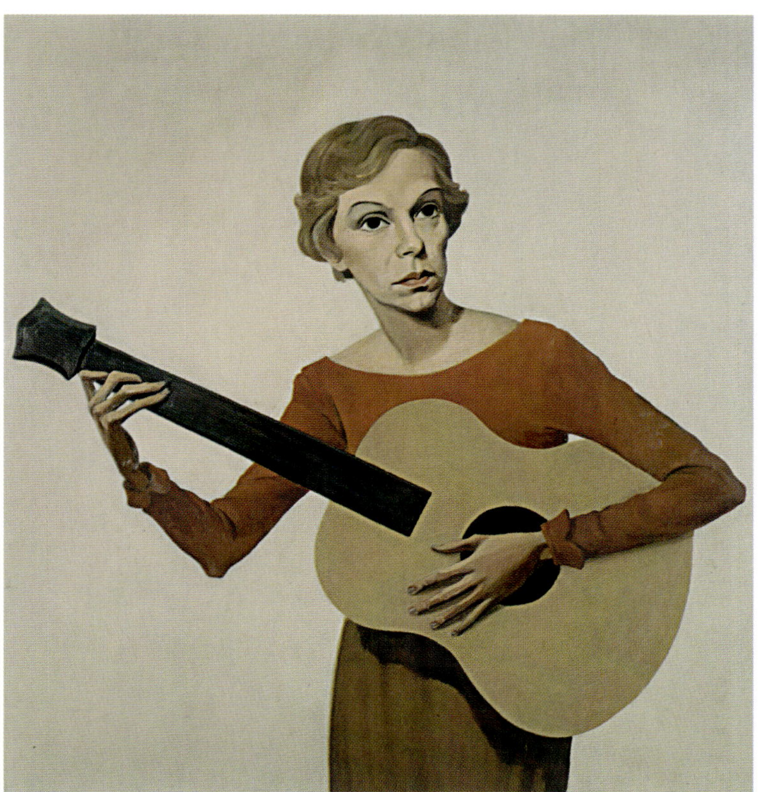

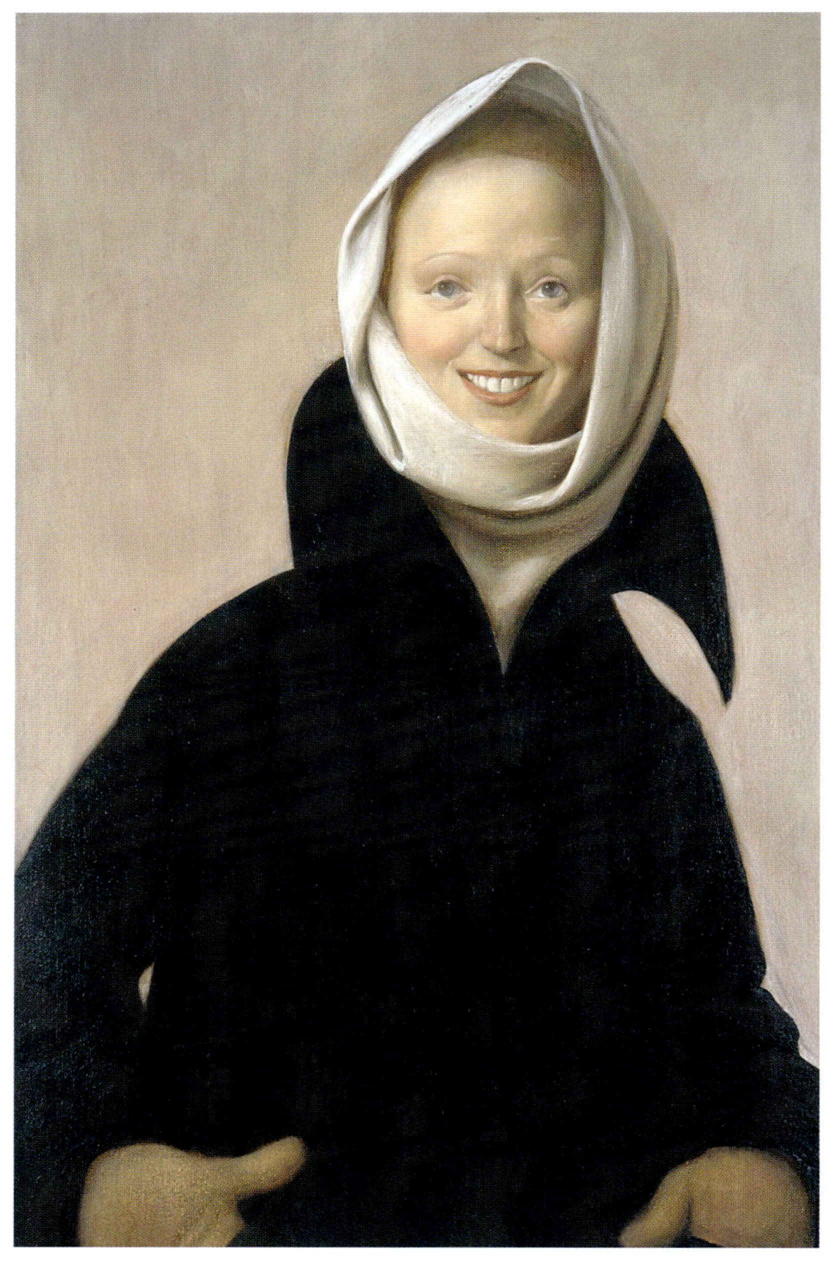

JOHN CURRIN, THE CUDDLER, 2000, oil on canvas, 38 x 24" /
DIE VERSCHMUSTE, Öl auf Leinwand, 96,5 x 61 cm. (PHOTO: ANDY KEATE)

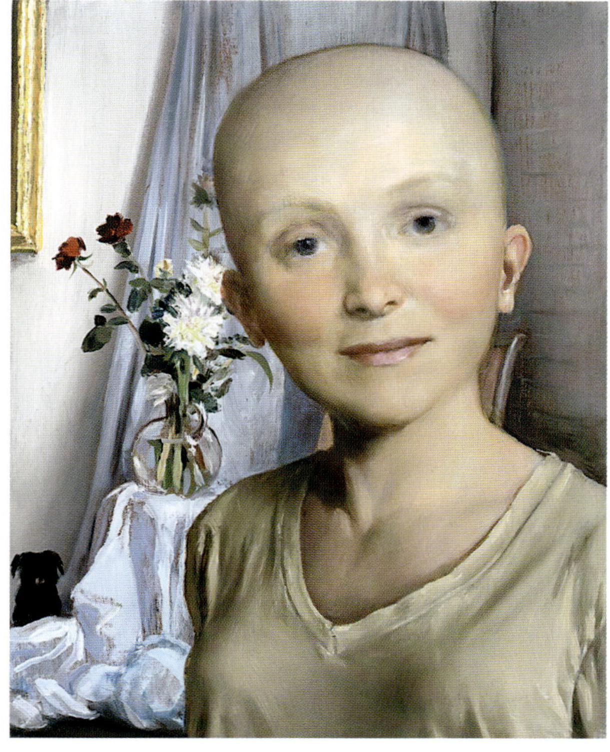

JOHN CURRIN, PORTRAIT OF CHEWY, 2001, oil on canvas, 18 x 14" / PORTRÄT VON CHEWY, Öl auf Leinwand, 45,7 x 35,6 cm. (PHOTO: OREN SLOR)

show you and you don't even get suspicious when you start going to parties and standing in the corner, tears in your eyes, your throat sore because you smoke and drink too much, shattered because parties are so boring and no one talks to you or anything. And the problem with life after youth is that you think you know how everything should feel and you look for it and never find it because ideas are always better than truths.

You're not young anymore and not old yet and that's the longest time that you spend and without noticing it people start treating you like a grown-up. Then I started working. I thought that would give me the feeling. There was always the feeling there. It was like hunger and not knowing for what.

Work.

It was getting up every morning. Much too early and always cold, the alarm clock ringing, the coffee on the kitchen table, and wanting to cry and not knowing why.

It was only the fear of being late, of not being good enough, of the interview with the boss, of wearing the wrong shirt, of giving the wrong answers, of the clock ticking and waiting for Sunday, and not knowing what to do and waiting for Monday and not knowing why, because Monday was fear. It was plodding to the crowded subway, walking into a building that smells wrong and saying hello to people who were never close, it was: being fired when I was too old.

I was never my friend—that's for sure.

I've found no one to love me. There was only love at night before I was with a person that I chose for myself.

Who was to make me unhappy.

I lay there nights when it was always bright before love and thought: how I would keep, the person, my person, playing with little animals under the covers. And I would sing to the person until she laughs and would laugh with her, until he fell out of bed, wake him up at night when the first snow falls and run outside, and hold her until he got warm. I wanted to walk all the paths with him that I had walked in my loneliness and the paths were new. I wanted to feed her mashed potatoes and run on cold fields, not speaking because my face was frozen and into bed at home and under the covers, play with little animals. I wanted to look at the person at night, never sleep again, full only from looking at her arms, wanted to eat his tears, to say: you don't have to cry anymore, I don't have to cry anymore, because we aren't alone anymore, wanted to build sand castles. To read books to him and kiss her fingertips, all one hundred one after the other. That's what I thought during the nights with the idea of a person and was so excited, as if I'd been given a present.

And then the person came, she was made of flesh and thoughts of his own and was mine for a while, and it never felt like the nights when I dreamed.

It was only silence and skin that was cold and alien to me and thoughts that I didn't understand and hostility, mine and his, because it felt so different to both of us, the idea had been so different.

And then the silence got too big, at some point, the smell too bad and then I left or she did, who cares.

It hurt for a while, a dead idea like that isn't much fun, until I distracted myself again and dreamed of the person who would rescue me. Never came true.

And no consolation from living in the time after love, we are all alone and only looking for someone who loves us and will find no one ever, no one. Because for everyone who seeks, there's one who is sought, and I didn't want to love anyone who wanted me. Never.

Please don't go, they said, the wrong people and I left, I thought I've got to go because the right person is waiting out there for me. Nobody was waiting. Love was sitting in my apartment and I closed the door.

I no longer found as many and they didn't get any younger, not me I thought and couldn't cope with their old flesh because it reminded me of what had to come.

It's not getting cold. At the edge of the street. And lights are coming on in the buildings. In the buildings, listen: they're screaming at each other, they're drinking and beating each other up beating up the kids fucking the kids fucking each other, beating each other up, they fall silent and weep because they're so sad, because they've failed, because they realize that their beautiful life is worthless, because they sense that it's not going to get any better, but worse, but don't know what to do about it. And the person they have is never the one to rescue them, is always only a person and never the one they could really love, but honestly, it was just bad luck and she's to blame, they say: I hate the way you eat, the way you walk, the way you smell, and they really mean themselves. The disappointment when they slowly see the light.

The day I saw myself in a mirror when I was not counting on myself in a mirror. Saw an unattractive man, overweight, bald patches glistening, when I realized: waiting for something big is a waste of time. The day I started drinking and taking sausages to bed with me, just so they'd be there when I woke up, the day I got cancer and noticed that I didn't have any friends, when I realized that I was a loser, the day I sensed that nothing was going to happen anymore, when I realized that I didn't know how to fill the time left, and what with.

Look at how I'm lying here now. Look at how I have no one to touch me once more, my heart, rolled up in my arms, but cheating won't work, it's my arms that are holding my legs.

Not afraid, not sad. But won't make it home anymore.

Too tired.

And now, now it's starting to snow and I never found anyone and it's getting dark.

(Translation: Catherine Schelbert)

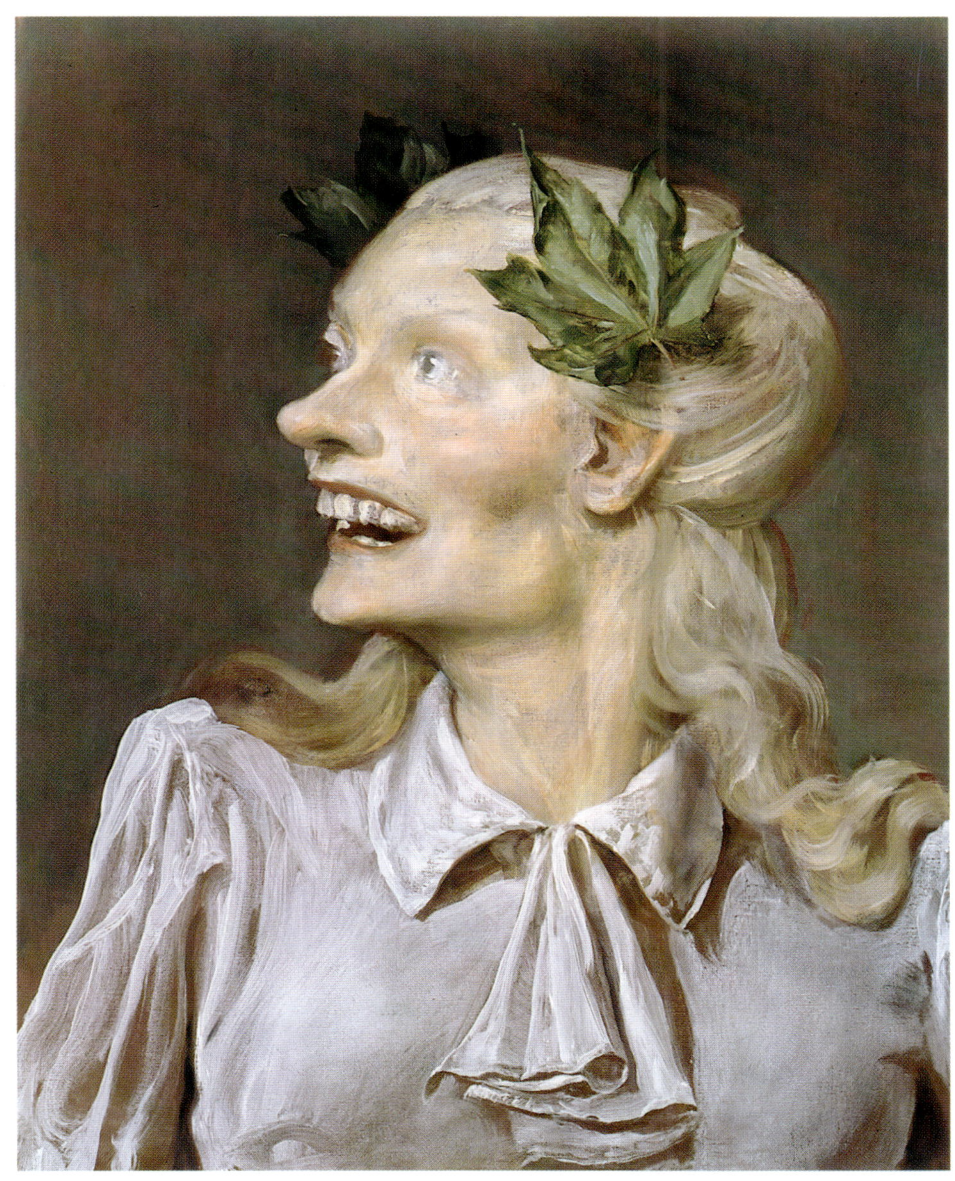

JOHN CURRIN, MINERVA, 2000, oil on canvas, 28 x 22" / Öl auf Leinwand, 71 x 56 cm.
(PHOTO: FRED SCRUTON)

THE BEGGAR'S ALMS, 2002
Etching with aquatint, sugarlift, spitbite,
and drypoint on Somerset soft white textured, 250gsm
Paper size 23½ x 18½", image 10½ x 8½"
Printed by Greg Burnet, Burnet Editions, New York
Edition of 70, signed and numbered

DAS ALMOSEN DER BETTLERIN, 2002
Radierung mit Aquatinta, Zuckertusche,
Pinselätzung und Kaltnadel auf Somerset soft white
mit leichter Textur, 250 g/m^2
Blatt 59,8 x 47,2 cm, Druck 26,5 x 21,5 cm
Gedruckt bei Greg Burnet, Burnet Editions, New York
Auflage: 70, signiert und nummeriert

(PHOTO: MANCIA/BODMER, FBM STUDIO, ZÜRICH)

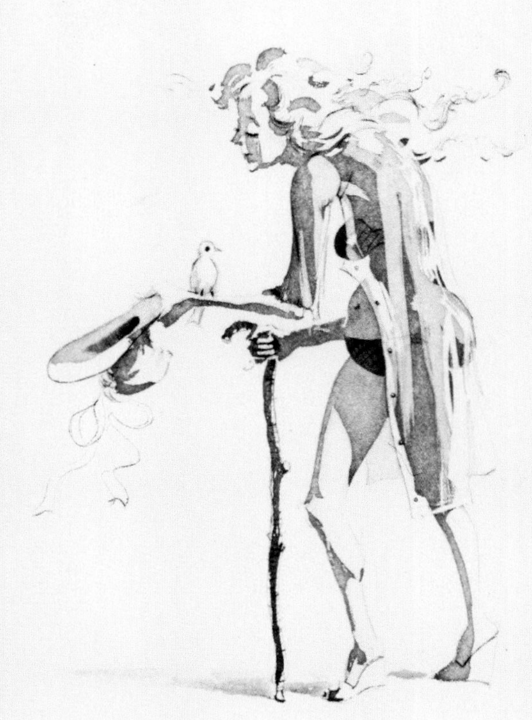

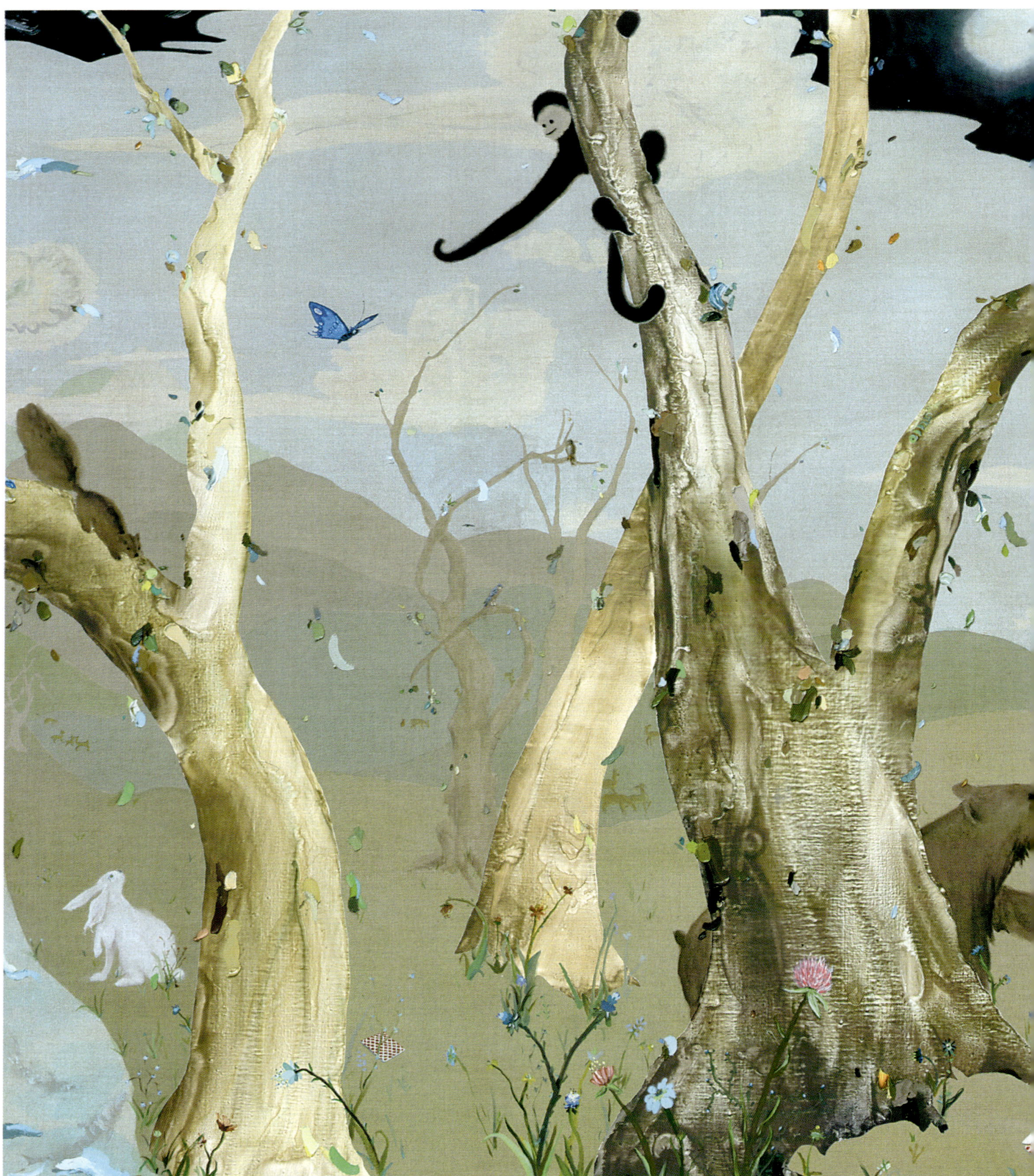

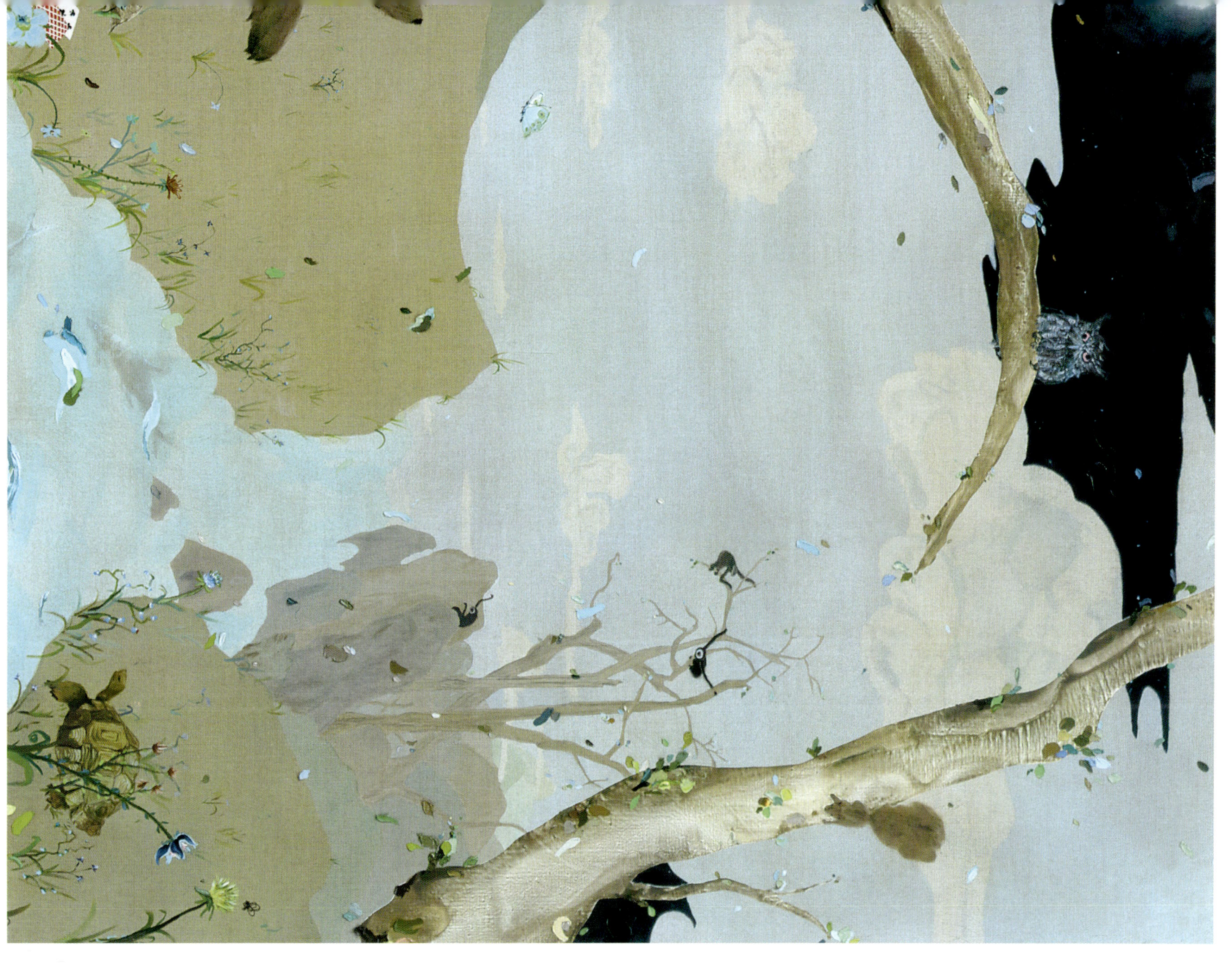

LAURA OWENS

Laura Owens
Paints a Picture

RUSSEL FERGUSON

My title is taken, of course, from the old series in *Art News,* which followed the progress of a painting in the studio of a well-known artist. On one hand the series reinforced the traditional idea of the artist's studio as a place of almost alchemical transformation, yet at the same time it partially de-mystified it by lifting the veil a bit on the prosaic work of making a painting. With some contemporary artists, such a title would be ironic, and the text would feature an account of the artist on the telephone while fabricators labored on the piece. But Laura Owens really does paint the old-fashioned way. Mostly, she is alone in the studio, with only occasional help from an assistant on tasks like stretching canvas and applying masking tape. She doesn't paint to a deadline. On any given day she is just "trying to make the best painting I can make at that moment."[1] There is an old handwritten sign on the studio wall: "Make stuff." Whatever she makes, though, "it's definitely going to be a painting."

Owens recently made a big painting (UNTITLED, like all of her work). It's seven feet high by eleven feet long, and it depicts an Edenic landscape, with

trees and flowers, and a river. There are animals everywhere: a bear and monkeys, squirrels and rabbits. Fish frolic in the river; butterflies fill the air. It is the making of this painting that will be my focus here.

The work has a double life, the parts of which are separate, yet deeply connected. On one level, it's a picture of a better world: a peaceable kingdom where all of nature co-exists in idyllic harmony. On another, simultaneous, level, it's a painting: an elaborately composed arrangement of paint on canvas that is inevitably part of a complex dialogue with the whole history of the medium. There is a constant back and forth between the creation of a pictorial world and the act of painting itself. For the work to be successful, a certain harmony needs to be achieved that will encompass both elements.

Harmony, in fact, is the real theme of the painting. It provides the motif: even when a monkey reaches for a butterfly, it is playful rather than predatory. And the same theme pervades the construction of the composition in which each of the many animals has a certain independence: none dominates. The largest animals—a monkey and a bear—are discreetly half-hidden behind a tree trunk. The trees themselves are dispersed across the canvas so that they leave the visual frame on all sides, while a single trunk arches ambiguously into the relatively empty space at the upper right. Empty space is as important

---

RUSSELL FERGUSON is Deputy Director for Exhibitions and Programs and Chief Curator at The UCLA Hammer Museum, Los Angeles. He is currently working on a survey of Christian Marclay's work that will open at the Hammer in the summer of 2003.

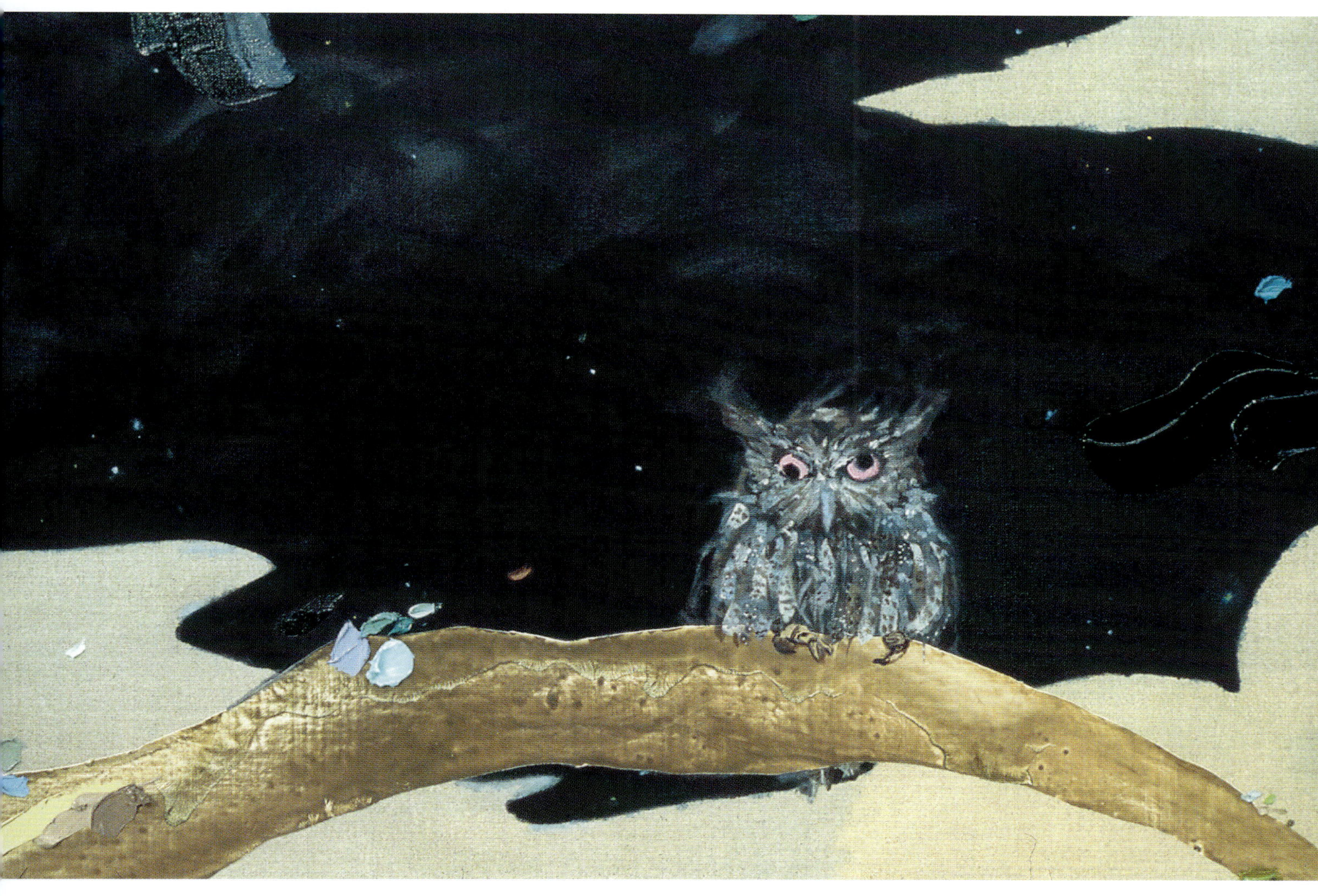

LAURA OWENS, UNTITLED, 2002, oil and acrylic on linen, 84 x 132", detail; full image on preceding double page. /
OHNE TITEL, 213 x 335 cm, Ausschnitt; ganzes Bild siehe vorangehende Doppelseite.
(PHOTO: DOUGLAS M. PARKER STUDIO)

here as occupied space. Among the animals, a lat-ticework of cross-directed looks serves to send the viewer's eye roaming in turn all over the huge canvas. The landscape in which the activity plays out is divided into sectors, but remains surprisingly uni-fied. Owens works with apparently unmodulated fields of color that nevertheless resolve themselves into a convincingly deep space, punctuated by unex-pected incident.

In the studio, when Owens is not painting, as she prepares to paint, she is often thinking about solu-tions that others have used to address issues as they emerge in her own work. Tiepolo's *Tasso Cycle* (1743–45) in the Art Institute of Chicago has been a recent inspiration, not just because of the paintings' sumptuous palette, but also for their sudden shifts in tone, and the seemingly isolated passages that both disrupt and confirm the compositions. It was these paintings that taught her to think of a painting's back, middle and foreground as related, but also as potentially discrete parts.

The process begins with drawings. There are tra-ditional drawings, but also collages. Any of these might also be scanned, and then manipulated with PhotoShop to find the right scale for a number of disparate elements. There are also experiments with color. Sometimes an entire drawing will be covered with numbers, corresponding to her own home-made color chart, until it looks like a paint-by-num-bers kit. For the big new painting she made a full-sized cartoon, although she did not pounce it. In-stead she moved it around, back and forth in front of and sometimes behind the painting as she worked on it. In many ways this intimate, tactile relationship be-tween preparatory drawing and finished painting echoes the way in which de Kooning used his draw-ings to trace over and alter a composition that was al-ready underway on canvas.

The drawings are followed by a number of studies on canvas that explore either a color combination or a particular motif from the proposed composition. Just as importantly, these studies delay the actual start of work on the large canvas, which requires the slow build-up of momentum. All the delays, Owens says, are like "a trick of the brain to make you think it's failsafe. It also wears you out, so that you can do

it. If I just start, I'm a little too self-aware." Psycho-logically, before beginning a big painting like this, there has been "a whole month of freaking out, but also getting excited."

That mental process is followed by a number of physical preparations that are simultaneously prac-tical and somewhat ritualistic. She mixes huge amounts of pigment—Pompeii reds, Italian pinks—loading up dozens of the tinfoil lasagna trays that serve as her palettes. "It's like revving your engines, getting psyched up," she says, although it is also true that "You can pass the moment to make a painting." There is always the right moment, just as in other areas of life.

Athletes often have elaborate rituals that they must carry out before their events. Their purpose is not merely to appease superstition; they also serve to calm nerves and empty out the mind, so that when the time comes to perform, action will not be im-peded by too much conscious effort. Paradoxically, this state can only be achieved through years of gru-eling practice. For Owens, all the freaking out and all the physical preparation are the stages she has to go through before getting to the point at which she can work confidently, in the zone where "'good' or 'bad' doesn't make sense." Yet this sense of building up to the action of painting has little in common with Harold Rosenberg's famous fifties formulation of the canvas "as an arena in which to act," his hymn to the unforeseen inspiration that must be found in "the painter's muscles and in the cream-colored sea into which he dives."[2] For Owens, the canvas is not an arena in which to fight. Rather, her preparation serves to imbue her with a spirit of strategic calm.

The first decisive mark on a white canvas will reg-ister immediately, setting the tone for whatever de-velopment the painting will undergo. But Owens no longer uses the white or cream-colored canvas that has been the norm since the era of action painting. Instead, she has begun painting with a dark brown linen as her support. Like the old masters, she now works slowly from dark into light.

Her first work on the canvas itself was to block out the silhouettes of the smaller trees and their branches with masking tape. Then the first painting: the monkey, brushed in with a dark water-based ink.

OWENS, UNTITLED, 2002, oil and acrylic on linen, 84 x 132", detail / OHNE TITEL, 213 x 335 cm, Ausschnitt.
(PHOTO: DOUGLAS M. PARKER STUDIO)

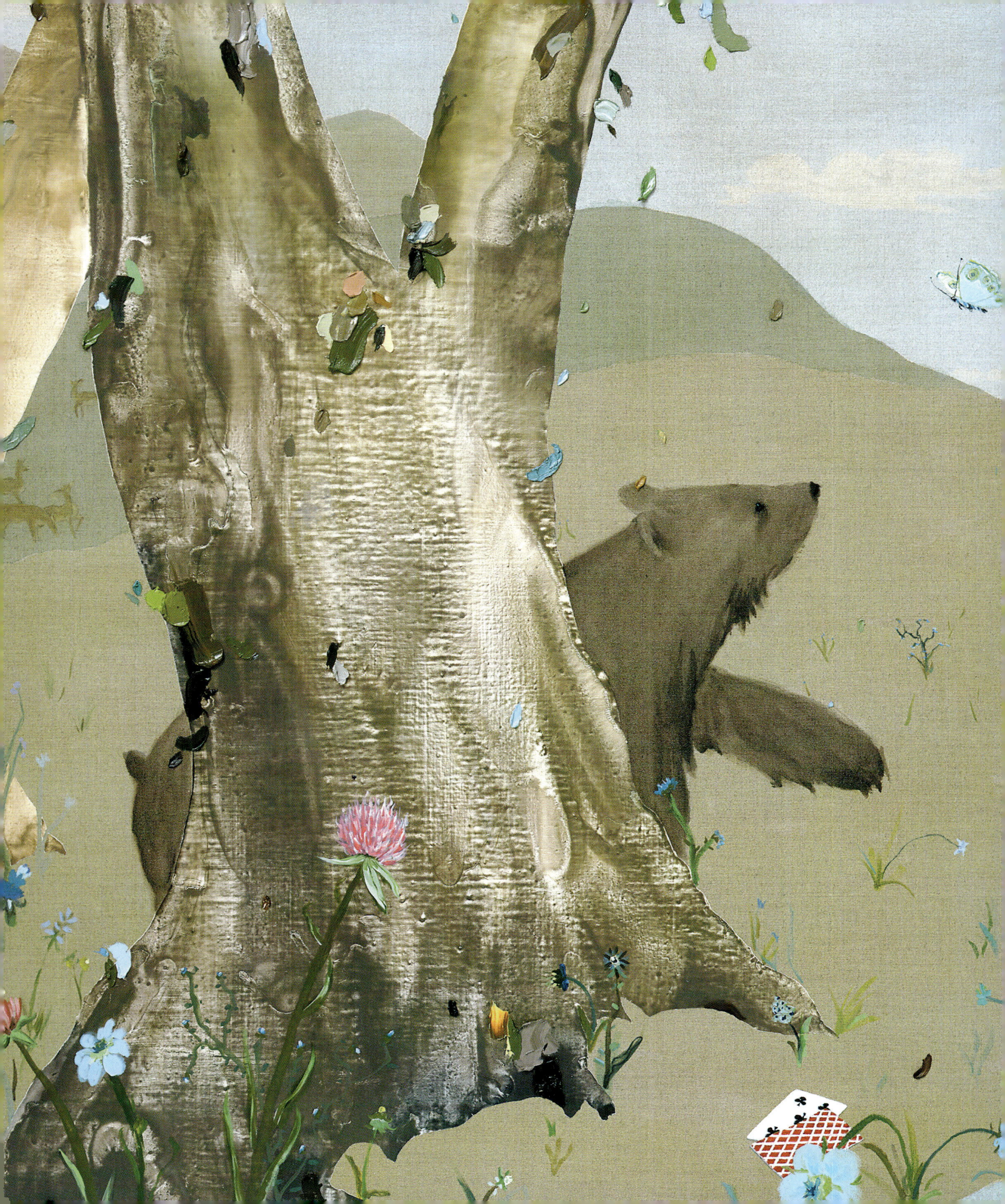

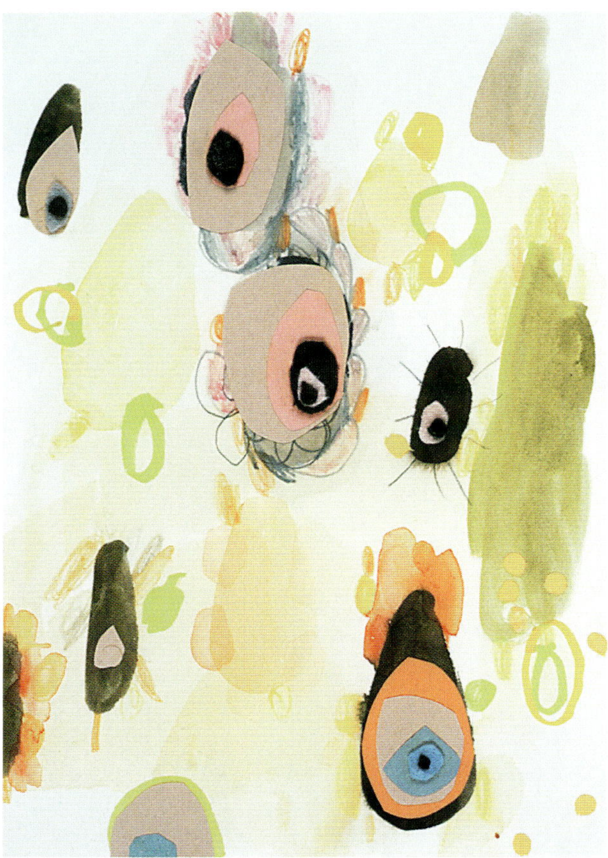

LAURA OWENS, UNTITLED, 2000, collage, watercolor, and pencil on colored paper, 10 x 7" / OHNE TITEL, Collage, Wasserfarbe und Farbstift auf farbigem Papier, 25,4 x 17,8 cm.

By wetting the canvas before applying the ink, she can achieve a satisfactorily fuzzy, furry edge to the silhouette. She's been painting monkeys for about three years now. They derive from those of the anonymous eleventh-century Chinese painter known as the Gibbon Master, in particular his MONKEYS IN A LOQUAT TREE, a large hanging scroll that belongs to the Palace Museum in Taipei. Chinese painting is clearly important to Owens, not just for particular models such as the monkey, but more broadly for its ability to create depth out of flatness, and for the alternative it provides to Western perspectival systems.

The next stage was to apply very thin acrylic washes: green and brown for the earth, dark blue and white for the sky. Then the clouds were loosely masked out and a light blue wash added. A greener blue was used for the stream below. The rabbits, the bear, and the squirrels were painted in acrylic. Then the monkey was masked out before a clear matt medium was laid down over everything that had been done so far.

After the medium had dried, the bigger trees were painted, using cutout paper as a template. First they were built up with as many as twenty layers of thin gesso, sanded down between each layer. Then they were painted with house paint, about ten different colors mixed by Owens and thinned-out with Floetrol, which makes the paint more flexible and slower to dry. This watery house paint was nevertheless applied quickly over the dry, chalky gesso, in about half an hour, with the rest of the canvas masked out. Then, painting in oil, Owens added the small monkeys, some more squirrels, turtles, and butterflies. Unusually for Owens, she re-painted the butterflies four or five times, in search of the right overall balance for the painting. At the same time, she went back over the whole surface with oil paint, thinly in the landscape, more thickly in certain details. Most of the flowers were painted in at this point, and the work was, finally, almost complete.

All the time she is painting, Owens is referring back to her drawings and studies, yet also to her original conception of the entire work. Sometimes she can misplace part of the original image she had in mind, "like when you tell your dream in words, you lose track of it." When she began the painting she was thinking about a kind of Rousseau jungle, but, as she puts it, "it ended up a bit more French countryside."

The hand of cards at the center of the bottom edge was added last, to hold the foreground, when it seemed that everything had become perhaps too equalized, too much in harmony. Even after such extensive preparation, and such intensive work on the canvas itself, it seems that spontaneity, and indeed chance, still have their part to play too.

1) Unless otherwise noted, all quotations by Owens are from a conversation at her studio on April 8, 2002.
2) Harold Rosenberg, "The American Action Painters" in *The Tradition of the New* (New York: McGraw Hill, 1952), p. 25.

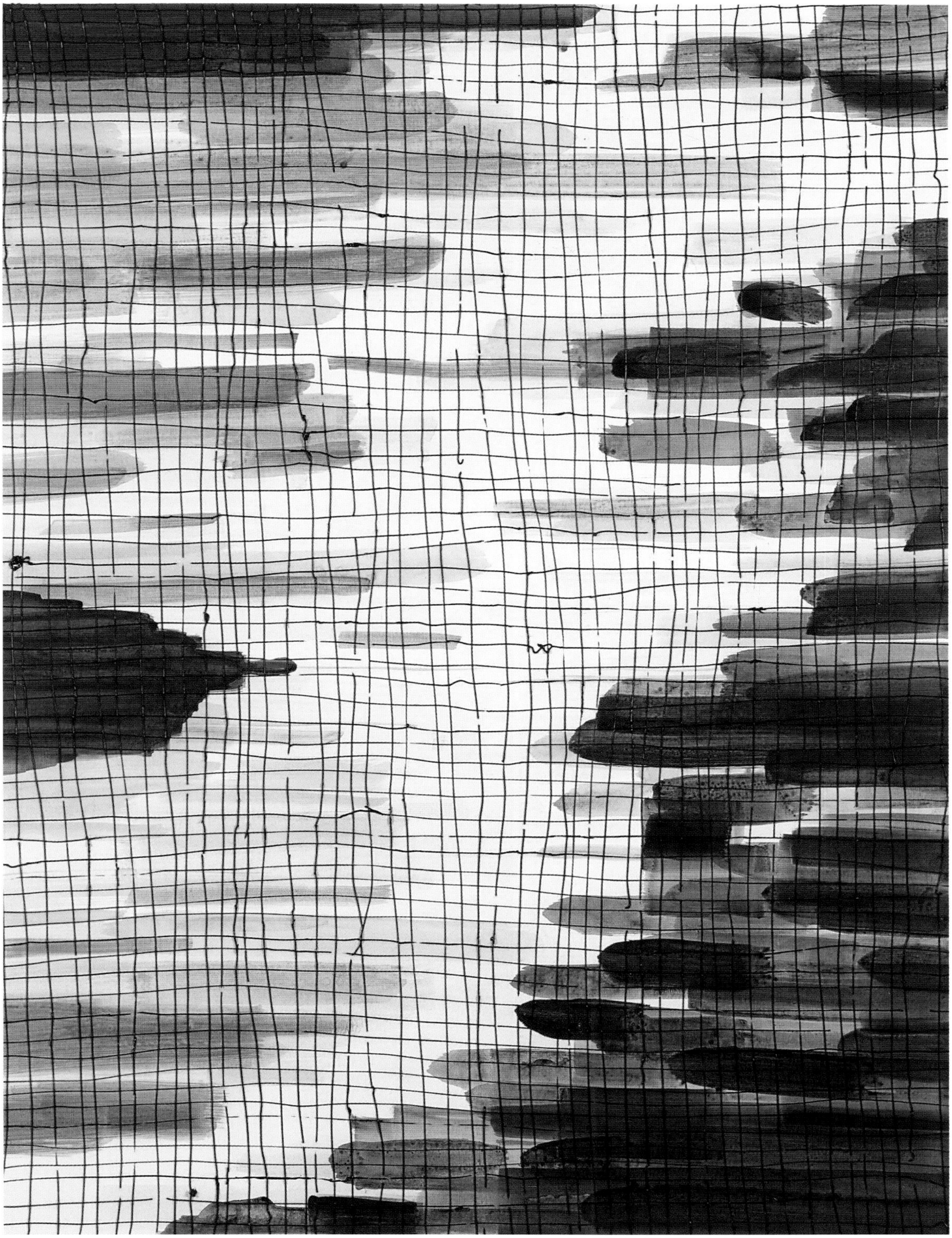

LAURA OWENS, UNTITLED, 1999, acrylic on canvas, 64¹/₂ x 49¹/₂" / OHNE TITEL, Acryl auf Leinwand, 164 x 126 cm.

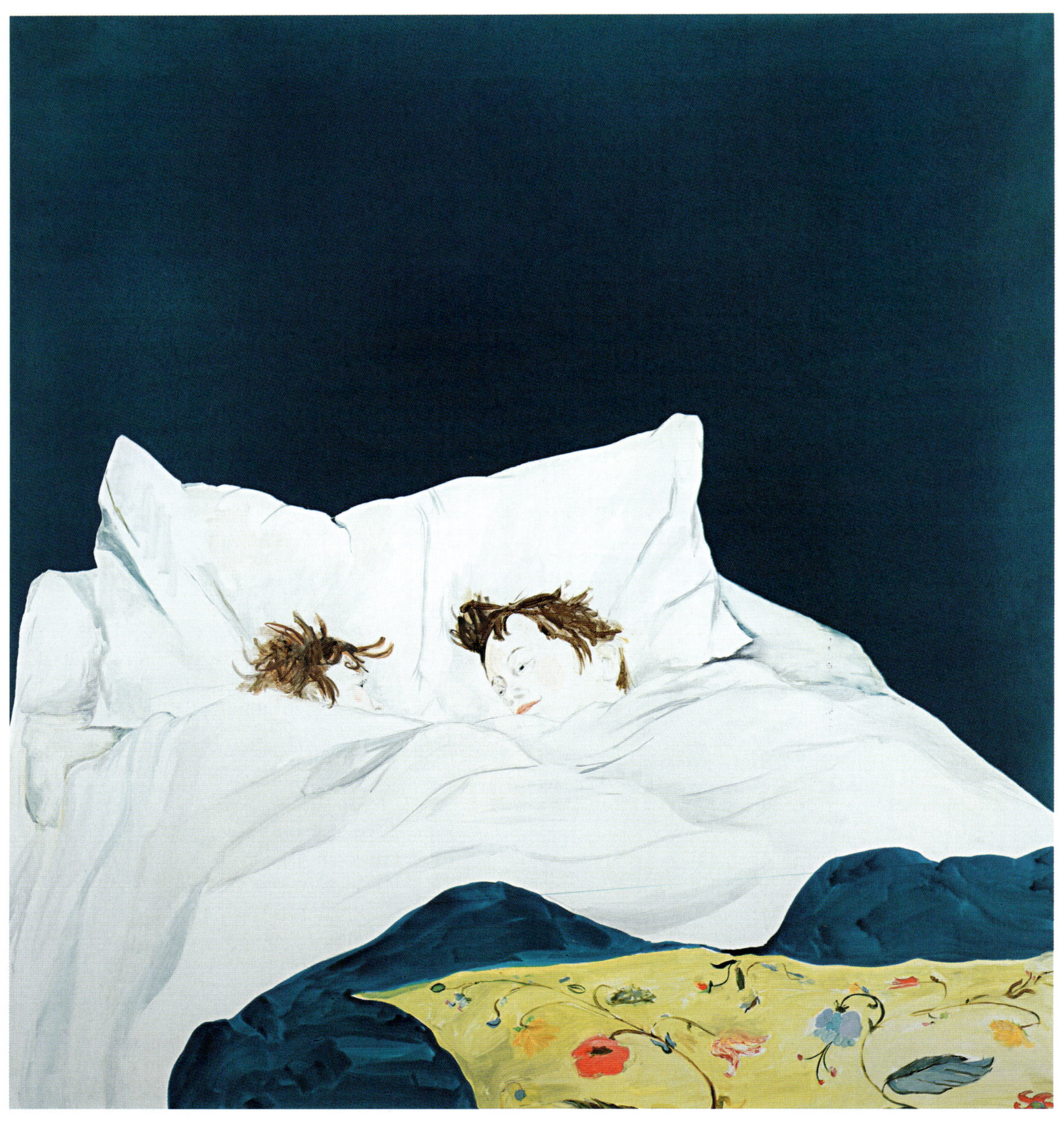

LAURA OWENS, UNTITLED, 2000, acrylic, oil, and watercolor on canvas, 66¹/₂ x 72" /
OHNE TITEL, Acryl, Öl und Wasserfarbe auf Leinwand, 169 x 183 cm.

Laura Owens malt ein Bild

RUSSEL FERGUSON

Mein Titel ist natürlich dieser alten Serie in *Art News* entliehen, die jeweils im Atelier eines bekannten Künstlers die Entstehung eines Bildes verfolgte. Einerseits bestätigte diese Serie die traditionelle Vorstellung vom Atelier als Ort beinah alchimistischer Transformationen, andererseits hat sie diese aber auch entmystifiziert, indem sie den Schleier etwas lüftete und die prosaische Arbeit des Bildermalens sichtbar machte. Auf gewisse zeitgenössische Künstler gemünzt, könnte ein solcher Titel nur ironisch wirken, und im Text wäre zu lesen, wie der Künstler telefoniert, während irgendwelche Spezialisten an seinem Werk arbeiten. Laura Owens hingegen malt auf ganz altmodische Art. Meistens ist sie allein in ihrem Atelier, nur gelegentlich hilft ihr jemand beim Aufziehen der Leinwand oder beim Abdecken. Sie setzt sich keinen Termin. Der Tag spielt keine Rolle: «Ich versuche einfach, das beste Bild zu machen, das ich in diesem Augenblick machen kann.»[1] An der Wand des Ateliers hängt ein altes, von Hand geschriebenes Schild: *Make stuff* (etwa: «Mach was und mach es selbst»). Aber was immer sie macht, «es wird mit Sicherheit ein Bild».

Owens hat vor kurzem ein grosses Bild fertig gestellt (UNTITLED, wie alle ihre Arbeiten). Es ist rund 214 Zentimeter hoch und 335 Zentimeter breit und zeigt eine paradiesische Landschaft mit Bäumen, Blumen und einem Fluss. Überall sind Tiere: ein Bär, Affen, Eichhörnchen und Kaninchen. Im Fluss tummeln sich Fische und darüber gaukeln Schmetterlinge. Die Entstehung dieses Bildes möchte ich im Folgenden etwas genauer betrachten.

Die Arbeit hat ein Doppelleben, und die einzelnen Teile, aus denen sie sich zusammensetzt, sind zwar separat, bilden aber trotzdem eine Einheit. Einerseits ist es das Bild einer besseren Welt: eines friedlichen Königreichs, in dem die ganze Natur in idyllischer Harmonie zusammenlebt. Andrerseits ist es einfach nur ein Bild: eine komplexe Farbkomposition auf Leinwand und damit auch Teil eines komplexen Dialogs mit der Geschichte des Mediums. Es ist ein dauerndes Hin und Her zwischen dem Schaffen einer Bildwelt und dem Akt des Malens selbst. Damit das Bild gelingt, muss eine gewisse Harmonie erreicht werden, die beide Elemente einschliesst.

Und Harmonie ist in der Tat das Thema des Bildes. Sie liefert das Motiv: Selbst wenn ein Affe nach einem Schmetterling greift, wirkt das eher verspielt als aggressiv. Dasselbe Thema bestimmt auch den Aufbau der Komposition, in der jedes Tier eine gewisse Unabhängigkeit besitzt: Keines dominiert. Die grössten Tiere – ein Affe und ein Bär – haben sich diskret hinter einen Baum zurückgezogen. Die Bäume selbst sind so über die Leinwand verteilt, dass sie an den Seiten über den Bildrand hinausreichen, während ein einzelner, seltsam gekrümmter Stamm in den relativ leeren Raum rechts oben hineinragt. Leerer Raum hat denselben Stellenwert wie ausge-

RUSSEL FERGUSON ist Chefkurator und stellvertretender Direktor für Ausstellungen und Programmgestaltung am UCLA Hammer Museum in Los Angeles. Er bereitet eine Gesamtschau von Christian Marclays Werk vor, die im Sommer 2003 im Hammer-Museum eröffnet werden soll.

füllter. Das dichte Geflecht der sich kreuzenden Tierblicke veranlasst auch den Betrachter, seinen Blick über die riesige Leinwand schweifen zu lassen. Die Landschaft, in der die Aktivitäten stattfinden, ist zwar mehrfach unterteilt, bleibt aber trotzdem erstaunlich einheitlich. Owens arbeitet mit anscheinend nicht modulierten Farbfeldern, die sich dennoch zu einem überzeugend tief wirkenden Raum auflösen, der von überraschenden Ereignissen akzentuiert wird.

Wenn Owens im Atelier nicht malt, sondern sich erst darauf vorbereitet, denkt sie oft über die Lösungen nach, die andere Künstler für dieselben Probleme gefunden haben, mit denen sie sich konfrontiert sieht. In jüngster Zeit fand sie Inspiration in Tiepolos *Tasso-Zyklus* (1743–45) im Chicagoer Art Institute, nicht nur wegen der überwältigend reichen Farbpalette der Gemälde, sondern auch wegen der abrupten Wechsel der Tonwerte und der scheinbar isolierten Passagen, die die Komposition gleichzeitig aufbrechen und zusammenhalten. Von diesen Gemälden hat sie gelernt, den Hinter-, Mittel- und Vordergrund eines Bildes sowohl als zusammengehörige wie auch als potenziell für sich stehende Teile zu sehen.

Die Arbeit beginnt mit Zeichnungen, traditionellen Zeichnungen und auch Collagen. Diese können auch eingescannt und mit Photoshop bearbeitet werden, um den richtigen Massstab für die unterschiedlichen Elemente zu finden. Auch mit Farben wird experimentiert. Manchmal ist die ganze Zeichnung gemäss Owens' ganz persönlicher Farbskala mit Zahlen bedeckt und sieht aus wie eine Malvorlage mit nummerierten Farbfeldern für ein *painting by numbers*. Für das neue grosse Bild fertigte Owens einen Entwurf in Originalgrösse an, den sie jedoch nicht durchpauste. Stattdessen schob sie ihn während der Arbeit vor, manchmal auch hinter dem Bild hin und her. In vielerlei Hinsicht erinnert diese innige, taktile Beziehung zwischen Skizze und fertigem Bild an de Koonings Verwendung seiner Skizzen beim Überarbeiten und Korrigieren der auf der Leinwand im Entstehen begriffenen Komposition.

Auf die Zeichnungen folgen verschiedene Studien auf Leinwand, die entweder eine Farbkombination oder ein bestimmtes Motiv der geplanten Komposition untersuchen. Mindestens so wichtig aber ist, dass diese Studien den Arbeitsbeginn auf der grossen Leinwand hinauszögern, der einen solchen langsamen Spannungsaufbau voraussetzt. Diese ganzen Verzögerungen, sagt Owens, sind wie «eine List des Gehirns, die einem das Gefühl gibt, dass nichts mehr schief gehen kann. Sie führen auch eine gewisse Erschöpfung herbei, die erst die Umsetzung erlaubt. Wenn ich mich direkt an die Arbeit mache, bin ich zu befangen.» Vor Beginn der Arbeit an einem so grossen Bild liegt «ein ganzer Monat verstörten Herumflippens, aber auch der freudigen Erwartung».

Auf diesen geistigen Prozess folgen ganz konkrete Vorbereitungen, die sowohl praktischen wie rituellen Charakter haben. Owens mischt enorme Farbmengen – Variationen in Pompejanischrot, Italian Pink – und füllt damit Dutzende von Lasagne-Schalen aus Alufolie, die sie als Paletten verwendet. «Es ist, als würde man die Motoren voll durchstarten, sich irgendwie aufputschen», meint sie, obwohl es auch vorkommen kann, dass «man den richtigen Augenblick für ein Bild verpasst.» Wie sonst im Leben geht es auch hier immer um den richtigen Moment.

Sportler haben oft komplizierte Rituale, die sie vor dem Wettkampf durchspielen müssen. Diese dienen nicht nur dazu, abergläubische Ängste zu beschwichtigen, sondern beruhigen auch die Nerven und machen den Kopf frei, damit die Leistung im entscheidenden Augenblick nicht durch zu viel bewusste Anstrengung behindert wird. Paradoxerweise kann dieser Zustand nur durch jahrelanges mühsames Training erreicht werden. Für Owens sind die Verstörung und die konkreten Vorbereitungen Stadien, die sie durchlaufen muss, um den Punkt zu erreichen, an dem sie sich zuversichtlich an die Arbeit machen kann, in einem Bereich, in dem es «kein ‹gut› oder ‹böse› gibt». Doch ihr sich in den Akt des Malens Hineinsteigern unterscheidet sich grundsätzlich von Harold Rosenbergs berühmter Formulierung aus den 50er Jahren, wonach die Leinwand «eine Arena» sei, «in der es zu agieren gilt», dieser Hymne an die unberechenbare Inspiration, die «in den Muskeln des Malers und dem cremefarbenen Meer, in das er abtaucht» gefunden werden müsse.[2] Für Owens ist die Leinwand keine Kampfarena. Ihre

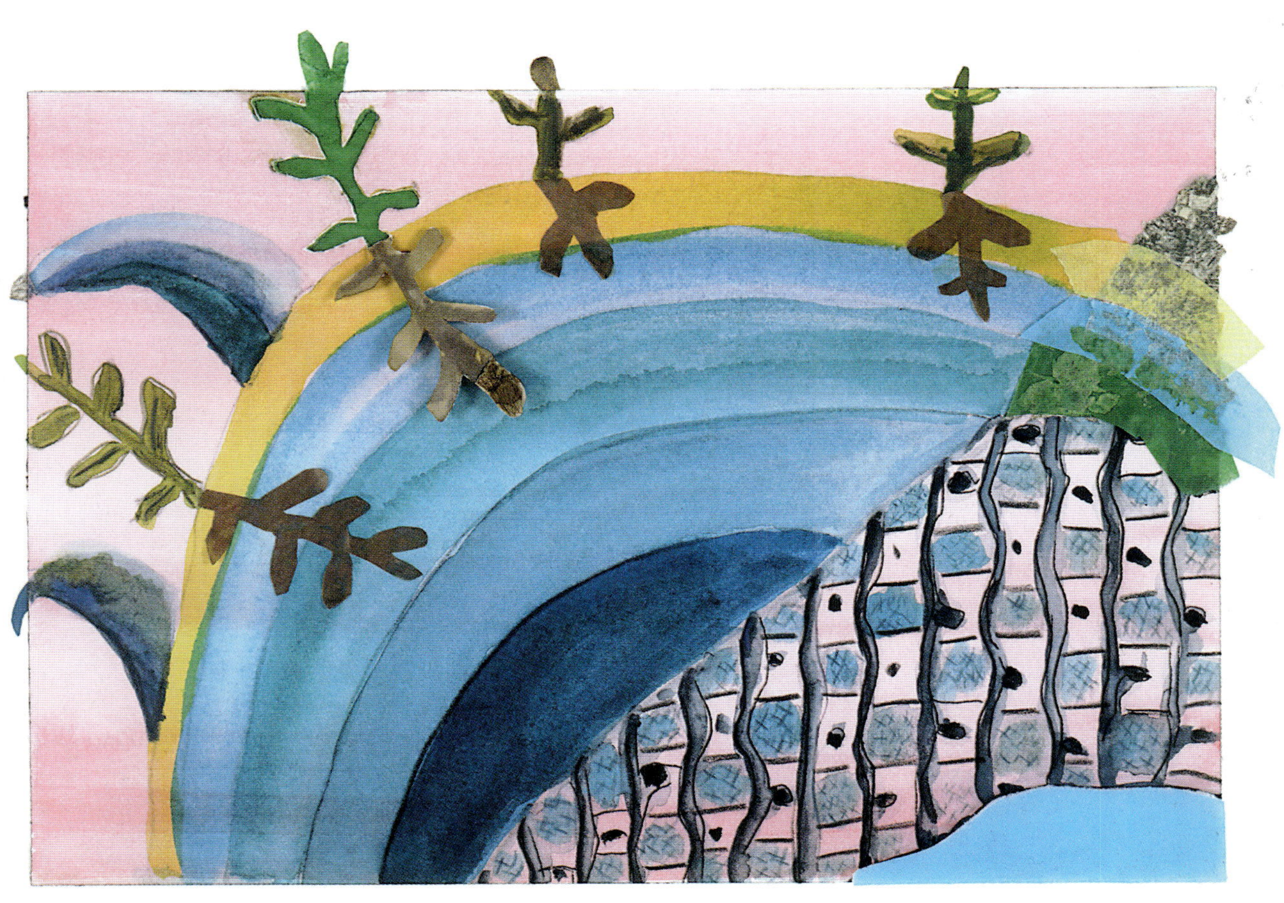

LAURA OWENS, UNTITLED, 2001, watercolor, tissue paper, and felt on paper, 7 x 10” /
Wasserfarbe, Seidenpapier und Filz auf Papier, 17,8 x 25,4 cm.

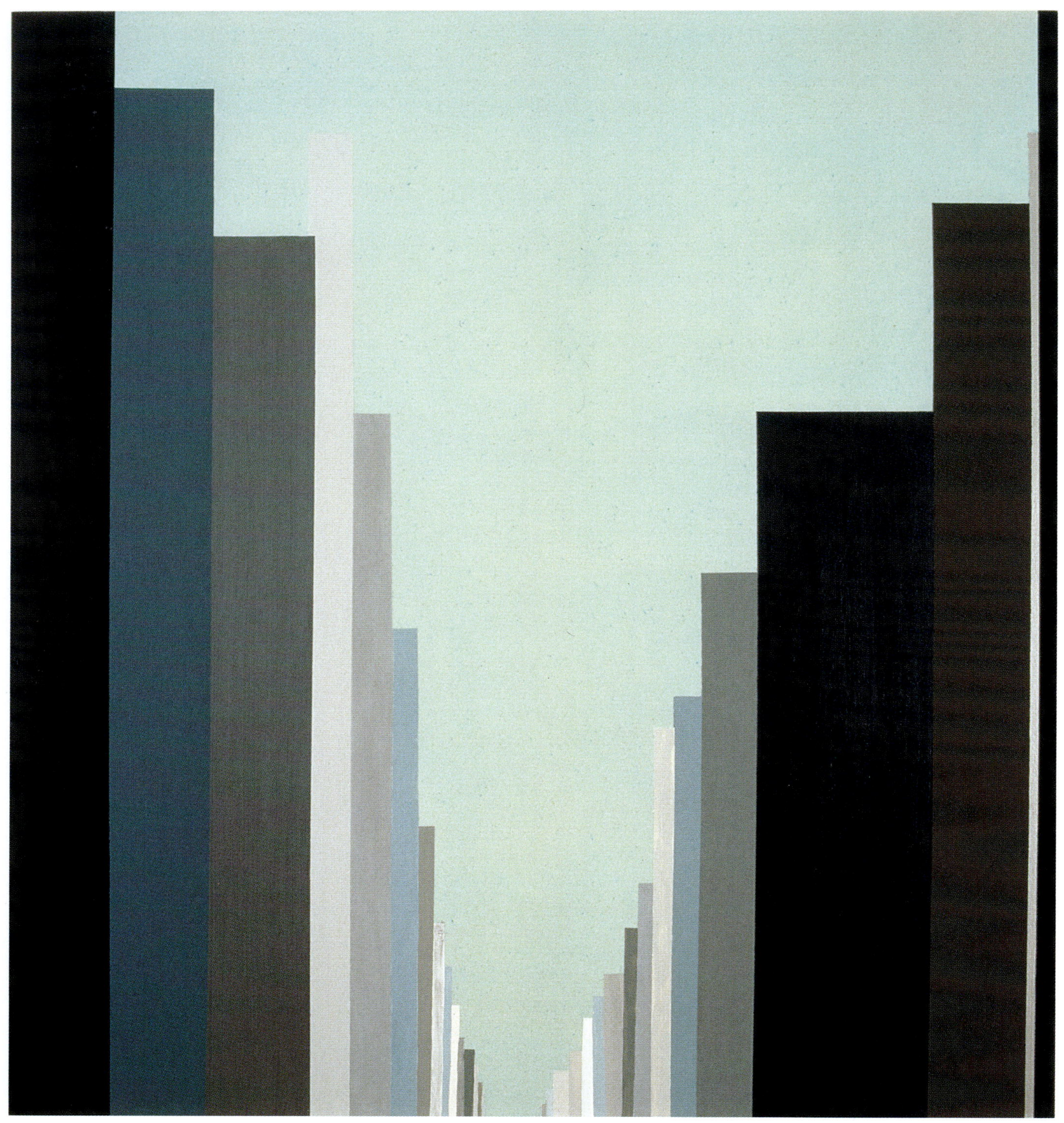

LAURA OWENS, UNTITLED, 1997, oil and acrylic on canvas, 49 ¾ x 45 ½" / OHNE TITEL, Öl und Acryl auf Leinwand, 126,4 x 115,6 cm.

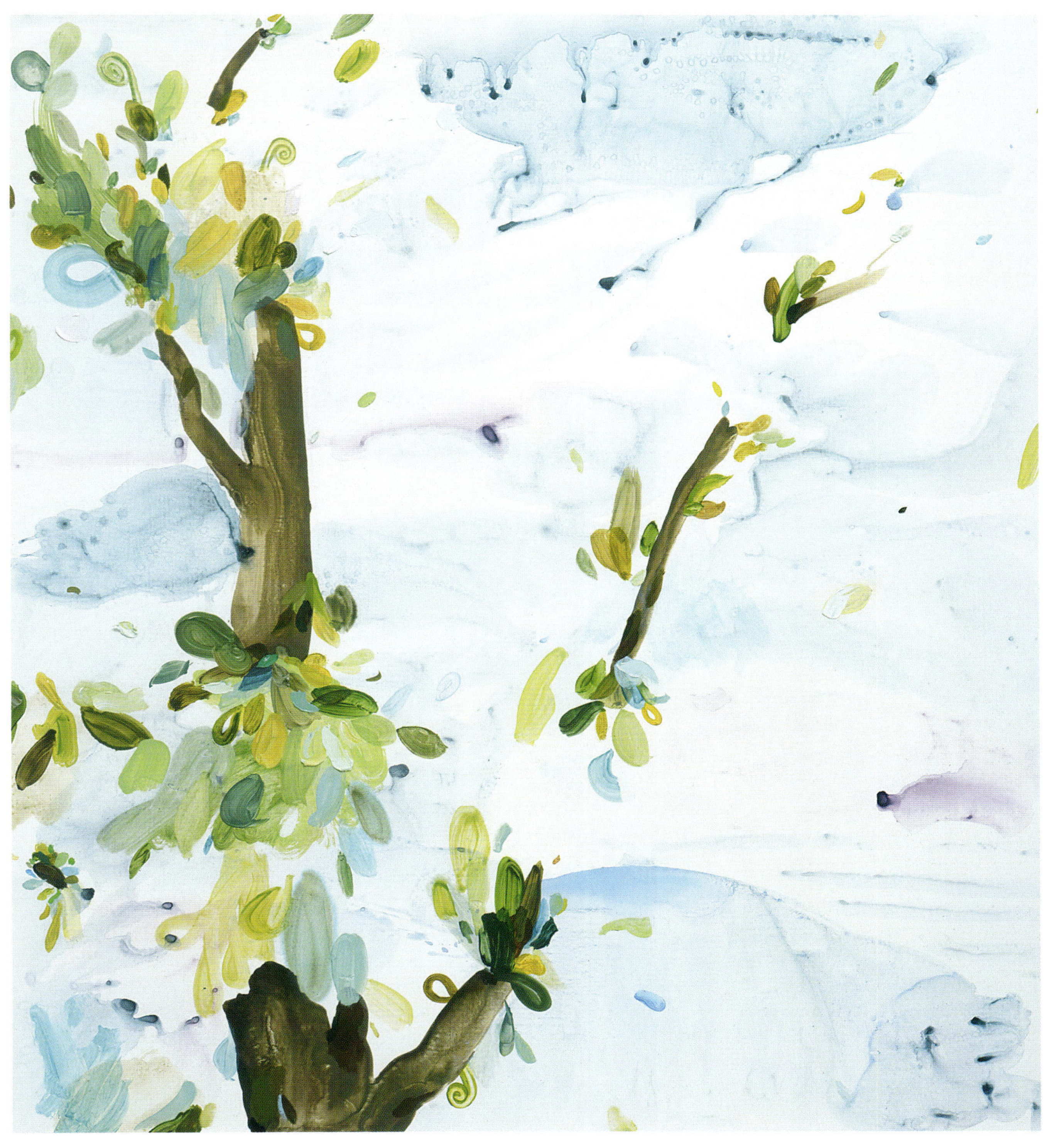

LAURA OWENS, UNTITLED, 2002, oil and acrylic on linen, 54 x 48" / OHNE TITEL, Öl und Acryl auf Leinen, 137,2 x 122 cm.
(PHOTO: DOUGLAS M. PARKER STUDIO)

Vorbereitungen haben vielmehr den Zweck, sie mit einem Geist zielgerichteter Ruhe zu erfüllen.

Die erste entscheidende Markierung auf einer weissen Leinwand schlägt sofort zu Buche und bestimmt jede weitere Entwicklung, die das Bild durchmacht. Aber Owens benutzt nicht mehr die weisse oder cremefarbene Leinwand, die seit der *action painting*-Ära die Norm war. Sie hat sich vielmehr auf dunkelbraune Leinwand als Untergrund verlegt. Wie die alten Meister arbeitet sie sich langsam vom Dunkel ins Licht.

Auf der Leinwand deckte sie zunächst mit Abdeckband die Umrisse der kleineren Bäume und Zweige ab. Dann malte sie das erste Bild: den Affen, hingepinselt in dunkler, wasserlöslicher Tusche. Indem sie die Leinwand vor dem Auftragen der Tinte befeuchtet, erreicht sie den gewünschten weichen, pelzigen Umriss. Inzwischen malt sie schon seit drei Jahren Affen. Ihr Vorbild ist ein anonymer chinesischer Meister aus dem elften Jahrhundert, auch der Gibbon-Meister genannt, der vor allem durch sein Bild AFFEN IN EINEM MISPELBAUM berühmt wurde, eine grosse hängende Rolle im Besitz des Palastmuseums in Taipei. Die chinesische Malerei bedeutet Owens offensichtlich viel, nicht nur was einzelne Motive wie die Affen angeht, sondern auch wegen ihrer Eigenschaft, Tiefe aus der Fläche entstehen zu lassen, und weil sie eine Alternative zur Perspektivenlehre der abendländischen Malerei bietet.

In der nächsten Phase wurden Acrylfarben in starker Verdünnung aufgetragen: Grün und Braun für die Erde, Dunkelblau und Weiss für den Himmel. Die Wolken wurden lose abgedeckt und eine helle Blauschicht aufgetragen. Für den Fluss darunter nahm sie ein Blau mit etwas mehr Grün darin. Die Kaninchen, der Bär und die Eichhörnchen wurden in Acryl gemalt. Dann deckte sie den Affen ab und überzog alles bis dahin Entstandene mit einer transparenten Mattschicht.

Nachdem diese Zwischenschicht getrocknet war, wurden mit Hilfe einer Papierschablone die grösseren Bäume ins Bild gesetzt. Dafür schichtete sie bis zu zwanzig hauchdünne Lagen Kalkgrund übereinander, die vor jedem neuen Auftrag wieder aufgeraut wurden. Darauf wurden sie mit normaler Dispersion bemalt; Owens hatte ungefähr zehn verschiedene Farbtöne gemischt und mit Floetrol verdünnt, was die Farbe geschmeidiger macht und langsamer trocknen lässt. Die wässrige Dispersion wurde dennoch rasch, in nur rund dreissig Minuten auf den trockenen Kalkgrund aufgetragen, der Rest der Leinwand war abgedeckt. Dann fügte Owens in Öl die kleineren Affen und noch ein paar Eichhörnchen, Schildkröten und Schmetterlinge hinzu. Und – eher ungewöhnlich bei Owens – die Schmetterlinge wurden vier bis fünf Mal übermalt, um das Bild auszubalancieren. Gleichzeitig ging sie noch einmal mit Ölfarbe über die ganze Bildfläche, etwas dünner in den Landschaftspartien, kräftiger bei bestimmten Einzelheiten. Dabei kamen auch die meisten Blumen hinzu, und die Arbeit war nun beinahe vollständig.

Wenn Owens malt, greift sie unentwegt auf ihre Zeichnungen und Studien zurück, aber auch auf ihre ursprüngliche Vorstellung des fertigen Bildes. Manchmal landen Teile der ursprünglichen Vorstellung auch an einem ganz anderen Ort, «wie wenn man einen Traum erzählt und dabei den Faden verliert». Zu Beginn der Arbeit hatte sie eine Art Rousseauschen Dschungel vor Augen, aber, so Owens, «dann wurde daraus eher eine französische Landschaft».

Die Spielkarten am unteren Rand in der Mitte wurden zuletzt hinzugefügt, um den Vordergrund zu halten, weil alles plötzlich zu ausgeglichen, zu harmonisch erschien. Aber selbst nach einer so gründlichen Vorbereitung und so intensiver Arbeit an der Leinwand bleibt offenbar noch genügend Spielraum für Spontaneität und sogar für den Zufall.

(Übersetzung: Goridis/Parker)

1) Sofern nicht anders vermerkt, stammen die Zitate aus einer Unterhaltung mit Owens, die am 8. April 2002 in ihrem Atelier stattfand.
2) Harald Rosenberg, «The American Action Painters», in: *The Tradition of the New*, New York, McGraw Hill, 1952, S. 25.

LAURA OWENS, UNTITLED, 1998, *acrylic on canvas, 66 x 72" / OHNE TITEL, Acryl auf Leinwand, 168 x 183 cm.*

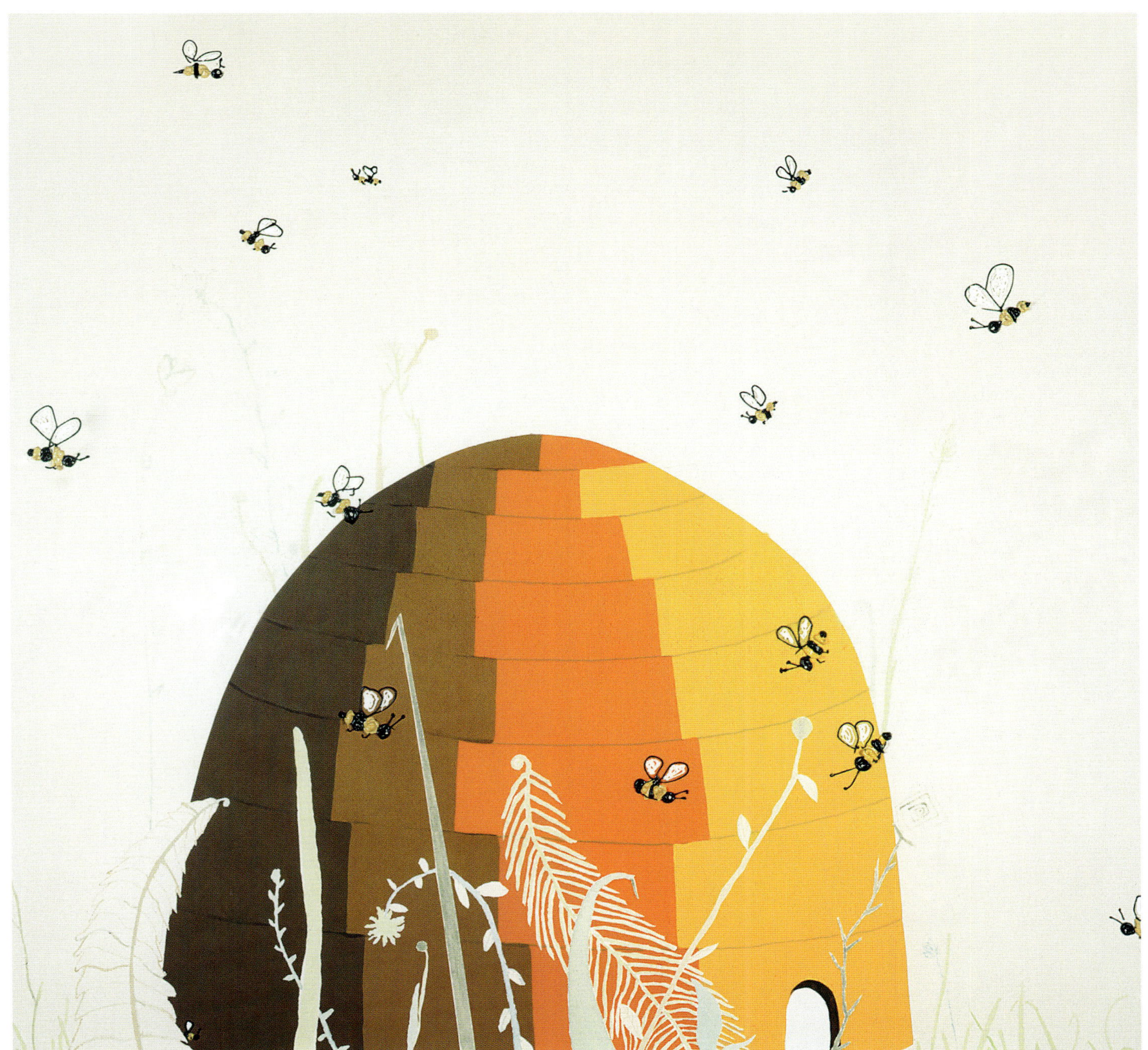

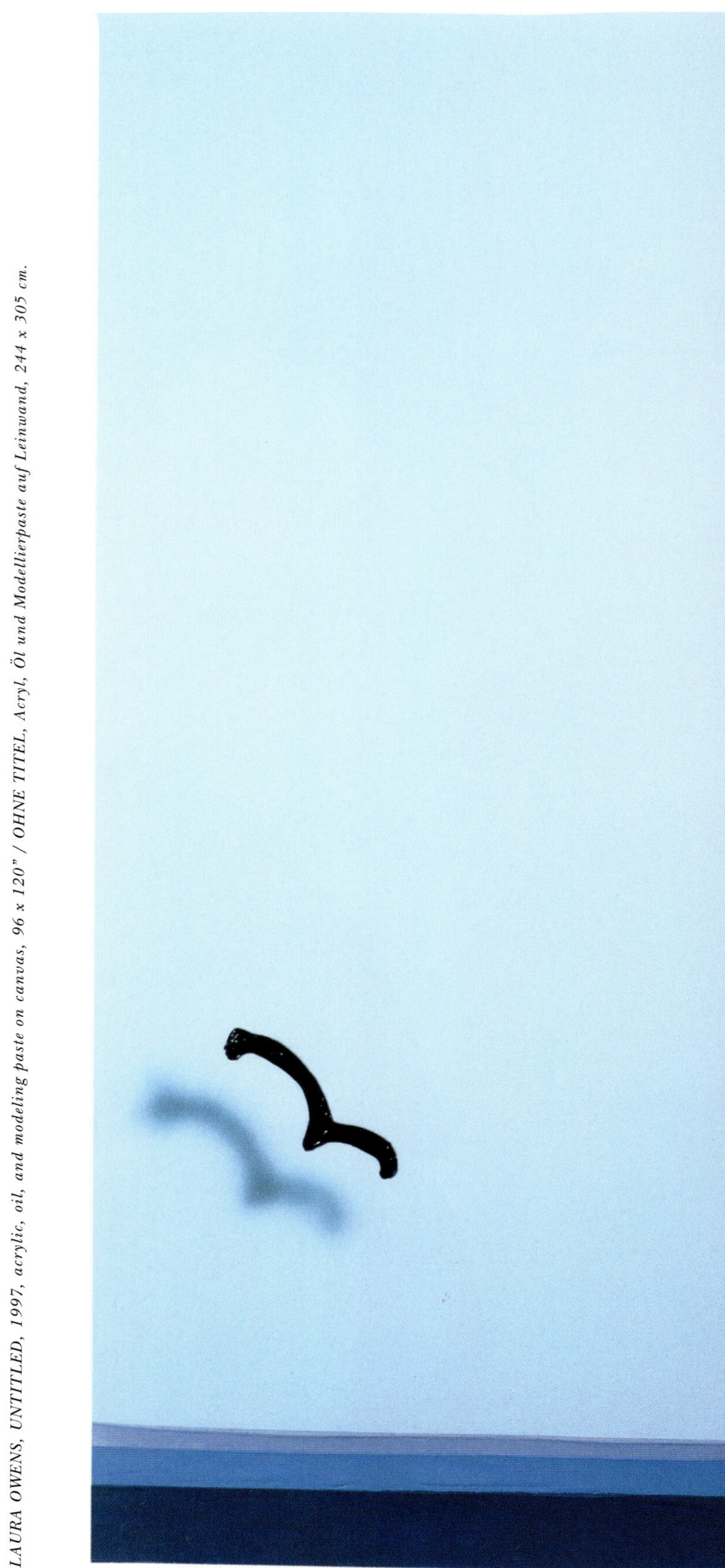

LAURA OWENS, UNTITLED, 1997, acrylic, oil, and modeling paste on canvas, 96 x 120" / OHNE TITEL, Acryl, Öl und Modellierpaste auf Leinwand, 244 x 305 cm.

MONKEY MAN KILLER

BENJAMIN WEISSMAN

High anxiety sweeps through the hamlet of Frost Heave as the Monkey Man killer claimed another victim, this time a postman, who was found impaled on one of his ski poles, mail satchel strapped to his back, no letter disturbed, three claw marks streaked across his frightened frozen face, a bloody carrier indeed. A modest pile of cash, not enough to really change one's life, but a decent amount to make days and nights pass with greater ease, is being offered by the police to the citizen who supplies info leading to capture.

I was reading the newspaper on the green tongue, our L-shaped sectional couch that has absorbed many years of coffee, whiskey, mango puree, drool, dog ass, kimchee, a sampling of some of the best music ever recorded, leaky ball point pens and a porcupine quill. And then it happened: my roommate, Dan, appeared out of nowhere. First no sign of life and then, abracadabra, twitchy itchy Dan, dressed head to toe in black Carhartt, eyes blackened with baseball makeup but no league games scheduled in winter with snow covering the ground like thick cake frosting.

Fleeing the notorious Monkey Man killer who swung from a vine above the Fountain of the Bashful Explorer, a bride and her sisters plus one aunt ran with flowers in their hair down a steep flight of stairs. The groom, trailing his future wife by only a few steps, suffered greatly for his slower feet by tripping on a fallen scarf, losing his balance, tumbling down a hundred stairs, striking his head numerous times. Similar sadness occurred when a Frost Heave baker, fearing attack, jumped to his death from the roof of his bakery. Lonely, yeasty dough rose without the powerful kneading hands of its maker as police detectives scoured the white, flour filled area for clues.

He made wicked buttermilk donuts. Maybe if I comfort his sexy slutty daughter at the funeral she will want to have sex with me.

Groups of frustrated men are taking to the streets waving sticks, scissors, swords, tridents and scimitars. Hoping to entice MMK who might very well be an alien from a planet that sneaks glances at Earth, the vigilantes also carry perfectly ripe bananas with a faint streak of green on the skin as bait.

A confident chef turns his back on the flame and multi-tasks, which is why I was grilling onions but wasn't physically in the kitchen.

"What are you cooking?" Dan asked, "What are you doing with the onions?"

"Potatoes Lyonnaises," I said.

We're rarely in the same room together because we work different shifts at the same restaurant. We conversed about caramelizing onions, how important it is to allow them time to break down, to be patient and not incessantly stir or flip the translucent 'fellas which look like wiggly worms when tripping on acid, to give them their own private time with the heated

---

BENJAMIN WEISSMAN is the author of *Dear Dead Person* (New York: High Risk Books/Serpent's Tail, 1994). He teaches writing at Art Center College of Design in Pasadena.

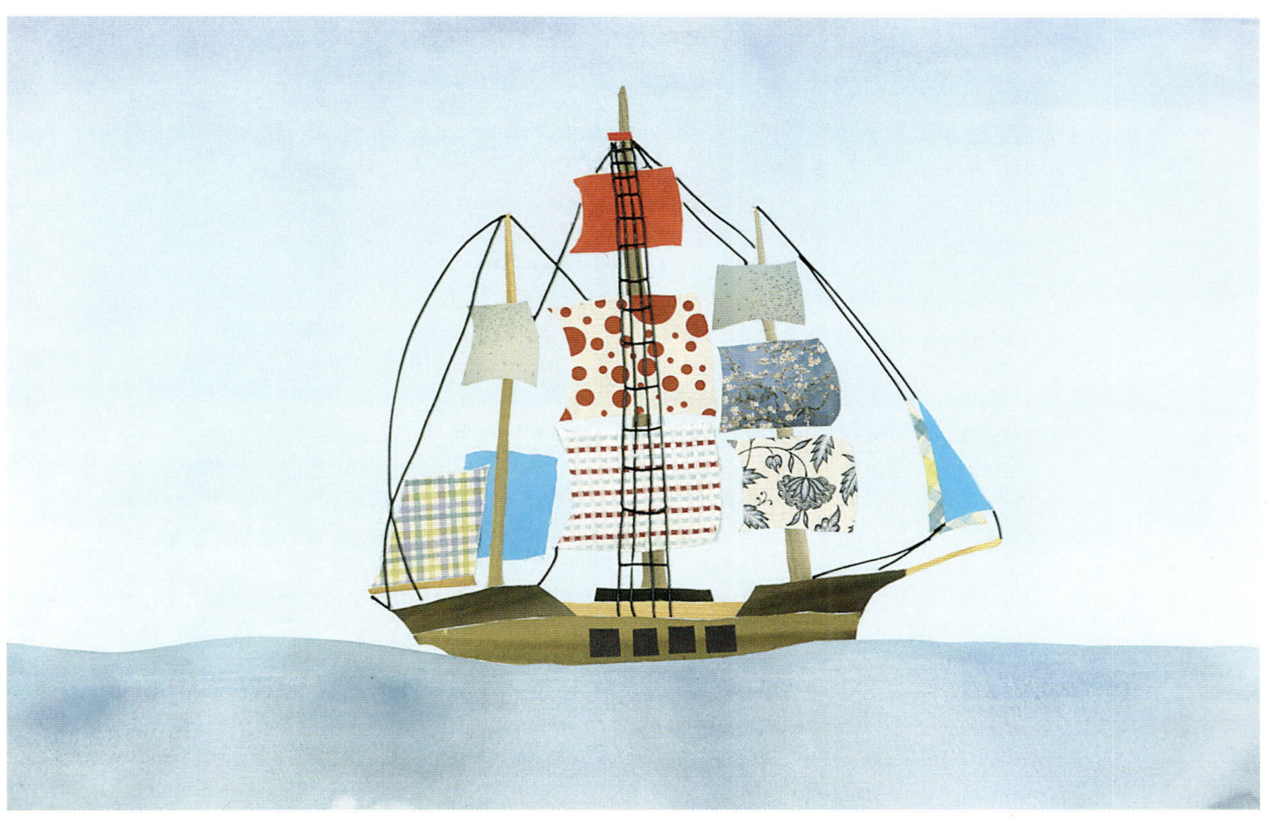

LAURA OWENS, UNTITLED 2000, acrylic, watercolor, paper, fabric, collage on paper, 26 x 40½" /
OHNE TITEL, Acryl, Wasserfarbe, Papier, Stoff, Collage auf Papier, 66 x 103 cm.

oil to brown in a skillet without distraction; otherwise the eater will not experience the remarkable transformation from harsh, tear-inducing bulb to silky sweet vegetable candy. We
tapped knucks on that shared dream. Word to the onion.

I take my dog Leslie, who was born without a fourth leg, out for a walk. She hobbles grace-
fully on three. Her fur is the color of wet sand. She likes the feel of snow on her paws. When
we approach the Fountain of Mystical Formulations I realize I am walking in my sleep, that I
have not officially woken up from the previous night's slumber. I say to myself, "Sleepwalker,
take yourself home now," but I just stand there. Once the perverse aroma of night blooming
jasmine enters my nostrils and my eyes flutter open. Awake, I bear witness to a little gentleman performing an unusual act, but my frozen blood and trembling arms cause temporary
inaction on my part. Was the little gentleman Dan?

The Monkey Man has three buttons on its chest. One makes it turn into a monkey, the second gives it
extra strength, and the third makes it invisible. When he touches a locked door, it falls off and breaks.

Dan and I first bonded over the divinely inspired bouillabaisse, and how it was originally
brought by angels to the Three Marys when they were shipwrecked on the bleak shores of the
Camargue. We know our bouillabaisse sucks because our lame ass frozen rock fish lacks the
high gelatin content necessary in creating that slightly cloudy look not to mention all the microscopic finny tidbits too small for market.

Some citizens, believing that you can rob the Monkey Man killer of his powers, are standing by ready to throw water on his chest. The creature's motherboard heart, concealed beneath its thick black coat of hair, gets short-circuited by liquid. Nonetheless, it is springtime and showy butterflies are on display, floating from flower to flower in an effort never to forget their previous lives as caterpillars. The police struggle with their homicidal instincts suggesting that we all shoot MMK on sight. This of course has led to mistakes.

I punched my mechanic in the neck thinking he was Monkey Man. He fell to the snow and cried out for help. I felt very bad but he looked so much like the simian marauder when he rolled out from under my truck. So terribly hairy, wearing black greasy clothes.

It is Sunday, snowflakes falling gently from the sky, a day to chill on the green tongue, alternate bong hits, and watch *The Naked Chef* on the food channel.

"Dude," I say, "did you know that a chef's hat is called a toque?"

"What do you mean, liar?" Dan reaches into his crotch, peers inside, and begins to scratch.

"I mean that the classic chef's hat was invented by French stoners who were toking burly weed and they named their big hat the toque."

Without warning Dan lunges at me. I receive minor abrasions. Fearing infection I walk through snow and visit my doctor who offers me an overly priced rabies shot, which I refuse. I opt for the modest tetanus shot.

Some people say MMK is painted silver; others have stated that he dresses all in white and is covered with bandages like a mummy. Only his bulging eyes are visible. Sometimes he wears safety goggles. There are also Monkey Man copy cats who don monkey masks and take advantage of the "fear-psychosis" of citizens so they may scuffle and loot.

My doctor described the maniac's mind to me: MMK, he said, is probably suffering from frustrations. He continued to freely espouse that the sufferer takes on a role that allows him to exercise control over people who would otherwise treat him as a failure. No one wants to touch him.

Then there was the poor little girl who was beaten because residents said that the devilish soul of a Monkey Man had inverted her body. She appeared upside down, bouncing on her head.

The phone rings. I answer. A halting voice on the other end. Dan's Hungarian love interest. Her name is very similar to o n i o n, but without the consonants. Before I have a chance to communicate a warm greeting Dan grabs the phone from me, turns his back and emits an "ooh ooh," then waits and laughs when he hears her make the same primal sound, i.e., their not so secret monkey code. Dan's incisors come to fine points. My teeth are all rounded for softer foods: oatmeal, ice cream, and éclairs. His teeth are for removing bottle caps. He and his insect-eating girlfriend make a date to go bouldering. I've seen Oouioo pull down fir branches and snack on pine needles. Dan drops the phone. Conversation done. He leaps into a handstand possession, his hairy toes wiggling freely. I have seen him draw pictures of Mary and the Baby Jesus with those long-fingered feet.

"Save some potatoes for me, dude," he says, and then vanishes in an unexplained manner. Suddenly there is a fire in the kitchen, oh no, the onions, followed by an explosion. I fly through the air and I land on my head on the street but when I right myself, I am happy to find nothing broken.

A bicycle rolls by. A projectile hits our front door. The Sunday paper.

The headline mirrors my exact thoughts: *HOW DO YOU KNOW WHEN TO BLOW THE WHISTLE?*

DER MONKEY-MAN-KILLER

BENJAMIN WEISSMAN

Entsetzen macht sich breit im Weiler Frost Heave. Der Monkey-Man-Killer hat wieder zugeschlagen. Diesmal ist das Opfer ein Briefträger, man hat ihn auf einem seiner Skistöcke aufgespiesst gefunden, seine Umhängetasche auf dem Rücken festgeschnallt, die Briefe darin unangetastet, und quer über seinem angstverzerrten, steif gefrorenen Gesicht drei blutige Krallenspuren. Ein echt blutiger Bote. Für nützliche Hinweise, die zur Ergreifung des Täters führen, setzt die Polizei eine kleinere Geldsumme aus, die zwar nicht ausreicht, um ein neues Leben anzufangen, aber immerhin so gross ist, dass man sich seine Tage und Nächte angenehmer gestalten könnte.

Ich las Zeitung auf unserer grünen Zunge, einem L-förmigen Couch-Element, das im Lauf der Jahre Unmengen an Kaffee, Whisky, Mangopüree, Speichel, Hundearsch, Kimtschi, eine Auswahl der besten Musik, die je aufgenommen wurde, schmierende Kugelschreiber und den Stachel eines Stachelschweins absorbiert hat. Da passierte es, mein Mitbewohner Dan tauchte plötzlich aus dem Nichts auf. Zuerst kein Lebenszeichen weit und breit, und dann, Abrakadabra, superduper Dan, von Kopf bis Fuss in schwarzer Arbeitskluft und mit schwarzen Baseball-Markierungen unter den Augen, obwohl im Winter, wenn der Schnee den Boden wie eine dicke Schicht Zuckerguss bedeckt, gar keine Ligaspiele stattfinden.

In wilder Flucht vor dem berüchtigten Monkey-Man-Killer, der sich an einer Liane vom Brunnen des Schüchternen Entdeckungsreisenden herunterschwang, rannte eine Braut mit ihren Schwestern und einer Tante mit Blumen im Haar die steilen Stufen einer Treppe hinunter. Der Bräutigam, der nur wenige Schritte hinter seiner zukünftigen Frau herlief, musste seine Langsamkeit schwer büssen: Er rutschte auf einem zu Boden geglittenen Schal aus, verlor das Gleichgewicht, stürzte hundert Treppenstufen hinunter und schlug dabei mehrmals mit dem Kopf auf. Nicht besser erging es einem Bäcker aus Frost Heave, als er aus Angst angefallen zu werden vom Dach seiner Bäckerei in den Tod sprang. Der einsam gärende Hefeteig ging ohne das kraftvolle Kneten der Bäckerhände auf, während Detektive der Kriminalpolizei das weisse, mehlstiebende Grundstück nach Indizien absuchten.

Er machte verteufelt gute Buttermilch-Donuts. Wer weiss, vielleicht geht seine Tochter, eine verdammt heisse Schlampe, mit mir ins Bett, wenn ich mich auf der Beerdigung ein bisschen um sie kümmere.

BENJAMIN WEISSMAN ist der Autor von *Dear Dead Person* (High Risk Books/Serpent's Tail, New York 1994). Er unterrichtet kreatives Schreiben am Art Center College of Design in Pasadena.

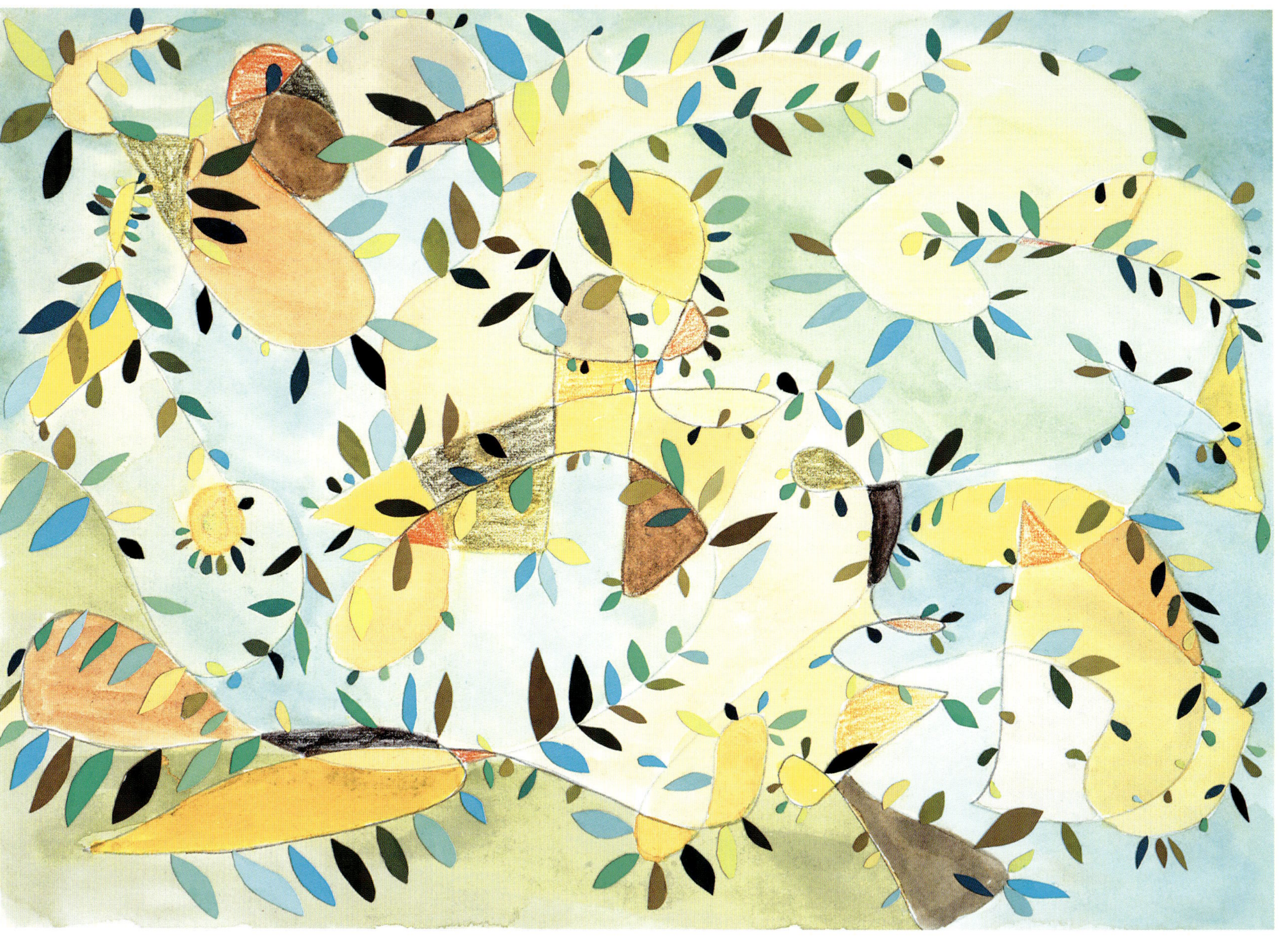

LAURA OWENS, UNTITLED, 2001, watercolor, pencil, and collage on paper, 10¼ x 7" / OHNE TITEL, Wasserfarbe, Farbstift und Collage auf Papier, 26 x 17,8 cm.

Frustrierte Männer strömen auf die Strasse und fuchteln mit Stöcken, Scheren, Schwertern, Dreizacken und Krummsäbeln herum. Als Köder hat die Bürgerwehr auch noch reife Bananen mit einem blassgrünen Streifen auf der Schale mitgebracht, um den MMK anzulocken; vielleicht ist er ja ein Ausserirdischer von einem Stern, auf dem man mit der Erde liebäugelt.

Ein selbstbewusster Koch dreht der Kochplatte und dem multifunktionalen Herd auch mal den Rücken zu; das machte es möglich, dass ich dabei war, Zwiebeln zu rösten, obwohl ich selbst nicht in der Küche war.

«Was kochst du?», fragte Dan. «Was machst du mit den Zwiebeln?»

«Pommes Lyonnaises», sagte ich.

Wir sind selten zusammen im gleichen Raum, da wir im Restaurant nicht in derselben Schicht arbeiten. Wir unterhielten uns über das Karamelisieren von Zwiebeln, darüber, wie wichtig es ist, ihnen beim Andämpfen genügend Zeit zu lassen, dass man geduldig sein muss und die glasigen Dinger, die sich winden wie Würmer in Säure, nicht ständig umrühren oder wenden darf, sondern sie im heissen Öl in Ruhe lassen muss, damit sie in der Pfanne ungehindert Farbe annehmen können. Andernfalls wird der Gast diese erstaunliche Verwandlung der scharfen, beissenden Zwiebel in ein süsses, seidenweiches Gemüsebonbon nicht erleben können. Wir gönnten uns einen kurzen Schlagabtausch zu diesem gemeinsamen Traum. Lasst Zwiebeln sprechen.

Ich führe meine Hündin Leslie spazieren, die ohne viertes Bein geboren wurde. Graziös hoppelt sie auf ihren drei Beinen herum. Ihr Fell hat die Farbe von nassem Sand. Sie mag das Gefühl von Schnee an den Pfoten. Als wir beim Brunnen der Zauberformeln ankommen, merke ich, dass ich schlafwandle, dass ich eigentlich seit letzter Nacht noch nicht aufgewacht bin. Ich sage mir: «Schlafwandler, geh jetzt nach Hause», aber ich bleibe einfach stehen. Bis mir der perverse Duft des nächtlich blühenden Jasmins in die Nase steigt und mich die Augen aufschlagen lässt. Kaum wach geworden werde ich Zeuge der merkwürdigen Handlung eines kleinen Herrn, aber mein stockendes Blut und meine zitternden Arme lassen mich tatenlos zuschauen. War der kleine Herr Dan?

Der Monkey-Man hat drei Knöpfe auf der Brust. Der erste verwandelt ihn in einen Affen, der zweite verleiht ihm Riesenkräfte und der dritte lässt ihn unsichtbar werden. Eine verriegelte Tür braucht er nur zu berühren, schon fällt sie berstend aus den Angeln.

Dan und ich haben erstmals über der Bouillabaisse, diesem Geschenk des Himmels, zueinander gefunden: Sie wurde ja ursprünglich von Engeln zu den an den verlassenen Gestaden der Camargue gestrandeten drei Marien gebracht. Wir wissen natürlich, dass unsere Bouillabaisse zu wünschen übrig lässt, weil der fade, gefrorene Kabeljau nicht den für das wolkige Aussehen der Suppe wichtigen Gelatinegehalt aufweist, vom Fehlen der mikroskopischen, für den Markt viel zu kleinen Delikatessfischchen ganz zu schweigen.

Ein paar Bürger, die glauben, man könnte den Monkey-Man-Killer seiner Kräfte berauben, lauern darauf, ihm Wasser auf die Brust zu schütten. Das hätte einen Kurzschluss in der unter dem dichten schwarzen Pelz verborgenen Schaltzentrale der Kreatur zur Folge. Trotz allem ist es Frühling und man sieht prächtige Schmetterlinge von Blüte zu Blüte gaukeln, immer bemüht, ihr früheres Raupendasein nicht zu vergessen. Die Polizei hat mit Mordgelüsten zu kämpfen und schlägt vor, wir alle sollten auf den MMK schiessen, sobald er sich blicken lässt. Das führte natürlich zu Missverständnissen.

Ich versetzte meinem Mechaniker einen Schlag ins Genick, weil ich ihn für Monkey-Man hielt. Er fiel in den Schnee und schrie um Hilfe. Es war mir gar nicht recht, aber für einen Moment hatte er tatsächlich wie dieser marodierende Affe ausgesehen, als er total behaart in seiner schwarzen, ölverschmierten Kluft unter meinem Kleinlaster hervorschoss.

Es ist Sonntag. Schneeflocken rieseln leise vom Himmel, ein Tag, um auf der grünen Zunge zu entspannen, den Joint kreisen zu lassen und sich auf dem Gourmetkanal *The Naked Chef* reinzuziehen.

«Mensch», sage ich, «hast du gewusst, dass eine Kochmütze *toque* heisst?»
«Was erzählst du da, du Lügenmaul?» Dan greift sich in den Schritt, schaut in seine Hose und beginnt sich zu kratzen.

«Ich sage, dass die klassische Kochmütze von französischen Kiffern erfunden wurde, die sich mit Killergras bedröhnten und ihre Riesentüten *toques* nannten.»

Ohne Vorwarnung holt Dan aus. Ich trage ein paar Schrammen davon und stapfe aus Angst vor einer Infektion durch den Schnee zu meinem Arzt, der mir eine viel zu teure Spritze gegen Tollwut verpassen will. Ich winke ab und entscheide mich für die billigere Tetanusspritze.

Manche behaupten, der MMK sei silbern bemalt, andere sagen, er sei ganz in Weiss gekleidet und wie eine Mumie in Bandagen eingewickelt. Zu sehen sind nur seine hervorquellenden Augen. Gelegentlich trägt er auch eine Schutzbrille. Es gibt eine ganze Reihe von Trittbrettfahrern, die sich Affenmasken aufsetzen und die allgemeine «Angstpsychose» zum Raufen und Plündern ausnützen.

Mein Arzt hat mir die geistige Verfassung dieses Irren erklärt: Der MMK sei wahrscheinlich hochgradig frustriert, und – so fabulierte er weiter – einer der leide, lege sich gern eine Rolle zu, die es ihm erlaube, andere Menschen unter seine Kontrolle zu bringen, Menschen, die ihn sonst als Versager betrachten würden. Niemand will mit ihm zu tun haben.

Dann war da noch dieses arme kleine Mädchen, das verprügelt wurde, weil die Hausbewohner behaupteten, dass die vom Teufel besessene Seele eines Affenmenschen ihren Körper auf den Kopf gestellt habe. Man sah sie nämlich immer nur auf dem Kopf herumhüpfen.

Das Telefon klingelt. Ich nehme ab. Eine stockende Stimme am anderen Ende. Dans ungarische Flamme. Ihr Name klingt wie «Onion» (Zwiebel), aber ohne Konsonanten. Bevor ich ein paar herzliche Worte zur Begrüssung mit ihr tauschen kann, entreisst mir Dan das Telefon, dreht mir den Rücken zu und stösst ein «Uuhuuh» aus, dann wartet er und lacht, als er denselben Urlaut in ihrem ganz und gar nicht geheimen Affencode, von ihr hört. Dans Schneidezähne laufen spitz zu. Meine Zähne sind dagegen durch das weiche Essen, das ich zu mir nehme – Haferschleim, Eiscrème und Liebesknochen –, gleichmässig abgerundet. Er kann mit den seinen sogar Flaschen öffnen. Er und seine Insekten essende Freundin verabreden sich zum Felsenklettern. Ich habe schon erlebt, wie Oioo die Zweige von Kieferbäumen herunterzog, um sich an den Nadeln zu verlustieren. Dan lässt den Hörer fallen. Das Gespräch ist beendet. Er macht einen Handstand und wackelt hemmungslos mit seinen haarigen Zehen. Ich hab auch schon gesehen, wie er mit diesen langen Zehen Bilder von Maria und dem Jesuskind gemalt hat.

«Heb ein paar Kartoffeln für mich auf, Alter», sagt er und verschwindet auf unerklärliche Weise. Jetzt brennt es plötzlich in der Küche – nicht doch, die Zwiebeln! –, dann folgt eine Explosion. Ich fliege durch die Luft und lande kopfüber auf der Strasse, doch als ich mich wieder aufrichte, stelle ich fest, dass ich mir zum Glück nichts gebrochen habe.

Ein Fahrrad rollt vorbei. Ein Projektil schlägt gegen unsere Haustür. Die Sonntagszeitung. Die Schlagzeile sagt genau, was ich denke: *WOHER WEISS MAN, WANN ABPFEIFEN?*

(Übersetzung: Goridis/Parker)

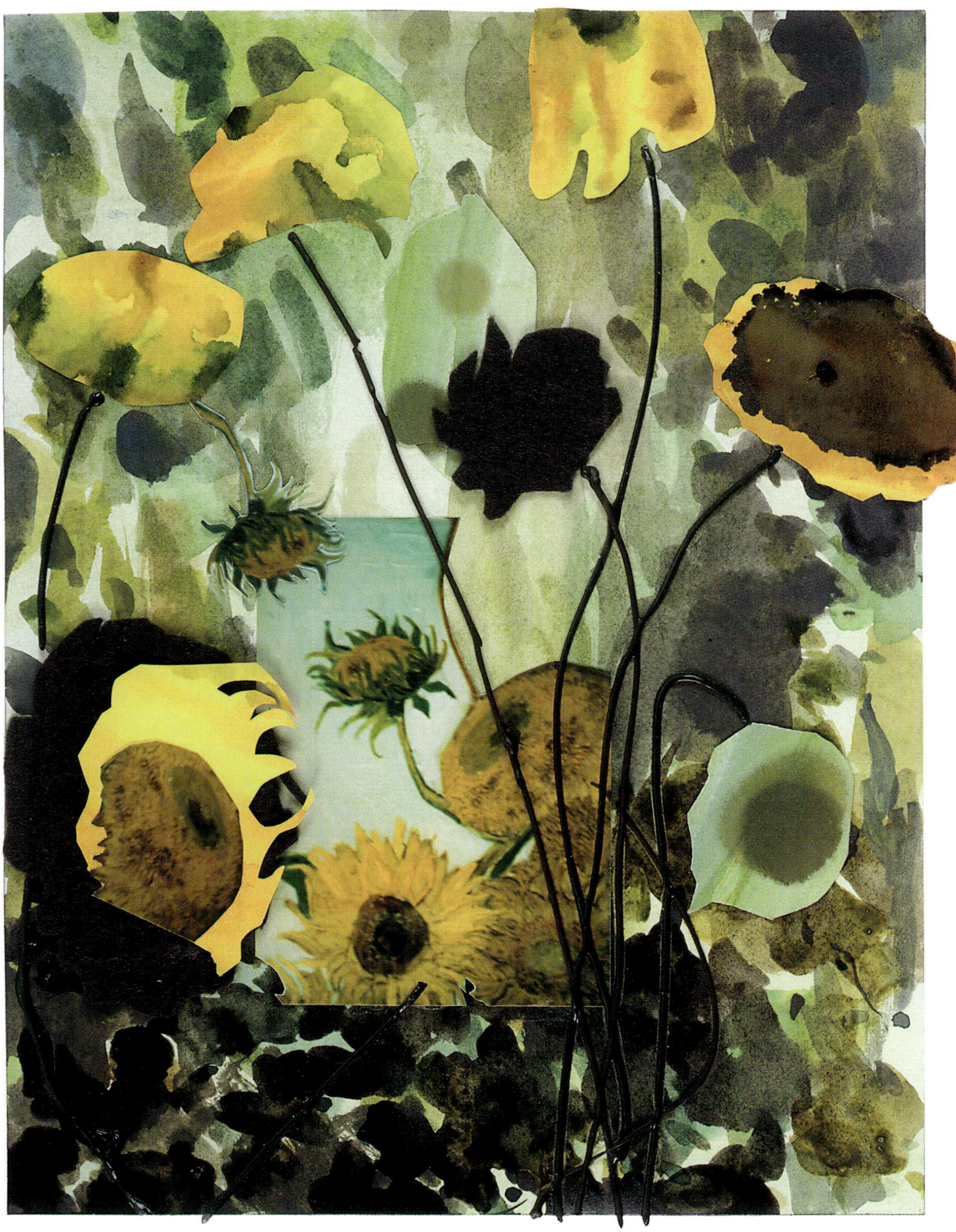

LAURA OWENS, UNTITLED, 2001, watercolor, felt, photo, collage on paper, 12 x 9½" / OHNE TITEL, Wasserfarbe, Filz, Photo, Collage auf Papier, 30,5 x 24 cm.

From my Junkyard to Yours

MUNGO THOMSON

I met Laura Owens and her work at the same time, at a show she had at ACME Gallery in Los Angeles in 1998. The exhibition was a nearly empty, nearly white space with a few nearly empty, nearly white canvases hovering around the edges of the room. The paintings (landscapes, more or less) had been installed so as to echo the scale and atmosphere of the gallery. They lurked around corners and hugged the walls as if they were hiding. The largest painting w a s one of the walls—built to fit snugly, and stretched, gessoed, and painted (a little) on site.

Each painting in the exhibition was itself a wall-like support for a few speedy pencil marks, stretches of monochrome, passages of stain and dry brush-work, airbrush, and knifed-on smears, that here co-hered into a yellow tree, and there into moonlit clouds that might have been an undersea scene. The mood of the work was somewhere between referential and reverential; between Lichtenstein's Chinese landscape paintings and Chinese landscape painting. They displayed a deliberated-upon spontaneity and a

(masterful) flaunting of non-mastery that felt democratic rather than bratty.

The work was very aware of its own existence. Its self-consciousness suggested an acute presence in the making, and seemed to recommend an acute presence in the viewing. The show demonstrated an interest in issues of immersion and phenomenology common to the history of L.A. art, but it was also c o m i c—ultimately the paintings called attention to the whole w a y o u t endeavor of producing such immense objects to generate such slight effects. Laura later told me that she had been "out of ideas," so she let the exact dimensions of the gallery determine the size of her paintings and proceeded from there, making picture windows for ACME.

Later I was at a dinner where people were talking about the show and I wasn't sure we'd seen the same show at all. I felt like I had been inside some kind of decorative Michael Asher. They discussed it as a straightforward exhibition of paintings, holding it to the kind of "Art" standard (think Janson's) that in my view the show was deliberately tweaking. The canvases were so contingent on the space that you couldn't talk about one without the other, and I

MUNGO THOMSON is an artist working and living in Los Angeles.

LAURA OWENS, UNTITLED, 1999, acrylic and oil on canvas, 122 x 102" / OHNE TITEL, Acryl und Öl auf Leinwand, 310 x 259 cm.

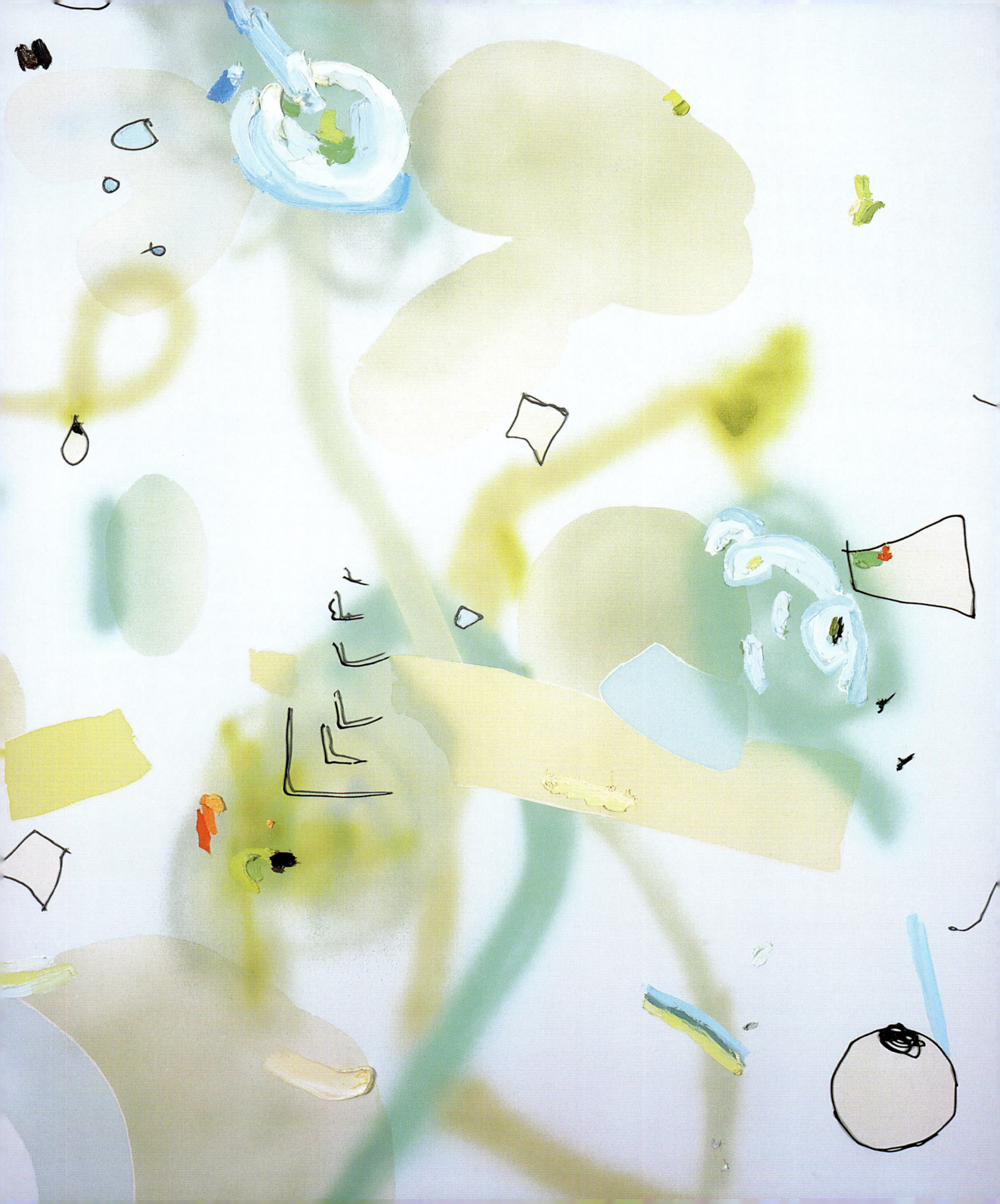

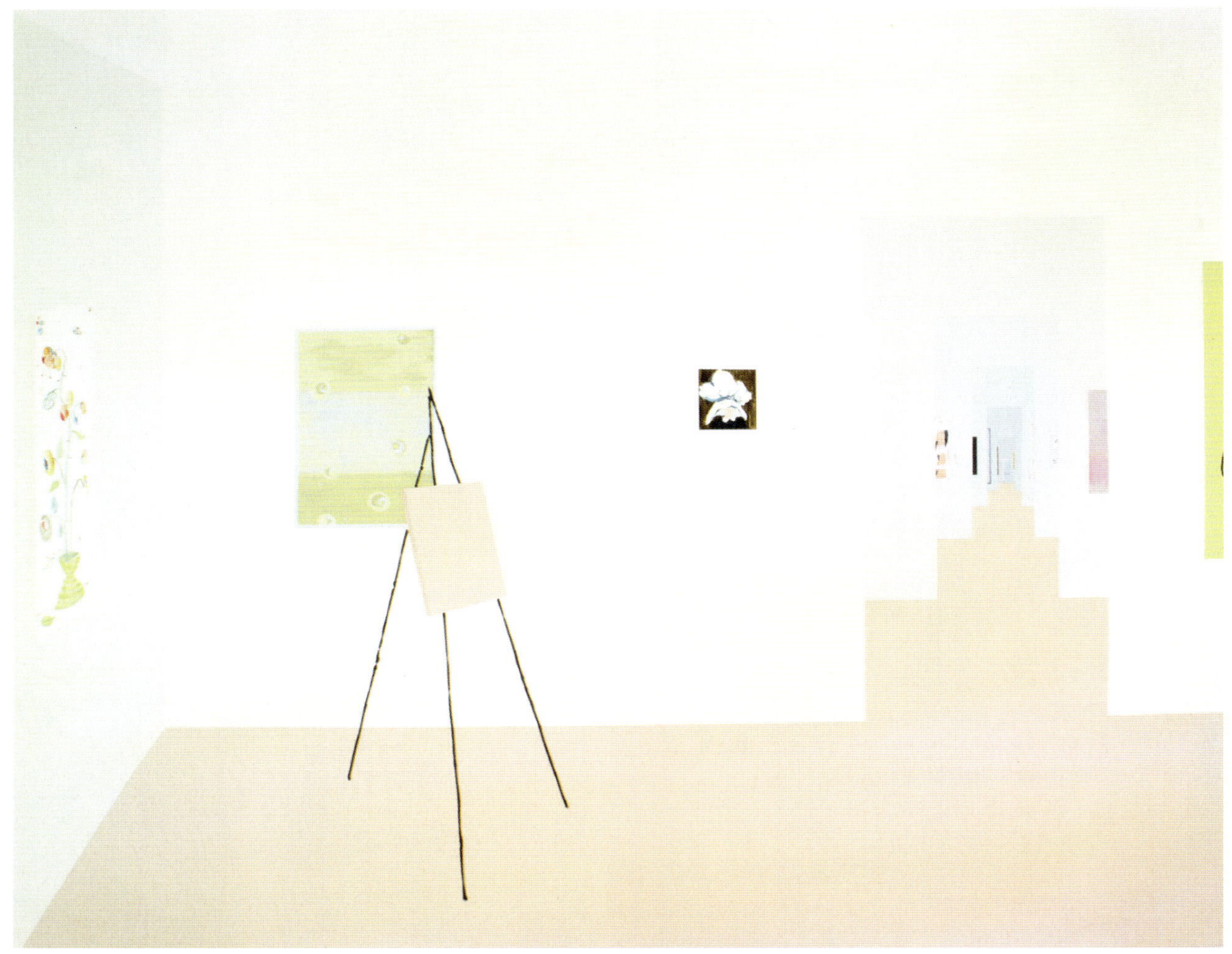

loved this about the work: it was anecdotal and expansive; it didn't stop at its edges. Here was the private mania of painting with a sociable side, addressing the specific circumstances of its production and display.

As time wore on and we became friends, I became familiar with Laura's special relationship to popular principles of "Art" and their role in her practice. Not long after the ACME show, after doing a weary round of studio visits at an art school, she told me, "The best stuff doesn't look like art." Not long after t h a t, when I was installing my own show up the road, she told me, "Don't be afraid of it looking too much like art." What these contradicting kernels of wisdom demonstrate is that, to Laura's (very West Coast third eye) way of seeing things, "Art" can be abandoned or embraced, but should never be cause for apprehension; for all the deliberation I see in her work, there remains above all a will for adventure (since it's all a path to discovery anyway, and each work makes way for the next and we create the world in every moment, and as you dream, so shall it be).

To me the work is a farcical representation, rendered with pathological sincerity, of what art is supposed to look like. All the cues are present to signal "painting": if the raw materials of the medium aren't being trotted out—unpainted canvas and pigment straight from the tube—then the historical record is being used as raw material. Clichés abound in Laura's paintings; allusions to the traditions and archetypes of Modernist abstraction, landscape, figuration, assemblage, the romantic, the maritime, and the postmodern, all figure in. The work seems to want to see how deeply the tropes of painting, and of looking at paintings, have been culturally absorbed; how well-traveled the path is from original to standard to generic. Laura's work stirs the idea of art that perches like a gargoyle in the collective unconscious (literally a gargoyle: it must look like a composite of Michelangelo's DAVID, Van Gogh's SELF-PORTRAIT WITH EAR BANDAGE, and the horse in Picasso's GUERNICA). For me the paintings recall the junkyard in my own brain where all of the how-to books, museum posters, and thrift-store paintings I've ever looked at have been dumped. (And they don't just recall specific articles in the junkyard, they recall the j u n k y a r d.) Still, for all the jadedness I read into the work, it seems enormously invested in getting past my own. That's where the pathological sincerity comes in. Laura goes to great lengths to deliver the perfect "painting," preferably outside of quotation marks.

With all the open-ended practices out there, I think it's hard to make open-ended paintings (I mean the edges are right t h e r e), but Laura manages it by diversifying: one painting rarely follows logically upon the last, except by a logic of inclusiveness and eclecticism. This is painting that's not only self-conscious, but conscious of its surroundings, right down to the wall that it's on and the room that it's in. This is the condition and the conundrum of Laura's practice—intense reverence for the histories and conventions of the production and display of paintings on the one hand, toying with them on the other hand, and the explicit transformation of this conversation into content: How to make a painting now? What to do with it? and even, What's the point? Not as in, Is painting dead?—something that would never occur

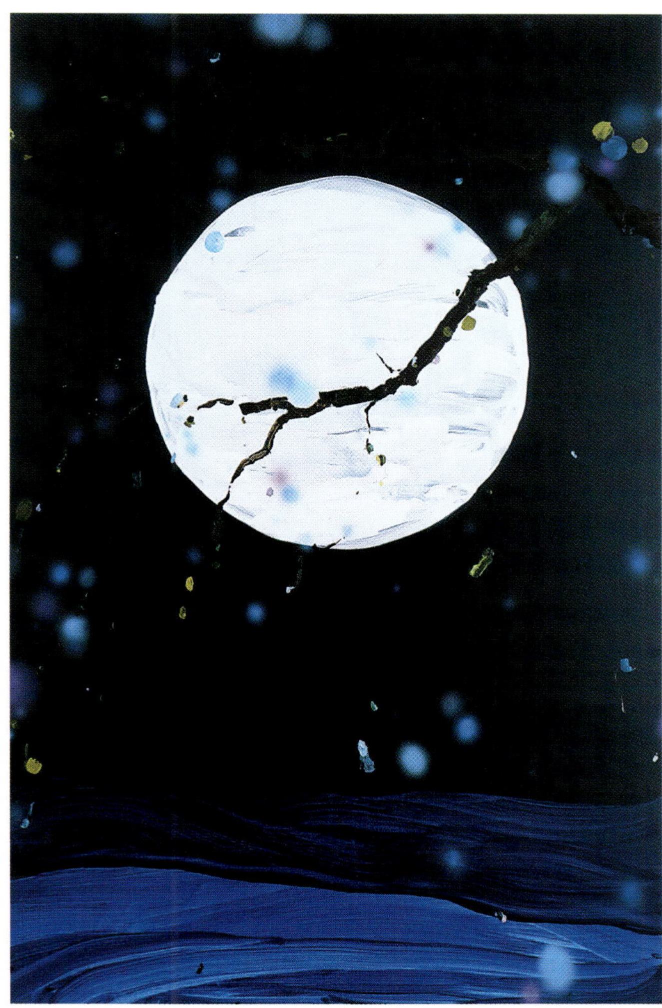

LAURA OWENS, UNTITLED, 2000, acrylic and oil on canvas,
110 x 72" / OHNE TITEL, Acryl und Öl auf Leinwand, 280 x 183 cm.

to her—but as in: Why do a n y t h i n g, given the nature of the work of art in the age of mechanical reproduction and the march of the culture industry and other paralyzing considerations ad infinitum, not to mention the looming presence of war and other major bummers? Is a painting capable of redeeming any of that? (Laura calls me up from time to time to ask things like, "Can we start a revolution?")

Ultimately the art that I care about in Los Angeles is given to consider the physical, social, and existential conditions of its own existence. It tends to be

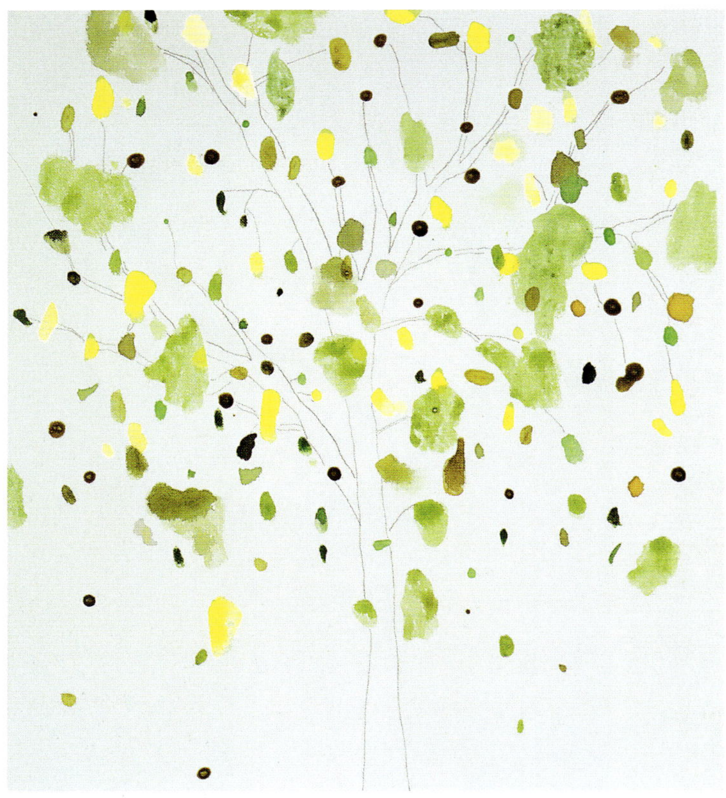

LAURA OWENS, UNTITLED, 1998, acrylic on canvas, 20 x 17½" / OHNE TITEL, Acryl auf Leinwand, 50,8 x 44,5 cm.

conversational and suggestive and to wear its doubts outright. It displays a certain nihilistic utopianism and is comfortable with oxymorons. It's not the kitsch and fiberglass of a dystopic Disneyland, but the spaced-out rigor of spending the day in the garden. It is interested in the bright light and negative space that is everywhere here and yet difficult to locate, and in prying out of the ether (now smog) some of the humor and pathos that was floated up there by Bas Jan Ader and John Baldessari circa 1970 (the year Laura was born).

Laura's work has a feel for the f e e l of this negative space. Her paintings soak up and reflect the atmosphere of L.A.—that of relationships (romantic, collegial, professional); thick hazes and cartoonish sunsets; glass skyscrapers peeking over hills; yoga classes and self-realization seminars; building gar-

dens of eucalyptus, palm, and bonsai trees (all non-native); metallic paint-jobs and restaurant aquariums; computer, TV, and movie screens; going to galleries and going to the park; and numerous fantasies of enlightenment, of ships sailing and cherry branches groping the moon. But further, an atmosphere of the permissive and inclusive, of "whatever" and "okay" and the up-for-anything pervades her practice, as it does this city. Laura's work seizes all the tropes of both painting and living in L.A., all the ups and downs of working and being here—trying to do something new, or failing that, interesting, or failing that, amusing; one day following the next like an exact copy (if a luminous one)—and twists these ambivalences into virtues. All these divergent experiences under one endless blue canopy, and a painting for every experience.

LAURA OWENS, UNTITLED, 2000, acrylic, oil, and watercolor on canvas, 96 x 84" / OHNE TITEL, Acryl, Öl und Wasserfarbe auf Leinwand, 244 x 213,4 cm.

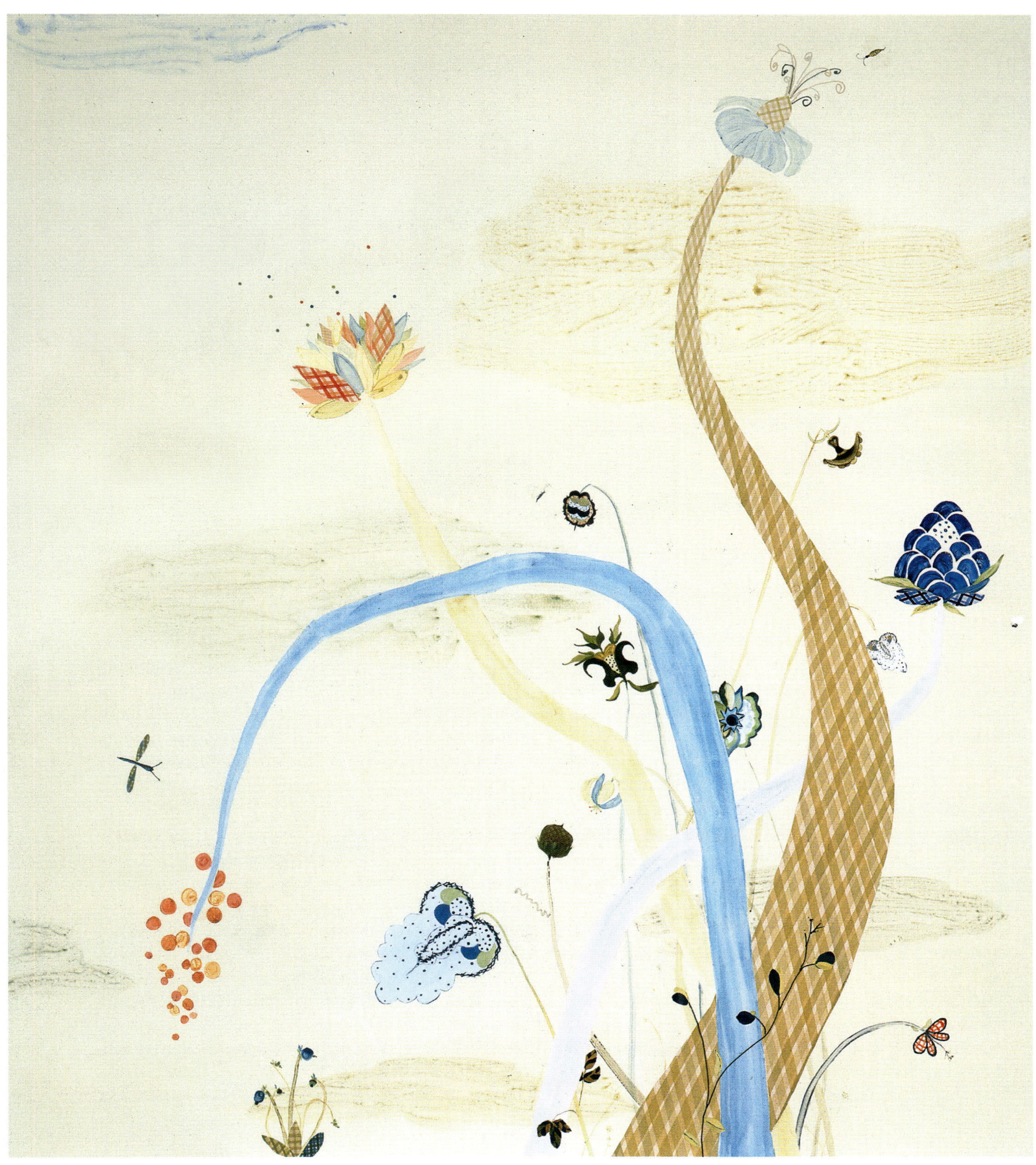

Von meinem Schrotthaufen zu deinem eigenen

MUNGO THOMSON

Ich lernte Laura Owens und ihr Werk gleichzeitig kennen, und zwar anlässlich ihrer Ausstellung in der ACME Gallery in Los Angeles 1998. Die Ausstellung bestand aus einem beinah leeren, beinah weissen Raum mit ein paar wenigen beinah leeren, beinah weissen, am Rand des Raumes schwebenden Leinwänden. Die Bilder (mehr oder weniger alles Landschaften) waren so gehängt, dass sie die Grösse und Atmosphäre des Galerieraumes aufnahmen und hervorhoben. Sie lauerten hinter jeder Ecke und drängten sich an die Wand, als wollten sie sich verstecken. Das grösste Bild war eine ganze Wand; es hatte genau die passende Grösse und war an Ort aufgespannt, grundiert und (ein bisschen) bemalt worden.

Jedes der Bilder in dieser Ausstellung war selbst ein wandähnlicher Träger für ein paar flüchtige Bleistiftzeichen, monochrome Partien, Stellen mit Flecken und trockenen Pinselstrichen, Airbrush-Flächen und aufgespachtelte Kleckse, die einmal

zu einem gelben Baum zusammenfanden, einmal zu Wolken im Mondlicht; es hätte aber auch eine Unterwasserlandschaft sein können. Die Stimmung in diesen Arbeiten schillerte zwischen Anspielung und Reverenz; zwischen Lichtensteins chinesischen Landschaftsbildern und Chinesischer Landschaftsmalerei. Sie waren auf wohl überlegte Art spontan und stellten (souverän) die Abwesenheit jeglicher Souveränität zur Schau, was weniger rotzfrech als vielmehr demokratisch wirkte.

Diese Kunst war sich ihrer eigenen Existenz durchaus bewusst. Dieses Selbstbewusste deutete auf eine wache Präsenz während des Entstehungsprozesses und liess auch eine entsprechend wache Präsenz beim Betrachten empfehlenswert erscheinen. Die ganze Ausstellung zeugte von einem Interesse für die Fragen des «sich in etwas Versenkens» und der Phänomenologie, die in der Geschichte der Kunst von Los Angeles geläufig sind. Aber sie hatte auch eine komische Seite; schliesslich lenkten die Bilder die Aufmerksamkeit auf das aufwändige Unterfangen, derart grosse Objekte herzustellen, um so unmerkliche Effekte zu erzielen. Laura erzählte mir später, dass ihr damals

MUNGO THOMSON is an artist working and living in Los Angeles.

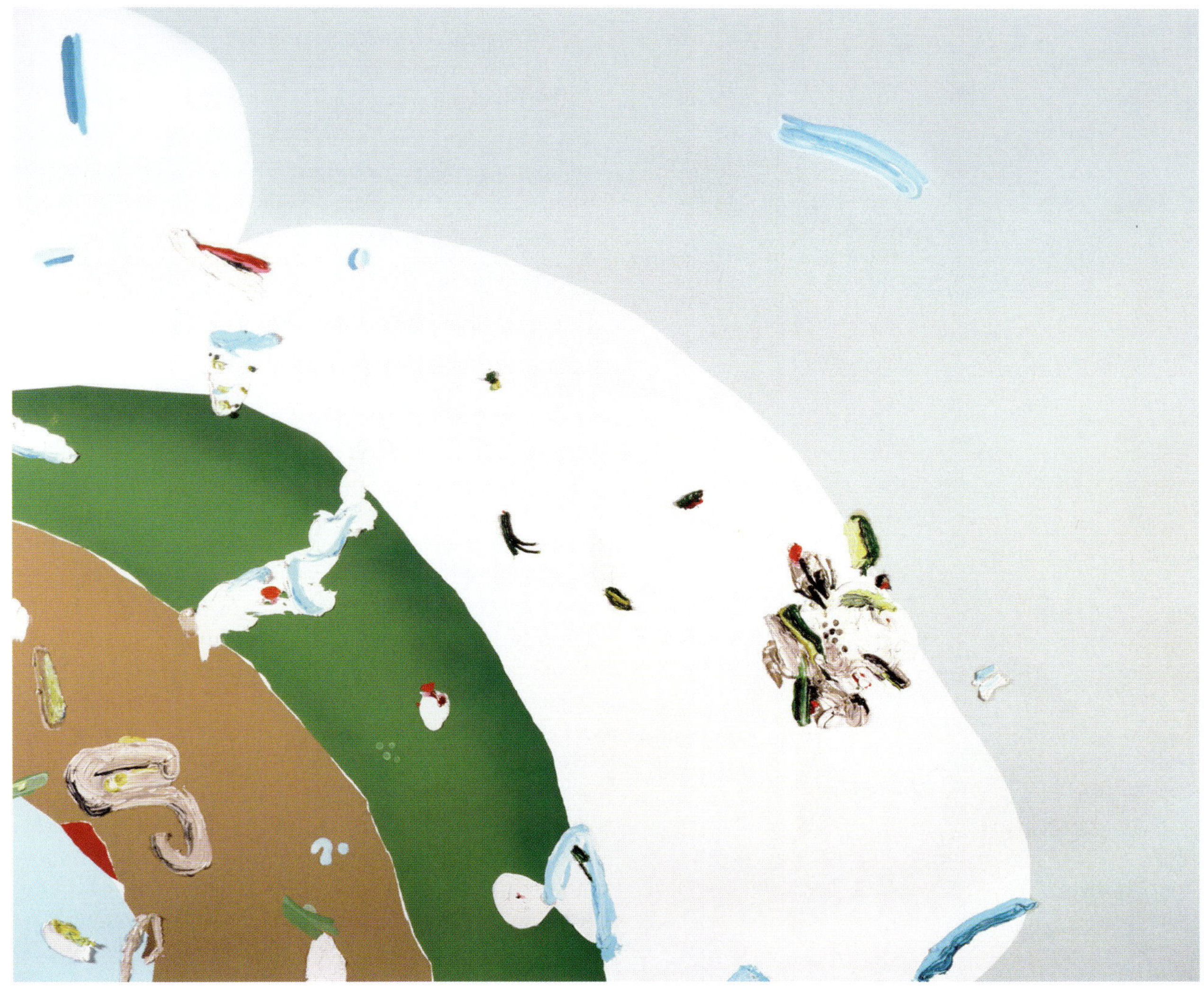

LAURA OWENS, UNTITLED, 1998, oil and acrylic on canvas, 84 x 96" / OHNE TITEL, Öl und Acryl auf Leinwand, 213,4 x 244 cm.

«die Ideen ausgegangen» seien, deshalb hatte sie die exakten Dimensionen der Galerie als Ausgangspunkt genommen und exakt passende Bilderfenster für ACME gemacht.

Später war ich bei einem Abendessen, wo die Leute über die Ausstellung sprachen, und hatte das Gefühl, wir hätten überhaupt nicht dieselbe Ausstellung gesehen. Mir war, als hätte ich eine Art dekorativen Michael Asher gesehen. Sie fanden, es sei eine ehrliche Malerei-Ausstellung gewesen, und schrieben es einer bestimmten Auffassung von «Kunst» zu

(wohl Jansons), dass ich die Ausstellung für eine bewusste Provokation hielt. Die Leinwände waren so raumgebunden, dass man nicht über sie reden konnte, ohne vom Raum zu reden, und das gefiel mir an dieser Arbeit: Sie war anekdotisch und expansiv; sie hörte nicht an den Bildrändern auf. Hier bekam die private Bildbesessenheit etwas Geselliges, das die spezifischen Umstände der Entstehung und des Ausstellens der Bilder zur Sprache brachte.

Nach einiger Zeit, als wir Freunde geworden waren, wurde mir auch Lauras besonderes Verhältnis

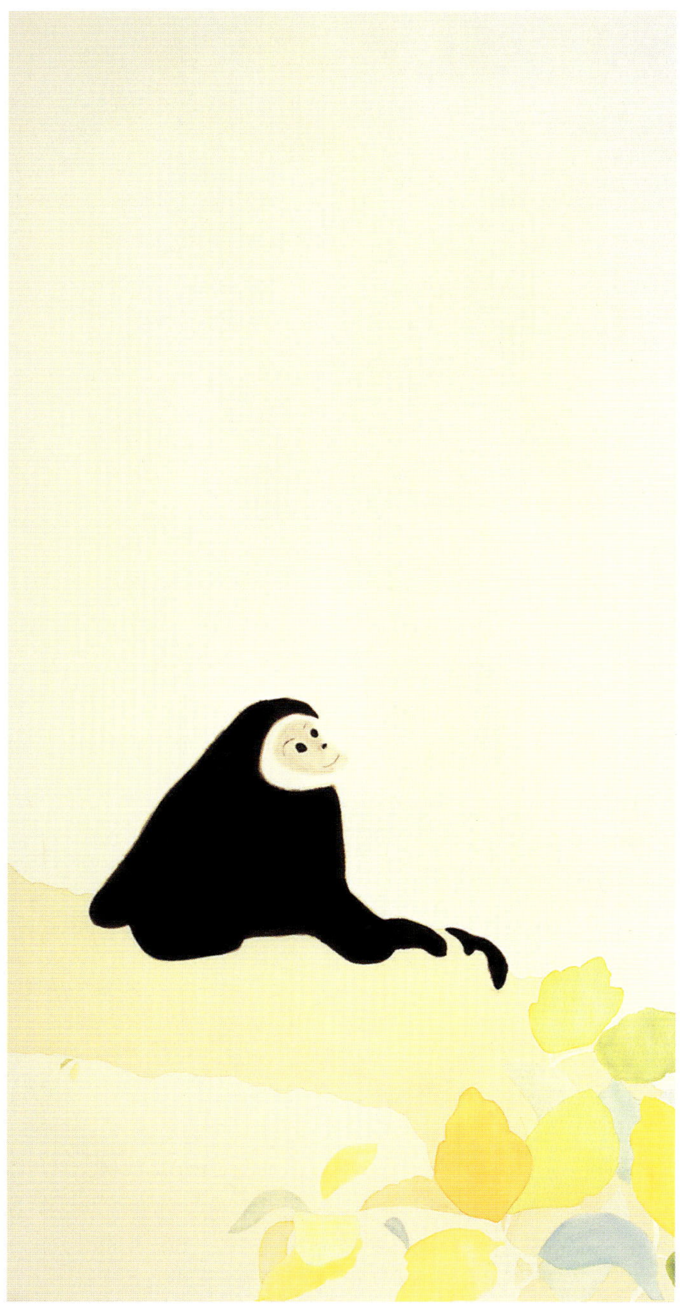

LAURA OWENS, UNTITLED, 1999, acrylic and ink on canvas,
2 parts, 122 x 60" each / OHNE TITEL, Acryl und Tusche auf Leinwand,
2-teilig, je 310 x 152,4 cm.

zu den geläufigen Vorstellungen von «Kunst» vertraut sowie deren Bedeutung für ihre eigene künstlerische Tätigkeit. Als sie – nicht lange nach der ACME-Ausstellung – an einer Kunstschule etwas lustlos eine Reihe von Atelierbesuchen absolvierte, meinte sie: «Das Beste sieht gar nicht aus wie Kunst.» Und wieder etwas später, als ich am Einrichten meiner eigenen Ausstellung war, sagte sie: «Hab keine Angst, dass es zu sehr nach Kunst aussieht.» Diese widersprüchlichen Weisheiten zeigen, dass «Kunst» in Lauras Augen (oder in ihrem sehr kalifornischen «dritten Auge») entweder aufgegeben oder aufgenommen werden kann, aber nie ein Grund zur Angst sein sollte; all der Überlegtheit in ihrer Arbeit zum Trotz steht über allem doch immer eine Lust am Abenteuer. (Das Ganze ist sowieso eine Entdeckungsreise und jedes Werk macht einem nächsten Platz; wir erschaffen die Welt in jedem Moment neu und wie wir sie uns erträumen, so wird sie sein.)

Mir erscheint dieses Werk als farcenhafte – mit geradezu pathologischer Aufrichtigkeit ausgeführte – Darstellung von etwas, was so aussieht, wie man es von Kunst erwartet. Alle Indizien, die auf «Malerei» schliessen lassen, sind vorhanden: Wo nicht die Rohmaterialien des Mediums ausgebreitet werden – unbemalte Leinwand und Farbe direkt aus der Tube –, kommt der historische Hintergrund als Rohmaterial zum Einsatz. Lauras Bilder wimmeln nur so von Klischees; Anspielungen auf Traditionen und Archetypen der Abstrakten Moderne, der Landschafts- und der figürlichen Malerei, der Assemblage, des Romantischen, Maritimen und Postmodernen, all das spielt mit hinein. Es ist, als ob diese Kunst überprüfen wollte, wie weit die rhetorischen Formeln der Malerei und der Betrachtung von Malerei in die allgemeine Kultur eingegangen sind; wie ausgetreten der Pfad vom Original zum Standardprodukt und zum beliebig Reproduzierbaren eigentlich ist. Lauras Arbeiten stören jene Vorstellung von Kunst auf, die wie eine dämonische Missgeburt im kollektiven Unbewussten lauert (buchstäblich eine Missgeburt, denn sie muss aussehen wie eine Kreuzung von Michelangelos DA-

VID, Van Goghs SELBSTPORTRÄT MIT VERBUNDENEM KOPF und dem Pferd aus Picassos GUERNICA). Mich bringen ihre Bilder auf den Schrotthaufen in meinem eigenen Hirn, wo all die Ratgeberbücher, Museumsplakate und Flohmarktbilder, die ich je gesehen habe, gelandet sind. (Und sie erinnern nicht nur an einzelne Dinge in diesem Schrotthaufen, sondern an den Schrotthaufen selbst.) Aber trotz dieser Übersättigung, die ich in Owens Werk sehe, hat es offenbar das Zeug dazu, mein eigenes weit hinter sich zu lassen. Und hier kommt ihre krankhafte Aufrichtigkeit ins Spiel: Laura nimmt sehr viel auf sich, um das vollkommene «Gemälde» zu schaffen, am liebsten ohne Anführungszeichen.

Bei all den gegenwärtigen Anstrengungen um eine offene Kunst, die keine Grenzen kennt, halte ich es für schwierig, wirklich offene Bilder zu malen (der Bildrand ist ja immer schon da), aber Laura gelingt es, indem sie diversifiziert: Ein Bild ist selten die logische Folge des vorangegangenen, es sei denn in einer Logik des Miteinschliessens und der Wiederaufnahme. Es ist eine Malerei, die sich nicht nur ihrer selbst bewusst ist, sondern auch ihrer Umgebung, bis hin zur Wand, an der sie hängt, und zum Raum, in dem sie sich befindet. Das ist die Voraussetzung und das Rätsel von Laura Owens Kunst; eine tiefe Hochachtung gegenüber dem Historischen und den Konventionen der Produktions- und Ausstellungspraxis auf der einen Seite, und auf der anderen Seite ein Spielen damit, und ein explizites Umsetzen dieses Dialogs im Inhaltlichen: Wie kann man heute malen? Was kann man damit anfangen? Ja sogar: Wozu überhaupt? Und zwar nicht wie in: «Ist die Malerei tot?», das würde ihr nicht im Traum einfallen, sondern wie in: Warum überhaupt etwas tun, angesichts der Natur des Kunstwerks im Zeitalter der technischen Reproduzierbarkeit, dem unaufhaltsamen Siegeszug der Kulturgüterindustrie und endloser weiterer lähmender Gedanken, gar nicht zu reden von der bedrohlichen Gegenwart von Krieg und anderen Tiefschlägen? Kann ein Bild irgendetwas von all dem auflösen oder wieder gutmachen? (Von

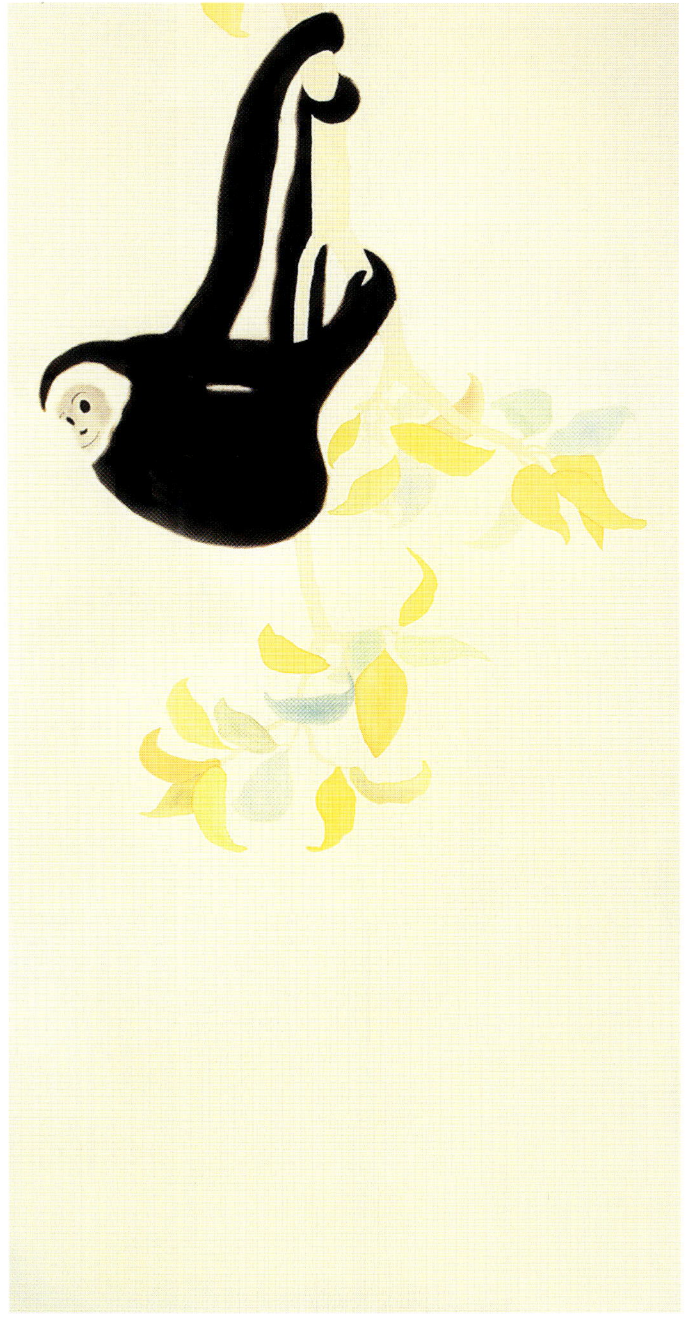

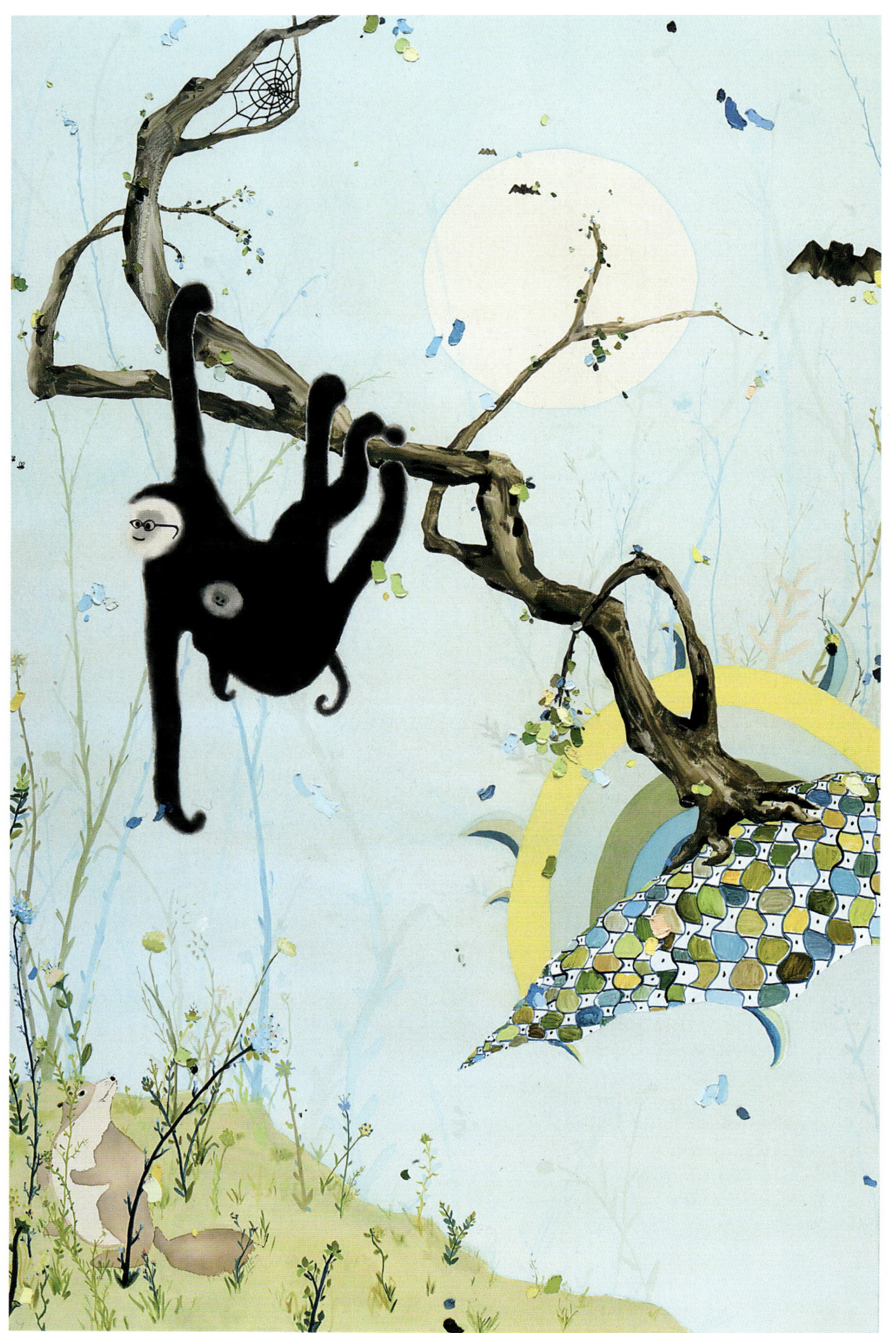

LAURA OWENS, UNTITLED, 2001, oil and acrylic on canvas, 106 x 67½" / OHNE TITEL, Öl und Acryl auf Leinwand, 269,2 x 171,5 cm. (PHOTO: DOUGLAS M. PARKER STUDIO)

LAURA OWENS, UNTITLED, 1998, acrylic and photo collage on watercolor paper, 9½ x 12½" / OHNE TITEL, Acryl und Photocollage auf Aquarellpapier, 24,1 x 31,8 cm.

Zeit zu Zeit ruft Laura mich an, um mir Fragen zu stellen wie diese: «Könnten wir nicht eine Revolution anzetteln?»

Letztlich ist alle Kunst in Los Angeles, an der mir etwas liegt, auf nihilistische Art utopisch (und steht auf gutem Fuss mit Oxymora); sie bezieht ihre physischen, sozialen und existenziellen Bedingungen mit ein. Sie ist diskussionsfreudig, geistig anregend und legt ihre Unsicherheiten gern offen dar. Es ist nicht der Kitsch und das Fiberglas eines überfüllten Disneyland, sondern die träumerisch sture Entschlossenheit, den Tag im Garten zu verbringen. Sie interessiert sich für das grelle Licht und den neutralen Raum, den es hier überall gibt und der dennoch schwer auszumachen ist. Und sie versucht dem Äther (bzw. dem Smog) etwas von jenem Humor und Pathos zu entreissen, welche Leute wie Bas Jan Ader und John Baldessari um 1970 (Lauras Geburtsjahr) herum hier aufsteigen liessen.

Lauras Werk lässt uns diesen neutralen Raum spüren. Ihre Bilder saugen die Atmosphäre von Los Angeles förmlich auf und reflektieren sie – eine Atmosphäre der Beziehungen (romantischer, kollegialer, beruflicher Art); dichte Nebelschwaden und cartoonwürdige Sonnenuntergänge; gläserne Wolkenkratzer, die hinter Hügeln hervorspähen; Yoga- und Selbsterfahrungskurse; Gebäudegärten mit Eukalyptus, Palmen und Bonsaibäumen (alles nicht einheimische Gewächse); metallisch glänzende Farbanstriche und Restaurants mit Aquarien; Computer- und TV-Bildschirme, Kinoleinwände; Galerien- und Parkbesuche; und zahlreiche Erleuchtungsphantasien von Schiffen mit geblähten Segeln und Kirschbaumzweigen, die nach dem Mond greifen. Aber auch die für Los Angeles typische Atmosphäre des Permissiven und alles Zulassenden, des Was-auch-Immer, O.K. und Für-alles-zu-haben-Seins ist in ihrer Kunst präsent. Lauras Werk nimmt sämtliche Tropen der Malerei und des Lebens in Los Angeles in sich auf, dieses ständige Auf und Ab, das mit dem hiesigen Leben und Arbeiten verbunden ist: Sie versucht etwas Neues zu machen, und falls das nicht gelingt, etwas Interessantes, und wenn auch das fehlschlägt, etwas Lustiges; ein Tag folgt dem nächsten wie eine exakte (allerdings glänzende) Kopie des vorangegangenen. Laura Owens macht aus diesen Ambivalenzen Tugenden. All die widersprüchlichen Erfahrungen unter demselben endlosen blauen Himmelszelt, und zu jeder Erfahrung ein Bild.

(Übersetzung: Susanne Schmidt)

EDITION FOR PARKETT LAURA OWENS

UNTITLED, 2002
Handprinted 10-color lithograph on tan BFK Rives with
three collage elements: one handpainted with watercolor on
blue Magnani Pescia, two on white BFK Rives, the color of the
moon will vary with each print, 18 x 12"
Printed by Ed Hamilton, Hamilton Press, Venice, California
Edition of 70, signed and numbered on the back

OHNE TITEL, 2002
Handgedruckte 10-Farben-Lithographie auf getöntem BFK Rives mit
drei Collage-Elementen: eines handbemalt mit Wasserfarbe auf
Magnani Pescia (Blau), zwei auf weissem BFK Rives, die Farbe des
Mondes variiert von Blatt zu Blatt, 45,8 x 30,6 cm
Gedruckt bei Ed Hamilton, Hamilton Press, Venice, Kalifornien
Auflage: 70, rückseitig signiert und nummeriert

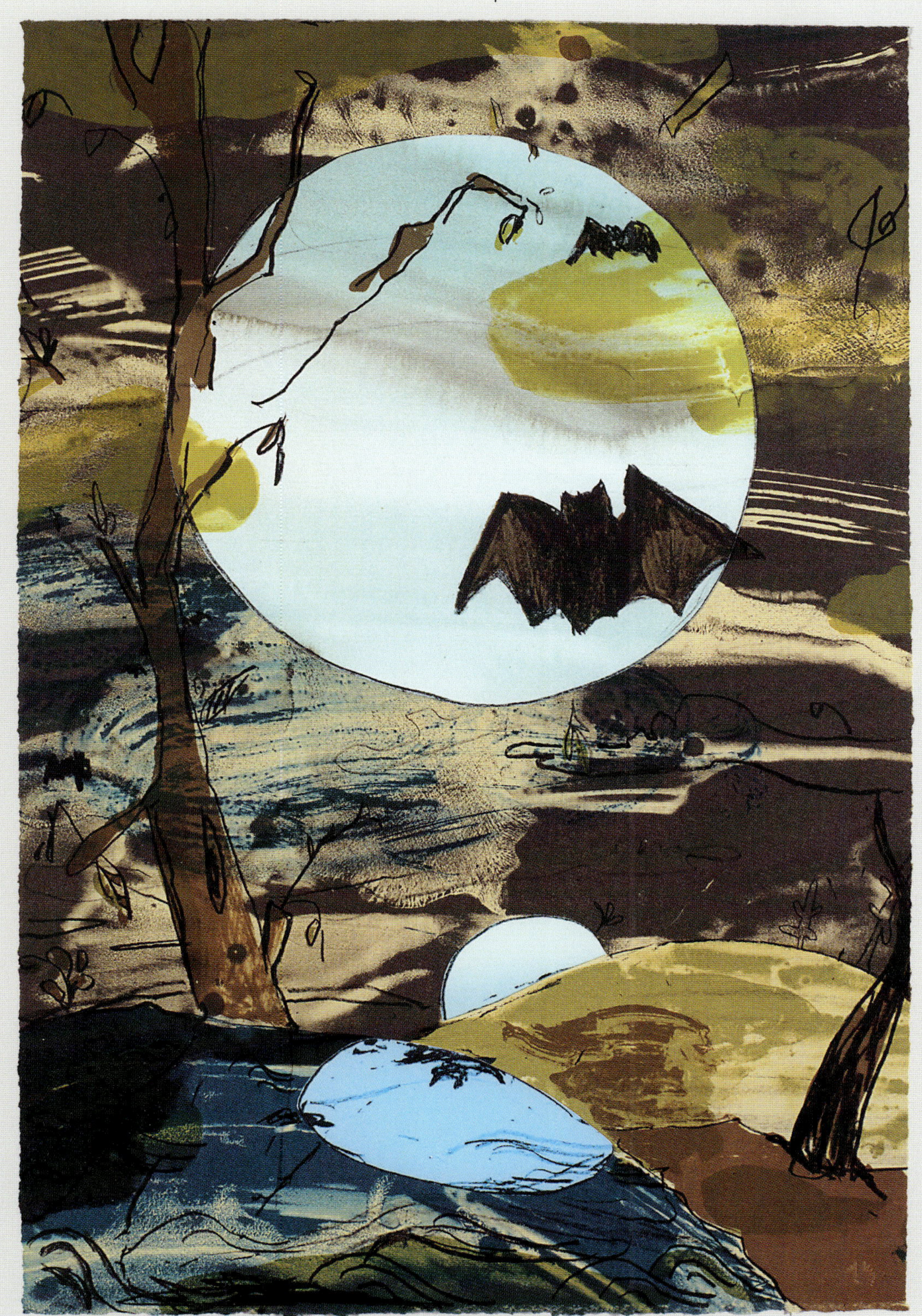

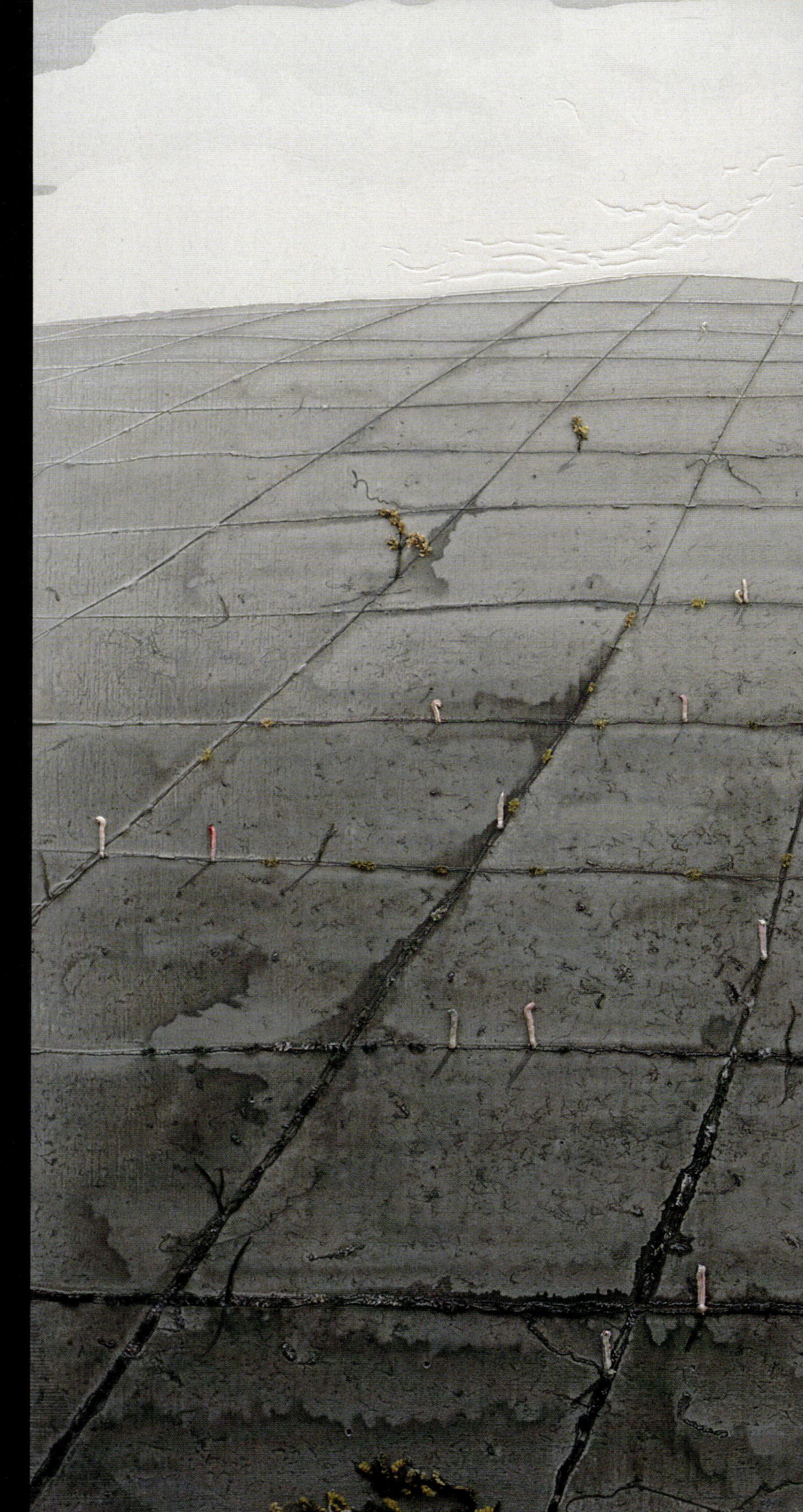

MICHAEL RAEDECKER

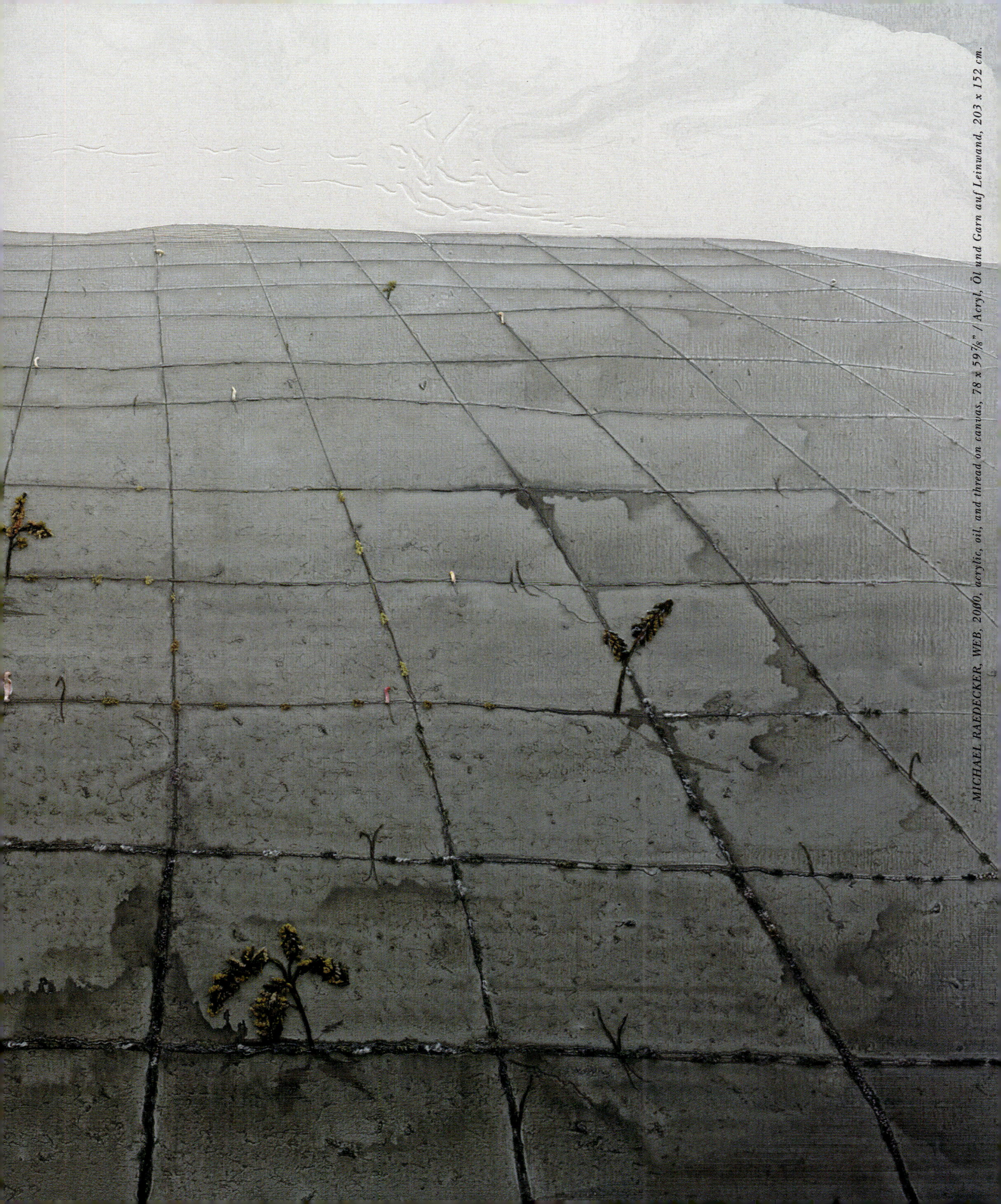

MICHAEL RAEDECKER, WEB, 2000, acrylic, oil, and thread on canvas, 78 x 59⅞" / Acryl, Öl und Garn auf Leinwand, 203 x 152 cm.

DIRTY PICTURES

BART VERSCHAFFEL

Viewed from the proper distance every painting becomes flat. When the picture is reproduced, this flatness remains. In the copy the painting obviously loses its materiality and its scale. But in addition, an entire array of viewing possibilities is reduced and simplified, as it were, to a single view: in contrast to studying paintings in "real life," their reproduction remains the same no matter how you look at them. Michael Raedecker's often large-scale paintings also turn into the "beautiful" flat images seen in reproductions when viewed from the right distance. However, his works revolve around what ensues by not looking from the proper distance, that is, by standing too close and hence seeing what happened in the process of making the picture.

In very realistic or illusionistic painting the image stays clear and sharp up to the shortest distance: the image sticks on the canvas; one sees the things portrayed just like one sees real objects in daily life. In many other and practically all modern paintings, the image gradually dissolves as one approaches. The image turns to "matter": roughly structured patches of

paint and color that signify nothing more than just paint and color. Just one step backwards allows miraculous recovery of the image from the magma, a witnessing of how order and meaning emerge out of the original chaos, and this bestows on the aesthetic experience a mythical depth... In the first case the artist is a master artisan or illusionist, who hides behind the realistic effect of his skillfully created images, in the second case he operates as an alchemist constructing form and definition from primal elements. Are image-makers extraordinary people?

It has rightly been said that Michael Raedecker's paintings are "unsettling": we do not readily comprehend what is actually happening in them nor do they offer us an ideal viewing distance from which we might feel that the image coalesces into an accessible whole. The paint, the various kinds of threads, and the other materials sometimes pasted and painted over, work at cross purposes. At the distance where, for example, the paint still yields an immaterial "image" and forms readable figures, the threads already break away from the whole and turn into "wool" and "hairs" that undermine the image. On closer examination, loose hairs and threads stuck into the paint, along with protruding lumps of paint, evoke miniature landscapes, which then again approximate the

BART VERSCHAFFEL is a philosopher teaching Architectural Theory at Ghent University, Belgium. He is also on the board of the Dutch art magazine *De Witte Raaf.*

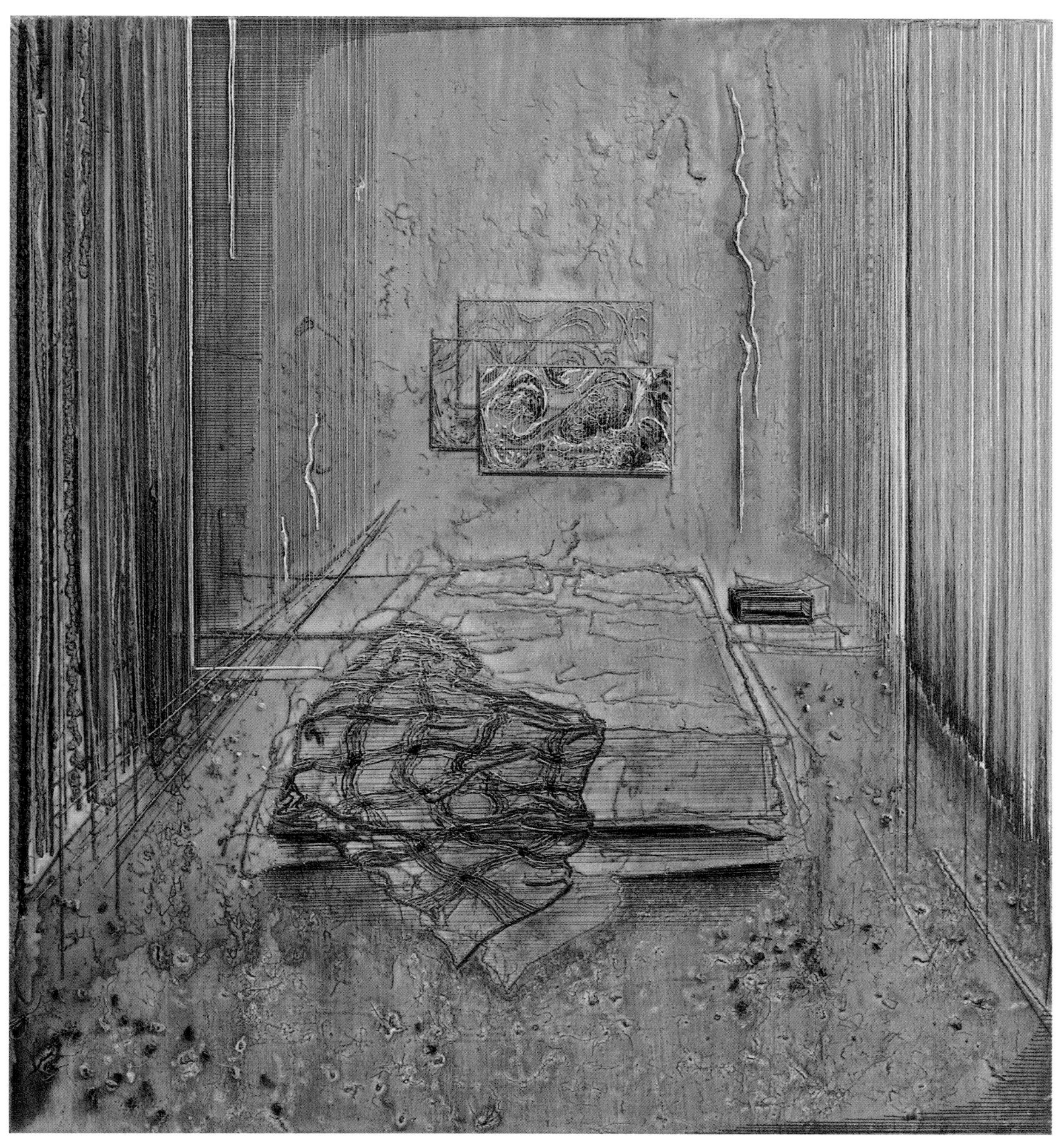

MICHAEL RAEDECKER, DIM, 2001, acrylic and thread on canvas, 28 x 31⅛" / Acryl und Garn auf Leinwand, 71 x 79 cm.

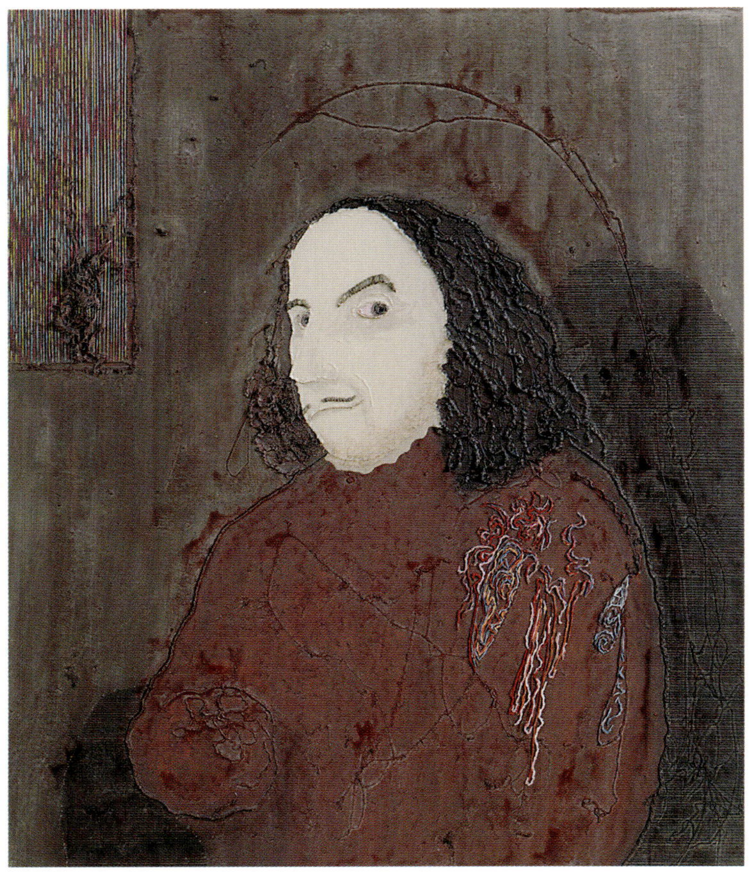

MICHAEL RAEDECKER, OPERATOR (AFTER GIORGIONE), 2002,
acrylic and thread on canvas, 35$^7/_{16}$ x 29$^1/_2$" / Acryl und Garn auf Leinwand, 90 x 75 cm.

complete image first seen in the painting, and so on. The embroidery and plaiting that Raedecker uses to imitate painterly effects never blend into the image evenly. The painting is never consistently "image" and the image never dissolves completely into paint. The image actually stays "messy" at all times; Raedecker's technique always generates the appearance of sloppy patchwork. The painter in this case is not a conjuror and not a magician, but a craftsman and a *bricoleur*. Seen from the right distance or in front of the camera the painting obviously does become "image"; yet, from (too) nearby the visual information transmits contradictory messages and the picture proves to be half made of noise. The paint-

ings are like worn-out vinyl LPs, with a scarcely discernible voice or melody amidst the many hisses and scratches, being played to an audience accustomed to a flawless and clean rendition.

Raedecker's strategy can also be read in the details of his images. In MIRAGE (1999) there are two tiny tree trunks to the left. And to the left again of these trunks a shadow line runs straight upwards, alongside the stem; this way, the tree-thread slightly detaches itself from the picture plane, yet simultaneously it treats the painting itself as a plane on which the shadow is cast. However, at the foot of the trunks the shadow of the stems starts sloping to the right, deep into the "landscape" of the image. Hence, the literal reading of the thread on the plane and the reading of the image as a surreal landscape are both evoked and yet mutually opposing. How could one look at such an image and not feel unsettled?

Raedecker's paintings evoke a recognizable basic imagery, taken from the tradition of painting or popular visual culture. His images are never entirely strange or original—they seem familiar, easy to label and to classify. Thus, most of his pictures to date show landscapes and interiors. A number of landscapes clearly allude to the oriental landscape tradition: a few lines and some threads pasted into the pale, primer-like ground suffice to evoke depth in the desiccated paint soil. There are various surrealistic landscapes, deep spaces with no horizon or sky, over which nameless shapes, marked by sharp shadows, are spread out. Since the objects elude identification, the scale of the depiction remains uncertain: Is it microscopic, is it cosmic? Surrealism is often just around the corner: the way in which the shapes are placed in the empty spaces and the confrontation of woolly, almost immaterial figures and objects with solid and yet amorphous ones are reminiscent of Magritte in his early work and even more so of Tanguy. Particularly innovative are some landscapes in which the world is folded or rolled up or forms a ring enclosing a vortex or hole. Raedecker's interiors—in fact the interiors of a type of house he also uses for his suburban exteriors—do not refer to a traditional painting theme or genre, yet they are very recognizable: It is the suburban home of the B-movie or police series, shot at the moment when the telephone starts ringing or the first car pulls up, and the story begins. In addition to these landscapes and domestic scenes, Raedecker also painted a few extremely spatial still lifes and a few portraits. In all these pictures the spectators will easily recognize the genre and be able to name what they see. However, at the same time it is evident that such naming or such references are secondary and do not reveal what is really happening in Raedecker's work.

Raedecker does not paint stories or situations but places. These places are like small boxes or cases. When we discover a lovely box we want to open it even if we know that it is empty; we want to see the bare interior, to smell it and give free rein to our dreams before closing it and turning it upside down in search of a sign or a name. To me that is the way in which Raedecker's paintings work: They seem to be made in order to put something in them, to save something preciously small and intimate, but they feel empty somehow. They are storage locations, the *topoi* of the classical *ars memoriae*. This even applies to the still lifes: The depicted objects naturally behave like actors who know they are being watched and address the viewers. But the spatiality of the pictures is more powerful than the single objects in them; the objects-actors do not perform on a stage but in a landscape, and the spectator's gaze passes through them into the depths.

The two portraits recently made by Raedecker radically reverse the spatiality and landscape setting of his earlier works. His mode of working remains the same inasmuch as there is initial recognition: "Ah, Giorgione!" However, instead of portraying sitters of his own, he remodels classical portraits using his own techniques. The choice of a painting by Giorgione as his source image is obviously not motivated by the sentimental desire to make a faithful, "true" picture of a face, but rather by the wish to revise the genre of the portrait. Not even Giorgione himself was primarily interested in rendering a face when he painted his PORTRAIT OF A GENTLEMAN (ca. 1510), now in the National Gallery in Washington. The Renaissance painter turns the head of his model in partial profile so that the "hole" of the left eye becomes central to the face and heightens the piercing impact of the gaze, hence imparting it with—in Deleuze's words—*visagéité* or faceness. Giorgione experiments with the pose of the fist and the eyes as a means to strengthen the artificial nature of the portrait (frontality, juxtaposition, presence…). It is exactly this "hole" of the eye and gaze that serves as the point of departure and even takes the focal position in Raedecker's OPERATOR (AFTER GIORGIONE) (2002). These portraits are not spatial or poetical like "spaces" or like the small empty boxes, and unlike conventional portraits they do not arouse "human interest" in faces. They are laboratory tests demonstrating the existence of the pure, immoral, meaningless force of the image.

(Translation: Jo Pollet)

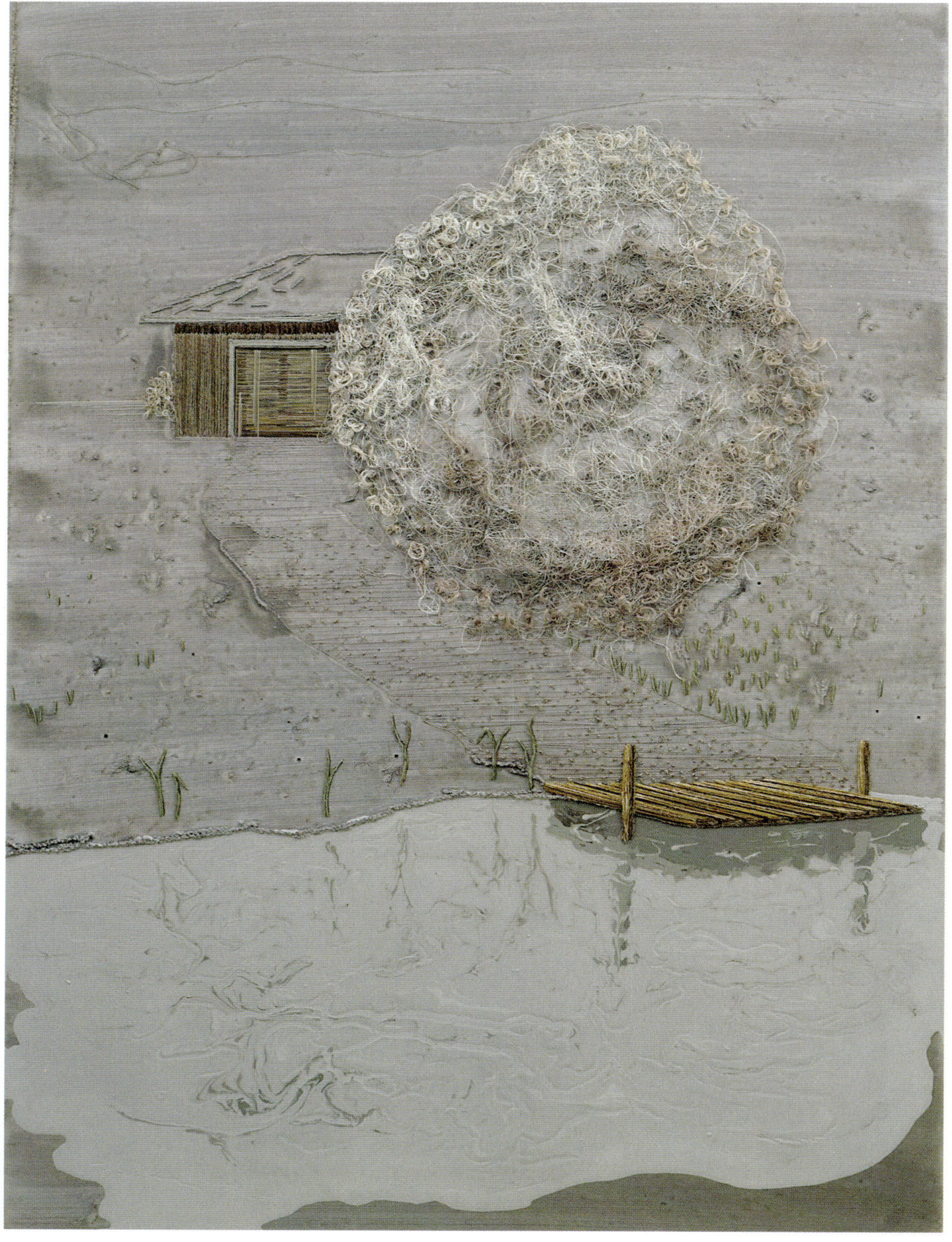

MICHAEL RAEDECKER, BLIND SPOT, 2000, acrylic and thread on canvas, 46 x 34" / Acryl und Garn auf Leinwand, 117 x 86,5 cm.

SCHMUTZIGE BILDER

BART VERSCHAFFEL

Aus einer gewissen Entfernung betrachtet wird jedes Gemälde flach. Reproduziert man es, bleibt diese Fläche übrig. In der Reproduktion verliert das Gemälde natürlich jegliche Materialität und seine ursprünglichen Grössenverhältnisse. Die Reproduktion kann nur noch einen Bruchteil des Originals vermitteln, nämlich jene visuellen Informationen, die auf einer Ebene zusammenkommen und ein Bildganzes ergeben. Betrachtet man eine Reproduktion aus der Nähe, bleibt das Bild, was es ist – ganz anders beim Original. Auch Michael Raedeckers meist grosse Gemälde werden aus der «richtigen» Entfernung betrachtet zu «schönen» flachen Bildern, wie man sie auf Reproduktionen sehen kann. Aber seine Arbeiten handeln gerade davon, was passiert, wenn man nicht in dieser «richtigen» Entfernung steht, sondern viel näher und deshalb sieht, was im Lauf der Entstehung des Bildes geschehen ist.

Bei sehr realistischer oder illusionistischer Malerei bleibt das Bild auch aus sehr grosser Nähe klar und scharf: Das Bild liegt unmittelbar auf der Leinwand und man nimmt die gemalten Dinge wahr wie Dinge im realen Leben. Bei vielen anderen und in

---

BART VERSCHAFFEL ist Philosoph und lehrt Architekturtheorie an der Universität Gent in Belgien. Er ist Mitherausgeber der holländischen Kunstzeitschrift *De Witte Raaf*.

fast allen modernen Bildern löst sich das Bild dagegen beim Näherkommen allmählich auf. Es wird zu reiner Materie: rauh strukturierte Farbflecken, die ausserhalb ihrer Stoff- und Farbqualität nichts bedeuten. Aber ein einziger Schritt rückwärts lässt das Bild wunderbarerweise wieder aus dem Magma hervortreten, zeigt auf, wie sich Ordnung und Inhalt aus dem ursprünglichen Chaos herauskristallisieren, und verleiht dem ästhetischen Ritual mythische Tiefe. Der Künstler ist zunächst einmal ein virtuoser Handwerker oder Illusionist, der sich hinter dem Realitätseffekt seiner kunstvoll hergestellten Bilder verbirgt, er ist aber auch ein Alchimist, der aus Urelementen erkenn- und benennbare Formen bildet. Sind Bildermacher vielleicht besondere Menschen?

Man sagt zu Recht, dass die Bilder von Michael Raedecker etwas «Ungemütliches» haben: Man sieht nicht sofort, was darin eigentlich passiert, und es ist nicht sofort klar, aus welcher Entfernung man sie betrachten muss, damit ein Ganzes erfassbar wird. Die Farbe, die verschiedenen Garnsorten und die anderen Materialien, die manchmal hinzugefügt und übermalt werden, arbeiten einander entgegen. Aus einer Entfernung, wo die Farbe immer noch ein immaterielles Bild liefert und lesbare Figuren bildet, lösen sich die Garnfäden schon aus dem Bild und werden zu «Wolle» und «Haaren», die das Bild stören. Bei näherem Hinsehen bilden lose in der Farbe klebende Haare und Fäden in Kombination mit sich aufwerfenden Farbklumpen eigene Miniaturlandschaften, die dann doch wieder sehr in die Nähe jenes Bildes kommen, das man zuerst gesehen hat, und so fort. Die Stickerei und das Flechtwerk, mit denen Raedecker malerische Effekte erzeugt oder nachahmt, fügen sich niemals schön und regelmässig ein. Das Gemälde ist nie ganz «Bild» und dieses wiederum löst sich auch nie ganz in Materie auf. Das Bild bleibt irgendwie immer ungepflegt; Raedeckers Technik ist immer ein wildes Durcheinander. Der Maler ist hier weder Zauberkünstler noch Magier, sondern ein *bricoleur*. Aus der «richtigen Entfernung» oder durch die Kamera gesehen, wird das Gemälde natürlich doch zum Bild und lässt sich anschauen, aber aus (zu) grosser Nähe betrachtet, behindern sich die visuellen Informationen gegenseitig und lassen das Bild erscheinen, als bestehe es zur Hälfte aus störenden Elementen. Die Bilder sind wie verschlissene Vinyl-Schallplatten, auf denen unter viel Gekratze und Gekrache Stimm- oder Melodiefetzen zu vernehmen sind, gespielt für ein Gehör, das an perfekte und saubere Wiedergabe gewöhnt ist.

Raedeckers Strategie ist auch in Details seiner Bilder zu erkennen. In MIRAGE (1999) stehen links zwei winzige Baumstämme. Gleich daneben laufen die Schattenstreifen den Stamm entlang nach oben, wodurch sich der Baumfaden leicht von der Fläche löst und das Relief betont. Gleichzeitig wird das Gemälde aber als Fläche behandelt, auf die dieser Schatten fällt. Vom Fusse der beiden Stämme läuft aber noch ein weiteres Schattenpaar vom Stamm aus schräg nach rechts oben, tief in die Bildlandschaft hinein. Der buchstäbliche Faden auf der Fläche und die Auffassung des Bildes als surreale Landschaft werden gleichzeitig angesprochen und gegeneinander gesetzt. Wie soll man da «gemütlich» schauen können?

Raedeckers Gemälde beschwören ein wieder erkennbares Grundvokabular aus der Tradition der Malerei oder der populären Bildkultur. Auf den ersten Blick wirken sie nie ganz fremd oder neu; man fühlt sich unmittelbar an etwas erinnert und meint, sie leicht benennen oder zuordnen zu können. So hat Raedecker, zum Beispiel, bisher vor allem Landschaften und Interieurs präsentiert und viele dieser Landschaften erinnern an asiatische Landschaftsmalerei: Wenige Linien oder Fäden in die bleiche Grundiermasse geklebt genügen, um im trockenen Farbgrund landschaftliche Tiefe hervorzurufen. Es gibt einige surreale Landschaften, tiefe Räume ohne Horizont und Licht, in denen namenlose Formen von scharfen Schatten begleitet verteilt sind. Weil keines dieser Objekte identifiziert beziehungsweise keine tatsächliche Grösse ausgemacht werden kann, bleibt der Massstab ungewiss: Ist er mikroskopisch oder kosmisch? Der Surrealismus ist nicht weit: Die Art, wie die Formen in diese leeren Räume gesetzt sind, und die Kombination von flauschigen, beinah immateriellen und harten, aber dennoch amorphen Figuren und Objekten erinnern an frühe Bilder von Magritte und vielleicht mehr noch von Tanguy. Ganz ungewöhnlich und nie gesehen erscheinen einige Landschaften, in denen die Welt zusammengefaltet oder aufgerollt wird oder sich um einen Wirbel oder ein Loch krümmt. Raedeckers Interieurs – ganz besonders die Interieurs jenes Haustyps, den er auch in seinen Aussenansichten verwendet – knüpfen nicht an ein traditionelles Thema oder Genre der Malerei an und sind uns doch vertraut: das Vorstadthaus aus dem B-Movie oder der Krimiserie, unmittelbar bevor das Telefon klingelt oder das erste Auto vorfährt und die Geschichte beginnt. Neben diesen Landschaften und häuslichen Szenen gibt es von Raedecker einige extrem räumlich wirkende Stillleben und etliche Porträts. Bei all diesen Bildern ist das Genre problemlos erkennbar und das Dargestellte lässt sich leicht benennen. Gleichzeitig wird aber auch deutlich, dass diese Benennungen oder Referenzen nebensächlich sind und letztlich nicht erschliessen, worum es in diesem Werk wirklich geht.

Raedecker malt weder Geschichten noch Situationen, sondern Orte. Diese sind wie kleine Dosen oder Kästchen. Findet man aber eine schöne Dose, so wird man sie öffnen und sich das leere Innere anschauen wollen, auch wenn man weiss, dass sie leer ist. Man schnuppert daran, lässt seiner Phantasie freien Lauf, um dann die Dose wieder zu schliessen, sie umzudrehen und auf der Unterseite nach einem Zeichen oder Namen zu suchen. Genau so scheinen mir Raedeckers Bilder zu funktionieren: Sie sind gemacht, um etwas aufzubewahren, etwas Kleines, Intimes,

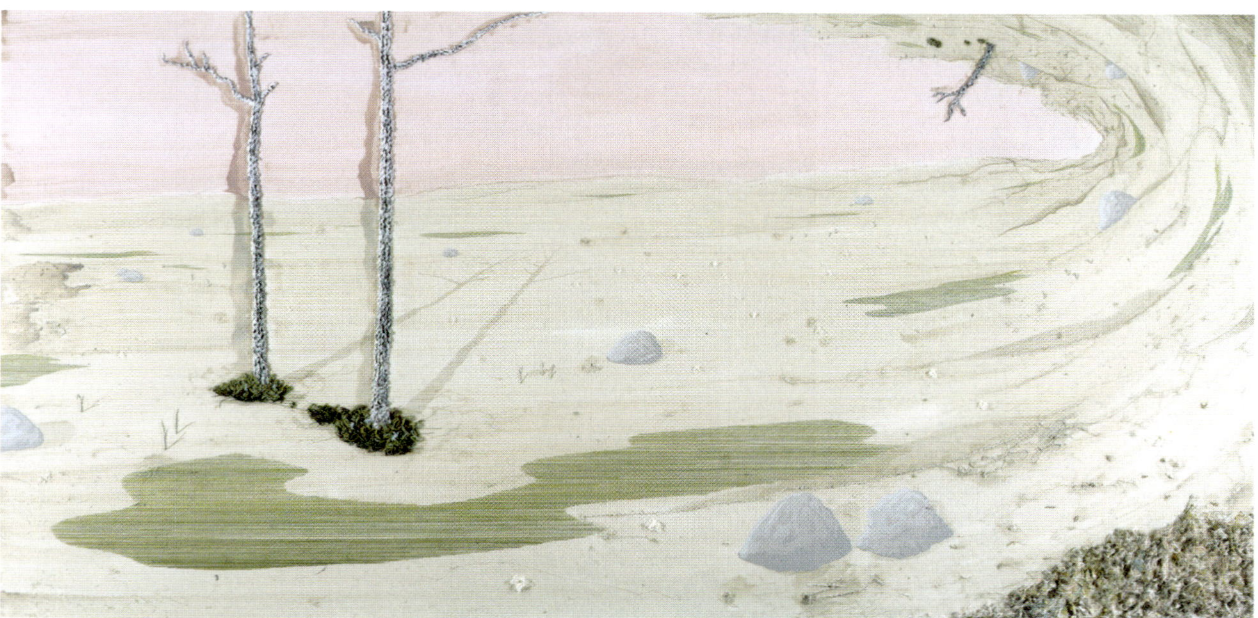

aber sie sind leer. Es sind Aufbewahrungsorte, *topoi* der klassischen *ars memoriae*. Das gilt selbst für seine Stillleben: Die dargestellten Objekte verhalten sich ganz natürlich, wie Schauspieler, die wissen, dass man ihnen zusieht, und sich auch an ihr Publikum wenden. Aber die Räumlichkeit der Bilder ist stärker als die gezeigten Gegenstände, die Objekte/Darsteller stehen nicht auf einer Bühne, sondern in einer Landschaft, und der Blick geht zwischen ihnen hindurch in die Tiefe.

Zwei erst jüngst entstandene Porträts verkehren die Räumlichkeit und Landschaftlichkeit der bisherigen Arbeiten in ihr Gegenteil. Raedecker bleibt bei der bisherigen Arbeitsweise: Der erste Moment ist wieder ein Aha-Erlebnis: «Ah, Giorgione!» Er porträtiert keine eigenen Modelle, sondern nimmt historische Porträts und verwandelt sie mit Hilfe seiner Techniken. Im Falle des Bildes, das von Giorgione ausgeht, ist klar, dass es hier nicht darum geht, ein Gesicht getreulich abzubilden, sondern darum, das Porträt als Genre unter die Lupe zu nehmen. Beim PORTRÄT EINES EDELMANNES (ca. 1510, National Gallery, Washington) ging es übrigens schon Giorgione nicht mehr um die getreue Wiedergabe eines Gesichts. Der Maler dreht den Kopf und Blick des Modells so, dass der linken Augenhöhle zentrale Bedeutung zukommt, was das Durchdringende des Blicks steigert und ihm so – mit Deleuze's Worten – *visagéité*, Gesichtlichkeit, verleiht. Giorgione experimentiert mit der Haltung der Faust und den Augen, um den Bildcharakter des Porträts (Frontalität, Gegenüberstellung, Gegenwärtigkeit...) zu verstärken. Es ist genau diese Augenhöhle, die Raedecker in seinem OPERATOR (AFTER GIORGIONE) (Spekulant/Nach Giorgione, 2002) als Ausgangspunkt nimmt und buchstäblich ins Zentrum rückt. Diese Porträts sind nicht räumlich und auch nicht poetisch wie Orte oder leere Dosen. Es steht auch kein «menschliches Interesse» an Gesichtern dahinter. Es sind Laborversuche, die die Existenz der puren, unmoralischen, sinnlosen Kraft des Bildes selbst demonstrieren.

(Übersetzung aus dem Niederländischen:
Marie-Luise Flammersfeld)

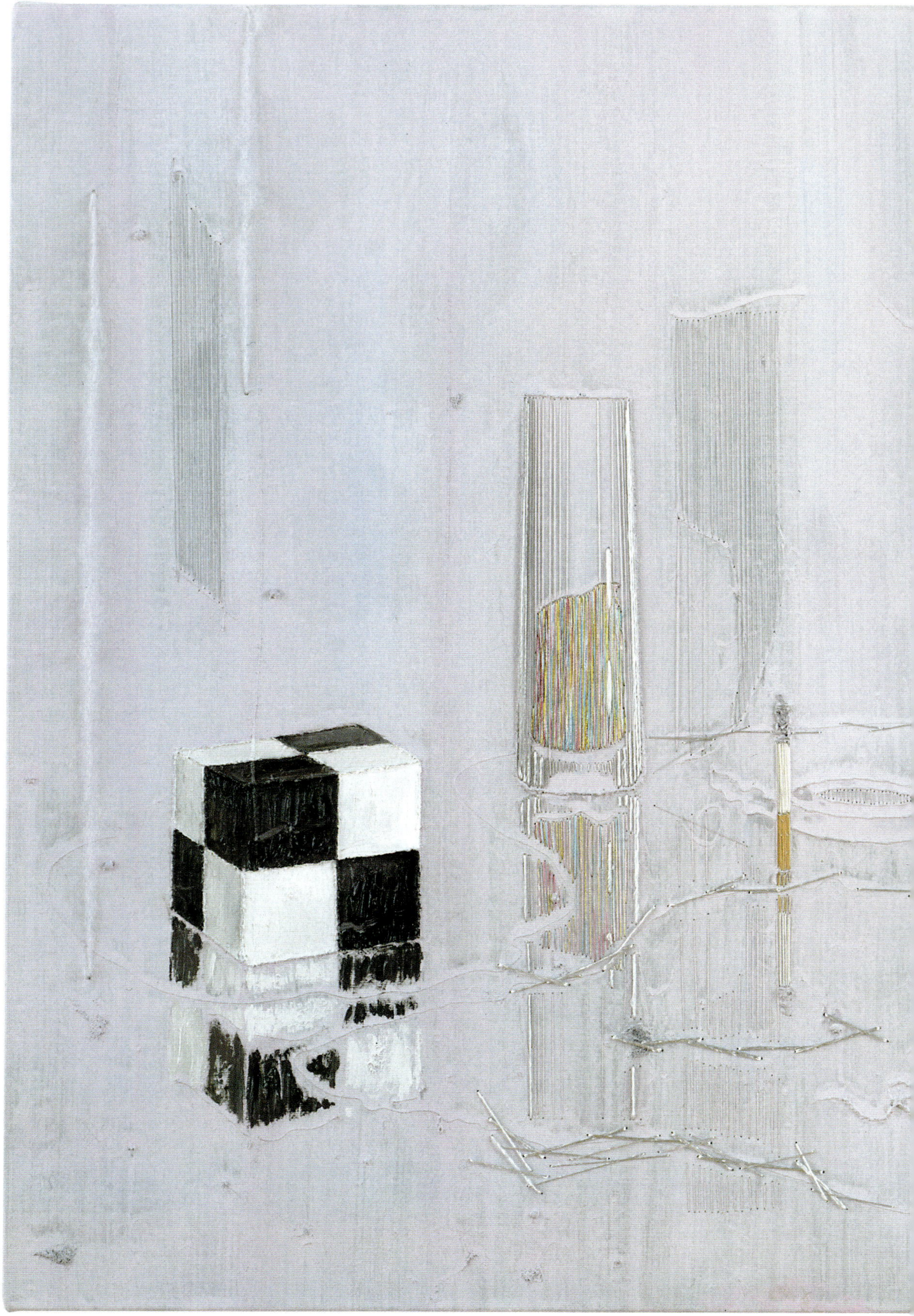

Michael Raedecker

MICHAEL RAEDECKER, PLACEBO, 2002, oil, acrylic, and thread on canvas, 25⅝ x 37⅞" / Öl, Acryl und Garn auf Leinwand, 65 x 96 cm.

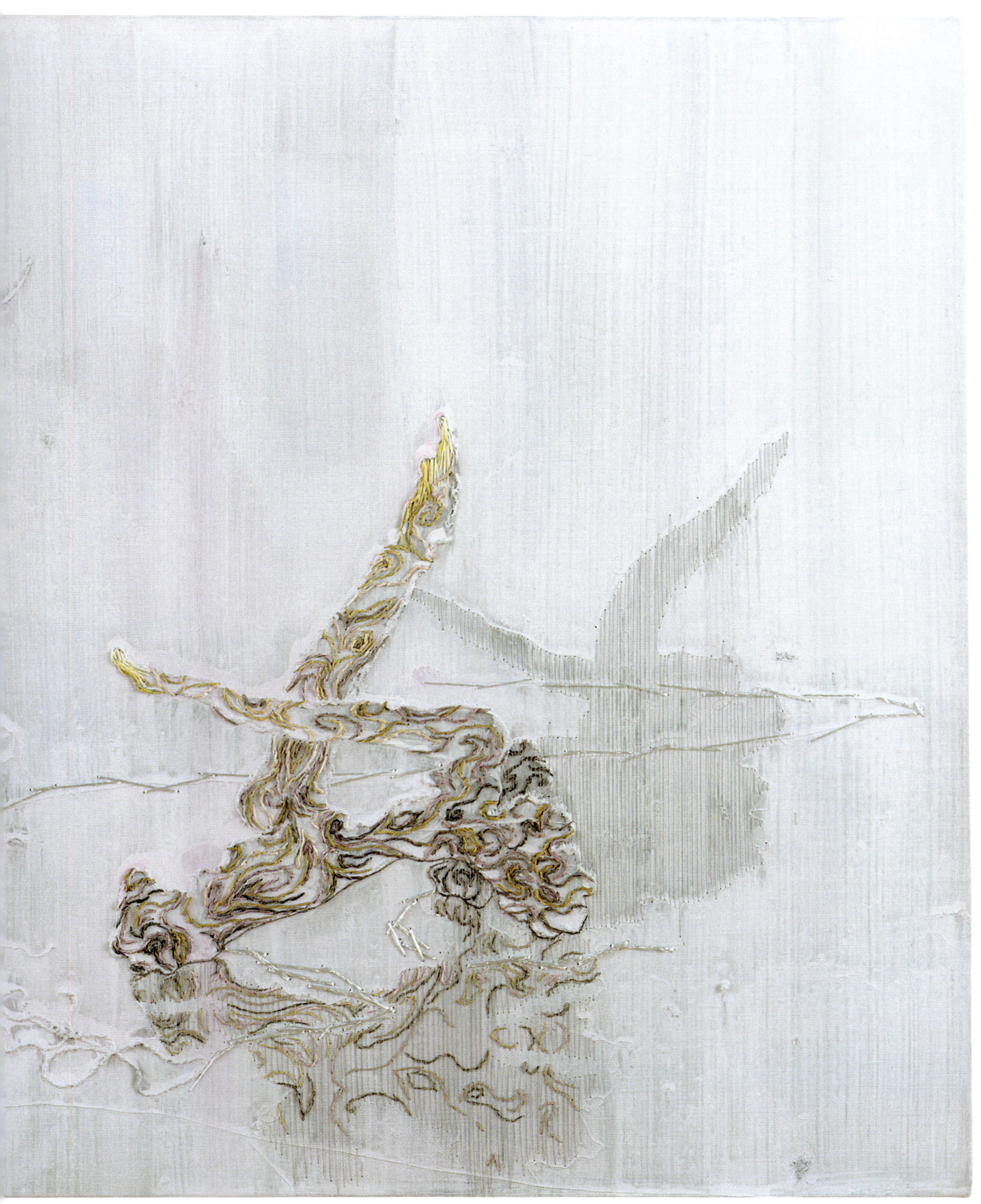

TERRY R. MYERS

No Place Like Homeless

No doubt these paintings are unlivable. But there is a lot of there there, in the form of rather weird things or substances that obviously have found a supportive, fecund home. This is a contradiction, but it is more specifically a productive discrepancy that initiates what appears to be an almost natural offsetting of terms rather than a gratuitous gesture of altercation (e.g. a sign of painting as a "struggle"). The overwhelming sense of calm that emerges from this balancing act is the primary reason why the resulting bleakness is so satisfying, filling, and even funny. All of the paint and all of the other materials that have been distributed across or planted in the surface of these canvases look as if they have been able to take root and take up all available space due to some type of fermentation or fertilization process. The implied growth potential of this abundance is poignantly negotiated by a visual barrenness that has been very specifically distributed (rationed?) amongst the necessary components of image: line, shape, and color. The illusion is that these abandoned rural or suburban homes, rooms, and landscapes pictured in these paintings do not have what is necessary for our survival only because all of the "home improvement" stuff—paint, yarn, thread, veneer, wood stain, etc.— has moved in and taken over the place. And why not? After all, this is painting, not a house.

But, of course, painting is often a home, albeit one that is rarely comfortable. There is compelling evidence that Michael Raedecker believes this to a certain degree, especially since he also makes it clear that he has productively invested (like all interesting

TERRY R. MYERS is a critic and independent curator who lives in Los Angeles. He is currently working on an exhibition project with the Pet Shop Boys.

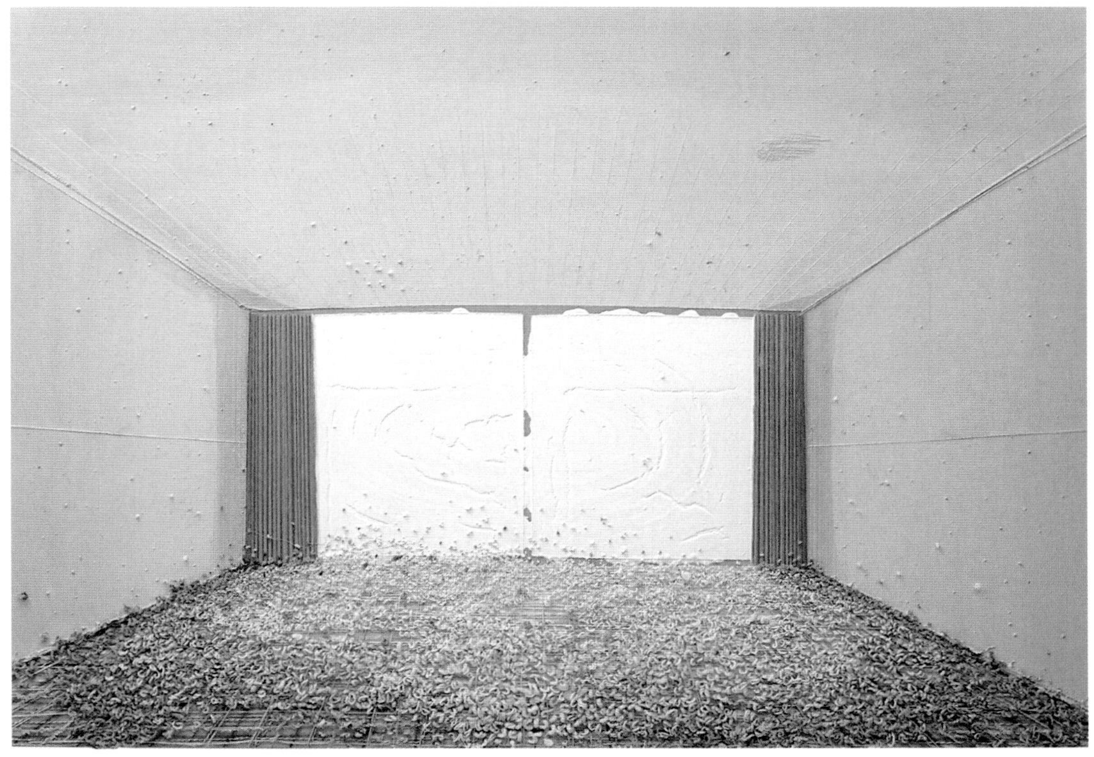

MICHAEL RAEDECKER, RADIATE, 2000, acrylic, wool, and thread on canvas, 70¼ x 50³/₁₆" /
Acryl, Wolle und Garn auf Leinwand, 178,5 x 127,5 cm.

painters) in the alienating aspects of his chosen activity, most of which have to do with an inability to leave the material as it is. In other words, it has never been easy to keep paint going for very long a s p a i n t, to maintain "painting" as "just painting." In 1962, even Clement Greenberg had to admit something like this, if somewhat begrudgingly: "as the fifties wore on, a good deal in Abstract Expressionist painting began fairly to cry out for a more coherent illusion of three-dimensional space, and to the extent that it did this it cried out for representation, since such coherence can be created only through the tangible representation of three-dimensional objects."[1] Identifying de Kooning's *Women* paintings of 1952–1955 as a watershed moment, the critic went on to coin the phrase "homeless representation," which he defined as "a plastic and descriptive painterliness that is applied to abstract ends, but which continues to suggest representational ones." With this definition on hand (and keeping Raedecker's paintings in mind), it makes perfect sense that for Greenberg an artist like Richard Diebenkorn "found a home for de Kooning's touch," when he returned to representation via Matisse. For "homeless representation," however, there was a need for some visible (and tangible) tension, a "dialectical" pressure that would transpose the ways and means of abstraction and representation. Enter the early work of Jasper Johns, who, for Greenberg, sang "the swan song of 'homeless representation,'" in his bait-and-switch approach to painting.

Forty years later, this song is still being sung provocatively in painting, even if today it is much more about sampling, or even—particularly in Raedecker's case—the sampler. Like music, painting has been completely rescued by sampling and its hands-on

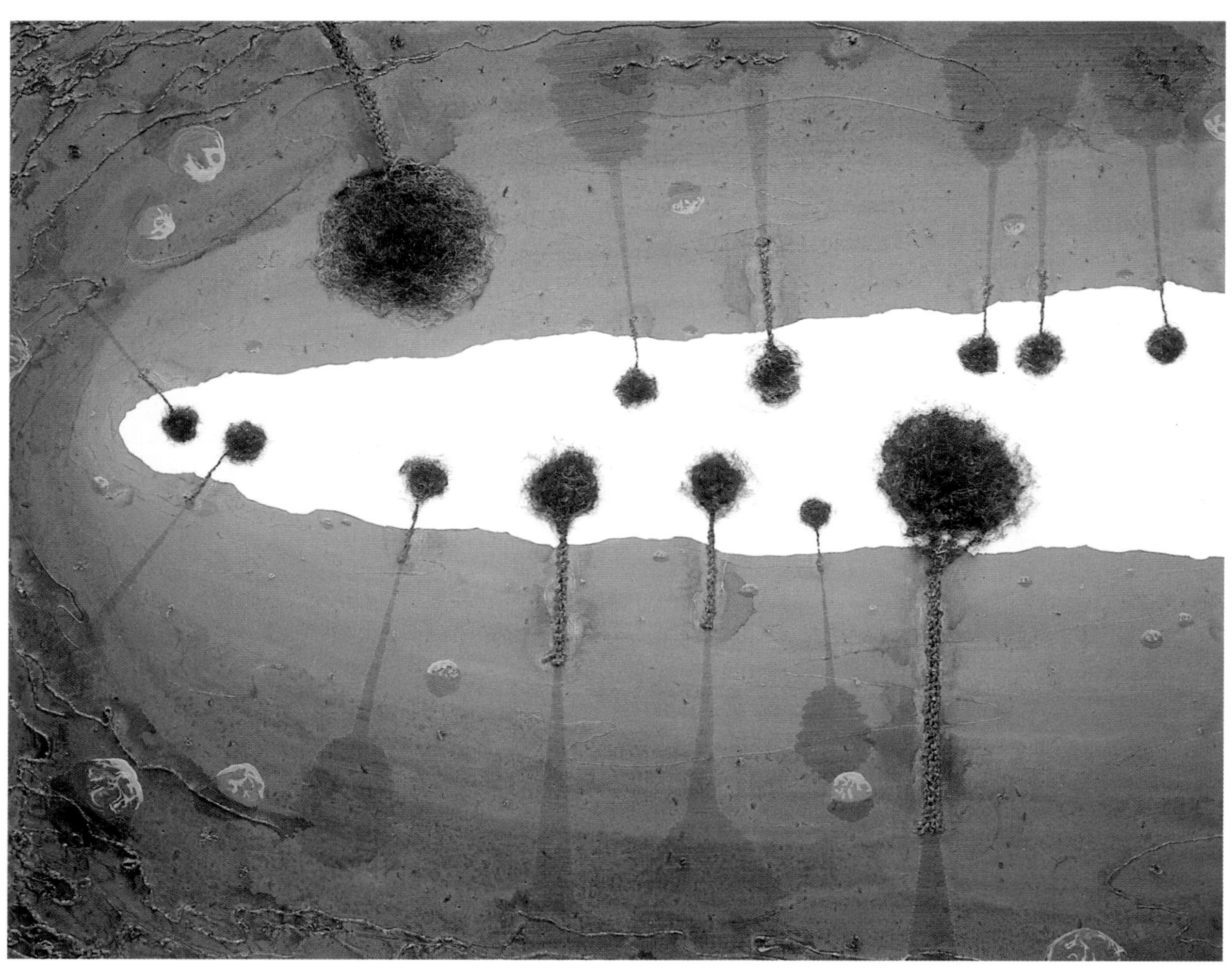

MICHAEL RAEDECKER, KISMET, 1999, acrylic and thread on canvas, 80⁷/₈ x 98⁷/₁₆" /
Acryl und Garn auf Leinwand, 205 x 250 cm. (PHOTO: PETER COX)

(even craft-like) approach—much of painting's history is now available without the baggage of nostalgia or the antagonism of appropriation. Raedecker gets it, and not only because he used to be a DJ. His paintings remind us that the only home any image has anymore is the one we make for it using things like the movies we will never forget or the songs we will never stop loving. Titling some of his paintings after songs by the likes of, for example, Elvis Presley or Spandau Ballet, Raedecker gives clues that everything in his paintings is directly tapping into the kind of collective memories that never leave us since they are perpetually re-woven into our brains because we want them to be. This is the part of painting that is very much n o t alienating.

Speaking of weaving, Raedecker's move from fashion to painting has been sufficiently written into his back-story, despite his assurances that his experiences in the former industry are not directly responsible for his use of some of its materials and techniques in the latter. In his early work embroidery was a practical and efficient way in which to make it clear that he considered painting to be most valid as a pastime (his early paintings were a sort of deconstruction of the paintings of Winston Churchill via photomechanical reproduction and thread that was used to "write" their context on their surfaces): "I wanted to use a technique which let me enjoy what I was doing, maybe listening to some music, and let my mind drift away."[2] Regardless of the explanation behind it (don't forget, after all, that Jasper Johns claims he had a dream in which he made a painting of an American flag), at the very least Raedecker's sewing technique literally grounds what comes across as his complete comfort with exploring and analyzing the relationship between materiality and "look" in his paintings. It could be said that all of the fibers in his work give him and us something to come home to, loose threads that actually anchor our shared experience of what should remain an impermeable painting.

It is just as likely that Raedecker's use of embroidery gives him an effectual way to get started or get something in or on the painting quickly during any moment of its making. It surely also makes it easier for him to rip or unravel something out of the picture if it isn't working.[3] The flexibility of Raedecker's needlework is what gives many of the images in his paintings the appearance of something that could easily be changed, particularly in works from a few years ago like REVERB (1998). In this painting (made with very little paint) "lines" of white thread dart like streaks of light or scratches across the surface of a schematic image of a living room that seems to have a floor made of water (or is the room slightly flooded?) that "reflects" the ceiling, walls, a window with a view of distant mountains, and—most boldly—an open curtain made with a dense stitching of yellow and brown embroidery thread that is the most physical thing in the work. (It is much more "present" in both material and color than the scattering of loose, frayed threads that hug the perimeter of the room like dust bunnies.) Since 1998, Raedecker's paintings have become much denser, creating a slowness in both image and material that has guaranteed that the work is seen fundamentally as painting instead of drawing or craft.

Of course, craft in the "handicraft" sense of the term (rather than, for example, the "Dutch landscape painting" sense of the term) is a relatively new issue in painting, and I'd imagine that if I were to only have Raedecker's paintings described to me that I might jump to some conclusion about their having a problematic relationship to the well-rehearsed ideological battles of art versus craft in gender or class terms. In his most recent paintings, Raedecker has successfully side-stepped this issue by conceptually opening up his use of fiber, not only by moving beyond a more "conventional" application of stitching and sewing, but also by enabling more of it to act like paint while remaining very much not paint. For example, in a painting like RADIATE (2000), the fibers on the floor of the depicted room are like tiny worms of paint. Other parts of this painting contain paint that has a lot more body than in other works: often the depleted paint in Raedecker's paintings looks like the residue left behind after a flood; in this instance, it has impossibly been able to wet through the window of another empty-yet-very-full room. Maybe a rather liquid avalanche has buried this house? A window in a similar painting, BLOCK (2001), has literally been boarded up with veneer. In its conceptual and physical melding of fiber and paint, Raedecker's work has much in common with the mid-seventies paintings of Joe Zucker. Well-known for his "cotton-ball" paintings from the late sixties, in which each puff was dipped in a different color of paint and placed on the painting in even rows, Zucker went on to produce a series that he called the *Reconstruction* paintings which grandly depicted the history of cotton production in the United States in cotton and paint. Rather than simply coating cotton balls with paint, in this series Zucker employed something akin to Greenberg's "descriptive and plastic painterliness": the fibers became part of the paint, fusing art and craft inextricably together. Zucker's statement at the time works nicely for Raedecker: "My selection of subject matter in relation to kinds of surfaces is important. Pictorial content becomes an iconography to discuss the topography of the painting."[4]

I would argue that it has been Raedecker's increasing attention to the topography of his paintings as paintings that has allowed him to open up the iconography of this work in terms of its content as well as its orientation. Exploring a considerable re-orientation first in major paintings like KISMET (1999) and UP (1999), and extending it in paintings like JOURNEYS TO GLORY (2001/2002) and EXPO-SURE (2001/2002), Raedecker has demonstrated his willingness to move beyond the conventional spatial relationship between an image and the painting it inhabits, to make representation "homeless" in more ways than one. Now he has us flat on our backs looking up into the sky or who knows where, rather than standing upright gazing out of a window or across a field. Disoriented and more than a little dazed, we are definitely not in Kansas any more, and it's very likely that we never were.

1) This quote from Clement Greenberg and all that follow are taken from his essay "After Abstract Expressionism" in *Clement Greenberg: The Collected Essays and Criticism. Modernism with a Vengeance, 1957–1969*, ed. John O'Brian (Chicago: The University of Chicago Press, 1993), pp. 124–125. First published in *Art International*, October 25, 1962.
2) Louisa Buck, "UK artist Q&A: Michael Raedecker," *The Art Newspaper*, no. 104 (June 2000), p. 67.
3) The beginning of Johns's first FLAG painting was a disaster: starting with enamel paint on a bed sheet he made a mess so he switched to encaustic. Rauschenberg then asked if he could paint one of the stripes and used red encaustic where he should have used white, and several of its collage elements needed to be stitched on to hold them in place. In fact, the entire painting is rather desperately stapled to at least one edge of its plywood support because the sheet was barely large enough to cover it. Moreover, the painting is awkwardly dated 1954–55 not because it took that long to complete it but because it was damaged at a party and had to be repaired. My point here in direct relationship to Raedecker's work is that interesting paintings are usually put through hell.
4) Joe Zucker, artist's statement in Richard Marshall, *New Image Painting* (New York: Whitney Museum of American Art, 1978), p. 68.

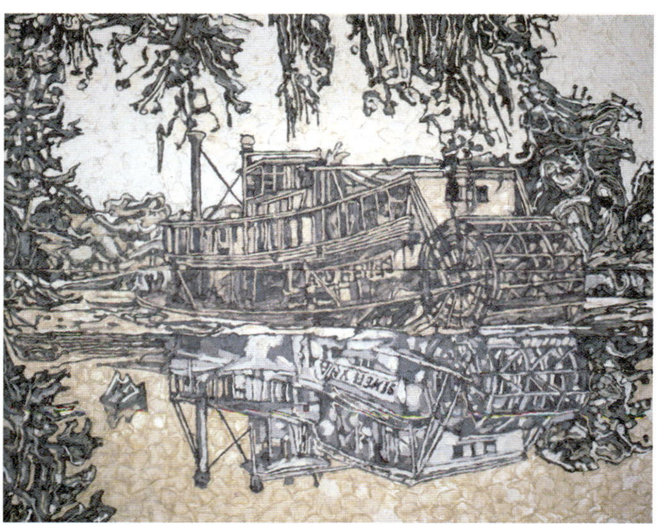

JOE ZUCKER, AMY HEWES, 1976,
acrylic and cotton on canvas, 96 x 120" /
Acryl und Baumwolle auf Leinwand, 243,8 x 304,8 cm.
(PHOTO: D. JAMES DEE)

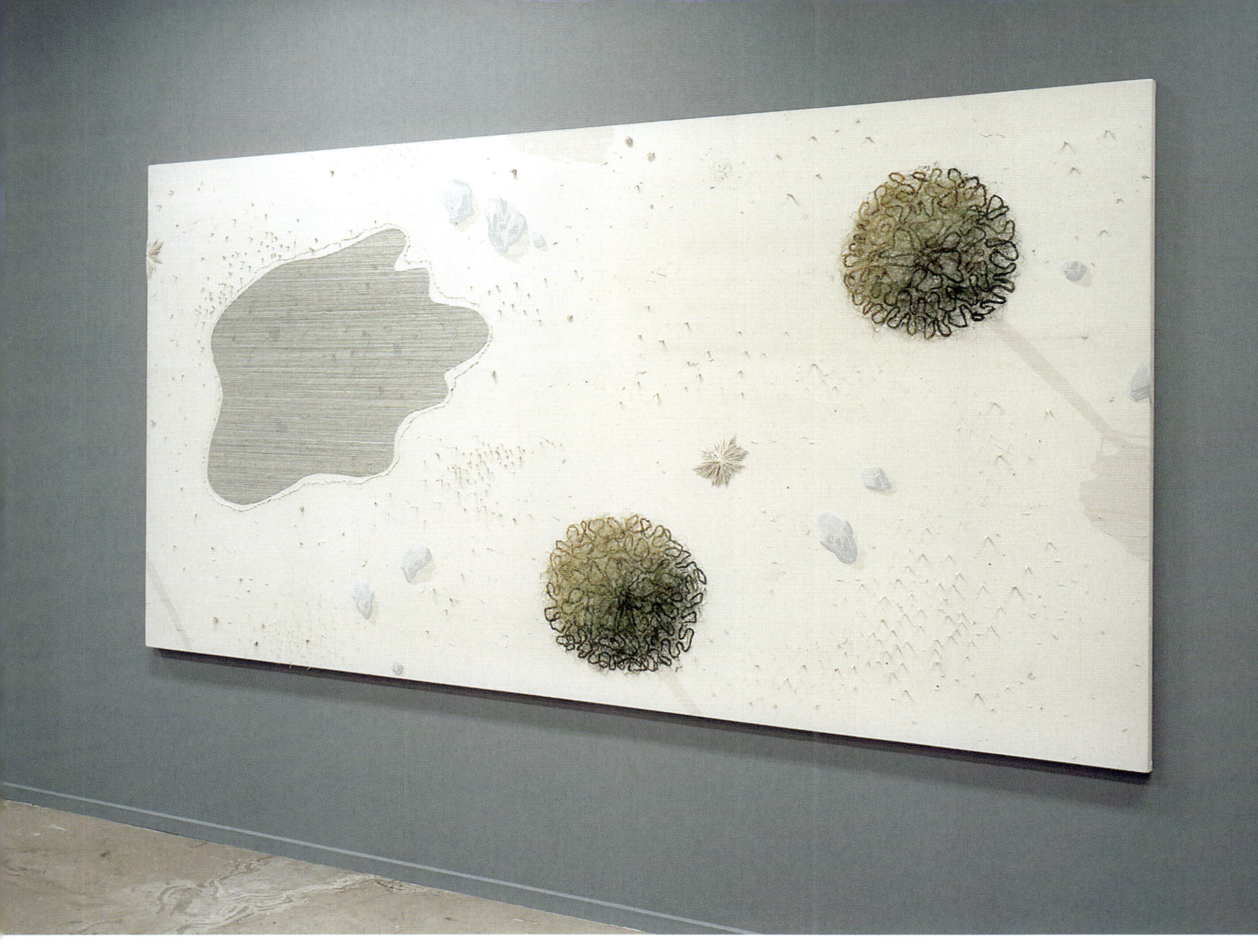

MICHAEL RAEDECKER, UP, 1999,
acrylic, oil, and thread on canvas, 67 x 134¹/₄" /
Acryl, Öl und Garn auf Leinwand, 170 x 341 cm.

113

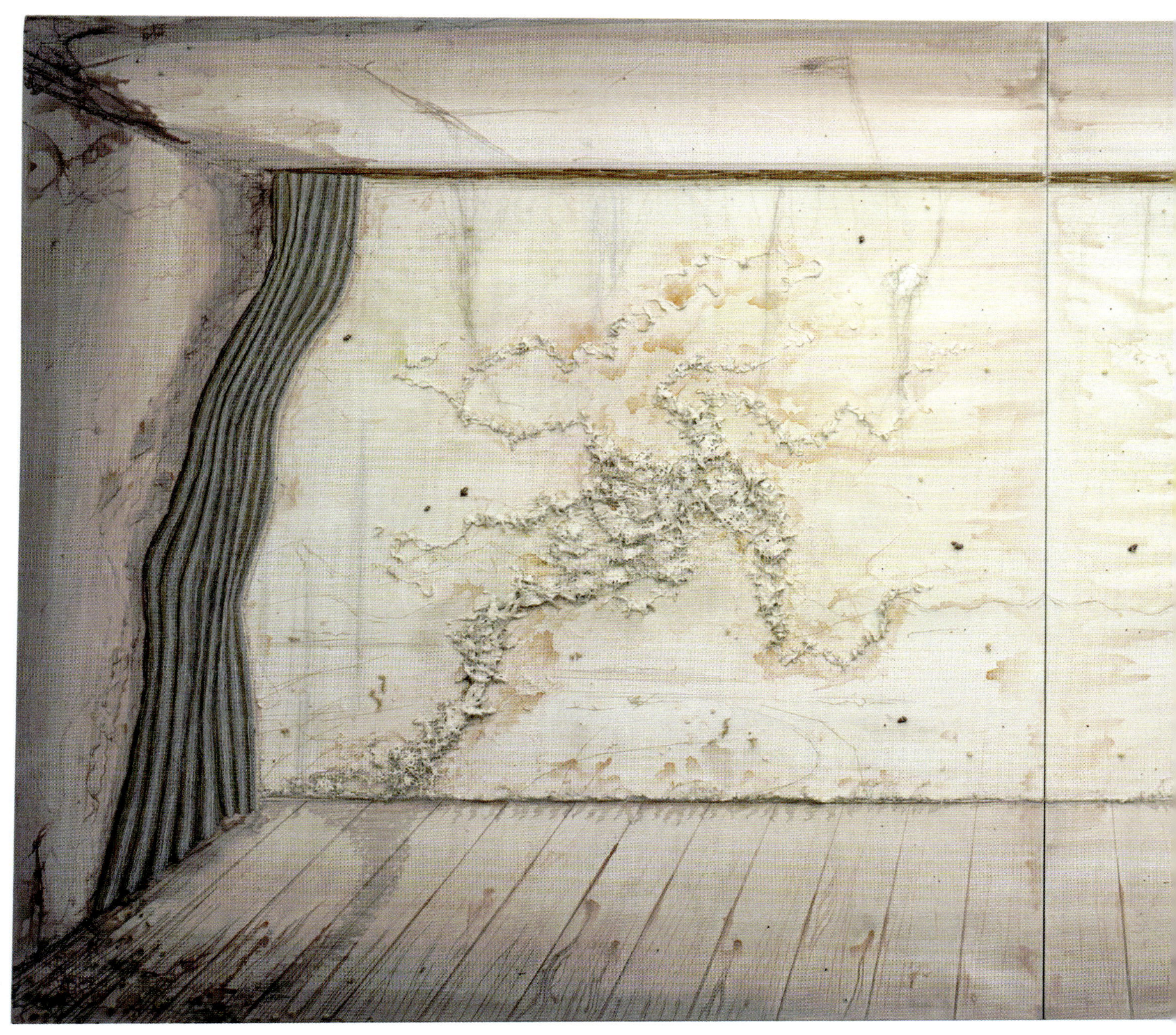

MICHAEL RAEDECKER, TO CUT A LONG STORY SHORT, 2001, acrylic and thread on canvas, 78 x 178" / Acryl und Garn auf Leinwand, 198 x 452 cm.

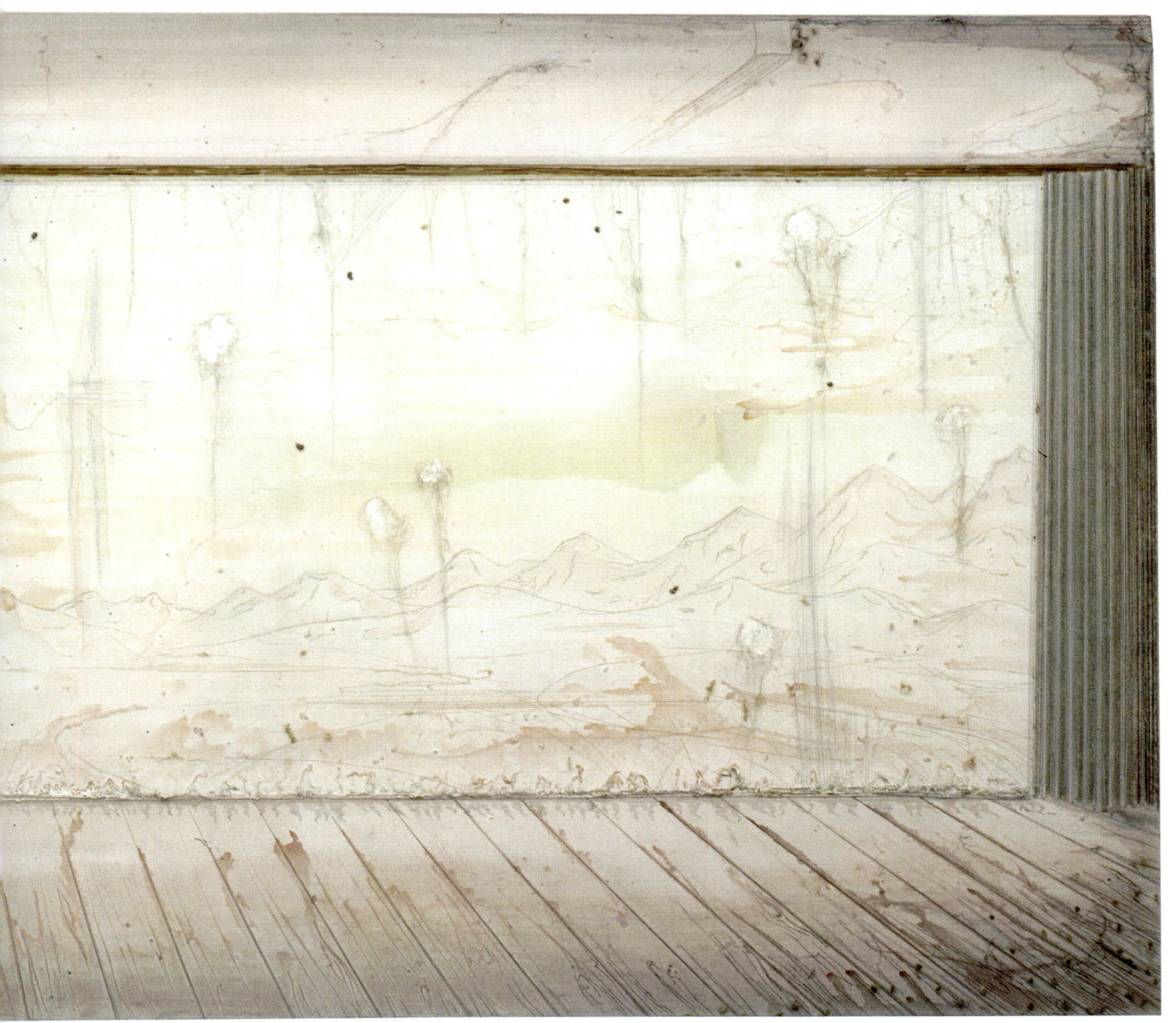

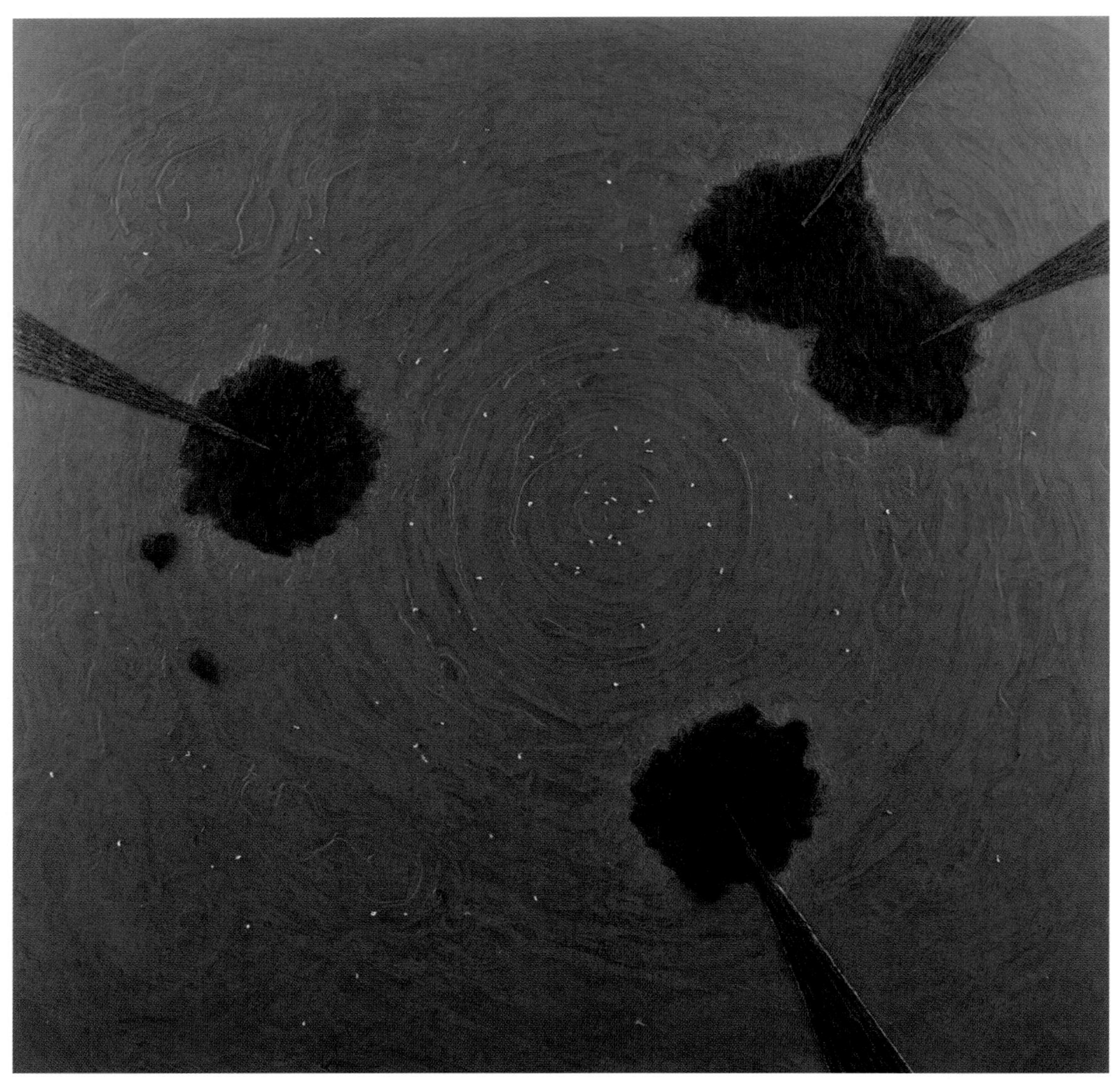

MICHAEL RAEDECKER, EXPOSURE, 2001/2002, oil, acrylic, and thread on canvas, 70 x 70" /
Öl, Acryl und Garn auf Leinwand, 178 x 178 cm.

TERRY R. MYERS

Unvergleichlich heimatlos

Diese Bilder haben nichts Wohnliches. Und doch findet man darin zahlreiche Stellen und Nischen, in Gestalt von ziemlich merkwürdigen Dingen und Materialien, die hier offenbar ein ihnen wohl gesinntes, fruchtbares Zuhause gefunden haben. Dies ist zwar ein Widerspruch, doch genau besehen ist es eine produktive Diskrepanz, die etwas in Gang setzt, was eher ein beinah natürliches Kompensieren von Gegebenheiten zu sein scheint als ein willkürlicher Ausdruck heftiger Auseinandersetzung (etwa ein Signal, dass Malen «Kampf» bedeute). Das überwältigende Gefühl der Ruhe, das aus diesem Balanceakt erwächst, ist der Hauptgrund, weshalb die entstehende Ödnis so befriedigend und erfüllend, ja komisch ist. Die Farben und alle anderen Materialien, die auf diesen Leinwänden verteilt oder auf ihrer Oberfläche angebracht wurden, sehen aus, als hätten sie Wurzeln geschlagen und aufgrund irgendei-

nes Gärungs- oder Befruchtungsprozesses den ganzen verfügbaren Raum überwuchert. Das implizierte Wachstumspotenzial dieser Fülle steht in entschiedenem Gegensatz zu der visuellen Kargheit, die ganz auf die für jedes Bild notwendigen Grundkomponenten verteilt (oder beschränkt?) ist, nämlich auf Linienführung, Form und Farbe. Die Illusion, dass die in diesen Bildern dargestellten, verlassenen ländlichen oder vorstädtischen Häuser, Räume und Landschaften nicht das zum Überleben Notwendige bereithalten, beruht allein darauf, dass das ganze «Heimverschönerungs»-Material – Farbe, Garn, Faden, Furnier, Holzbeize usw. – gewissermassen selbst hier eingezogen ist und alles in Beschlag genommen hat. Und wieso auch nicht? Schliesslich handelt es sich hier um Malerei und nicht um ein Haus.

Aber natürlich ist die Malerei oft ein Zuhause, wenn auch selten ein gemütliches. Es gibt überzeugende Anhaltspunkte dafür, dass Michael Raedecker dies bis zu einem gewissen Grad glaubt, vor allem, da er klar zum Ausdruck bringt, dass er (wie alle interessanten Maler) schöpferisch in die befremdlichen

---

TERRY R. MYERS ist Kunstkritiker und freier Kurator. Er lebt in Los Angeles und arbeitet gegenwärtig an einem Ausstellungsprojekt mit den Pet Shop Boys.

Aspekte seiner gewählten Tätigkeit verstrickt ist, die zumeist mit der Schwierigkeit zusammenhängen, das Material so zu belassen, wie es ist. Mit anderen Worten, es war nie einfach, Farbe längere Zeit a l s F a r b e und das «Malen» «einfach nur als Malen» bestehen zu lassen. 1962 musste selbst Clement Greenberg, wiewohl nur widerstrebend, etwas Ähnliches eingestehen: «…im Lauf der 50er Jahre begann ein Grossteil der abstrakt-expressionistischen Malerei geradezu nach einer kohärenteren Illusion des dreidimensionalen Raums zu schreien, und damit

tion (und mit Raedeckers Bildern im Hinterkopf) leuchtet es vollkommen ein, dass für Greenberg ein Künstler wie Richard Diebenkorn «eine Heimat für de Koonings Malweise gefunden» hat, als er über Matisse zur Gegenständlichkeit zurückkehrte. Für die «heimatlose Gegenständlichkeit» brauchte es jedoch eine sichtbare (und greifbare) Spannung, einen «dialektischen» Druck, der die Mittel und Wege von Abstraktion und Gegenständlichkeit transponierte. Das gilt auch für das Frühwerk von Jasper Johns, der laut Greenberg mit seiner Lockvogelstrategie «den

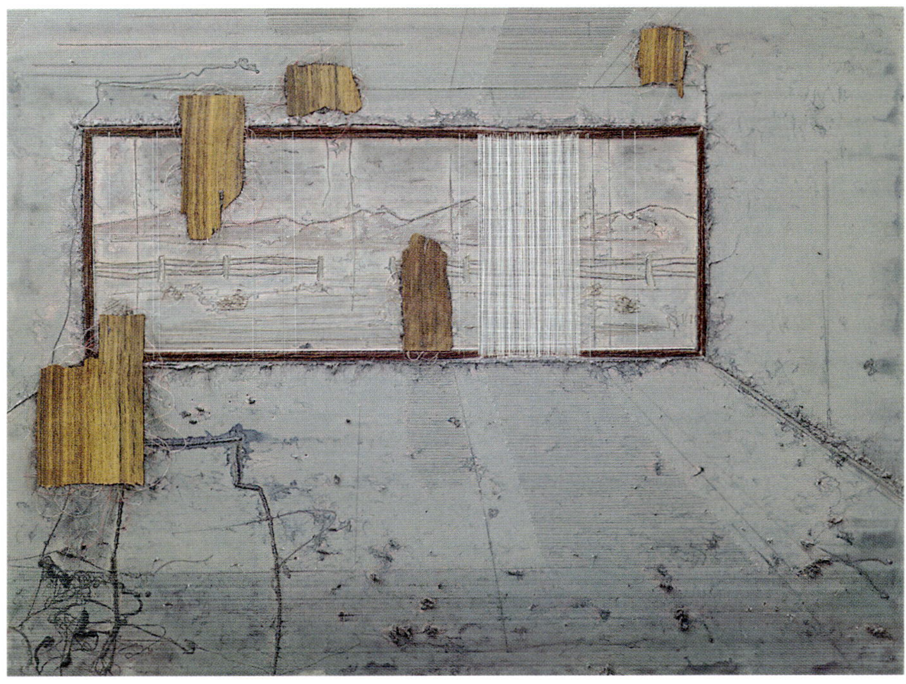

verlangte sie zugleich nach Gegenständlichkeit, denn eine solche Kohärenz lässt sich nur mittels der greifbaren Darstellung dreidimensionaler Gegenstände erzeugen.»[1] Der Kritiker verstand de Koonings Bilderserie *Women* (1952–1955) als Wendepunkt und prägte den Begriff der «heimatlosen Gegenständlichkeit», welche er definiert als «eine betont malerische Darstellung, die das Plastische und Beschreibende zugunsten abstrakter Zielsetzungen einsetzt, jedoch weiterhin eine gewisse Gegenständlichkeit suggeriert». Angesichts dieser Defini-

Schwanengesang der ‹heimatlosen Gegenständlichkeit›» sang.

Vierzig Jahre später erklingt dieser provokative Gesang in der Malerei noch immer, auch wenn es heute viel eher um das Sampeln oder sogar – gerade im Fall von Raedecker – den Sampler geht. Genau wie die Musik wurde die Malerei allein durch das Sampeln und seinen praktischen (ja handwerklichen) Ansatz gerettet; ein Grossteil der Geschichte der Malerei ist nun ohne nostalgischen Ballast und die antagonistische Haltung der Appropriation ver-

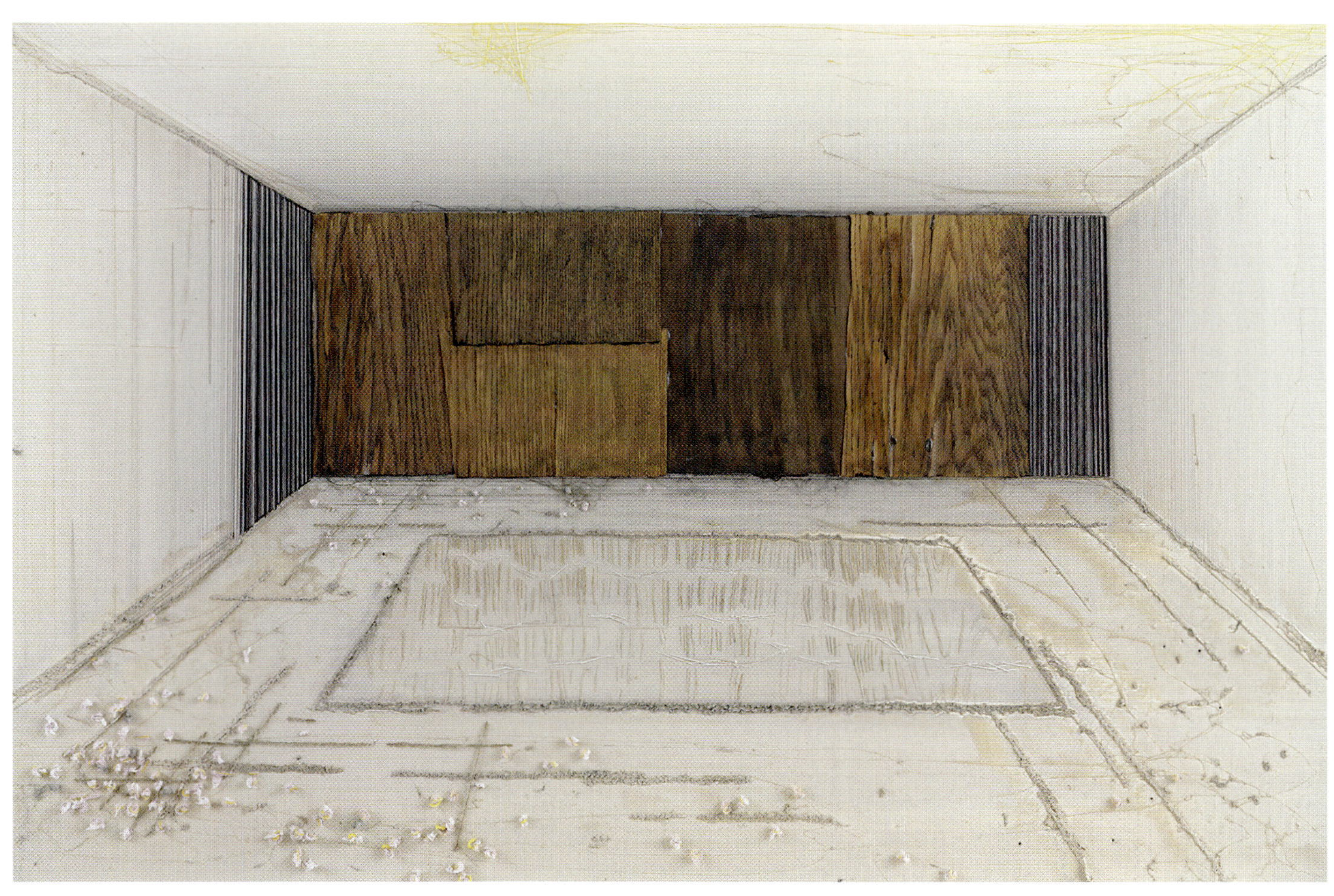

MICHAEL RAEDECKER, BLOCK, 2001, acrylic, woodstain, veneer, and thread on canvas, 47¼ x 70⅞" /
Acryl, Holzbeize, Furnierholz und Garn auf Leinwand, 120 x 180 cm.

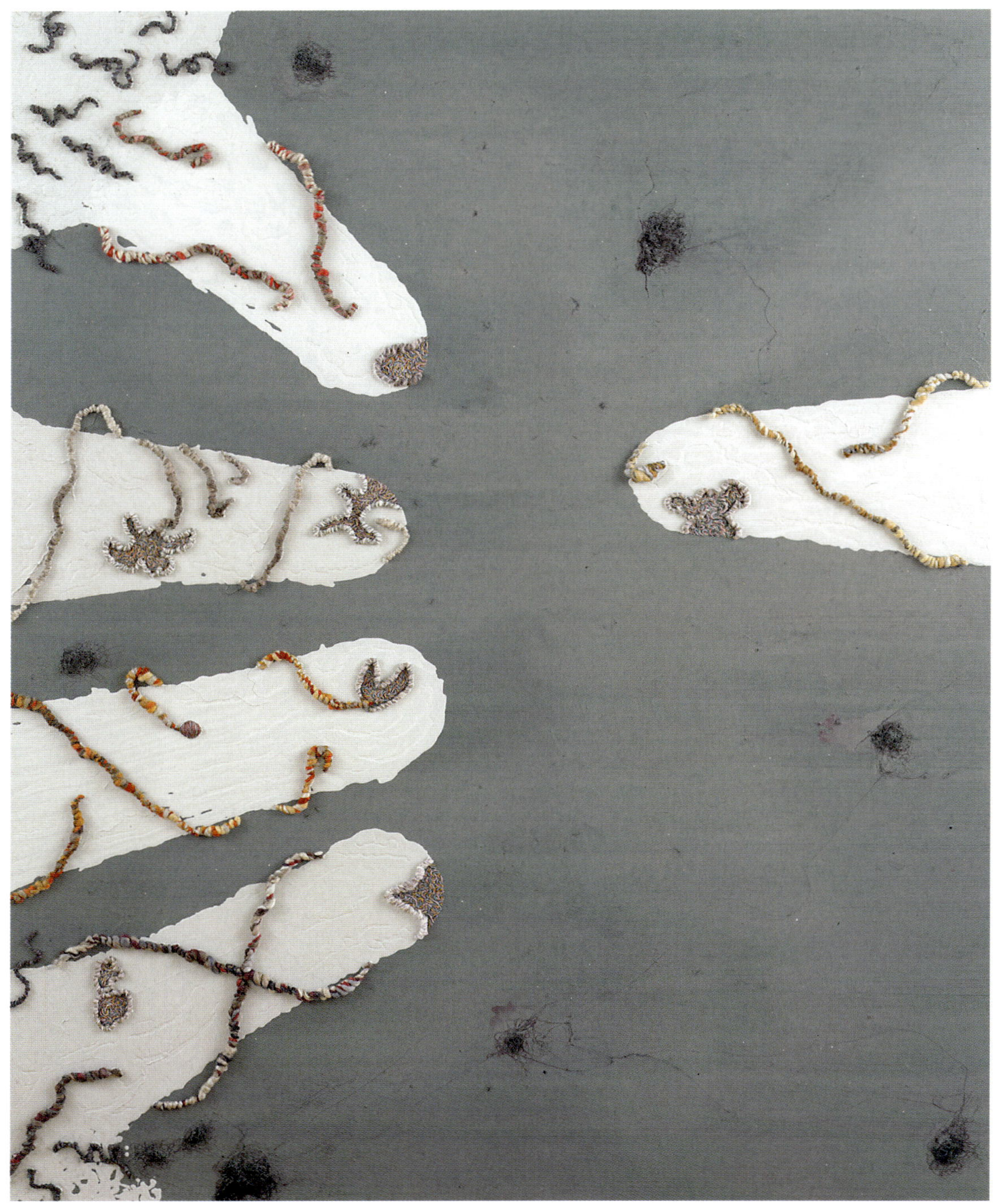

MICHAEL RAEDECKER, JOURNEYS TO GLORY, 2001/2002, acrylic and thread on canvas, 82 $^{11}/_{16}$ x 66 $^{1}/_{8}$" /
Acryl und Garn auf Leinwand, 210 x 168 cm.

fügbar. Raedecker hat das erfasst und nicht nur weil er früher DJ war. Seine Bilder erinnern uns daran, dass die einzige Heimat, die ein Bild noch hat, jene ist, die wir ihm schaffen, indem wir Dinge verwenden wie Filme, die wir nie vergessen, oder Songs, die wir immer lieben werden. Wenn Raedecker einige seiner Bilder nach Songs von Musikgrössen wie Elvis Presley oder Spandau Ballet betitelt, liefert er Hinweise, dass in seinen Bildern direkt kollektive Erinnerungen angezapft werden, die uns nie abhanden kommen, da sie sich uns immer wieder neu ins Gedächtnis weben, weil wir es so wollen. Dieser Teil der Malerei ist ganz und gar n i c h t entfremdend.

Apropos Weben: Raedeckers Wechsel von der Mode zur Malerei erscheint angesichts seines Hintergrunds als logischer Schritt, obschon er beteuert, dass seine früheren Erfahrungen in der Modebranche nicht direkt dafür verantwortlich sind, dass er heute zum Teil deren Materialien und Techniken einsetzt. In seinen frühen Arbeiten war die Stickerei eine praktische und effiziente Möglichkeit, zum Ausdruck zu bringen, dass er die Malerei als sehr sinnvollen Zeitvertreib betrachtete (seine frühen Bilder waren eine Art Dekonstruktion der Porträts von Winston Churchill mit Hilfe von photomechanischer Reproduktion und Faden, mit welchem er ihren Kontext auf die Bildfläche «schrieb»): «Ich wollte eine Technik anwenden, die es mir erlaubte, meine Tätigkeit zu geniessen und dabei vielleicht Musik zu hören und die Gedanken schweifen zu lassen.»[2] Egal, welche Erklärung dahinter steht (denken wir nur daran, dass Jasper Johns behauptet, er habe einen Traum gehabt, in welchem er eine amerikanische Flagge malte), zumindest zeigt Raedeckers Nähtechnik, dass es ihm anscheinend ungemein wohl dabei ist, die Beziehung zwischen Materialität und «Look» in seinen Bildern zu erkunden und zu analysieren. Man könnte sagen, dass alle Fasern, die er in seinen Arbeiten verwendet, bei ihm und uns eine Art Heimatgefühl auslösen, lose Fäden, die tatsächlich unser gemeinsames Erleben eines Bildes verankern, das als solches undurchdringlich bleiben soll.

Es ist ebenso wahrscheinlich, dass die Stickerei Raedecker eine wirksame Möglichkeit bietet, einen Anfang zu finden oder jederzeit rasch etwas Neues ins Bild einzuarbeiten. Bestimmt erleichtert es ihm auch, etwas aufzutrennen oder ganz aus dem Bild zu entfernen, falls es nicht funktioniert.[3] Dank der Flexibilität von Raedeckers Stickerei wirken viele Bilder innerhalb seiner Gemälde so, als könnten sie mühelos verändert werden, das trifft vor allem bei einigen vor wenigen Jahren entstandenen Werken zu, etwa REVERB (Nachhall, 1998). In diesem Bild (das mit sehr wenig Farbe gemacht ist) flitzen weisse Fadenlinien wie Lichtstrahlen oder Kratzer über die schematische Darstellung eines Wohnzimmers, dessen Fussboden anscheinend aus Wasser besteht (oder ist der Raum leicht überschwemmt?), so dass sich verschiedene Dinge darin «spiegeln»: die Decke, die Wände, ein Fenster mit Fernsicht auf die Berge und – besonders auffällig – ein offener Vorhang, der mit dichten Stichen aus gelbem und braunem Garn aufgestickt ist und das körperlich greifbarste Element des Ganzen darstellt. (Er ist materiell und farblich weitaus «präsenter» als all die losen, ausgefransten Fäden, die den Raum wie Staubflocken umgeben.) Seit 1998 sind Raedeckers Gemälde viel dichter geworden, in Bilder und Materialien ist eine gewisse Langsamkeit eingezogen, die bewirkt, dass das Werk in erster Linie als Gemälde und nicht als Zeichnung oder Handarbeit wahrgenommen wird.

Natürlich ist Kunstfertigkeit im «handwerklichen» Sinn des Wortes (im Gegensatz etwa zum Begriff, wie er in der niederländischen Landschaftsmalerei verwendet wird) in der Malerei ein relativ neues Thema, und ich könnte mir vorstellen, dass ich, würde man mir Raedeckers Gemälde bloss beschreiben, den voreiligen Schluss ziehen könnte, sie hätten eine problematische Beziehung zur altbekannten ideologischen Auseinandersetzung zwischen Kunst und Kunsthandwerk auf dem Hintergrund des Geschlechter- oder Klassenkampfes. In seinen neuesten Arbeiten weicht Raedecker diesem Thema erfolgreich aus, indem er den Gebrauch der Fasern konzeptuell erweitert, und zwar nicht nur, indem er sich über «konventionellere» Anwendungen des Stickens und Nähens hinausbewegt, sondern auch, indem er verschiedene Materialien zunehmend wie Farbe wirken lässt, ohne ihnen ihren Materialcharakter zu nehmen. So muten zum Beispiel in einem Bild wie RADIATE (Strahlen, 2000) die Fasern auf dem Boden des abgebildeten Raums wie winzige Farbwürmchen an. Andernorts ist in diesem Bild Farbe aufgetragen, die weit mehr Volumen besitzt als in anderen Werken: Oft wirken die ausgewaschenen Farben in Raedeckers Gemälden wie Rückstände, die nach einer Überschwemmung zurückgeblieben sind. In diesem Fall schaffte die Farbe es unglaublicherweise, durch das Fenster eines weiteren leeren und doch sehr vollen Raums zu sickern. Vielleicht ist eine ziemlich flüssige Lawine auf dieses Haus niedergegangen? Ein Fenster auf einem ähnlichen Bild – BLOCK (2001) – ist buchstäblich mit Furnierholz zugenagelt. Durch die konzeptuelle und tatsächliche Vermischung von Fasern und Farbe haben Raedeckers Arbeiten viel mit den Mitte der 70er Jahre entstandenen Bildern von Joe Zucker gemein. Zucker, der sich mit seinen *Wattebausch*-Bildern (in denen er Wattebällchen in unterschiedliche Farben tauchte und in regelmässigen Reihen auf dem Bild anordnete) in den späten 60er Jahren einen Namen gemacht hatte, schuf danach unter dem Titel *Reconstruction* eine Bilderserie, die mittels Watte und Farbe in prachtvoller Weise die Geschichte der Baumwollproduktion in den USA darstellte. Er überzog in dieser Serie nicht einfach Wattebällchen mit Farbe, sondern bediente sich einer Technik, die Greenbergs plastischer und beschreibender malerischen Darstellungsweise nahe kam: Die Fasern wurden T e i l der Farbe, so dass Kunst und Handwerk untrennbar miteinander verschmolzen. Was Zucker damals sagte, lässt sich auch auf Raedecker anwenden: «Meine Themenwahl im Verhältnis zu den möglichen Oberflächen ist wichtig. Der Bildinhalt wird zu einer Ikonographie, um die Topographie des Bildes zur Sprache zu bringen.»[4]

Es war wohl Raedeckers zunehmende Aufmerksamkeit für die Topographie seiner Gemälde als Ge-

MICHAEL RAEDECKER, IS THIS IT, 2001, acrylic and thread on canvas, detail, overall size 60¼ x 40⅜" / Acryl und Garn auf Leinwand, Ausschnitt, ganzes Bild 153 x 102,5 cm.

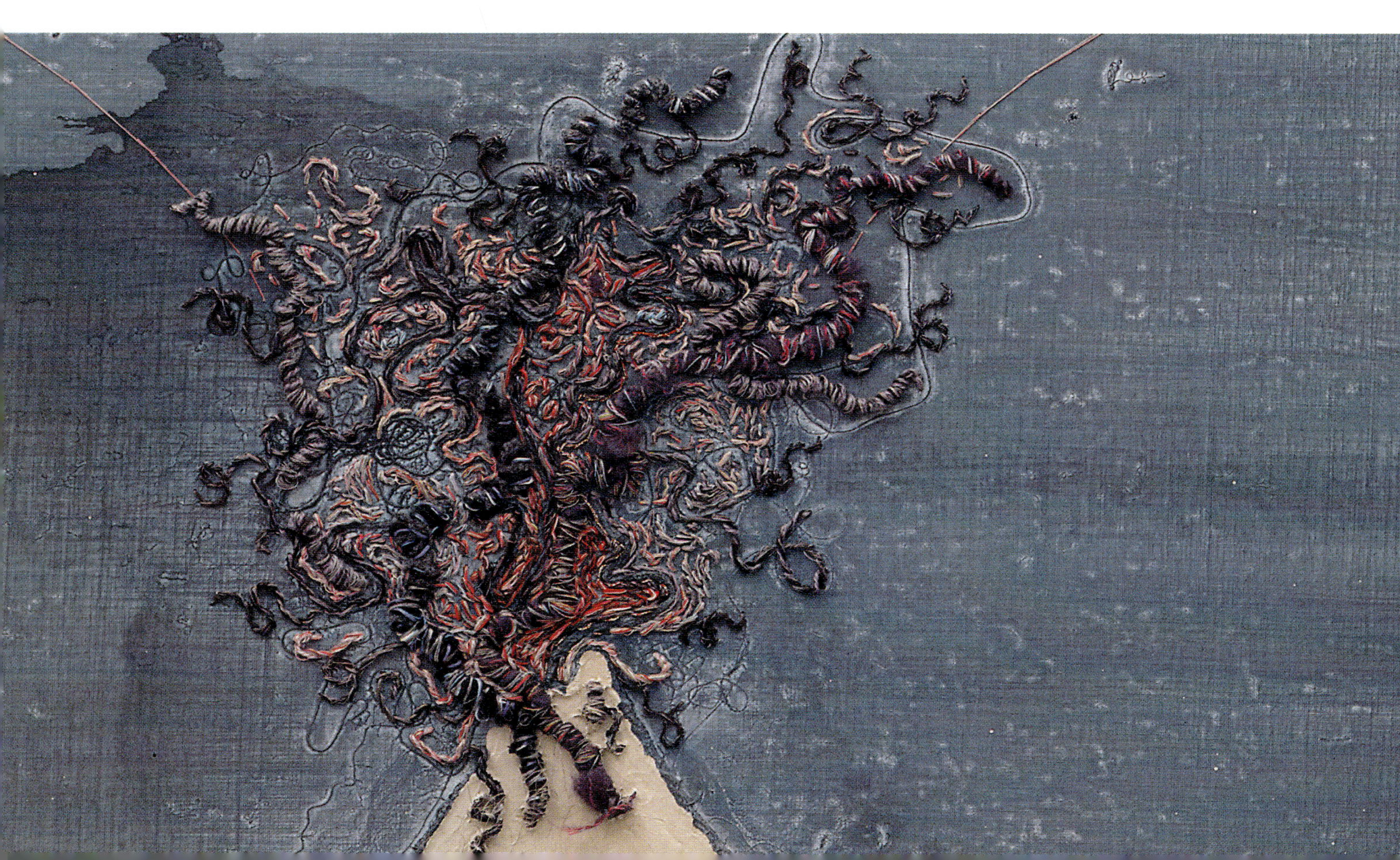

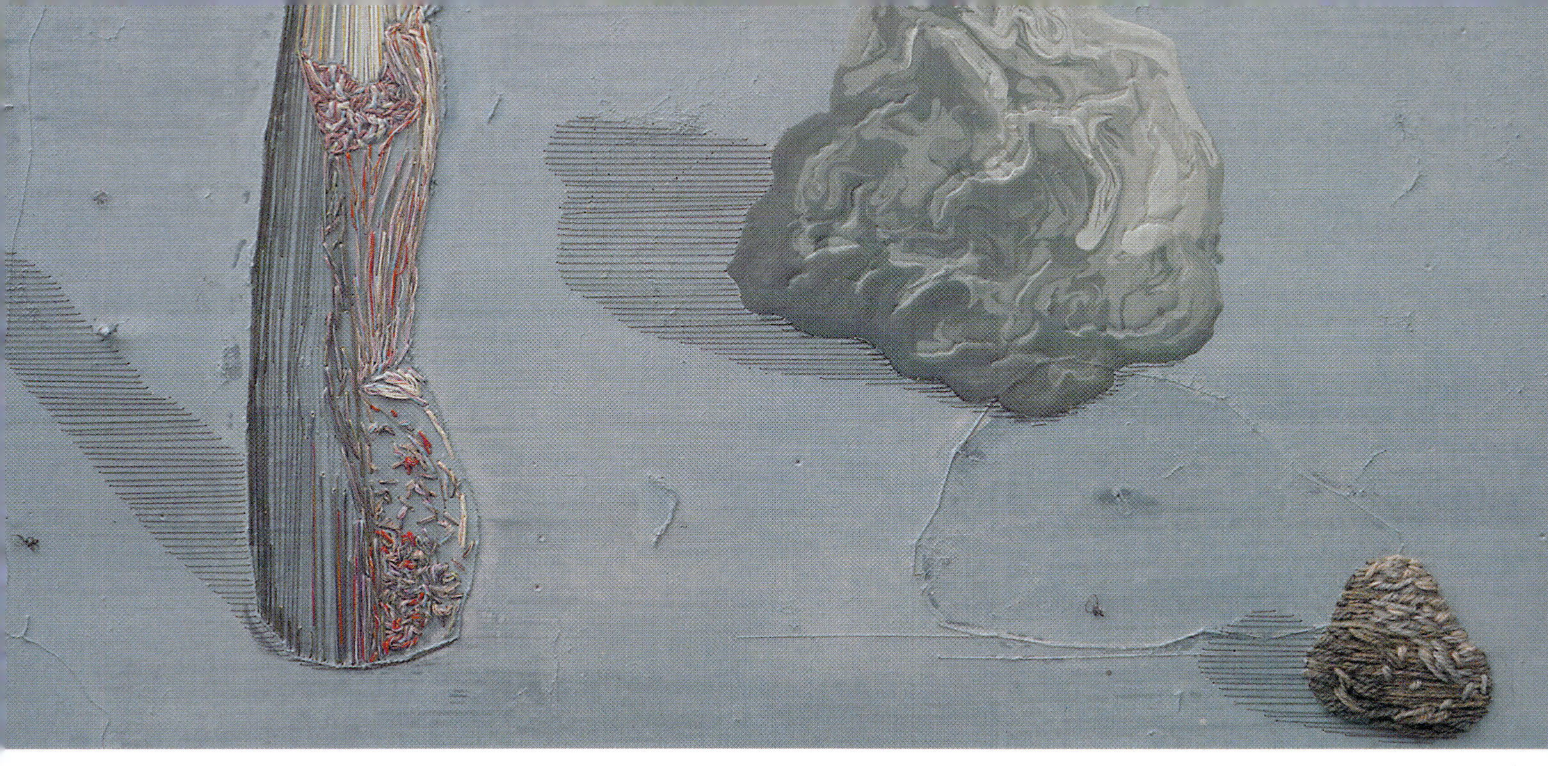

mälde, die es ihm ermöglichte, die Ikonographie seiner Werke sowohl inhaltlich als auch im Hinblick auf ihre Ausrichtung auszuweiten. Indem er in bedeutenden Bildern wie KISMET (1999) und UP (Auf, 1999) eine beachtliche Neuausrichtung vornahm, die er in Werken wie JOURNEYS TO GLORY (Wege zum Ruhm) und EXPOSURE (Ausgesetzt sein), beide 2001/2002, noch erweiterte, hat Raedecker seine Bereitschaft gezeigt, sich über die traditionelle räumliche Beziehung zwischen einem Bild und dem Gemälde, in dem es beherbergt ist, hinauszubewegen und die Darstellung auf mehr als eine Weise «heimatlos» werden zu lassen. Nun hat er uns so weit, dass wir flach auf dem Rücken liegen und zum Himmel oder wohin auch immer aufschauen, statt aufrecht stehend aus einem Fenster oder über ein Feld zu blicken. Orientierungslos und mehr als nur ein bisschen benommen, befinden wir uns eindeutig nicht mehr in Kansas, und es steht zu vermuten, dass wir gar nie dort waren.

(Übersetzung: Irene Aeberli)

1) Dieses und alle folgenden Zitate von Clement Greenberg stammen aus seinem Essay «Nach dem Abstrakten Expressionismus», in: Clement Greenberg, *Die Essenz der Moderne. Ausgewählte Essays und Kritiken*, hg. v. Karlheinz Lüdeking, übers. v. Christoph Hollender, Fundus-Bücher, Verlag der Kunst, Amsterdam/Dresden 1997, S. 314–335. (Englisch erstmals erschienen in der Zeitschrift *Art International*, 6. Jg., Nr. 8, 25. Oktober 1962, S. 24–32.)
2) Louisa Buck, «UK artist Q&A: Michael Raedecker», *The Art Newspaper*, Nr. 104, Juni 2000, S. 67.
3) Johns' erstes *Flaggen*-Bild begann als Fiasko. Da seine Versuche mit Lackfarbe auf einem Bettlaken in einem Schlamassel endeten, ging er zu Enkaustik über. Dann bat ihn Rauschenberg, einen der Streifen malen zu dürfen, und verwendete rote Wachsfarbe statt weisser. Ausserdem mussten mehrere Collage-Elemente festgenäht werden, damit sie überhaupt hielten. Tatsächlich wurde das ganze Bild mindestens an einer Kante auf ziemlich verzweifelte Art auf den Bildträger aus Sperrholz getackert, da das Laken nur knapp gross genug war. Zudem ist das Bild etwas umständlich mit 1954–55 datiert, aber nicht etwa, weil seine Fertigstellung so lange gedauert hätte, sondern weil es bei einer Party beschädigt wurde und wieder repariert werden musste. Was ich hier mit Blick auf Raedeckers Arbeiten zum Ausdruck bringen will, ist, dass interessante Bilder gewöhnlich Höllisches durchmachen müssen.
4) Joe Zucker, Statement des Künstlers, in: Richard Marshall, *New Image Painting*, Whitney Museum of American Art, New York 1978, S. 68.

Their Second Home

DAVE EGGERS

Hollis and his father broke the upper crust with each step. Below the crust the snow was dry and granular, a feel of both cotton and sand. Hollis and his father were walking home from his grandmother's house, where they had turned her over and washed her.

Hollis's family was now in a new house. Two months ago they had moved from their grandmother's house, where they had lived the nine years of Hollis's life, to this new house, about three miles away. The air was heavy with cold, and breathing it in felt to Hollis like inhaling glass and expelling wool.

Sixteen inches of snow had fallen in two days and nothing had been plowed. The car Hollis's father drove would not make it through this, so they had walked. Their grandmother was alone but for the neighbor girl, Kelly, who was fine but sometimes needed relief. They were walking up a hill in the park, a shortcut that would take them under the highway and to a field that led through the incorporated area and to their house.

"I figured out how to scare your mom," Hollis's father said.

It was the first thing Hollis or his father had said during the walk.

"How do you mean?" Hollis said.

"You know that window next to her desk?"

Hollis did. His mother's office was on the second floor. He nodded.

"Well, she's not used to anything happening right out her window, right?"

Hollis nodded again. His mother's window, over her desk where she did bookkeeping and tax returns, overlooked the backyard, and beyond it, the unincorporated land.

"Well, I've been thinking that a great way to really scare her would be to jump out right there and yell like crazy. She'd scream like a banshee."

Hollis didn't know what a banshee was, but his father had said this before, so he assumed a banshee was either someone who screamed a lot, or screamed loudly and well. Hollis pic-

---

DAVE EGGERS is the author of a new novel, untitled at press time, and the editor of *McSweeney's*.

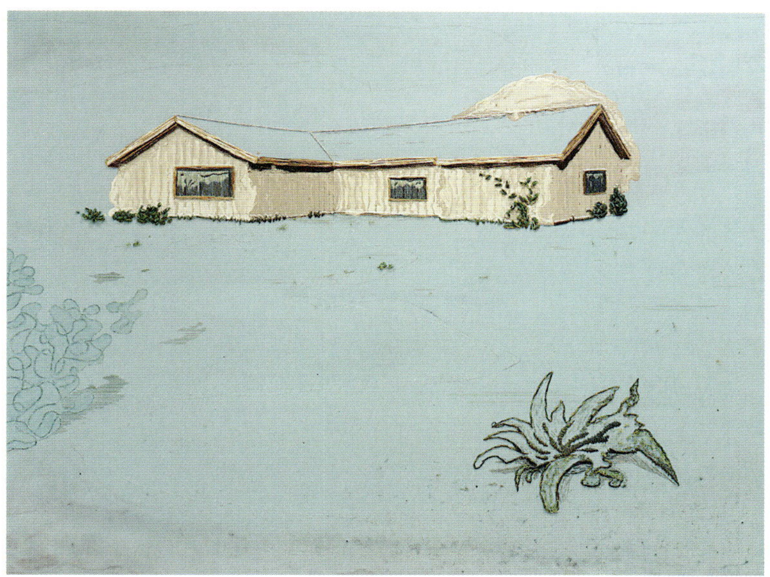

MICHAEL RAEDECKER, MONUMENT, 1998,
acrylic and thread on canvas, 55⅞ x 72" /
Acryl und Garn auf Leinwand, 142 x 183 cm.

tured his mother screaming. "I would just get up on the ladder and pop out, and yell Wah!" his father said.

They were walking under the highway now and his father's voice was louder, and his Wah! stayed in the underpass for some time.

As they were passing through the dim corridor Hollis wondered how loudly his mother would scream, and how long afterward she would calm down. He wondered if his mother would find the scaring funny, or if she would be angry.

Hollis wanted to scare his mother.

"I want to scare her," he said.

"You can watch me do it," his father said. They were now in the light again. "Actually, maybe it's not such a great idea. Your mom doesn't like being scared."

Hollis took in a quick breath.

"She does!" Hollis said.

"No, I don't think she does. That one time I did it she was mad for a pretty long while."

Hollis remembered hearing about that afterward. After seeing a suspenseful movie on TV, his father had hidden in the back seat of the car. He knew Hollis's mom would go to the convenience store, which she did every night to get fresh bagels for the next morning, so he snuck out to the car and had hidden in the back seat. He had stayed there, in the back seat, while she started out on the highway and then exited onto the frontage road. He waited until the third stop light, when the road was dark and quiet. Then he jumped up and yelled "Wah!"

They had stayed there, at the intersection, for an hour afterward.

"She'll like it this time," Hollis said.

"No, I don't think so," his father said. "It was a bad idea."

Hollis was furious. He couldn't believe this possibility was being taken from him. The scaring was something that was about to happen, the event looming ahead like a holiday, and

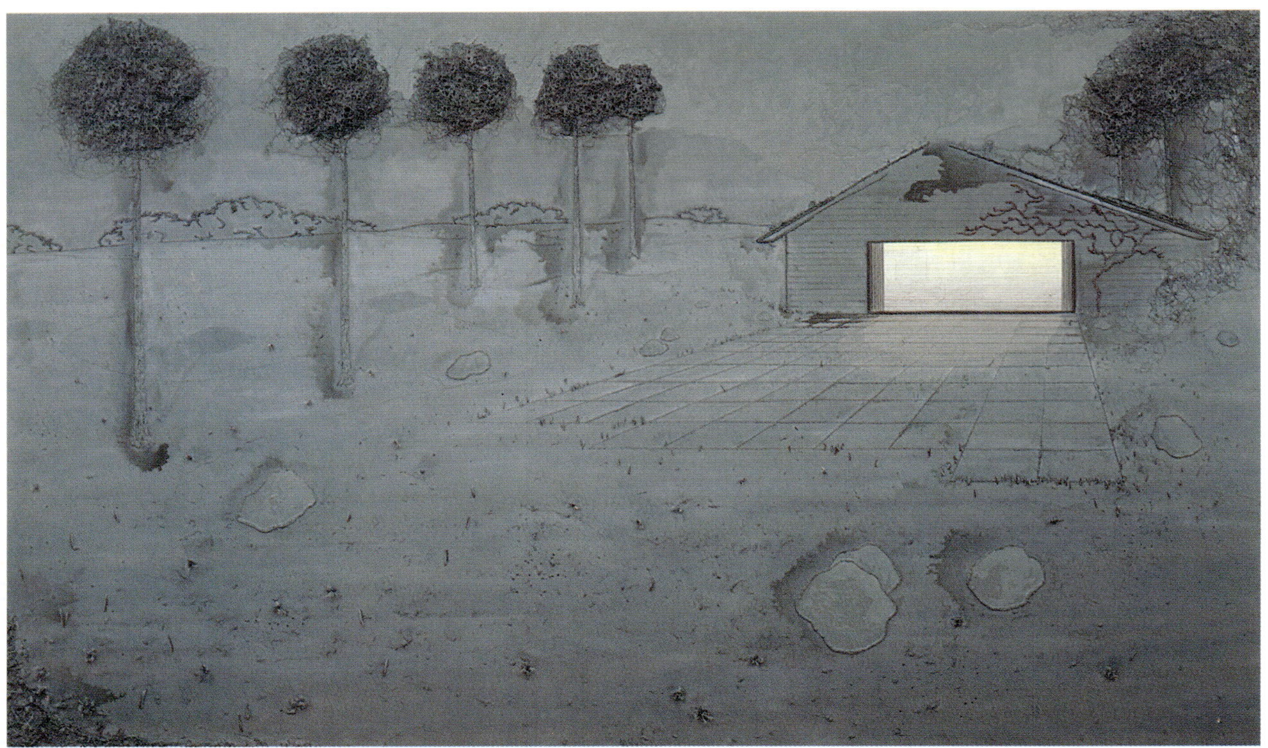

MICHAEL RAEDECKER, INS AND OUTS, 2000, acrylic and thread on canvas,
130 x 78" / Acryl und Garn auf Leinwand, 330 x 198 cm.

now it would not happen. He felt dizzy. He would have to argue with his father to ensure any possibility of it happening, and even then it probably would not happen.

As they walked, the snow breaking underfoot, Hollis explored other ways he could jump in front of his mother's window. He could do it himself, but the ladder was too heavy for him to lift and raise. He could jump from the tree nearby, but that was too far. He could somehow swing from the rooftop from a rope, perhaps tied to the chimney. He couldn't remember if they had any rope that would be strong enough.

As they came across the field and saw the house in the distance, Hollis pleaded with his father to scare his mother. His father told him to drop it. Hollis begged. His father stopped responding. He was finished with the subject.

When they pushed through the hedge at the perimeter of their yard, they could see Hollis's mother in her second-floor window, her soft oval face painted in ochre. She was reading something under her grandfather's ancient lamp, steam from her tea rising around her face like creeping ivy.

Hollis's father went inside, stomping his feet on the porch, releasing the snow. Hollis went to the garage and found the dead frog he'd been keeping in a jar. He dropped it onto his father's worktable and cut its belly stem to stern.

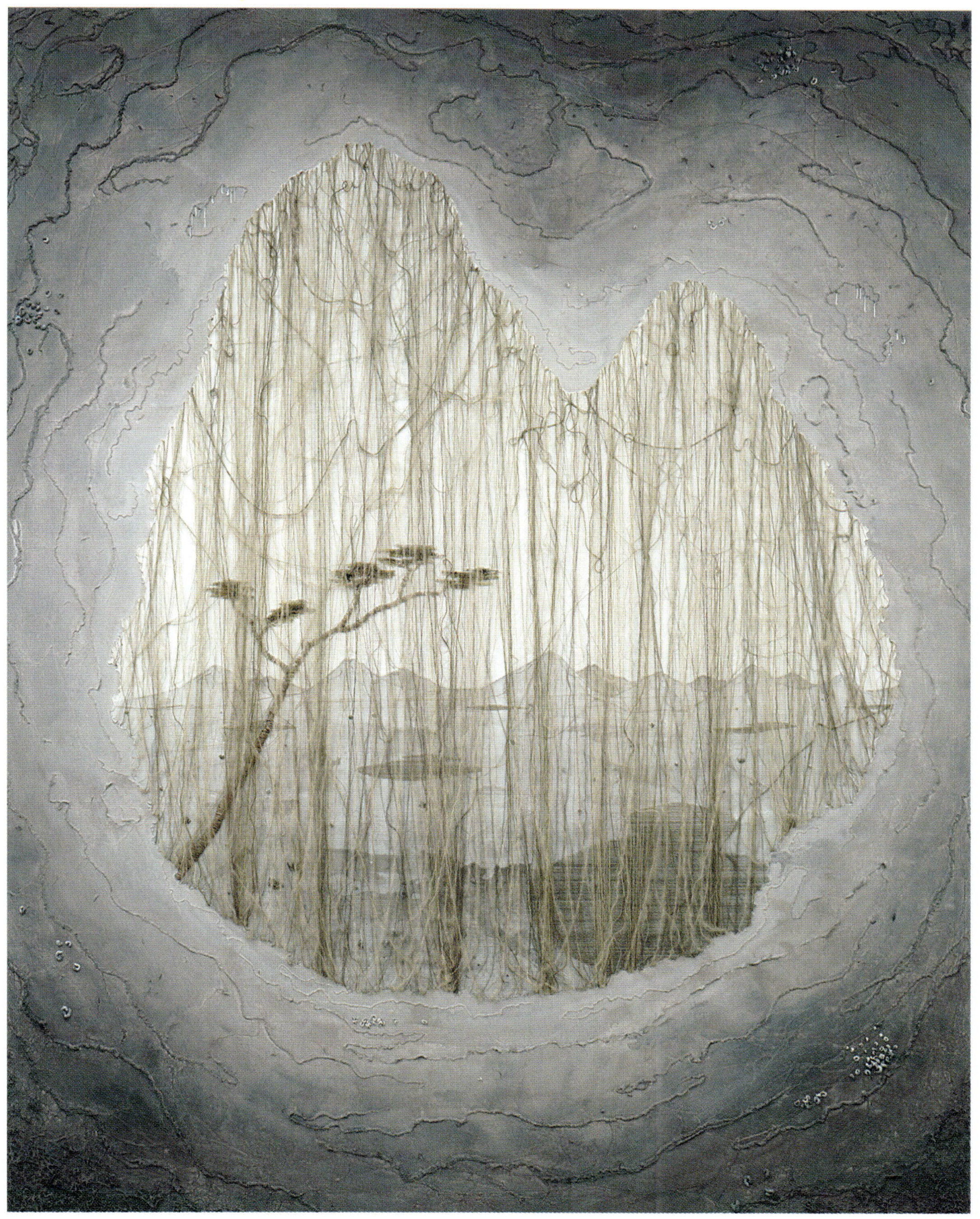

*MICHAEL RAEDECKER, ECHO, 2000, acrylic and thread on canvas,
100 x 78" / Acryl und Garn auf Leinwand, 254 x 198 cm.*

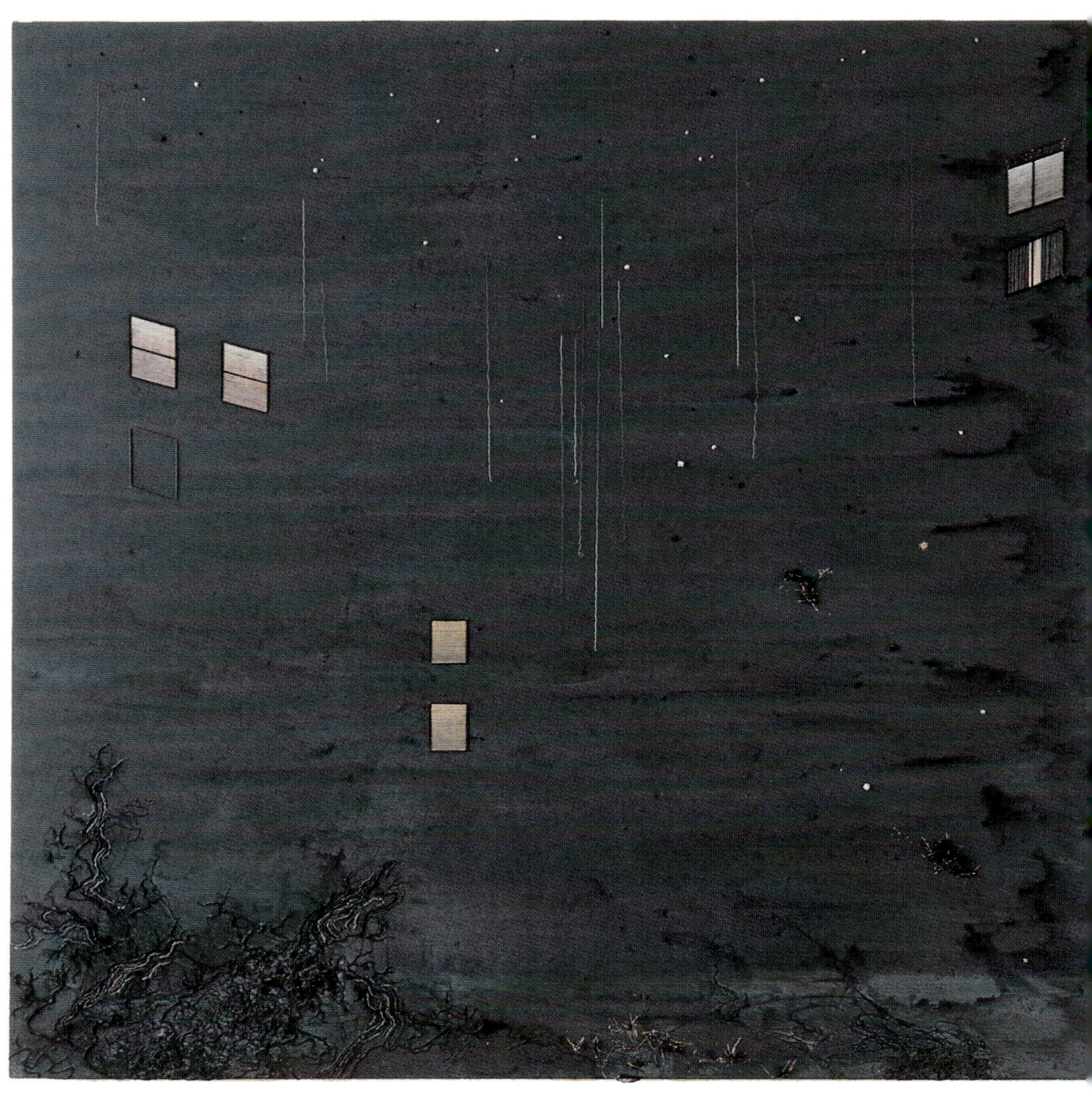

MICHAEL RAEDECKER, SYNCHRONICITY, *acrylic and thread on canvas, diptych, 67 x 149⅝" /*
Acryl und Garn auf Leinwand, Diptychon, 170 x 380 cm.

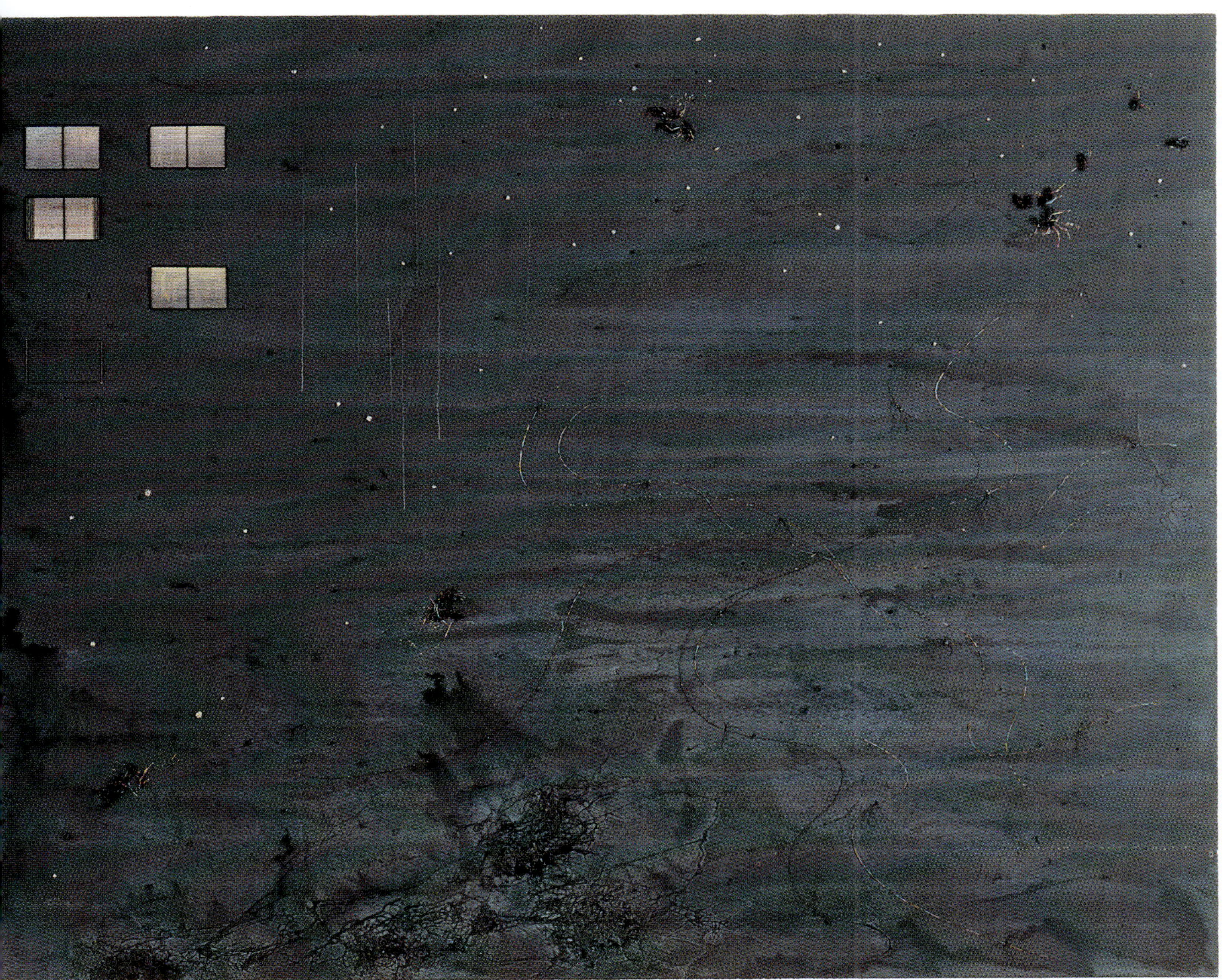

Michael Raedecker

Das zweite Zuhause

DAVE EGGERS

Mit jedem Schritt durchbrachen Hollis und sein Vater die verharschte Schneedecke. Darunter war der Schnee körnig trocken und fühlte sich an wie Baumwolle und Sand zugleich. Hollis und sein Vater waren auf dem Heimweg. Sie kamen vom Haus der Grossmutter, die sie im Bett gewendet und gewaschen hatten.

Hollis' Familie lebte jetzt in einem neuen Haus. Vor zwei Monaten waren sie aus dem Haus der Grossmutter, wo sie die ganzen neun Jahre, die Hollis auf der Welt war, gewohnt hatten, in dieses neue, etwa drei Meilen entfernte Haus umgezogen. Die Kälte lastete schwer in der Luft und Hollis kam es bei jedem Atemzug vor, als würde er Glas ein- und Wolle ausatmen.

In zwei Tagen waren gut vierzig Zentimeter Schnee gefallen und die Strasse war nicht geräumt worden. Mit dem Auto, das Hollis' Vater fuhr, war an ein Durchkommen nicht mehr zu denken, deshalb waren sie zu Fuss gegangen. Die Grossmutter lebte allein, bis auf das Nachbarmädchen Kelly, das zwar gut zu ihr schaute, aber manchmal etwas Entlastung brauchte. Jetzt stiegen sie im Park eine Anhöhe hinauf, eine Abkürzung, die unter dem Highway hindurch auf eine Wiese und dann quer über Gemeindegebiet schliesslich zu ihrem Haus führte.

«Ich weiss, wie wir deine Mama erschrecken könnten», sagte Hollis' Vater.

Es waren die ersten Worte, die Hollis und sein Vater wechselten, seit sie auf dem Heimweg waren.

«Wie denn?»

«Du kennst doch das Fenster, hinter dem ihr Schreibtisch steht?»

Klar doch. Hollis nickte. Das Büro seiner Mutter war im oberen Stock.

«Und sie ist nicht darauf gefasst, dass direkt vor ihrem Fenster was los ist, oder?»

Wieder nickte Hollis. Vom Fenster über dem Schreibtisch, an dem seine Mutter ihre Buchhaltungsarbeit erledigte und Steuererklärungen ausfüllte, sah man den Garten hinter dem Haus und das Brachland dahinter.

«Ich glaube, man könnte ihr wirklich einen wahnsinnigen Schreck einjagen, wenn man direkt vor dem Fenster plötzlich hervorschnellen und wie verrückt schreien würde. Sie würde kreischen wie ein Banshee.»

DAVE EGGERS hat einen neuen Roman geschrieben, dessen Titel zurzeit noch nicht feststeht, und ist Herausgeber der Zeitschrift *McSweeney's*.

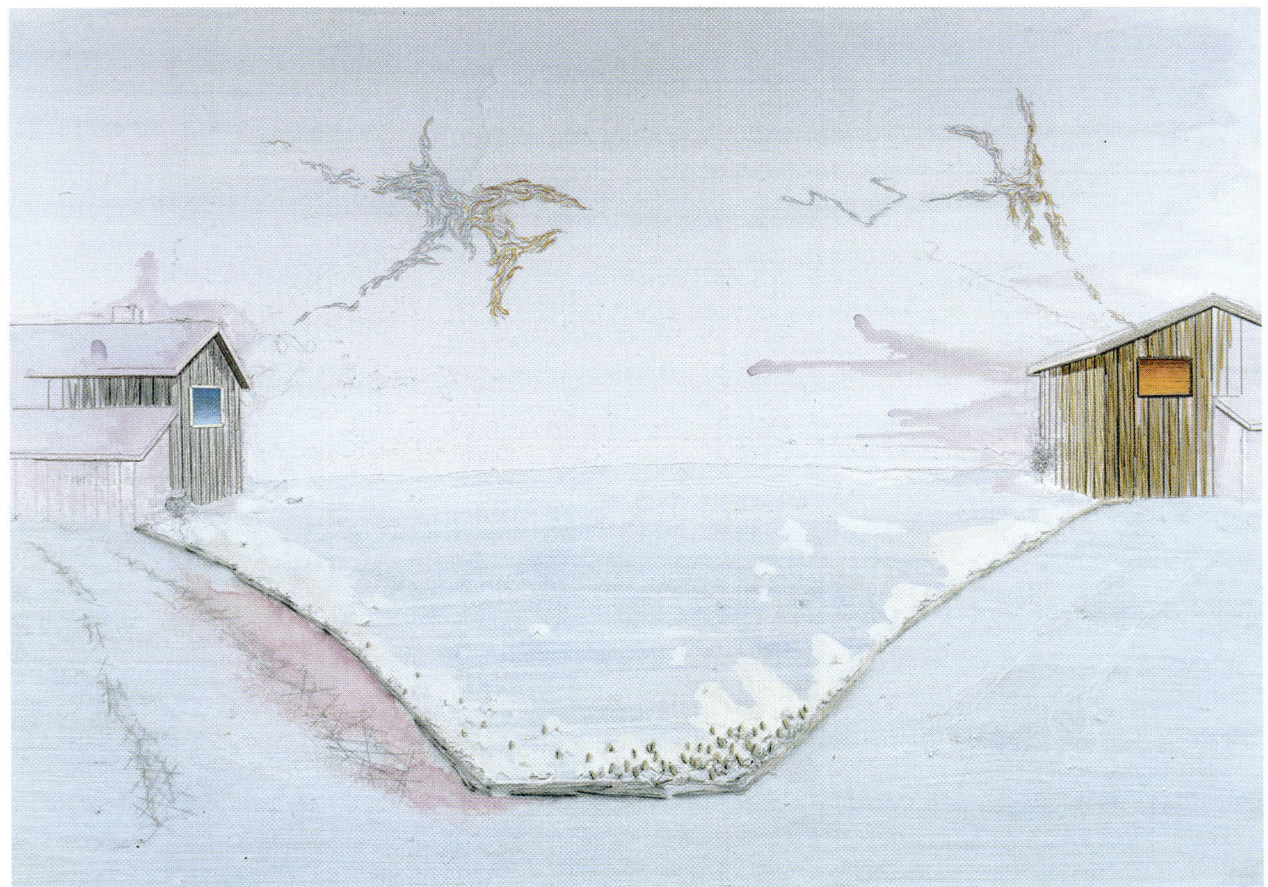

Hollis wusste zwar nicht, was ein Banshee war, aber sein Vater hatte das schon öfter gesagt, also nahm er an, dass ein Banshee entweder jemand war, der dauernd schrie oder aber besonders gut und laut schrie. Hollis stellte sich vor, wie seine Mutter schreien würde. «Ich würde einfach die Leiter hinaufsteigen, den Kopf hervorstrecken und ‹buh› schreien!», meinte der Vater.

Sie waren jetzt direkt unter dem Highway, die Stimme des Vaters klang lauter und sein «Buh» hallte längere Zeit in der Unterführung nach.

Während sie die dunkle Passage durchquerten, fragte sich Hollis, wie laut seine Mutter wohl schreien würde und wie lange es ginge, bis sie sich wieder beruhigt hätte. Er überlegte, ob die Mutter es lustig fände, erschreckt zu werden, ober ob sie wütend würde.

Hollis wollte die Mutter erschrecken.

«Ich will sie erschrecken», sagte er.

«Du kannst mir dabei zusehen», sagte sein Vater. Sie waren jetzt wieder am Tageslicht. «Aber vielleicht ist die Idee doch nicht so gut. Deine Mama mag es nämlich nicht, wenn man sie erschreckt.»

Hollis schnappte nach Luft.

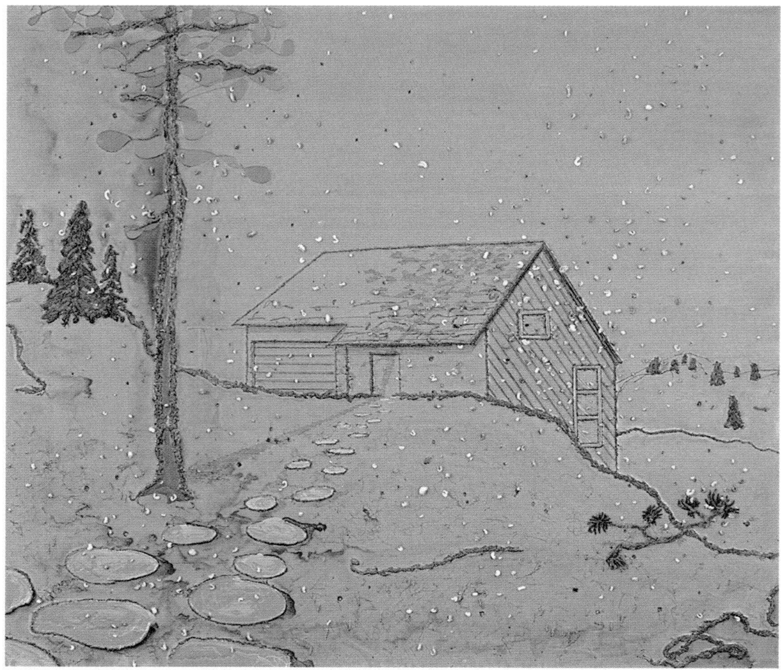

«Doch, sie mag es!», sagte er.

«Nein, ich glaube nicht, dass sie es mag. Das eine Mal, als ich es tat, war sie ziemlich lange verschnupft.»

Hollis erinnerte sich, dass er damals erst nachträglich davon gehört hatte. Nach einem spannenden Fernsehkrimi hatte sich sein Vater auf dem Rücksitz des Autos versteckt. Er wusste, dass Hollis' Mutter wie jeden Abend zum nächsten Lebensmittelgeschäft fahren würde, um frische Bagels für den nächsten Morgen zu besorgen. Also schlich er zum Auto hinaus und versteckte sich auf dem Rücksitz. Dort auf dem Rücksitz harrte er während der Fahrt auf dem Highway aus und auch noch, als sie die Ausfahrt zur Strasse mit den Geschäften nahm. Er wartete bis zum dritten Rotlicht, wo die Strasse dunkel und ruhig war. Dort sprang er auf und brüllte: «Buh!».

Danach waren sie eine ganze Stunde lang an der Kreuzung stehen geblieben.

«Diesmal wird sie es mögen», sagte Hollis.

«Nein, ich glaube nicht», sagte sein Vater. «Es war keine gute Idee.»

Hollis war wütend. Er konnte nicht glauben, dass man ihn dieses Abenteuers berauben wollte. Die Aussicht seine Mutter zu erschrecken war schon so greifbar geworden, es war ein Ereignis, das unmittelbar bevorstand und seine Schatten vorauswarf wie ein Feiertag, und nun sollte es nicht stattfinden. Ihm wurde schwindlig. Er würde mit seinem Vater streiten müssen, damit es wenn irgend möglich doch noch zustande käme, aber selbst das nützte wohl nichts mehr.

Während sie über den brüchigen Schnee gingen, dachte sich Hollis weitere Varianten aus, wie er vor das Fenster seiner Mutter springen könnte. Er könnte es selbst tun, aber die Leiter war zu schwer, er konnte sie nicht allein anheben und aufstellen. Er könnte vom nächststehenden Baum springen, aber der stand zu weit weg. Er könnte sich irgendwie vom

Dach schwingen, vielleicht an einem Seil, das am Kamin festgemacht wäre. Aber er war nicht einmal sicher, ob sie ein Seil hatten, das dafür stark genug war.

Als sie über die Wiese gingen und das Haus in der Ferne sichtbar wurde, flehte Hollis seinen Vater an, die Mutter doch bitte zu erschrecken. Der Vater sagte, er solle damit aufhören. Hollis bettelte. Der Vater antwortete nicht mehr. Für ihn war die Sache erledigt.

Als sie sich an der Grenze zum eigenen Garten durch die Hecke zwängten, konnten sie Hollis' Mutter hinter dem Fenster im ersten Stock erkennen, ockerfarben zeichnete sich das weiche Oval ihres Gesichts ab. Unter der alten Lampe des Grossvaters las sie etwas, während aus ihrer Teetasse feiner Dampf aufstieg und sich wie Efeu um ihr Gesicht rankte.

Hollis' Vater stampfte sich auf der Veranda den Schnee von den Füssen und ging ins Haus. Hollis ging in die Garage und holte den toten Frosch, den er dort in einem Glas aufbewahrte. Er knallte ihn auf den Arbeitstisch seines Vaters und schlitzte dem Tier mit einem einzigen langen Schnitt Bauch und Kehle auf.

(Übersetzung: Parker/Aeberli)

MICHAEL RAEDECKER, HAZE, 1998, acrylic and thread on canvas, 54 x 70" / Acryl und Garn auf Leinwand, 137 x 178 cm.

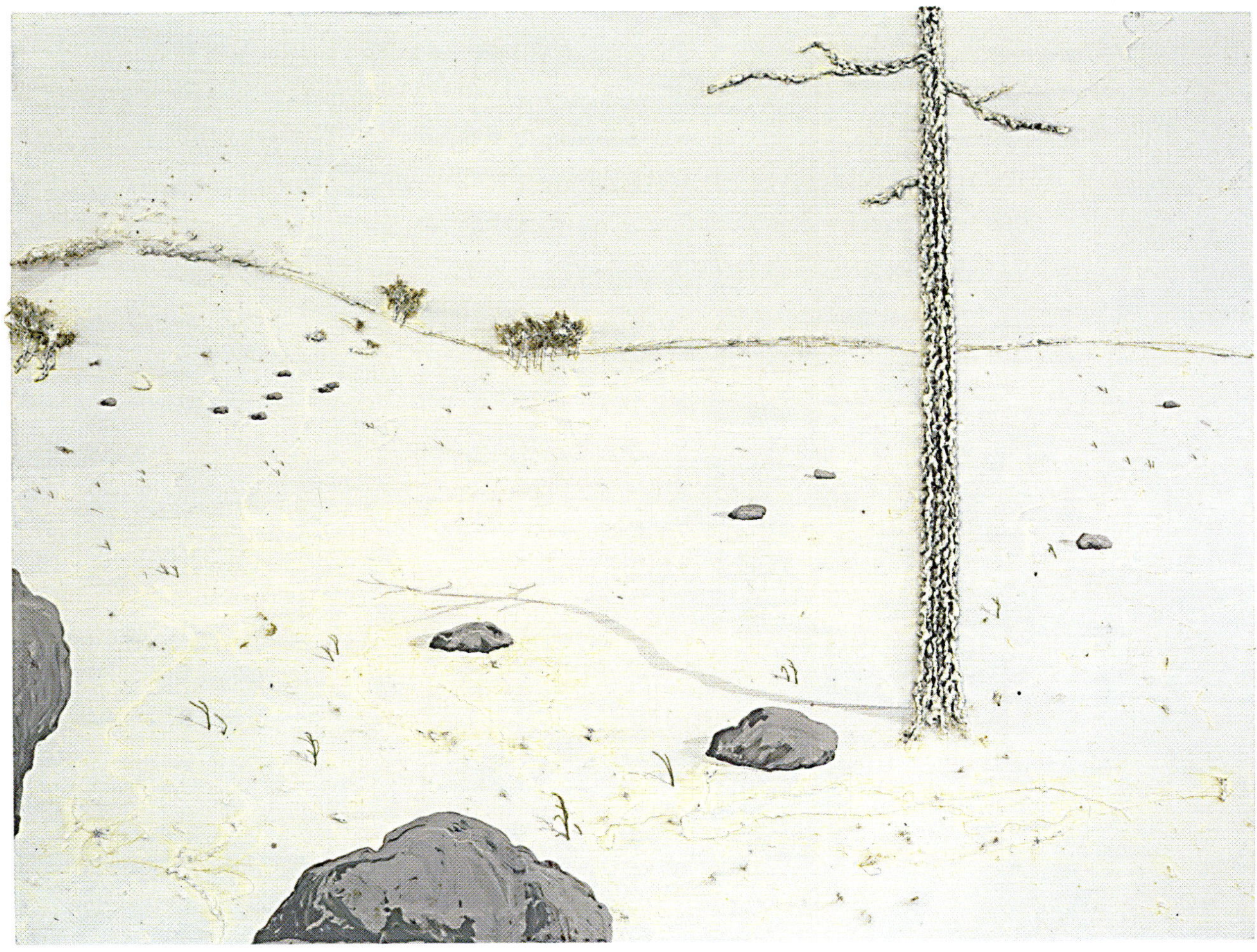

THE OTHER SIDE, 2002
10-color silkscreen print on pure silk satin scarf with
handrolled border, 33½ x 33½"
Detail from the back of the painting INCOMPLETE (2002)
Produced by Fabric Frontline, Zurich
Edition of 99, signed and numbered certificate

10-Farben-Siebdruck auf Seidensatinfoulard,
handrouliert, 85 x 85 cm
Ausschnitt der Rückansicht des Bildes INCOMPLETE (2002)
Produktion: Fabric Frontline, Zürich
Auflage: 99, signiertes und nummeriertes Zertifikat

(PHOTO: MANCIA/BODMER FBM STUDIO, ZÜRICH)

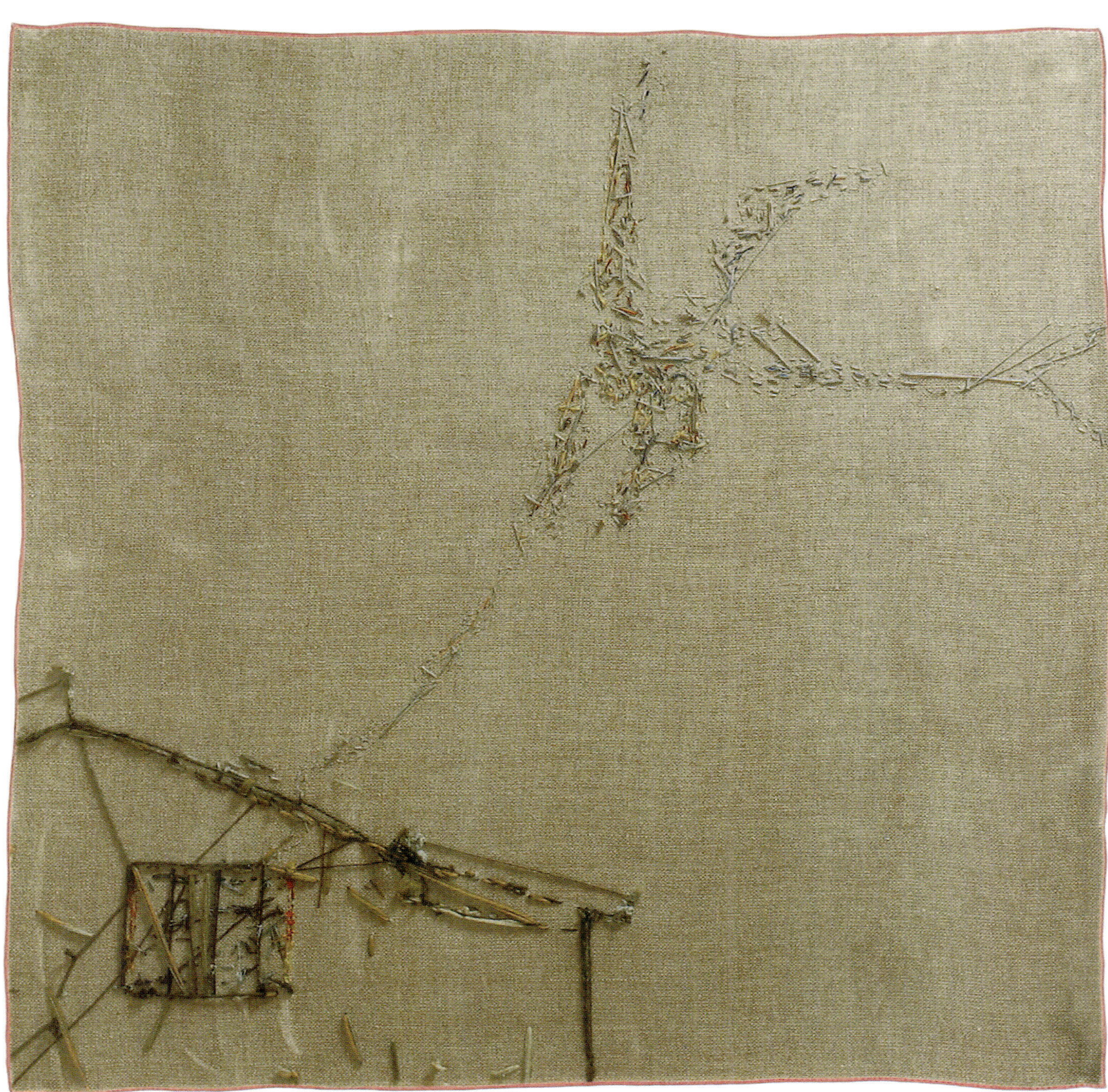

LOVESICKNESS

THE CORRESPONDENCE BETWEEN
DIETER ROTH & DOROTHY IANNONE

ROBERT STORR

You're not supposed to read other people's mail. That traditional bourgeois taboo adds piquancy to both the inadvertent and surreptitious invasion of someone else's privacy. It also prompts anguished confessional types as well as guiltless exhibitionists to divulge their secrets along with those of their perhaps unwitting correspondents. To these sources we owe a wealth of epistolary literature and much of what we will ever know about the intimate unfolding of history.

However, the worst punishment for violating this widely ignored injunction is not public blame or private moral pangs, but the disappointment that comes from learning too much about people. And if not disappointment, exactly, then sadness at the discovery that those we admire for what they do are just as helpless, inconsistent, and unreliable in their everyday existence as the reader, and frequently more so.

Dieter and Dorothy: Dieter Roth and Dorothy Iannone—Their Correspondence in Words and Works 1967–1998 inspires these cautionary thoughts and triggers these mixed emotions.[1] Handsomely laid out and lavishly printed, its 256 pages contain the texts and images that survive from both sides of a thirty-year postal romance between the polymath, polymorphous, polynomial, polynational Swiss artist best known as Dieter Roth, and his expatriate Ameri-

can paramour—and "lioness," so he called her—Dorothy Iannone. To be sure, their meeting in Reykjavik, her sudden abandonment of a marriage in New York, and the first seven years of six-months-on, six-months-off cohabitation were passionate and heartily physical, as Iannone's drawings attest. Combining the decoratively schematic look of Indian Folk painting with cheerful *Yellow Submarine* cartoon-ness and her own earthy scenarios and gender codes—there is plenty of graphic good-time sex between women who have swollen, almost testicular pudenda and men who sport ever-ready penises and lots of body hair—her art is colorful, confidentially sentimental, and stylistically unchanging.

With Iannone's illuminations setting the tone, and her elaborate picture-stories of their adventures in bohemia filling many of the narrative gaps in the account of their lives together and apart, the book as a whole comes to resemble a time capsule of the sixties, but prolonged into the seventies, eighties, and nineties, complete with near penniless nomadism, spontaneous bursts of creative energy ultimately consumed by the constant work of keeping patrons and collaborators on side and on track, opportunistic infidelities on both sides rationalized as the proof of trust within an open relationship, and, in lieu of the period's mind-expanding drugs, lots of mind-numbing drink.

Like most romances, Roth and Iannone's seems to have been lopsided. All in all there are a few extended letters from Roth to his partner, and those reproduced are, for the most part, forlorn if not self-absorbed, as if Roth only wrote when he was unhappy

---

ROBERT STORR is an artist and critic, and a Senior Curator in the Department of Painting and Sculpture at The Museum of Modern Art, New York. He has recently been appointed Rosalie Solow Professor of Modern Art at the Institute of Fine Arts, New York University.

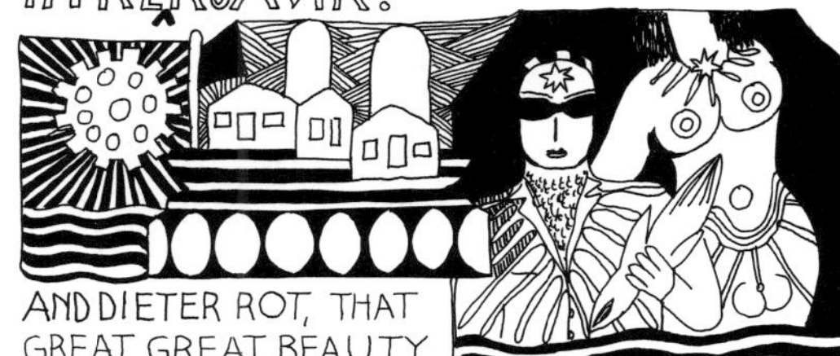

AND DIETER ROT, THAT GREAT, GREAT BEAUTY, IS ON THE PIER WAITING FOR US, WITH A VERY FRESH FISH, WRAPPED IN NEWSPAPER, UNDER HIS ARM. DIETER, SO FRESH HIMSELF, SO IMMERSED IN RESPONSIBILITY, SO IMMERSED IN THE URGENCY OF HIS ART, DIETER, NONETHELESS, A LOVER OF BEAUTIES, IS THERE WAITING FOR US.

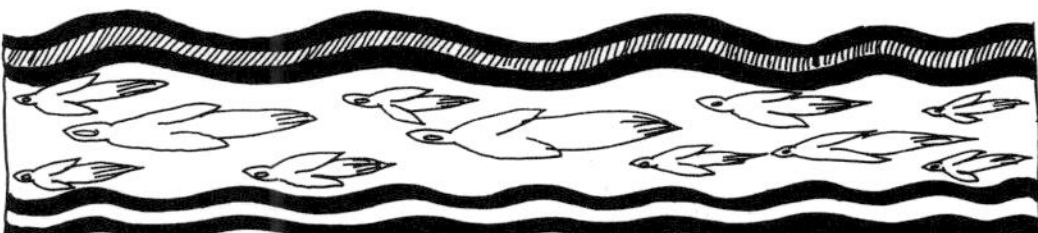

AND WHEN I SAW DIETER I KNEW I WOULD CHANGE MY LIFE.

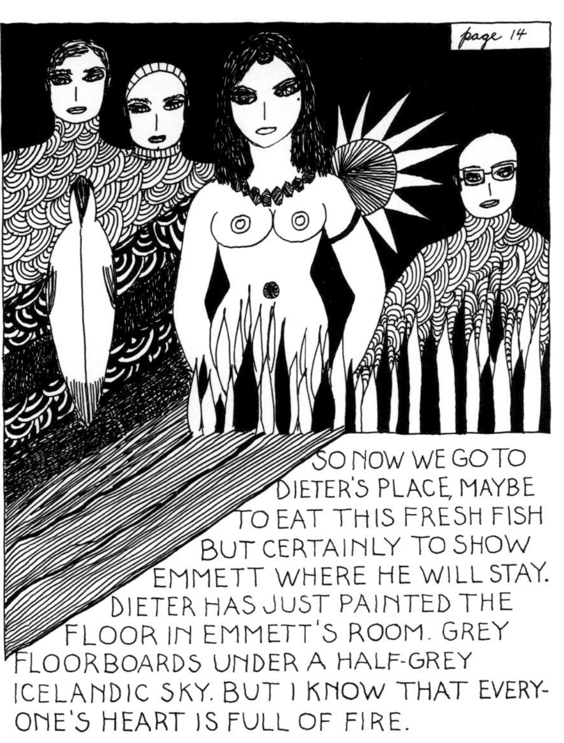

SO NOW WE GO TO DIETER'S PLACE, MAYBE TO EAT THIS FRESH FISH BUT CERTAINLY TO SHOW EMMETT WHERE HE WILL STAY. DIETER HAS JUST PAINTED THE FLOOR IN EMMETT'S ROOM. GREY FLOORBOARDS UNDER A HALF-GREY ICELANDIC SKY. BUT I KNOW THAT EVERY-ONE'S HEART IS FULL OF FIRE.

THAT NIGHT WE SET OUT FOR A RESTAURANT. DIETER IS WEARING A SHIRT WITH NO TIE. HE HAS SOME SAFETY PINS HOLDING HIS SHIRT TOGETHER. (A FEW WEEKS AGO, NORMAN MAILER, HEARING THIS PARTICULAR SARTORIAL DETAIL, REMARKED HOW PUNK DIETER WAS WAY BACK THEN.) WE STROLL THROUGH THE REYKJAVIK STREETS.

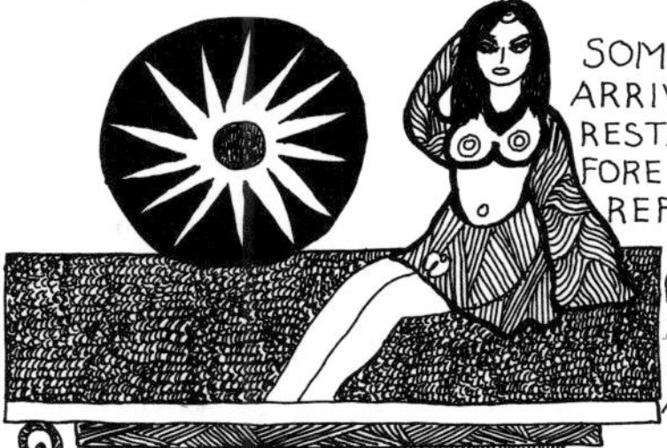

SOMEHOW DIETER ARRIVES AT THE RESTAURANT BE-FORE US AND IS REFUSED AD-MITTANCE, BECAUSE, I SUPPOSE, OF HIS APPEAR-ANCE.

JAMES, MY TRADITIONAL BOSTON JAMES, CAN'T FORGIVE THIS. HE SAYS HARSH AND UNFAIR THINGS WHICH HURT DIETER AND EMMETT AND ME. SO DIETER AND EMMETT SPLIT AND, AFTER A FEW MOMENTS, ASKING DOROTHY TO FOLLOW HIM, JAMES GOES OFF IN THE OPPOSITE DIRECTION.

DOROTHY SITS ON THE SIDEWALK PONDERING, HER STANDARDS (ANOTHER WORD FOR LOVE?) CHALLENGING HER LOYALTY.

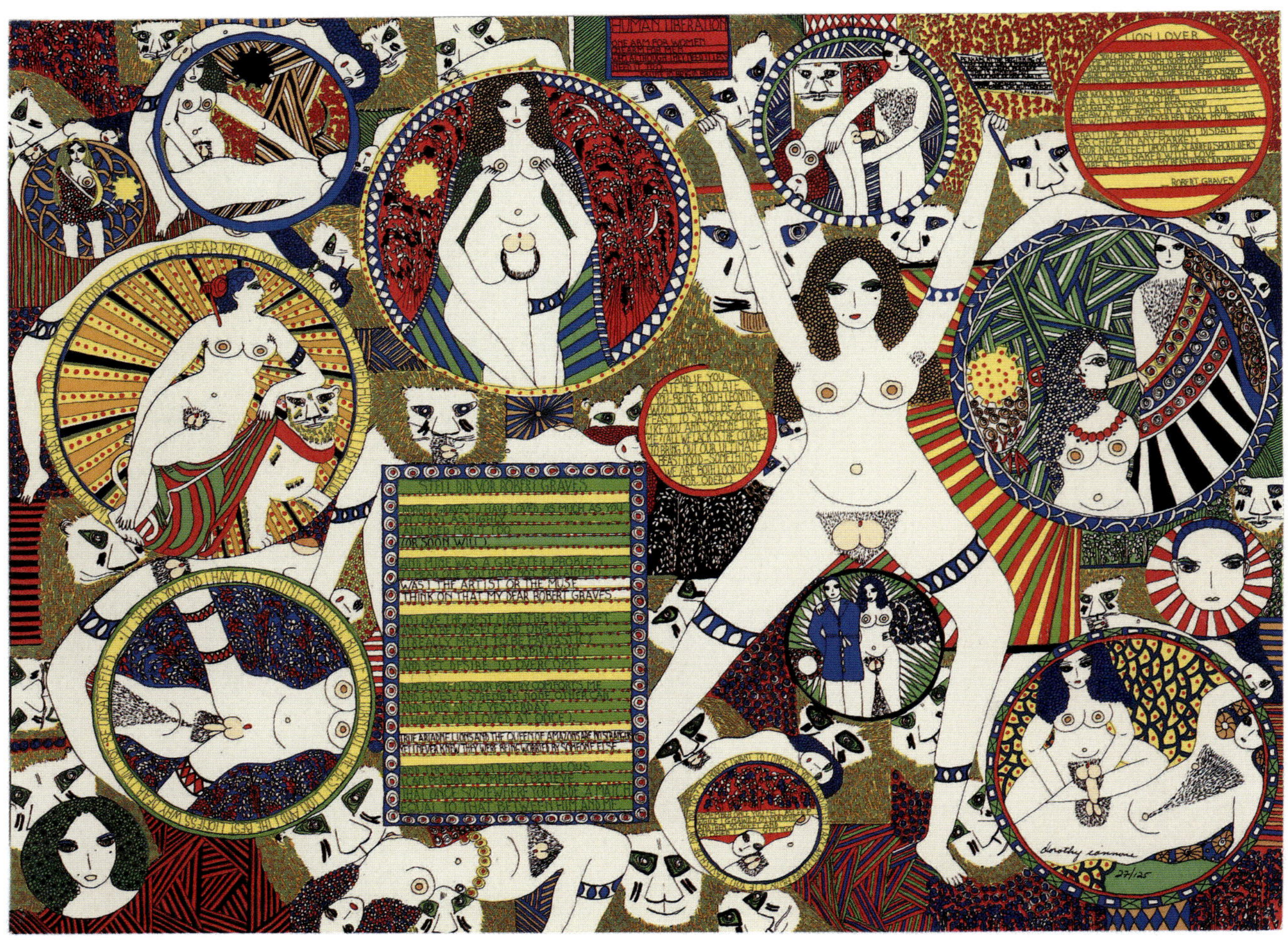

DOROTHY IANNONE, HUMAN LIBERATION, 1972, silkscreen print, 20 x 27¹/₈", edition of 125 /
MENSCHLICHE BEFREIUNG, Siebdruck, 51 x 69 cm.

or when he finally felt obliged to respond to Iannone's stream of alternately wistful and lustful entreaties. In sum, their exchange makes for depressing reading, though no more so than would be the case in going through any batch of letters left over from a once smoldering, but ultimately doomed encounter between two needy but mismatched people who retained a gentle and regretful affection for one another.

So why linger over this volume?

First, for the flashes of wordplay and typographical whimsy that flare up in the ashes of life's trivia and love's exhaustion. Roth was a punster and manic alliterator in every language he spoke and in every mood he experienced, including regular bouts of deep, hung-over melancholy. On the back of a vintage postcard picturing a village railroad station over which Roth painted a window sill, curtains, and a flower pot, he writes "Maybe, this is from someone that said, 'Maybe this is from someone that sad?'" On the more upbeat side, another postcard shows a faded sepia photograph pasted to the front with bas-relief thick gobs of acrylic paint depicting a blue figure mounting a red figure from the rear, on which

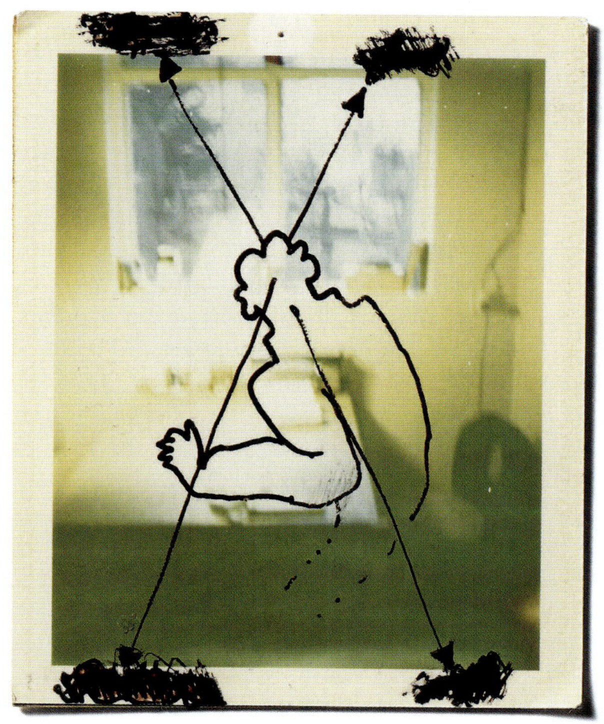

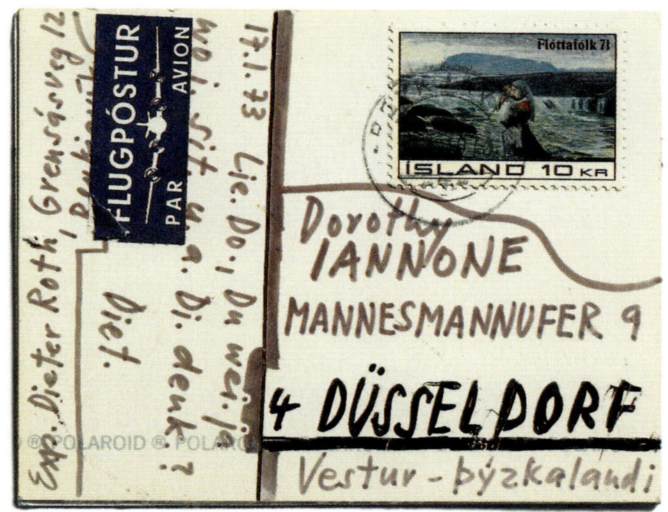

Dieter Roth, Reykjavik, 17 January 1973,
Lie. do., du wei. ja wo. i. sit. u. a. Di. denk.? Diet. /
De. Do., You kn. where. i. sit. a. think. o. y. right.? Diet.

Roth inscribed the words "MY BRAMMSIEST (per favore), ONE, MOST MIGHTY MOUSE, allow me, to put YOU, MY MOUSIEST MOST, MIGHTY MEMOUSE, and SOME like ME ontopof YOU, on the little PICTURE of my little BED. Longingwise?" This missive elicits a vividly unshy, memory—or promise—of favorite pleasures from Iannone, just as a subsequent letter does in a picture (generously offered for solitary use) of her nude legs and backside with her upper body bent forward and out of sight. Poor Roth answers with a woebegone admission of impotence while "sitting in my house by the sea, looking at your great behind." *Post coitum omne animal triste,* the saying goes. Can this be raised to an aesthetic principle—without coitus or even self-stimulation? Maybe.

And the second reason for savoring these pages? The even more remarkable, though sometimes somber drawings, collages, text montages, and minipaintings that constitute Roth's most fully engaged half of these bittersweet interchanges. Wonderfully reproduced so that the tone and textures of the paper on which he worked, the thrust of his mark-making—the flow of ink, drag of pencil, the specific sheen and density of pigment—are faithfully registered, and his images assume their true object quality. Roth was among the most ingenious and prolific designer-draftsman of the postwar era. Starting as a precocious master of the waning neo-constructivism of the fifties, then becoming an elegant stylist in a delicate sixties Pop manner that recalls Jim Dine, David Hockney, Peter Max, and a host of rock-and-roll illustrators but nonetheless veers into Lewis Carroll-like absurdity without benefit of magic mushrooms, though tending toward extravagant molds, Roth ended up the trickster par excellence of a kind of graphic materialism that evokes arte povera while wreaking havoc with that school's mystical lyricism. As an avowed anti-master of off-hand special effects, Roth was generally at his best in ephemeral formats from biodegradable objects made of or incorporat-

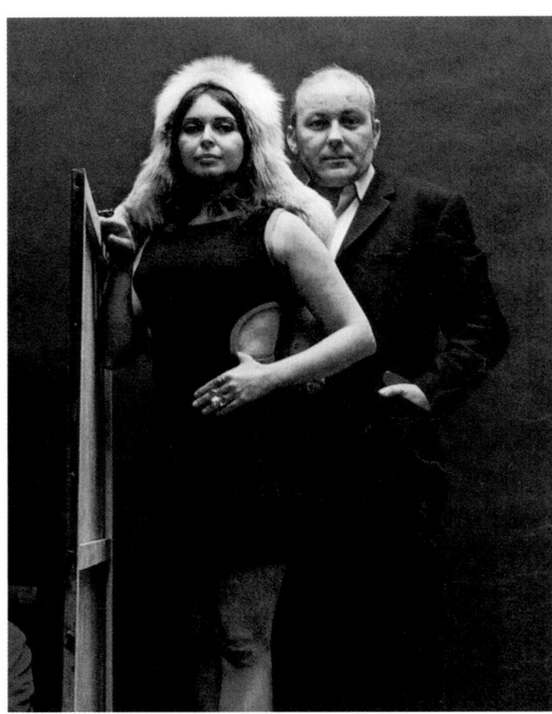

*Dorothy & Dieter, Ausschnitt aus einem Photo in «Die Zeit»,
1971 / detail from a photograph in "Die Zeit," 1971.
(PHOTO: CHARLES WILP)*

ing cheese and chocolate to throwaway notes, which, of course, no one who received them ever considered throwing away.

We can be grateful that Iannone saved hers not just for personal reasons but for art. Doodling has rarely reached such exquisiteness—no one has been more alert than Roth to the different inflections of a fountain pen and a felt-tip pen, nor has anyone until Franz West made more of the variable opacities of straight out of the tube brown, black, white, and gray. Moreover with the superposition of flat contoured sheets of cardboard and tactilely rich, but sometimes repugnant, layers of paint, Roth brought correspondence art to the edge of sculpture that suggests at times the sensibility of a brooding Richard Tuttle or a Beuys who has long since given up on making the world a better place, not to mention making himself completely at home in any corner of it. In that context his verbal and visual jokes are a matter of sprightly whistling in the dark, and his self-

portraits, of which there are many, are the reflection of a Narcissus mesmerized not by his actual beauty, but by vestiges of the balding, increasingly puffy visage he captures in Polaroids or turns via swooping lines into genuinely funny caricatures. Roth was a virtuoso of minor modes, too proud to make anything that couldn't stand up to careful scrutiny—hence the inherent interest and authority of even the paltriest scraps he touched—and too disdainful of fine art pretensions to compete directly with major artists of his day, though he did distinguish himself in collaborations with Richard Hamilton and others. These letters between Roth and Iannone do not, in that sense, really constitute collaboration, but they do provide valuable, if fleeting, insight into a man—at the cost of too much exposure to the messiness and corniness of Iannone's only partially-requited devotion to him—along with much aesthetic pleasure. In effect the last judgment on the wisdom of Iannone's publishing details of her relationship with Roth belongs to Roth himself who, on the occasion of an exhibition of his work and that of his son, Björn, held one year before Roth's death, wrote: "And though a rather well-known German magazine *(art)* wrote once—some ten years ago, I have seen the letter—: 'A journalist does not write about her lover in a public review!' I say, now June 1997, 'the better the (artistic) work of your lover is, the better you can love him/her, and the better you have a chance to grow (as an artist).' Good work of a lover makes good talk for her/his lover."[2] Such prickly reciprocity seems to have been the essence of their bond, and the poignancy of this book has everything to do with how fragile, yet how durable, but above all how ordinary that bond fundamentally was. Exceptional artists are that way by virtue of what they make; however, the emotions they sublimate in the process may not be exceptional at all. The assumption that they are is a residue of Romanticism that this thirty year liaison lays to rest in an autumnal pile of dried, but still brilliant leaves.

1) *Dieter and Dorothy: Dieter Roth and Dorothy Iannone – Their Correspondence in Words and Works 1967 – 1998,* ed. by Dorothy Iannone (Zürich: bilgerverlag, 2001). All images are taken from that book.
2) Quoted ibid., p. 241

LIEBESKUMMER

DER BRIEFWECHSEL ZWISCHEN DIETER ROTH UND DOROTHY IANNONE

ROBERT STORR

Fremde Briefe soll man nicht lesen. Das ist ein alt-vertrautes gutbürgerliches Tabu, welches die versehentliche wie die bewusst unerlaubte Verletzung der Privatsphäre nur umso reizvoller erscheinen lässt. Deshalb fühlen sich verzweifelt Geständnishungrige und schuldlose Exhibitionisten dazu veranlasst, zusammen mit den eigenen Geheimnissen vielleicht auch jene ihrer nichts ahnenden Briefpartner auszuplaudern. Solchen Quellen verdanken wir eine reiche Briefliteratur und eine Menge von dem, was wir über die privaten Hintergründe der Geschichte wissen.

Die schlimmste Strafe für die Übertretung dieses oft missachteten Gebots ist jedoch nicht der öffentliche Tadel oder das eigene schlechte Gewissen, sondern die Enttäuschung, die man erlebt, wenn man allzu viel über seine Mitmenschen in Erfahrung bringt; und wenn nicht direkt Enttäuschung, so doch die traurige Entdeckung, dass die von uns Bewunderten in ihrem Alltag genauso hilflos, widersprüchlich und unzuverlässig sind wie wir heimlichen Leserinnen und Leser ihrer Briefe, ja oft noch in weit grösserem Masse.

Das Buch *Dieter and Dorothy: Dieter Roth and Dorothy Iannone – Their Correspondence in Words and Works 1967–1998* löst diese Art von Bedenken und gemischten Gefühlen aus.[1] Die 256 Seiten des wundervoll gestalteten und verschwenderisch ausgestatteten Bandes enthalten die Texte und Bilder einer dreissig Jahre dauernden Briefromanze zwischen dem vielsei-

tigen, vielschichtigen, vielnamigen und multinationalen Schweizer Künstler Dieter Roth und seiner ebenfalls ausgewanderten amerikanischen Geliebten – und «Löwin», wie er sie nannte – Dorothy Iannone. Mit Sicherheit waren ihre Begegnung in Reykjavik, Iannones abrupte Auflösung ihrer Ehe in New York und die ersten sieben Jahre, die sie jeweils sechs Monate getrennt, sechs Monate gemeinsam verbrachten, von Leidenschaft und Sinnlichkeit bestimmt, wie Iannones Zeichnungen bezeugen. In diesen verbindet sich das Dekorativ-Abstrakte indianischer Volkskunst mit einem heiteren, an *Yellow Submarine* erinnernden Cartoon-Stil und ihren eigenen derben Szenarien und Geschlechter-Codes – es wimmelt nur so von lustvoll gezeichneten Sexszenen zwischen Frauen mit schwellenden, beinah hodenartigen Geschlechtsteilen und dicht behaarten Männern mit stets bereiten Penissen. Ihre Kunst ist farbenfroh, vertraulich-gefühlsbetont bei gleich bleibendem Stil.

Iannones stimmungsvolle Illustrationen und ihre kunstvoll ausgearbeiteten Bildgeschichten der gemeinsamen Boheme-Abenteuer füllen manche inhaltlichen Lücken dieser Dokumentation ihres gemeinsam und getrennt verbrachten Lebens und machen das Buch zu einer Art Zeitkapsel aus den 60er Jahren, die bis in die 70er, 80er und 90er Jahre reicht. Dazu gehören ein mausarmes Wanderleben; spontane Ausbrüche kreativer Energie, die schliesslich von dem unablässigen Bemühen aufgerieben werden, Mäzene und Mitarbeiter bei der Stange zu halten; gelegentliche Seitensprünge auf beiden Seiten, die als Vertrauensbeweis innerhalb einer offenen Beziehung rationalisiert werden, sowie – anstelle der damals so beliebten bewusstseinserweiternden Drogen – das Bewusstsein vernebelnde Saufereien.

ROBERT STORR ist Künstler und Kritiker sowie Kurator für Malerei und Bildhauerei am Museum of Modern Art in New York. Vor kurzem wurde er zum Rosalie Solow-Professor am Institute of Fine Arts der New York University ernannt.

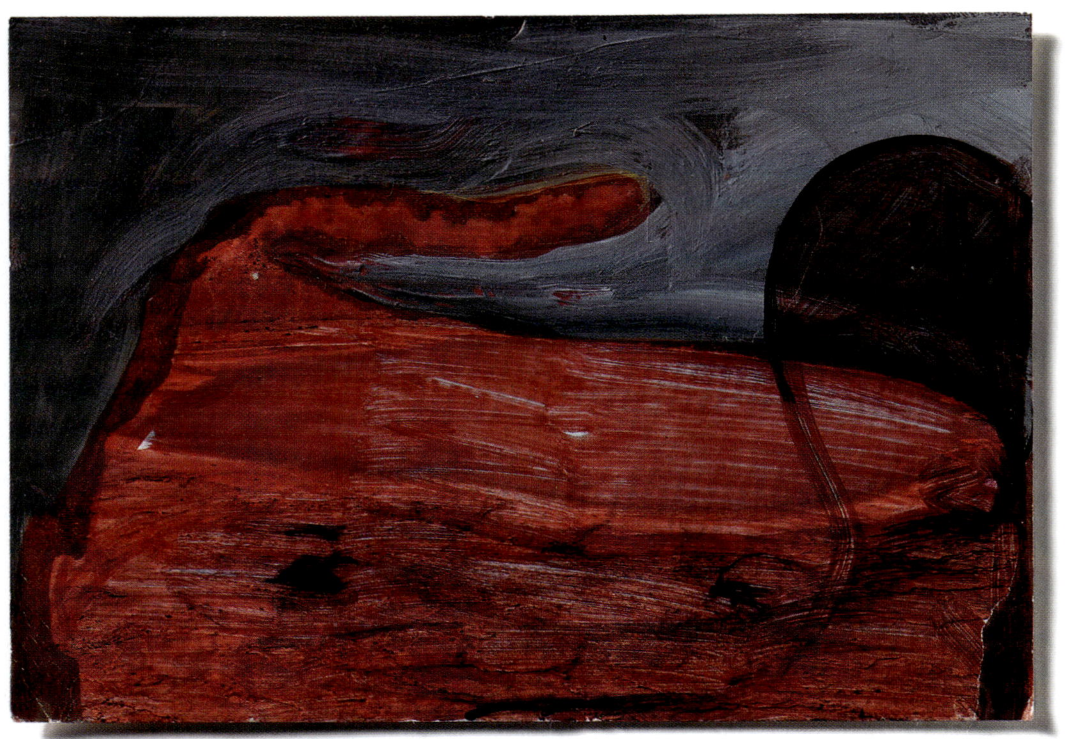

Dieter Roth, Mosfellssveit, 10. Dezember 1976: Hallo Doro, dein Brief klang traurig! Ich hoffe, er klingt nur so, weil du getrunken hast? Ein Jackpot ist schwer zu finden, besonders wenn man ihn bei Menschen sucht (Jack the Pot gibt es nicht, es sieht nur manchmal so aus, jeder/jede ist sein (oder ihr) eigener J.P. (oder in deinem Fall; Janepot) – vielleicht. Was kann ich sagen? Nichts, glaube ich. Wie lange wirst du in Berlin bleiben? Kuss, v. Dieter.

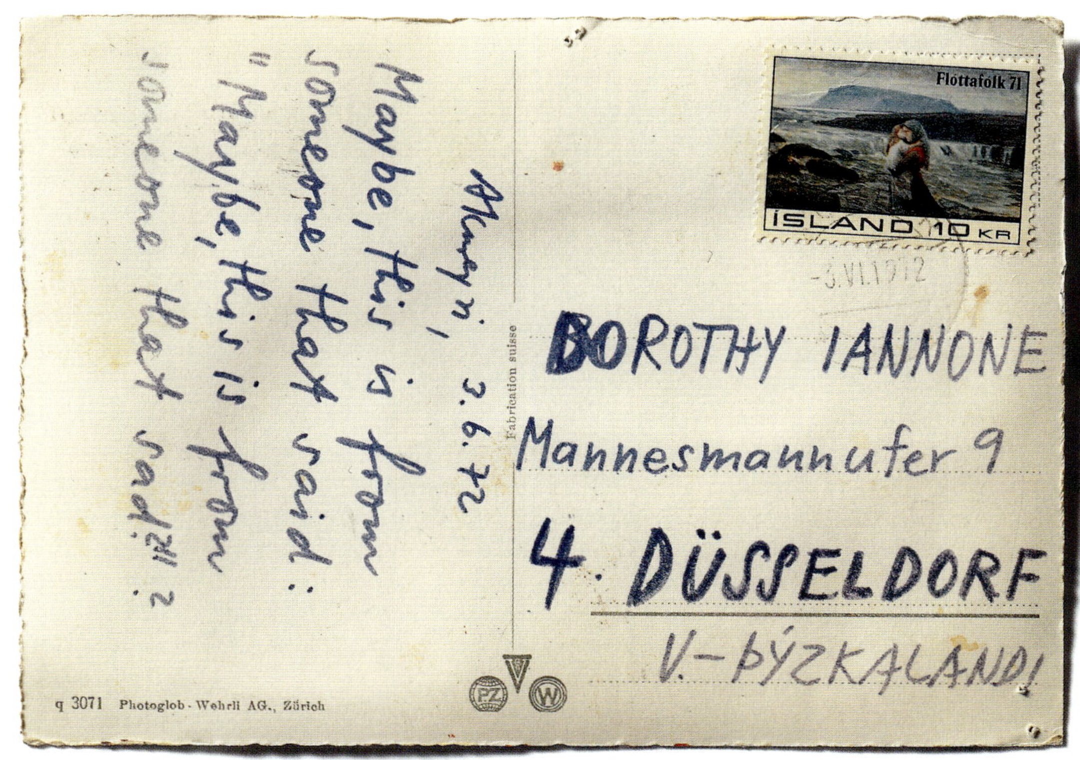

Dieter Roth, Akureyri, 3 June 1972: Maybe, this is from someone that said: "Maybe, this is from someone that sad?"? /
Vielleicht ist dies von jemandem, der sagte: «Vielleicht ist dies von jemandem, der so traurig ist?»? (ALLE ABBILDUNGEN STAMMEN AUS DEM BUCH «DIETER ROTH &
DOROTHY IANNONE: THEIR CORRESPONDENCE IN WORDS AND WORKS 1967–1998»)

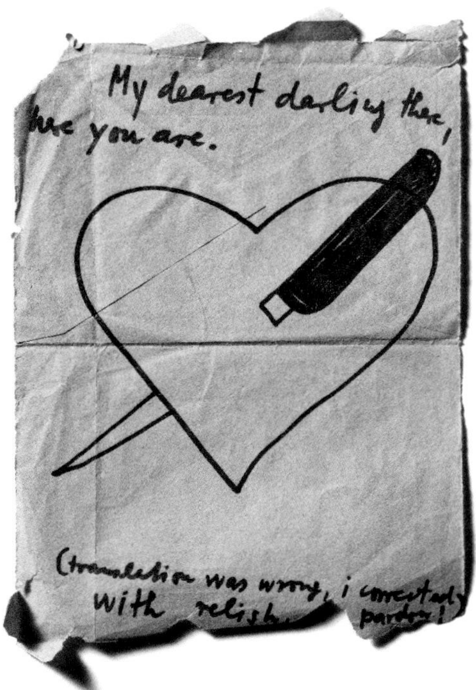

Dieter to Dorothy, Düsseldorf 1971: Dorothy asked Dieter to make this
drawing for her to copy, because she needed a more three-dimensional
rendition of a heart being penetrated by a knife than she would have
been able to make herself. In his parenthesis Dieter Roth is referring to
a friend's German translation of a text by Dorothy / Dorothy bat Dieter
um diese Zeichnung, damit sie sie kopieren könnte, weil sie eine drei-
dimensionalere Darstellung eines von einem Messer durchbohrten
Herzens brauchte, als sie selbst zuwege brachte. In der Klammer
nimmt Dieter Roth Bezug auf die missratene deutsche Übersetzung
eines Textes von Dorothy, die er «genüsslich» korrigiert habe.

Wie die meisten Liebesgeschichten scheint auch die
von Roth und Iannone nicht ganz symmetrisch gewesen zu sein. Von Roth gibt es insgesamt eher wenige
ausführliche Briefe an seine Partnerin, und die im
Buch wiedergegebenen sind, wenn nicht rein selbst-
bezogen, meistens verzweifelt, als hätte Roth nur
geschrieben, wenn er unglücklich war oder einfach
nicht mehr anders konnte, als auf Iannones Strom
abwechselnd sehnsüchtiger und wollüstiger Be-
schwörungen zu antworten. Alles in allem ist ihr
Austausch eine eher deprimierende Lektüre, so de-
primierend, wie eben jede Lektüre von Briefen ist,
die von einer grossen, aber letztlich zum Scheitern

verurteilten Leidenschaft zurückbleiben, Briefe von
zwei ebenso liebesbedürftigen wie nicht zueinander
passenden Menschen, die sich jedoch eine von Be-
dauern und Zärtlichkeit geprägte Zuneigung be-
wahrt haben.

Warum also bei diesem Buch verweilen?

Zunächst einmal wegen der funkelnden Wort-
spiele und typographischen Verrücktheiten, die aus
der Asche alltäglicher Trivialitäten und einer erlo-
schenen Liebe emporlodern. Roth war in jeder Sprache, die er beherrschte, und in jeder Verfassung, in
der er sich befand, einschliesslich der regelmässig
auftretenden Anfälle existenziellen Katzenjammers,
ein alliterationsbesessener Wortakrobat. Auf der
Rückseite einer alten Postkarte mit dem Bild eines
Dorfbahnhofs, den Roth mit einem Fensterbrett,
Vorhängen und einem Blumentopf übermalt hatte,
schreibt er: «Maybe, this is from someone that said,
‹Maybe this is from someone that sad?›?» Etwas opti-
mistischer eine andere Karte mit einem verblassen-
den sepiafarbenen Photo auf der Vorderseite: Darauf
kleisterte Roth reliefartig dicke Acrylfarbklumpen,
die eine blaue Figur zeigen, welche eine rote Figur
von hinten besteigt. Der Begleittext lautet: «MY
BRAMMSIEST (per favore), ONE, MOST MIGHTY
MOUSE, allow me, to put YOU, MOUSIEST MOST
MIGHTY MEMOUSE and SOME like ME ontopof YOU,
on the little PICTURE of my little BED. Longingwise?»
Diese Botschaft entlockt Iannone eine sehr leben-
dige, offenherzige Erinnerung an ihre Lieblings-
spiele, die vielleicht auch ein Versprechen war. Und
in einem späteren Brief schickt sie ihm ein (gross-
zügig für einsame Stunden vermachtes) Bild, eine
Rückansicht ihrer nackten Beine und ihres Hinter-
teils mit nach vorne gebeugtem, nicht sichtbarem
Oberkörper. Der arme Roth antwortet mit einem
traurigen Eingeständnis seiner Impotenz: «Ich sitze
in meinem Haus am Meer und blickte auf dein wun-
derbares Hinterteil.» *Post coitum omne animal triste,*
sagt das Sprichwort. Kann das – auch ohne Koitus
und Selbststimulierung – zum ästhetischen Prinzip
erhoben werden? Vielleicht.

Aber gibt es noch weitere Gründe, an diesen Seiten Gefallen zu finden? Da sind die vielleicht noch
bedeutenderen, wenn auch manchmal düsteren
Zeichnungen, Collagen, Textmontagen und Mini-

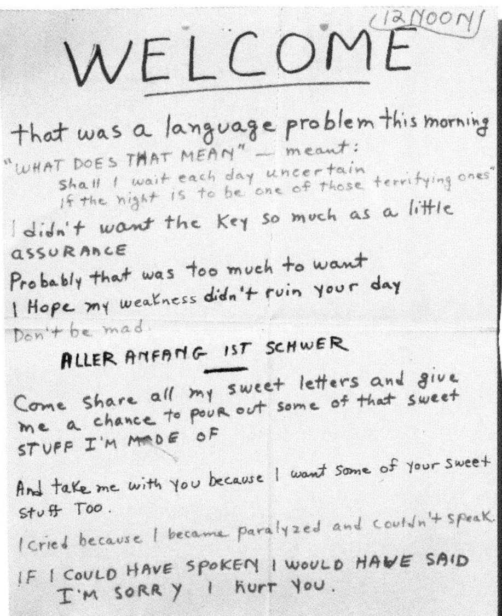

From Dorothy to Dieter, Basel, Autumn 1967, 12 o'clock noon / Dorothy an Dieter, Basel, Herbst 1967, 12 Uhr mittags.

der 60er, die an Jim Dine, David Hockney, Peter Max und zahlreiche weitere Rock-and-Roll-Illustratoren denken lässt; gleichzeitig hatte er jedoch einen Hang zum Absurden à la Lewis Carroll – zwar ohne Zauberpilze, aber mit einem starken Faible für ausgefallene Formen – und wurde schliesslich zum trickreichen Vertreter eines graphischen Materialismus, der an die Arte Povera erinnert, mit dem mystischen Lyrismus dieser Schule aber rückhaltlos aufräumt. Als eingeschworener Anti-Meister improvisierter Spezialeffekte erwies sich Roth im Umgang mit kurzlebigen Materialien als besonders einfallsreich; das reichte von biologisch abbaubaren Gegenständen aus Käse und Schokolade bis zu Wegwerf-Nachrichten, die natürlich keiner der Empfänger je weggeworfen hat.

Wir können Iannone dankbar sein, dass sie seine Botschaften nicht nur aus persönlichen Gründen, sondern auch der Kunst zuliebe aufbewahrt hat. Selten sind Kritzeleien zu solcher Vollkommenheit gediehen; keiner achtete so aufmerksam auf die variablen Möglichkeiten eines Füllhalters oder Filzstiftes wie Roth, und bis Franz West auftauchte, hat auch keiner so viel aus den Braun-, Schwarz- und Grautönen direkt aus der Tube gemacht. Ausserdem brachte Roth – mit dem Aufeinanderkleben von dünnen, passend zugeschnittenen Kartons und seinem haptisch erlebbaren, wenn auch manchmal abstossend wirkenden Farbauftrag – die Kunst der Korrespondenz in die Nähe der Skulptur; eine Skulptur, die an die Sensibilität eines grüblerischen Richard Tuttle erinnert oder eines Beuys, der längst nicht mehr die Welt verbessern, geschweige denn sich in

bilder, die Roths engagiertesten Beitrag zu diesem bittersüssen Zwiegespräch ausmachen. Die Reproduktionen sind so perfekt, Ton und Struktur des verwendeten Papiers, aber auch Roths Duktus – der Fluss der Tinte, der Bleistiftstrich, Glanz und Konsistenz der Farben – derart getreu wiedergegeben, dass man meinen könnte, die Originale vor sich zu haben. Roth war einer der einfallsreichsten und produktivsten Graphiker und Zeichner der Nachkriegszeit. Er begann als früh vollendeter Meister des bereits abflauenden Neokonstruktivismus der 50er Jahre und entwickelte sich zu einem äusserst eleganten Stilisten einer sensiblen Pop-Manier

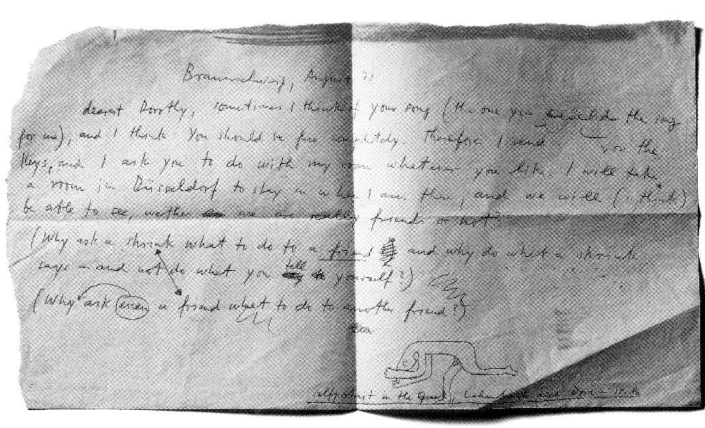

From Dieter to Dorothy, Braunschweig, August 1971, with his "selfportrait in the Greek, Lehmbruck and Doro-Stile" / Dieter an Dorothy, Braunschweig, August 1971, mit einem «Selbstporträt im griechischen, Lehmbruck- und Doro-Stil».

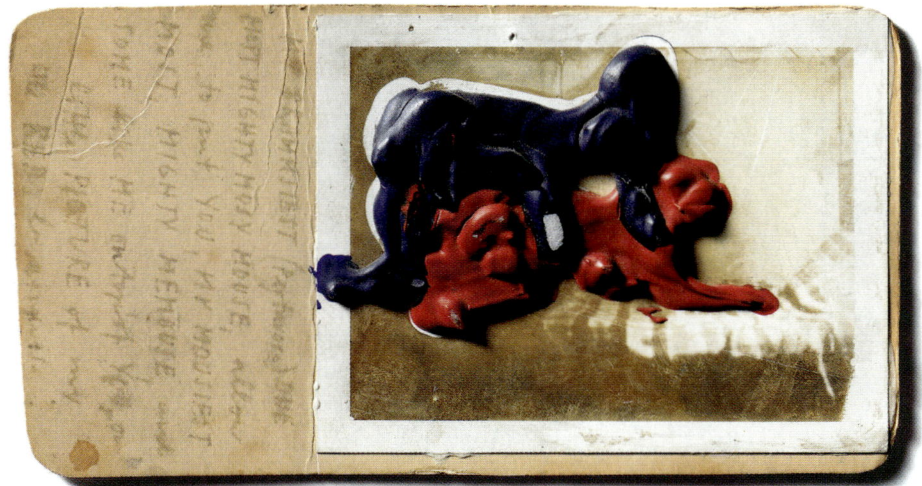

Dieter Roth, Reykjavik, August 1968:
MY BRAMMSIEST (per favore), ONE
MOST MIGHTY MOSY MOUSE, allow
me, to put YOU, MY MOUSIEST MOST,
MIGHTY, MEMOUSE, and SOME like
ME ontopof YOU, on the little PICTURE
of my little BED. longingwise?

ihr einrichten wollte. Auf diesem Hintergrund entpuppen sich Roths verbale und visuelle Scherze als eine Art munteres Pfeifen im Dunkeln und seine zahllosen Selbstporträts als Spiegelbilder eines Narziss, der nicht von seiner aktuellen Schönheit fasziniert ist, sondern von den Überresten eines zunehmend kahlen und aufgedunsenen Gesichts, das er in Polaroidbildern festhält oder mit Hilfe schwungvoller Linien in umwerfend komische Karikaturen verwandelt. Roth war ein Virtuose der kleinen Form, zu stolz, etwas zu machen, was dem kritischen Blick nicht standhalten konnte – daher die Bedeutung und Gültigkeit noch der kleinsten Papierfetzen, die er benützte –, und künstlerischen Prätentionen zu sehr abhold, um direkt mit bekannten Künstlern seiner Zeit zu wetteifern, obwohl er sich auf gemeinsame Projekte mit Richard Hamilton und anderen durchaus einliess. Den Briefwechsel zwischen Roth und Iannone kann man nicht in diesem Sinn als *Collaboration* bezeichnen, doch er vermittelt wichtige, wenn auch flüchtige Einblicke in das Leben eines Mannes und einen erheblichen ästhetischen Genuss – allerdings auf Kosten einer rücksichtslosen Blosslegung des Chaotischen und Sentimentalen von Iannones nur teilweise erwiderter Zuneigung. Ob der Schritt Iannones, die Einzelheiten ihrer Beziehung zu Roth zu veröffentlichen, weise war, kann in letzter Instanz nur Roth selbst beurteilen, der ein Jahr vor seinem Tod, anlässlich einer gemeinsamen Ausstellung mit seinem Sohn Björn bemerkte: «Obwohl eine bekannte deutsche Zeitschrift *(art)* – vor etwa zehn Jahren, ich hab den Brief gesehen – meinte: ‹Eine Journalistin schreibt nicht über ihren Geliebten in einer für die Öffentlichkeit bestimmten Rezension!›, sage ich, jetzt, im Juni 1997: ‹Je besser die (künstlerische) Arbeit eines/einer Geliebten ist, desto besser kann man ihn/sie lieben und desto besser stehen seine/ihre Chancen, selbst (als Künstler) zu wachsen.› Die gute Arbeit des/der Geliebten ist für den Partner/die Partnerin ein guter Gesprächsstoff.»[2] Diese verzwickte Reziprozität scheint die Grundlage ihrer Beziehung gewesen zu sein, und das Spannende an diesem Buch liegt gerade in der Fragilität, aber auch im Dauerhaften und Normalen dieser Verbindung. Aussergewöhnliche Künstler zeichnen sich durch ihre Werke aus; die Emotionen, die sie dabei sublimieren, müssen überhaupt nicht aussergewöhnlich sein. Die Vorstellung, sie seien es, ist ein romantisches Relikt, das von dieser dreissig Jahre dauernden Liaison unter einem Häufchen trockener, aber nach wie vor leuchtender Herbstblätter zur letzten Ruhe gebettet wird.

(Übersetzung: Goridis/Parker)

1) *Dieter and Dorothy: Dieter Roth and Dorothy Iannone – Their Correspondence in Words and Works 1967–1998*, hg. v. Dorothy Iannone, bilgerverlag, Zürich 2001. (Alle hier gezeigten Bilder stammen aus diesem Buch.)
2) Zitiert ebenda, S. 241.

Dorothy's birthday card for Dieter, Berlin, 21 April 1998, felt pen and collage (1972) on cardboard, 11 13/16 x 8 5/8" / Dorothys letzte Geburtstagskarte für Dieter, Filzstift und Collage (1972) auf Karton, 30 x 22 cm.

Schwebende Bilder – rätselhafte Narrationen

Zu den aktuellen Videoarbeiten von Hubbard/Birchler

KONRAD BITTERLI

In einem endlos erscheinenden Bildersog durchmisst die Kamera einen spärlich beleuchteten Wellblechschuppen und registriert alle Gegenstände, die sich da angesammelt haben: Maschinen, Werkzeuge, herumliegende Bierflaschen, ein Sofa und dazwischen ein Schlagzeug sowie mehrere Gitarren. Die mit Grillengezirpe unterlegte Sequenz endet unvermittelt im Raum, um dann in steter Gegenbewegung an ihren Ausgangspunkt im Dunkel der Aussenwand zurückzukehren. Allein, die Bewegung stoppt nicht, sondern gleitet ohne Unterbrechung nach draussen in die Nacht, wo eine junge Frau vor den beleuchteten Fenstern ins Bild tritt. In einem sanften Bogen erfasst die Kamera die Figur, wie sie Steine aufhebt, diese gegen ein verlassenes Haus wirft. Dabei hört man ein Fenster zu Bruch gehen und einen Hund anschlagen. Vom Aussenraum schwenkt die Kamera wieder ins Innere der Hütte, wo sich vier junge Männer zum Musizieren versammelt haben. Einer davon spielt auf einer Bassgitarre, während die drei andern zuhören beziehungsweise miteinander plaudern. Die Szene wird in derselben ruhigen Bewegung ge-

filmt wie zuvor. Danach führt die Kamera kurz durch die dunkle Mauerzone hinters Haus, wo die junge Frau inzwischen verschwunden ist und nur mehr das Zirpen und der leise Sound der Gitarre zu hören sind. Diese Bewegungen wiederholen sich, bis die Kamera schliesslich auf die Fenster draussen schwenkt, in denen die Jugendlichen sich deutlich abzeichnen. Beim erneuten Durchdringen der Grenzlinie zwischen Innen- und Aussenraum beginnt der Videoloop in der leeren Hütte von vorne...

DETACHED BUILDING lautet der Titel der aktuellen Videoarbeit des schweizerisch-amerikanischen Künstlerpaares Teresa Hubbard (1965 in Dublin/Irland geboren) und Alexander Birchler (1962 in Baden/Schweiz geboren). Konzipiert als Schleife ohne Anfang oder Ende und realisiert als im abgedunkelten Ausstellungsraum sanft schwebende Projektion, besticht sie durch eine Kameraführung, die behutsam die zum Proberaum umfunktionierte Werkstatt durchmisst. Dabei werden in Grossformat all die kleinen Ereignisse und Dinge erfasst, die zur atmosphärischen Verdichtung der fünfminütigen Sequenz beitragen. Verstärkt durch die unterlegte Tonspur – drinnen ist das Zirpen der Grillen, draussen der Klang der Gitarre zu hören –, wird die formale und

KONRAD BITTERLI ist Kurator am Kunstmuseum St. Gallen. Er lebt und arbeitet in St. Gallen und Daiwil.

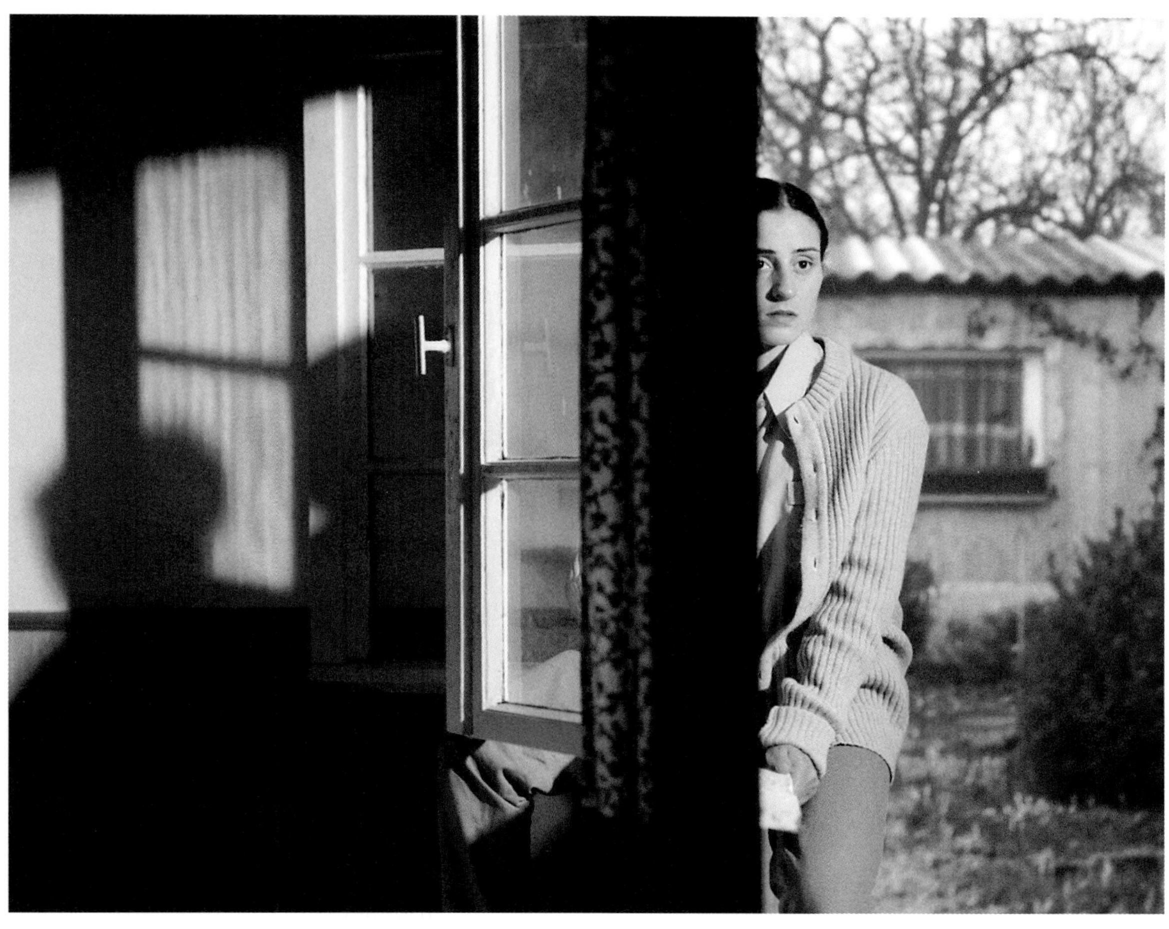

inhaltliche Verklammerung von Innen- und Aussenraum evident. Diese Konzentration unterscheidet
das Werk von all den massenhaft produzierten Mu-
sikvideo-Clips in gängiger MTV-Ästhetik. Während
Letztere in wenigen Minuten mittels dichter Bild-
folgen und schneller Schnitte oft belanglose Geschichten zu erzählen suchen, eröffnen sich in
Hubbard/Birchlers Videosequenz unterschiedliche
Handlungsstränge: Musiker und Frau scheinen in
keiner ersichtlichen Beziehung zueinander zu
stehen. Verhalten deuten sich dennoch Gegensätze
an: Innen/Aussen, Licht/Dunkel, Mann/Frau, Indi-
viduum/Gruppe… Sie legen zwar potenzielle Erzählungen nahe, verfestigen sich jedoch nie zu einer
Geschichte und provozieren im Gegenteil Fragen
zur narrativen Anlage, die nicht zu beantworten
sind: Welches Verhältnis besteht zwischen den jungen Männern und zwischen ihnen und der Frau?
Weshalb wirft sie Steine? Spielt der Gitarrist aus
reiner Freude oder wird er einer Prüfung unterzo-
gen? Wie auch immer, stets schwingt in Hubbard/
Birchlers Arbeiten eine sanfte Melancholie mit,
scheinen sich unter der vermeintlich vertrauten
Oberfläche emotional geladene Erfahrungen und
existenzielle Konflikte sachte abzuzeichnen: *Letzten
Endes geht es immer darum, eine Geschichte zu erzählen.*

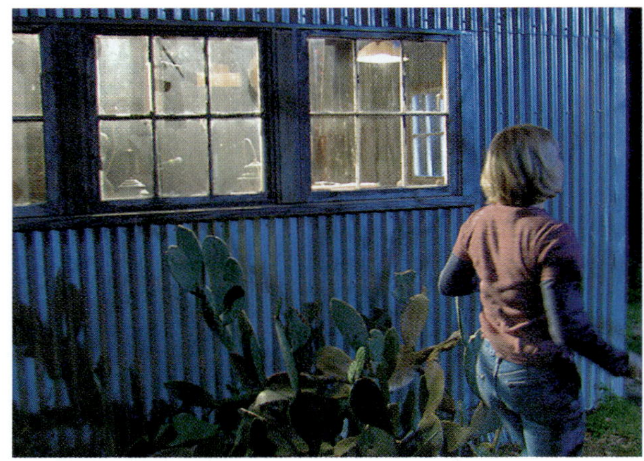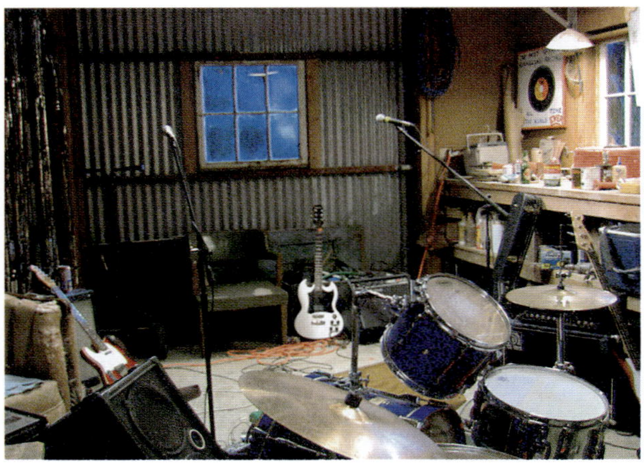

Wenn wir eine narrative Struktur erfinden, gehört dazu in den meisten Fällen auch, dass wir einen physischen Raum konstruieren. Einen Raum, der eine psychische Spannung suggeriert, in dem es gleitende Übergänge zwischen Innen und Aussen oder Vergangenheit und Gegenwart gibt.[1]

Mit «Wild Walls» betitelten Hubbard/Birchler ihre bisher umfassendste Ausstellung, die nach dem Museum Haus Lange und Haus Esters in Krefeld, im Amsterdamer Zentrum für Photographie, im Kunstmuseum St. Gallen und in der Kunsthalle zu Kiel zu sehen war und erstmals die aktuellen Videoarbeiten ins Zentrum rückte, nachdem in den vergangenen Jahren in zahlreichen Ausstellungen in Zürich, Frankfurt, Berlin und Chicago sowie an den Biennalen von Venedig und Montreal ihre Photoarbeiten einem breiten Publikum zugänglich gemacht worden waren. Der Titel der aktuellen Präsentation, «Wild Walls», verweist konsequent auf die Welt des Films und des Kinos. Der Bezug zum Filmischen ist allerdings bereits in frühen Werken spürbar, angefangen beim Nachbau von Modellen in der Installation CONTESTANTS IN A BIRDHOUSE COMPETITION (1991), über die eindrückliche Photoserie *Stripping* (1998), für die die Künstler eigens Kulissenarchitekturen bauten, um den Moment des Übergangs zwischen Innen- und Aussenraum zu bespielen, bis hin zu den so genannten *Filmstills* (2000), die sinni-

gerweise nicht Filmszenen photographisch wiedergeben, sondern Fassaden von Lichtspielhäusern abbilden.

Für das Verständnis der Videoarbeiten von Hubbard/Birchler spielen die Filmgeschichte und namentlich der notorische Alfred Hitchcock eine zentrale Rolle. Für einmal ist es nicht die bezaubernde Kim Novak, die in *Vertigo* die Zuschauer in ihren Bann zieht, es ist die in einer Truhe versteckte Leiche im 1948 entstandenen Streifen *Rope (Cocktail für eine Leiche)*. Um eine Cocktailparty handelt es sich bei der Filmhandlung in der Tat, wobei das Buffet auf derselben Truhe serviert wird, in der die Leiche ruht. *Rope* ist ein mit den üblichen Hitchcock-Ingredienzien angerichteter Film, unterscheidet sich von andern Regiearbeiten des Meisters jedoch durch die experimentelle Anlage, die ihn erst zum cineastischen Meisterwerk werden lässt. Gedreht wurde er nämlich in minutenlangen, ununterbrochenen Kameraeinstellungen. Dazu wurden so genannte «Wild Walls» verwendet, verschiebbare Kulissenwände, die ein Inszenieren ohne nachträgliche Schnitte ermöglichten. Die Kulissen wurden während des Drehs einfach hin und her geschoben, um der Kamera die Verfolgung der Protagonisten durch mehrere Räume zu erlauben. Mit diesem inszenatorischen Trick lenkt Hitchcock die Aufmerksamkeit von der Erzählung des Films – der Aufdeckung eines vermeintlich perfekten Mords – auf dessen ansonsten verdeckte Produktionsprozesse. Dabei leistet der Meister des Suspense trotz des offensichtlichen Bemühens, die Fiktion der Geschichte aufrechtzuerhalten, der Demaskierung des Films als Konstruktion von Wirklichkeiten Vorschub. Eine vergleichbare, in diesem Falle jedoch bewusst intendierte Enttarnung filmischer Illusionen prägt auch Hubbard/Birchlers Videoarbeiten DETACHED BUILDING und EIGHT (beide 2001). Vordergründig erzählen sie von vertrauten Begebenheiten, thematisieren indes entschieden die Auflösung filmischer Konventionen und linearer Narrationen.

Beide Strategien scheinen in EIGHT zugespitzt, die psychologischen Momente verdichtet. Der Titel spielt auf den Geburtstag eines Mädchens an, dessen Gartenparty sprichwörtlich ins Wasser gefallen ist. Übrig geblieben sind die Reste eines fröhlichen Kinderfestes mit bunten Dekorationen und verlassenem Buffet. Ins detailreich inszenierte Ensemble tritt ein Mädchen, schneidet sich ein Stück Kuchen ab und geht ins Haus zurück, wobei ihr die Kamera stets

folgt. Wiederum verbindet die Kamerafahrt Aussen- und Innenraum in einer Sequenz. Einzig gelegentliche Close-ups und zwei Gegenschnitte unterbrechen den Lauf der Dinge: Der eine zeigt das Gesicht des Mädchens draussen, während der andere das Kind beim Blick durch das «weinende Fenster»[2] in den Garten erfasst. Im Gegensatz zu DETACHED BUILDING ist das räumliche Dispositiv, obwohl durch eine Kamerafahrt zur Einheit zusammengezogen, nicht zu klären: Innen- und Aussenraum sind kompliziert ineinander verschachtelt, die Einheit von Ort und Handlung in Frage gestellt. Das im Film suggerierte Raumkontinuum lässt sich nur mehr als gedankliche Konstruktion, als brüchige Fiktion aufrechterhalten. Die Illusion wirkt um so fragiler, als die zeitliche Abfolge der Handlung in der endlosen Wiederholung der dreiminütigen Szene permanent unterlaufen wird: Lineare Zeit wird in zyklische Zeit überführt, in der weder ein Vorher und Nachher noch Kausalitäten existieren.

In DETACHED BUILDING und EIGHT hintertreiben Hubbard/Birchler den «Schein des Wahren»[3], der das klassische Kino wie die Massenkultur ins-

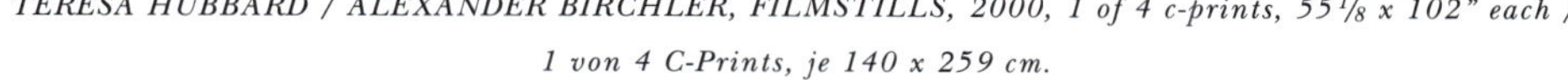

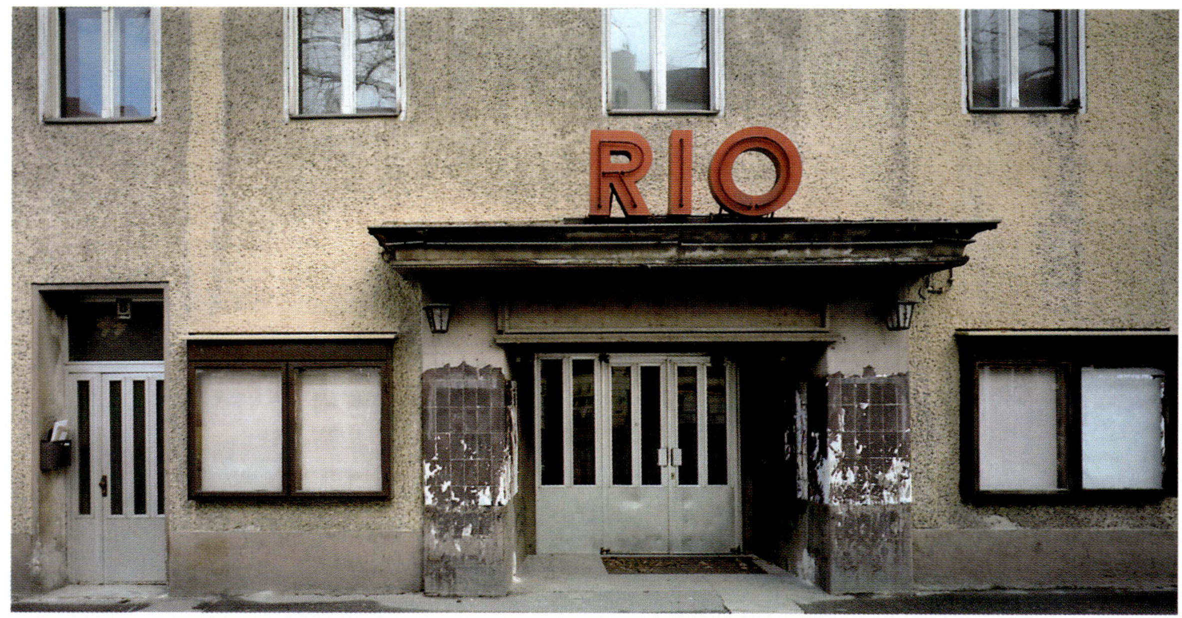

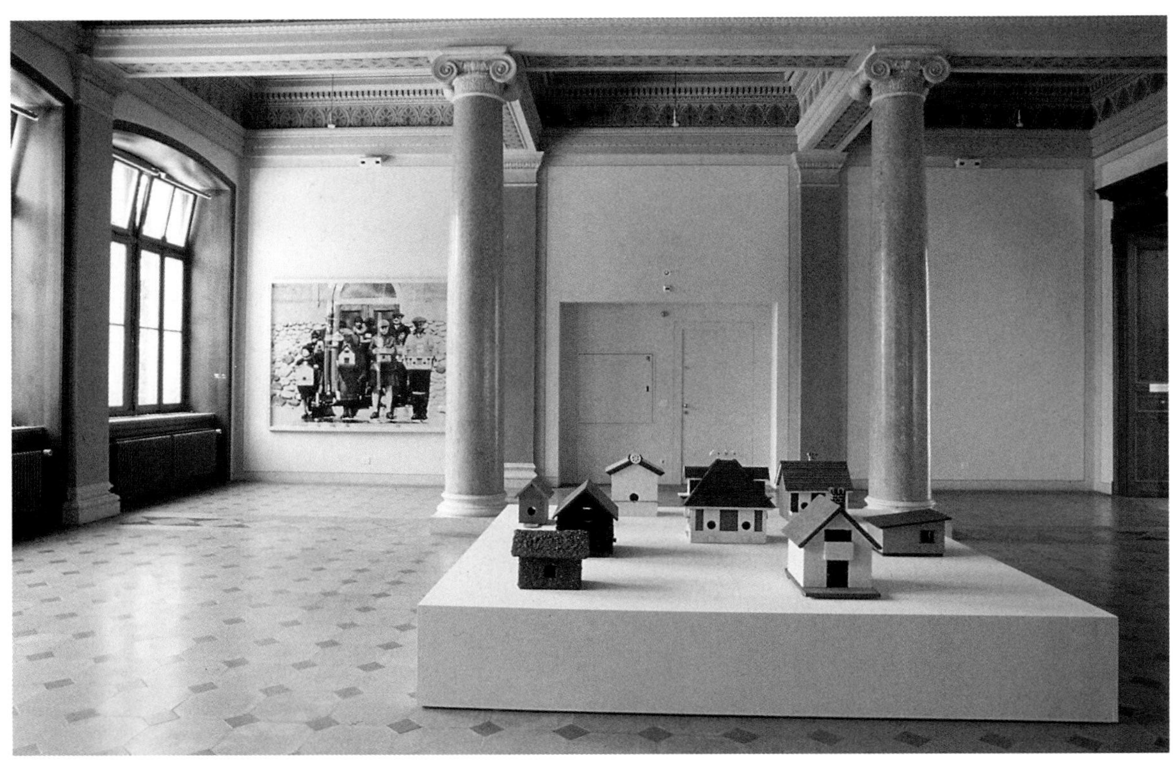

gesamt prägt und damit eine Form der glatten Oberflächen und der linearen Erzählungen fördert, die ihre Produktionsprozesse permanent ausblendet. Dieser Fiktionalisierung arbeiten heute zahlreiche Kunstschaffende entgegen. Eine weit verbreitete Methode der zeitgenössischen Videokunst ist dabei die Aufsplitterung linearer Erzählweisen in multiple Projektionen, wie sie beispielsweise Pipilotti Rist oder Doug Aitken virtuos umgesetzt haben. Teresa Hubbard und Alexander Birchler hingegen verzichten in ihren Arbeiten auf die Zersplitterung der Wahrnehmung, sie vertrauen vielmehr der Suggestionskraft langsamer Kamerafahrten und endloser Videoschleifen in eindrücklichen Grossprojektionen. Aber auch sie thematisieren die Konstruktionen von Wirklichkeit, indem sie mittels Zeitzyklen und Raumverschachtelungen die Bedingungen des narrativen Films, die Illusion kausaler Zusammenhänge, zeit-

licher Abfolgen oder räumlicher Einheiten permanent unterwandern. Und dabei erzählen sie in einprägsamen Bildern jene alltäglichen Geschichten von räumlichen und psychologischen Grenzen, von Verletzlichkeiten, von Trauer und Verlust, Geschichten aus der vertrauten Lebenswirklichkeit, die in einer rätselhaften Möglichkeitsform verharren und gerade aufgrund ihrer Offenheit so unmittelbar berühren – als schwebende, nichtlineare Narrationen mit dem Betrachter als Teilhaber am endlosen Prozess potenzieller Sinnstiftungen.

1) Alexander Birchler im Gespräch mit Martin Hentschel, in: Martin Hentschel (Hrsg.), *Wild Walls*, Kerber Verlag, Bielefeld 2001, S. 76.
2) Ebenda, S. 76.
3) Vilém Flusser, *Gesten. Versuch einer Phänomenologie*, Fischer Taschenbuch Wissenschaft, Frankfurt 1994, S. 120.

Floating Images – Enigmatic Narratives

Recent Videos by Hubbard/Birchler

KONRAD BITTERLI

In a seemingly endless stream of pictures the camera paces off a dimly lit tin hut and registers all the things that have accumulated there: machines, tools, scattered beer bottles, a sofa, and somewhere in between a set of drums and several guitars. This sequence, with its soundtrack of chirping crickets, comes to an abrupt end inside the room and then slowly, steadily moves backwards to its starting point in the darkness of the outside wall. But the movement does not stop there; it glides without interruption out into the night, where a young woman comes into view in front of the illuminated window. The camera captures her in the process of picking up stones and throwing them at a deserted house. The panes of a window are heard shattering in the background and a dog begins to bark. The camera pans back to the inside of the shed, where four young men have assembled to make music. One of them is playing a bass guitar while the other three listen to him or talk to each other. The scene is filmed with the same quiet movement as before. Then the camera takes us through the dark zone of the wall and behind the house. The young woman has vanished; only the chirping and the soft strumming of the guitar are heard. These movements are repeated until the camera finally pans outside to the window through which the young people inside are clearly

outlined. On crossing the borderline between inside and outside once again, the video loop starts pacing off the shed again.

The Swiss-American artist duo Teresa Hubbard (born in 1965 in Dublin/Ireland) and Alexander Birchler (born in 1962 in Baden/Switzerland) call their latest video piece DETACHED BUILDING. It is designed as an ongoing loop and executed as an image floating in the darkened gallery. One is struck by the extremely gentle movement of the camera, pacing off the workshop. All of the unassuming events and objects are captured in large-format and contribute to the compressed atmosphere of the five-minute sequence. The soundtrack—inside, the chirping of the crickets; outside, the sound of the guitar—underscores the formal and contextual framing of the interior and exterior spaces. The concentrated atmosphere of the work distinguishes it from the masses of music videos produced with conventional MTV aesthetics. While the latter attempt to tell often trivial stories in the space of a few minutes by means of compressed sequencing and fast cuts, Hubbard/Birchler's video loop suggests various narrative strands. Although the musicians and the woman do not appear to be related to each other in any way, a subtext of dichotomies, such as inside/outside, light/dark, man/woman, or individual/group, hints at potential narratives. These do not consolidate into a story but instead provoke unanswered questions: What is the relationship among the musicians and

---

KONRAD BITTERLI is the curator of the Kunstmuseum in St. Gallen; he lives and works in St. Gallen and Daiwil.

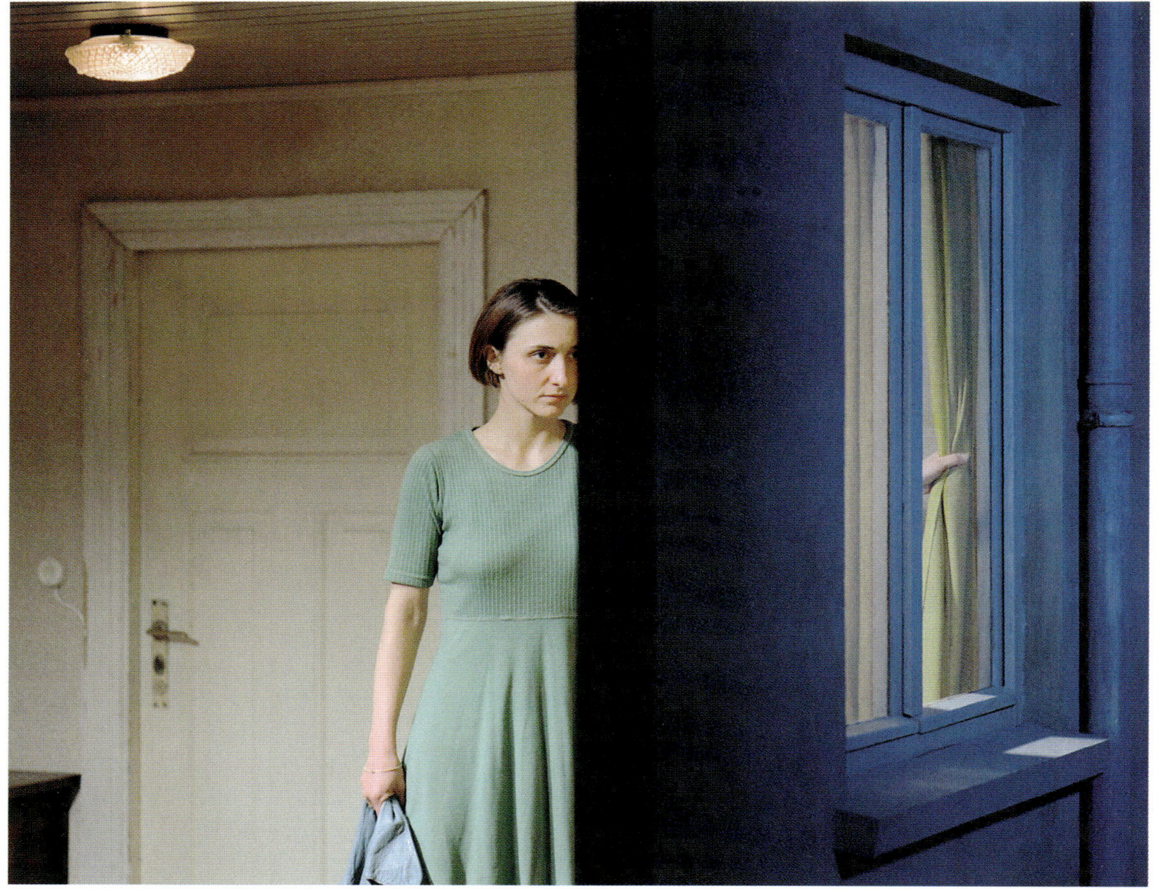

between them and the woman? Why is she throwing stones? Is the guitarist playing for fun or is he being tested? Whatever the case, a touch of gentle melancholy always resonates in Hubbard/Birchler's works. Emotionally charged experiences and existential conflict seem about to ruffle the familiarity of surface appearances. *It always comes down to telling a story. For us, constructing a narrative most often involves the process of physically building a space. We build spaces that suggest psychological tension, where there is a slippage between inside and outside, past and present.*[1]

Hubbard/Birchler's largest exhibition to date, "Wild Walls," began at the Museum Haus Lange und Haus Esters in Krefeld before moving on to the Amsterdam Center of Photography, the Kunstmuseum St. Gallen, and the Kunsthalle zu Kiel. It was the first exhibition to highlight their current video work, following numerous exhibitions in Zürich, Frankfurt, Berlin, and Chicago, and also at the biennials in Venice and Montreal, where their photo works reached a wide audience. The title of the current presentation, "Wild Walls," refers explicitly to the cinema and the world of movie theaters. Filmmaking had already played a role in the artists' early works, starting with the reconstruction of models in the installation CONTESTANTS IN A BIRDHOUSE COMPETITION (1991), in the impressive photo series *Stripping* (1998), for which the duo built their own stage sets to study the transition between indoor and outdoor spaces, and more recently in the so-called *Filmstills* (2000), which belie expectations by depicting the façades of movie houses instead of scenes from films.

The history of film and specifically one of its most renowned directors, Alfred Hitchcock, are central to an understanding of Hubbard/Birchler's videos. For once the subject of investigation is not the irresistibly charming Kim Novak, who captivates the audience in *Vertigo*; it is the corpse hidden in a chest in the film *Rope*. During the cocktail party in the film, the hors d'oeuvres are served on the very chest in which the corpse has been hidden. *Rope* contains all the ingredients that made Hitchcock famous, but it stands out from the great director's other films because of an experimental approach which was to make it a masterpiece of cinema. It was shot in ten-minute long takes. In order to shoot a scene that would need no editing, so-called "wild walls" were constructed. These movable flats were simply shifted around during the take in order to enable the camera to track the protagonists through several rooms. Through this trick of staging, Hitchcock shifts the attention from the plot of the film—the study of a supposedly perfect murder—to the film's ordinarily hidden processes of production. Thus, despite the obvious effort to sustain a narrative fiction, the master of suspense actually lays the groundwork for the treatment of film as constructed reality. A comparable but, in this case, intentional revelation of cinematic illusion also marks Hubbard/Birchler's video works DETACHED BUILDING and EIGHT (both 2001). On the face of it, they show ordinary, familiar things, while actually undermining film conventions and linear narration with great determination.

In EIGHT, the two strategies seem even more pointed, and the psychological aspects more condensed. The title refers to a girl's birthday garden party which has literally ended up all wet. Only the colorful decorations of a cheerful children's party and a deserted buffet have been left behind. Into this scene, staged in great detail, walks a girl, who cuts off a piece of cake and goes back into the house, steadily followed by the camera. Once again the tracking camera links interior and exterior space in a single sequence. The take is interrupted only by the occasional close-up and two reverses: one shows the face of the girl outdoors, while the other captures her looking at the garden through the "weeping window."[2] In contrast to DETACHED BUILDING, the geography of this scene remains puzzling although it is united through the tracking camera. Inside and outside spaces are complex and convoluted, the unity of place and action is called into question. The spatial continuum suggested in the film proves to be sustainable only as a mental construct, as a fragile fic-

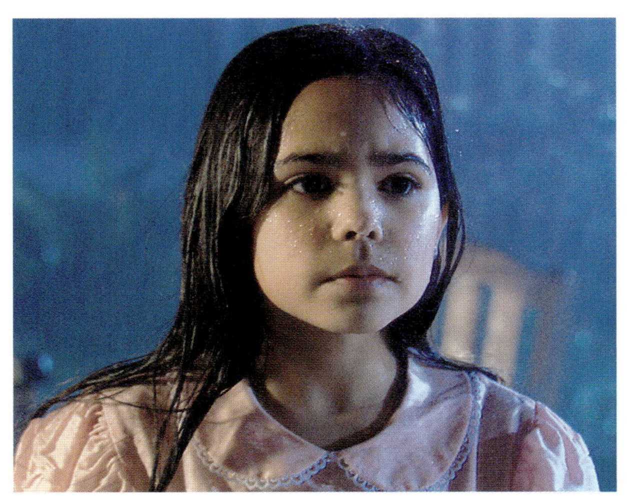

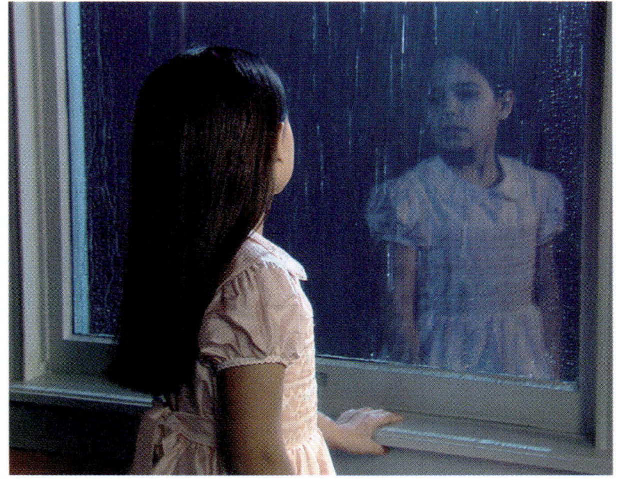

TERESA HUBBARD / ALEXANDER BIRCHLER, EIGHT, 2001, stills from high definition video with sound transferred to DVD, loop of 3 mins. 35 secs. / ACHT, Video in hoher Auflösung mit Ton auf DVD übertragen, Dauer 3 Min. 35 Sek., Endlosschlaufe.

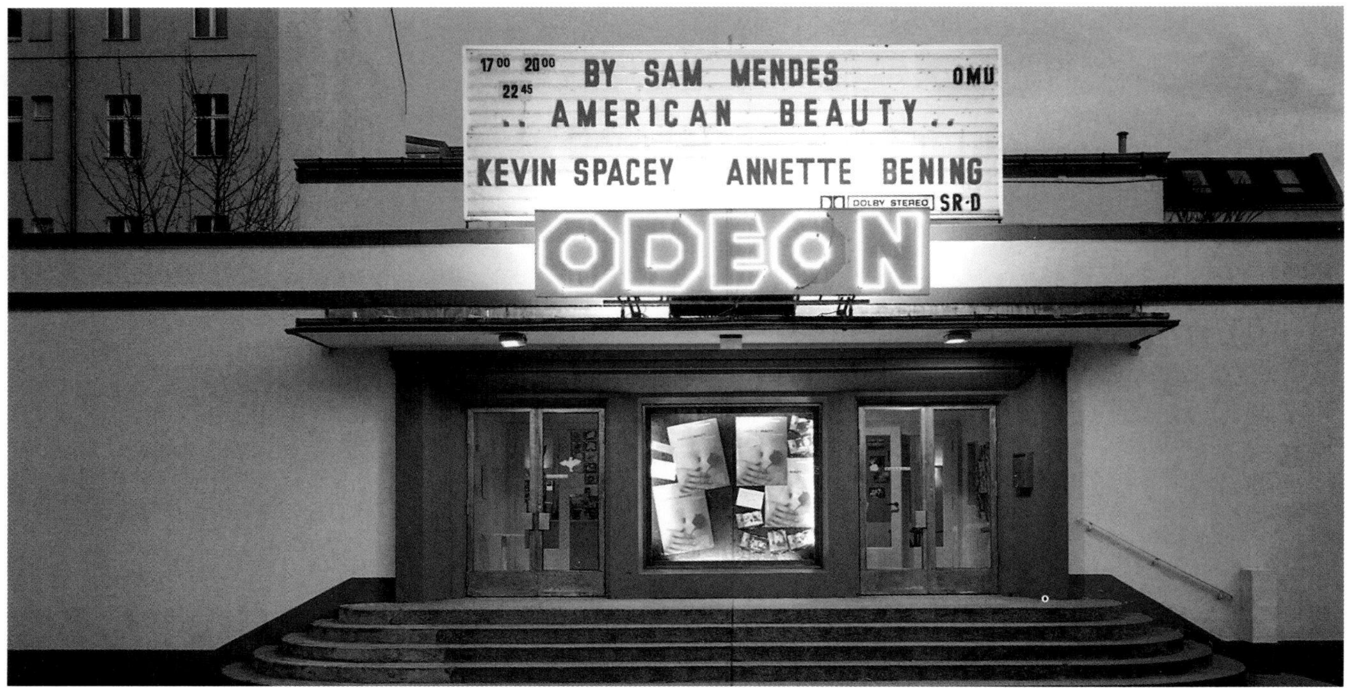

TERESA HUBBARD / ALEXANDER BIRCHLER, FILMSTILLS, 2000, 1 of 4 c-prints, 55 1/8 x 102" each /
1 von 4 C-Prints, je 140 x 259 cm.

tion. The fragility of the illusion is underscored by the endless repetition of the three-minute sequence which undermines any conventional understanding of time passing. Linear time becomes cyclical; there is no before, no after, and no causality.

In DETACHED BUILDING and EIGHT, Hubbard/Birchler thwart the "semblance of truthfulness,"[3] characteristic of classical cinema and mass culture, with their smooth surfaces, linear narratives, and persistent concealment of the process of production. Art practitioners today frequently seek to subvert the conventions of fictionalization. A widespread method in contemporary video art, for example, is to split up linear narrative modes in multiple projections, a method practiced with great mastery by such artists as Pipilotti Rist or Doug Aitken. In contrast, Teresa Hubbard and Alexander Birchler do not split up perception in their work, but rather rely on the suggestive power of the slowly tracking camera and endless video loops in impressive large-scale projec-

tions. But they also interrogate constructions of reality by constantly undermining the premises of the narrative film, the illusion of causal connections, temporal sequences or spatial unities by means of time cycles and rooms within rooms. Their memorable images recount ordinary tales of spatial and psychological constraints, of vulnerability, of mourning and loss, stories from familiar, daily lives, arrested in enigmatic subjunctives whose poignancy rests on the very fact that they are entirely open-ended—as floating, non-linear narratives with the viewer as a participant in the never-ending process of devising potential meanings.

(Translation: Catherine Schelbert)

1) Alexander Birchler in conversation with Martin Hentschel in: Martin Hentschel (ed.), *Wild Walls* (Bielefeld: Kerber Verlag, 2001), p. 77.
2) Ibid., p. 77.
3) Vilém Flusser, *Gesten. Versuch einer Phänomenologie* (Frankfurt: Fischer Taschenbuch Wissenschaft, 1994), p. 120.

INSERT
LOU
REED

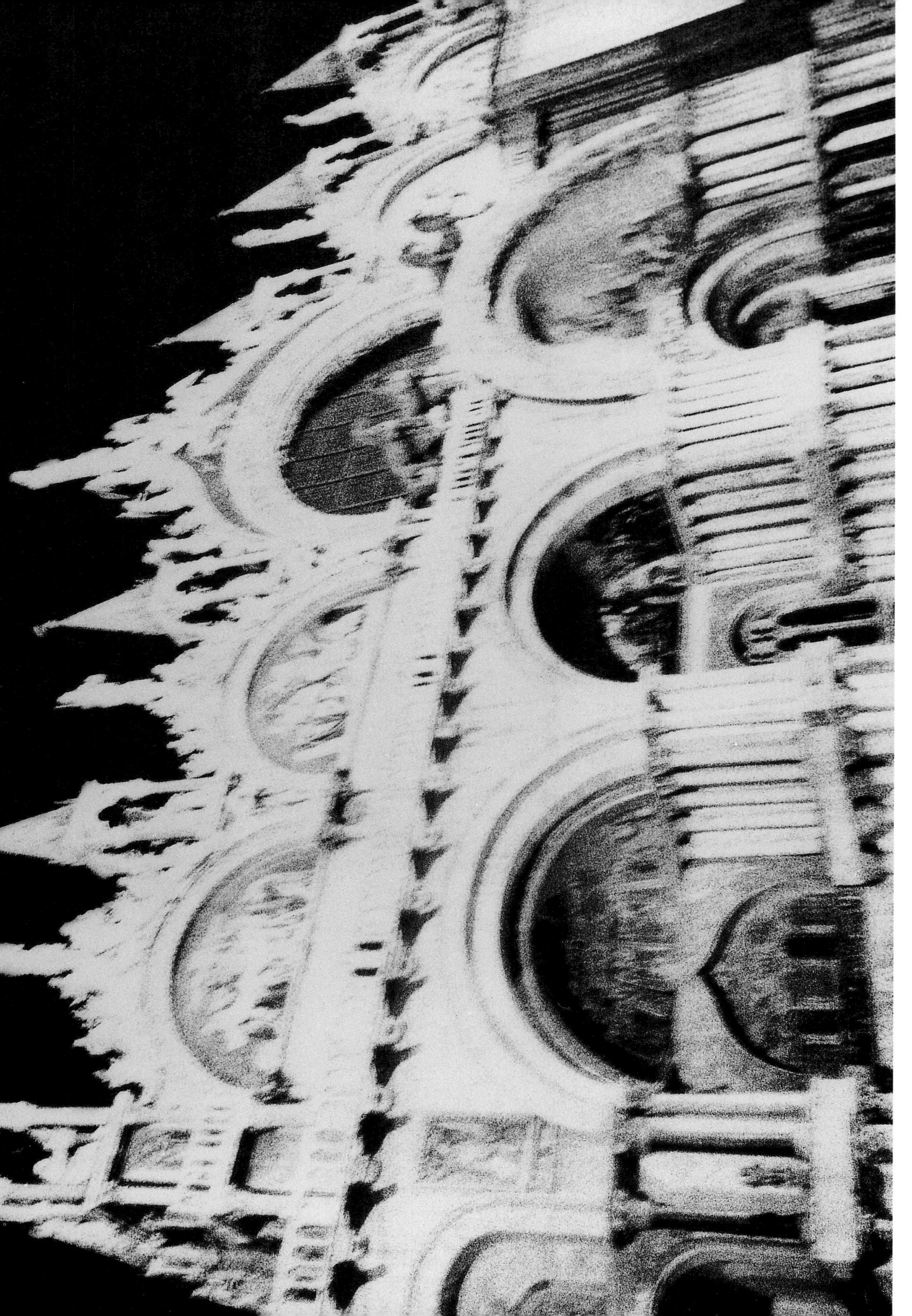

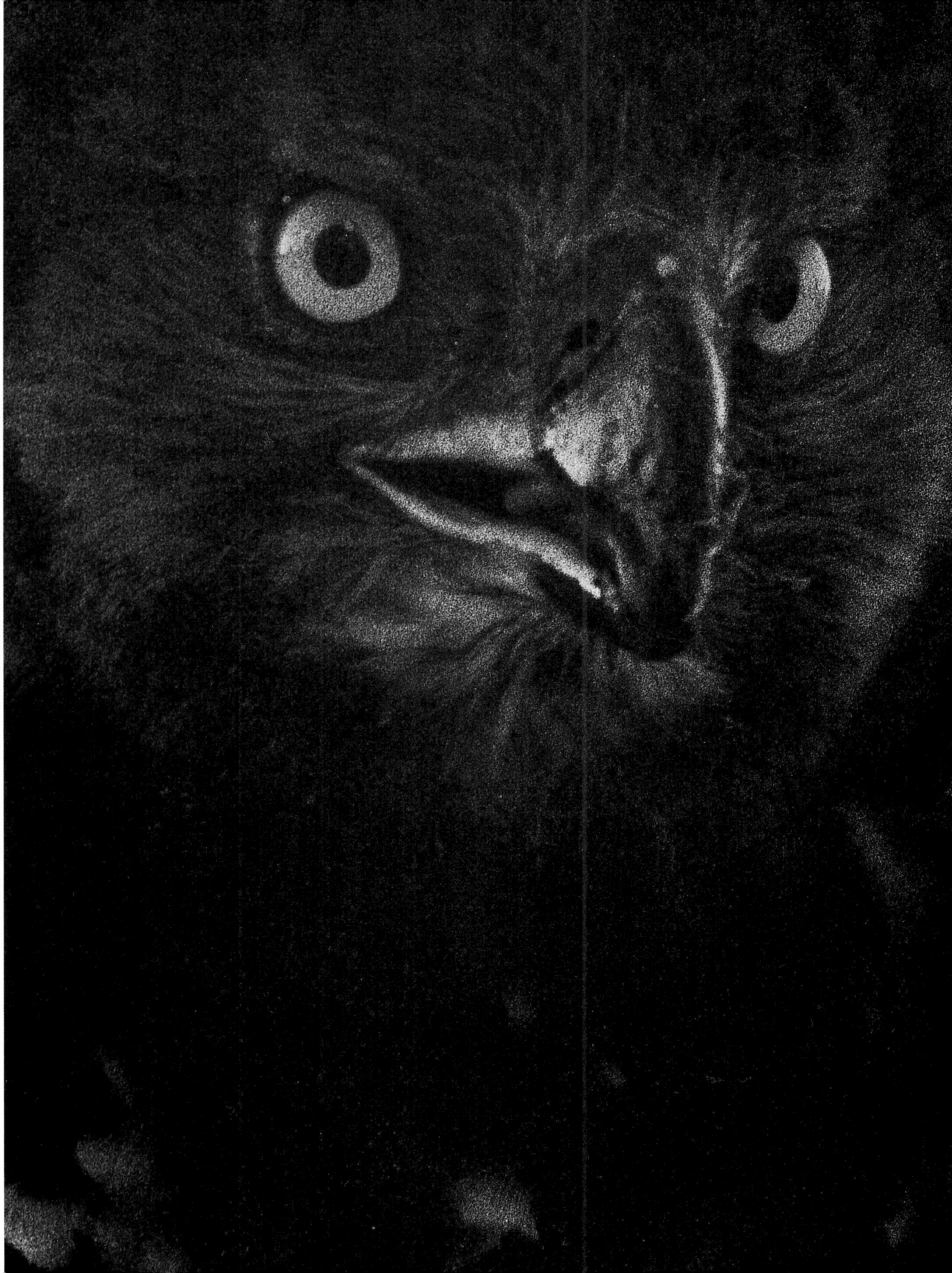

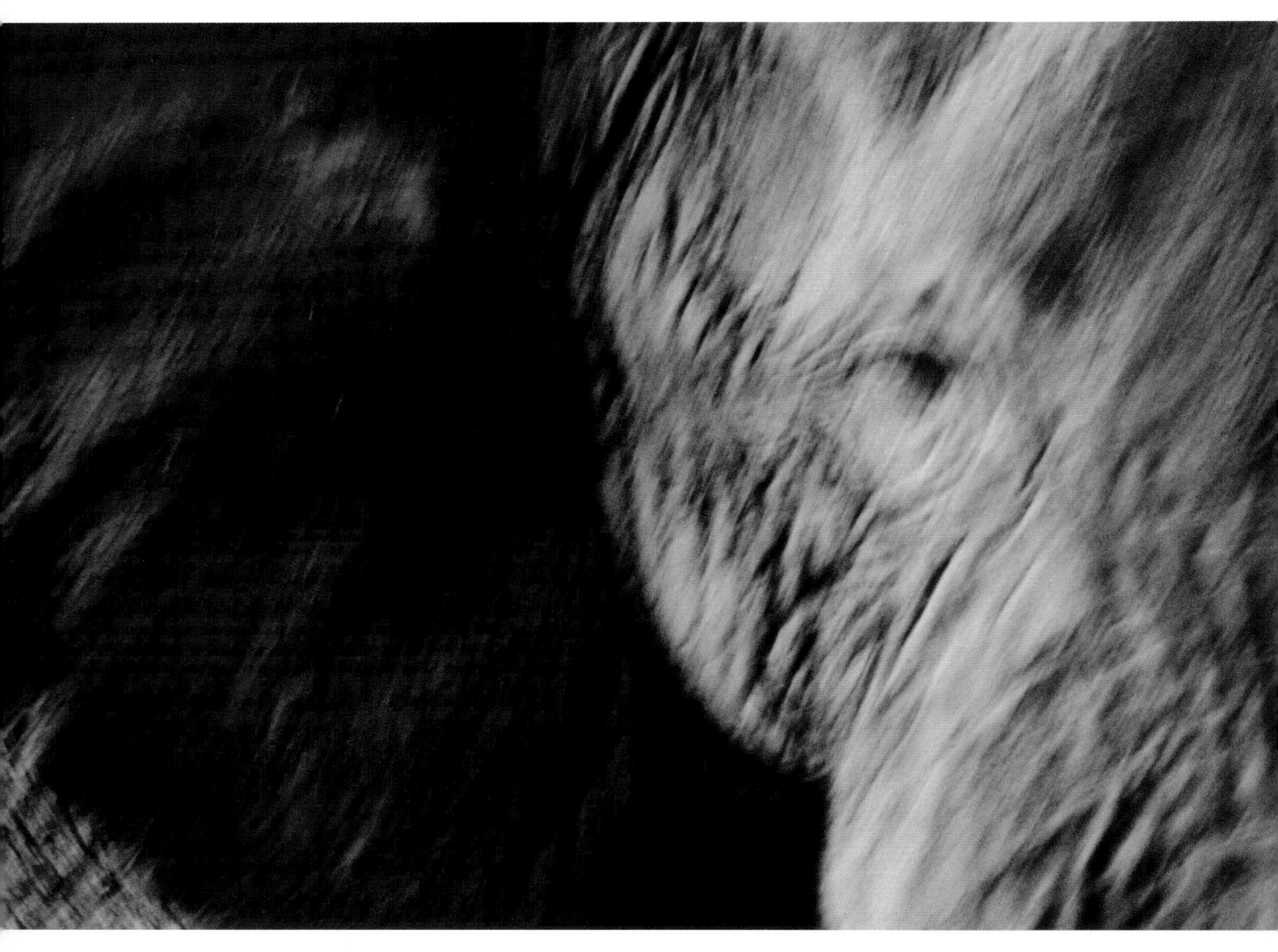

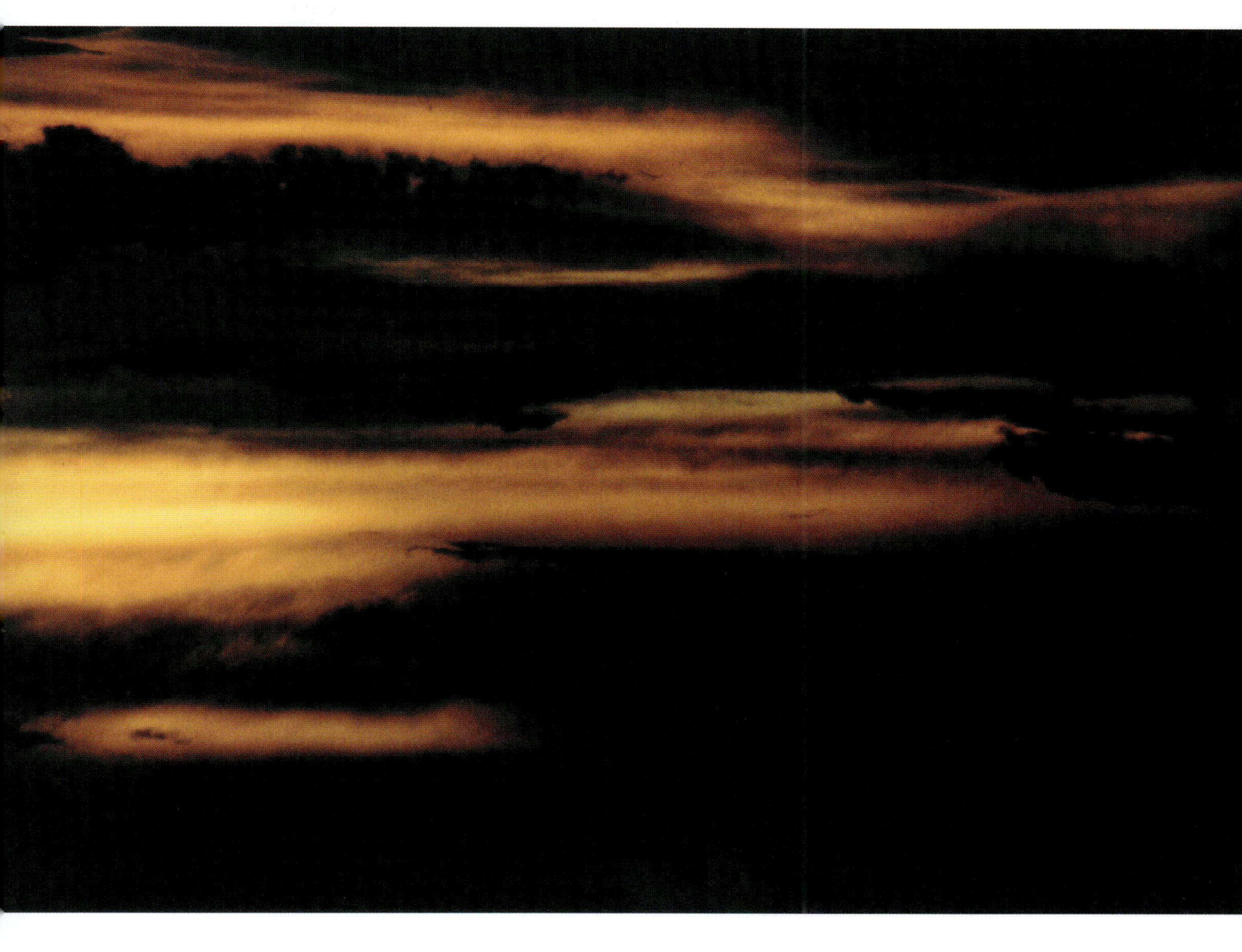

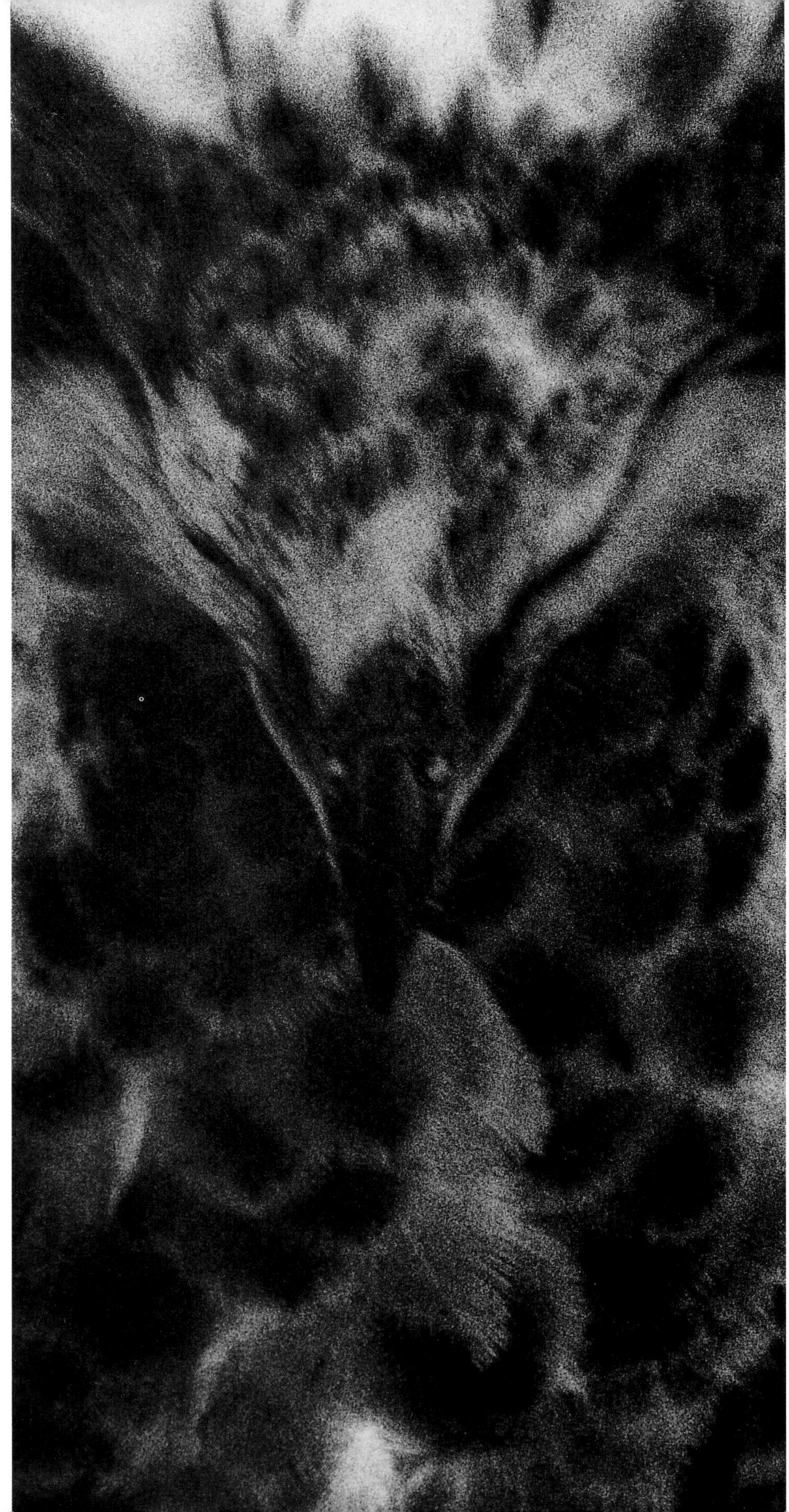

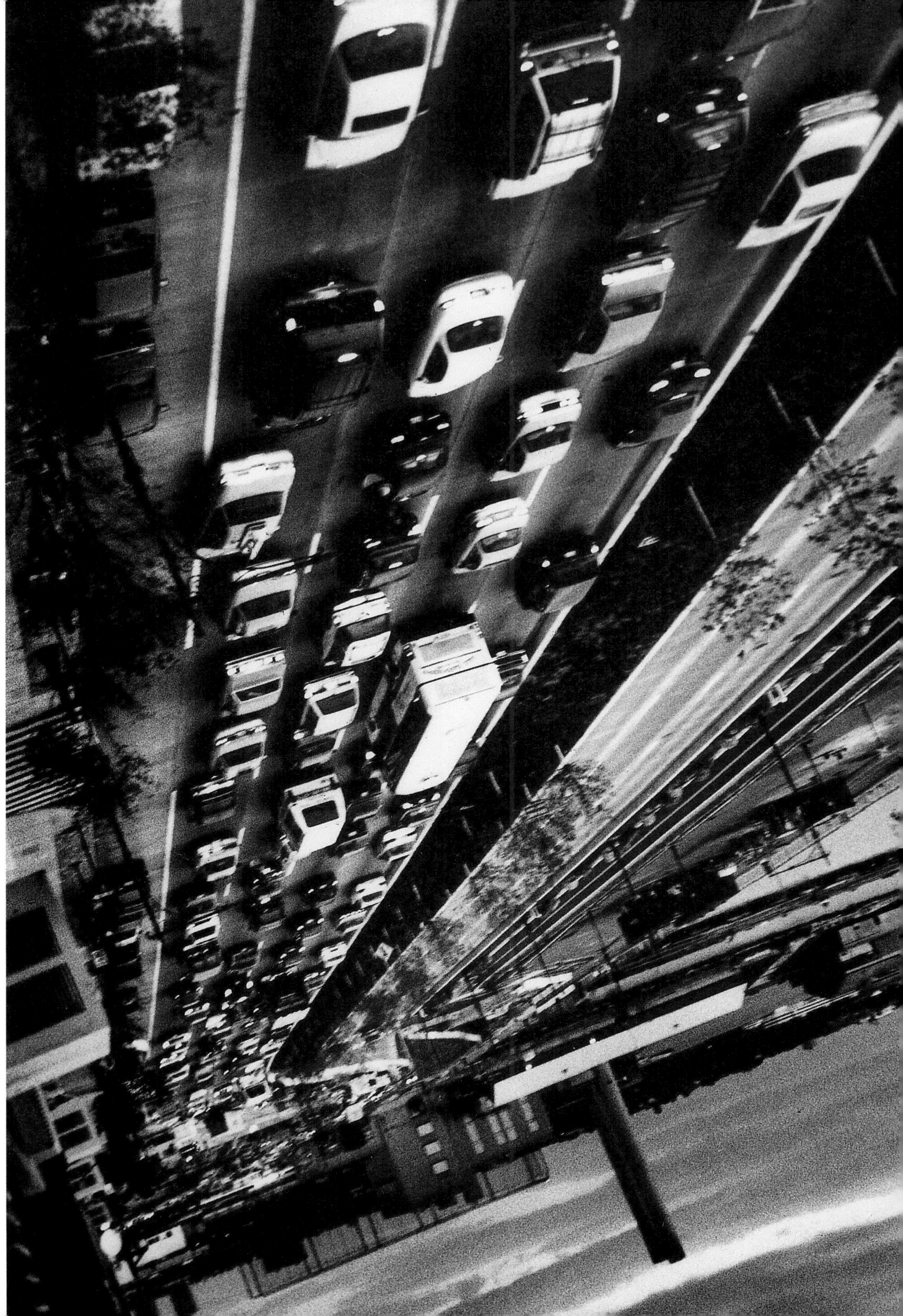

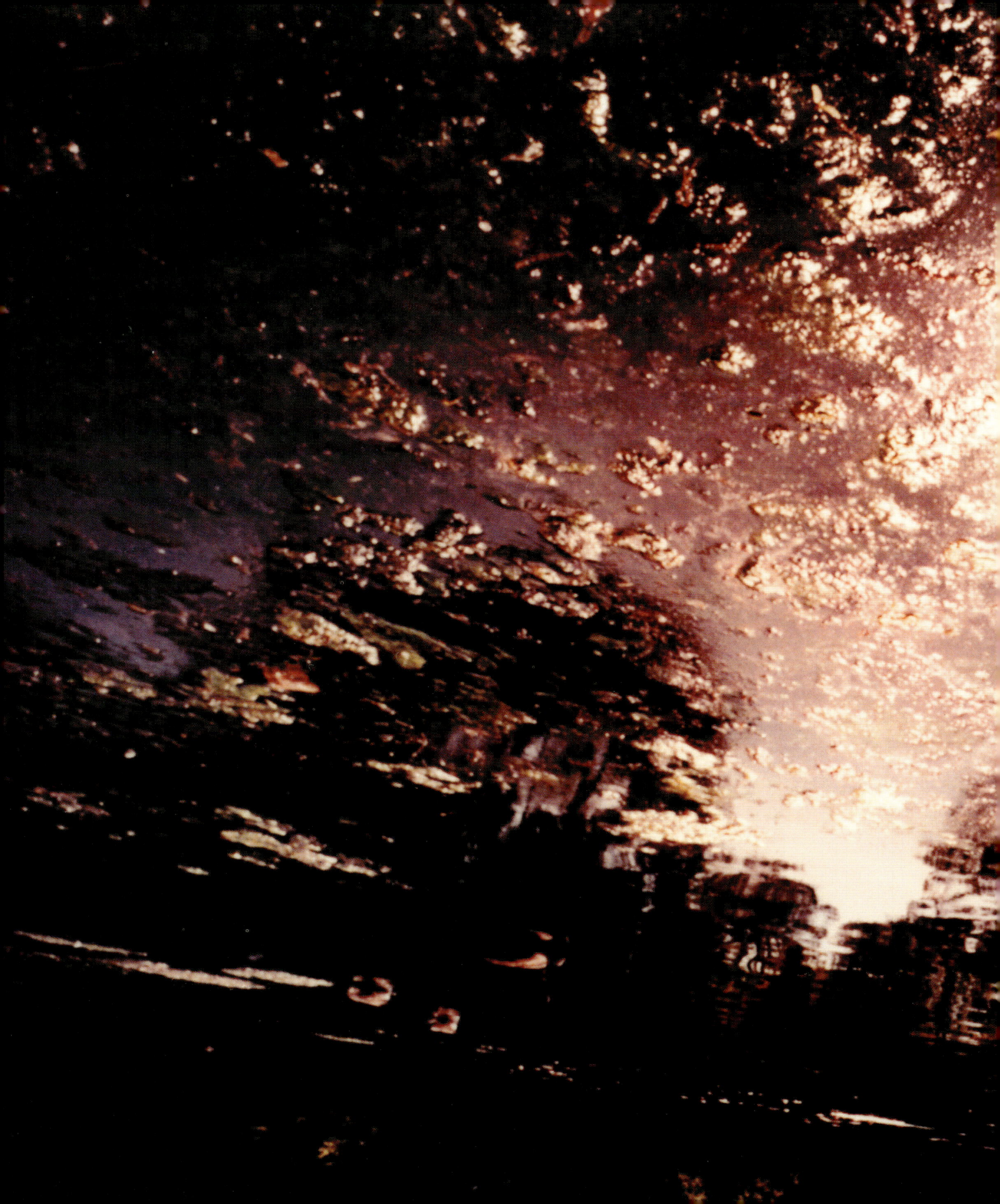

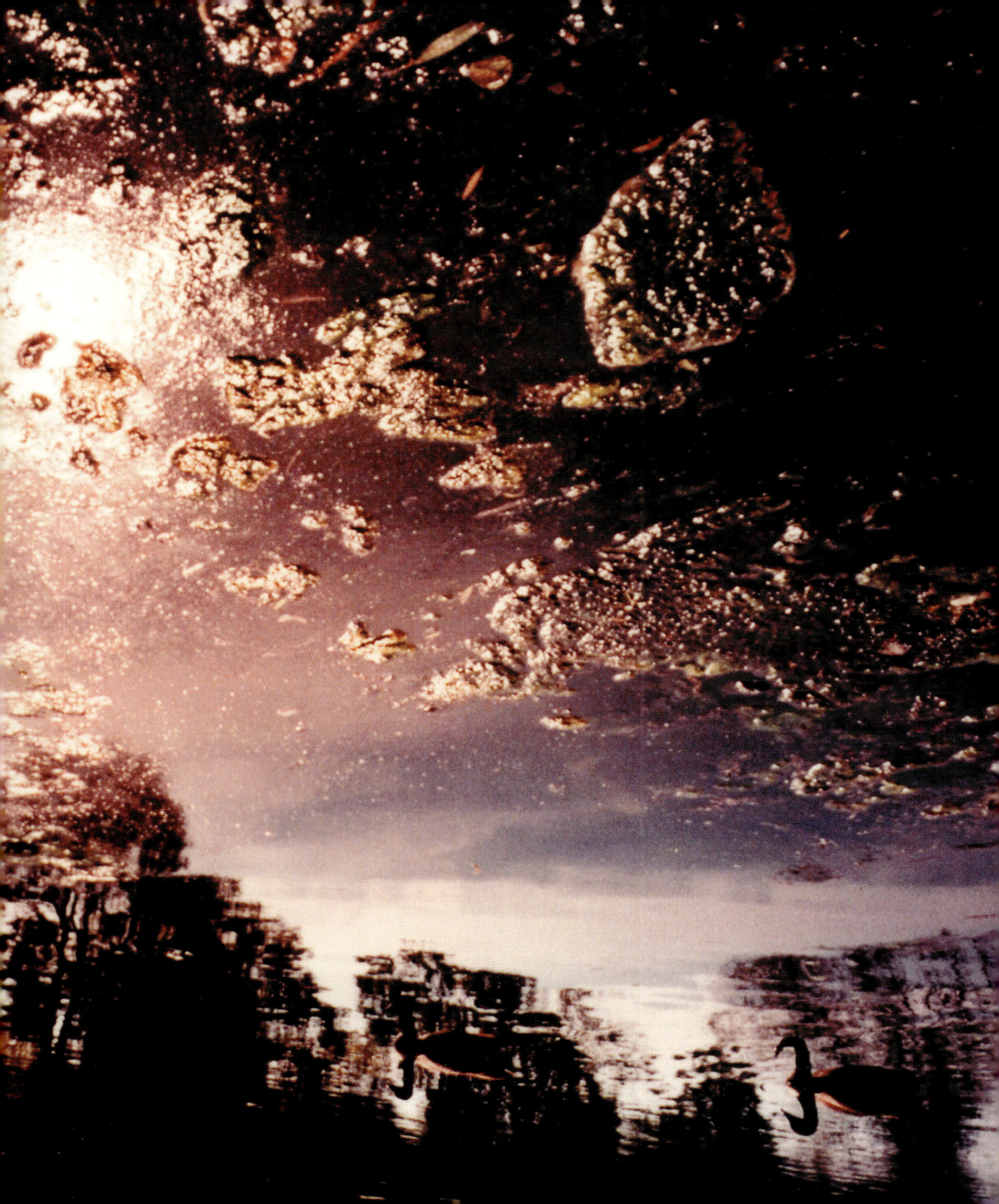

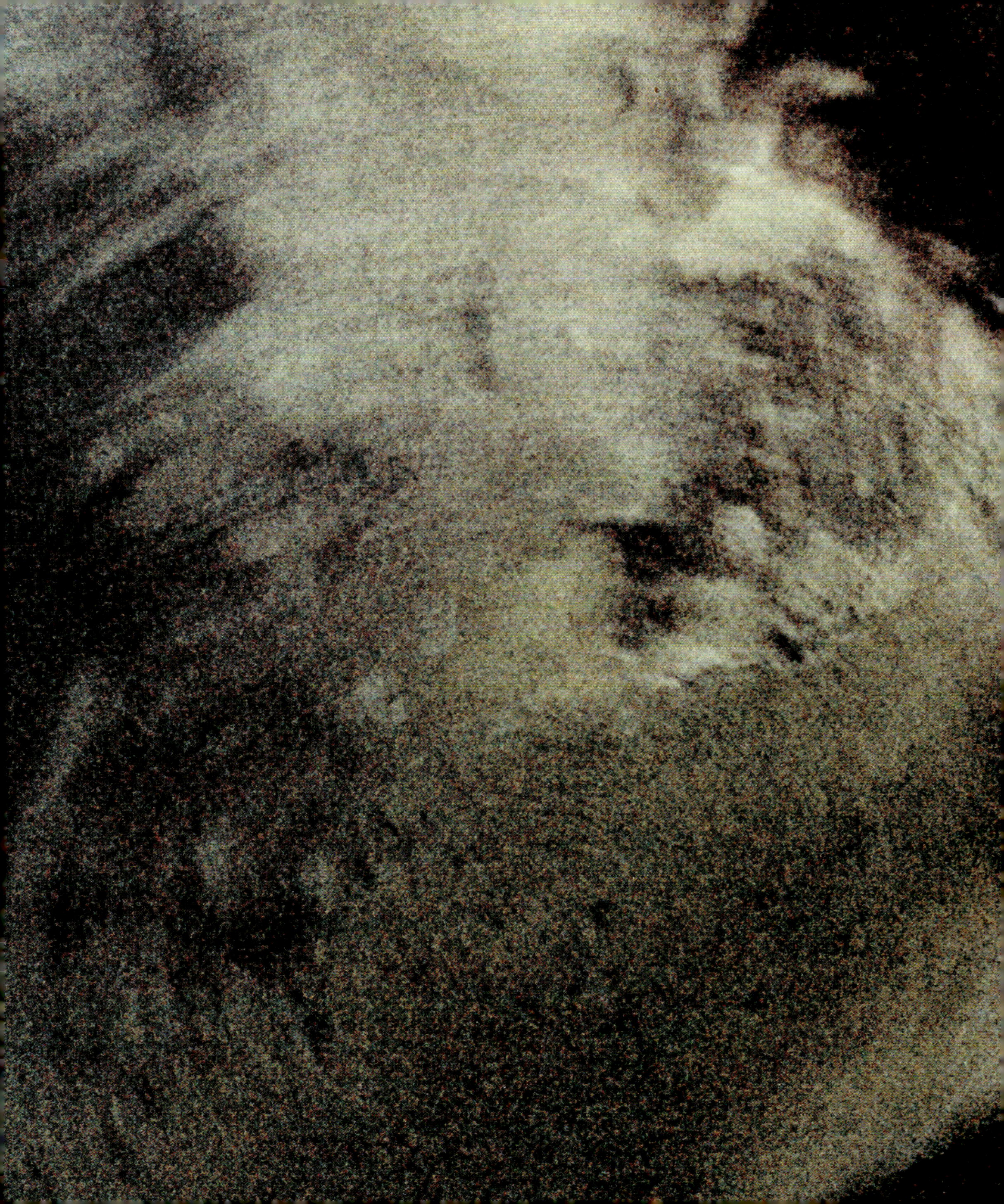

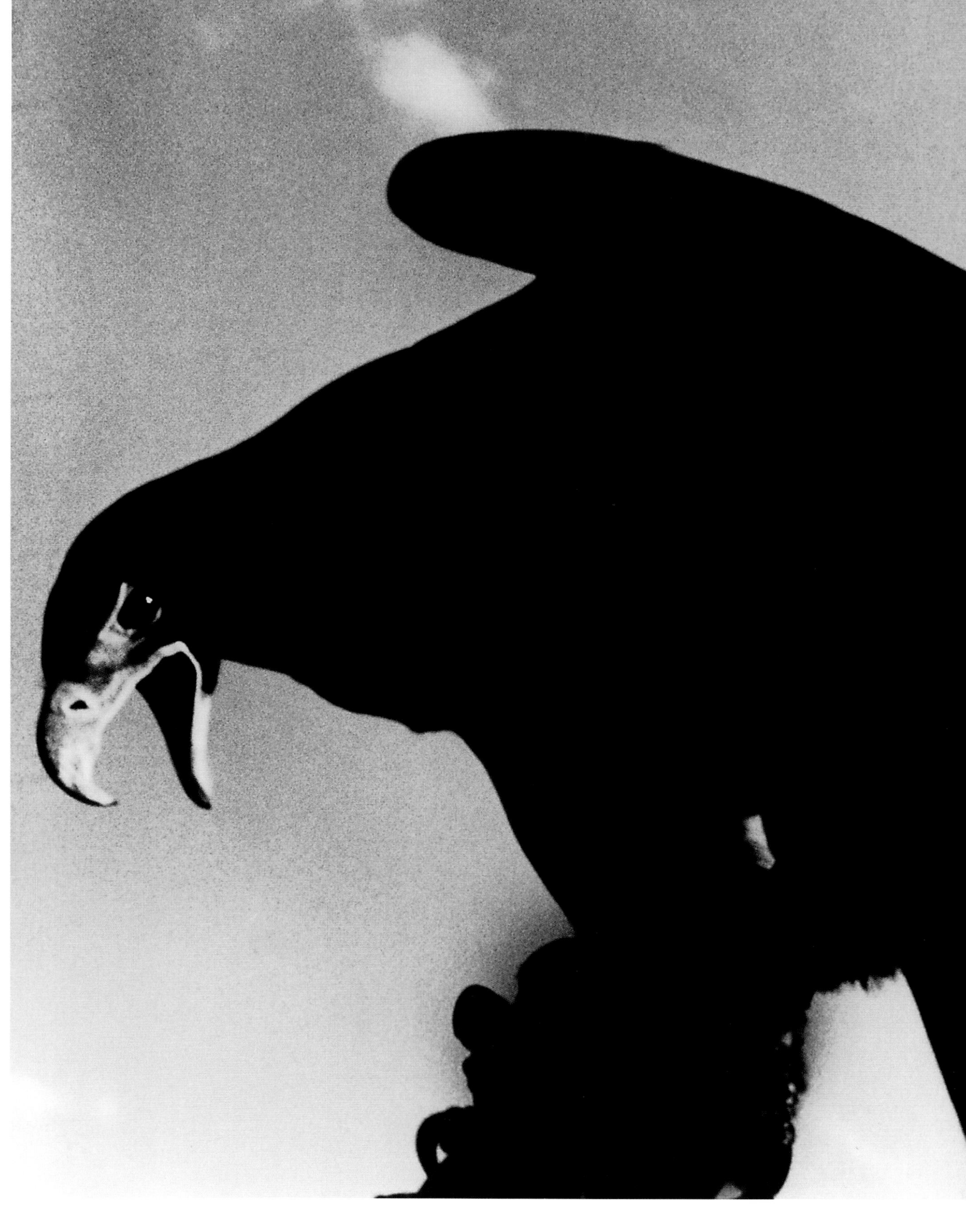

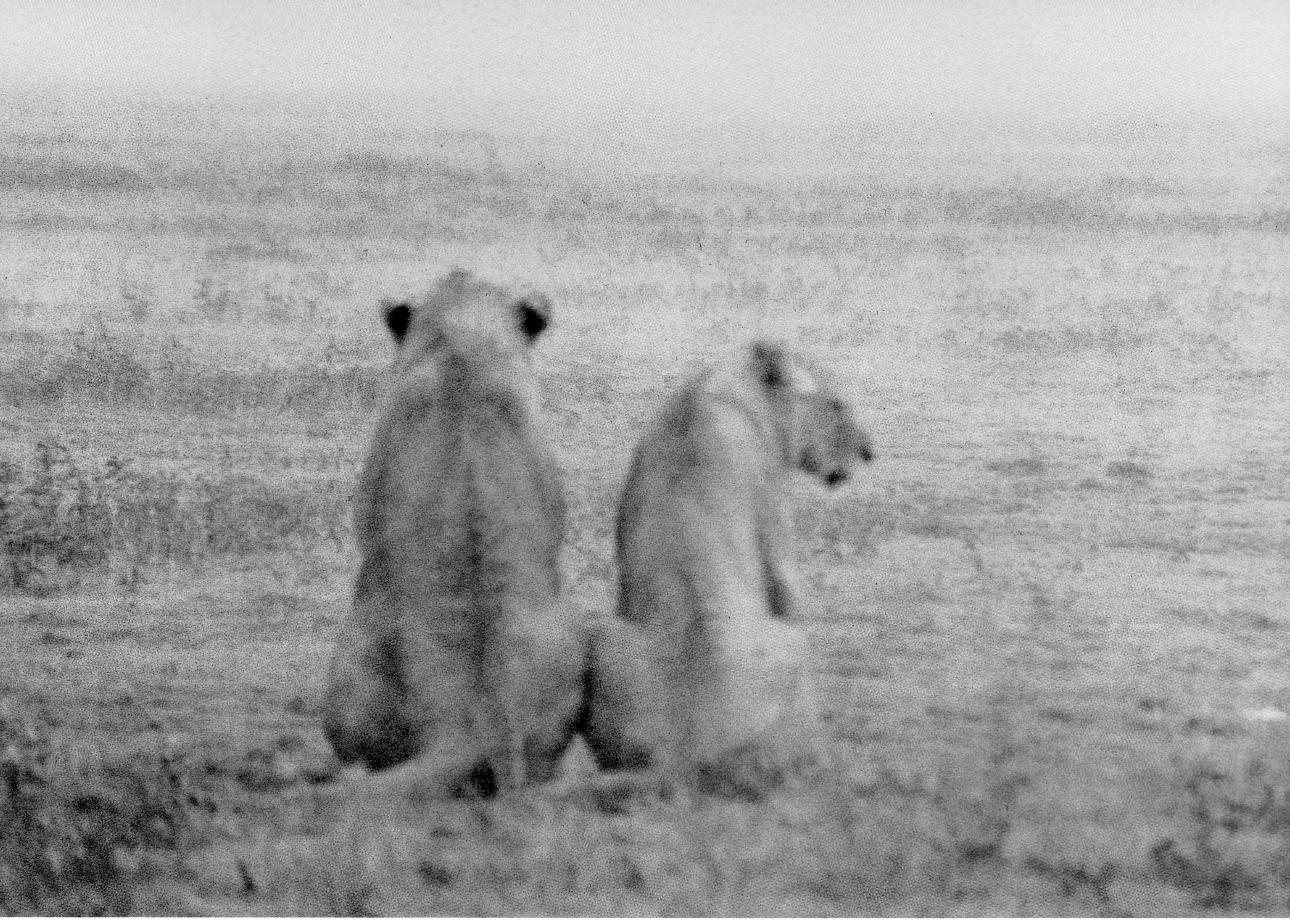

LOU REED, INSERT FOR PARKETT NO. 65, 2002

MARKÉTA OTHOVÁ:

Traumwandeln in eine erzählte Stille

CHRISTINA VÉGH

Odjezd – Abfahrt. Wohin? Der Blick fällt auf den Schriftzug einer Bahnhofstafel. Die Schwarzweiss-Aufnahme wird oben durch einen horizontal verlaufenden Fries, unten von zwei, jeweils zur Hälfte angeschnittenen Fensterbogen abgeschlossen. Der mit einer Abfahrt implizierten Dynamik steht ein in sich ruhender Bildaufbau entgegen. Bewegung und Stillstand in einem.

ODJEZD (Abfahrt, 1997) ist eine von wenigen Aufnahmen, die die tschechische Künstlerin Markéta Othová als Einzelbild zum Werk erhebt. Ihr Blick richtet sich auf unterschiedlichste alltägliche Phänomene. Stadt und Land, Architektur und Körper, Aussenraum und Innenraum, Stillleben und menschliche Figur. Bei ihrer Motivwahl scheint sie sich nicht festlegen zu wollen. Meist entstehen die Aussenaufnah-

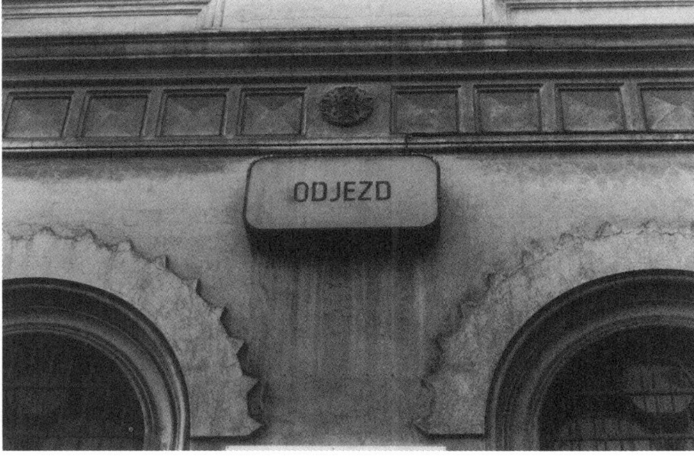

MARKÉTA OTHOVÁ, ODJEZD / DEPARTURE, 1997, black-and-white photograph, 43 5/16 x 63" / ABFAHRT, Schwarzweissphoto, 110 x 160 cm.

men unterwegs auf Reisen; zu Hause in Prag ist ihr Blick introvertierter, hier beobachtet sie Innenhöfe, Zimmer oder Objekte. Ihr eigentliches Werk entsteht jedoch erst in einem zweiten Schritt, wenn sie den stetig wachsenden Bilderfundus konsultiert, einzelne Aufnahmen auswählt und immer im selben Format von 110 x 160 cm entwickelt. Im Falle von ODJEZD handelt es sich um ein Bild von 1995, das erst

zwei Jahre später den Weg aus ihrem Archiv gefunden hat.

Seit 1994 präsentiert Othová ihre Bilder meist in Gruppen. Im Zusammenschluss suggerieren sie einen Handlungsablauf. So beispielsweise in WHILE YOU WERE SLEEPING (2001), einer sechsteiligen Arbeit, die mit einer Aufnahme einer schlafenden jungen Frau beginnt und über einen feierlich gedeckten Tisch hin zu Parkansichten

---

CHRISTINA VÉGH, Kuratorin an der Kunsthalle Basel, lebt in Basel und Zürich.

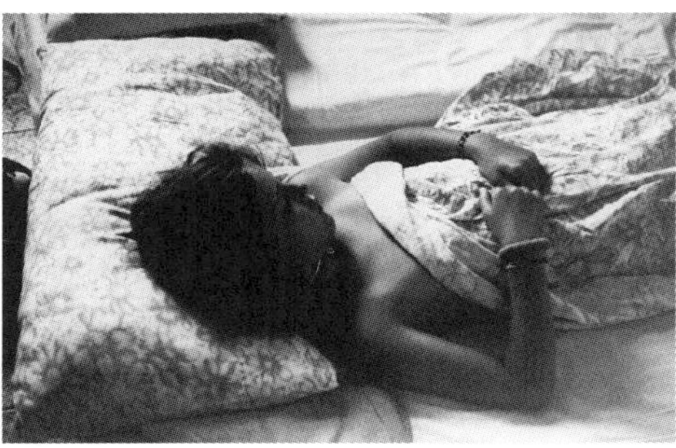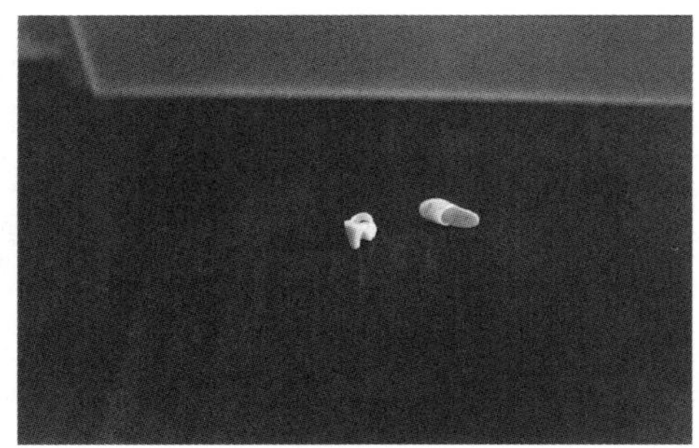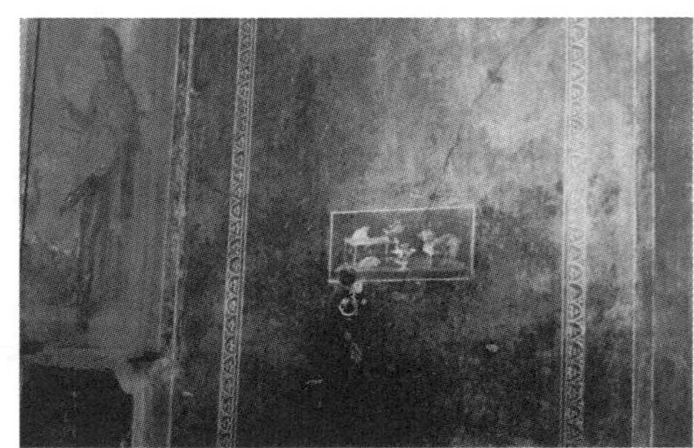

MARKÉTA OTHOVÁ, WHILE YOU WERE SLEEPING, 2001, 6 black-and-white photographs, 43 5/16 x 63" each / WÄHREND DU SCHLIEFST, 6 Schwarzweissphotos, je 110 x 160 cm.

führt. Die Abfolge der unspektakulären Aufnahmen lässt nach einer Geschichte suchen: ausgiebiger Schlaf, durchtanzte Nacht, herrschaftlicher Landsitz, gediegenes Mahl am Tag danach, Ausklinken im frühsommerlichen Park. Oder verweist der Titel auf die viel gerühmte «Poetik des Augenblicks» (Cartier-Bresson); handelt es sich um Bilder der Abwesenheit, um vom Schlaf geraubte Momente? Die Bilderreihe bleibt offen, der Werktitel schafft einen zusätzlichen Interpretationsraum. Othová vergleicht ihre Aufnahmen mit Worten, die im Nebeneinander einen Satz bilden.[1] Nicht die korrekte Grammatik verbindet ein Bild mit dem anderen, sondern die Suggestionskraft, die vom einzelnen Bild-Wort ausgeht und diffuse Bedeutungsfelder zwischen ihnen entstehen lässt. Wie bei ODJEZD, wo allein der Schriftzug den Widerstreit zwischen Stillstand und Bewegung, zwischen Augenblick und Narration auslöst, bleibt bei WHILE YOU WERE SLEEPING die Spannung gegensätzlicher Lesarten unauflösbar. Die Kategorie der Zeit ist dabei von tragender Bedeutung. Das eine Mal scheint sie angehalten, das andere Mal nimmt sie ihren Lauf. Jede Erzählung gründet auf einer zeitlichen Abfolge, das eine kann nur nach dem anderen gesagt

werden. Markéta Othová erzählt Stille: Wie ist es möglich, zum Erzählen einer Geschichte anzuheben und dabei die Stimme nicht klingen zu lassen?

Der allgemeinen lauten und effekthascherischen Bilderflut begegnet die Künstlerin mit unspektakulären, stillen Aufnahmen.[2] So gesehen erfüllen ihre Arbeiten den von Vilém Flusser geforderten Anspruch an eine kritische Photographie: dem Abstumpfen der Bewohner des «photographischen Universums» entgegenzuwirken. Wir sind von immer mehr und immer neuen, die technischen Möglichkeiten nutzenden Bildfindungen umgeben. Das photographische Bild nehmen wir kaum mehr wahr, da es von «Gewohnheit verdeckt», gewöhnlich geworden ist.[3] Othová durchbricht die alltägliche Redundanz des photographischen Bildes mit Mitteln, die in mancherlei Hinsicht mehr ans neunzehnte als ans zwanzigste oder gar einundzwanzigste Jahrhundert denken lassen. Sie hat sich der Schwarzweiss-Photographie verschrieben und kommt ohne manipulative Eingriffe aus. Weder bearbeitet sie das Photonegativ oder den Abzug, noch inszeniert sie die photographisch festgehaltene Realität.

Die einzelnen Bilder scheinen zufällig, alltäglich, nichtssagend. Othová

führt uns keine neuen Bilder der Welt vor Augen, sondern Bilder, mit denen wir so innig verbunden sind, dass wir uns ihrer nicht bewusst sind. Sie sucht sie aus ihrem Bilderarchiv heraus und spricht unser eigenes Bildgedächtnis an. In der künstlerischen Dramaturgie der Bilderreihen manifestiert sich eine von Georges Didi-Hubermann ins Feld geführte Gemeinschaft, die alles umfasst:

Fragmente, Zusammenfügungen, Verquickungen, Entstellungen. Die Szenen unserer Träume lassen uns nicht nur allein, verwaist, sondern sie selbst in ihrer ganzen Vielzahl erscheinen wie eine wimmelnde Masse von absolut verwaisten, zusammenhanglosen Bildern. Tatsächlich jedoch verhält es sich anders. Denn diese Bilder formen eine Gemeinschaft, wenn auch eine verworrene und lückenhafte, eine Gemeinschaft, deren Sinn derselbe ist wie der aller Verwirrungen und all dessen, was uns das Leben vorenthält.[4]

Oft begegnen wir Bildern vom Transfer, vom Unterwegssein: Wolken oder Landschaften ziehen vorbei, Autos und Schiffe passieren, Schuhe stehen zum Weggehen bereit oder sind gerade nach der Heimkehr abgestreift, Personen kommen an, gehen weg, kehren zurück. Die Wanderschaft des Lebens, das Reisen von Ort zu Ort, der

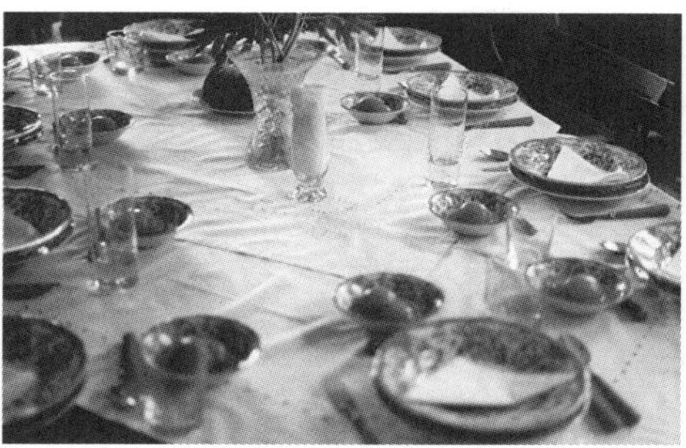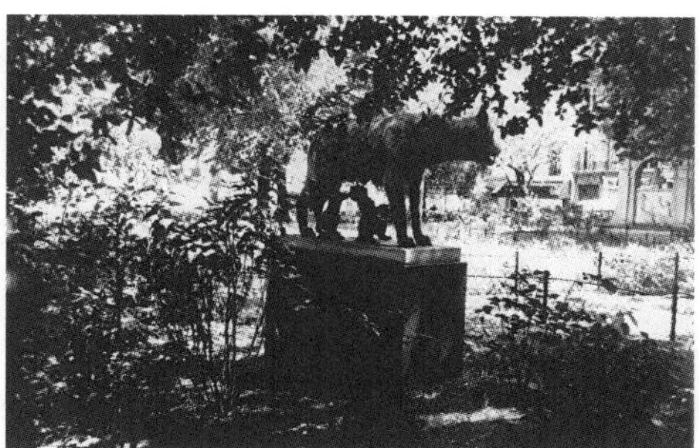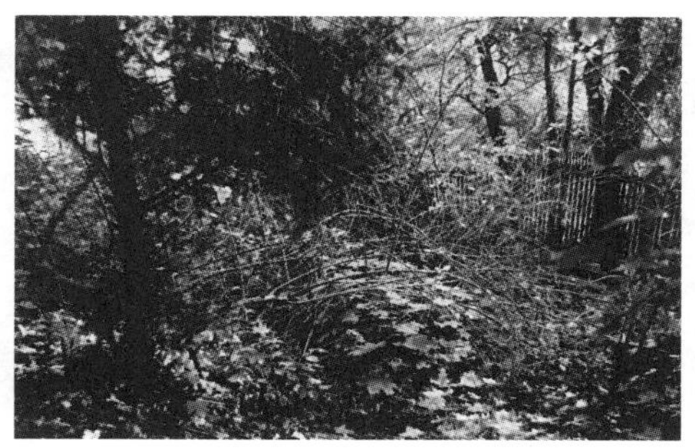

Flux zwischen tatsächlich Erlebtem und Geträumtem. Unvermittelt stehen Bilder wie Bruchstücke der Erinnerung nebeneinander. Diese Reisen werden mit Aufnahmen des Stillstandes angehalten; Wartesäle, Wohnzimmer, Vasen, Parkplätze, Fassaden schieben sich in den Fluss der Bewegung. Die einzelne Aufnahme scheint aus einem Handlungszusammenhang gerissen, wird zum Fragment. Als solches bewegt sie sich in der neuen Korrelation gleichsam traumwandlerisch.

Die Strategie, durch abrupte Brüche neue Assoziationsfelder zu schaffen, wendet die Künstlerin manchmal auch bei den Werktiteln an. Ein Buch, dessen Seiten bis auf wenige Aussparungen weiss übermalt sind, bildet einen Speicher für neue Bedeutungszusammenhänge. Der Grammatik entrissen, entsteht wie im Falle von FIRE FOR POCKETS! (1997) eine neue Syntax. Meist wählt die Künstlerin jedoch Titel, die uns als Phrasen bekannt sind, etwa PARIS–TEXAS (1998), SONY MUSIC (1999) oder EXCALIBUR (1999). Diese stimulieren im Betrachter Stimmungen und Bilder der Erinnerung, die sich mit den präsentierten photographischen Bildgruppen überlagern. In EXPERIENCE DREAM (1998) manifestiert sich die angestrebte Fusion von

Sehen und Erinnern exemplarisch: Links aus dem Dunkeln schimmernde Laternen, rechts eine weisse Hausfassade mit den schwarzen Konturen eines Graffito; die Aufforderung Träume real zu erfahren, das Verbinden von Hell und Dunkel, Tag und Nacht, Realität und Traum.

Othová hält sich nicht dogmatisch an ihre selbst auferlegten Regeln. Bei UTOPIA (2000) handelt es sich um neun Aufnahmen, die vor Ort in Serie entstanden sind. Sie gewähren einen Blick in einen Innenhof, wo Kinder auf abenteuerliche Weise aus dem Fenster eines Hauses mit Vordach klettern. Die Abfolge erinnert an Filmstills, jedoch ist der Handlungsablauf auch hier unterbrochen. Othová behält die tatsächlich stattgefundene zeitliche Abfolge bei, setzt Pausen ein, indem sie Aufnahmen der Serie «entfernt» und als Coda ein Bild derselben Situation hinzufügt, das einen Tag später entstanden ist. Selbst hier, in offensichtlicher Nähe zur Reportagephotographie, wird die Empfindung des Vorher und Nachher irritiert, springt der Blick zwischen Fern- und Nahsicht hin und her. Die Bilder erscheinen wie unsystematisch aufflackernde Erinnerungsfetzen. Vielleicht ist dies der Grund für die leise, melancholische Atmosphäre,

die sämtliche Arbeiten Othovás umgibt. Wenn präzise und auf immer andere Weise der Eindruck von Erinnerung wachgerufen wird, spitzt sich der Topos, wonach alles mit der Kamera Festgehaltene bereits Vergangenheit und Tod bedeutet (Barthes) zu.

Und doch bleibt der Blick in den Schwarzweiss-Aufnahmen nüchtern. Die «absichtsvolle Absichtslosigkeit» in den Bildern steht in einer Tradition, die mit Edward Ruscha (TWENTYSIX GASOLINE STATIONS, 1963), Dan Graham (HOME FOR AMERICAS, 1966/67) oder Robert Smithson (THE CRYSTAL LAND, 1966) ihren Anfang nahm.[5] Im Gegensatz zu den Begründern der konzeptuellen Photographie lässt Othová den Betrachter jedoch emotional stärker partizipieren. Das lakonische Festhalten der Welt ist Mittel, Erinnerungen wachzurufen, und äussert sich in der Intimität, die alles Abgelichtete durchdringt. *French Connection* (2001), ein Buchprojekt von Markéta Othová und Pierre Daguin fragt gerade nach der viel gerühmten Objektivität des photographischen Bildes.[6] Ist es möglich, dass zwei Personen unabhängig voneinander gleiche Bilder machen? Es sind 28 Bildpaare vereint, die bei aller Ähnlichkeit doch unterschiedlicher nicht sein könnten. Die beiden Künst-

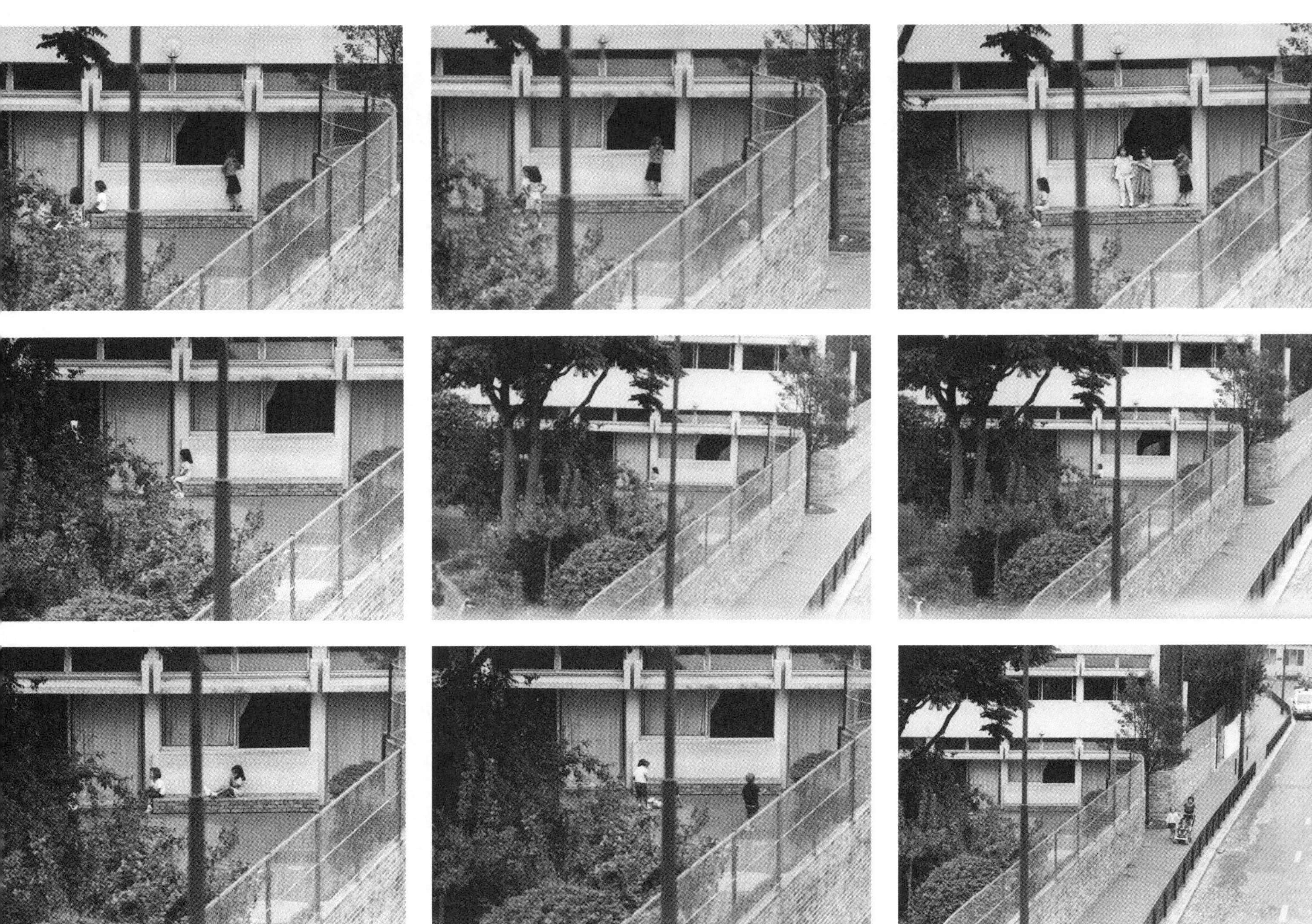

MARKÉTA OTHOVÁ, UTOPIA, 2000, 9 black-and-white photographs, 43⁵⁄₁₆ x 63" each / 9 Schwarzweissphotos, je 110 x 160 cm.

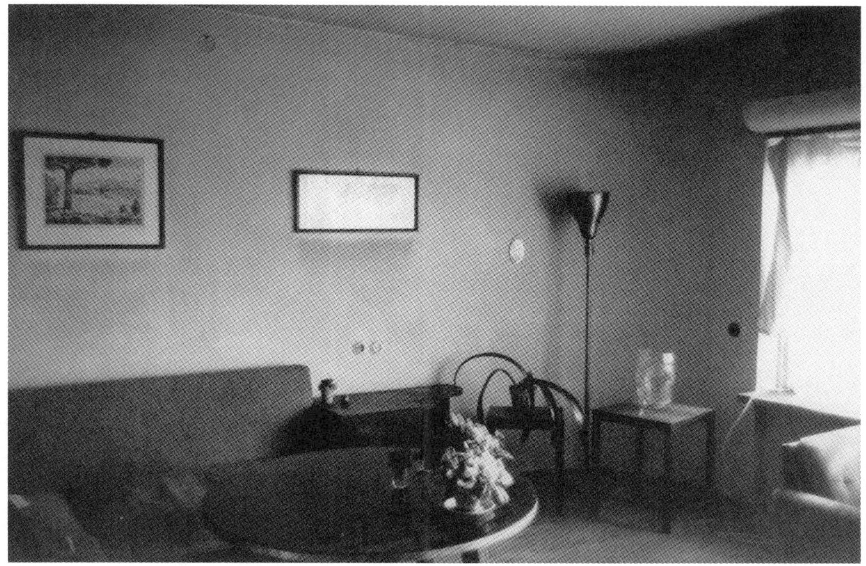

ler haben ihre Bildarchive nach «verwandten» Aufnahmen durchforstet. Schnörkellose, ja spröde Bilder unspektakulärer Alltäglichkeit – links in Farbe (Daguin), rechts in Schwarzweiss (Othová) – stehen einander gegenüber. Verwaiste Parkbänke, geparkte Autos, Büsche am Stadtrand. Sobald die Motive nicht dieselben sind, stellen formale Aspekte eine Parallele her; ein Getränkeautomat steht neben einem Kühlschrank, eine diagonal verlaufende niedrige Balustrade neben einem schmalen Pflanzentrog aus Beton. Je mehr Ähnlichkeit, desto geschärfter der Blick für die Differenz: Eine gleichnishafte Annäherung zweier Personen, zweier Blickwinkel. Ein Kulturaustausch zwischen Ost und West? Gerade im Nebeneinander fällt die Innerlichkeit der Bilder Othovás besonders ins Auge. Sie lassen an den tschechischen Poetismus eines Josef Sudek denken, der seine Aufnahmen explizit als Erinnerungen bezeichnete.[7] Othová fängt Bilder der Welt ein, die Anschluss suchen an so etwas wie das diffuse Un-

bewusste. SOMETHING I CAN'T REMEMBER (2000) lässt darauf schliessen, dass Traumwandeln zwischen Erleben und Erinnern nicht einfach ist.

1) Die Künstlerin im Gespräch mit der Autorin, Ende Januar 2002. Sofern nicht anders vermerkt, sind sämtliche Informationen zur Werkgenese diesem Gespräch entnommen.
2) Vgl. Gerry Badger, «Die Kunst, die sich verbirgt. Anmerkungen zum stillen Wesen der Fotografie», in: *How you look at it. Fotografien des 20. Jahrhunderts* (Kat.), Thomas Weski, Heinz Liesbrock (Hg.), Oktagon Verlag, Köln 2000, S. 60–81.
3) Vilém Flusser, *Für eine Philosophie der Fotografie*, European Photography, Göttingen 1983, S. 59 ff.
4) Georges Didi-Huberman, *Phasmes: Essays über Erscheinungen von Photographien, Spielzeug, mystischen Texten, Bildausschnitten, Insekten, Tintenflecken, Traumerzählungen, Alltäglichkeiten, Skulpturen, Filmbildern...*, Dumont, Köln 2001, S. 25.
5) Vgl. Rosalind Krauss, «Die Neuerfindung der Fotografie», in: *Das Versprechen der Fotografie. Die Sammlung der DG Bank*, Sabau, Luminita (Hg.), München/London/New York 1998. Und Jeff Wall, «Zeichen der Indifferenz: Aspekte der Photographie in der, oder als, Konzeptkunst

(1995)», in: Ders., *Szenarien im Bildraum der Wirklichkeit: Essays und Interviews Jeff Wall*, Stemmrich, Gregor (Hg.), Amsterdam/Dresden 1997, S. 375–434.
6) Eine Fortsetzung des Buchprojektes ist geplant. Andere Zusammenarbeiten mit Pierre Daguin waren: *33*, ein Buchprojekt mit Texten von Daguin und Illustrationen von Othová (1994), die gemeinsamen Ausstellungen «Bazar», organisiert von Divus, Prag (1995), «Apollo 13», Ruce Gallery, Prag (1996), «Team Spirit», Vaclav Spala Gallery, Prag (1998), sowie *The Nude*, ein Buch mit Photographien von Daguin, gestaltet von Othová (1998).
7) Die bekannten Aufnahmen Sudeks aus seinem Atelierfenster (1940–54) können als Schau aus und in das Innere gesehen werden. Das Atelier bedeutete ihm während des Krieges mehr als ein einfaches Refugium. Intimität wird in den Bildern Othovás nicht nur spürbar, wenn sie ihren eigenen Körper oder ihre persönlichen Belange porträtiert, sondern auch bei den vielen Ansichten von Innenhöfen, die einen Aufnahme- und Betrachterstandpunkt in einer Wohnung implizieren. Die meisten Innenhofansichten entstehen denn auch in ihrer Heimatstadt Prag, manche auch in ihrer eigenen Wohnung (SONY MUSIC, 1999, EXCALIBUR, 1999). Vgl. *Josef Sudek, Das stille Leben der Dinge*, Kunstmuseum Wolfsburg (Kat.), 7. März – 24. Mai 1998, S. 24.

MARKÉTA OTHOVÁ:

Sleepwalking in Narrated Silence

CHRISTINA VÉGH

Odjezd—departure. Where to? The gaze is focussed on the lettering of a railroad station sign. The black-and-white shot shows a horizontal frieze at the top and the cropped arches of two windows at the bottom. The self-contained calmness of composition counteracts the dynamic implied by departure. Movement and stasis in one.

ODJEZD (1997) is one of the few single shots that the Czech artist Markéta Othová elevates to the status of a work. Her attention is directed towards a wide variety of ordinary phenomena: city and country, architecture and volume, exterior and interior, still life and human figure. She seems to avoid narrowing down her choice of motif. Most of her outdoor shots are taken when she's traveling, but at home in Prague her gaze is more introverted, aimed at inner courtyards, rooms or objects. The actual oeuvre, however, is the product of a second step in which Othová consults her steadily growing stock of photographs, chooses certain shots and develops them, always in the same format of 110 x 160 cm / 43 x 63". ODJEZD is a picture that she took in 1995, two years before she made use of it.

Since 1994, Othová has generally presented her pictures in groups. In combination they suggest a sequence of action, as in WHILE YOU WERE SLEEPING (2001), a suite of six pictures, which begins with a shot of a woman sleeping, moves on to a formally set table, and ends with views of a park. The sequence of unspectacular shots encourages narrative invention: extended sleep, dancing all night, patrician residence, formal dinner the day after, topped off by an early summertime stroll in the park. Or does the title refer to the much-lauded "decisive moment" (Cartier-Bresson) or do the pictures speak of absence, of moments robbed by sleep? The suite is open-

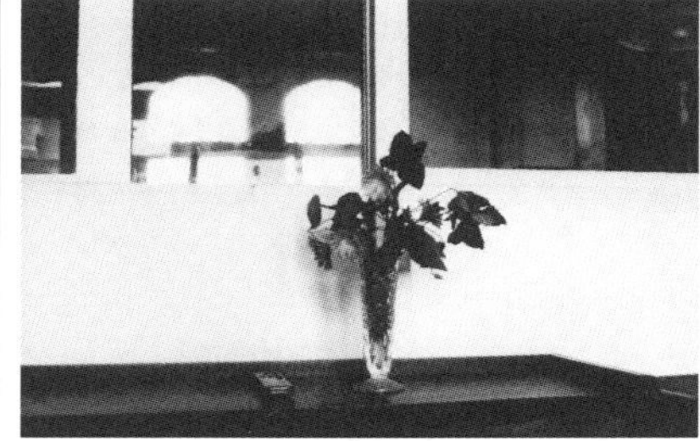

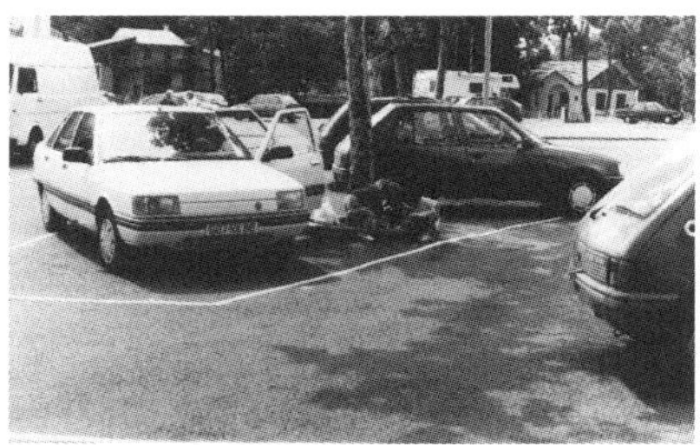

MARKÉTA OTHOVÁ, PARIS–TEXAS, 1998,
2 black-and-white photographs, 43⁵/₁₆ x 63"
each / 2 Schwarzweissphotos, je 110 x 160 cm.

ended; the title adds another interpretive dimension. Othová compares her pictures to words placed next to each other to form a sentence.[1] It is not the correct grammar that links one picture

CHRISTINA VÉGH, Curator at the Kunsthalle Basel, lives in Basel and Zurich.

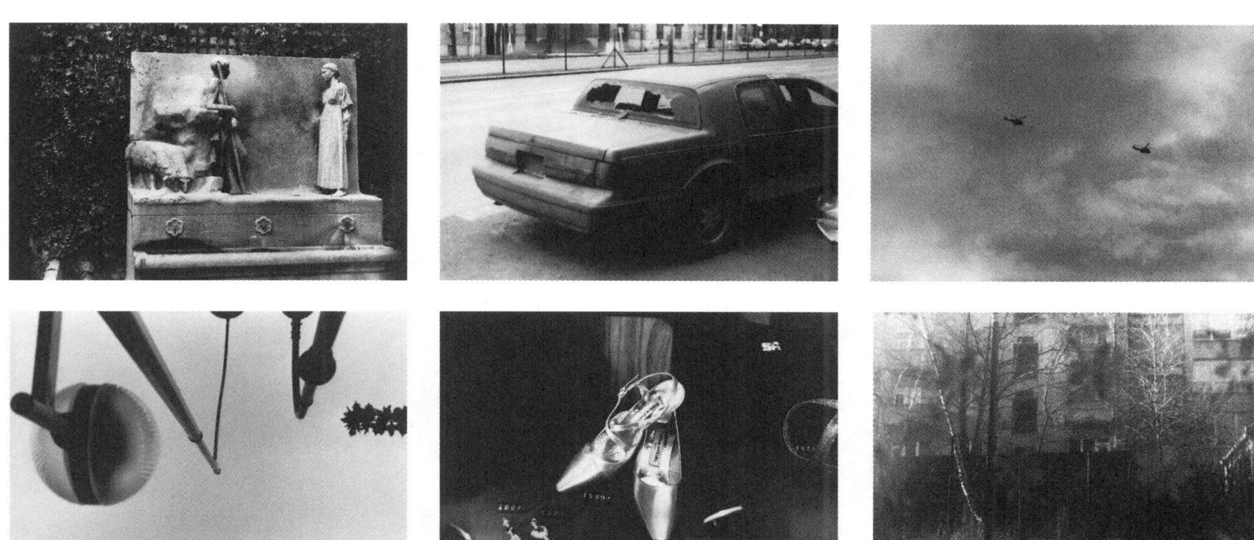

MARKÉTA OTHOVÁ, EXCALIBUR, 1999, 6 black-and-white photographs, 43⁵/₁₆ x 63" each / 6 Schwarzweissphotos, je 110 x 160 cm.

with another but rather the suggestive power of the picture-words, which produces diffuse fields of meaning between them. As in ODJEZD, where the mere lettering is enough to conjure opposition between standstill and movement, between moment and narrative, the tension in WHILE YOU WERE SLEEPING is not and cannot be resolved. In this, the category of time plays an essential role. At times it is arrested; at others it takes its course. Every narrative takes place in time, things can only be said in a temporal sequence, one after the other. Markéta Othová tells silence: How is it possible to scommence telling a story and not make use of one's voice?

The artist responds to the generally loud, USP-ish flood of pictures with unspectacular, quiet photographs.[2] In this respect, her works satisfy the conditions of Vilém Flusser's call for critical photography to counteract the dulling of the inhabitants of the "photographic universe." We are surrounded by ever more and incessantly new visual inventions, a phenomenon abetted by technological advances in picture-making. We barely take note any more of the photographed picture for it is buried under habit, it has become ordinary.[3] Othová breaks through the daily redundancy of the photograph by exploiting means which are more reminiscent of the nineteenth than the twentieth or even twenty-first century. She manipulates neither the negative nor the print; nor does she stage the reality she shoots.

The single pictures seem accidental, banal, unexpressive. Othová does not offer us new pictures of the world but rather pictures that are so much a part of us that we are not aware of them. She selects them from her archives and thereby nudges dormant, almost innately personal pictorial memories. The artistic dramaturgy of the suites corroborates Georges Didi-

Huberman's idea of an all-encompassing community.

Fragments, assemblages, entanglements, distortions. The scenes of our dreams not only leave us abandoned, alone, but themselves appear in all their abundance like a swarming mass of utterly abandoned, disconnected images. But the situation is actually different. For these pictures form a community, albeit a confused and disjunctive one, a community whose meaning is the same as all confusion and all of that which life withholds from us.[4]

We often encounter pictures captured in transit, while on the road: clouds or landscapes passing by, moving cars and ships, shoes standing ready for departure or just kicked off on coming home, people arriving, leaving, returning. Life's meanderings, traveling from place to place, the flow between real and dreamed experience. Pictures, like shards of memory, suddenly appear side by side. The journeys come to a halt in these shots of stand-

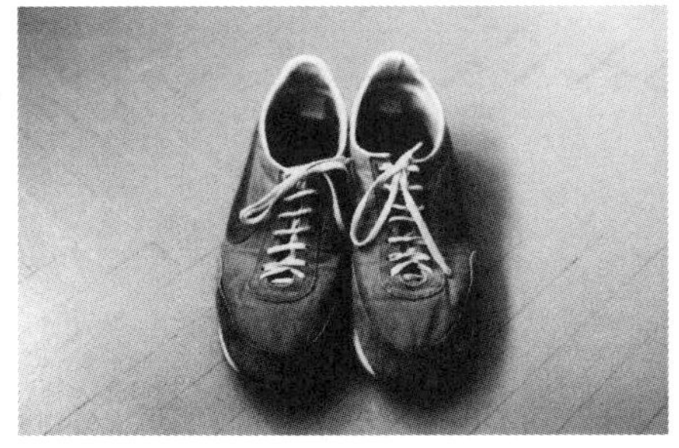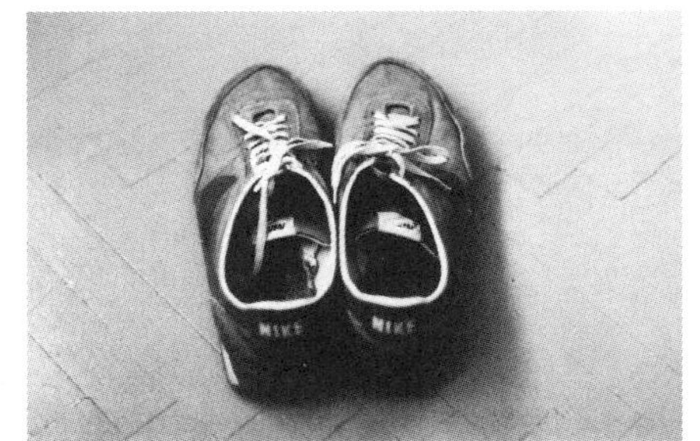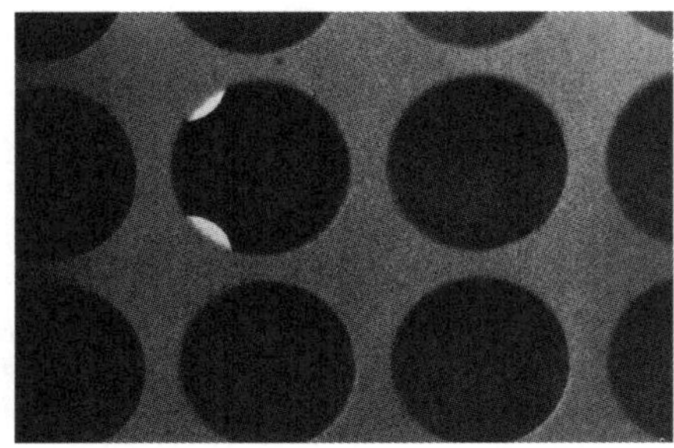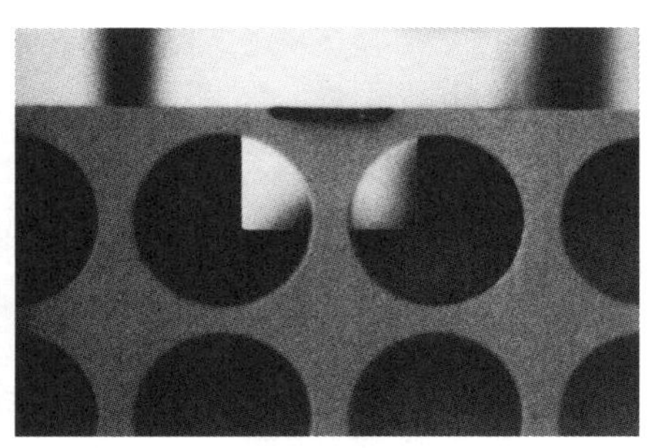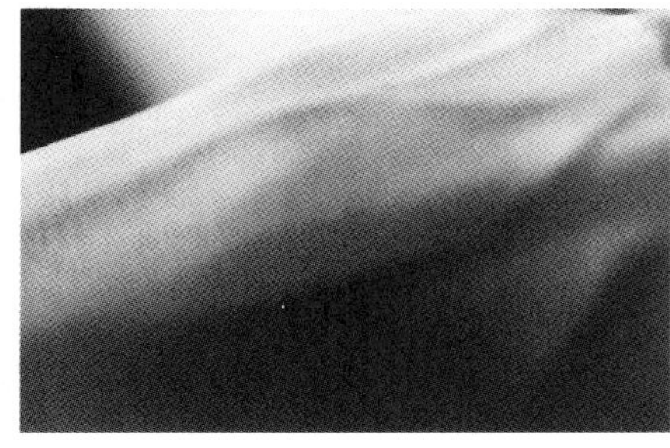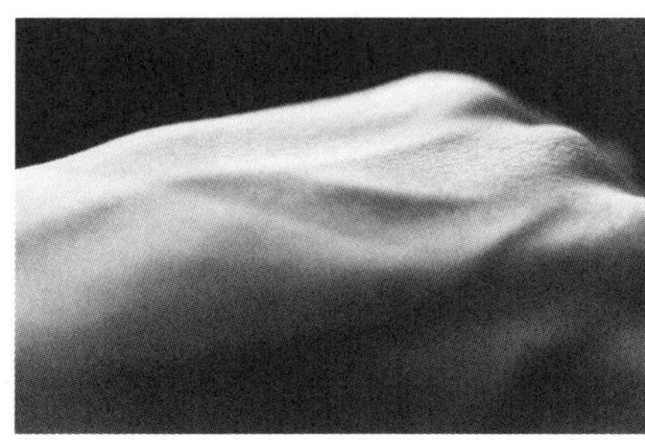

MARKÉTA OTHOVÁ, POWER OF DESTINY, 1999, 10 black-and-white photographs, 43⁵/₁₆ x 63" each / MACHT DES SCHICKSALS, 10 Schwarzweissphotos, je 110 x 160 cm.

still; waiting rooms, living rooms, vases, parking spaces, facades cut across the flow of movement. The single shot seems to have been torn out of the context of action; it becomes a fragment that moves in its new context as if it were sleepwalking.

The strategy of creating new fields of association by means of abrupt breaks sometimes crops up in the artist's titles as well. A book, most of whose pages have been overpainted in white, provides a storeroom for new combinations of meaning. Deprived of grammar, a new syntax emerges, as in the case of FIRE FOR POCKETS! (1997). As a rule, however, the artist chooses titles that ring a bell: PARIS–TEXAS (1998), SONY MUSIC (1999), or EX-CALIBUR (1999). These conjure moods and visual memories, which merge with the presented suites of photographs. An example par excellence of the fusion of seeing and remembering is found in EXPERIENCE DREAM (1998): lanterns shimmering in the darkness to the left, a white facade with black contours like graffiti to the right challenge us to experience dreams as reality in the unity of darkness and light, day and night, reality and dream.

Othová does not rigidly adhere to these self-imposed rules. In UTOPIA (2000), she shot a series of nine pictures of an inner courtyard where children are seen in the daredevil act of climbing out of the window of a building onto a dangerously narrow roof. The sequence looks like film stills but once again there are gaps in the course of the action. Although she retains the temporal order of the pictures, Othová removes shots in the series and adds a coda: a picture of the same situation, which she took the following day. Even here, in official proximity to reportage, sensations of before and after are undermined; the gaze jumps between long-shot and close-up. The pictures appear unsystematic, like flashing scraps of memory. Perhaps this explains the soft, melancholy atmosphere that pervades most of Othová's work. When impressions of memory are aroused with precision and in so many different ways, the topos of photographic content as representation of the past and death (Barthes) becomes increasingly inescapable.

Nonetheless, the gaze in these black-and-white prints remains matter of fact. The "intentional lack of intent" in these pictures reflects a tradition that began with Edward Ruscha (TWENTYSIX GASOLINE STATIONS, 1963), Dan Graham (HOME FOR AMERICAS, 1966/67), and Robert Smithson (THE CRYSTAL LAND, 1966).[5] In contrast to the founders of conceptual photography, Othová allows her viewers stronger emotional participation. Her laconic record of the world is a means of tapping memories and is expressed in the intimacy that permeates all of her work. *French Connection* (2002), a book project by Markéta Othová and Pierre Daguin, examines the much-vaunted objectivity of the photographed image.[6] Is it possible for two people to shoot identical pictures independently of each other? The twenty-eight pairs of pictures which the authors present could hardly be more dissimilar. The two artists combed their archives for 'related' photographs. Straightforward,

even aloof pictures of unspectacular ordinariness are juxtaposed: Daguin's in color to the right, Othová's black-and-whites to the left. Deserted park benches, parked cars, bushes on the city outskirts. If the subject matter is not the same, then formal aspects establish parallels: a vending machine for drinks next to a refrigerator or a low balustrade running diagonally across the picture next to a narrow, concrete planting trough. The greater the similarity, the more receptive we are to the difference: two people who look alike, two vantage points. A cultural exchange between East and West? The combination underscores the intimacy of Othová's pictures even more. One is reminded of the Czech poeticism of Josef Sudek who explicitly called his photographs memories.[7] Othová captures pictures of the world that seek contact with something akin to a diffuse unconscious. SOMETHING I CAN'T REMEMBER (2000) suggests that sleepwalking between living and remembering is not effortless.

(Translation: Catherine Schelbert)

1) The artist in conversation with the writer at the end of January 2002. Unless otherwise indicated, all information on the genesis of Othová's oeuvre stems from this conversation.

2) See Gerry Badger, "The Art That Hides Itself—Notes on Photography's Quiet Genius" in: Thomas Weski, Heinz Liesbrock (eds.), *How you look at it. Photographs of the 20th Century* (London: Thames & Hudson, 2000), pp. 60–81.

3) Vilém Flusser, *Für eine Philosophie der Fotografie* (Göttingen: European Photography, 1983), pp. 59ff.

4) Georges Didi-Huberman, *Phasmes: Essais sur l'apparition* (Paris: Editions de Minuit, 1998). [Quote translated from German version, *Phasmen* (Köln: Dumont), p. 25]

5) Cf. Rosalind Krauss, "Reinventing 'Photography'" in: Luminita Sabau (ed.), *The Promise of Photography. The DG Bank Collection* (Munich, London, New York: Prestel, 1998), pp. 33ff.; and Jeff Wall, "Marks of Indifference: Aspects of Photography in, or as, Conceptual Art" in: Ann Goldstein and Anne Rorimer, *Reconsidering the Object of Art: 1965–1975*, ex. cat. (Los Angeles: The Museum of Contemporary Art, 1995), pp. 247–267.

6) A sequel to the book project is planned. Other joint projects with Pierre Daguin include: *33*, text by Daguin, illustrations by Othová (1994); joint exhibitions "Bazar," organized by Divus in Prague (1995); "Apollo 13," Ruce Gallery, Prague (1996); "Team Spirit," Vaclav Spala Gallery, Prague (1998), and *The Nude*, a book with photographs by Daguin, book design by Othová (1998).

7) Sudek's famous pictures taken from the window of his studio (1940–54) can be viewed as looking both out of and into an inner world. The studio meant more to him during the war than a simple sanctuary. Intimacy is felt in Othová's pictures not only when she portrays her own body or personal concerns but also in her many shots of inner courtyards, which imply a view or a shot taken from an apartment. In fact, she took most of the courtyard pictures in her native Prague, many from her own apartment (SONY MUSIC, EXCALIBUR). Cf. *Josef Sudek, Das stille Leben der Dinge*, ex. cat., Kunstmuseum Wolfsburg, March 7 – May 24, 1998, p. 24.

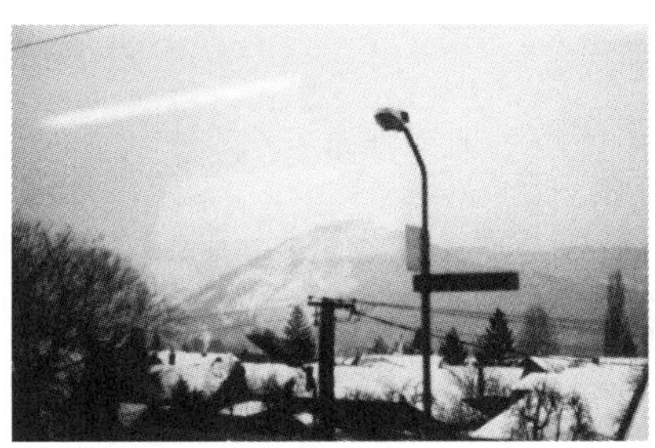
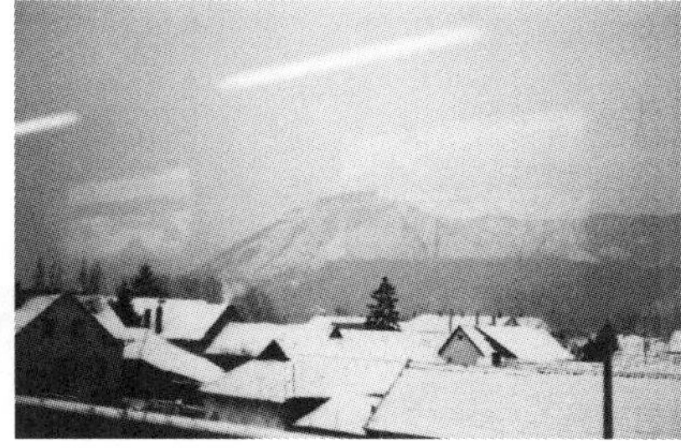
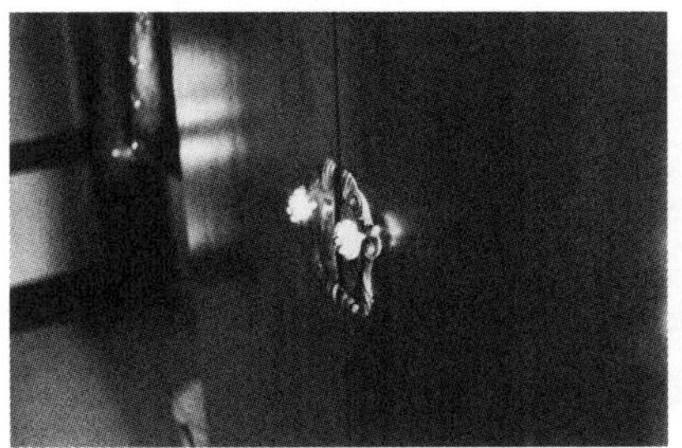
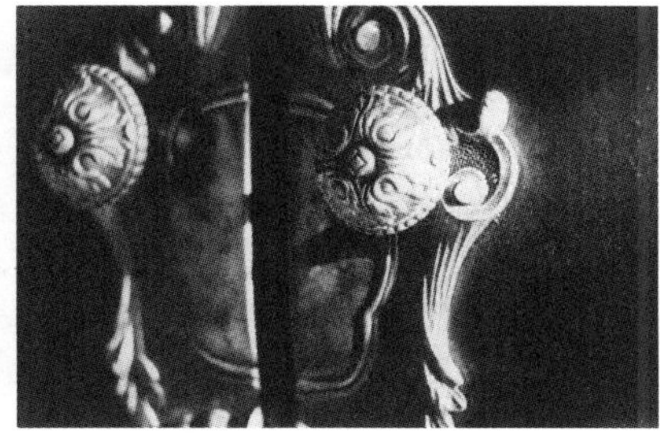

From America

IN EVERY EDITION OF PARKETT, TWO CUMULUS CLOUDS, ONE FROM AMERICA, THE OTHER FROM EUROPE, FLOAT OUT TO AN INTERESTED PUBLIC. THEY CONVEY INDIVIDUAL OPINIONS, ASSESSMENTS, AND MEMORABLE ENCOUNTERS—AS ENTIRELY PERSONAL PRESENTATIONS OF PROFESSIONAL ISSUES.

OUR CONTRIBUTORS TO THIS ISSUE ARE GERMAN ARTIST OLAV WESTPHALEN WHO LIVES AND WORKS IN NEW YORK, AND THOMAS HAHN, A PARIS BASED CRITIC WITH A SPECIAL INTEREST IN DANCE, THEATER, AND CIRCUS.

Veiled Controversy

OLAV WESTPHALEN

Months before it opened, the recent exhibition "Mirroring Evil" at the Jewish Museum in New York, a show of contemporary art employing fascist imagery, caused a sizable public stink. At the time, few had actually seen any of the art in the show. The controversy was largely based on reports of what was going to be shown, rather than on the impact of the actual art works. First and foremost, they existed in an arena of rumors and hearsay. And it was in this realm that they caused a fuss. Many of them, it turns out, only function there; they make for better gossip than art.

Take Tom Sachs' PRADA DEATH CAMP (1998). When described in writing, the fact that Sachs built a Nazi death camp from a Prada hatbox sounds provocative to a lot of people. Yet the actual object, when seen in the gallery, is entirely underwhelming. It's painfully obvious that it only exists so that it can be said (and printed) that Tom Sachs built a death camp out of a Prada hatbox. There's nothing wrong with provocation. But there's nothing right with it either. It depends on who is being provoked to what end, and maybe also on how low you have to stoop to upset someone. Provocation has been the workhorse of the avantgarde for too long to be a virtue in and of itself anymore. These days the notion that art needs to shock usually goes along with a conservative desire to confine artists to an eccentric, entertaining and ultimately harmless role. If the works in this show were meant to stir up a debate, they were certainly successful. If they aimed at not just any debate, but a relevant one, if they wanted, as Gertrude Stein once phrased it, something "that makes a difference a difference,"[1] their success seems doubtful at best.

In broad strokes, the controversy went like this: Those opposing the exhibition insisted that Nazism and its aesthetic manifestations could only be viewed with unequivocal criticism and that they had to be condemned at all times. To them, the idea that fascist im-

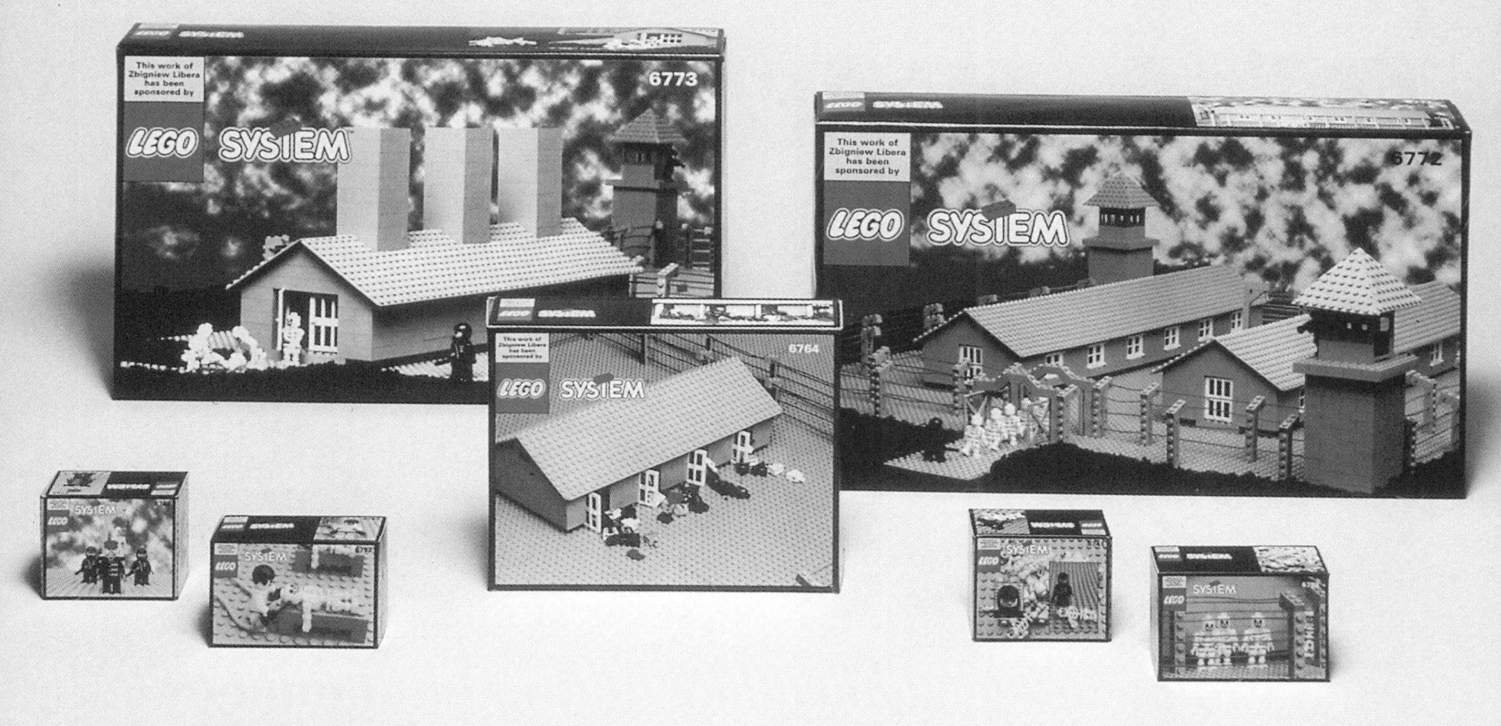

ZBIGNIEW LIBERA, LEGO CONCENTRATION CAMP SET, 1996, cardboard boxes and photographic reproductions, part of the exhibition "Mirroring Evil," March 17 to June 30, 2002, The Jewish Museum New York / LEGO-KONZENTRATIONSLAGERSET, Kartonschachteln und Photoreproduktionen, Ausstellung «Mirroring Evil», 17.–30. Juni 2002. (PHOTO: DAVID HEALD)

agery could become the material for ambivalent, even playful art not only meant an intolerable insult to the victims but also an irresponsible and dangerous belittling of the most immense of crimes. The supporters argued that we can only confront fascism effectively if we admit to its seductive potential. They also put forward the notion that taboos generally fetishize what they suppress, and that it's therefore healthy to violate them, even if they protect us from painful material. And finally, there was a kind of Frankfurt-School reasoning, mostly conjured up around the work of Tom Sachs and Maciej Toporowicz, suggesting that con-

sumer capitalism with its ability to exert normative pressure on its subjects may resemble fascist oppression more closely than we'd like to think.

While these are interesting ideas, they are far from being new ones, which makes museum director Joan Rosenbaum's claim that this show is "about raising questions" less than convincing.[2] If anything, this show is about reiterating well-established questions. Of course one could counter that even if a concept has been mulled over by intellectuals and the interested public for decades, museums still have a mission to educate those who haven't been exposed to it. That's a valid point.

But it is not what the artists in "Mirroring Evil" do. They don't address the broad public, instead they employ a decidedly anti-populist language, namely that of academically taught, later generation, conceptual art. It's a useful language for some purposes, but it severely limits the audience, and thus it raises the bar. Initiated viewers will expect more than just illustrations of received ideas. And they will recognize when artists use the trappings of discourse merely to protect themselves from the public's harsh judgments.

If someone was interested, for example, in the investment of sexual desire in fascist violence, s/he probably

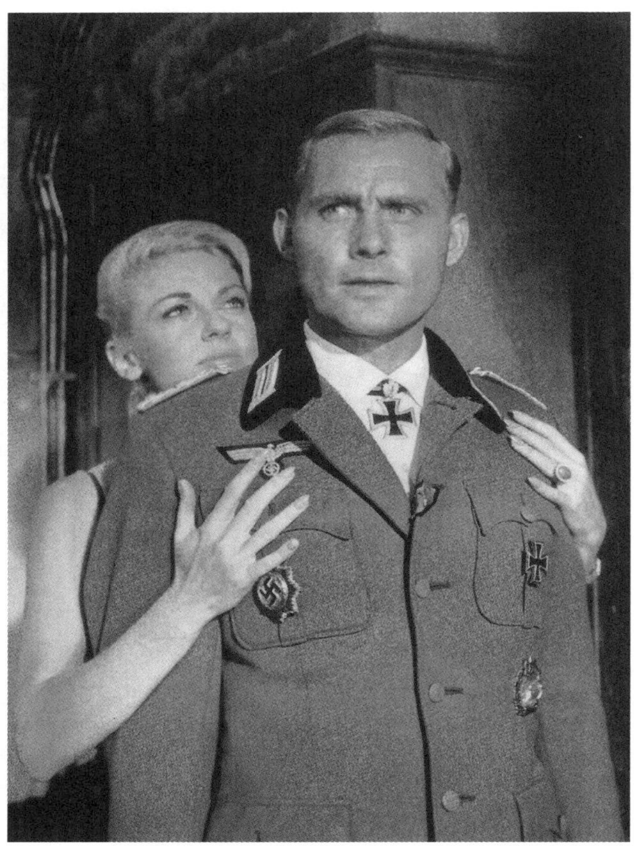

swastikas, etc. We know the method. It's the rhetorical figure of the gag, made up of two opposing scripts, set-up and punch line, that dominates the show. Boaz Arad is the only successful artist in this category. For his video HE-BREW LESSON (2000) he took propaganda footage of Hitler speaking at mass rallies, cut it up into minute fragments and spliced them together again in such a way that the demagogue suddenly seems to speak shaky Hebrew. "Shalom Jerusalem! I apologize!" he says as he jumps and jerks from one syllable to the next, from Nuremberg to Munich to Berlin. The idea is simple, and it is a joke too, but it exceeds the one-liner. It is hilarious to see Hitler turned into a spastic stutterer. Yet at the same time the imposing images and the roar of the crowd, chopped up but still enormous, convey a clear sense of the perverse sublime which the original footage evoked, without ever allowing it to unfold.

A few good works notwithstanding, "Mirroring Evil" remains a weak show. But it's by no means a fascist show, or one that unwittingly propagates fascism. It doesn't warrant the controversy created around it. Just as the works in it don't warrant the exhibition that was made of them. And this is more or less where the art critical coverage ended. Right after "Mirroring Evil" opened, reviews in publications ranging from *The New York Times* to *The New Yorker* to *Flash Art* trashed the show for its mediocre artistic quality, and then left it there, almost as though the quality argument offered a welcome exit from a messy situation. It does, however, leave some questions unanswered: If the aesthetics and the discourse were indeed unremarkable, and if the majority of the works were mere academic

wouldn't wait for Maciej Toporowicz and his heavy-handed juxtaposition of Riefenstahl-footage with Calvin Klein ads. Instead, s/he might have picked up *Male Fantasies*, Klaus Theweleit's study on the emergence of fascist masculinity (and s/he could have picked it up as early as 1977). Or s/he might take Elias Canetti's 1960 *Crowds and Power*, which betrays far deeper insight into the dehumanizing and exhilarating mechanisms of power and violence than anything in this exhibition; or s/he could read Bataille or Foucault on the matter. The list is long and it isn't limited to theorists. (Martin Kippenberger, Rainer Werner Fassbinder, Hans Jürgen Syberberg, among many others, have made valid artistic contributions.) Most of the art in "Mirroring Evil" poses as theory-inspired and critical, yet much of it seems plainly clueless. Neither the use of Nazi material nor the arguments developed, sketchily, around it are new or surprising. What's new is only that works like these are shown in a Jewish institution.

"Mirroring Evil" is a smallish show as far as contemporary group shows go. There are only thirteen artists in the exhibition. Still, it feels redundant. One especially overused formula is the conflation of things we like with things we abhor; Prada fashion with concentration camps, Calvin Klein ads with Nazi Propaganda, film classics with exercises, why did the museum curate "Mirroring Evil" in the first place? And why did a mediocre show meet such harsh opposition?

The other day, I rifled through a friend's CD collection and came upon *The Alibi CD*, a compilation of background soundtracks for phone conversations. It allows you to call home and pretend you're stuck at the airport or in traffic while you do other, covert things. What if both the exhibition and the controversy around it were something like an "Alibi CD"? It is at least conceivable that what comes across as a staged debate on fascist aesthetics may, knowingly or not, serve to veil a related but altogether different conflict. Again, the main bone of contention weren't any of the ideas expressed, but the fact that they were presented in a renowned Jewish institution.

Perhaps, what's really at stake here is not a discussion of Nazi glamour, but a struggle over conflicting concepts of Jewish identity. On the one hand there is a static, post-war self-image, rooted in the memory of the Holocaust, assumed inherently innocent, but also limited by the confines of victimhood. On the other hand a more ambiguous model seems to emerge, exemplified by the artist's mimicry of fascist techniques and by the Jewish Museum's validation of such work, a self-image that includes an option to—at least speculatively—identify with power, violence, and even with the role of the perpetrator.

The notion of exemption from moral fallibility is a dangerous one, and it is becoming very common. We are quickly getting used to wartime-rhetoric and simplistic polarizations into "us" and "them," into "good" and "evil." One of the prerequisites of any ethical conduct is the recognition of one's own capability of evil and wrong-doing. It is the basis of moral dilemma and of ethical choice. And it is in this regard, as a show that questions not the historic truth of the holocaust, but current assumptions of moral exceptionalism and inherent goodness, that "Mirroring Evil" is an important and, given the current political climate, courageous enterprise. It would have been better, had the art been better. But just as an ugly brush can sometimes paint a beautiful picture, perhaps dumb art can be employed towards a wise cause.

As I left the Jewish Museum I bumped into a boy of about eight-years old waving an Israeli flag twice his size. Across Fifth Avenue, Central Park was buzzing with demonstrators who had come for the Israel Day Parade and a subsequent rally in support of Israel. Even without such coincidences, it would be hard to contemplate "Mirroring Evil" without thinking of the current hostilities in the Middle East.

When Paul Wolfowitz, one of the staunchest and most hawkish supporters of Israel in the US-administration, spoke at a pro-Israel rally in Washington in April, he was booed by the crowd for stating the obvious, namely that "innocent Palestinians are suffering and dying in great numbers as well."[3] In a *New York Times* Op-Ed piece centered on this incident, Frank Rich noted: "Anti-Semitism is at a low ebb in America. (…) If someone like Paul Wolfowitz can be counted by some Jews among our enemies, we're looking for new ones in all the wrong places."[4] And, one could add, there might even be a deep psychic investment in the notion of being under permanent attack from all sides. Tony Judt, a professor of European History at New York Univer-sity, wrote in *The New York Review of Books* as follows: "Most Israelis are still trapped in the story of their own uniqueness. … The problem for the rest of the world since 1967 is that Israel has changed in ways that render its traditional self-description absurd. It is now a regional colonial power, by some accounts the world's fourth-largest military establishment. … But Israelis themselves are blind to this. In their own eyes they are still a small victim-community, defending themselves with restraint and reluctance against overwhelming odds."[5]

Historical relativism in regard to the holocaust is unacceptable. At the same time the notion that past suffering exempts anyone from present ethical responsibility is absurd. This goes not only for Israel, but for everybody, including the US. After all, Bush's "War on Terrorism" provided the language for the latest escalation of the Middle East conflict. A long time ago, in his "Lecture on Nothing" John Cage expressed the hope that some day "America will be just another country. No more, no less."[6] Israel and Palestine too, one might add.

1) Gertrude Stein, "Composition as Explanation" (1926) in Carl van Vechten (ed.), *The Selected Writings of Gertrude Stein* (New York: The Modern Library, 1962), p. 513.
2) Joan Rosenbaum, exhibition text, "Mirroring Evil: Nazi Imagery/Recent Art" (New York: The Jewish Museum, March 17 – June 30, 2002).
3) Paul Wolfowitz quoted in Frank Rich, "The Booing of Wolfowitz," *The New York Times*, May 11, 2002, Op-Ed, p. 17.
4) Ibid.
5) Tony Judt, "The Road to Nowhere," *The New York Review of Books*, May 9, 2002 (Vol. 49, issue 8).
6) John Cage, "Lecture on Nothing," at the Artists' Club in New York City, 1949, reprinted in John Cage, *Silence: Lectures & Writings* (Hanover: Wesleyan University Press, 1961).

Verschleierte *Kontroverse*

OLAV WESTPHALEN

Bereits Monate vor ihrer Eröffnung führte «Mirroring Evil», die jüngste Schau im Jewish Museum in New York, zu einigem Aufruhr in der Öffentlichkeit. Zu diesem Zeitpunkt hatten nur wenige die Ausstellung über Gegenwartskunst, die sich faschistischer Motive bedient, überhaupt gesehen. Ausgangspunkt für die Kontroverse waren vor allem Berichte darüber, was gezeigt werden sollte, und weniger der Eindruck, den man von den Kunstwerken selbst gewonnen hatte. Zunächst einmal existierten sie lediglich in Form von Gerüchten und Hörensagen, und in diesem Bereich verursachten sie denn auch einen Riesenwirbel. Viele der Werke, so stellte sich bald heraus, funktionieren auch nur dort: Zum Klatsch taugen sie besser als zur Kunst.

Nehmen wir zum Beispiel Tom Sachs' PRADA DEATH CAMP (Prada-Vernichtungslager, 1998). Schildert man den Leuten die Tatsache, dass Sachs ein NS-Vernichtungslager aus einer Prada-Hutschachtel gebaut hat, wirkt das provozierend. Sieht man das konkrete Objekt jedoch im Ausstellungsraum, so lässt es einen völlig kalt. Es ist allzu offensichtlich nur dazu da, damit man verkünden (und drucken) kann, Tom Sachs habe ein Vernichtungslager aus einer Prada-Hutschachtel gebaut. An sich ist nichts gegen Provokation einzuwenden. Aber es spricht auch

nichts dafür. Es hängt davon ab, wer zu welchem Zweck provoziert wird, und vielleicht auch davon, zu wie billigen Mitteln man greifen muss, um jemanden in Aufregung zu versetzen. Die Provokation ist von der Avantgarde schon viel zu lange beinah zu Tode geritten worden, als dass sie noch ein Wert an sich wäre. Heutzutage geht die Vorstellung, dass Kunst schockieren müsse, meist mit dem konservativen Wunsch einher, dem Künstler eine ausschliesslich exzentrische, unterhaltsame, letzten Endes harmlose Rolle zuzuschieben. Falls die Werke in dieser Ausstellung in erster Linie eine Diskussion anregen sollten, so ist ihnen das zweifellos gelungen. Wenn sie dagegen nicht bloss irgendeine, sondern eine relevante Diskussion anstrebten, und es ihnen darum zu tun war, einen Unterschied zu machen, der einen Unterschied macht (so ähnlich hat es Gertrude Stein einmal ausgedrückt), so ist ihr Erfolg im besten Falle zweifelhaft.[1]

In groben Zügen spielte sich die Kontroverse wie folgt ab: Die Gegner der Ausstellung stellten sich auf den Standpunkt, der Nationalsozialismus und seine ästhetischen Erscheinungsformen erlaubten nur eine ungeteilt kritische Betrachtung und seien grundsätzlich immer zu verurteilen. Für sie bedeutete die Vorstellung, dass die

Bildsprache des Faschismus Stoff für eine ambivalente, ja sogar verspielte Kunst liefern könnte, nicht nur eine unerträgliche Verunglimpfung der Opfer, sondern auch eine unverantwortliche und gefährliche Bagatellisierung eines in seiner Ungeheuerlichkeit unübertroffenen Verbrechens. Die Befürworter meinten, man könne dem Faschismus nur dann wirkungsvoll begegnen, wenn man sich dessen Verführungspotenzial eingestünde. Darüber hinaus vertrat diese Partei die Ansicht, dass Tabus in der Regel das, was sie verdrängen, fetischisieren und es deshalb heilsam sei, sie zu brechen, selbst wenn sie uns vor schmerzlichen Dingen schützen. Und schliesslich gab es eine Argumentationsweise getreu der Frankfurter Schule: Sie wurde hauptsächlich im Zusammenhang mit dem Werk von Tom Sachs und Maciej Toporowicz dahingehend bemüht, dass der Kapitalismus der Konsumgesellschaft mit dem normativen Druck, den er auf jene ausübte, die unter ihm lebten, der faschistischen Unterdrückung vielleicht ähnlicher sei, als man glauben möchte.

So interessant diese Überlegungen sind, so sind sie doch alles andere als neu, was die Behauptung der Direktorin des Museums, Joan Rosenbaum, dass es der Ausstellung darum ginge, Fragen aufzuwerfen, nicht gerade überzeugend erscheinen lässt.[2]) Wenn es in dieser Ausstellung überhaupt um etwas geht, so darum, altbekannte Fragen noch einmal aufzugreifen. Darauf liesse sich erwidern, dass, auch wenn eine Idee seit Jahrzehnten von Intellektuellen und der interessierten Öffentlichkeit durchgekaut worden sei, Museen nach wie vor die Aufgabe hätten, jene aufzuklären, die damit noch nicht in Berührung gekommen seien. Das ist an sich ein stichhaltiges Argument, nur erfüllen die Künstlerinnen und Künstler in «Mirroring Evil» diese Aufgabe nicht. Sie wenden sich nicht an die breite Öffentlichkeit, sondern bedienen sich eines entschieden antipopulistischen Vokabulars, nämlich jenes der Konzeptkunst der zweiten Generation, das an Kunstakademien unterrichtet wird. Es ist eine Sprache, die für manche Zwecke durchaus brauchbar ist, aber sie ist nur einem begrenzten Publikum zugänglich und legt die Latte damit entsprechend hoch. Diese Eingeweihten werden jedoch mehr erwarten als die blosse Illustration allgemein bekannter Vorstellungen. Und es wird ihnen nicht entgehen, wenn Künstler das Blendwerk des Diskurses lediglich dazu verwenden, um sich vor dem strengen Urteil der Öffentlichkeit zu schützen.

Wenn sich jemand etwa für die libidinöse Besetzung faschistischer Gewalt interessiert, so hat er wohl kaum auf Maciej Toporowicz und seine umständliche Gegenüberstellung von Leni Riefenstahls Filmbildern und Calvin-Klein-Werbung gewartet. Statt dessen hätte er längst (und zwar schon 1977) Klaus Theweleits *Männerphantasien*, eine umfassende Studie über den Männlichkeitswahn des Faschismus, zur Hand nehmen können. Oder er hätte zu Elias Canettis *Masse und Macht*

von 1960 greifen können, einem Buch, das eine wesentlich tiefere Einsicht in die entmenschlichenden und stimulierenden Mechanismen der Macht und Gewalt verrät als irgendein Werk in dieser Ausstellung. Auch Bataille oder Foucault kann man zu diesem Thema beiziehen. Die Liste ist lang und beschränkt sich nicht nur auf theoretische Denker. (Es gibt auch überzeugende künstlerische Beiträge, etwa von Martin Kippenberger, Rainer Werner Fassbinder, Hans-Jürgen Syberberg und zahlreichen anderen.) Der Grossteil der Kunst in «Mirroring Evil» gibt vor, theoretisch inspiriert und kritisch zu sein, wirkt jedoch schlicht unbedarft. Weder die Einbeziehung nationalsozialistischen Materials noch die

Argumente, die, skizzenhaft, darauf aufgebaut werden, sind neu oder überraschend. Neu ist lediglich, dass solche Werke in einem jüdischen Institut gezeigt werden.

Für eine Gruppenausstellung ist «Mirroring Evil» eher klein: Es sind lediglich 13 Künstlerinnen und Künstler vertreten. Dennoch wirkt das Gezeigte redundant. Ein übermässig bemühter Topos ist die Verknüpfung von Dingen, die wir mögen, mit solchen, die wir verabscheuen: Prada-Mode mit Konzentrationslagern, Calvin-Klein-Werbung mit Nazipropaganda, Filmklassiker mit Hakenkreuzen usw. Man kennt dieses Verfahren. Es ist die rhetorische Figur des Gags dank zwei gegensätzlichen Handlungsabläufen, Aufbau versus auf-

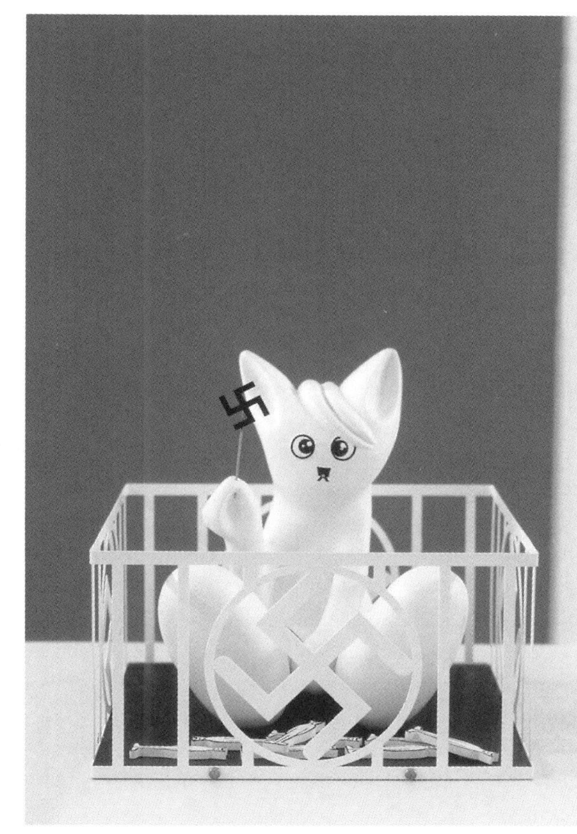

ALAIN SÉCHAS, ENFANTS GÂTÉS / SPOILED CHILDREN, 1997, detail, plywood, aplastic, mirrors / VERWÖHNTE KINDER, Ausschnitt, Sperrholz, Plastik, Spiegel. (PHOTO: GALERIE EMMANUEL PERROTIN, PARIS)

lösende Pointe, die die Ausstellung dominiert. Boaz Arad weiss als Einziger in dieser Kategorie zu überzeugen. Für seine Videoarbeit HEBREW LESSON (Hebräischstunde; 2000) zerschnitt er Propagandafilmmaterial von Hitlerreden bei Massenveranstaltungen in winzige Fragmente und klebte sie dergestalt wieder zusammen, dass der Demagoge plötzlich ein holpriges Hebräisch zu sprechen scheint: «Schalom Jerusalem! Ich bitte um Entschuldigung!», sagt er, während er ruckartig von einer Silbe zur nächsten und zwischen Nürnberg, München und Berlin hin und her springt. Die Idee ist simpel und das Ganze ist zwar auch ein Gag, geht jedoch über die kurzlebige Pointe hinaus. Es ist urkomisch zu sehen, wie Hitler zum spastischen Stotterer wird. Dennoch vermitteln die spektakulären Bilder und das zerhackte, aber immer noch gewaltige Tosen der Massen eine klare Vorstellung von der perversen Erhabenheit, die das ursprüngliche Filmmaterial beschwor, ohne diese jemals wirklich zum Tragen kommen zu lassen.

Trotz einiger weniger gelungener Arbeiten ist «Mirroring Evil» insgesamt eine schwache Ausstellung. Sie ist jedoch keineswegs faschistisch oder propagiert gar ungewollt den Faschismus. Sie rechtfertigt den Streit nicht, der sich an ihr entzündet hat; genauso wenig wie die gezeigten Werke die Ausstellung, die mit ihnen veranstaltet wurde, rechtfertigen. Hier hörte auch die Auseinandersetzung der Kunstkritik mit der Ausstellung mehr oder weniger auf. Unmittelbar nach der Eröffnung prangerten Rezensionen in Blättern wie *The New York Times* und *The New Yorker* bis zu *Flash Art* die mediokre Qualität der Kunst in der Ausstellung an und liessen es dabei bewenden, fast

so, als biete das Qualitätsargument einen willkommenen Ausweg aus einer vertrackten Situation. Dennoch bleiben einige Fragen offen: Wenn die künstlerische Qualität und der Diskurs tatsächlich nicht weiter bemerkenswert und die Werke in der Mehrzahl blosse akademische Übungen waren, weshalb organisierte das Museum dann überhaupt diese Ausstellung? Und weshalb stiess eine so mittelmässige Ausstellung auf derart scharfen Widerstand?

Neulich durchstöberte ich die CD-Sammlung eines Freundes und stiess auf *The Alibi CD*, eine Sammlung von Hintergrundgeräuschen für Telefongespräche. Damit kann man zu Hause anrufen und so tun, als sitze man am Flughafen oder im Verkehr fest, während man heimlich etwas ganz anderes treibt. Was ist, wenn sowohl die Ausstellung als auch die Kontroverse um sie so etwas wie eine «Alibi CD» wären? Der Gedanke lässt sich zumindest nicht ohne weiteres von der Hand weisen, dass eine inszeniert wirkende Debatte über faschistische Ästhetik bewusst oder unbewusst dazu dienen könnte, einen damit zusammenhängenden, aber völlig anderen Konflikt zu verschleiern. Damit ginge es wiederum nicht um die Ideen, die dabei zum Ausdruck kamen, sondern um die Tatsache, dass sie in einem prominenten jüdischen Museum vorgestellt wurden.

Vielleicht geht es hier im Grunde nicht um die Auseinandersetzung mit dem Faszinosum Nationalsozialismus, sondern um einen Streit über gegensätzliche Auffassungen von jüdischer Identität. Auf der einen Seite gibt es das statische Selbstbild der Nachkriegszeit, das in der Erinnerung an den Holocaust wurzelt und ursprünglich unschuldig aufgegriffen wurde, aber gleichzeitig auf die Opferrolle einge-

engt ist. Auf der anderen Seite scheint sich ein weniger einseitiges Modell herauszukristallisieren: Die Imitation faschistischer Strategien durch Künstler und die Anerkennung solcher Kunst durch das Jewish Museum sind Beispiele für dieses Selbstverständnis, das auch die Möglichkeit einer – zumindest spekulativen – Identifikation mit Macht, Gewalt, ja sogar mit der Täterrolle einschliesst.

Der Gedanke, man sei selbst von moralischer Fehlbarkeit ausgenommen, ist eine gefährliche Vorstellung und eine, die immer mehr um sich greift. Wir gewöhnen uns schnell an Kriegsrhetorik und allzu simple Polarisierungen à la «wir» und «sie», «gut» und «böse». Eine der Voraussetzungen für moralisch einwandfreies Verhalten ist die Erkenntnis, dass man selbst zum Bösen und zu Verfehlungen fähig ist. Das ist die Grundlage jedes moralischen Dilemmas und jeder ethischen Entscheidung. In eben dieser Hinsicht – als Ausstellung, die nicht die historische Wahrheit des Holocausts, sondern eine heutige Mentalität in Frage stellt, die von einer moralischen Ausnahmestellung und grundsätzlicher Rechtschaffenheit ausgeht – ist «Mirroring Evil» ein wichtiges und in Anbetracht des aktuellen politischen Klimas mutiges Unterfangen. Es hätte der Ausstellung gut getan, wäre die Kunst besser gewesen, aber so, wie ein unansehnlicher Pinsel manchmal ein wunderschönes Bild malt, lässt sich dümmliche Kunst vielleicht in den Dienst einer vernünftigen Sache stellen.

Beim Verlassen des Jewish Museum lief mir ein etwa achtjähriger Junge über den Weg, der eine israelische Flagge schwenkte, die doppelt so gross war wie er selbst. Auf der gegenüberliegenden Seite der Fifth Avenue wim-

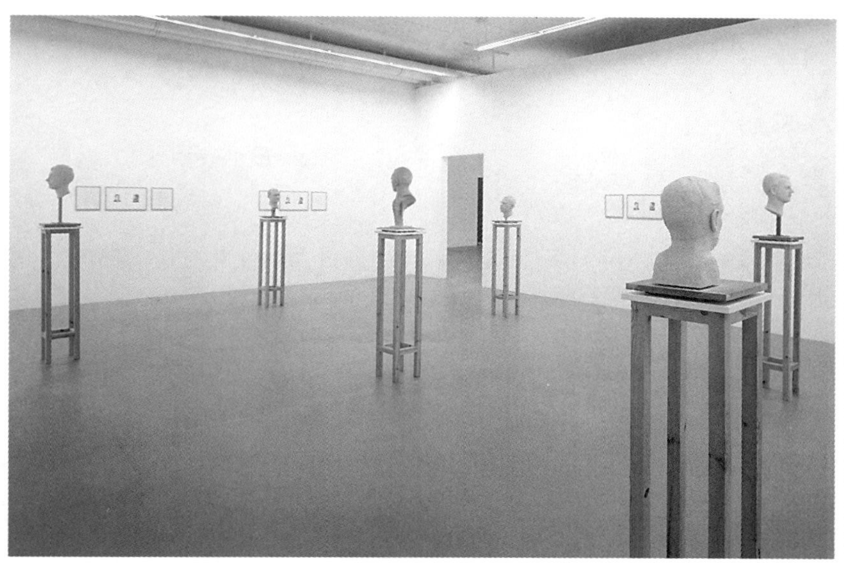

CHRISTINE BORLAND, L'HOMME DOUBLE, 1997, 6 clay heads on plinths (Mengele portrayed by 6 different sculptors after blurred photographs), framed documents, installation view at the migros museum of contemporary art, Zurich / 6 Tonköpfe auf Sockeln (Mengele porträtiert von 6 verschiedenen Künstlern anhand schlechter Photographien), gerahmte Dokumente, Installation im Museum für Gegenwartskunst, Zürich.

melte der Central Park von Demonstranten, die sich zur Israel Day Parade und einer anschliessenden Massenkundgebung zur Unterstützung Israels eingefunden hatten. Selbst ohne Zufälle dieser Art täte man sich schwer, über «Mirroring Evil» zu reflektieren, ohne dabei an die gegenwärtigen Feindseligkeiten im Nahen Osten zu denken.

Als Paul Wolfowitz, einer der erbittertsten Falken und treuesten Freunde Israels in der Regierung Bush, im April bei einer proisraelischen Grosskundgebung in Washington eine Rede hielt, wurde er von der Menge ausgebuht, weil er eine Binsenwahrheit aussprach, nämlich dass «auch unschuldige Palästinenser in grosser Zahl leiden und sterben».[3] In einem Artikel auf der Meinungsseite der *New York Times*, der sich um diesen Vorfall drehte, meinte

Frank Rich: «Der Antisemitismus ist in Amerika auf einem Tiefstand (…) Wenn einer wie Paul Wolfowitz von manchen Juden zu unseren Feinden gerechnet werden kann, bedeutet das, dass wir an den völlig falschen Stellen nach neuen Feinden suchen.»[4] Ja, in die Vorstellung, man werde ständig von allen Seiten angegriffen, mag sogar ein tiefes psychisches Bedürfnis hereinspielen. Tony Judt, Professor für Europäische Geschichte an der New York University, äusserte sich in der *New York Review of Books* wie folgt: «Die meisten Israelis sind nach wie vor in der Geschichte, in der Erzählung ihrer eigenen Einzigartigkeit gefangen. (…) Seit 1967 besteht das Problem für den Rest der Welt darin, dass Israel sich in einer Weise gewandelt hat, die seine traditionelle Selbstdefinition ad absurdum führt. Es ist heute eine regionale Kolo-

nialmacht, manchen Darstellungen zufolge die viertstärkste Militärmacht der Welt. (…) Doch die Israelis selbst sind dieser Tatsache gegenüber blind. In ihren Augen sind sie weiterhin eine kleine Gemeinschaft von Opfern, die sich zurückhaltend und widerwillig verteidigt, obwohl sich alles gegen sie verschworen zu haben scheint.»[5]

In Bezug auf den Holocaust ist jeder historische Relativismus inakzeptabel. Gleichzeitig ist die Vorstellung, wonach vergangenes Leiden einen in der Gegenwart von moralischer Verantwortung befreie, absurd. Das gilt nicht nur für Israel, sondern für alle, die USA eingeschlossen. Schliesslich lieferte Bush's «Krieg gegen den Terrorismus» das Stichwort für die jüngste Eskalation des Nahostkonflikts. Vor langer Zeit verlieh John Cage in seiner «Lecture on Nothing / Vorlesung über nichts» der Hoffnung Ausdruck, ·Amerika möge eines Tages «einfach ein Land sein wie jedes andere. Nicht mehr und nicht weniger.»[6] Dasselbe, so möchte man hinzufügen, wäre Israel und Palästina zu wünschen.

(Übersetzung: Bram Opstelten)

1) Gertrude Stein, «Composition as Explanation" (1926) /«Komposition als Erklärung», in: *Lesebuch zum allmählichen Kennenlernen von Gertrude Stein*, Suhrkamp, Frankfurt am Main 1994, S. 155.
2) Joan Rosenbaum, Text zur Ausstellung «Mirroring Evil: Nazi Imagery/Recent Art», The Jewish Museum, New York, 17. März bis 30. Juni 2002.
3) Paul Wolfowitz, zit. bei Frank Rich, «The Booing of Wolfowitz», in: *The New York Times*, 11. Mai 2002, Op-Ed (Meinungsseite), S. 17.
4) Ebenda.
5) Tony Judt, «The Road to Nowhere», in: *The New York Review of Books*, Nr. 49/8 (9. Mai 2002).
6) John Cage, «Lecture on Nothing», 1949 im Artist's Club in New York, abgedruckt in John Cage, *Silence: Lectures & Writings*, Wesleyan University Press, Hanover 1961.

CUMULUS

Aus Europa

IN JEDER AUSGABE VON PARKETT PEILT EINE CUMULUS-WOLKE AUS
AMERIKA UND EINE AUS EUROPA DIE INTERESSIERTEN KUNSTFREUNDE
AN. SIE TRÄGT PERSÖNLICHE RÜCKBLICKE, BEURTEILUNGEN UND
DENKWÜRDIGE BEGEGNUNGEN MIT SICH – ALS JEWEILS GANZ EIGENE
DARSTELLUNG EINER BERUFLICHEN AUSEINANDERSETZUNG.

IN DIESEM BAND ÄUSSERN SICH THOMAS HAHN AUS PARIS, EIN KRITIKER MIT
DEM SPEZIALGEBIET TANZ, THEATER UND ZIRKUS, SOWIE DER DEUTSCHE KÜNSTLER
OLAV WESTPHALEN, DER IN NEW YORK LEBT UND ARBEITET.

BAUHAUS DER MANEGE

THOMAS HAHN

Immer schwieriger wird es, beim Streifzug durch Frankreichs Kunstszene nicht Jongleuren, Artisten oder Clowns zu begegnen. Der Zirkus ist zu einer blühenden Landschaft geworden, zu einem Laboratorium avantgardistischer Experimente. Mobil, offen, unberechenbar. Es ist, als sollten Oskar Schlemmer, Fernand Léger, Xanti Schawinsky oder László Moholy-Nagy

THOMAS HAHN ist als Kulturkritiker mit Schwerpunkt Tanz, Theater, Körpertheater, Zirkus und Strassentheater tätig. Er lebt in Paris und ist Frankreichkorrespondent mehrerer deutscher Kulturzeitschriften, u. a. auch von *ballet-tanz*.

bald dem Rund verfallende Nachfolger finden. Als in den 20er und 30er Jahren Zirkus und Variété intensiv mit der Kunst des Körpers flirteten, schöpften Pioniere wie Oskar Schlemmer oder die Dadaisten aus dem Potenzial des Zirkus, um dem Körper einen neuen Stellenwert zu verleihen und die Dominanz des Textes auf der Bühne zu durchbrechen.

Aktuell findet Daniel Buren unter einer blauen Kunststoffkuppel die Freiheit, seine Konzepte zur destabilisierenden Wirkung von Farbe *in situ* anzuwenden, unbeleckt von dem ihm lästigen Etikett des offiziellen, staatstragenden Designkünstlers. Farbige Para-

vents verstellen die Sicht auf weisses Pferd und schwarze Tänzerin. Buren irritiert den Blick des Zuschauers, der nach oben in die Spiegel schauen muss, um die Musiker im Inneren eines senkrecht gestreiften Zylinders zu sehen. Der Bauhaus-Riege hätte dieses *in situ* närrischen Spass gemacht. Das Buren-Zelt versteckt sich in einem Niemandsland zwischen der Pariser Ringautobahn und der Bibliothèque François Mitterrand hinter verfallenden Industriebauten. «Buren Cirque» heisst das von Dan Demuynck mit Artisten, Voltigeuren, Jongleuren, Tänzern, Clowns und Musikern ausgestattete Programm. Die Auseinandersetzung mit der Architektur eines geschlossenen, definierten Raumes und dessen Unterteilung in kleine Einheiten, die den Betrachter zwingen, seinen Standpunkt zu definieren, praktiziert Buren sinnigerweise auch im Centre Pompidou, in welchem er gleichzeitig mit der Premiere von «Buren Cirque» hochoffiziell seine Installation LE MUSÉE QUI N'EXISTAIT PAS eröffnet.

Dem Centre Pompidou gleich gegenüber liegt das IRCAM (Institut de Recherche et Coordination Acoustique/ Musique), das sich mit musikalischer Recherche befasst. Roland Auzet vereint in einer Person die verschiedenen Welten, hat Zirkusschulen durchlaufen und experimentiert am IRCAM. Er setzt Artisten zusammen mit «Cyber-Zoo», Ultraschall-Handschuh oder Videokunst in Szene, kombiniert Tanz mit virtueller Jonglage oder Akrobatik mit der Lautmalerei in einem Gedicht von Gherasim Luca, «Héros-limite». Da findet der *saut périlleux* im Munde statt, als Zungenbrecher. Auzet ist Perkussionist und nennt seine Gesamtkunstwerke «Le Cirque du Tambour».

Es muss nicht immer die neueste Musik sein, die neue Pisten erschliesst. Bernard Kudlak, einer der Pioniere des Nouveau Cirque, Gründer und Leiter des Cirque Plume, inszenierte Ende 2001 eine neue Version von Mauricio Kagels *Variété (Opéra-cirque)*, das 1977 uraufgeführt wurde. Ein Werk, das einen gewissen Einfluss auf die Erneuerung des Zirkus gehabt haben mag. Selbst das Variété, in Frankreich Music-Hall geheissen, war einst ein Ort der Recherche, sagt Nadège Maruta, vor ein paar Jahren noch Solistin am Moulin Rouge, heute Choreographin und, so hofft sie, bald Mitarbeiterin eines neu eröffneten Variété-Theaters in Paris, in dem Akrobatik sich wieder mit Avant-

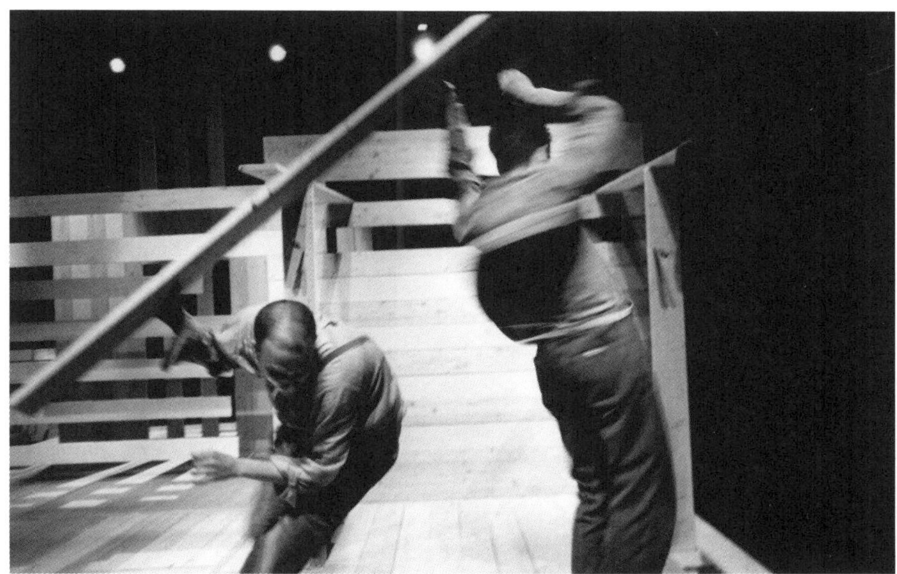

METZGER/ZIMMERMANN/DE PERROT, HOI , Gregor Metzger,
Martin Zimmermann, Théâtre Vidy-Lausanne, September 2001.
(ALLE PHOTOS: MARIO DEL CURTO, LAUSANNE)

garde reimen soll, so wie schon vor der Bauhaus-Zeit mit Loïe Fuller.

Zirkus ist heute nicht d i e , aber e i n e Art nouveau, die ganz selbstverständlich die Genres vermischt. Der Jongleur ist gleichzeitig Clown und der Akrobat Schauspieler. Der Rappe Zingaro wurde zur lebendigen Skulptur und nach seinem betrauerten Tod in *Triptyk* durch skelettartige Pferdeskulpturen von Jean-Lois Sauvat ersetzt. Hela Fattoumi choreographierte 1999 *Vita Nova*. Die Artisten mussten sich dabei einer ganz neuen Art von Geräten bedienen, gestaltet von Raymond Sarti und, wiederum, Les Bains Douches. Sanft geschwungene Skulpturen aus Edelstahl machten – nach Art von Daniel Buren – das Kunststück zum Kunst-Stück. Und die Compagnie Les Arts Sauts eröffnete einen völlig neuen

Blickwinkel auf die Trapezflieger, als sie die Zuschauer zu *Kayassine* in Liegestühlen Platz nehmen liess. Über den Köpfen erstreckte sich eine gigantische Stahlträgerstruktur von Patrick Claudy. Ob gerade wie ein Kran oder geschwungen wie ein Brückenträger, an ihr illustrierten die Trapezkünstler ein romantisches Sternenmärchen.

Noch ist die tiefe Recherche zum Bezug zwischen Zirkus und zeitgenössischer Kunst Sache einiger Individuen, doch auch die heute allgegenwärtige Vermengung von Artistik und Tanz begann mit dem Forschungsdrang einiger Visionäre. Hervorheben muss man hier aber, dass die Verbindung von Tanz und Zirkus nicht nur den Künstlern zu verdanken ist, sondern auch der Institution, die bewusst bekannte Choreographen dazu einlud, mit Abschlussjahrgängen der staatlichen französischen Zirkusakademie Bühnenwerke zu kreieren. Bildende Künstler müssen sich mit ihrer Faszination für die Welt der Artisten bescheiden. Daniel Buren kassiert nicht einen Euro Honorar für seinen Zirkus *in situ.* Ihn trieb der Wunsch ein Experiment zu Ende zu führen, das er vor zwei Jahren mit Dan Demuynck und Adrienne Larue (Compagnie Foraine) begonnen hatte. Damals gestaltete er die Anfangssequenz, den Einzug der Artisten. Die anderen «Zirkusnummern» gestalteten Christian Boltanski, Jannis Kounellis, Giulio Paolini, Claude Acquart vom Kunstzentrum Les Bains Douches in Montbéliard und andere. «Et qui libre?» hiess das Programm.

Frei ist der Zirkus. Frei davon, sich vom traditionellen Familienbetrieb mit seinen Pailletten und Dressurnummern absetzen zu müssen. Frei davon, diese immer aufs Neue zu parodieren, was viele trotzdem weiter tun. Frei davon, ein Thema, eine Geschichte oder sonst einen Zusammenhang zu konstruieren, was oft genug künstlich, verkrampft und überflüssig wirkte. Frei davon, sich die Aufteilung in Nummern zu untersagen, weil der Nouveau Cirque vor nunmehr zwanzig Jahren angetreten war, die Solidarität des Kollektivs zu preisen und Dressur als politisch unkorrekte Quälerei zu brandmarken. Inzwischen darf man auch wieder mit echten Tieren arbeiten, ohne als reaktionär zu gelten. Die Compagnie Foraine liess schon 1993 vier Elefanten in ihrer Bearbeitung von *King Lear* auftreten, bevor sie ihre Folgewerke Marcel Duchamp widmete.

Heute ist der Zirkus selbst ein Bauhaus. Alle Elemente liegen bereit, von mutigen Abenteurern beliebig kombiniert zu werden: Tanz, Theater, Artistik, zeitgenössische Musik und Kunst, Abstraktion und Narration, neue Technologien, Tiere, Schweiss und Sägespäne. In Zelten, in Theatern oder im öffentlichen Raum.

In diesem Umfeld des Aufbruchs agieren auch drei Schweizer Künstler, deren Erfolg scheinbar aus dem Nichts genau diese Bauhaus-Freiheit illustriert. Vor fünf Jahren tanzte Gregor Metzger bei Béjart, bevor er mit La Fura dels Baus das Bilderstürmen explorierte, und Martin Zimmermann tourte als Mitbegründer mit der Compagnie Anomalie. *Le cri du caméléon,* eine Zusammenarbeit zwischen Anomalie und Josef Nadj wurde ein Welterfolg. Es war die erste grosse Produktion eines Choreographen mit dem Abschlussjahrgang des Centre National des Arts du Cirque (CNAC) in Chalons-en-Champagne. Dessen Leiter, Bernard Turin, wagte das Experiment, das sich bisher jährlich wiederholte, zuletzt mit Philippe Decouflé. Zu Metzger und Zimmermann gehört auch Dimitri de Perrot, Komponist und DJ, der in Zürich mit Sendak, in London im Blue Note auftrat und regelmässig mit dem australischen Gitarristen Hugo Race zusammenarbeitet. Gemeinsam haben die drei ein Künstlerkollektiv gegründet. Metzger / Zimmermann / de Perrot heissen sie.[1] Damit war das Schicksal des DJ besiegelt. In jedem Dokument wird er als Letzter genannt. Dabei war gerade die Erweiterung der Kombination Zirkus/Tanz durch DJ-ing und Scratch der Paukenschlag, der ihrem ersten Werk, *Gopf,* zu fast ebensolchem Ruhm verhalf, wie er *Le cri du caméléon* beschieden war. Denn so brillant die Verrenkungen, der Slapstick und die Tanzzitate von Metzger und Zimmermann auch sind, gerade der konzeptuelle Geniestreich, die sechs Platten-

spieler des Musikers de Perrot in ihre Bühnenbilder zu integrieren, liess die Zirkuswelt aufhorchen. So verbindet sie mit Werken wie *Le Cirque du Tambour* oder *Variété (Opéra-cirque)* die Suche nach der Körperlichkeit des Klanges und der Klanglichkeit des Körpers. Auch ihr merkwürdiger Bandwurmname hob sie heraus aus der Masse der sich bildenden Kompanien, die als Duos, Trios und manchmal sogar solo mit ihrer Artistik den Tanzboden erobern.

Man riet ihnen, sich «Gopf» zu nennen, wie ihr erstes Stück. Sie lehnten ab. Ihre Kompanie ist kein Selbstzweck, keine Selbst-Aufgabe; kein Endprodukt, sondern die Permanenz einer ständig neu enstehenden Begegnung dreier Individuen, Symbol der Freiheit der Mitglieder eines Kollektivs, das erweiterbar bleibt, reduzierbar und variabel wie das Variété. Schon die Gründung des Kollektivs und der explizite Ausruf seiner Mobilität sind als Kunstwerk zu verstehen. Offenlegung des sonst Versteckten ist das Handwerkszeug des Clowns. Auch diese Traditionsfigur hat sich von alten Klischees befreit. Man kann Clownfestivals besuchen, ohne einer einzigen roten Nase zu begegnen. Chaplin war ein Mime, was aber sind Metzger/Zimmermann/de Perrot? Clowns irgendwo ganz bestimmt, Tänzer eventuell, Performer ganz sicher, ein Schritt in der Entwicklung der aufführenden Künste ganz offensichtlich, denn wer so neu ist, dass man ihn nicht einordnen kann, dem gehört die Zukunft. Mit *Gopf* konnte man sie noch der Kategorie Josef Nadj zuordnen, der allerdings selber Graphik studiert hat, Skulpturen fertigt (und das ebenso faszinierend wie Jan Fabre) und zugibt, dass er sich nur deshalb als Choreograph klassifizieren

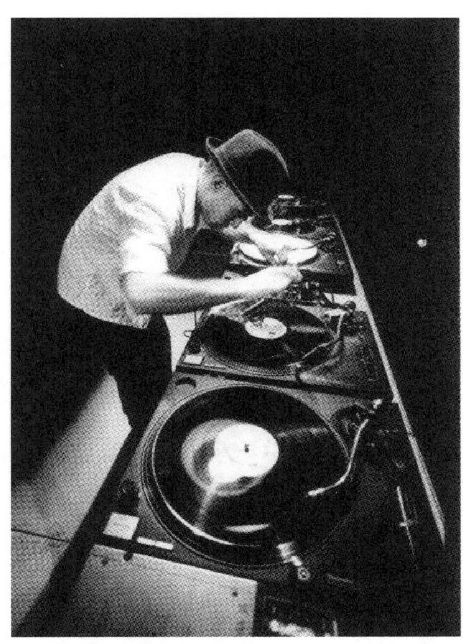

liess, weil er unter diesem Etikett am ehesten Subventionen erhoffen konnte.

Nach *Gopf* kreierten Metzger/Zimmermann/de Perrot *Hoi*, das endgültig eine ausschliesslich ihnen eigene Handschrift trägt. Noch wörtlicher ist hier der Bezug des kollektiv gestalteten Bühnenbilds zum Bauhaus zu nehmen. Drei Urschweizer Kreaturen und universelle Eigenbrötler nutzen den Bretterwald, der anfänglich noch als Parkett und glatt wie ein Bergsee daliegt, um Berge, Hütten, Forst und Furcht entstehen zu lassen. Die mobile Skulptur ist in ihrer Funktion für das Stück und in ihrem Stellenwert als Kunstwerk mit Burens *in situ*-Gestaltung oder Sartis Geräten in *Vita Nova* vergleichbar. Wie in *Gopf* hat de Perrot seine sechs Plattenspieler dabei, die jetzt aber senkrecht stehen und trotzdem funktionieren. Wenn das nicht zirkusreif ist! Abwechselnd tauchen sie aus der Unterwelt auf. Wie in *Gopf* ist die Bühne in ständiger Bewegung, quasi als vierte Figur, welche die Akteure verschlingt, ausspeit, schlägt oder narrt.

Der internationale Erfolg von Metzger/Zimmermann/de Perrot gründet sich auch darauf, dass ihre Figuren profunde Fragen an das Zusammenleben der Menschen und an die *condition humaine* stellen und in verschiedenen Situationen ganz unterschiedliche Reaktionen erzeugen. Den Ruf nach Freiheit zum Beispiel. Da stand nach einer Aufführung von *Gopf* in Belgrad, kurz vor den Wahlen, das Publikum mit erhobener Faust im Raum. So unmittelbar kann die Botschaft der Freiheit empfangen werden, die entsteht, wenn Künstler sich aller Genrezwänge entledigen und sich durch ein kafkaeskes Labyrinth kämpfen.

Über den Disziplinen steht die Disziplin, die man erwirbt, wenn man bei Béjart zum Solisten avanciert oder jahrelang mit Zirkusproduktionen tourt. Dort lernt man den Umgang mit dem Körper – dem eigenen und dem der Partner. De Perrot, der DJ, brauchte dafür ein Warm-up mit *Gopf*. In *Hoi* partizipiert er nun aktiv am Perpetuum mobile der Berggestalten. Sie bezeichnen sich als Band, in der jeder auf jeden eingehen muss, damit das Zusammenspiel funktioniert.

Konzeptkunst liegt ihnen nahe. So werden sie für die nächste Ausgabe des Festivals «Iles de danses» zusammen mit dem Aktionskünstler San Keller ein Event zelebrieren. Hundertzwanzig Stunden lang haben sie nun ihren Hit *Gopf* gespielt, und um diese Zeit noch einmal ablaufen zu lassen, werden sie hundertzwanzig Stunden am Stück aktiv sein.

Der Zirkus destabilisiert erstarrende Kunstformen und schafft neue Dynamik. So sah es schon Fernand Léger, als er schrieb: «Geh in den Zirkus! Nichts ist so rund wie der Zirkus. (…) Das Publikum wird zum mobilen Dekor. Es bewegt sich mit dem Ablauf der Handlung. (…) Geh in den Zirkus, weg von der Geometrie rechteckiger Fenster, hinein ins Wunderland sich drehender Kreise.»[2]

Bei so viel Drang zur Innovation stellt sich die Frage, wie es überhaupt dazu kommen konnte, dass Zirkus über einige Nachkriegsdekaden als rückständige Kunstform angesehen wurde. Vor dem Krieg noch als soziokultureller Katalysator verstanden, wurde der Familienzirkus ab den 70er Jahren ein Opfer der allgemeinen Beschleunigung. Ein Hort der Traurigkeit, finanziell gebeutelt, behaftet mit einem begrenzten Programm aus vererbten Kunststücken, die im Lauf der Zeit immer schlechter wurden. So war es oder so wollte man es sehen, als Jack Lang 1984 das Centre National des Arts du Cirque (CNAC) in Chalons-en-Champagne gründete. Schon vorher deuteten Pioniere wie Christian Taguet (Le Puits aux images, heute: Le Cirque Baroque) oder Bernard Kudlak (Cirque Plume) an, dass sich, wie im Tanz, eine neue Ästhetik gegen die alte durchsetzen sollte. Bis wohin dieser Weg einstweilen geführt hat, demonstrieren Metzger/Zimmermann/de Perrot oder *Le Cirque du Tambour*, gleich ob man sie nun als Motor oder als vorläufig neuestes Produkt einer Bewegung ansieht. Wohin die noch führen wird, darauf dürfen wir gespannt sein wie ein Hochseil.

1) Metzger/Zimmermann/de Perrot finden Sie im Internet unter: www.mzdp.ch
2) Fernand Léger, «Zirkus», in: *Mensch, Maschine, Malerei*, übers. v. Robert Füglister, Benteli, Bern 1971, S. 177. (Original: *Fonctions de la Peinture*, Paris 1965.)

BAUHAUS IN THE ARENA

THOMAS HAHN

It is becoming increasingly difficult, on touring the art scene in France, not to meet up with jugglers, artistes, or clowns. The circus has become a blossoming landscape, a laboratory of avant-garde experiments. Mobile, open, unpredictable. It looks as if successors to Oskar Schlemmer, Fernand Léger, Xanti Schawinsky, or László Moholy-Nagy have succumbed to the ring. In the twenties and thirties, when circus and vaudeville began flirting intensely with the art of the body, pioneers like Oskar Schlemmer or the Dadaists exploited the potential of the circus, lending new significance to the body and parrying the dominance of the spoken word on stage.

Currently, under a blue plastic dome, Daniel Buren has found the freedom to implement his concepts on the destabilizing effect of color *in situ*, unsullied by the annoying label of official state designer. Colorful screens obstruct the view of the black dancer and her white horse. Buren forces us to look up at mirrors overhead in order to see the musicians inside a vertically

THOMAS HAHN writes on dance, theater, physical theater, circus, and street theater. He lives in Paris and is the French correspondent for several German-language publications, including *ballet-tanz*, Europe's leading dance magazine.

striped cylinder. The Bauhaus crew would have been thoroughly delighted by this *in situ* event. The Buren tent is tucked away behind abandoned industrial buildings in a no man's land between the ring-road around Paris and the Bibliothèque François Mitterrand. *Buren Cirque* is what Dan Demuynck calls his program fitted with acrobats, trapeze artistes, jugglers, dancers, clowns, and musicians. Experimentation with the architecture of a closed, defined room, and its subdivision into small units that compel viewers to define their standpoint, also tellingly characterizes Buren's presentation at Centre Pompidou, where the highly official opening of his installation, LE MUSÉE QUI N'EXISTAIT PAS, took place at the same time as the premier of *Buren Cirque*.

Directly opposite the Centre Pompidou is the musical research center, IRCAM (Institut de Recherche et Coordination Acoustique/Musique). Roland Auzet unites discrete worlds in one person, has trained at circus academies, and is now experimenting at the IRCAM. He incorporates artists in a cyber zoo and in video art, has them work with ultrasonic gloves, combines dance with virtual juggling, or acrobatics with the onomatopoeia of a poem by Gherasim Luca, *Le Héros-limite*. There, the salto mortale is a tongue twister, a

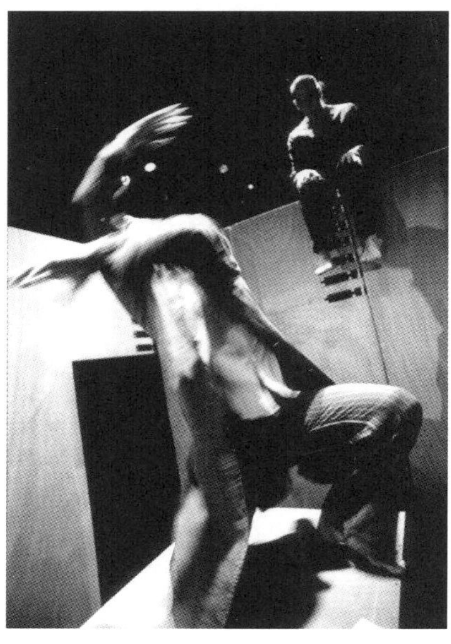

METZGER/ZIMMERMANN/DE PERROT, GOPF, Gregor Metzger, Martin Zimmermann, Kaserne Basel, März 2000.

feat of lips and mouth. Auzet is a percussionist and calls his gesamtkunstwerks *Le Cirque du Tambour.*

It doesn't always have to be the latest music in order to chart new territory. At the end of 2001, Bernard Kudlak, one of the pioneers of the Nouveau Cirque and founder-cum-director of the Cirque Plume, staged a new version of Mauricio Kagel's *Variété (Opéra-cirque)*, first performed in 1977—a work that may well have had a say in the revival of the circus. Even music hall, as it is also called in France, was once a place for research, according to Nadège Maruta. A few years ago Maruta was still a soloist at Moulin Rouge; she is now a choreographer and soon hopes to be working at a new vaudeville theater about to open in Paris, where acrobatics will once again rub shoulders with the avant-garde, as it did with Loïe Fuller even before the advent of the Bauhaus.

Today circus is quite literally an art nouveau, where mixing up genres comes naturally. The juggler is also the clown and the acrobat the actor. Black Zingaro was a living sculpture and after his deeply mourned death, skeletal horse sculptures by Jean-Lois Sauvat replaced him in *Triptyk*. In 1999 Hela Fattoumi choreographed *Vita Nova*. The artistes had to cope with an entirely new kind of equipment designed by Raymond Sarti and by Les Bains Douches. Softly sweeping sculptures of stainless-steel turned the artistry of the feat into the artistry of art, à la Daniel Buren, while the Compagnie Les Arts Sauts created an entirely new vision of the flying trapeze, when spectators at *Kayassine* were invited to take their "seats" in loungers. A gigantic load bearing structure of steel by Patrick Claudy was spread out overhead. Looking like a crane at one moment and a graceful bridgehead the next, it provided the airy foundations for a romantic fairy tale of stars on the flying trapeze.

In-depth exploration of the relationship between circus and contemporary art is still the domain of a select few, but today's omnipresent blend of circus artistry and dance was also originally inspired by the experimental drive of only a few, rare visionaries.

Significantly, the connection between dance and circus is indebted not only to the artists involved, but also to the institution that chose to invite well-known choreographers to create works for the stage with the graduating classes of the State Circus Academy in France. For fine artists, the only reward is their fascination with the world of artistes. Daniel Buren is not earning a single Euro for his circus, *in situ*. He was motivated by the desire to complete an experiment that he had begun two years earlier with Dan Demuynck and Adrienne Larue (Compagnie Foraine). At the time he had designed the opening parade of artistes. The other "circus numbers" were designed by Christian Boltanski, Jannis Kounellis, Giulio Paolini, Claude Acquart of the art center Les Bains Douches in Montbéliard, and others. The program was called *Et qui libre*?

The circus is free in spirit. Free of the need to pit itself against traditional family operations with their sequins and tamed animals. Free of the need to caricature them, though many continue to do so. Free of the need to construct a theme, a story, or a red thread of some kind, which may sometimes seem phony, labored, and superficial anyway. Free of the need to renounce the presentation of numbers because Nouveau Cirque took the leap, nigh on twenty years ago, to champion the solidarity of the collective and to condemn the taming of animals as politically incorrect and cruel. In the meantime, groups can work with real animals again without being written off as reactionary. In 1993, the Compagnie Foraine flaunted four elephants on stage in their production of *King Lear*, before devoting themselves in their later productions to Marcel Duchamp.

Circus has become its own Bauhaus. All of the elements are at hand, ready to be combined at will by daring adventurers: dance, theater, artistry, contemporary music and art, abstraction and narration, new technologies, animals,

METZGER/ZIMMERMANN/DE PERROT, HOI, Gregor Metzger, Dimitri de Perrot, Théâtre Vidy-Lausanne, September 2001.

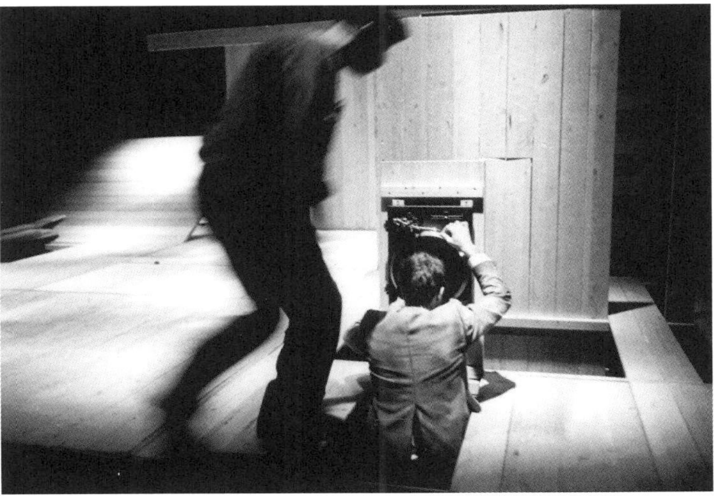

sweat, and sawdust. In tents, in theaters, in public spaces.

In this open-ended atmosphere of change and renewal, three Swiss artists have burst upon the scene, instantly chalking up successes out of thin air, in perfect illustration of Bauhaus freedom. Five years ago Gregor Metzger was dancing with Béjart before he started exploring iconoclasm with La Fura dels Baus, and Martin Zimmermann was touring with the Compagnie Anomalie. *Le cri du caméléon,* the internationally acclaimed collaboration between Anomalie and Josef Nadj, was the first major production of a choreographer with the graduating class at the Centre National des Arts du Cirque (CNAC) in Chalons-en-Champagne. Its director, Bernard Turin, hazarded the

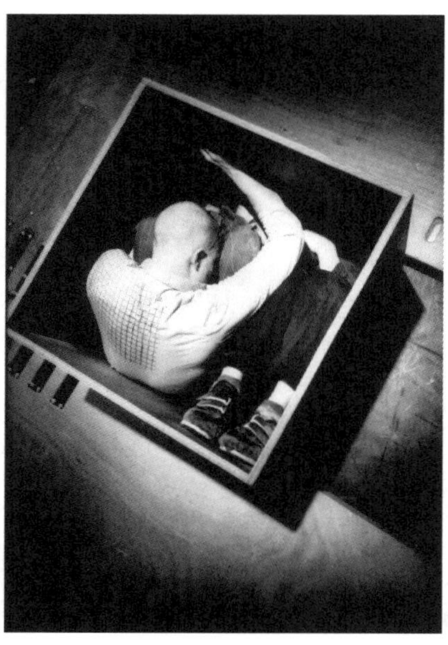

initial experiment; it has been repeated annually ever since, most recently with Philippe Decouflé. The third member of the group, after Metzger and Zimmermann, is Dimitri de Perrot, composer and DJ, who has performed with Sendak in Zurich and at the Blue Note in London as well as collaborating regularly with Australian guitarist Hugo Race. The three founded an artist's collective: Metzger/Zimmermann/de Perrot.[1] The DJ's fate was thereby sealed; he is the last-named member of the trio in every document—this one included. But the fusion of DJing and scratch with the circus/dance combination actually tipped the scales in making their first piece, *Gopf,* nearly as famous as *Le cri du caméléon*. The brilliance of the contortions, the slapstick, and the dance citations of Metzger and Zimmermann are uncontested, but the idea of integrating the musician' six record players in their stage set was a conceptual stroke of genius that made the circus world sit up and take notice. Thus, their inquiry into the physicality of sound and the tonality of the body shows an affinity with such works as *Le Cirque du Tambour* or *Variété (Opéra-cirque)*. And their odd, drawn-out name set them off against the mushrooming companies that are struggling to take the dance world by storm as duos or trios or even solo performers.

It was suggested that the trio call themselves "Gopf" after their first show. They refused. Their company is not an end in itself, not a self-imposed task; it is not an end product but rather the permanence of ceaselessly new encounters among three individuals, the symbol of the freedom of members of a collective that remains as expandable, reducible, and variable as vaudeville.

Even the founding of the collective and the explicit proclamation of its mobility are to be understood as an artwork. The exposure of things ordinarily concealed is the handicraft of the clown. This traditional figure has now jettisoned ingrained clichés. One can attend clown festivals without seeing a single red nose. Chaplin was a mime but what is Metzger/Zimmermann/de Perrot? Most certainly a manner of clown, possibly dancers, definitely performers, and obviously a step in the evolution of the performing arts, because any group so new that they can't be pigeonholed have the future in their pockets. *Gopf* was still more or less classifiable as belonging to the category Josef Nadj, although Nadj himself studied graphic arts, produced sculptures (easily as fascinating as those of Jan Fabre), and admits that he only allowed himself to be called a choreographer because that label was useful in applying for funds.

After *Gopf,* Metzger/Zimmermann/de Perrot created *Hoi.* The group now had a production unmistakably stamped with a full-fledged signature of their own. Even more literal is the relationship of the collectively designed stage set to Bauhaus. Three primeval Swiss creatures and universal eccentrics belabor a gathering of planks, which starts out as parquetry and lies there as smooth as a mountain lake, to conjure mountains, huts, forests, and fear. Their mobile sculpture, as it functions in the piece and as a work of art, is comparable to Buren's *in situ* design or Sarti's gear in *Vita Nova.* As in *Gopf,* de Perrot has his six record players, which now appear upended on stage but they still work. Now there's a circus trick for you! The performers emerge alternately out of the underworld. Once again the stage is constantly moving, in effect a fourth performer, who devours, spews out, beats up, or makes fools of the three protagonists.

The international success of Metzger/Zimmermann/de Perrot is also indebted to the fact that the three figures raise profound questions about human cohabitation and the *condition humaine* and manage to generate startlingly different reactions in various situations. The call for freedom, for example. After a performance of *Gopf* in Belgrade, shortly before the elections, the spectators rose to their feet with fists raised. That is how immediate the response can be to the message of freedom that emerges when artists completely ignore the constraints of genre and fight their way through a Kafkaesque labyrinth.

Disciplines are eclipsed by the discipline acquired when one becomes a soloist under the tutelage of Béjart or spends years touring with circus productions. There one learns how to master the body—one's own and that of one's partner. De Perrot, the DJ, used *Gopf* to warm up. By the time *Hoi* hit the road, he was already an active participant of the mountain imps' *perpetuum mobile*. They describe themselves as a band, in which they all have to be attuned to each other for the ensemble to work.

Conceptual art appeals to them. The next time the "Iles de danses" festival rolls around, they will celebrate an event with Swiss action artist San Keller, to last 120 hours in honor of the fact that *Gopf* has so far played 120 times.

Circus destabilizes entrenched art forms and creates a new dynamics. Fernand Léger had already recognized

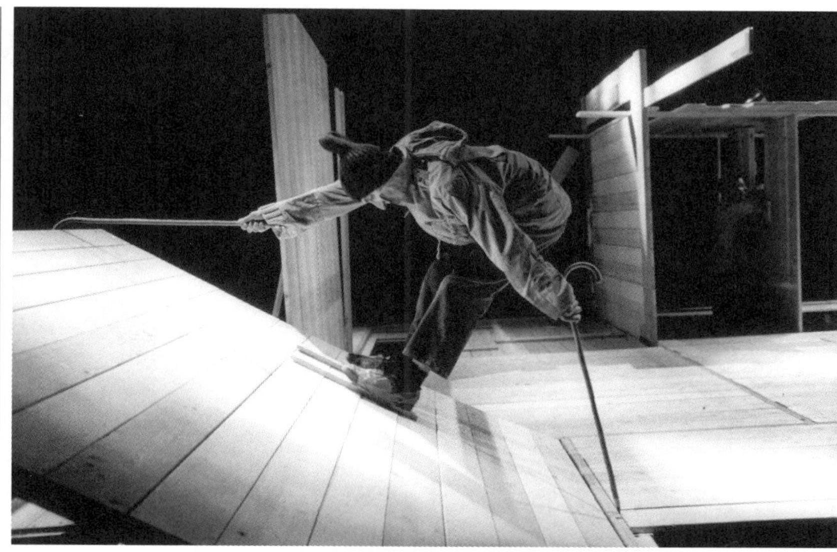

METZGER/ZIMMERMANN/DE PERROT, HOI,
Martin Zimmermann, Théâtre Vidy-Lausanne, September 2001.
(PHOTOS: MARIO DEL CURTO, LAUSANNE)

this when he wrote: "Go to the circus! Nothing is as round as the circus. The audience is mobile embellishment, following the movement of the artistes. This is the end of your rectangles, your geometrical windows; you have entered the land of revolving action."[2]

With so much innovative drive, one wonders how it was possible to view the circus as a backward art form for so many decades after the Second World War. Still considered a sociocultural catalyst before the war, the family circus fell victim to the acceleration that prevailed from the seventies onwards. A sanctuary of sadness, financially battered, saddled with a limited program of inherited numbers that kept getting worse: That was the official view in 1984, when Jack Lang founded the Centre National des Arts du Cirque (CNAC) in Chalons-en-Champagne.

But, as in dance, a new aesthetic was already testing its wings as indicated by such pioneers as Christian Taguet (Le Puits aux images, now called Le Cirque Baroque) or Bernard Kudlak (Cirque Plume). Metzger/Zimmermann/de Perrot or *Le Cirque du Tambour* brilliantly demonstrate the consequences of these early attempts to oppose the old forms, regardless of whether they are seen as the driving force or the latest product of a movement. We are as taut as a tightrope in anticipation of future developments.

(Translation: Catherine Schelbert)

1) You will find Metzger/Zimmermann/de Perrot's homepage at: www.mzdp.ch
2) Fernand Léger, "Le cirque" in *Fonctions de la peinture* (Paris: Gallimard, 1997), p. 267. Also published in English: *Functions of Painting* (London: Thames & Hudson / New York: Viking, 1973).

BALKON

Weltering in Blood
ARTEMISIA GENTILESCHI (1593–1653)

SHEENA WAGSTAFF

The savage and bloody spectacle of Judith in the act of murdering Holofernes is one of the iconographic paintings with which the name Artemisia Gentileschi has come to be associated. Gentileschi painted two versions: one at the beginning of her career in about 1612, the other when she had established herself, in 1620, as an important history painter in Rome and Florence.[1] To chance upon these works in uptown Manhattan on a spring morning in 2002 is at once a profoundly unsettling and revelatory experience.[2] Both paintings have an extraordinary authority and facility, given potency by the terrible impact of Judith's horrifying deed. Not until the calculated bloodbaths of the Vienna Actionists (Rudolf Schwarzkogler, Otto Mühl, Hermann Nitsch, and Günter Brus) in the sixties and seventies did the gory slashing and severance of a vital appendage to a body trunk carry such shock value. More contemporary versions in which bodily fluids define

SHEENA WAGSTAFF is Director of Exhibitions & Displays at Tate Modern, London.

works of performative art can be seen generally as oblique homages to, or sanitized ideologically feeble attempts to emulate, the intense taboo-breaking rituals of their elders. These include the pseudo-martyrdom of Sebastian Horsley's recent crucifixion in the Philippines; the portentous mutilations, bandagings, and bleedings of Franko B; and David Blaine's unique form of popular entertainment in ghoulish, bloody sleights of hand or body.

The painting JUDITH SLAYING HOLOFERNES has come to be linked inextricably to the events of Gentileschi's personal life. Partly through its recurrent reference in popular cultural forms such as novels[3] and films during the last decade, this powerful emblematic image has become a ubiquitous indicator of Gentileschi's physically violated state and assumed emotional trauma. The tendency to associate the artist Gentileschi with the biblical Judith and her grisly deed has been further perpetuated by a large amount of critical literature produced in the past 25 years, devoted variously to substantiating, refuting or diffusing a biographically-related appreciation of the work.

Only recently has this formidable painting been liberated from a hermetic, self-referential and spiky academic fest of psychoanalytic, feminist and semiological readings—though these have been crucial to establishing a serious scholarly interpretation of Gentileschi's work—by a refreshingly broader historic cultural assessment of seventeenth-century Baroque Italy.

The ghastly demise of Holofernes at the hand of Judith was not an unusual topic for the Baroque period. Indeed, biblical stories from the Old Testament as raw material for narrative painting were highly popular in the sixteenth and seventeenth centuries with patrons and artists alike. Some of the better known artists who took up the challenge to explore the dramatic potential of Judith's tale include Mantegna, Botticelli, Rubens, Caravaggio, and Orazio Gentileschi.

Not unlike the Ann Lee manga character, bought and then co-opted by a group of contemporary artists including Pierre Huyghe and Liam Gillick, Judith became separated from her original context by becoming a kind of performative cipher, resulting in an inordinate number of divergent versions of the story. Indeed, the differing interpretive and artistic means by which Judith was repeatedly represented over the years necessarily changed the meaning of its emblematic representation each time. As with the Ann Lee character in a different medium, Judith carries rich potential for both explicit formal expression as well as implicit response to the conditions and time of its making.

The original story of why Holofernes had to be murdered is an apocryphal one. It dates from the second century B.C. and describes how the merciless Assyrian army, led by their general Holofernes, was besieging Judith's city of Bethulia. Judith's plan to deliver her countrymen from this potentially fatal scourge was simple but highly dangerous. Donning her most elegant clothing, she set out for the enemy's settlement, accompanied by her maidservant, Abra. Offering to serve Holofernes and his king, the women were given entry to the camp. Holofernes was then so captivated by Judith's beauty that he invited her to dine with him. Thereupon, rather surprisingly, he drank himself into a stupor and passed out. Seeing her opportunity, Judith seized her host's sword and, with the help of Abra, who restrains the convulsive flailing arms of the semi-conscious Holofernes, hacked through the sinew and bone of his neck and decapitated him. The two women then concealed the grisly trophy in a basket, escaped the camp and returned to Bethulia where they triumphantly displayed Holofernes' head to the Israelite army—demonstrating at one stroke both the emasculated and literally head-less condition of the Assyrian army. Thus the besieged troops

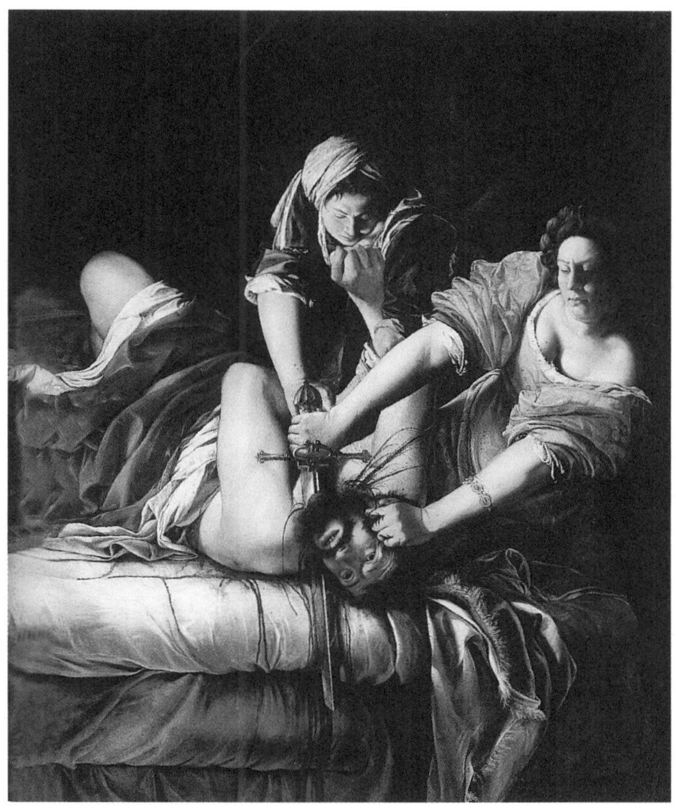

ARTEMISIA GENTILESCHI, JUDITH SLAYING HOLOFERNES, ca. 1620, oil on canvas, 64 x 39³/₈" / JUDITH ENTHAUPTET HOLOFERNES, Öl auf Leinwand, 162,5 x 100 cm, Galleria degli Uffizi, Firenze.

were galvanized to victory—and Judith is acclaimed for having saved both her city and nation.

The theme of women killing men was popular in the middle ages as an admonitory tale illustrating the unnatural reversal of the divine order of the hierarchy of the sexes. By the sixteenth century, this representation of a subverted social order had come to have a sexual dimension alongside the political meaning of the original, apocryphal text with the assumption that Judith had gained access to Holofernes because of her beauty rather than the potency of Israelite military secrets she was feigning to offer.

Artemisia Gentileschi made her artistic debut in Rome in about 1610 (the year of Caravaggio's death) at the age of 17—and embarked about a year later on her first version of JUDITH SLAYING HOLOFERNES. Like the best of the seventeenth-century artists, Gentileschi had elected to compete at the loftiest level as a history painter of instructional, inspirational and elevating religious, historical and mythological scenes. By choosing to depict in this early work the very act of Holofernes' homicide, however, Gentileschi departed from the traditional prototypes of the theme that depicted the aftermath of the nasty deed, usually the two women furtively leaving the camp and carrying the basket in which Holofernes' head rests.

A determining factor in Artemisia's training as an artist was her father, Orazio Gentileschi, whose encounter with Caravaggio in 1600 was the central event of his life. Gentileschi was to become the most singular of those artists who were directly influenced by Caravaggio. Although Artemisia's knowledge of Caravaggio was indirect, she understood the revolutionary qualities of Caravaggio's vision through her father's work as well as that of other painters in Rome. The subversive axiom of Caravaggio lay in his demand for a radical rethinking of the relationship between the imagined and the real, the artist and model. In the critical language of the day, he proposed a "truth" in painting, *il vero*, which prized a direct observation against the imaginative "verisimilitude" of Renaissance painting which extolled the exemplary and ideal. It was Caravaggio's unprecedented and ultimate achievement to transform the verity of the ordinary everyday scene and imbue it with extraordinary drama.

While Orazio's (at least four)[4] depictions of Judith and her Maidservant followed the dominant prototype of the period—the moments after the killing—it was Caravaggio's JUDITH DECAPITATING HOLOFERNES of 1599 which was crucial to Artemisia's conception of the theme.[5] The winsome Judith is portrayed as well-progressed with her task, having already gingerly sawn through half of Holofernes' neck at arm's length. She draws back, frowning with effort and repugnance as she considers her act, passively observed by a geriatric Abra. Notwithstanding the dramatic contrast of light and shadow and his careful and penetrating illumination of Judith in her harrowing act, Caravaggio's scene is nevertheless an arrested action. It allows the viewer to linger over detail and form, almost like scanning a still life—indeed, a stilled life.

Although Artemisia's version emulates the awkwardly outstretched arms of Caravaggio's Judith, her Judith is entirely credible as an assassin, further aided by a complicitly active Abra who uses her weight to control the frenzied Holofernes, his eyes taking on the agonized glaze of dying, as Judith finishes up her mutilation.

Artemisia amplifies Caravaggio's vision by showing what violence really looks like. Brought to the very edge of the bed where the white sheets are already stained with rivulets of blood coursing down the side of the mattress, the viewer—drawn directly into the action—senses the physical effort required to slash skin, rip through flesh, shatter bone, and smell the hot sweet stickiness of freshly spurting blood. Artemisia's strongly expressive presentation of the story—through an unrefined naturalism of firm or flayed flesh and muscle, through keenly observed details of determined or tormented physiognomies, through the tangible physicality of three people struggling for life or death—is enhanced by the bold drama of Caravaggist lighting, and results in an extraordinarily visceral and psychologically vivid work. It depicts and defines the actual moment of death. It is the ultimate portrait of a killing, a politically expedient execution.

When Artemisia Gentileschi embarked on her first version of the heroic Judith in 1612, her career was just beginning at a vital time in early-Baroque Rome during the Counter-Reformation. Her second version of Judith was completed the same year as the Battle of the White Mountain (near Prague, 1620), an early skirmish of the Thirty Years' War, in which the Catholics won a decisive victory over the Protestants.[6] As the historian Richard Spear describes it, people in Rome must have been aware that this great conflict was tearing Latin Christianity apart, not least because the Vatican was trying, with little success, to appear neutral and broker peace between the two sides. As a Catholic, Artemisia Gentileschi must have known of these affairs, though it is impossible to know how much she cared.

Although Italy was then at the conflux of Counter-Reformation Catholicism on the one hand and the development of the modern formation of the secular nation-state on the other, the systems of patronage from the Renaissance still prevailed: Artemisia's second version of JUDITH SLAYING HOLOFERNES (1620) was commissioned by Cosimo II de Medici.

Undoubtedly made as a variant of the earlier image of Holofernes' murder, this later painting is notable for its even more vicious and horrific evocation of the story. Its most exceptional features are the viscous spurts of blood which spray out from Holofernes' lacerated neck as Judith pierces and ruptures his arteries. Other rivers of blood gushing from the open wound cascade over the edge of the bed or course along folds in the linen, sullying its whiteness with seeping red gore. Judith is splashed by the arcing deep red spouts of Holofernes' lifeblood, staining her dress with ruby beads of sanguine, which mark and identify her as the perpetrator of the deed.

Many psychoanalytic and feminist analyses to explain such paroxysmal violence have been proposed over the past two decades: they include references to castration and childbirth, a simplistic causal connection between Artemisia's own sexual experience and her penchant for depicting strong heroines as vengeful victorious women, and a more complex argument that the painting should be read as an encoding of the artist's sublimated responses to the events of her life and the historical context in which she worked. It is also assumed that in making adjustments to the previous composition Artemisia was demonstrating the development of her artistic prowess over the previous years and also according with the wishes of her patron. This is indicated by the fact that Artemisia signed the work prominently on the blade of the sword. Thus the work is larger in scale, a rigorously symmetrical arrangement of the figures places Holofernes' head more centrally in the composition and the color combinations have been refined so that the luscious red of Holofernes' coverlet emphasizes the rich dense crimson of his blood. It is also true that in the later version the viewer is not so involved with the action, seeing it at further remove and having a higher vantage point from which to view the decapitation. Being less involved spatially with the harrowing bloody drama, yet still transfixed by the compelling horror of the extreme carnage and its entirely believable evocation of the splinter and squelch of bone and blood, the viewer (and Gentileschi's patron) is better placed to appreciate the artist's virtuosity. The two paintings offer differing relationships between subject and viewer, reality and dramatic staging, believability and stylistic virtuosity—and thus, slightly shift the significance of the story of Judith.

It is useful to note that the dominant pictorial interpretation of the biblical story over the centuries has focused less on the fact that a man loses his life in a most terrible way than on the events featuring the woman and her servant either before or after the murder. Gentileschi co-opts—and reveals in action for the first time—an emergent kind of woman, whose deed is never measured against the rigid moral teachings of the Catholic Church. Judith's face reflects no remorse or sense of wrong-doing in her quiescent self-possessed determination to achieve her goal. Indeed, it seems as if Judith's world has a kind of moral relativity, where good and evil are not the same thing at all times and in all places. Like de Sade's Justine, Judith is contrived to represent a moral absolute in a world where it could be seen that no moral absolutes exist.[7]

More than this however, Gentileschi's vivid portrayal of psychological and intellectual violence suggests her recognition of the power of the Judith story, and the particular moment of causing death, as a potent carrier of different kinds of meaning. Moreover, taking the visualization of physical violence to its limits without overt threat to the institutional establishment, to art society and patronage, was a brilliant achievement for Gentileschi. That she also contrived to make two compelling manifestations of the formidable Judith character convey different kinds of formal virtuosity and vision, along with an understanding of the time in which they arose, confirms the superiority of Artemisia's artistry. It goes some way to explain why encountering the paintings four centuries later is still such an utterly shocking experience.

1) There are at least four versions of the story in Artemisia Gentileschi's oeuvre: JUDITH SLAYING HOLOFERNES (1612–13); JUDITH AND HER MAIDSERVANT (1618–19); JUDITH SLAYING HOLOFERNES (1620); JUDITH AND HER MAIDSERVANT (1625–27).

2) The exhibition "Orazio and Artemisia Gentileschi: Father and Daughter Painters in Baroque Italy," was presented at The Metropolitan Museum of Art, New York, February 14–May 12, 2002, and at the Saint Louis Art Museum, June 14–September 15, 2002.

3) The Italian novel, *Artemisia* by Anna Banti (1947), originally translated into English in 1988, ensured a particularly eager American readership when it was reissued in 1995. A more recent fictional account, *The Passion of Artemisia* by Susan Vreeland, entangles the reader in an excruciatingly girls-own confessional tale of unreconstructed female masochism which one reviewer described as "Artemisia in Hollywood."

4) Orazio Gentileschi rendered many versions of the subject: JUDITH AND HER MAIDSERVANT (1608–9); JUDITH AND HER MAIDSERVANT ABRA WITH THE HEAD OF HOLOFERNES (1610–12); JUDITH AND HER MAIDSERVANT WITH THE HEAD OF HOLOFERNES (1611).

5) As well as her dependence on prototypes by other artists working in Rome at the same time, other sources from whom Artemisia borrowed included Peter Paul Rubens' painting THE GREAT JUDITH (now lost), Gerrit van Honthorst, and the Caravaggesque Dutch master, Simon Vouet.

6) The war (1618–48) was a complex political struggle for European hegemony drawing every European power into bloody conflict.

7) It is tempting to equate Gentileschi's painting of violent dismembering as a pictorial metaphor for the tearing apart of Latin Christianity in her native Rome in the early part of the century—just as the crumbling of institutionalized Christianity sometime near the end of the seventeenth century, when its mythology no longer proved capable of controlling and revivifying the imagination of its followers, as well as the revolutionary politics of the period, have come to be seen as a causal factor in de Sade's art. Similarly, an equivalence can be made between the ritualistic immolations of the Vienna Actionists arising from the religious ferment and political turmoil of post-war Austria.

Ein Blutbad

ARTEMISIA GENTILESCHI (1593 – 1653)

SHEENA WAGSTAFF

Das grausame, blutrünstige Spektakel der Enthauptung des Holofernes durch Judith ist eines der Sujets, das sich mit dem Namen Artemisia Gentileschi verbindet. Gentileschi malte das Motiv in zwei Versionen: die erste ganz am Anfang ihrer Laufbahn als Malerin, um 1612, die andere 1620, als sie in Rom und Florenz bereits als bedeutende Historienmalerin anerkannt war.[1] Die unerwartete Begegnung mit diesen beiden Werken an einem Frühlingsmorgen in uptown Manhattan im Jahr 2002 war jedenfalls sehr bewegend und aufschlussreich.[2] Beide Gemälde zeugen von einer aussergewöhnlichen Autorität und Souveränität und hinterlassen einen starken Eindruck durch die erschreckend detailgetreue Wiedergabe von Judiths Bluttat. Bis zu den bewusst inszenierten Blutbädern der Wiener Aktionisten (Rudolf Schwarzkogler, Otto Mühl, Hermann Nitsch und Günter Brus) in den 60er und 70er Jahren des zwanzigsten Jahrhunderts hat es seither keine derart

SHEENA WAGSTAFF ist Direktorin für Ausstellungen und Aktivitäten der Tate Modern, London.

schockierende Darstellung einer blutigen Schlächterei oder des Abtrennens eines lebensnotwendigen Körperteils mehr gegeben. Neuere Spielarten desselben, wenn etwa Performance-Künstler mit Körperflüssigkeiten arbeiten, sind in der Regel heimliche Hommagen an ihre Vorgänger oder sterile und wenig durchdachte Versuche, die heftigen Tabuverletzungsrituale derselben noch zu überbieten. Dazu muss auch das Scheinmärtyrertum von Sebastian Horsleys jüngster Kreuzigungsaktion auf den Philippinen gerechnet werden, sowie das symbolträchtige Verstümmeln, Einbandagieren und Blutvergiessen bei Franko B, oder David Blaines spezielle Art der Volksbelustigung durch entsetzlich blutige Geschicklichkeitsspiele mit den Händen oder anderen Körperteilen.

Das Gemälde JUDITH ENTHAUPTET HOLOFERNES gilt allgemein als untrennbar mit Ereignissen aus Gentileschis Privatleben verbunden. Die Allgegenwart dieses eindrucksvollen symbolischen Bildes hat zum Teil wohl damit zu tun, dass es in den letzten zehn Jahren in Romanen und Filmen immer wieder als Indiz für Gentileschis Ver-

gewaltigung und das damit verbundene emotionale Trauma gedeutet wurde. Die Tendenz, die Künstlerin Gentileschi mit der biblischen Judith und ihrer Gräueltat zu identifizieren, wurde zudem auch von einem Grossteil der kunsthistorischen Literatur der letzten fünfundzwanzig Jahre gepflegt, welche sich abwechselnd auf die wissenschaftliche Untermauerung, Ablehnung oder Verbreitung einer biographisch ausgerichteten Interpretation des Werkes verlegte. Erst in jüngster Zeit wurde die rein hermetische, selbstreferenzielle und trocken akademische Betrachtungsweise dieses Bildes – samt den damit verbundenen psychoanalytischen, feministischen und semiologischen Deutungen, die allerdings für die seriöse wissenschaftliche Interpretation des Werkes von zentraler Bedeutung waren – abgelöst von einer erfrischenden, viel umfassenderen Betrachtung des barocken Italien des siebzehnten Jahrhunderts.

Das schreckliche Ende des Holofernes durch Judiths Hand war im Barock durchaus kein ungewöhnliches Sujet. Tatsächlich waren Bibelgeschichten aus dem Alten Testament im sechzehn-

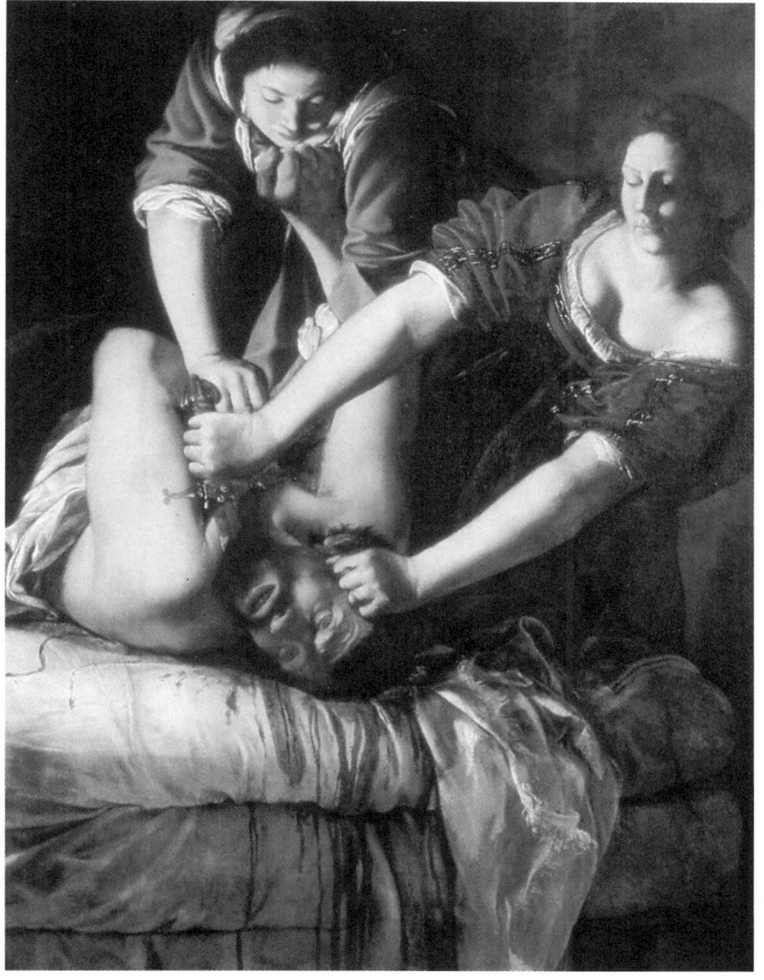

ten und siebzehnten Jahrhundert als Stoff der Historienmalerei bei Auftraggebern wie Künstlern äusserst beliebt. Einige der bekannteren Künstler, die das dramatische Potenzial der Judith-Geschichte anzugehen wagten, waren Mantegna, Botticelli, Rubens, Caravaggio und Orazio Gentileschi. Ähnlich wie die Manga-Figur der AnnLee, die von zeitgenössischen Künstlern (u.a. Pierre Huyghe und Liam Gillick) gekauft und für die eigene Kunst einge-

spannt wurde, hatte man auch Judith aus ihrem ursprünglichen Kontext isoliert; sie war zu einer Art Chiffre für eine bestimmte Handlung geworden, wodurch unzählige, ganz unterschiedliche Versionen ihrer Geschichte entstanden. Die verschiedenen Deutungs- und Darstellungsweisen des Judith-Stoffes veränderten seinen symbolischen Gehalt von Mal zu Mal. Ebenso wie in der Figur der AnnLee, wenn auch in einem ganz anderen Medium,

steckt auch in der Judith ein riesiges Potenzial formaler Ausdrucksweisen, aber auch impliziter Reaktionsmöglichkeiten auf Zeit und Umstände der Entstehung ihrer jeweiligen Darstellung.

Die Geschichte der Ermordung des Holofernes stammt ursprünglich aus den Apokryphen. Sie entstand im zweiten vorchristlichen Jahrhundert und schildert die gnadenlose Belagerung von Judiths Heimatstadt Bethulia

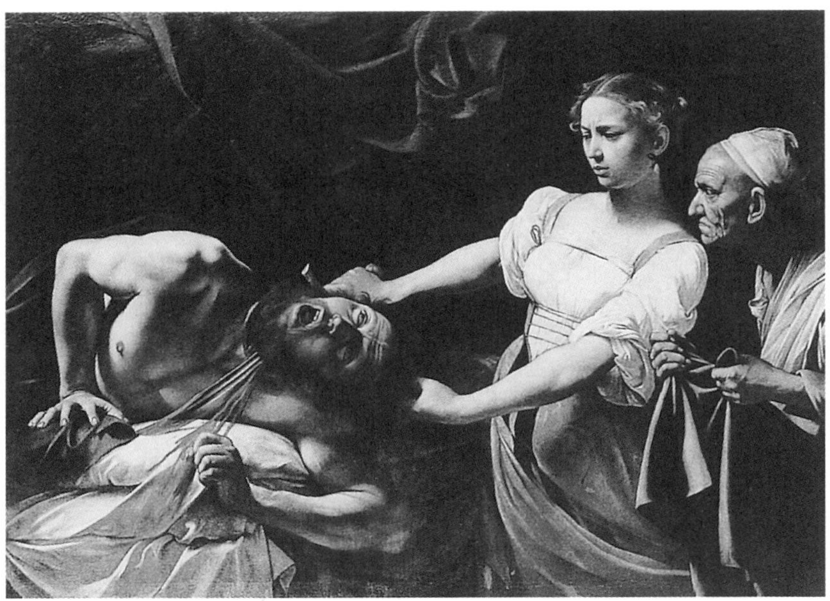

durch die assyrische Armee unter Führung von General Holofernes. Judiths Plan, ihre Landsleute aus dieser tödlichen Zwangslage zu befreien, war einfach, aber höchst gefährlich. In ihren schönsten Kleidern, nur von der Magd Abra begleitet, machte sie sich auf den Weg ins feindliche Lager. Da sie Holofernes und seinem König ihre Dienste anboten, gewährte man den Frauen Zutritt. Holofernes war von Judiths Schönheit derart angetan, dass er sie einlud mit ihm zu speisen. Dabei betrank er sich erstaunlicherweise bis zur Bewusstlosigkeit. Judith erkannte ihre Gelegenheit, ergriff das Schwert des Gastgebers und enthauptete Holofernes, indem sie seinen Hals samt Nackenmuskulatur und Wirbelsäule durchtrennte, während Abra die unkontrolliert zuckenden Arme des halb Ohnmächtigen niederhielt. Darauf versteckten die beiden Frauen ihre grässli-

che Trophäe in einem Korb, flohen aus dem Lager und kehrten nach Bethulia zurück, wo sie der Armee der Israeliten triumphierend das Haupt des Holofernes zeigten und offenbarten, dass die assyrische Armee mit einem Schlag entmannt worden war und ihr Oberhaupt verloren hatte. So wurden die belagerten Truppen zu Siegern und Judith wurde der Ruhm zuteil, sowohl ihre Stadt wie ihr Volk gerettet zu haben.

Männer mordende Frauen waren im Mittelalter ein beliebtes Thema erbaulicher Geschichten zur Illustration des widernatürlichen Verstosses gegen die gottgewollte Geschlechterhierarchie. Im sechzehnten Jahrhundert hatte die Darstellung der Unterhöhlung der Gesellschaftsordnung in der Judith-Geschichte, neben der ursprünglichen politischen Bedeutung des Bibeltextes, bereits eine sexuelle Dimension hinzugewonnen (weil Ju-

dith eher dank ihrer Schönheit Zutritt zu Holofernes erhält, als wegen allfälliger militärischer Geheimnisse, die sie verraten könnte).

Artemisia Gentileschi begann ihre künstlerische Laufbahn mit siebzehn Jahren in Rom, also 1610 (im Jahr von Caravaggios Tod). Etwa ein Jahr später begann sie mit der Arbeit an ihrer ersten Version von JUDITH ENTHAUPTET HOLOFERNES. Wie die besten Künstler des siebzehnten Jahrhunderts wollte Gentileschi die Konkurrenz auf höchstem Niveau antreten, nämlich als Historienmalerin von inspirierten und erhabenen religiösen, historischen und mythologischen Szenen, die der Erbauung dienen sollten. Indem sie sich in diesem frühen Werk dazu entschloss, direkt den Akt des Mordes an Holofernes darzustellen, entfernte sich Gentileschi jedoch von den traditionellen Vorbildern zu diesem Thema, die gewöhnlich die Szene unmittelbar nach der Bluttat abbildeten, nämlich, wie die beiden Frauen mit dem Korb, in dem das Haupt des Holofernes liegt, heimlich das Lager verlassen.

Eine wesentliche Rolle in Artemisias künstlerischer Ausbildung spielte ihr Vater, Orazio Gentileschi. Für Orazio wiederum war die Begegnung mit Caravaggio um 1600 das entscheidende Ereignis seines Lebens. Danach wurde er zur herausragenden Figur unter den vielen von Caravaggio beeinflussten Künstlern. Obwohl Artemisia Caravaggio nur indirekt kannte, lernte sie das Revolutionäre seiner Sichtweise durch das Werk ihres Vaters kennen, aber auch durch die Arbeiten anderer in Rom lebender Künstler. Das Subversive an Caravaggios Lehre lag in seiner Forderung das Verhältnis zwischen Imagination und Realität, Maler und Modell radikal zu überdenken. Entsprechend dem kritischen Vokabular seiner Zeit verlangte er eine «Wahrheit» in der Malerei, welche die direkte Beobachtung der imaginierten «Wahrscheinlichkeit» der Renaissancemalerei vorzog, die das Exemplarische und Ideale bevorzugte.

Caravaggios revolutionäre und entscheidende Leistung war, dass er die Wahrheit der gewöhnlichen Alltagsszene nahm, um sie dann mit unerhörter Dramatik aufzuladen.

Während Orazios Bilder (mindestens vier) von JUDITH UND IHRER MAGD den geläufigen Vorbildern der Zeit entsprechen und eine Szene nach dem Mord zeigen,[3] gab Caravaggios JUDITH ENTHAUPTET HOLOFERNES (1599) offenbar den entscheidenden Anstoss zu Artemisias Behandlung des Themas[4]: Die siegreiche Judith hat ihre Tat schon fast zu Ende gebracht, Holofernes' Hals ist bereits zur Hälfte durchgesäbelt. Die Heldin lehnt sich zurück, die Stirn in Falten vor Anstrengung und Abscheu angesichts ihrer Tat, während die alte Abra untätig zuschaut. Trotz des dramatischen Kontrastes von Licht und Schatten und der sorgfältigen Illumination von Judith bei ihrer Gewalttat, zeigt Caravaggios Szene eigentlich eine unterbrochene Handlung. Sie erlaubt dem Betrachter sich in Einzelheiten zu vertiefen und zeigt – beinah wie beim Studium eines Stilllebens – ein zum Stillstand gebrachtes Leben. Obwohl Artemisia den merkwürdig gestreckten Arm von Caravaggios Judith verändert hat, ist ihre Judith als Mörderin vollkommen glaubhaft, was noch unterstützt wird durch eine komplizenhaft aktive Abra, die ihr ganzes Gewicht einsetzt, um den entsetzten Holofernes zu bändigen; dessen Augen nehmen den glasigen Ausdruck eines Sterbenden an,

während Judith die Enthauptung zu Ende bringt.

Artemisia nimmt Caravaggio beim Wort, indem sie zeigt, wie Gewalt in Wahrheit aussieht. Der Betrachter ist ganz nah am Bettrand, wo die weissen Betttücher fleckig sind und Blutbäche seitlich an der Matratze hinunterrinnen; er kann in solch unmittelbarer Nähe zum Geschehen förmlich die körperliche Anstrengung spüren, die nötig ist, um Haut und Sehnen zu durchtrennen und schliesslich den Wirbelknochen zu zertrümmern; ja, er kann förmlich das heisse, süssklebrig sprudelnde Blut riechen. Artemisias äusserst expressive Darstellung der Geschichte – mit ihrer ungeniert naturalistischen Wiedergabe des festen oder bereits abgetrennten Fleisches, den scharf beobachteten Details der entschlossenen oder gequälten Mienen und der greifbaren Körperlichkeit dieser drei Menschen in ihrem Kampf auf Leben und Tod – wird noch unterstrichen durch die kühne caravaggeske Lichtgebung und ergibt insgesamt ein aussergewöhnlich lebendiges und psychologisch überzeugendes Bild. Es zeigt und definiert zugleich den Moment des Todes. Es ist das ultimative Porträt eines Mordes, einer politisch erfolgreichen Exekution.

Als Artemisia Gentileschi 1612 die erste Version der heroischen Judith in Angriff nahm, begann ihre Karriere gerade mitten in einer bewegten Zeit im frühbarocken Rom; die Gegenreformation war in vollem Gange. Die zweite Version der Judith beendete sie 1920, dem Jahr der Schlacht am Weissen Berg (bei Prag), einem frühen, aber entscheidenden Scharmützel des Dreissigjährigen Krieges, welches die katholische Seite für sich entscheiden konnte. Wie der Historiker Richard

Spear schreibt, müssen die Menschen in Rom damals erkannt haben, dass dieser Konflikt drohte, die abendländische Christenheit zu entzweien, nicht zuletzt, weil der Papst zunächst mit wenig Erfolg versuchte, neutral zu erscheinen und zwischen den Kriegsparteien zu vermitteln. Als Katholikin muss Artemisia Gentileschi um diese Dinge gewusst haben, obwohl wir nicht wissen können, ob und wie sehr sie sich dafür interessierte.

Auch wenn Italien sich damals irgendwo zwischen dem Katholizismus der Gegenreformation und der Entwicklung der modernen Form des säkularisierten Nationalstaates befand, bestanden die Fürstentümer der Renaissance noch immer: So entstand Artemisias zweite Version von JUDITH ENTHAUPTET HOLOFERNES (1620) im Auftrag von Cosimo II. von Medici.

Die spätere Variante des Mordes an Holofernes zeichnet sich durch eine noch wildere und schrecklichere Wiedergabe des Geschehens aus. Besonders auffällig ist, wie das Blut aus Holofernes' malträtiertem Hals spritzt, während Judith die Arterien durchtrennt. Ströme von Blut schiessen aus der offenen Wunde und ergiessen sich über die Bettkante oder entlang den Falten des Bettzeugs und tränken das weisse Leinen blutrot. Judith ist besudelt von Holofernes' Lebenssaft, der in rotem Strahl emporschiesst, ihr Kleid mit rubinroten Blutstropfen übersät und sie als Täterin brandmarkt.

In den letzten zwei Jahrzehnten gab es zahlreiche psychoanalytische und feministische Erklärungsversuche für die ausserordentliche Gewalttätigkeit dieser Darstellung: Man bezog sich auf Kastration und Geburt, machte eine allzu vereinfachende kausale Verknüpfung zwischen Artemisias eigener sexueller Erfahrung und ihrer Vorliebe für starke Frauen und siegreiche Rächerinnen oder führte das etwas komplexere Argument an, das Bild sei zu lesen als Verschlüsselung der sublimierten Reaktion der Künstlerin auf Ereignisse ihres Lebens und den historischen Kontext, in dem sie arbeitete. Man darf wohl annehmen, dass Artemisia mit den Veränderungen gegenüber der früheren Version sowohl ihre fortgeschrittene Entwicklung und Kunstfertigkeit acht Jahre später demonstrieren wollte als auch den Wünschen ihres Auftraggebers nachkam. Dafür spricht auch die Tatsache, dass sie das Bild besonders gut sichtbar signierte: auf der Klinge des Schwertes. Das spätere Bild zeigt alles in etwas grösserem Massstab, die Figuren sind streng symmetrisch angeordnet, wobei der Kopf des Holofernes in der Komposition eine zentrale Stellung einnimmt und die Farben raffinierter gewählt sind. So verstärkt etwa das elegante Rot von Holofernes' Bettdecke das Dunkelrot des strömenden Blutes. Es trifft auch zu, dass der Betrachter in der späteren Version nicht mehr so sehr in die Handlung eingebunden ist; er steht etwas weiter entfernt vom Geschehen und sieht die Enthauptung von weiter oben. Da er zwar räumlich weniger nah dran ist, aber dennoch betroffen vom Schrecklichen dieses extremen Blutbades, welches das Blutvergiessen und Zersplittern der Wirbel völlig glaubhaft veranschaulicht, befindet sich der Betrachter (wie Gentileschis Auftraggeber) in einer guten (von der ersten Version völlig verschiedenen) Position, um die Virtuosität der Künstlerin begutachten zu können. Die beiden Gemälde unterscheiden sich demnach in den Beziehungen zwischen Sujet und Betrachter, Realität und dramatischer

Inszenierung, Glaubwürdigkeit und stilistischer Virtuosität; und damit verlagert sich auch die Bedeutung der Geschichte von Judith ein wenig.

Es mag nützlich sein, festzuhalten, dass die künstlerischen Darstellungen der biblischen Erzählung über Jahrhunderte hinweg weniger die Tatsache in den Vordergrund rückten, dass ein Mensch sein Leben auf schreckliche Weise verliert, sondern sich auf das Bild der Frauen vor oder nach der Mordtat beschränkten. Gentileschi greift einen bisher verborgenen Frauentypus auf und zeigt ihn erstmals in Aktion – eine Frau, deren Tat nicht den moralischen Massstäben der katholischen Kirche unterliegt. Judiths Gesicht zeigt keinerlei Gewissensnot oder Unrechtsbewusstsein, sondern lediglich ruhige, beherrschte Entschlossenheit. Es scheint in der Tat, als herrsche in Judiths Welt eine Art moralischer Relativität, derzufolge Gut und Böse nicht immer und überall dasselbe sind. Wie de Sades Justine ist Judith dazu gezwungen, eine moralische Absolutheit zu vertreten, in einer Welt, in der zu sehen war, dass es eine solche nicht gab.[5]

Aber mehr noch deutet Gentileschis lebhafte Schilderung der psychologischen und intellektuellen Gewalt darauf hin, dass sie erkennt, dass die starke Erzählung und der besondere Moment des Tötens mehrere mögliche Bedeutungen transportieren können. Dass es Gentileschi zudem gelang, die Darstellung physischer Gewalt derart auf die Spitze zu treiben, ohne dass sich die damalige Kunstwelt oder ihr Auftraggeber bedroht fühlten, muss man schlicht brillant nennen. Dass ihr schliesslich gleich zwei überzeugende Darstellungen der imposanten Figur der Judith gelangen, die beide vom

Verständnis der Künstlerin für die jeweilige Zeit ihrer Entstehung zeugen und in denen ihre formale Virtuosität und ihre Gestaltungskraft je verschieden zum Tragen kamen, bekräftigt Artemisias künstlerische Souveränität. Das mag ein Stück weit erklären, warum die Begegnung mit diesen Bildern selbst nach vierhundert Jahren noch immer eine durch und durch erschütternde Erfahrung ist.

(Übersetzung: Wilma Parker)

1) Es gibt mindestens vier Versionen dieser Geschichte in Artemisia Gentileschis Werk: JUDITH ENTHAUPTET HOLOFERNES (1612/13); JUDITH UND IHRE MAGD (1618/19); JUDITH ENTHAUPTET HOLOFERNES (1620); JUDITH UND IHRE MAGD (1625–27).
2) Die Ausstellung «Orazio und Artemisia Gentileschi: Father and Daughter Painters in Baroque Italy» im Metropolitan Museum of Art in New York dauerte vom 14. Februar bis 12. Mai 2002.
3) Orazio schuf mehrere Variationen zum Thema: JUDITH UND IHRE MAGD (1608/09); JUDITH UND IHRE MAGD ABRA MIT DEM KOPF DES HOLOFERNES (1610–12); JUDITH UND IHRE MAGD MIT DEM KOPF DES HOLOFERNES (1611).
4) Neben anderen in Rom lebenden Künstlern liess sich Artemisia u.a. auch von folgenden Künstlern inspirieren: Paul Rubens' (heute verlorenes) Gemälde DIE GROSSE JUDITH, ferner Gerrit van Honthorst sowie dem holländischen Caravaggio-Schüler Simon Vouet.
5) Man ist versucht Gentileschis Bild der gewaltsamen Zerstückelung als Gleichnis für die Entzweiung der abendländischen Christenheit zu Beginn des Jahrhunderts zu verstehen; parallel zum Zerfall der Macht der Kirche gegen Ende des siebzehnten Jahrhunderts, als der christliche Mythos nicht mehr in der Lage war, den Geist der Gläubigen in Schach zu halten und neu zu beleben, und genauso wie die revolutionären Zustände jener Zeit als auslösender Faktor für die Kunst des Marquis de Sade angesehen werden. Auch zwischen den Opferritualen der Wiener Aktionisten und den religiösen und politischen Zuständen im Österreich der Nachkriegszeit lässt sich eine solche Verbindung herstellen.

PROJEKT-WETTBEWERB
«ERLEBNISPFAD LANGETE»
Öffentliche Ausschreibung

Die Region Oberaargau plant auf Sommer 2003 die Eröffnung eines Erlebnispfades, der thematisch auf Oberaargauer Sagen beruht und dem Flüsschen Langete – von Eriswil bis Langenthal – entlang führt.

Auf den Sagenschauplätzen der Dörfer Eriswil, Rohrbach, Madiswil und der Stadt Langenthal sollen die entsprechenden Sagen gestalterisch umgesetzt und zu Publikumsmagneten der Region werden.

Kulturschaffende – kreative Einzelpersonen, Künstlergruppen, Schulen für Gestaltung, Kunst und Design, vorzugsweise mit Erfahrung in Projektmanagement – sind eingeladen, ein Gesamtkonzept mittels anzuforderndem Bewerbungsformular einzureichen.

Das künstlerische Gesamtkonzept wie auch dessen Umsetzung obliegen, im Sinne eines Gesamtleistungsauftrags, dem/der Wettbewerbsgewinner/-in.

Für die Realisierung des Projektes sind insgesamt Fr. 90'000 vorgesehen (pro Standort Fr. 20'000 sowie zusätzlich Fr. 10'000 für die Projektleitung. Preisgeld: 1. Rang: Fr. 1500; 2. Rang: Fr. 1000; 3. Rang: Fr. 500.
Eingabefrist bis 30.11.2002
Jurierung & Auftragserteilung bis 31.12.2002
Eröffnung des Sagen-Erlebnispfades: 1. August 2003.

Für weitere Informationen und Bewerbungsformulare wenden Sie sich an:
Frau Christine A. Jossen, Leiterin Tourismus & Marketing Region Oberaargau, Jurastrasse 22, 4900 Langenthal, Tel. 062-916 22 26, E-Mail: tourismus@oberaargau.ch oder besuchen Sie unsere Homepage www.oberaargau.ch

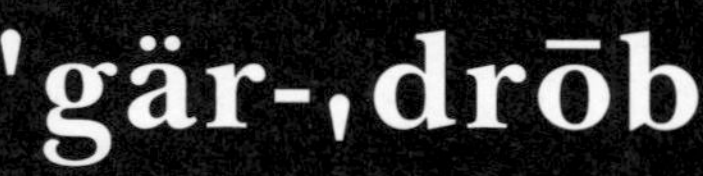

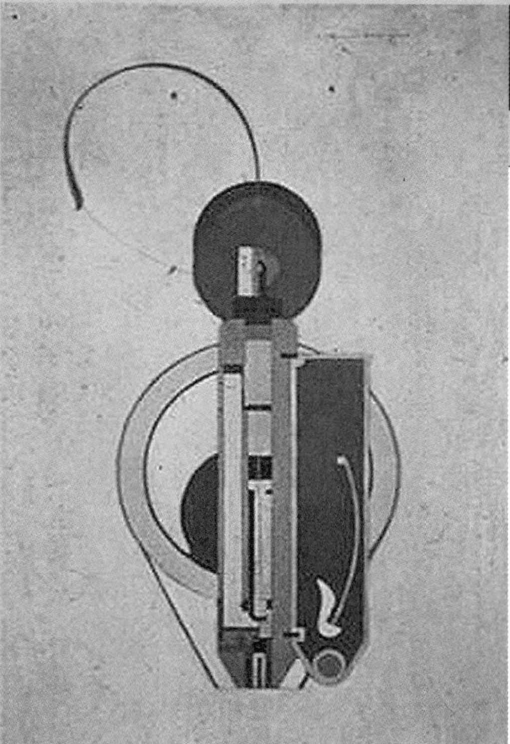

PARKETT-PREISFRAGE / PARKETT COMPETITION

Durchforsten Sie Ihr visuelles Gedächtnis! / Test your visual memory!

Erkennen Sie dieses Bild? Woran erinnert es Sie?

Die ersten 3 richtigen beziehungsweise originellsten Antworten gewinnen je 1 Exemplar des neuen Parkett-Postkarten-Sets (128 Farbpostkarten der Parketteditionen mit Textbüchlein zur Parkett-Ausstellung im MoMA, New York, 2001)

Can you identify the picture above? What does it remind you of?

The first three correct or most original answers will each win 1 copy of Parkett's New Postcard Set (featuring 128 color postcards of the special editions to date and text booklet on the Parkett exhibition at MoMA, New York, 2001).

Senden Sie Ihre Lösung per Post, Fax oder E-Mail an: / Send us your answer by mail, fax or e-mail:
Parkett Verlag, Garderobe, Quellenstrasse 27, 8031 Zürich, Fax: ++41 1 272 43 01, E-Mail: s.schmidt@parkettart.com or Parkett Publishers, Garderobe, 155 Ave. of the Americas, New York, NY 10013, fax: ++1 212 271 0704, e-mail: s.schmidt@parkettart.com

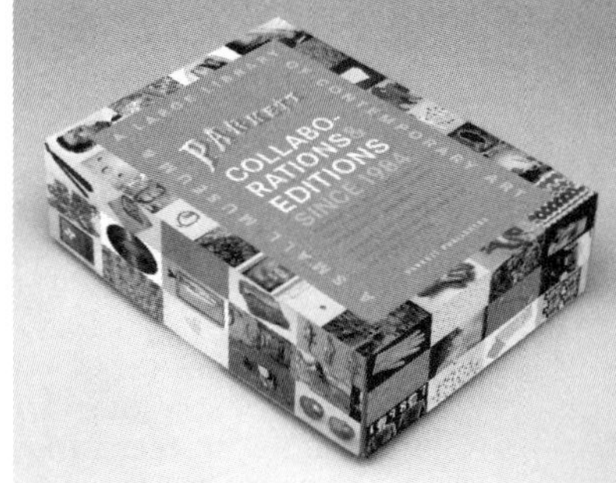

Parkett Postcard Set

COLLABORATIONS

ANGELA BULLOCH
DANIEL BUREN
PIERRE HUYGHE

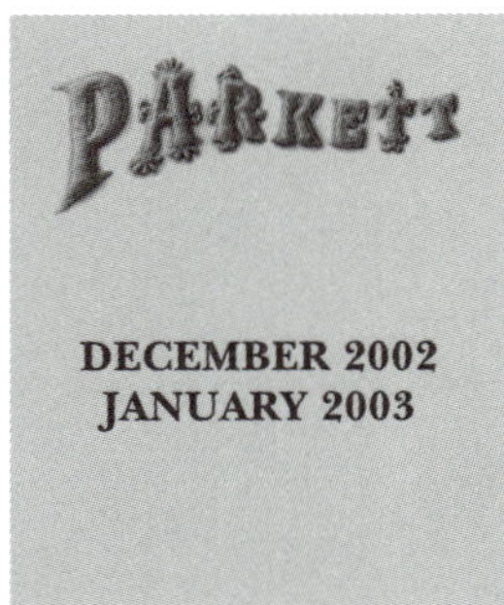

No. 66 - ISBN 3-907582-16-0

JOHN CURRIN
LAURA OWENS
MICHAEL RAEDECKER
SEWARD, VAN DE WALLE, BERG, FERGUSON, THOMSON, WEISSMAN, VERSCHAFFEL, MYERS, EGGERS
INSERT: **LOU REED**
KURT W. FORSTER: **JEFF WALL**
STORR: **DIETER ROTH & DOROTHY IANNONE**
KONRAD BITTERLI: **HUBBARD/BIRCHLER**
LES INFOS: CHRISTINA VÉGH
CUMULUS: OLAV WESTPHALEN, THOMAS HAHN
BALKON: SHEENA WAGSTAFF

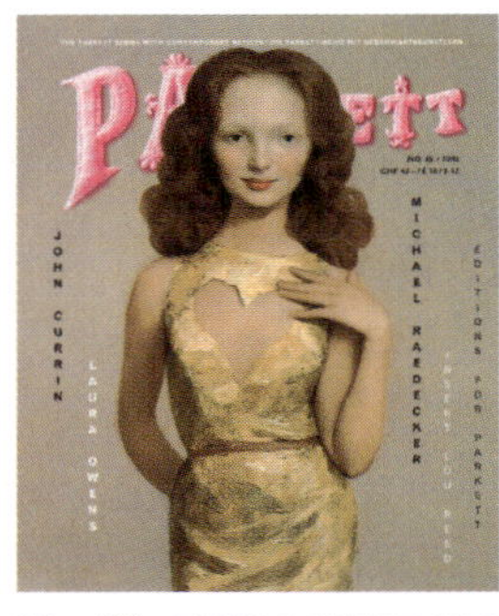

No. 65 - ISBN 3-907582-15-2

OLAFUR ELIASSON
TOM FRIEDMAN
RODNEY GRAHAM
BLOM, MORGAN, CAMERON, MATSUI, WATERS/FRIEDMAN, COOKE, HALE
INSERT: **AMY SILLMAN**
VÉRONIQUE D'AUZAC: **XAVIER VEILHAN**
A.M. HOMES: **CHRIS VERENE** (INTERVIEW)
HAKAN NILSSON: **ANNIKA LARSSON**
INQUIRY/UMFRAGE:
LEARNING FROM "DOCUMENTA"

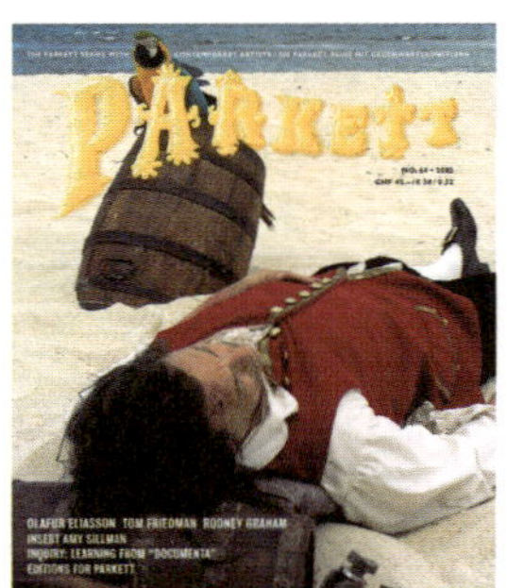

No. 64 - ISBN 3-907582-14-4

TRACEY EMIN
WILLIAM KENTRIDGE
GREGOR SCHNEIDER
BARBER, MUIR, PREECE, GUNNING, STEWART, GOLDBERG, PUVOGEL, LOOCK
INSERT: **JEREMY BLAKE**
CLAUDIA SPINELLI: **FABRICE GYGI**
RAINER FUCHS: **KATHARINA GROSSE**
ADRIAN DANNATT: **THE THREE**
CUMULUS: CH. RATTEMEYER, D. BIRNBAUM
BALKON: MICHAEL OPPITZ

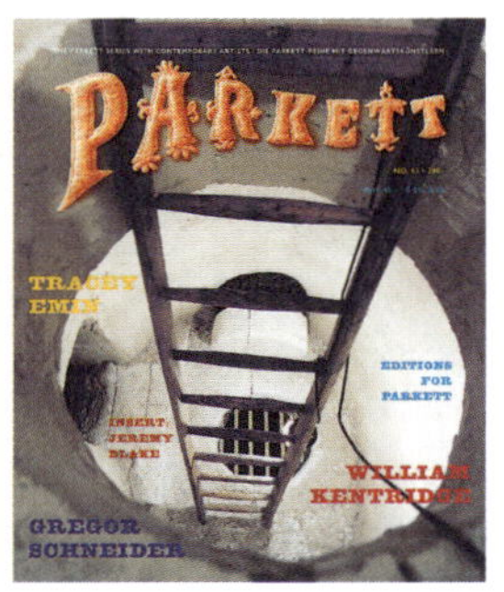

No. 63 - ISBN 3-907582-13-6

JOHN WESLEY
TACITA DEAN
THOMAS DEMAND
MILLAR, CARABELL, SCHWARZ
NORDEN, KÖNIG/STOCKEBRAND
HAINLEY, SEARLE, RUBY, HEISER
INSERT: **G. STEINER & J. LENZLINGER**
PHILIP URSPRUNG: **ALLAN KAPROW**
RUSSELL FERGUSON: **GLEN WILSON**
EDWARD A. SCHEER: **MIKE PARR**
LES INFOS: DAVID GREENBERG
CUMULUS: G. CARMINE, S. DIETZ

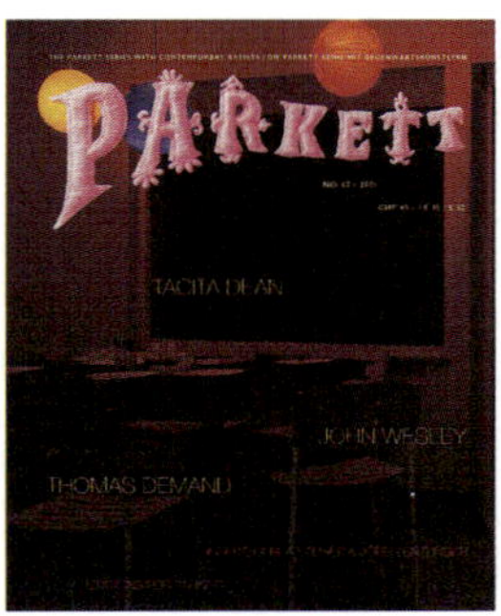

No. 62 - ISBN 3-907582-12-8

BRIDGET RILEY
LIAM GILLICK
SARAH MORRIS
MATTHEW RITCHIE
KUDIELKA, HICKEY
GILLICK, STEMMRICH, WOLLEN
NICHOLS GOODEVE, KLEIN, PRINZHORN
RABINOWITZ, GALISON/JONES, MARCUS
ELISABETH KLEY: **PAUL LINCOLN**
CUMULUS: O. ENWEZOR, M. WARNER
BALKON: STELLA ROLLIG

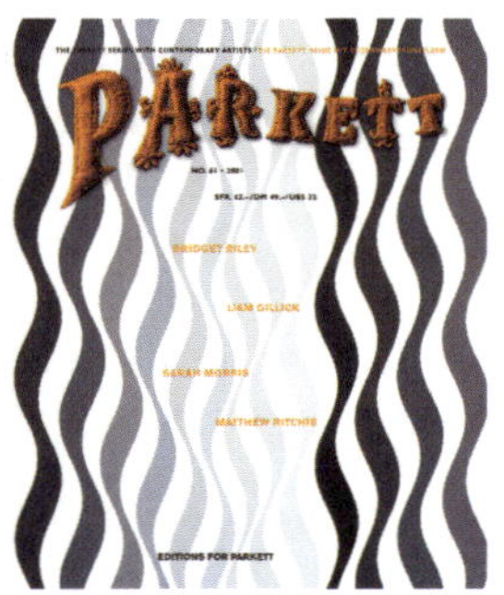

No. 61 - ISBN 3-907582-11-X

CHUCK CLOSE
DIANA THATER
LUC TUYMANS
PROSE, CLOSE/PEYTON, SHIFF,
CLOSE/CURIGER
ARRHENIUS, HASLINGER, GILBERT-ROLFE
HOPTMAN, MOSQUERA, REUST
INSERT: **SHIRANA SHAHBAZI**
GREG HILTY: **JEREMY DELLER**
HOWARD SINGERMAN: **DAVID BUNN**
LES INFOS: THIERRY DE DUVE—INTERVIEW
CUMULUS: FRAZER WARD, HANS ULRICH RECK

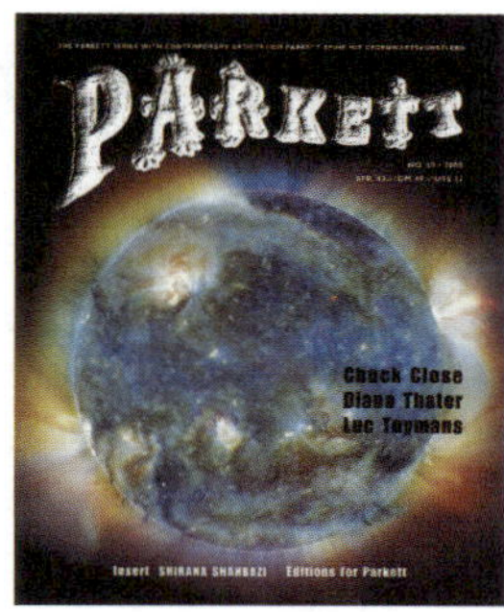

No. 60 - ISBN 3-907582-10-1

MAURIZIO CATTELAN
YAYOI KUSAMA
KARA WALKER
BOURRIAUD, GINGERAS, BONAMI
PANHANS-BÜHLER, MATSUI, POLLOCK
DUBOIS SHAW, JANUS, WALKER
INSERT: **ANDREAS ZÜST**
VINCENT KATZ,
ELISABETH BRONFEN: **ANNETTE MESSAGER**
JAN AVGIKOS: **ANNA GASKELL**
LES INFOS: ALI SUBOTNICK
CUMULUS: M. ROWELL, L. FÖLDENYI
BALKON: MICHELLE NICOL

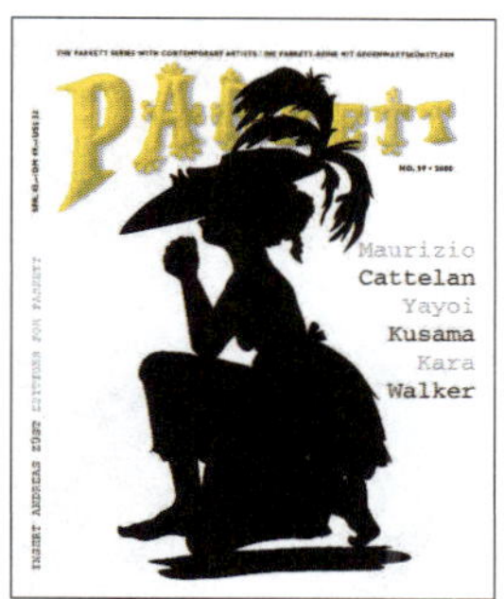

No. 59 - ISBN 3-907582-09-8

JAMES ROSENQUIST
SYLVIE FLEURY
JASON RHOADES
RUSSELL, KOONS/ROSENQUIST, HULTEN, FELIX
GLENN, LOBEL, DANNATT, RUF, KOETHER
FERGUSON, ORTH, SCHEIDEMANN/HERMANN
INSERT: **HENRY BOND**
GILDA WILLIAMS: **JANE & LOUISE WILSON**
SLAVOJ ZIZEK, PAUL D. MILLER & CHRIS OFILI
LES INFOS: ANNA HELWING
CUMULUS: DAVID ROBBINS, HILDE TEERLINCK
BALKON: KNUT EBELING

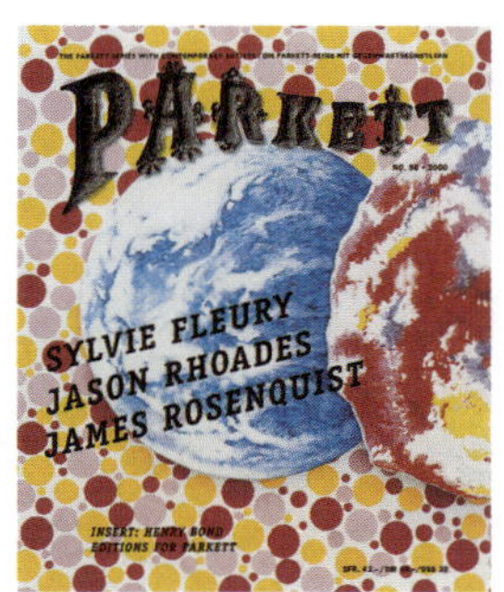

No. 58 - ISBN 3-907582-08-X

DOUG AITKEN
NAN GOLDIN
THOMAS HIRSCHHORN
ROBERTS, BONAMI, VAN ASSCHE, LEBOVICI
DANTO, LIEBMANN, FRIIS-HANSEN, HAKERT,
EISENBERG, FLECK, GINGERAS, VERGNE, STEINWEG
DAVID GREENBERG: **DONALD BAECHLER**
ANDREA KROKSNES: **LOUISE LAWLER**
LIONEL BOVIER: **JOHN MILLER**
LES INFOS: RUDOLF SCHMITZ
CUMULUS: H.U. OBRIST, CONNIE BUTLER
BALKON: JURI STEINER & ANNELISE COSTE

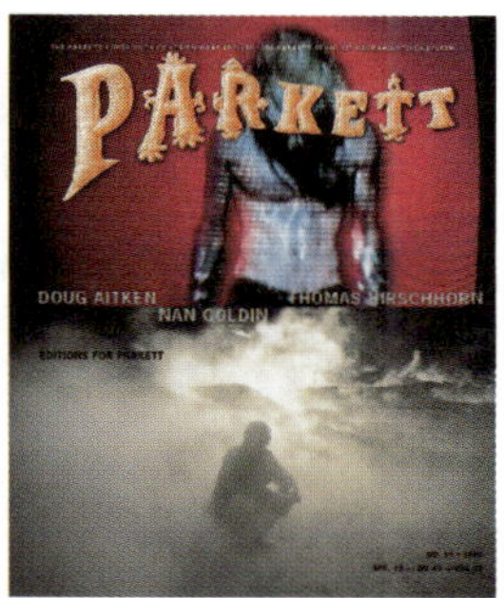

No. 57 - ISBN 3-907582-07-1

ELLSWORTH KELLY
VANESSA BEECROFT
JORGE PARDO
KELLEIN, FER, MAURER, RIMANELLI
BRYSON, TAZZI, SEWARD, AVGIKOS
FERGUSON, VÉGH, VAN WINKEL
FRANGENBERG, BUSH
GREG HILTY: **CERITH WYN EVANS**
THOMAS Y. LEVIN: **CHRISTIAN MARCLAY**
LYNNE COOKE: **DIANA THATER**
LES INFOS: DIANE LEWIS
CUMULUS: ADRIAN DANNATT, PETR NEDOMA

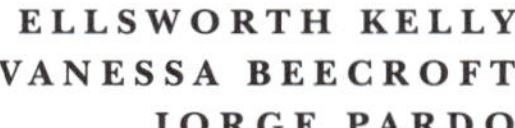
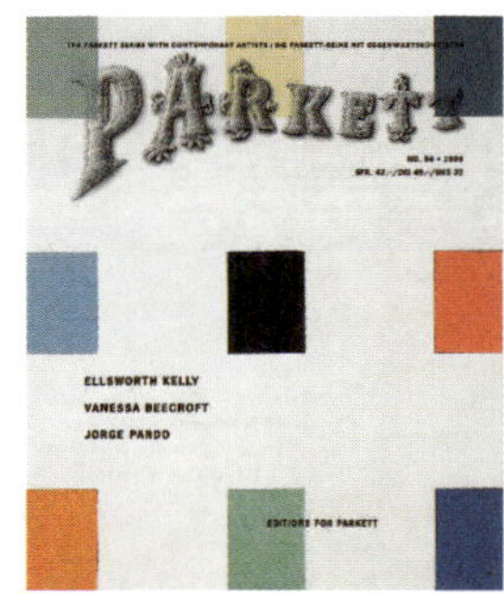

No. 56 - ISBN 3-907582-06-3

EDWARD RUSCHA
ANDREAS SLOMINSKI
SAM TAYLOR-WOOD
PERRONE, HIGGIE, SINGERMAN, SCHENKER
SCANLAN, SPECTOR, FREY, HEYNEN
GROYS/FUNCKE/HOFFMANN, BRONFEN
BONAMI, LAJER-BURCHARTH
INSERT: **KARA WALKER**
BORIS GROYS: **PAVEL PEPPERSTEIN**
RUDOLF SCHMITZ: **ALEXANDER KLUGE**
BEATRIX RUF: **EIJA-LIISA AHTILA**
CUMULUS: MICHELLE NICOL, SUELY ROLNIK

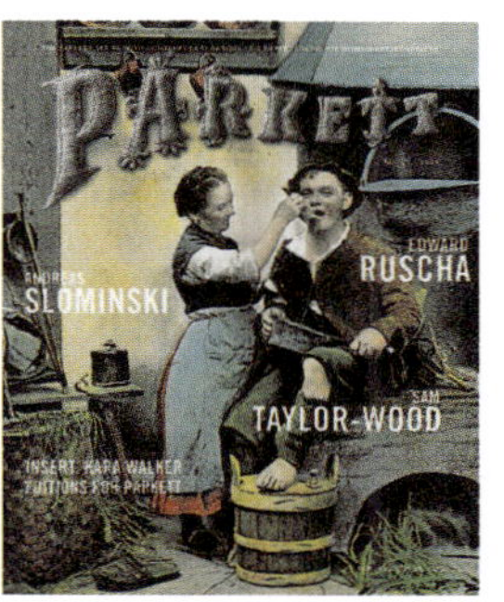

No. 55 - ISBN 3-907582-05-5

RONI HORN
MARIKO MORI
BEAT STREULI
SCHORR, GUNNARSSON, GOROVOY, LEWIS
SPECTOR, BRYSON, NAKAZAWA, NICHOLS
GOODEVE, STALS, DANTO, AMANO, SMITH
INSERT: **MATTHEW RITCHIE**
VINCENT KATZ: **ALEX KATZ**
HORST BREDEKAMP: **STEPHAN VON HUENE**
PAUL D. MILLER: **SHIRIN NESHAT**
LES INFOS:
OKWUI ENWEZOR & WILLIAM KENTRIDGE
CUMULUS: VALÉRIA PICCOLI, MARIA LIND

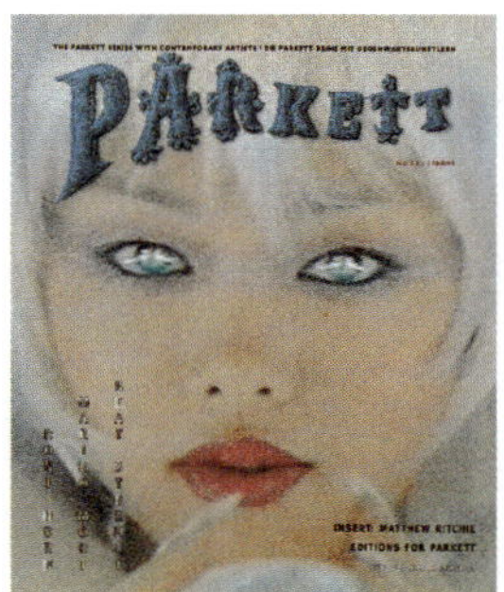

No. 54 - ISBN 3-907582-04-7

TRACEY MOFFATT
ELIZABETH PEYTON
WOLFGANG TILLMANS
MARTIN, LAJER-BURCHARTH, RIMANELLI
PILGRIM, URSPRUNG, LIEBMANN, MATSUI
WAKEFIELD, BUDNEY, NESBITT, ZIEGLER
INSERT: **DAVID SHRIGLEY**
CATHERINE BERNARD: **JOHAN GRIMONPREZ**
BERNARD MARCADÉ: **ROBERT GOBER**
LES INFOS DE L'ENFER: VALERIA LIEBERMANN
CUMULUS: BLESSING, AUPETITALLOT
BALKON: STEINER/MAGNAGUAGNO

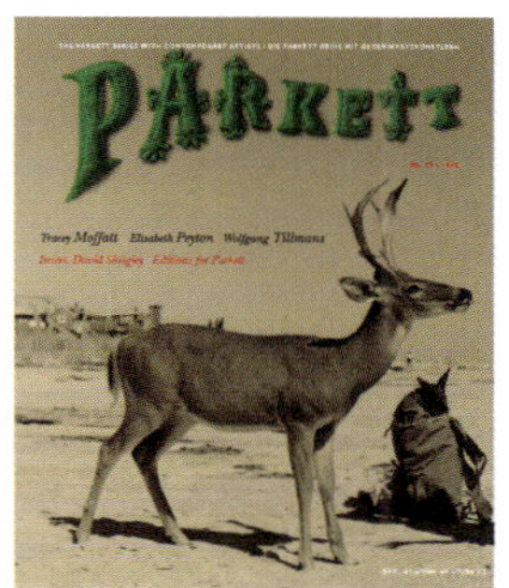

No. 53 - ISBN 3-907582-03-9

KAREN KILIMNIK
MALCOLM MORLEY
UGO RONDINONE
SCHORR, BÜRGI, JUNCOSA, MORLEY,
LEBENSZTEJN, BONAMI, VERWOERT, HOPTMAN,
INSERT: **THOMAS BAYRLE**
ED WHITE: **JEAN MICHEL OTHONIEL**
NEVILLE WAKEFIELD: **RICHARD SERRA**
GILDA WILLIAMS: **GILLIAN WEARING**
ROBERT GRESKOVIC: **MERCE CUNNINGHAM**
CUMULUS: WALKER, KURZMEYER
BALKON: CECILIA VICUÑA

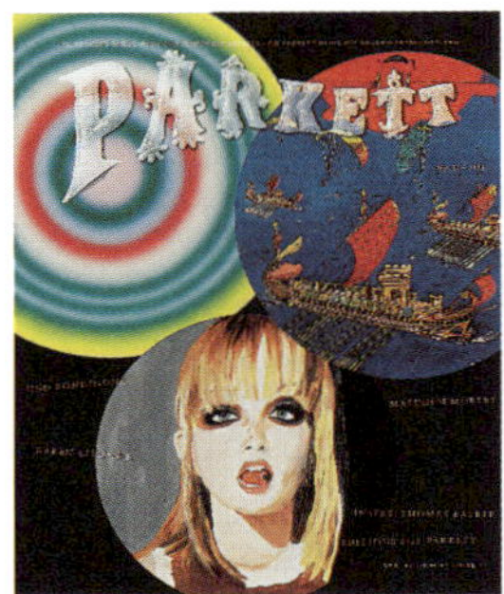

No. 52 - ISBN 3-907582-02-0

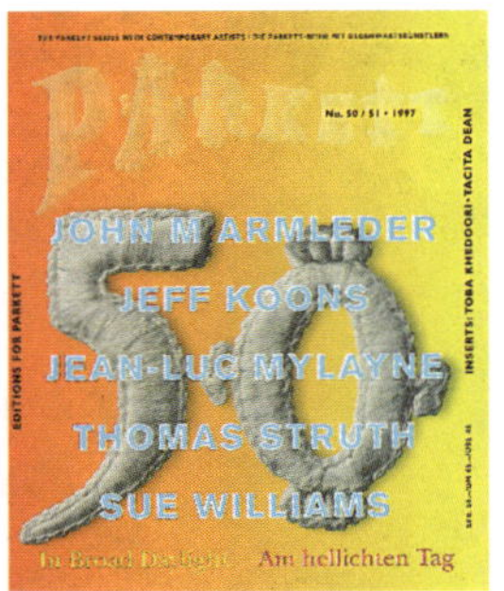

JOHN M ARMLEDER, JEFF KOONS
JEAN-LUC MYLAYNE
THOMAS STRUTH, SUE WILLIAMS
DI PIETRANTONIO, BOVIER, MUNIZ,
SEWARD, LOERS, NICHOLS GOODEVE,
COOKE, DION, ARNAUDET, MYLAYNE,
CURIGER, LINGWOOD, OKUTSU, BRYSON,
SCHJELDAHL, NESBIT, DANNATT, CAMHI
INSERTS: **TOBA KHEDOORI, TACITA DEAN**
ONFRAY: **HYACINTHE RIGAUD**, NICOL: **SAM SAMORE**
MURPHY, VAN DER WALLE, STEINER,
KURT W. FORSTER: **FRANK GEHRY**
CUMULUS: COLEMAN, BIRNBAUM

50/51 - ISBN 3-907582-00-4

LAURIE ANDERSON
DOUGLAS GORDON
JEFF WALL
FLOOD, BEZZOLA, FERGUSON
GILLICK/GORDON, BRYSON, PONTBRIAND
SCHORR, ANDERSON, BURCKHARDT, BUDNEY
INSERT: **SILVIA BÄCHLI**
COLIN DE LAND: **JOHN WATERS**
ROBERT STORR: **SEYDOU KEITA**
DANIELA SALVIONI: **CLEGG & GUTTMANN**
CUMULUS: KITTELMANN, MEYER

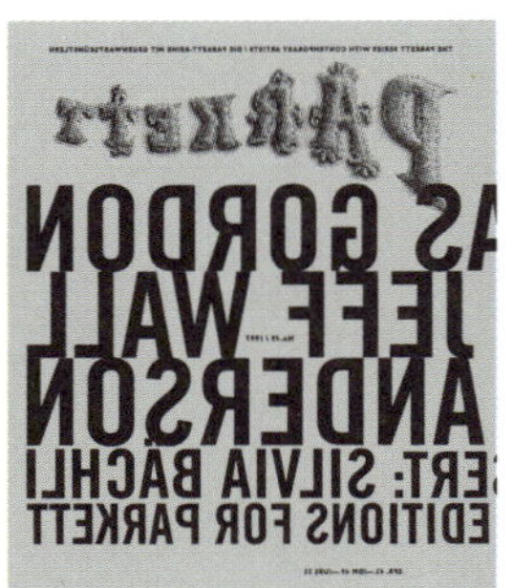

No. 49 - ISBN 3-907509-99-4

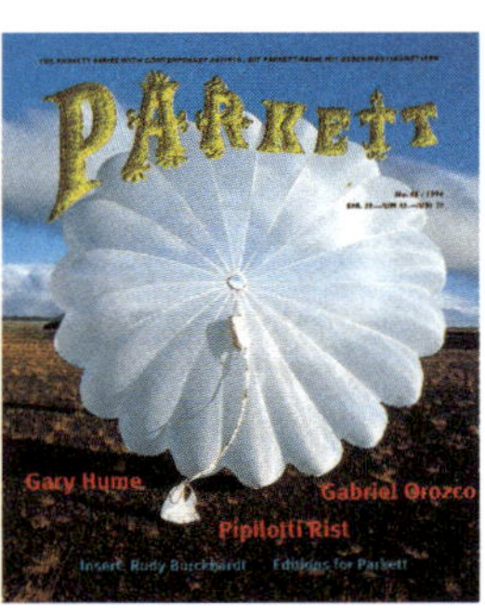

GARY HUME
GABRIEL OROZCO
PIPILOTTI RIST
BOVIER, MUIR, FOGLE, BONAMI
DE ZEGHER, SPECTOR, URSPRUNG
BABIAS, COLOMBO, ANDERSON
INSERT: **RUDY BURCKHARDT**
VINCENT KATZ: **RUDY BURCKHARDT**
VAN DER WALLE: **CHARLES LONG
& STEREOLAB**
FAYE HIRSCH: **BRUCE CONNER**
CHRISTOPH DOSWALD: **IAN ANÜLL**
CUMULUS: LEGGAT, SCHNEIDER

No. 48 - ISBN 3-907509-98-6

TONY OURSLER
RAYMOND PETTIBON
THOMAS SCHÜTTE
COOKE, RICHARD, NERI,
LEWIS, GROYS, ALS, RUGOFF,
GOODEVE, SEARLE, MARI, REUST,
WAKEFIELD, LOOCK, JANUS
INSERT: **ZOE LEONARD & CHERYL DUNYE**
JURI STEINER: **EMMA KUNZ**
MAX WECHSLER: **CHRISTOPH RÜTIMANN**
SUSAN MORGAN: **DIANE ARBUS**
CUMULUS: PRINCENTHAL, BOVIER/CHERIX

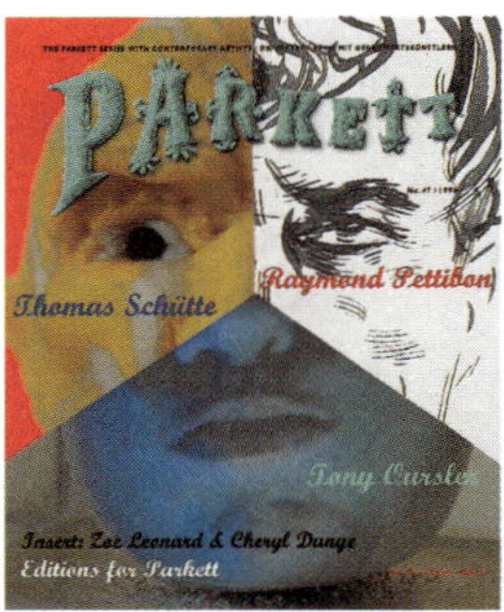

No. 47 - ISBN 3-907509-97-8

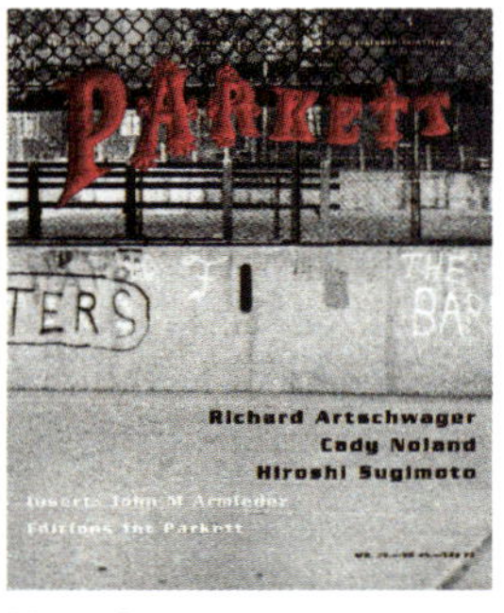

RICHARD ARTSCHWAGER
CADY NOLAND
HIROSHI SUGIMOTO
DEITCHER, SCHAFFNER, FORSTER, MUNIZ
ARMSTRONG, RELYEA, BOGDAN, GOODEVE
NICKAS, BRYSON, RUGOFF, DENSON
INSERT: **JOHN M ARMLEDER**
ROLAND WÄSPE: **ERWIN WURM**
DANIEL BIRNBAUM: **ÖYVIND FAHLSTRÖM**
LES INFOS DU PARADIS: ROBERT FLECK
CUMULUS: MILLER, VETTESE
BALKON: MARTIN HELLER

No. 46 - ISBN 3-907509-96-X

VIJA CELMINS
ANDREAS GURSKY
RIRKRIT TIRAVANIJA
PRINCENTHAL, LEWIS, SILVERTHORNE
SHIFF, CRIQUI, BURCKHARDT, WAKEFIELD
SCHORR, MELO, GILLICK, FLOOD, STEINER
INSERT: **HANS DANUSER**
LES INFOS: LIAM GILLICK & DOUGLAS GORDON
LYNNE COOKE, DAVID DEITCHER
DANIEL KURJAKOVIC: **MARIE JOSÉ BURKI**
NAN GOLDIN: **PETER HUJAR**
NOEMI SMOLIK: **ANDREAS SLOMINSKI**
JASON SIMON: **MARK DION**
LUK LAMBRECHT: **MARK LUYTEN**

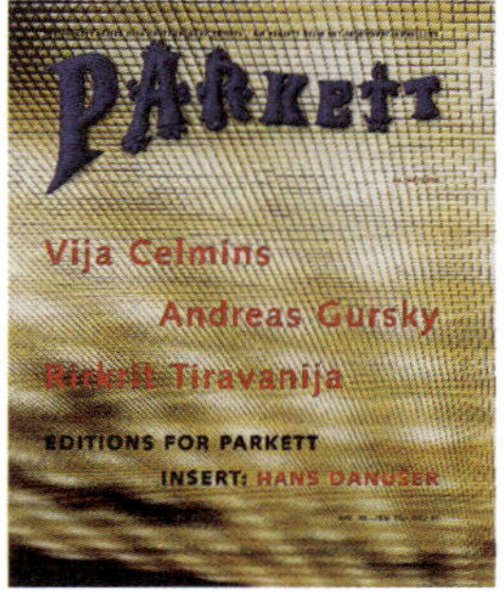

No. 44 - ISBN 3-907509-94-3

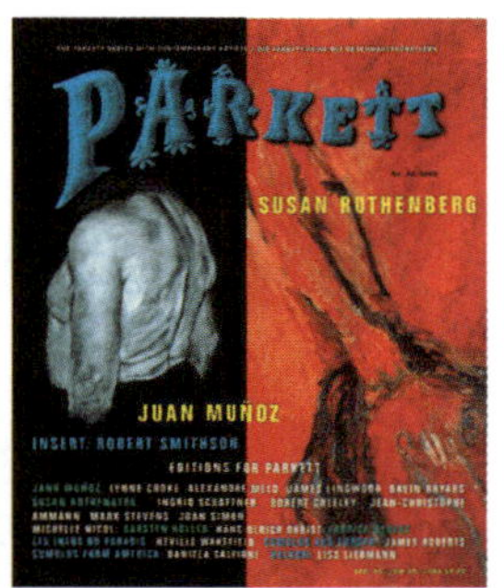

JUAN MUÑOZ
SUSAN ROTHENBERG
LYNNE COOKE, ALEXANDRE MELO
JAMES LINGWOOD, GAVIN BRYARS
ROBERT CREELEY, INGRID SCHAFFNER
JEAN-CHRISTOPHE AMMANN
MARK STEVENS, JOAN SIMON
INSERT: **ROBERT SMITHSON**
NEVILLE WAKEFIELD
MICHELLE NICOL: **CARSTEN HÖLLER**
HANS-ULRICH OBRIST: **FABRICE HYBERT**

No. 43 - ISBN 3-907509-93-5

LAWRENCE WEINER
RACHEL WHITEREAD
BROOKS ADAMS, FRANCES RICHARD
DIETER SCHWARZ, DANIELA SALVIONI
ED LEFFINGWELL, LANE RELYEA
NEVILLE WAKEFIELD, RUDOLF SCHMITZ
TREVOR FAIRBROTHER, SIMON WATNEY
INSERT: **NAN GOLDIN**
VINCE LEO: **ROBERT FRANK**
CLAUDE RITSCHARD: **MARKUS RAETZ**

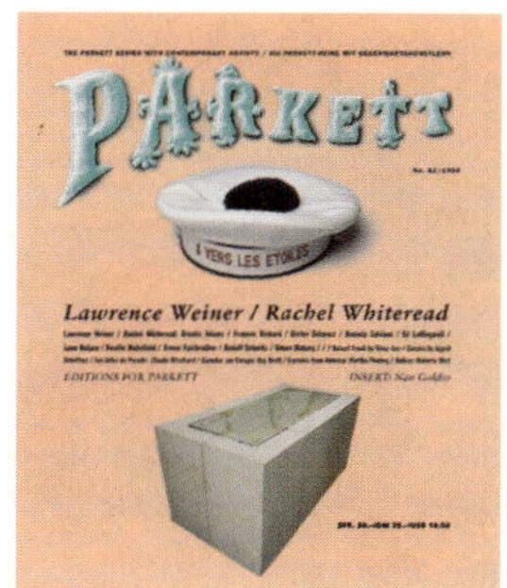

No. 42 - ISBN 3-907509-92-7

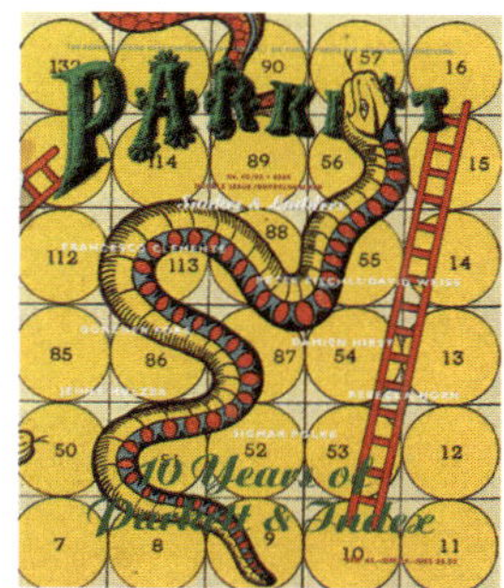

FRANCESCO CLEMENTE
GÜNTHER FÖRG
PETER FISCHLI / DAVID WEISS
DAMIEN HIRST
JENNY HOLZER
REBECCA HORN
SIGMAR POLKE
HOLLAND COTTER, BORIS GROYS
MAX WECHSLER, DAVID RIMANELLI
JOAN SIMON, GORDON BURN
GILBERT LASCAULT, WERNER SPIES
BICE CURIGER, JEFF PERRONE
G. ROGER DENSON, VIK MUNIZ
DAVE HICKEY

40/41 - ISBN 3-907509-90-0

FELIX GONZALEZ-TORRES
WOLFGANG LAIB
NANCY SPECTOR, SIMON WATNEY,
SUSAN TALLMAN, DIDIER SEMIN,
CLARE FARROW, JEAN-MARC AVRILLA,
THOMAS McEVILLEY
CLAUDE GINTZ: **GABRIEL OROZCO**
WALTER GRASSKAMP: **AXEL KASSEBÖHMER**
NEVILLE WAKEFIELD: **MATTHEW BARNEY**
INSERT: **RONI HORN**
LES INFOS DU PARADIS: **BURT BARR**
CUMULUS: **MEYER VAISMAN**

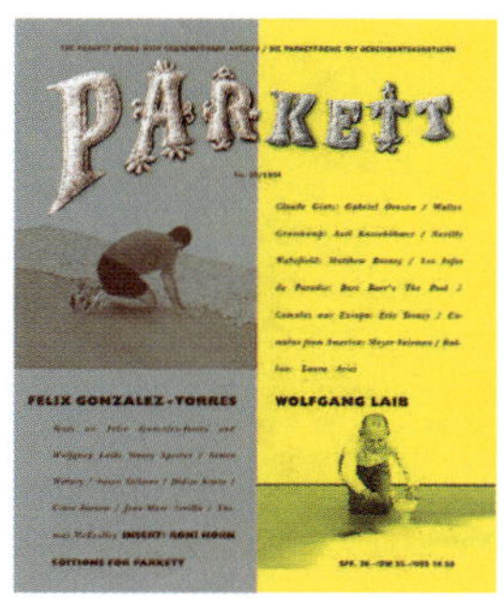

No. 39 - ISBN 3-907509-89-7

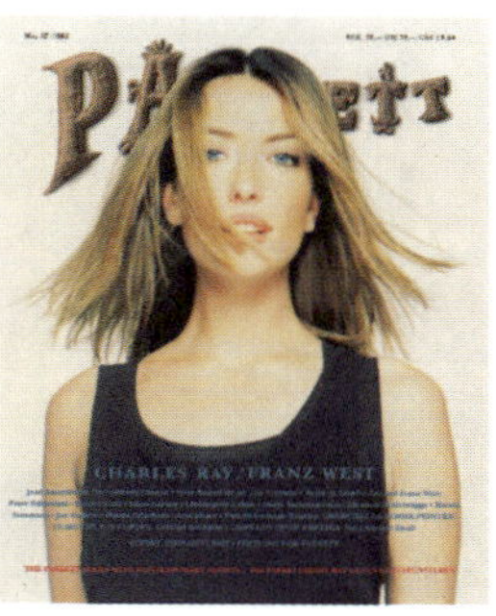

CHARLES RAY
FRANZ WEST
KLAUS KERTESS, CHRISTOPHER KNIGHT
PETER SCHJELDAHL, ROBERT STORR
JAN AVGIKOS, AXEL HUBER
MARTIN PRINZHORN, ELISABETH
SCHLEBRÜGGE, HARALD SZEEMANN,
DENYS ZACHAROPOULOS
INSERT: **PIPILOTTI RIST**
JEAN BAUDRILLARD
HANS RUDOLF REUST: **LUC TUYMANS**
PARKETT INQUIRY:
CHERCHEZ LA FEMME PEINTRE!

No. 37 - ISBN 3-907509-87-0

ILYA KABAKOV
RICHARD PRINCE
BORIS GROYS, ROBERT STORR
JAN THORN-PRIKKER
CLAUDIA JOLLES, EDMUND WHITE
SUSAN TALLMAN, DANIELA
SALVIONI, KATHY ACKER
INSERT: **TATSUO MIYAJIMA**
GUDRUN INBODEN: **ASTA GRÖTING**
LYNNE COOKE: **GARY HILL**
PATRICK McGRATH: **STEPHEN ELLIS**

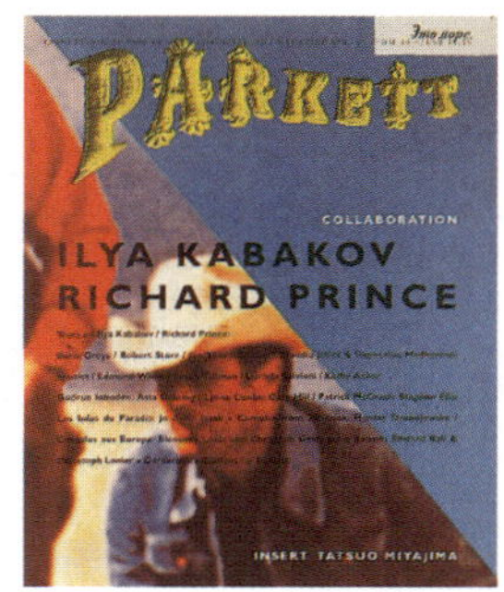

No. 34 - ISBN 3-907509-84-6

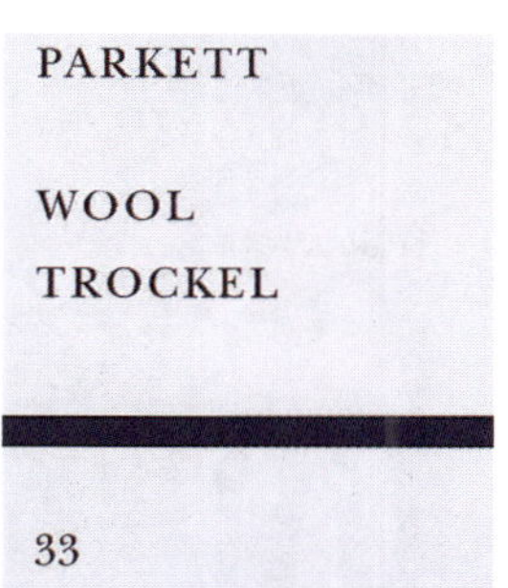

ROSEMARIE TROCKEL
CHRISTOPHER WOOL
VERONIQUE BACCHETTA,
BARRETT WATTEN,
ANNE WAGNER, JIM LEWIS,
GREIL MARCUS, JEFF PERRONE,
DIEDRICH DIEDERICHSEN
INSERT: **ADRIAN SCHIESS**
MARINA WARNER: **PENIS PLENTY**
G. ROGER DENSON:
DENNIS OPPENHEIM
CAMIEL VAN WINKEL

No. 33 - ISBN 3-907509-83-3

IMI KNOEBEL
SHERRIE LEVINE
RUDOLF BUMILLER
RAINER CRONE / DAVID MOOS
LISA LIEBMANN, DANIELA SALVIONI
ERICH FRANZ, HOWARD SINGERMANN
INSERT: **DAMIEN HIRST**
SHEENA WAGSTAFF: **VIJA CELMINS**
JIM LEWIS: **LARRY CLARK**
LIAM GILLICK: **BETHAN HUWS**
THOMAS KELLEIN: **WALTER DE MARIA**

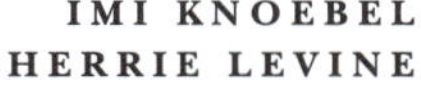
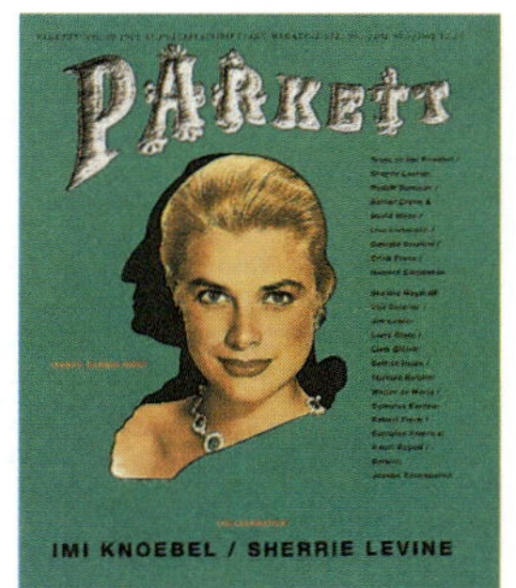

No. 32 - ISBN 3-907509-82-X

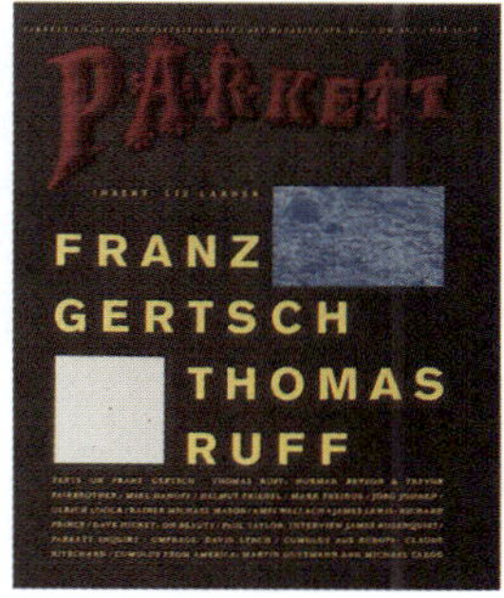

FRANZ GERTSCH
THOMAS RUFF
HELMUT FRIEDEL, ULRICH LOOCK
I. MICHAEL DANOFF, AMEI WALLACH
RAINER MICHAEL MASON
MARC FREIDUS, JÖRG JOHNEN
TREVOR FAIRBROTHER / NORMAN BRYSON
INSERT: **LIZ LARNER**
JAMES LEWIS: **RICHARD PRINCE**
DAVID HICKEY:
**THE INVISIBLE DRAGON /
DER UNSICHTBARE DRACHEN**
PAUL TAYLOR: **JAMES ROSENQUIST**

No. 28 - ISBN 3-907509-78-1

ALIGHIERO E BOETTI
JEAN-CHRISTOPHE AMMANN
GIOVAN BATTISTA SALERNO
RAINER CRONE & DAVID MOOS
FRIEDEMANN MALSCH
JEAN-PIERRE BORDAZ
ALAIN CUEFF
INSERT: **CINDY SHERMAN**
SHEENA WAGSTAFF:
SOPHIE CALLE
HERBERT LACHMEYER/
BRIGITTE FELDERER: **FRANZ WEST**
JUTTA KOETHER: **MIKE KELLEY**

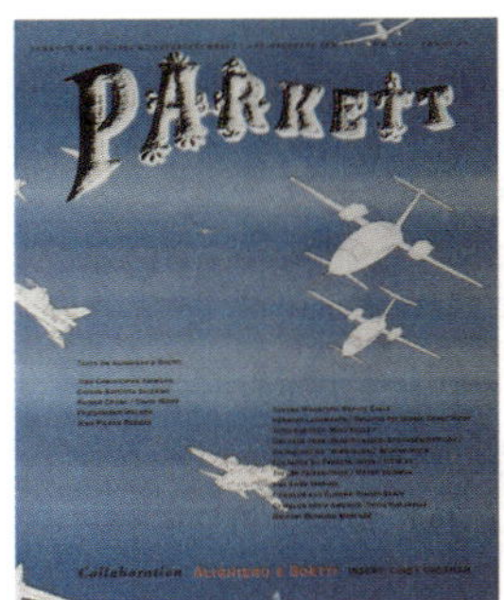

No. 24 - ISBN 3-907509-74-9

RICHARD ARTSCHWAGER
ARTHUR C. DANTO, GEORG KOHLER,
MARIO A. ORLANDO, JOYCE
CAROL OATES, WERNER OECHSLIN,
ALAN LIGHTMAN, PATRICK
McGRATH, DANIEL SOUTIF,
LASZLO F. FÖLDENYI, JEAN STROUSE
INSERT: **DAVID BYRNE**
RENATE PUVOGEL: **ANDRÉ THOMKINS**
ULRICH LOOCK: **THOMAS STRUTH**
NANCY SPECTOR: **MEREDITH MONK**

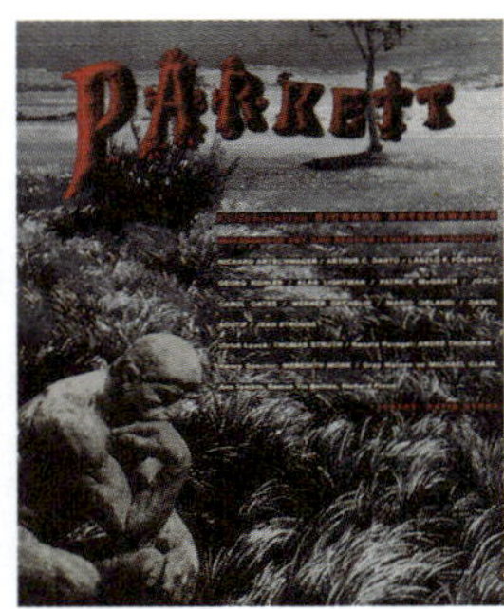

No. 23 - ISBN 3-907509-73-0

ALEX KATZ
JOHN RUSSELL, BROOKS ADAMS,
DAVID RIMANELLI, FRANCESCO
CLEMENTE, MICHAEL KRÜGER,
RICHARD FLOOD, PATRICK FREY,
CARL STIGLIANO, BICE CURIGER,
GLENN O'BRIEN
INSERT: **WILLIAM WEGMAN**
LISA LIEBMAN: **ROBERT GOBER**
JACQUELINE BURCKHARDT:
GIULIO ROMANO

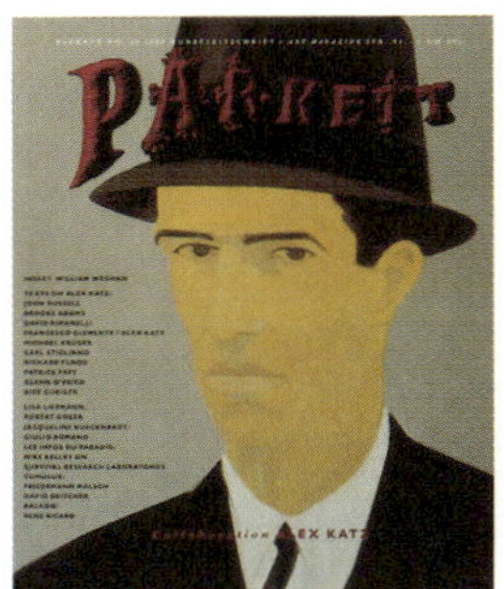

No. 21 - ISBN 3-907509-71-4

MARIO MERZ
MARLIS GRÜTERICH, JEANNE
SILVERTHORNE, DEMOSTHENES
DAVVETAS, HARALD SZEEMANN,
DENYS ZACHAROPOULOS
INSERT: **GENERAL IDEA**
MAX KOZLOFF: **GILLES PERESS**
FRIEDEMANN MALSCH:
GEORG HEROLD
BRUNELLA ANTOMARINI:
FRANCESCA WOODMAN

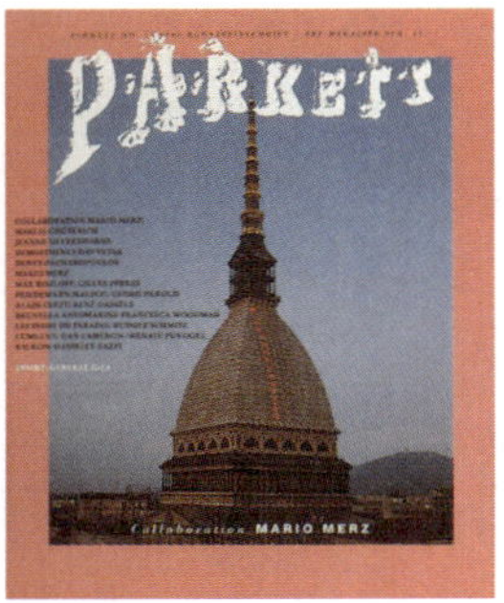

No. 15 - ISBN 3-907509-65-X

GILBERT & GEORGE
DUNCAN FALLOWELL, MARIO
CODOGNATO, JEREMY COOPER,
DEMOSTHENES DAVVETAS,
WOLF JAHN
INSERT: **ROSEMARIE TROCKEL**
ROBERT STORR: **NANCY SPERO**
HAIM STEINBACH: **MANIFESTO**
JÖRG ZUTTER: **THOMAS HUBER**

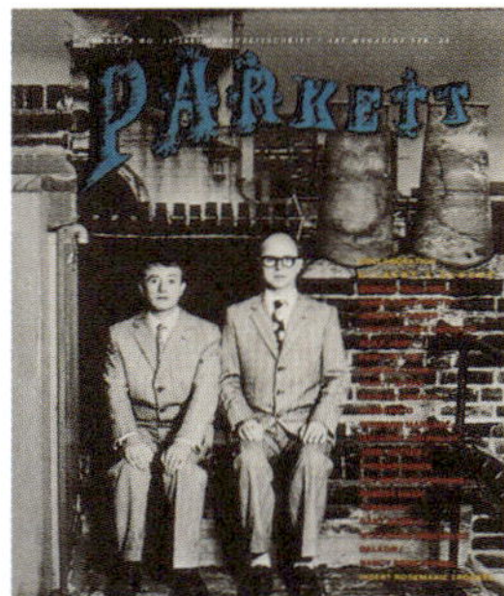

No. 14 - ISBN 3-907509-64-1

GEORG BASELITZ
REMO GUIDIERI, DIETER
KOEPPLIN, ERIC DARRAGON,
RAINER MICHAEL MASON, FRANZ
MEYER, JOHN CALDWELL
INSERT: **BARBARA KRUGER**
GRAY WATSON: **DEREK JARMAN**
CAROL SQUIERS:
PHOTO OPPORTUNITY
ROSETTA BROOKS:
TROY BRAUNTUCH

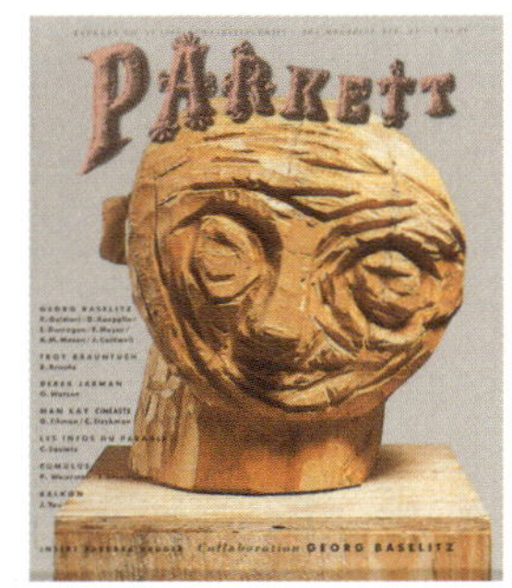

No. 11 - ISBN 3-907509-61-7

The PARKETT Series is created in collaboration with artists, who contribute an original work available exclusively to the subscribers in the form of a signed limited SPECIAL EDITION. The available works are also reproduced in each PARKETT issue.

Each SPECIAL EDITION is available by order from any one of our offices in New York or Zurich. Just fill in the details below and send this card to the office nearest you. Once your order has been processed, you will be issued with an invoice and your personal edition number. Upon receipt of payment, you will receive the SPECIAL EDITION. (Please note that supply is subject to availability. PARKETT does not assume responsibility for any delays in production of SPECIAL EDITIONS. Postage is not included.)

☐ As a subscriber to PARKETT, I would like to order the following Special Edition(s), signed and numbered by the artist.

PARKETT No.	ARTIST	NAME:
PARKETT No.	ARTIST	ADDRESS:
PARKETT No.	ARTIST	CITY:
PARKETT No.	ARTIST	STATE/ZIP:
PARKETT No.	ARTIST	COUNTRY:
PARKETT No.	ARTIST	PHONE:

☐ I have indicated my way of payment on the reverse side of this form.

Send this form to the PARKETT office nearest you:

PARKETT PUBLISHERS   155 AV. OF THE AMERICAS   NEW YORK, NY 10013   PHONE (212) 673-2660   FAX (212) 271-0704

PARKETT VERLAG   QUELLENSTRASSE 27   CH-8031 ZÜRICH   TELEFON +41-1-271 81 40   FAX +41-1-272 43 01

Visit our website: www.parkettart.com

KÜNSTLEREDITIONEN FÜR PARKETT-ABONNENTEN
WWW.PARKETTART.COM

65

Die PARKETT-Buchreihe entsteht in Zusammenarbeit mit Künstlern, die eigens für die Abonnenten einen Originalbeitrag in Form einer limitierten und signierten EDITION gestalten. Diese Editionen sind auch in der Zeitschrift abgebildet und können mit dieser Bestellkarte in jedem unserer Büros in Zürich, Frankfurt oder New York bestellt werden. Sie erhalten dann Ihre persönliche Editionsnummer und eine Rechnung. Sobald wir Ihre Zahlung erhalten haben, schicken wir Ihnen Ihre Edition(en). Lieferung solange Vorrat. PARKETT übernimmt keine Verantwortung für allfällige Verzögerungen bei der Herstellung der Vorzugsausgaben. Versandkosten und MwSt (Schweiz) nicht inbegriffen.

☐ Ich bin PARKETT-Abonnent(in) und bestelle folgende EDITION(EN), nummeriert und vom Künstler signiert:

PARKETT Nr.	KÜNSTLER/IN	NAME:
PARKETT Nr.	KÜNSTLER/IN	STRASSE:
PARKETT Nr.	KÜNSTLER/IN	PLZ/STADT:
PARKETT Nr.	KÜNSTLER/IN	LAND:
PARKETT Nr.	KÜNSTLER/IN	TEL.:

☐ Meine Zahlungsweise habe ich auf der Rückseite angegeben.

Senden Sie die Bestellkarte an das PARKETT-Büro in Ihrer Nähe:

PARKETT VERLAG   QUELLENSTRASSE 27   CH-8031 ZÜRICH   TELEFON +41-1-271 81 40   FAX +41-1-272 43 01

PARKETT PUBLISHERS   155 AV. OF THE AMERICAS   NEW YORK, NY 10013   PHONE (212) 673-2660   FAX (212) 271-0704

Besuchen Sie unsere Website: www.parkettart.com

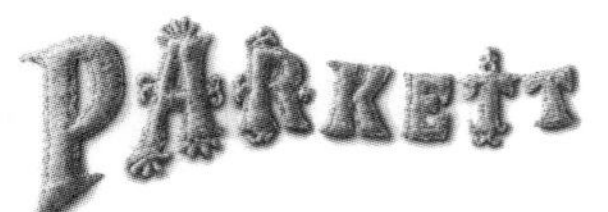

SUBSCRIBE, COMPLETE OR SEND A GIFT SUBSCRIPTION TO THE BEST BOOK SERIES ON CONTEMPORARY ARTISTS – WWW.PARKETTART.COM

☐ I wish to subscribe to the PARKETT Series, starting with issue no. _______
☐ I wish to send a gift subscription, starting with issue no. _______ (a gift card in my name will be sent to the recipient):

   ☐ for 1 year (3 issues) at US $ 80 (USA/Canada), € 82 (Europe), € 98 (Rest of the World)
   ☐ for 2 years (6 issues) at US $ 145 (USA/Canada), € 150 (Europe), € 188 (Rest of the World)
   ☐ for 3 years (9 issues) at US $ 205 (USA/Canada), € 212 (Europe), € 278 (Rest of the World)
   ☐ for 1 year (3 issues) at the special student discount (US $ 65 for USA/Canada, € 67 for Europe). A copy of my student ID is enclosed.
   Postage included. All prices subject to change.

☐ I wish to complete my PARKETT library and order the following issue(s):

No. ____
at € 30 each (up to no. 43: € 20; no. 44–48: € 28), postage not included. Within the USA & Canada $ 32 (up to no. 43: $ 22.50; no. 44–48: $ 29), add postage: $ 5 (USA), $ 10 (Canada). (Sold out: No. 1–10, 12, 13, 16, 17, 19, 22, 25, 26, 27, 29–31, 35, 36, 38, 45).

☐ I wish to order _______ copies of the New PARKETT Postcard Set with Text Booklet on MoMA Show. Featuring all artists' editions made for PARKETT since 1984 and a booklet with essays by Deborah Wye (Chief Curator Illustrated Books and Prints at MoMA) and Susan Tallman. 128 color postcards, booklet with 2 texts, color reproductions of all 64 PARKETT covers. 64 p., packed in a box, 6¼ x 4¾ x 2⅜", € 30 (USA $ 27) per set, plus postage.

NAME: ____

ADDRESS: ____

CITY: ____

STATE/ZIP/COUNTRY: __________________________________

TEL.: ______________________ FAX: ___________________

E-MAIL: ____

GIFT RECIPIENT: ______________________________________

ADDRESS: ____

CITY: ____

STATE/ZIP: ____

COUNTRY: ____

☐ Charge my Visa Card ☐ Mastercard ☐ AMEX

Card No. |_|_|_|_|_|_|_|_|_|_|_|_|_|_| Expiration date _______

☐ Payment enclosed (US check or money order) ☐ Bill me

DATE ____

SIGNATURE ____

Send this form to the PARKETT office nearest you:

PARKETT PUBLISHERS 155 AV. OF THE AMERICAS NEW YORK, NY 10013 PHONE (212) 673-2660 FAX (212) 271-0704
PARKETT VERLAG QUELLENSTRASSE 27 CH-8031 ZÜRICH TELEFON +41-1-271 81 40 FAX +41-1-272 43 01
Visit our website: www.parkettart.com

ABONNIEREN, VERVOLLSTÄNDIGEN ODER VERSCHENKEN SIE DIE UMFASSENDSTE BUCHREIHE ÜBER GEGENWARTSKÜNSTLER – WWW.PARKETTART.COM

☐ Ich abonniere die PARKETT-Reihe ab Nr. _______
☐ Ich verschenke ein PARKETT-Abonnement ab Nr. _______ (Der/die Beschenkte erhält eine Geschenkkarte in meinem Namen)

   ☐ für 1 Jahr (3 Bände) zu: € 78 (Deutschland), CHF 116.– (Schweiz), € 82 (übriges Europa)
   ☐ für 2 Jahre (6 Bände) zu: € 140 (Deutschland), CHF 216.– (Schweiz), € 150 (übriges Europa)
   ☐ für 3 Jahre (9 Bände) zu: € 200 (Deutschland), CHF 312.– (Schweiz), € 212 (übriges Europa)
   ☐ für 1 Jahr (3 Bände) zum Studenten-Sonderpreis (Deutschland: € 65 /Schweiz: CHF 96.– / übriges Europa: € 67). Eine Kopie meines gültigen Studentenausweises lege ich bei.
   Preise einschliesslich Versandkosten. Preisänderungen vorbehalten.

☐ Ich möchte meine PARKETT-Bibliothek vervollständigen und bestelle die folgenden noch erhältliche(n) Ausgabe(n):

Nr. ____
zu je € 30 / CHF 45.– (bis Nr. 43: € 20 / CHF 30.–; Nr. 44–48: € 28 / CHF 39.–), zzgl. Versandkosten (vergriffen: Nr. 1–10, 12, 13, 16, 17, 19, 22, 25, 26, 27, 29–31, 35, 36, 38, 45).

☐ Ich bestelle _______ Ex. des Neuen PARKETT-Postkarten-Sets mit Textbüchlein zur MoMA-Ausstellung. Mit Postkarten der seit 1984 von Künstlern für PARKETT geschaffenen Editionen. Das Textbüchlein enthält 2 Essays zur Ausstellung im MoMA, New York, von Deborah Wye (Chefkuratorin für illustrierte Bücher und Grafik am MoMA) und Susan Tallman. 128 Farbpostkarten, Büchlein mit zwei Texten, Farbabb. aller 64 PARKETT-Titelblätter u.a.m. 64 S., in bunter Schachtel, 16 x 12 x 6 cm. € 30 / CHF 45.– pro Set, zzgl. Versandkosten.

NAME: ____

STRASSE: ____

PLZ/STADT: ____

LAND: ____

TEL.: ______________________ FAX: ___________________

E-MAIL: ____

BESCHENKTE(R): ______________________________________

STRASSE: ____

PLZ/STADT: ____

LAND: ____

☐ Ich zahle mit Visa ☐ Eurocard/Mastercard ☐ AMEX

Karten Nr. |_|_|_|_|_|_|_|_|_|_|_|_|_|_| Gültig bis _______

☐ Mein Scheck über CHF/€ _____________________ liegt bei.

☐ Bitte senden Sie mir eine Rechnung.

DATUM ____

UNTERSCHRIFT ____

Senden Sie die Bestellkarte an das PARKETT-Büro in Ihrer Nähe:

PARKETT VERLAG QUELLENSTRASSE 27 CH-8031 ZÜRICH TELEFON +41-1-271 81 40 FAX +41-1-272 43 01
PARKETT PUBLISHERS 155 AV. OF THE AMERICAS NEW YORK, NY 10013 PHONE (212) 673-2660 FAX (212) 271-0704
Besuchen Sie unsere Website: www.parkettart.com

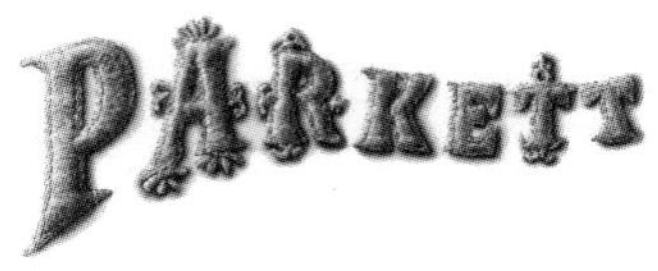

ARTISTS' MONOGRAPHS & EDITIONS / KÜNSTLERMONOGRAPHIEN & EDITIONEN

FOR AVAILABILITY SEE NEXT PAGE / LIEFERBARKEIT SIEHE FOLGENDE SEITE

Doug Aitken, vol. 57
Laurie Anderson, vol. 49
John Armleder, vol. 50/51
Richard Artschwager, vol. 23, vol. 46
John Baldessari, vol. 29
Stephan Balkenhol, vol. 36
Matthew Barney, vol. 45
Georg Baselitz, vol. 11
Vanessa Beecroft, vol. 56
Ross Bleckner, vol. 38
Alighiero e Boetti, vol. 24
Christian Boltanski, vol. 22
Louise Bourgeois, vol. 27
Angela Bulloch, vol. 66
Daniel Buren, vol. 66
Sophie Calle, vol. 36
Maurizio Cattelan, vol. 59
Vija Celmins, vol. 44
Francesco Clemente, vol. 9 & 40/41
Chuck Close, vol. 60
Enzo Cucchi, vol. 1
John Currin, vol. 65
Tacita Dean, vol. 62
Thomas Demand, vol. 62
Martin Disler, vol. 3
Marlene Dumas, vol. 38
Olafur Eliasson, vol. 64
Tracey Emin, vol. 63
Eric Fischl, vol. 5
Peter Fischli/David Weiss, vol.17, 40/41
Sylvie Fleury, vol. 58
Günther Förg, vol. 26 & 40/41
Tom Friedman, vol. 64
Katharina Fritsch, vol. 25
Liam Gillick, vol. 61
Franz Gertsch, vol. 28
Gilbert & George, vol. 14
Robert Gober, vol. 27
Nan Goldin, vol. 57
Felix Gonzalez-Torres, vol. 39
Douglas Gordon, vol. 49
Rodney Graham, vol. 64

Andreas Gursky, vol. 44
David Hammons, vol. 31
Thomas Hirschhorn, vol. 57
Damien Hirst, vol. 40/41
Jenny Holzer, vol. 40/41
Rebecca Horn, vol. 13 & 40/41
Roni Horn, vol. 54
Pierre Huyghe, vol. 66
Gary Hume, vol. 48
Ilya Kabakov, vol. 34
Alex Katz, vol. 21
Mike Kelley, vol. 31
Ellsworth Kelly, vol. 56
William Kentridge, vol. 63
Karen Kilimnik, vol. 52
Martin Kippenberger, vol. 19
Imi Knoebel, vol. 32
Jeff Koons, vol. 19, 50/51
Jannis Kounellis, vol. 6
Yayoi Kusama, vol. 59
Wolfgang Laib, vol. 39
Sherrie Levine, vol. 32
Sarah Lucas, vol. 45
Brice Marden, vol. 7
Mario Merz, vol. 15
Tracey Moffatt, vol. 53
Mariko Mori, vol. 54
Malcolm Morley, vol. 52
Sarah Morris, vol. 61
Juan Muñoz, vol. 43
Jean-Luc Mylayne, vol. 50/51
Bruce Nauman, vol. 10
Cady Noland, vol. 46
Meret Oppenheim, vol. 4
Gabriel Orozco, vol. 48
Tony Oursler, vol. 47
Laura Owens, vol. 65
Jorge Pardo, vol. 56
Raymond Pettibon, vol. 47
Elizabeth Peyton, vol. 53
Sigmar Polke, vol. 2, 30 & 40/41
Richard Prince, vol. 34

Michael Raedecker, vol. 65
Markus Raetz, vol. 8
Charles Ray, vol. 37
Jason Rhoades, vol. 58
Gerhard Richter, vol. 35
Bridget Riley, vol. 61
Pipilotti Rist, vol. 48
Matthew Ritchie, vol. 61
Tim Rollins & K.O.S., vol. 20
Ugo Rondinone, vol. 52
James Rosenquist, vol. 58
Susan Rothenberg, vol. 43
Thomas Ruff, vol. 28
Edward Ruscha, vol. 18 & 55
Gregor Schneider, vol. 63
Thomas Schütte, vol. 47
Cindy Sherman, vol. 29
Roman Signer, vol. 45
Andreas Slominski, vol. 55
Beat Streuli, vol. 54
Thomas Struth, vol. 50/51
Hiroshi Sugimoto, vol. 46
Philip Taaffe, vol. 26
Sam Taylor-Wood, vol. 55
Diana Thater, vol. 60
Wolfgang Tillmans, vol. 53
Rirkrit Tiravanija, vol. 44
Rosemarie Trockel, vol. 33
James Turrell, vol. 25
Luc Tuymans, vol. 60
Kara Walker, vol. 59
Jeff Wall, vol. 22 & 49
Andy Warhol, vol. 12
Lawrence Weiner, vol. 42
John Wesley, vol. 62
Franz West, vol. 37
Rachel Whiteread, vol. 42
Sue Williams, vol 50/51
Robert Wilson, vol. 16
Christopher Wool, vol. 33

vol.	Collaboration				vol.	Collaboration				vol.	Collaboration		
66	Angela Bulloch	m	e		50/51	John Armleder	m			32	Imi Knoebel	m	
	Daniel Buren	m	e			Jeff Koons	m	e			Sherrie Levine	m	
	Pierre Huyghe	m	e			Jean-Luc Mylayne	m			31	David Hammons		
65	John Currin	m	e			Thomas Struth	m			31	Mike Kelley		
	Laura Owens	m	e			Sue Williams	m			30	Sigmar Polke		
	Michael Raedecker	m	e		49	Laurie Anderson	m	e		29	John Baldessari		
64	Olafur Eliasson	m				Douglas Gordon	m			29	Cindy Sherman		
	Tom Friedman	m				Jeff Wall	m			28	Franz Gertsch	m	
	Rodney Graham	m			48	Gary Hume	m				Thomas Ruff	m	
63	Tracey Emin	m	e			Gabriel Orozco	m			27	Louise Bourgeois		
	William Kentridge	m	e			Pipilotti Rist	m				Robert Gober		
	Gregor Schneider	m			47	Tony Oursler	m			26	Günther Förg		
62	Tacita Dean	m	e			Raymond Pettibon	m				Philip Taaffe		
	Thomas Demand	m				Thomas Schütte	m	e		25	Katharina Fritsch	m	e
	John Wesley	m	e		46	Richard Artschwager	m				James Turrell	m	e
61	Liam Gillick	m				Cady Noland	m			24	Alighiero e Boetti	m	e
	Sarah Morris	m	e			Hiroshi Sugimoto	m			23	Richard Artschwager	m	
	Bridget Riley	m	e		45	Matthew Barney	m			22	Christian Boltanski		
	Matthew Ritchie	m	e			Sarah Lucas	m				Jeff Wall		
60	Chuck Close	m				Roman Signer	m	e		21	Alex Katz	m	e
	Diana Thater	m	e		44	Vija Celmins	m			20	Tim Rollins + K.O.S.	m	
	Luc Tuymans	m	e			Andreas Gursky	m			19	Martin Kippenberger		
59	Maurizio Cattelan	m				Rirkrit Tiravanija	m	e			Jeff Koons		
	Yayoi Kusama	m	e		43	Juan Muñoz	m			18	Ed Ruscha	m	
	Kara Walker	m				Susan Rothenberg	m	e		17	Fischli/Weiss		
58	Sylvie Fleury	m	e		42	Lawrence Weiner	m	e		16	Robert Wilson		
	Jason Rhoades	m	e			Rachel Whiteread	m			15	Mario Merz	m	
	James Rosenquist	m	e		40/41	Francesco Clemente	m			14	Gilbert & George	m	
57	Doug Aitken	m	e			Fischli/Weiss	m			13	Rebecca Horn		
	Nan Goldin	m				Günther Förg	m			12	Andy Warhol		
	Thomas Hirschhorn	m				Damien Hirst	m			11	Georg Baselitz	m	
56	Vanessa Beecroft	m				Jenny Holzer	m			10	Bruce Nauman		
	Ellsworth Kelly	m				Rebecca Horn	m			9	Francesco Clemente		
	Jorge Pardo	m	e			Sigmar Polke	m			8	Markus Raetz		
55	Edward Ruscha	m			39	Felix Gonzalez-Torres	m			7	Brice Marden		
	Andreas Slominski	m				Wolfgang Laib	m			6	Jannis Kounellis		
	Sam Taylor-Wood	m			38	Ross Bleckner				5	Eric Fischl		
54	Roni Horn	m	e			Marlene Dumas				4	Meret Oppenheim		
	Mariko Mori	m			37	Charles Ray	m			3	Martin Disler		
	Beat Streuli	m				Franz West	m	e		2	Sigmar Polke		
53	Tracey Moffatt	m			36	Stephan Balkenhol				1	Enzo Cucchi		
	Elizabeth Peyton	m				Sophie Calle							
	Wolfgang Tillmans	m			35	Gerhard Richter							
52	Karen Kilimnik	m	e		34	Ilya Kabakov	m						
	Malcolm Morley	m	e			Richard Prince	m						
	Ugo Rondinone	m	e		33	Rosemarie Trockel	m						
						Christopher Wool	m						

m = available monograph / erhältliche Monographie, e = available edition / erhältliche Edition
Delivery subject to availability at time of order / Lieferung solange Vorrat

EDITIONS FOR PARKETT

PARKETT 65

JOHN CURRIN

THE BEGGAR'S ALMS, 2002

Etching with aquatint, sugarlift, spitbite, and drypoint on Somerset
soft white textured, 250gsm
Paper size 23½ x 18½", image 10½ x 8½"
Printed by Greg Burnet, Burnet Editions, New York
Edition of 70, signed and numbered, **$ 1550 / € 1600**

DAS ALMOSEN DER BETTLERIN, 2002

Radierung mit Aquatinta, Zuckertusche, Pinselätzung und Kaltnadel
auf Somerset soft white mit leichter Textur, 250 g/m²
Blatt 59,8 x 47,2 cm, Druck 26,5 x 21,5 cm
Gedruckt bei Greg Burnet, Burnet Editions, New York
Auflage: 70, signiert und nummeriert, **CHF 2400.– / € 1600**

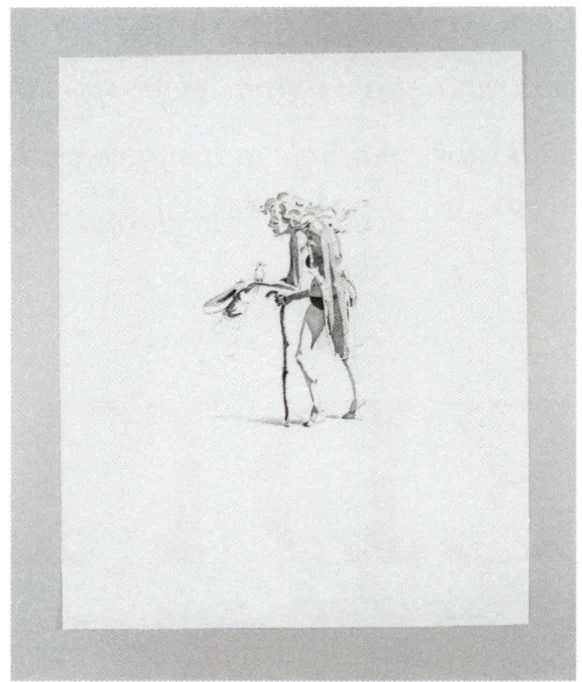

PARKETT 65

LAURA OWENS

UNTITLED, 2002

Handprinted 10-color lithograph on tan BFK Rives with three collage
elements: one handpainted with watercolor on blue Magnani Pescia, two on
white BFK Rives, the color of the moon will vary with each print, 18 x 12"
Printed by Ed Hamilton, Hamilton Press, Venice, California
Edition of 70, signed and numbered on the back, **$ 1250 / € 1300**

OHNE TITEL, 2002

Handgedruckte 10-Farben-Lithographie auf getöntem BFK Rives mit drei
Collage-Elementen: eines handbemalt mit Wasserfarbe auf Magnani Pescia
(Blau), zwei auf weissem BFK Rives, die Farbe des Mondes variiert von Blatt
zu Blatt, 45,8 x 30,6 cm
Gedruckt bei Ed Hamilton, Hamilton Press, Venice, Kalifornien
Auflage: 70, rückseitig signiert und nummeriert, **CHF 1900.– / € 1300**

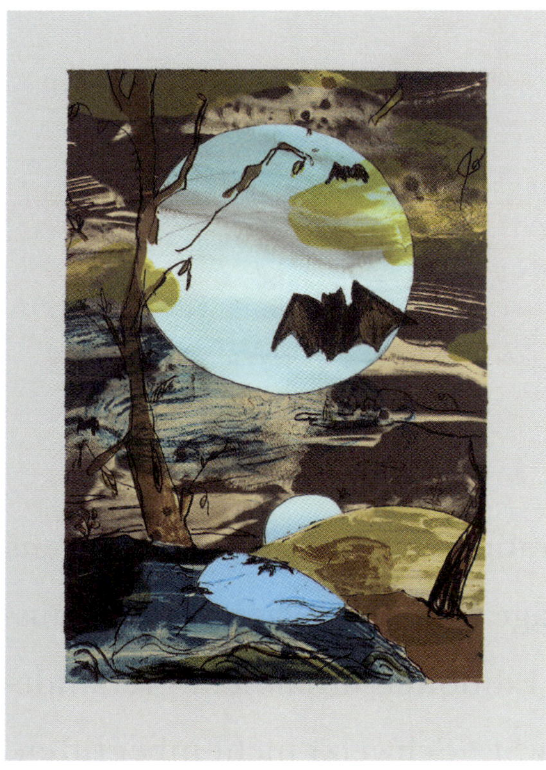

MICHAEL RAEDECKER
THE OTHER SIDE, 2002

10-color silkscreen print on pure silk satin scarf
with handrolled border, 33½ x 33½"
Detail from the back of the painting INCOMPLETE (2002)
Produced by Fabric Frontline, Zurich
Edition of 99, signed and numbered certificate,
$ 500 / € 550

10-Farben-Siebdruck auf Seidensatinfoulard,
handrouliert, 85 x 85 cm
Produktion: Fabric Frontline, Zürich
Ausschnitt der Rückansicht des Bildes INCOMPLETE (2002)
Auflage: 99, signiertes und nummeriertes Zertifikat,
CHF 770.– / € 550

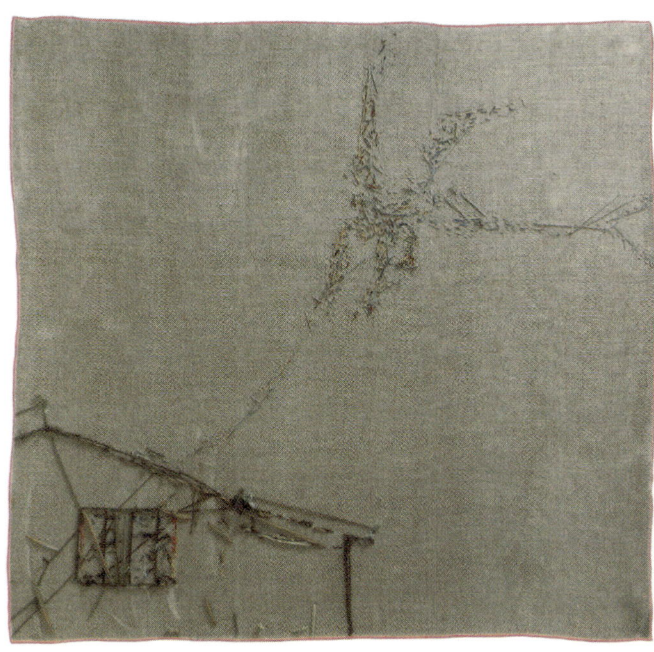

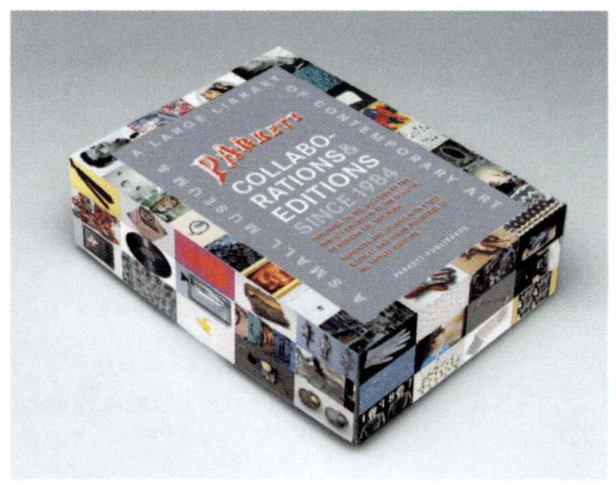

CHF 45.– / $ 27 / € 30
ISBN 3-907582-23-3

NEW PARKETT POSTCARD SET WITH
TEXT BOOKLET ON MOMA SHOW

Featuring the artists' editions made for PARKETT since 1984
and a booklet with essays by Deborah Wye (Chief Curator Illustrated Books
and Prints at MoMA) and Susan Tallman.
128 color postcards, booklet with 2 texts, color reproductions of all
64 PARKETT covers. 64 p., packed in a white box, 6¼ x 4¾ x 2⅜".

NEUES PARKETT-POSTKARTEN-SET MIT
TEXTBÜCHLEIN ZUR MOMA-AUSSTELLUNG

Mit Postkarten aller 128 seit 1984 von Künstlern für PARKETT geschaffenen
Editionen. Das Textbüchlein enthält zwei Essays zur Ausstellung im MoMA,
New York, von Deborah Wye (Chefkuratorin für illustrierte Bücher
und Grafik am MoMA) und Susan Tallman.
128 Farbpostkarten, Büchlein mit zwei Texten, Farbabb. aller
64 PARKETT-Titelblätter u.a.m. 64 S., in weisser Schachtel, 16 x 12 x 6 cm.

PARKETT IN BOOKSHOPS (Selection)

NORTH & SOUTH AMERICA, ASIA, AUSTRALIA

DISTRIBUTOR / VERTRIEB
D.A.P. (DISTRIBUTED ART PUBLISHERS)
155 AVENUE OF THE AMERICAS, 2ND FLOOR, NEW YORK, NY 10013

USA

AUSTIN, TX
BOOK PEOPLE
603 N. LAMAR

BERKELEY, CA
BERKELEY ART MUSEUM
2625 DURANT AVENUE
CODY'S BOOKS
2454 TELEGRAPHE AVENUE

BEVERLY HILLS, CA
RIZZOLI
9501 WILSHIRE BOULEVARD

BOSTON, MA
INSTITUTE OF CONTEMPORARY ART
955 BOYLSTON STREET
TRIDENT BOOKSELLERS
338 NEWBURY STREET

BUFFALO, NY
TALKING LEAVES
3158 MAIN STREET

CAMBRIDGE, MA
MIT PRESS BOOKSTORE
292 MAIN STREET

CHICAGO, IL
ART INSTITUTE OF CHICAGO
104 S. MICHIGAN
MUSEUM OF CONTEMPORARY ART
220 EAST CHICAGO AVENUE
QUIMBY'S
1854 W. NORTH AVENUE
SMART MUSEUM OF ART
5550 S. GREENWOOD AVENUE

CINCINNATI, OH
CONTEMPORARY ARTS CENTER
115 E. 5TH STREET

COLUMBUS, OH
COLUMBUS MUSEUM OF ART
372 COMMONS MALL
WEXNER CENTER BOOKSTORE
30 W. 15TH STREET

CORAL GABLES, FL
BOOKS & BOOKS
296 ARAGON ROAD

HOUSTON, TX
BRAZOS BOOKSTORE
2421 BISSONNET
CONTEMPORARY ARTS MUSEUM
5216 MONTROSE BOULEVARD
MENIL COLLECTION
1520 SUL ROSS

HUNTINGTON, WV
HUNTINGTON MUSEUM OF ART
2033 MCCOY ROAD

LOS ANGELES, CA
BOOKSOUP
8818 SUNSET BOULEVARD
MUSEUM OF CONTEMPORARY ART
250, S. GRAND
UCLA / ARMAND HAMMER MUSEUM OF ART
10899 WILSHIRE BOULEVARD

MIAMI, FL
BOOKS & BOOKS
296 ARAGON AVENUE, CORAL GABLES
MUSEUM OF CONTEMPORARY ART
770 N.E. 125TH STREET NORTH MIAMI

MINNEAPOLIS, MN
THE WALKER ART CENTER BOOKSTORE
VINELAND PLACE

NEW YORK, NY
GUGGENHEIM DOWNTOWN MUSEUM
575 BROADWAY
MUSEUM OF MODERN ART
11 W. 53RD STREET
NEW MUSEUM OF CONTEMPORARY ART
583 BROADWAY
RIZZOLI
454 WEST BROADWAY
SAINT MARK'S BOOKSTORE
31 3RD AVENUE

OAKLAND, CA
DIESEL, A BOOKSTORE
5433 COLLEGE AVENUE

OAK PARK, MI
BOOK BEAT LTD.
26010 GREENFIELD

OMAHA, NE
JOSLYN ART MUSEUM
2200 DODGE STREET

PHILADELPHIA, PA
AVRIL 50
3406 SANSOM STREET
WATERSTONE BOOKSELLERS
2191 HORNIG ROAD

PITTSBURGH, PA
CARNEGIE INSTITUTE
4400 FORBES AVENUE

PORTLAND, OR
POWELL'S BOOKS
7 NW 9TH STREET

PROVIDENCE, NY
ACCIDENT OR DESIGN
128 N. MAIN STREET
RHODE ISLAND SCHOOL OF DESIGN
2 COLLEGE STREET, 1765

SAN ANTONIO, TX
SLOAN / HALL SAN ANTONIO
5930 BROADWAY

SAN FRANCISCO, CA
A CLEAN WELL LIGHTED PLACE
601 VAN NESS AVENUE
CITY LIGHTS BOOKSHOP
261 COLUMBUS AVENUE
SAN FRANCISCO MUSEUM OF MODERN ART, MUSEUMBOOKS
151 3RD STREET, 1ST FLOOR

ST. LOUIS, MO
LEFT BANK BOOKS
399 NORTH EUCLID

SANTA MONICA, CA
ARCANA
1229 3RD STREET PROMENADE
HENNESSEY & INGALLS BOOKS
1254 3RD STREET PROMENADE

ST. PAUL, MN
HUNGRY MIND BOOKSTORE
1648 GRAND AVENUE

SEATTLE, WA
UNIVERSITY BOOKSTORE
4326 UNIVERSITY WAY

WASHINGTON D.C.
NATIONAL GALLERY OF ART
6TH STREET & CONSTITUTION AVENUE, NW

CANADA / KANADA

CALGARY
TREPANIER BAER GALLERY
105 999 8TH STREET SW

MONTREAL
ARTEXTE
3575 STREET LAURENT
OLIVIERI LIBRAIRIE BOOKSTORE
185 STREET CATHERINE WEST

TORONTO
ART GALLERY OF ONTARIO
317 DUNDAS STREET WEST
ART METROPOLE
788 KING STREET WEST
DAVID MIRVISH BOOKS ON ART
596 MARKHAM STREET

VANCOUVER
VANCOUVER ART GALLERY
750 HORNBY STREET

AUSTRALIA / AUSTRALIEN

DARLINGHURST
EAST SYDNEY BOOKSTORE
THE DOME, THE ELAN BUILDING
1 KINGS CROSS ROAD

SYDNEY
MUSEUM OF CONTEMPORARY ART
140 GEORGE STREET, CIRCULAR QUAY NORTH
GLEE BOOKS
191 GLEBE POINT ROAD, GLEBE

NEW ZEALAND / NEUSEELAND
AUCKLAND
PROPAGANDA
2 CARR ROAD, MT ROSKILL

ASIA / ASIEN

JAPAN

TOKYO
AOYAMA BOOK CENTRE, SHIBUYA-KU
COSMOS AOYAMA GARDEN FLOOR B2F
5-53-97, JINGUMAE
ART & BOOKS
2-1-13-307
TAKANAWA, MINATO-KU
WATARI MUSEUM OF CONTEMPORARY ART, ON SUNDAYS BOOKSHOP
376 JINGUMAE SHIBUYA-KU

SINGAPORE / SINGAPUR
PAGE ONE BOOKSTORE
20 KAKI BUKIT VIEW TECHPARK

GREAT BRITAIN / GROSSBRITANNIEN

DISTRIBUTOR / VERTRIEB
CENTRAL BOOKS
99, WALLIS ROAD
LONDON E9 5LN

BRISTOL
ARNOLFINI BOOKSHOP
16 NARROW QUAY

LONDON
BORDERS BOOKSHOP
120 CHARING CROSS ROAD

BORDERS BOOKSHOP
203–207 OXFORD STREET
CAMDEN ARTS CENTRE
ARKWRIGHT ROAD
HAYWARD GALLERY
SOUTH BANK
IAN SHIPLEY BOOKSHOP
70 CHARING CROSS ROAD
INSTITUTE OF CONTEMPORARY ARTS
12 CARLTON HOUSE TERRACE
THE MALL
SERPENTINE GALLERY
KENSINGTON GARDENS
TATE MODERN
BANKSIDE
ZWEMMER LTD. ART BOOKS
24 LITCHFIELD STREET

IRELAND / IRLAND
DUBLIN
DOUGLAS HYDE GALLERY
TRINITY COLLEGE

GERMANY / DEUTSCHLAND
DISTRIBUTOR / VERTRIEB
GVA VERLAGSSERVICE GÖTTINGEN
PF 2021
D-37010 GÖTTINGEN
BERLIN
BÜCHERBOGEN AM SAVIGNYPLATZ
STADTBAHNBOGEN 593
GALERIE 2000 KUNSTBUCHHANDLUNG
KNESEBECKSTRASSE 56/58
WALTHER KÖNIG BUCHHANDLUNG, MUSEUM FÜR
GEGENWARTSKUNST
IM HAMBURGER BAHNHOF INVALIDENSTRASSE 50–51
WIENS LADEN & VERLAG
LINIENSTRASSE 158 (HOF)
WASMUTH GMBH & CO.
PFALZBURGERSTRASSE 43–44
BREMEN
BEIM STEINERNEN KREUZ GMBH
BEIM STEINERNEN KREUZ 1
DÜSSELDORF
LITERATUR BEI RUDOLF MÜLLER
NEUSTRASSE 38
WALTHER KÖNIG BUCHHANDLUNG
HEINRICH-HEINE-ALLEE 15
FRANKFURT
KUNST-BUCH, KUNSTHALLE SCHIRN
RÖMERBERG 7
WALTHER KÖNIG BUCHHANDLUNG
DOMSTRASSE 6
HAMBURG
HELMUT VON DER HÖH BUCHHANDLUNG
GROSSE BLEICHEN 21
SAUTTER + LACKMANN BUCHHANDLUNG
ADMIRALITÄTSTRASSE 71/72
HANNOVER
MERZ KUNSTBUCHHANDLUNG
KURT-SCHWITTERS-PLATZ
KARLSRUHE
HANS MENDE BUCHHANDLUNG
KARLSTRASSE 76
KÖLN
SCHADEN.COM BUCHHANDEL
BURGMAUER 10
WALTHER KÖNIG BUCHHANDLUNG
EHRENSTRASSE 4
KIOSK-BUCH-EVENT GMBH
IM MEDIAPARK 7
MÜNCHEN
HANS GOLTZ BUCHHANDLUNG
FÜR BILDENDE KUNST
TÜRKENSTRASSE 54
ILKA KÖNIG BUCHHANDLUNG
MAXIMILIANSTRASSE 35

L. WERNER BUCHHANDLUNG
RESIDENZSTRASSE 18
NÜRNBERG
WALTHER KÖNIG BUCHHANDLUNG
LUITPOLDSTRASSE 5
STUTTGART
LIMACHER BUCHHANDLUNG
KÖNIGSTRASSE 28 / KÖNIGSBAU

SPAIN / SPANIEN
BARCELONA
LAIE – CAIXAFÒRUM
MARQUES DE COMILLAS 6–8
LAIE – CCCB (CENTRE DE CULTURA
CONTEMPORÀNIA DE BARCELONA)
MONTALEGRE 5
MADRID
MUSEO NACIONAL REINA SOFIA
C/ SANTA ISABEL, 52

FRANCE / FRANKREICH
PARIS
COLETTE
213, RUE SAINT-HONORÉ
CENTRE POMPIDOU, FLAMMARION 4
26, RUE JACOB
GALERIE NATIONALE DU JEU DE PAUME
1, PLACE DE LA CONCORDE
LIBRAIRIE DU MUSÉE D'ART MODERNE
9, RUE GASTON DE SAINT-PAUL

ITALY / ITALIEN
MILANO
A&M BOOKSTORE
30, VIA TADINO
ROMA
GALLERIA NAZIONALE D'ARTE MODERNA
131, VIA DELLE BELLE ARTI
GALLERIA PRIMO PIANO
203, VIA PANISPERNA

NORWAY / NORWEGEN
OSLO
THE NATIONAL MUSEUM OF CONTEMPORARY ART
BANKPLASSEN 4 / SKATTEFOG

PORTUGAL
LISBOA
MODULO CENTRO DIFUSOR DE ARTE
CALÇADA DOS MESTRES 34 A–B
PORTO
MODULO CENTRO DIFUSOR DE ARTE
AV. BOAVISTA 854

SWEDEN / SCHWEDEN
STOCKHOLM
KULTURHUSET KONSTIG
MEDIA & KONSTBOKHANDEL
SERGELS TORG 3
MODERNA MUSEET
SKEPPSHOLMEN
GÖTEBORG
GÖTEBORGS KONSTMUSEUM
GÖTAPLATSEN / AVENYN

TURKEY / TÜRKEI
ISTANBUL
ROBINSON CRUSOE BOOKS PUSULA PRODUCTIONS
389 ISTIKAL CADDESI BEYOGLU

**NETHERLANDS, BELGIUM
AND LUXEMBURG**
DISTRIBUTOR / VERTRIEB
IDEA BOOKS
NIEUWE HERENGRACHT 11
NL-1011 RK AMSTERDAM

NETHERLANDS / NIEDERLANDE
AMSTERDAM
ART BOOK
VAN BAERLESTRAAT 126
ATHENAEUM NIEUWSCENTRUM
SPUI 14–16

ROBERT PREMSELA BOOKSHOP
VAN BAERLESTRAAT 78
GRONINGEN
SCHOLTENS / WRISTERS BOOKSHOP
FULDENSTRAAT 20
ROTTERDAM
DONNER BOOKSHOP
LIJNBAAN 150

BELGIUM / BELGIEN
ANTWERPEN
F.N.A.C.
GROENPLAATS
BRUXELLES
TROPISMES LIBRAIRIES
GALERIE DES PRINCES 11
GENT
COPYRIGHT BOOKSHOP
JACOBIJNENSTRAAT 8

LUXEMBOURG / LUXEMBURG
LUXEMBOURG
CASINO LUXEMBOURG
41, RUE NOTRE-DAME

SWITZERLAND / SCHWEIZ
DISTRIBUTOR / VERTRIEB
B+I BUCH + INFORMATION
CENTRALWEG 16
CH-8910 AFFOLTERN A. A.
BASEL
FONDATION BEYELER
BASELSTRASSE 77, RIEHEN
GALERIE STAMPA
SPALENBERG 2
JÄGGI BUCHHANDLUNG
FREIE STRASSE 32
KUNSTHALLE BASEL
KLOSTERGASSE 5
BERN
HANS HUBER AG BUCHHANDLUNG
MARKTGASSE 59
STAUFFACHER BUCHHANDLUNG
IM KUNSTMUSEUM
HODLERSTRASSE 12
LUZERN
RÄBER BÜCHER AG
FRANKENSTRASSE 7-9
GENÈVE
LIBRAIRIE PAYOT
5, RUE DE CHANTEPOULET
MENDRISIO
GABRIELE CAPELLI LIBRERIA ARCHITETTURA
4, VIA NOBILI BOSIA
ST. GALLEN
RÖSSLITOR BÜCHER
WEBERGASSE 5
ZÜRICH
CALLIGRAMME BUCHHANDLUNG
HÄRINGSTRASSE 4
HOWEG BUCHHANDLUNG
WAFFENPLATZ 1
KUNSTGRIFF BUCHHANDLUNG
LIMMATSTRASSE 270
KUNSTHAUS ZÜRICH
HEIMPLATZ 1
KUNSTKIOSK
LIMMATQUAI 31
ORELL FÜSSLI KRAUTHAMMER
MARKTGASSE 12
ORELL FÜSSLI BUCHHANDLUNG
FÜSSLISTRASSE 4
SCALO BOOKS & LOOKS
WEINBERGSTRASSE 22 A
SEC 52 BUCHHANDLUNG
JOSEFSTRASSE 52

ZÜRICH

ARS FUTURA	Bleicherweg 45 8002 Zürich Tel. 01 201 88 10 www.arsfutura.ch arsfutura@bluewin.ch	TEN YEARS ARSFUTURA/ ZEHN JAHRE ARSFUTURA TORBJORN RODLAND: Black OLAF BREUNING	22.8.–21.9.2002 27.9.–16.11.2002 29.11.–1.2.2003
GALERIE ART ONE	Heinrichstrasse 239 8005 Zürich Tel. 076 55 99 88 2 www.stiftungartone.ch info@stiftungartone.ch	Galerieeröffnung, Vernissage ANINA SCHENKER, ANOUSH ABRAR, CÉDRIC BOBAY, EVER AFTER INGRID KÄSER & KATRIN HOTZ, JASON KLIMATSAS, KÖRNER UNION NINA AREGGER, REGULA J. KOPP	25.10.2002, 18–21 h 26.10.–30.11.2002
BOB VAN ORSOUW	Limmatstrasse 270 8005 Zürich Tel. 01 273 11 00 bobvanorsouw@access.ch	SHIRANA SHAHBAZI CALLUM INNES ART COLOGNE	24.8.–12.10.2002 19.10.–12.12.2002 30.10.–3.11.2002
ELISABETH KAUFMANN	Müllerstrasse 57 8004 Zürich Tel./Fax 043 322 01 15 elkauf@yahoo.com	ERWIN BOHATSCH ART FORUM BERLIN ART COLOGNE KÖLN	25.10.–19.12.2002 26.9.–30.9.2002 30.10.–3.11.2002
GALERIE LELONG	Utoquai 31 8008 Zürich Tel. 01 251 11 20 galerie.lelong@dplanet.ch	ARNULF RAINER: Bilder	14.9.–2.11.2002
MAI 36 GALERIE	Rämistrasse 37 8001 Zürich Tel. 01 261 68 80 www.artgalleries/mai36 mai36@artgalleries.ch	STEPHAN BALKENHOL ART COLOGNE MAGNUS VON PLESSEN ART | BASEL | MIAMI BEACH	4.10.–2.11.2002 30.10.–3.11.2002 8.11.–7.12.2002 5.12.–8.12.2002
MARK MÜLLER	Gessnerallee 36 8001 Zürich Tel. 01 211 81 55 www.markmueller.ch mark.mueller@dplanet.ch	ART FORUM BERLIN – KünstlerInnen der Galerie RETO BOLLER "Process Blue C" & im Guestroom: CHALET 5: BLOCK I JÜRG STÄUBLE "Skulpturen" & im Guestroom: A.D.S. DONALDSON ART COLOGNE – KünstlerInnen der Galerie	26.9.–30.9.2002 22.8.–12.10.2002 19.10.–14.12.2002 30.10.–3.11.2002
SEMINA RERUM IRÈNE PREISWERK	Cäcilienstrasse 3 8032 Zürich Tel. 01 251 26 39 www.seminarerum.ch ipreiswerk@bluewin.ch	CÉCILE WICK: Weisse Reiche AMI: Fotografie ERIK STEFFENSEN: Red Centre	bis 12.10.2002 19.10.–30.11.2002 8.12.–1.2.2003

E X H I B I T I O N S

GALERIE LEHMANN	Josefstrasse 53	room I	
LESKIW+SCHEDLER	8005 Zürich	STEPHEN BARKER, Restoration	**26.9.–2.11.2002**
	Tel. 01 440 61 20	room II	
	www.schedler.ch	JAMES SHEEHAN, new paintings	**26.9.–2.11.2002**
	zurich@schedler.ch	room I und II	
		MARGARET MORGAN, A Pictorial Guide	
		to Sanitary Defects	**7.11.–21.12.2002**
ANNEMARIE VERNA	Neptunstrasse 45	RITA McBRIDE	
	8032 Zürich	(in collaboration with MAI 36 GALLERY)	**3.10.–23.11.2002**
	Tel. 01 262 38 20		
	office@annemarie-verna.ch		
GALERIE	Waldmannstrasse 6	ALOIS LICHTSTEINER	**5.10.–16.11.2002**
JAMILEH WEBER	8001 Zürich		
	Tel. 01 252 10 66		
	www.jamilehweber.com		
	info@jamilehweber.com		
BRIGITTE WEISS	Müllerstrasse 67	ANDREAS RÜTHI	**bis 12.10.2002**
	8004 Zürich	DAVID N. CHIEPPO	**bis 12.10.2002**
	Tel. 01 241 83 35	ART FORUM BERLIN 2002	
	brigitteweiss@bluewin.ch	Halle/Stand 21a/18	**26.9.–30.9.2002**
	www.likeyou.com/brigitteweiss	CHRISTIAN VETTER	**Nov./Dez. 2002**

BASEL

NICOLAS KRUPP	Erlenstrasse 15	SONJA FELDMEIER	**22.8.–12.10.2002**
	4058 Basel	SHAHRYAR NASHAT	**17.10.–7.12.2002**
	Tel. 061 683 32 65	ARTISSIMA TORINO	**14.11.–17.11.2002**
	www.nicolaskrupp.com	STUDER/vd BERG	**12.12.–1.2.2003**
	nic@nicolaskrupp.com	PETER FRIEDL	**6.2.–29.3.2003**
GALERIE FRIEDRICH	Grenzacherstrasse 4	ANDRES LUTZ & ANDERS GUGGISBERG, I will rest	
	4058 Basel	in pieces (Gastkurator: Konrad Bitterli)	**7.9.–19.10.2002**
	Tel. 061 683 50 80	ANA AXPE, DOMINIQUE LÄMMLI,	
	galerie-friedrich@bluewin.ch	CHANTAL MICHEL	**26.10.–16.11.2002**
		on paper	**22.11.–10.1.2003**

ST. GALLEN

WILMA LOCK	Schmiedgasse 15	MARK FRANCIS – New Paintings	**14.9.–30.11.2002**
	9000 St. Gallen	F. E. WALTHER – STEPHEN WESTFALL –	
	Tel. 071 222 62 52	KELLY WOOD	**4.12.–1.2.2003**
	wilmalock@freesurf.ch	geschlossen/closed	**23.12.–7.1.2003**
SUSANNA KULLI	Davidstrasse 40	ADRIAN SCHIESS – neue Arbeiten	**Oktober 2002**
	9000 St. Gallen	ROLF GRAF – Fotografien	**Dez. 2002 – Jan. 2003**
	Tel. 071 223 59 58		
	www.susannakulli.ch		

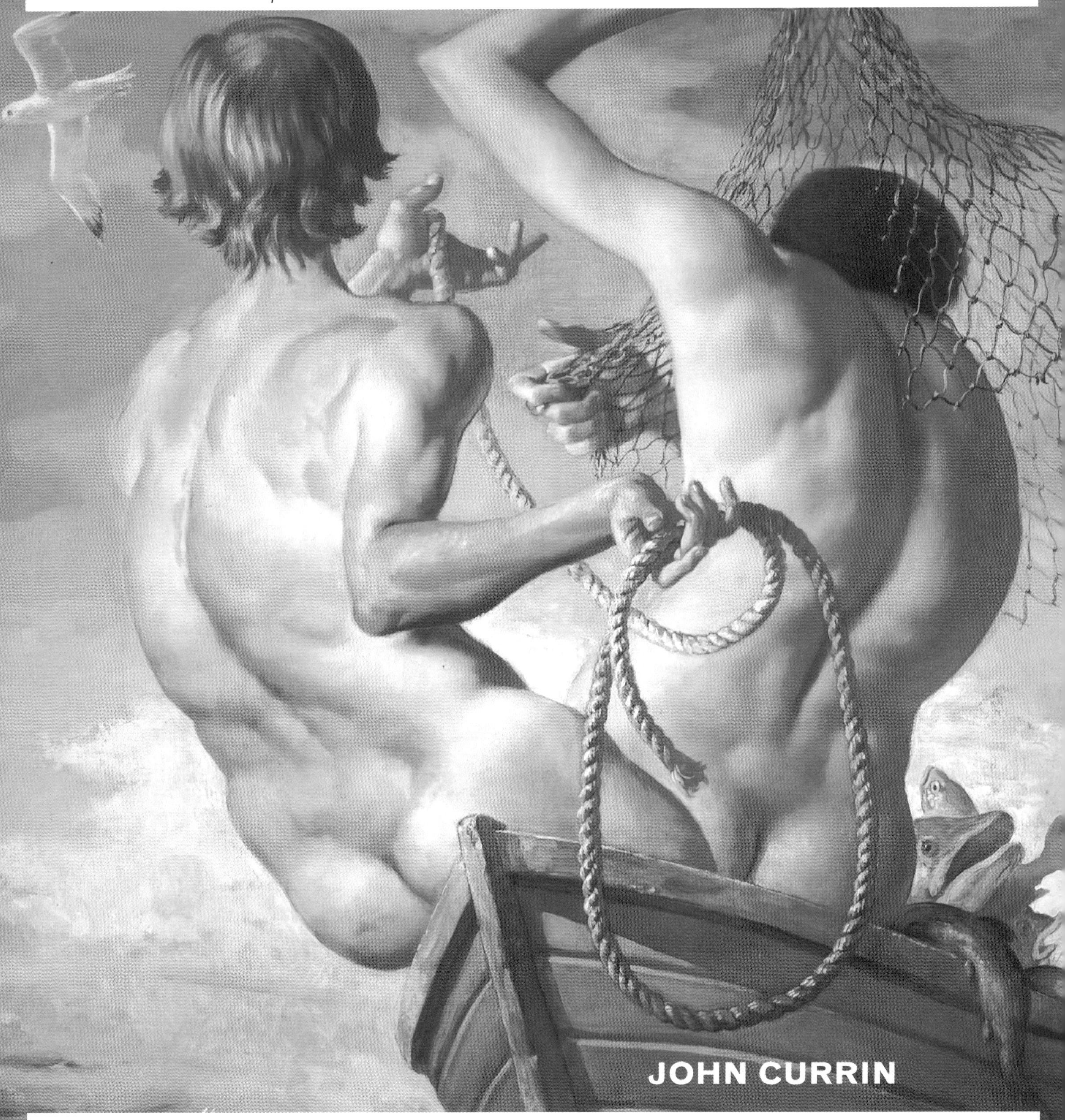
Andrea Rosen Gallery
JOHN CURRIN
525 West 24th St New York, NY 10011 telephone: 212 627 6000 fax: 212 627 5450 www.andrearosengallery.com
"Fishermen" © 2002

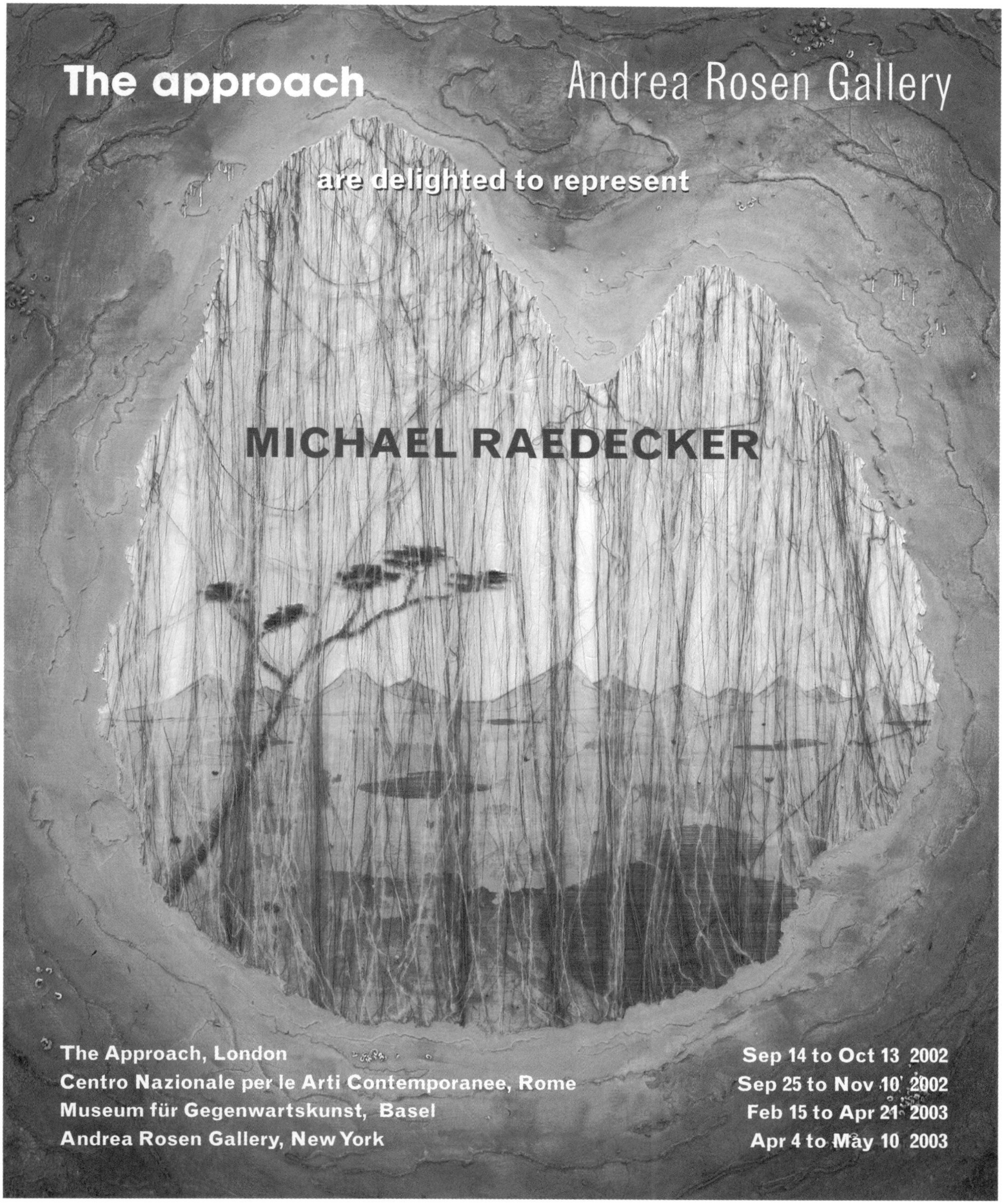

The approach
Andrea Rosen Gallery
are delighted to represent
MICHAEL RAEDECKER
The Approach, London
Centro Nazionale per le Arti Contemporanee, Rome
Museum für Gegenwartskunst, Basel
Andrea Rosen Gallery, New York
Sep 14 to Oct 13 2002
Sep 25 to Nov 10 2002
Feb 15 to Apr 21 2003
Apr 4 to May 10 2003

franz ackermann

james angus

dirk bell

martin creed

verne dawson

peter doig

urs fischer

dara friedman

mark handforth

udomsak krisanamis

mark leckey

aleksandra mir

chris ofili

laura owens

oliver payne & nick relph

elizabeth peyton

steven pippin

rob pruitt

rirkrit tiravanija

piotr uklanski

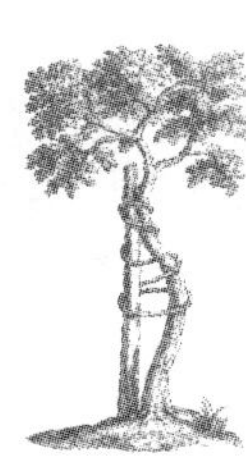

Gavin Brown's enterprise 436 W 15th St NY 10011 212 6275258 212 6275261 gallery@gavinbrown.biz

SEPTEMBER/NOVEMBER

PETER CAIN
MORE COURAGE LESS OIL

PAUL FEELEY
PAINTINGS AND SCULPTURE

SAM TAYLOR-WOOD
THE PASSION

NOVEMBER/JANUARY

JEAN-MARC BUSTAMANTE

PETER HUJAR
PORTRAITS IN LIFE AND DEATH

MATTHEW MARKS GALLERY
523 W 24 STREET
522 W 22 STREET
NEW YORK NEW YORK 10011
212 243 0200
WWW.MATTHEWMARKS.COM

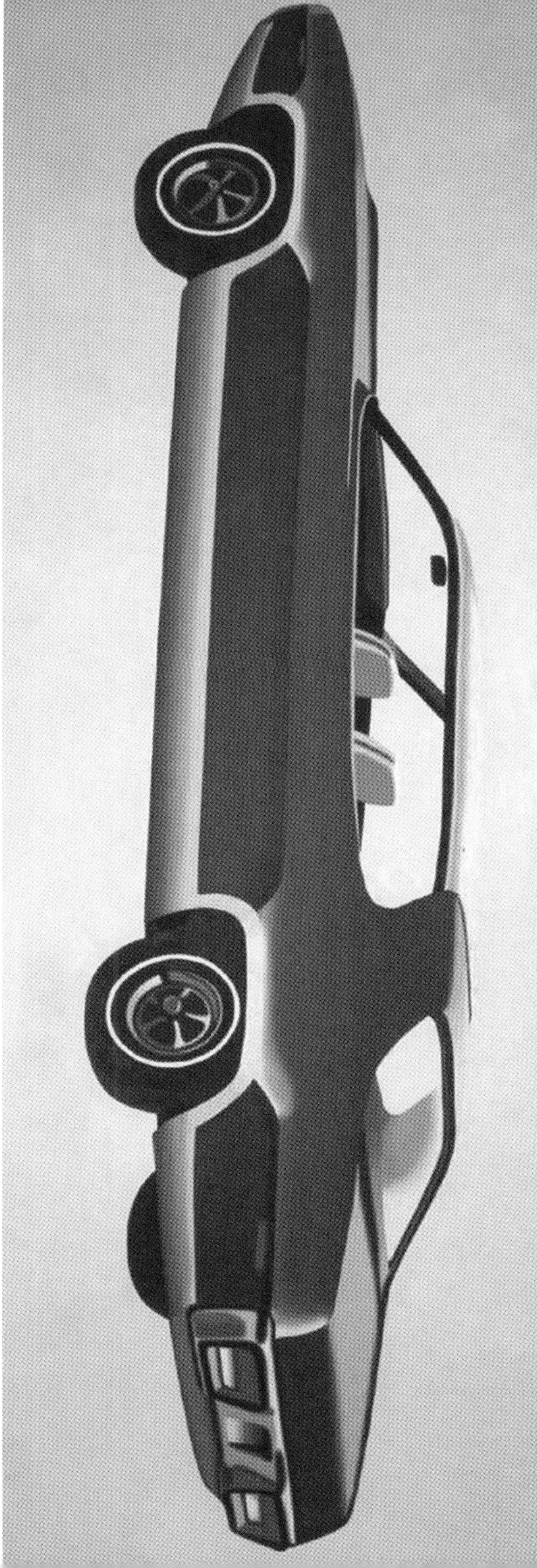

PETER CAIN UNTITLED 1988 OIL ON CANVAS 90 x 34 INCHES

JEFF WALL

SEPTEMBER 20 – NOVEMBER 2, 2002

WILLIAM KENTRIDGE

NOVEMBER 7, 2002 – JANUARY 4, 2003

MARIAN GOODMAN GALLERY

24 WEST 57TH STREET NEW YORK, NY 10019
TEL: 212-977-7160 FAX: 212-581-5187 WWW.MARIANGOODMAN.COM

3 SEPT – 12 OCT

JO BAER
DAN FLAVIN
SOL LEWITT
TONY SMITH

534 W 21

MICHAEL HURSON

521 W 21

19 OCT – 30 NOV

CARL ANDRE

534 W 21

SOL LEWITT

521 W 21

PAULA COOPER GALLERY

534/521 WEST 21ST STREET NEW YORK, NY 10011

TEL 212.255.1105 FAX 212.255.5156

GALERIA ▪ HELGA DE ALVEAR

DR. FOURQUET 12, 28012 MADRID.TEL:(34) 91 468 05 06 FAX:(34) 91 467 51 34
e-mail:galeria@helgadealvear.net   www.helgadealvear.net

September 19 - November 2

STAN DOUGLAS

November 2002 - January 2003

DANIEL CANOGAR

January - February

IMI KNOEBEL

March - April

MONTSERRAT SOTO

April - June

"REFLECTIONS"

June - July

FRANK THIEL

September 25 - 30

ART FORUM BERLIN

5 - 8 December

ART BASEL MIAMI BEACH

24. AUGUST BIS 12. OKTOBER 2002

ANDRÉ THOMKINS

26. OKTOBER BIS 21. DEZEMBER 2002

PAUL MCCARTHY / JASON RHOADES
SHIT PLUG

**LOUISE BOURGEOIS – DAN GRAHAM – MARY HEILMANN – THE ESTATE OF EVA HESSE – RICHARD JACKSON – ON KAWARA
RACHEL KHEDOORI – GUILLERMO KUITCA – PAUL MCCARTHY – JOHN MCCRACKEN – RAYMOND PETTIBON
JASON RHOADES – PIPILOTTI RIST – ANRI SALA – ROMAN SIGNER – DIANA THATER – THE ESTATE OF ANDRÉ THOMKINS**

GALERIE HAUSER & WIRTH

Limmatstrasse 270, 8005 Zürich / Tel: +41 1 446 80 50, Fax: +41 1 446 80 55 / www.ghw.ch / Öffnungszeiten: Di- Fr 12 - 18, Sa 11 - 16 Uhr

24. AUGUST BIS 12. OKTOBER 2002

SUE WILLIAMS

26. OKTOBER BIS 21. DEZEMBER 2002

BEAT STREULI

**DOUG AITKEN – EMMANUELLE ANTILLE – ANGELA BULLOCH – VERNE DAWSON – MARIA EICHHORN
URS FISCHER – PETER FISCHLI / DAVID WEISS – SYLVIE FLEURY – LIAM GILLICK – CANDIDA HÖFER – RONI HORN – KAREN KILIMNIK
GERWALD ROCKENSCHAUB – UGO RONDINONE – DIETER ROTH – JEAN-FRÉDÉRIC SCHNYDER – BEAT STREULI – FRANZ WEST – SUE WILLIAMS**

GALERIE HAUSER & WIRTH & PRESENHUBER

Limmatstrasse 270, 8005 Zürich / Tel: +41 1 446 80 60, Fax: +41 1 446 80 65 / www.ghwp.ch / Öffnungszeiten: Di- Fr 12 - 18, Sa 11 - 16 Uhr

WORKS AVAILABLE BY:

Josef Albers	Malcolm Morley
Richard Artschwager	Bruce Nauman
Louise Bourgeois	Yves Oppenheim
Jean-Marc Bustamante	Michelangelo Pistoletto
Alexander Calder	Peter Rogiers
John Chamberlain	Robert Ryman
Lili Dujourie	Julião Sarmento
William Eggleston	Ettore Spalletti
Barry Flanagan	Frank Stella
Lucio Fontana	Mitja Tušek
Adam Fuss	Cy Twombly
Antony Gormley	Patrick Vanden Eynde
Dianne Hagen	Jan Vercruysse
Roni Horn	Gert Verhoeven
Donald Judd	Didier Vermeiren
Robert Mapplethorpe	Andy Warhol
Allan McCollum	James Welling
Jürgen Meyer	Stephen Wilks

Xavier Hufkens

Sint-Jorisstraat 6–8 rue Saint-Georges

Brussel 1050 Bruxelles

TEL. 32 (0)2 639 67 30 – FAX 32 (0)2 639 67 38

info@xavierhufkens.com
http://www.xavierhufkens.com

Open Tuesday to Saturday, noon to 6 pm

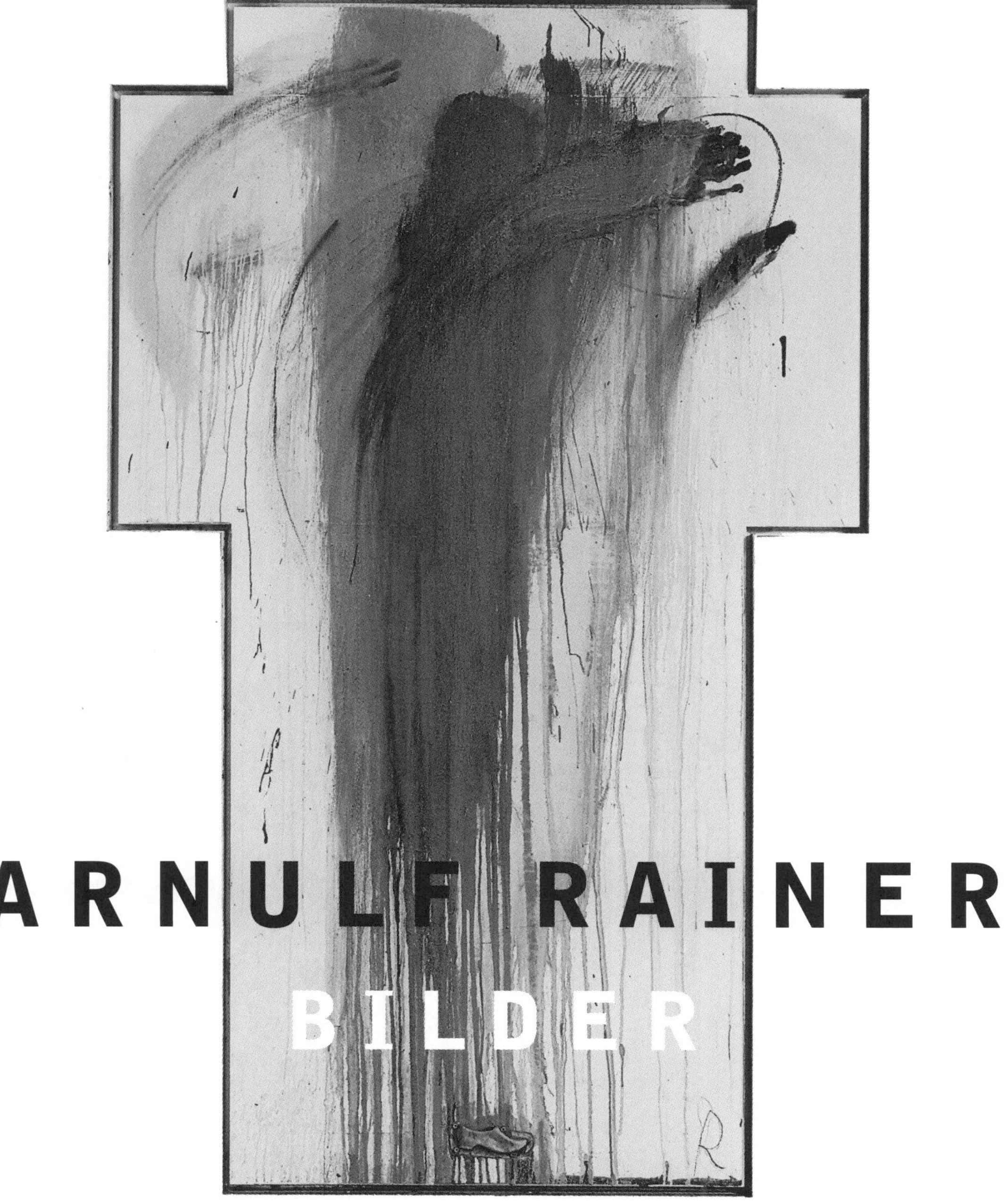

ARNULF RAINER

BILDER

14. SEPTEMBER – 2. NOVEMBER 2002

GALERIE LELONG ZÜRICH

UTOQUAI 31 • 8008 ZÜRICH • TEL. 01/251 11 20

GEORG KARGL

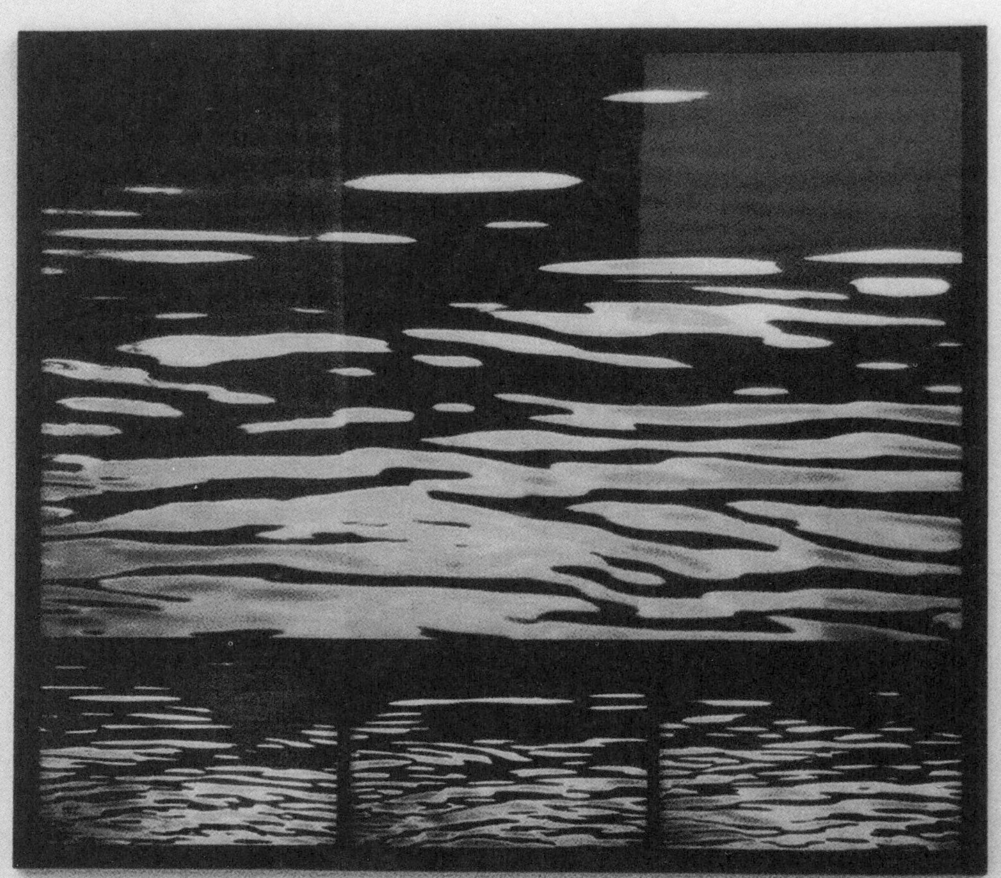

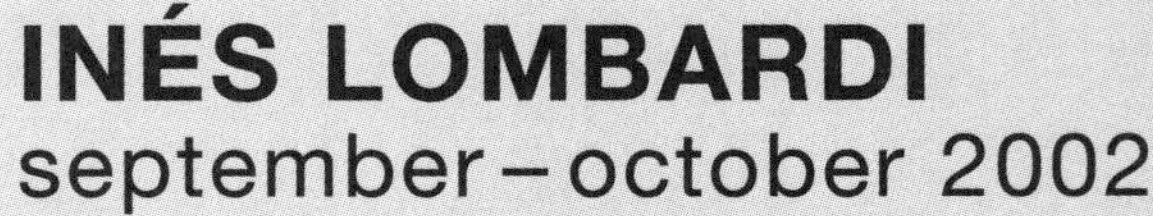

INÉS LOMBARDI
september – october 2002

SCHLEIFMÜHLGASSE 5 WIEN 1040
TEL 5854199 FAX 5854199

MAI 36 GALERIE

FRANZ ACKERMANN

IAN ANÜLL

JOHN BALDESSARI

MATTHEW BENEDICT

STEPHAN BALKENHOL

TROY BRAUNTUCH

ANKE DOBERAUER

PIA FRIES

ANDREAS GURSKY

RITA MCBRIDE

HARALD F. MÜLLER

MATT MULLICAN

MANFRED PERNICE

MAGNUS VON PLESSEN

GLEN RUBSAMEN

CHRISTOPH RÜTIMANN

THOMAS RUFF

JÖRG SASSE

PAUL THEK

LAWRENCE WEINER

RÉMY ZAUGG

STEPHAN BALKENHOL
October 4 – November 2, 2002

ART COLOGNE
October 30 – November 3, 2002

MAGNUS VON PLESSEN
November 8 – December 7, 2002

Art | Basel | Miami Beach
December 5–8, 2002

Rämistrasse 37, CH-8001 Zürich, www.artgalleries.ch/mai36
Tel. +41 1 261 68 80, Fax +41 1 261 68 81, mai36@artgalleries.ch

Galerie Edition Kunsthandel GmbH
Meisenburgstraße 169–173
45133 Essen
Tel. **+49 2 01 871 00-0**
Fax **+49 2 01 871 00-10**
INFO@2021ART.COM
WWW.2021ART.COM

Di–Fr 10–18 · Sa 11–16
und nach Vereinbarung

Andreas Slominski
21|9 – 23|11|2002

ab 30.11.2002 Zeitgenössische japanische Malerei

Ugo Rondinone   Sadie Coles HQ

Elizabeth Peyton   Sadie Coles HQ

Jonathan Horowitz   Sadie Coles HQ

JP Munro   Sadie Coles HQ

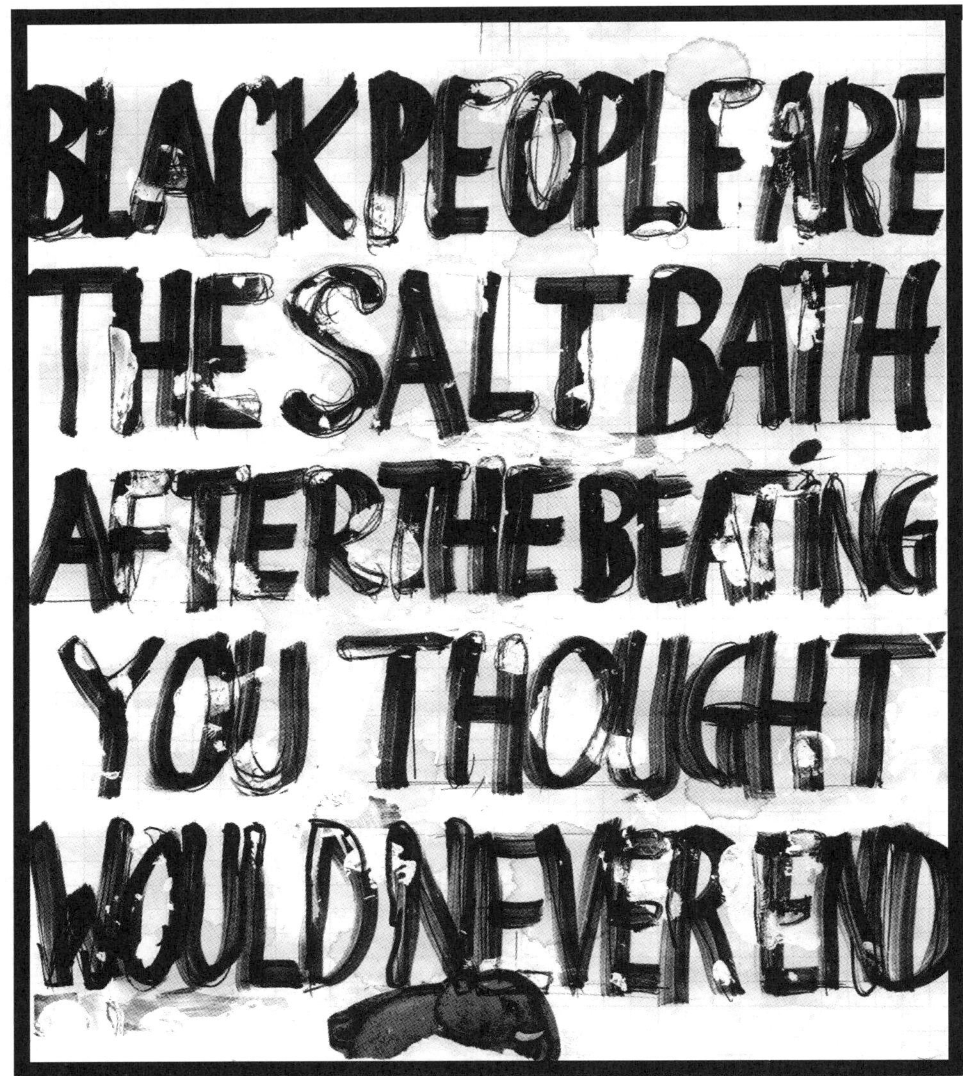

William Pope. L "Black Drawing" , 2002

427 West 126th St.
New York, NY 10027
Tel: +0 11 212 662.8610
Fax: +0 11 212 662.2800

www.elproyecto.com
mail@elproyecto.com

962 B East 4th St.
Los Angeles, CA 9001
Tel: +0 11 213 620.0692
Fax: +0 11 213 620.0743

Nader Ahriman   Janine Cirincione & Michael Ferraro   José Damasceno   Art Domantay   Maria Elena Gonzalez   Nic Hess   Glenn Kaino
Kim Sooja   Daniel Knorr   Daniel J. Martinez   Julie Mehretu   Aernout Mik   Kori Newkirk   Paul Pfeiffer   William Pope. L   Liza May Post
Tracey Rose   Peter Rostovsky   Jason Salavon   Bülent Sangar   Cristían Silva   Grazia Toderi   Uri Tzaig   Stephen Vitiello   Matthias Vriens   Martin Weber

info@zieglergalerie.com

SERGE ZIEGLER GALERIE

GALERIE BERND KLÜSER

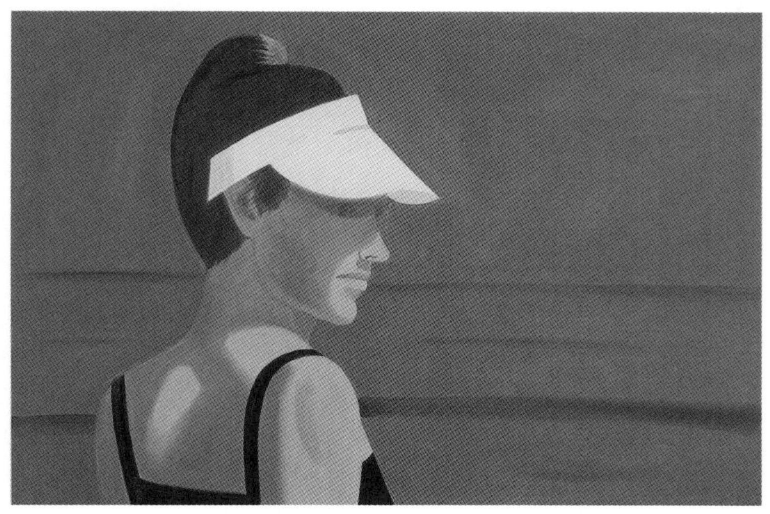

ALEX KATZ
Sep./Oct. 2002

GEORGENSTR. 15, D-80799 MÜNCHEN, TEL +49 89 384081-0, FAX +49 89 384081-20

GALERIE KLÜSER 2

NEW
ADDITIONAL
SPACE

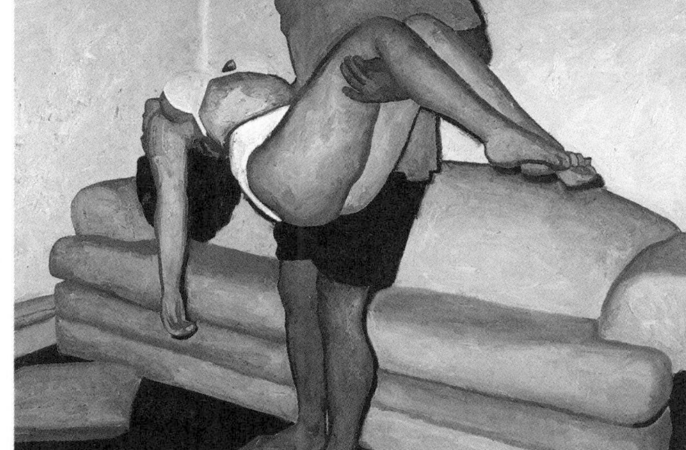

RYAN MENDOZA
Sep./Oct. 2002

TÜRKENSTR. 23, D-80799 MÜNCHEN, TEL +49 89 384081-23, FAX +49 89 384081-20

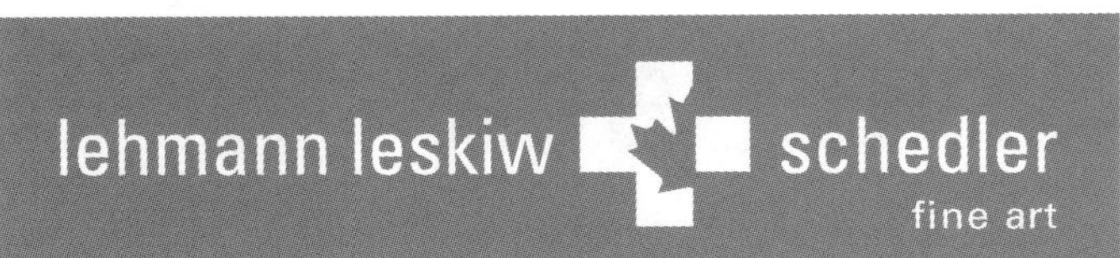

Lehmann Leskiw + Schedler
Josefstrasse 53
CH 8005 Zürich
T +41 1 440 61 20
F +41 1 440 61 21

Tuesday to Friday 12 - 6 p.m.
Saturday 11 a.m. - 4 p.m.

room I
Stephen Barker, Restoration
room II
James Sheehan, new paintings
26 September until 2 November 2002

opening soon
Lehmann Leskiw + Schedler, Toronto
Toronto, Canada

room I & II
Margaret Morgan, a pictorial guide to sanitary defects
8 November until 21 December 2002

zurich@l-l-s.com
www.l-l-s.com
Member of
Association of Swiss Galleries AGS

Peter Aspell, Stephen Barker, Jan Czerwinski, Matthew Dayler, Martin Fivian, Allen Frame, Max Grüter, Dieter Hall, Christoph Hänsli, Marcus Leatherdale, Attila Richard Lukacs, Margaret Morgan, Andrea Muheim, Richard Müller, Walter Pfeiffer, Mauro Restiffe, Heike Ruschmeyer, Eliane Rutishauser, Gyle Ryon, Hans Scheule, James Sheehan, Philipp Späti, Lee Wagstaff, Karlheinz Weinberger, Hans Witschi

---

Erwin Bohatsch → 25.10. bis 19.12.2002 Hanne Darboven Walter Dahn Silvie Defraoui Silvie und Chérif Defraoui Jan Fabre Gloria Friedmann → 22.8. bis 5.10.2002 James Hyde Olav Christopher Jenssen Jos Näpflin Shahryar Nashat Susanne Paesler Pavel Pepperstein Bojan Šarčević Anselm Stalder Daniel Schibli Estate Martin Disler

Art Forum Berlin 25. bis 30. September 2002
Art Cologne Köln 30. Oktober bis 3. November 2002

ELISABETH KAUFMANN

Müllerstrasse 57 CH-8004 Zürich, Telefon Fax Mail + 41 043 322 01 15 elkauf@yahoo.com
Dienstag bis Freitag 14 bis 18 Uhr, Samstag 11 bis 16 Uhr

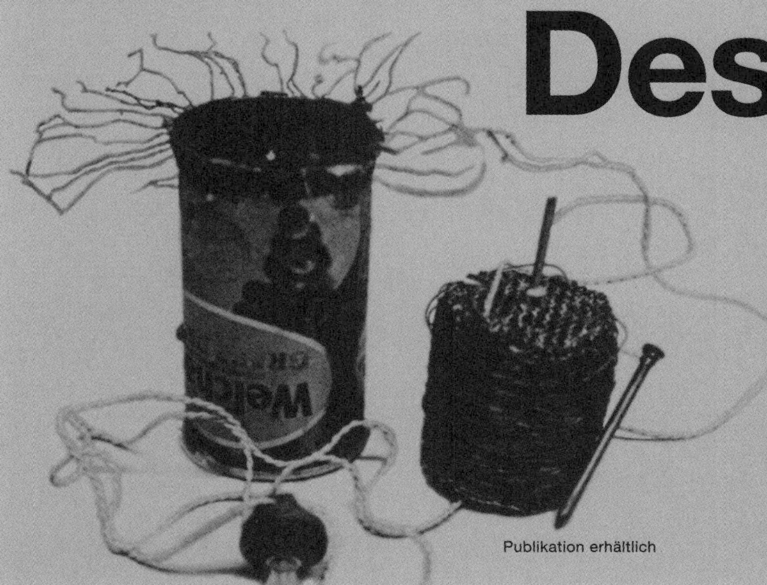

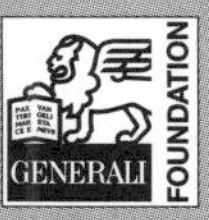

Julie Mehretu • Nedko Solakov • Hans Stalder

18.10.–1.12.2002

Kunstmuseum Thun

Kunstmuseum Thun, Thunerhof
Hofstettenstrasse 14, CH-3600 Thun
Öffnungszeiten:Di bis So 10–17 Uhr
Mi 10–21 Uhr, Mo geschlossen
www.kunstmuseumthun.ch

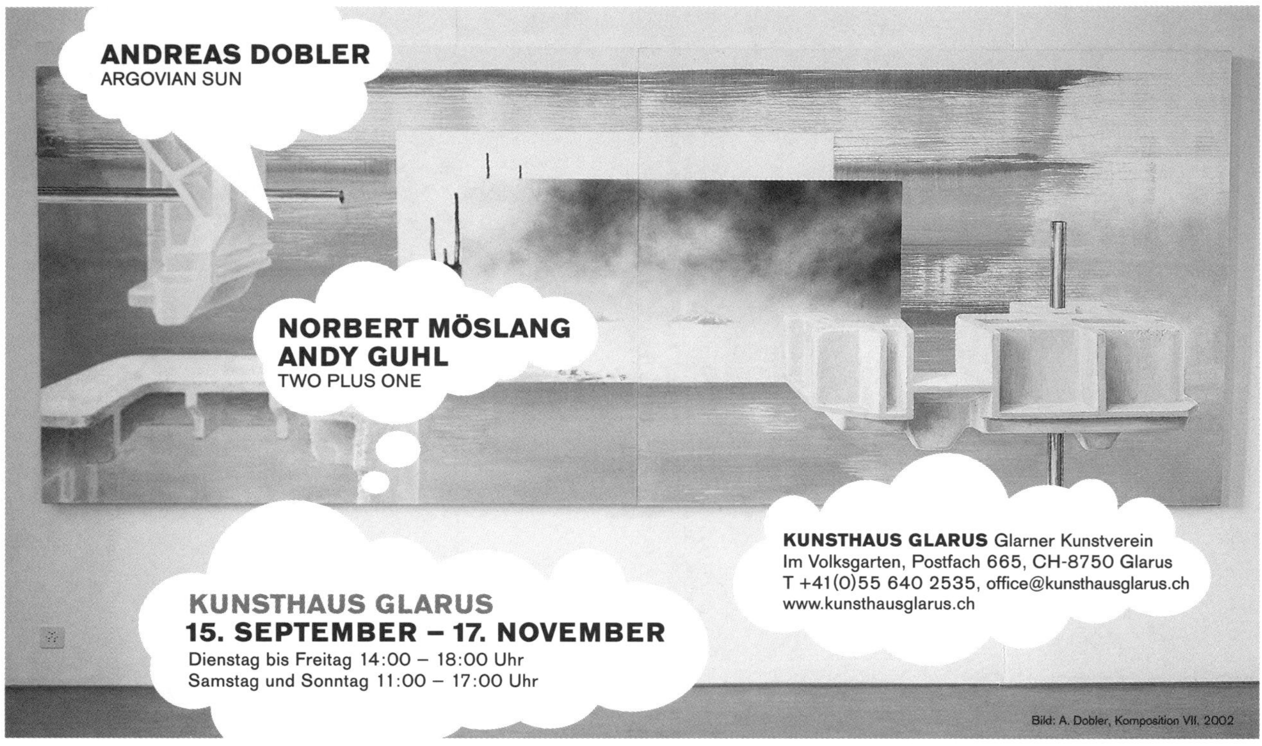

31.8. - 27.10.2002

Hans-Peter Feldmann Kunstausstellung

9.11.2002 - 5.1.2003

Joachim Brohm Areal

Valérie Jouve

FOTOMUSEUM WINTERTHUR

Grüzenstrasse 44
CH-8400 Winterthur
Tel: 052/233 60 86
www.fotomuseum.ch

Di – Fr 12 – 18 Uhr
Mi 12 – 19.30 Uhr
Sa/So 11 – 17 Uhr

Richard Paul Lohse
September 15, 2002 to January 12, 2003

Schweiz konkret 2: Clara Friedrich,
Verena Loewensberg, Sophie Taeuber-Arp
June 9, 2002 to February 2003

Re-opening: The Rockefeller Dining Room
from June 9, 2002 onward

haus **konstruktiv**

Wednesday–Friday 12 am–6 pm
Saturday/Sunday 11 am–6 pm
Closed Monday/Tuesday

Haus Konstruktiv
Selnaustrasse 25, CH-8001 Zurich
Phone +41 01 217 70 80, Fax +41 01 217 70 90
info@hauskonstruktiv.ch
www.hauskonstruktiv.ch

CATHY WILKES
HENRY J. DARGER

24. August bis 20. Oktober 2002
migros museum für gegenwartskunst
Limmatstrasse 270
CH-8005 Zürich
Di–Fr 12–18h, Sa/So 11–17h
T +411 277 20 50 F +411 277 62 86
www.migrosmuseum.ch

migros museum
Museum für Gegenwartskunst Zürich

The British Council

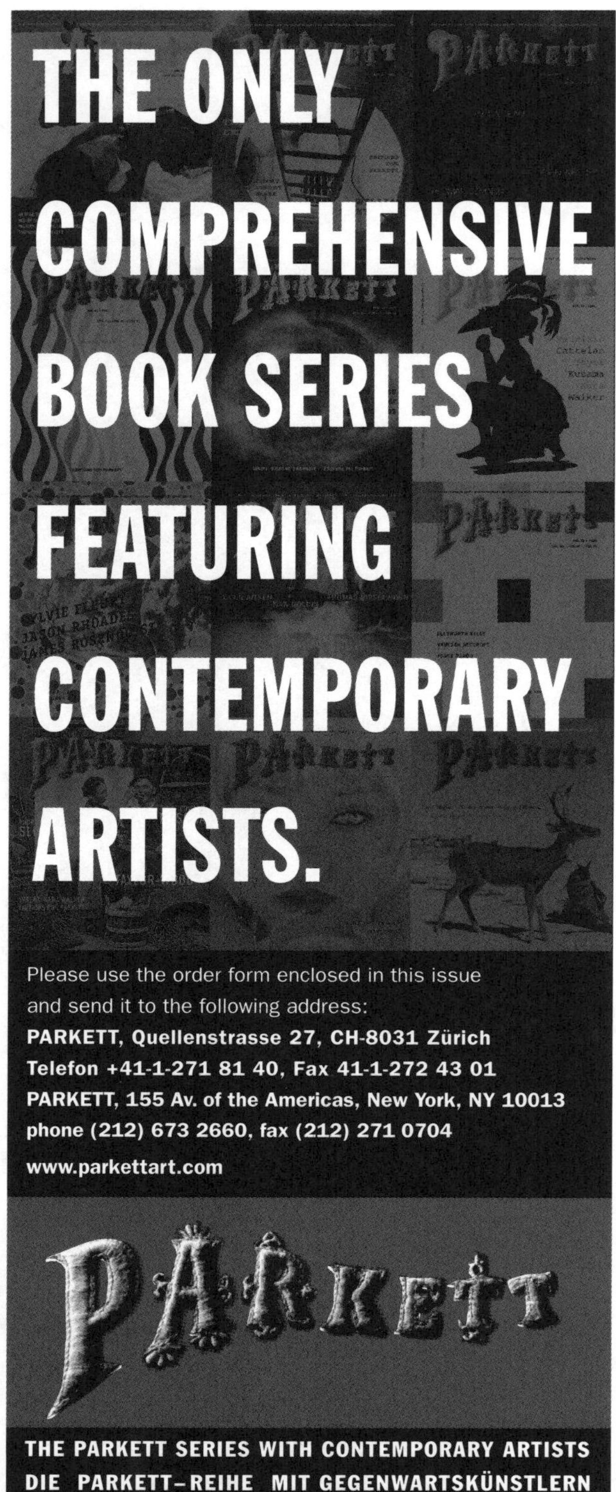

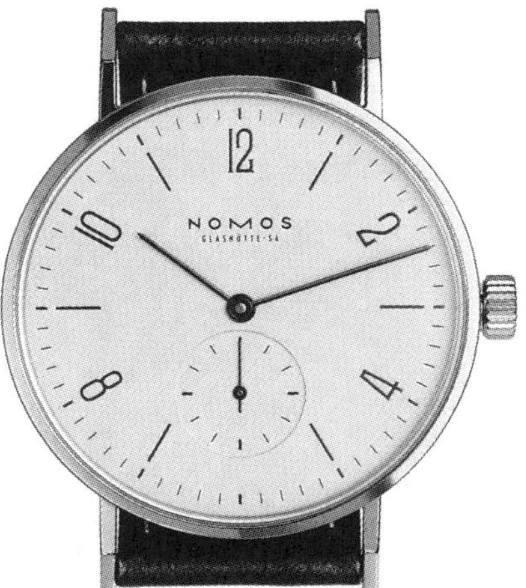

Tangente **690** € (unverb. Preisempf.)

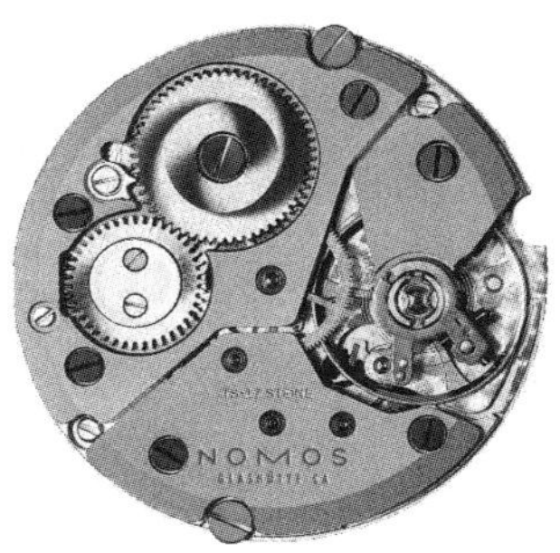

NOMOS Werk 1 TS

NOMOS
GLASHÜTTE·SA

etwa bei: Basel **Spinnler und Schweizer**; Bern **Uhrsachen**; Olten **Brunner**; Zürich **Bieri** ▪ Augsburg **Mayer**; Berlin **Lorenz**, **Wempe**; Bielefeld **Böckelmann**; Bonn **Kersting**, **Toussaint**; Dresden **Wempe**; Düsseldorf **Blome**, **Wempe**; Frankfurt **Christ Kaiserstraße**, **Wempe**; Halle **Schulz**; Hamburg **Ohle**, **Wempe**; Hannover **Wempe**; Karlsruhe **Christensen**; Koblenz **Hofacker**; Köln **Berghoff**, **Wempe**; Leipzig **Schneider**, **Wempe**; München **Huber**, **Kiefer**, **Wempe**; Münster **Freisfeld**; Wiesbaden **Hembd** ▪ Wien **Wempe** ▪ Paris **Wempe** ▪ Mailand **Rocca**; Turin **Rocca** ▪ Barcelona **BelClock**; Las Palmas **Olivin Canarias**; Madrid **Wempe** ▪ London **Watch Gallery**, **Wempe** ▪ Amsterdam **Hermann Benard**; Den Haag **van Willegen** ▪ Budapest **Poen** ▪ New York **D'Fly**, **Wempe** ▪ Singapur **Sincere** ▪ Tokyo **Osawa**

www.glashuette.com ▪ nomos@glashuette.com

La Mirada – Zeitgenössische Fotokunst aus Lateinamerika

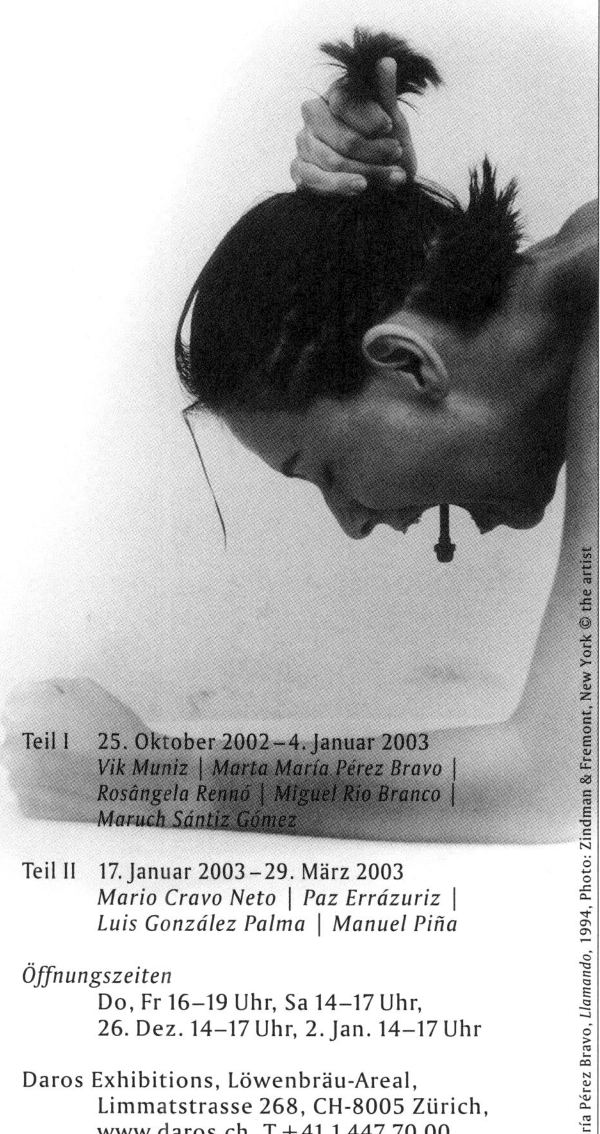

Marta María Pérez Bravo, *Llamando*, 1994. Photo: Zindman & Fremont, New York © the artist

Kunsttransporte in alle Erdteile

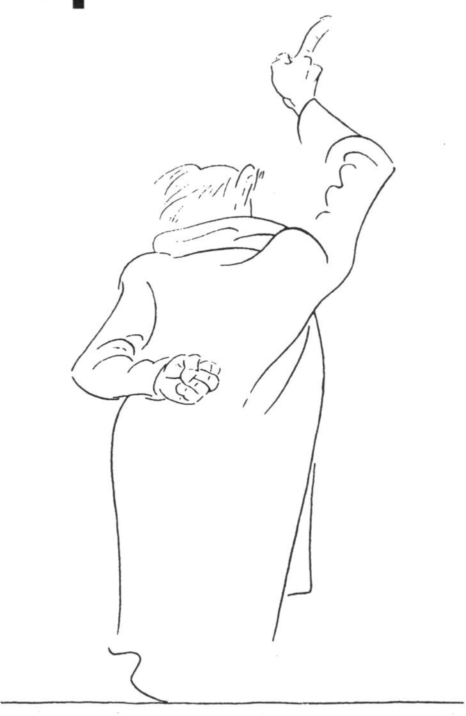

«In den Kunsttransporten, wer nicht das Beste hat, hat nichts»   *(frei nach Olaf Gulbransson)*

MÖBEL-TRANSPORT AG

für sorgfältige Transporte

Gaswerkareal
8010 Zürich
Tel. 01 733 51 11
Fax 01 730 88 80

Genuastrasse 14
4142 Münchenstein-Basel
Tel. 061 331 88 55
Fax 061 331 80 47

E-Mail: moebel@moebel-transport-ag.com
http://www.moebel-transport-ag.com
Filialen in Chiasso und Frankfurt Flughafen.

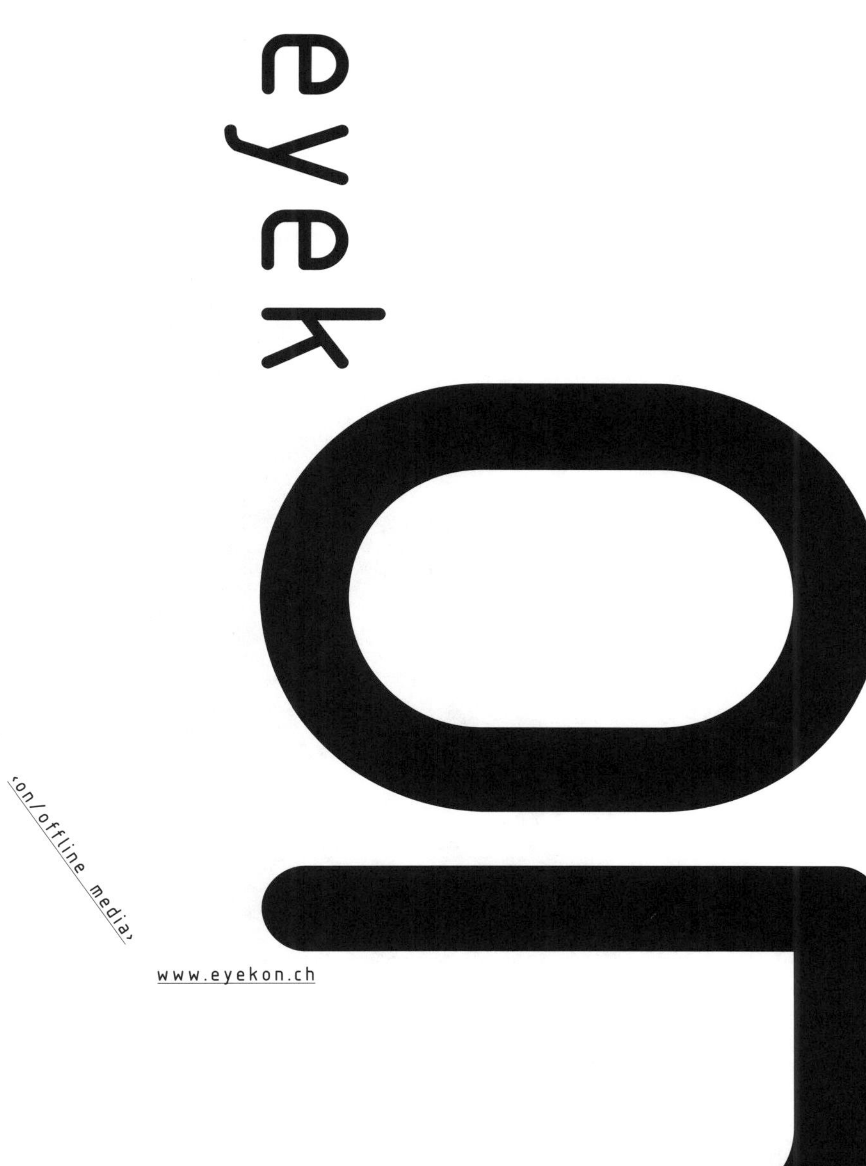

eyek
‹on/offline media›
www.eyekon.ch

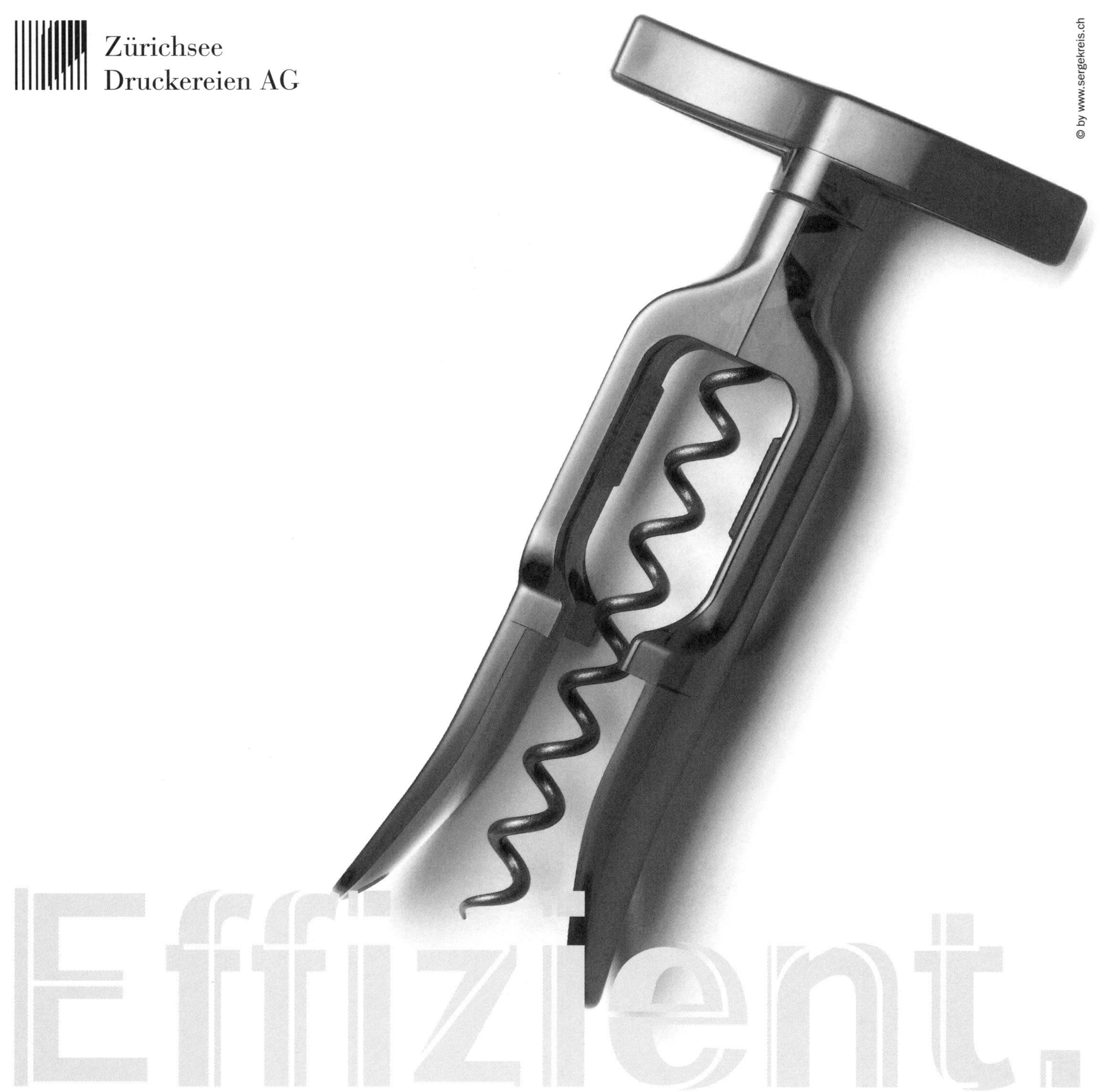

Zürichsee
Druckereien AG
© by www.sergekreis.ch
Effizient.
Für Sie öffnen wir neue Horizonte
Effizient: Zürichsee Druckereien AG • Seestrasse 86 • Postfach • 8712 Stäfa • Tel. 01 928 53 03 • Fax 01 928 53 10 • Internet www.zsd.ch

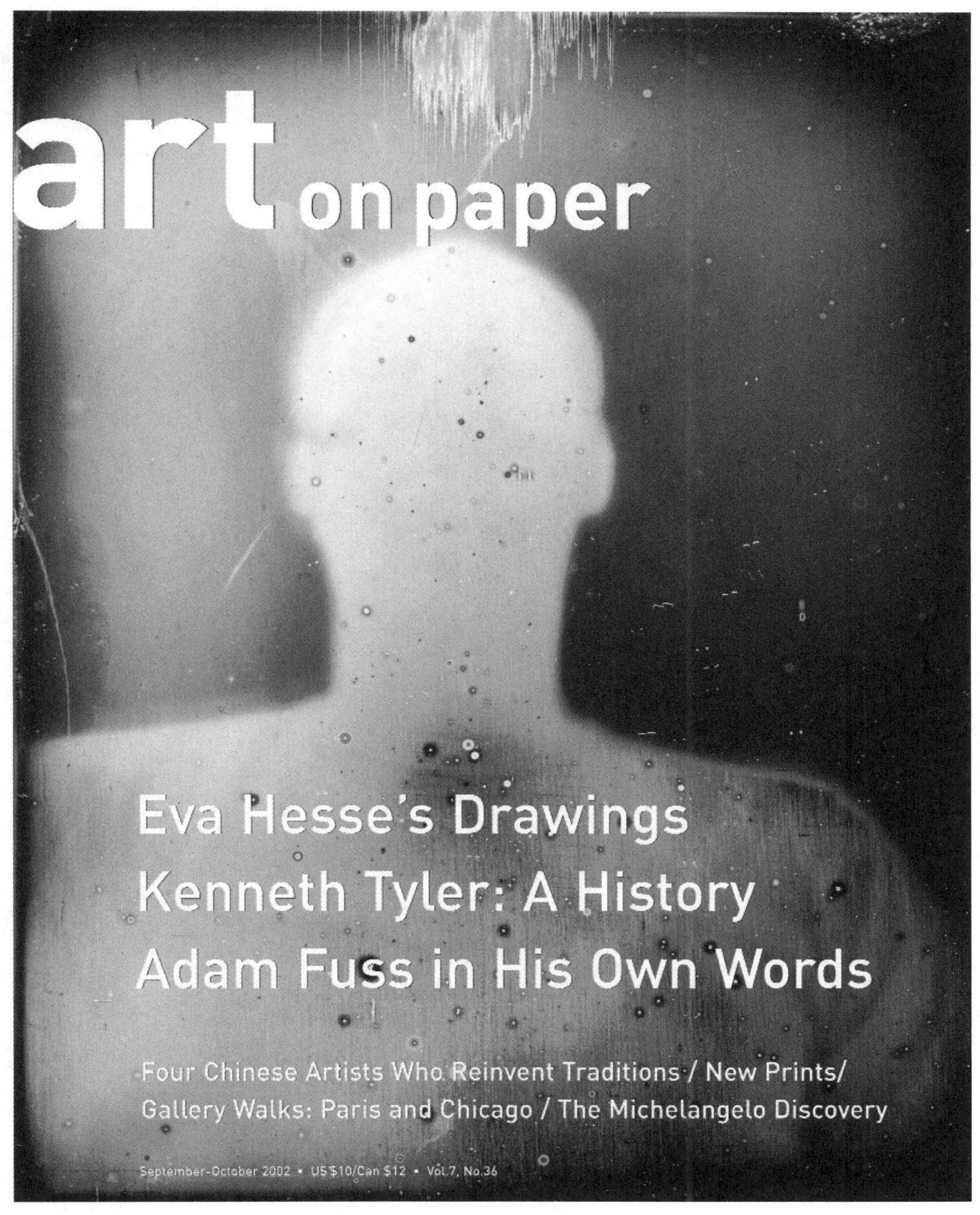

The International Art Magazine Dedicated to Prints, Drawings, and Photography

Galleries List at July 25, 2002/Elenco Gallerie al 25 Luglio 2002

⑨

ARTissima

THE INTERNATIONAL FAIR OF CONTEMPORARY ART

NOVEMBER 14 -17, 2002
TURIN, ITALY

Info: tel. +39/011/546284 fax +39/011/5623094 www.artissima.it info@artissima.it

Art|Basel|Miami Beach
5–8|Dec|02

Art Galleries | 20.21 Galerie D-Essen | **303 Gallery** New York | **A** | **Adelantado** Valencia | **Aeroplastics** Brussels | **Aizpuru** Madrid, Sevilla |
Alexander New York | **de Alvear** Madrid | **Ambrosino** Miami | **Ameringer/Howard/Yohe** New York | **Andriesse** Amsterdam |
Arndt & Partner Berlin | **Artcore** Toronto | **Asprey Jacques** London | **B** | **Barquet** New York | **von Bartha** Basel | **Benítez** Madrid |
Benzacar Buenos Aires | **Berggruen** San Francisco | **Bernier/Eliades** Athens | **Beyeler** Basel | **Blum** New York, Zurich |
Blum & Poe Santa Monica | **Boesky** New York | **Bonakdar** New York | **Bransten** San Francisco | **Brito Cimino** São Paulo |
Brownstone New York | **C** | **Capitain** Cologne | **de Carlo** Milano | **Casa Triângulo** São Paulo | **Cats** Brussels, Knokke |
Chac Mool West Hollywood LA | **Cobo** Sevilla | **Cohan** New York | **Contemporary Fine Arts** Berlin | **Continua** I-San Gimignano | **Corkin** Toronto |
Cowles New York | **Crane Kalman** London | **Crousel** Paris | **D** | **D'Amelio Terras** New York | **Deitch** New York | **Di Meo** Paris | **Díaz** Madrid |
F | **Faggionato** London | **Farber/La Serre** F-Trets | **Fortes Vilaça** São Paulo | **Freeman** Brooklyn | **Barry Friedman** New York |
Stephen Friedman London | **Frith** London | **G** | **Gagosian** New York, Los Angeles, London | **Galerie 1900-2000** Paris |
Gasser & Grunert New York | **Gering** New York | **Gladstone** New York | **Gmurzynska** Cologne, Zug | **Goodman James** New York |
Goodman Marian New York, Paris | **The Goodman Gallery** Johannesburg | **Gray** Chicago, New York | **Greve** Cologne, Milan, Paris, St. Moritz |
Grimes Santa Monica | **Christina Guerra** Lisboa | **Guerrero** Mexico City | **H** | **Haas & Fuchs** Berlin | **Hauser & Wirth** Zurich | **Hetzler** Berlin |
Hilger Vienna | **Nancy Hoffman** New York | **Rhona Hoffman** Chicago | **Hussenot** Paris | **Hufkens** Bruxelles | **Hutton** New York |
J | **Jablonka** Cologne | **Jacobson** London | **Janssen** Cologne | **Jopling** London | **Juda** London | **K** | **Kaplan** New York |
Karpio San José de Costa Rica | **Kasmin** New York | **Kelly** New York | **Klosterfelde** Berlin | **Leo König** New York | **Kohn** Los Angeles |
Krinzinger Vienna | **Krugier** Geneva | **Kukje** Seoul | **Kurimanzutto** Mexico City | **L** | **L.A.** Frankfurt am Main | **Lambert** Paris | **Landau** Montreal |
Leavin Los Angeles | **Lehmann Maupin** New York | **Lelong** New York, Paris, Zurich | **Lisson** London | **Locks** Philadelphia | **López** Madrid |
Lowenstein Buenos Aires, Miami Beach | **Luhring Augustine** New York | **M** | **Mai 36** Zurich | **Martin** New York |
Hans Mayer Düsseldorf, Berlin | **Menocal** Mexico City | **Metro Pictures** New York | **Marion Meyer** Paris | **Millan** São Paulo |
Robert Miller New York | **Miro** London | **Mitchell-Innes & Nash** New York | **Moeller** New York | **N** | **nächst St. Stephan** Vienna | **Nagel** Cologne |
Nelson Paris | **Neu** Berlin | **neugerriemschneider** Berlin | **Nordenhake** Berlin | **O** | **OMR** Mexico | **P** | **P.P.O.W.** New York |
PaceWildenstein New York | **Painter** Santa Monica | **Palix** Paris, Mexico City | **Park Ryu Sook** Seoul | **Parkett** New York, Zurich |
Perrotin Paris | **Petzel** New York | **Polígrafa** Barcelona | **Prats** Barcelona | **The Project** New York | **Protetch** New York |
R | **Regen Projects** Los Angeles | **Reynolds** London | **Ropac** Salzburg, Paris | **Rosen** New York | **S** | **Schipper & Krome** Berlin | **Schultz** Berlin |
Sikkema New York | **Skarstedt** New York | **Snitzer** Miami | **Sperone Westwater** New York, Rome, Milan | **Sprüth/Magers** Cologne |
Stähli Zurich, Cologne, Recife | **Steinbaum** Miami | **Stern** West Hollywood LA | **Strina** São Paulo | **Svestka** Prague, Berlin, London |
T | **Taka Ishii** Tokyo | **Timothy Taylor** London | **Team** New York | **Tega** Milan | **Torch** Amsterdam | **Tsingou** London | **V** | **Van de Weghe** New York |
Villepoix Paris | **W** | **Waddington** London | **Y** | **Young** Chicago | **Z** | **Zwirner** New York | **Zwirner & Wirth** New York |
Art Statements | **Candice Breitz** Kaufmann Milano | **Björn Dahlem** Campaña Cologne | **Chris Finley** Tilton New York |
Michel Groisman Baró Senna São Paulo | **Mark Handforth** Brown New York | **Hanspeter Hofmann** Wuethrich Basel |
Jim Lambie Modern Institute Glasgow | **Jonathan Meese** Contemporary Fine Arts Berlin | **Jason Middlebrook Meltzer** New York |
MR Koyama Tokyo | **Tim Noble + Sue Webster** Modern Art London | **Odili Donald Odita** Lynch New York | **Alessandro Pessoli** Kern New York |
Santiago Sierra Kilchmann Zürich | **Elisa Sighicelli** Marconi Milano | **Eliezer Sonnenschein Sommer** Tel-Aviv |
Hiroshi Sugito Klagsbrun New York | **Javier Téllez** Serge Ziegler Zürich | **David Thorpe** Interim Art London | **Costa Vece** Noero Torino |
Amir Zaki James Harris Seattle | **Art Positions** | **Air de Paris** Paris | **Bastide** Brussels | **Carlier Gebauer** Berlin |
China Art Objects Los Angeles | **Cohan Leslie and Browne** New York | **Espacio Mínimo** Madrid | **F A Projects** London | **Hanley** San Francisco |
Janda Vienna | **Kaufmann** Milan | **Kreps** New York | **Kuckei + Kuckei** Berlin | **Lombard-Freid** New York | **Maccarone** New York |
Meyer Riegger Karlsruhe | **Mizuma** Tokyo | **Rare** New York | **Sandroni Rey** Venice LA | **Thumm** Berlin | **Vedanta** Chicago | **Welters** Amsterdam |
Art Projects | **Art Sculpture Park** | **Art Video Lounge** | Index July 02

The International Art Show – La Exposición Internacional de Arte
Art Basel Miami Beach, P.O. Box, CH-4021 Basel
Fax +41 58 206 31 32, MiamiBeach@ArtBasel.com, www.ArtBasel.com

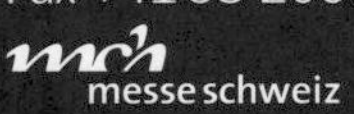

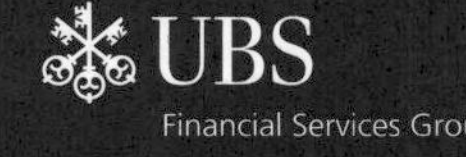

Kunst

2003

Zürich

9th International Contemporary Art Fair

28–31 March

ABB Hall 550

Zürich-Oerlikon

Phone +41 1 381 00 52

mail@kunstzuerich.ch

www.kunstzuerich.ch

ART
COLOGNE
ARTPOLE OF THE WORLD
30. Okt. - 3. Nov. 2002
36. Internationale Messe für Moderne Kunst
KölnMesse GmbH · Tel. (o)2 21/8 21-32 48
Fax (o)2 21/8 21-37 34 · www.artcologne.de
Köln Messe

A SMALL MUSEUM AND A LARGE LIBRARY WITH CONTEMPORARY ARTISTS

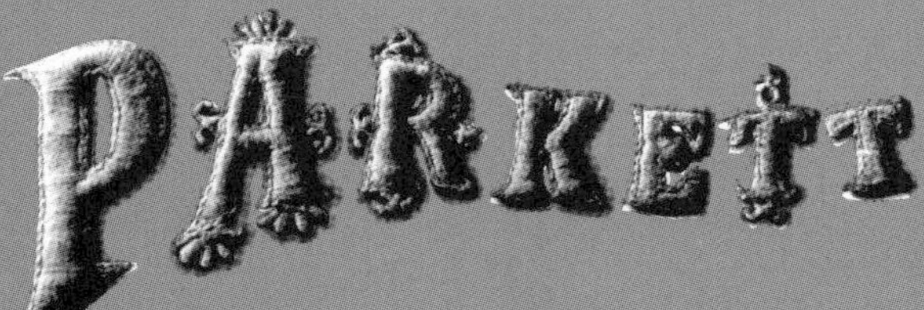

For further information on subscriptions,
back issues and editions, please contact the office nearest you:

PARKETT VERLAG · QUELLENSTR. 27 · 8031 ZÜRICH
TELEFON +41-1-271 81 40 · FAX +41-1-272 43 01

PARKETT · 155 AV. OF THE AMERICAS · N.Y. 10013
PHONE 212 - 673 2660 · FAX 212 - 271 0704

WWW. PARKETTART.COM

The *parergon* stands out [*se détache*] both from the *ergon* [the work] and from the milieu, it stands out first of all like a figure on a ground. But it does not stand out in the same way as the work. The latter also stands out against a ground. But the parergonal frame stands out against two grounds [*fonds*], but with respect to each of those two grounds, it merges [*se fond*] into the other. With respect to the work which can serve as a ground for it, it merges into the wall, and then, gradually, into the general text. With respect to the background which the general text is, it merges into the work which stands out against the general background. There is always a form on a ground, but the *parergon* is a form which has as its traditional determination not that it stands out but that it disappears, buries itself, effaces itself, melts away at the moment it deploys its greatest energy. The frame is in no case a background in the way that the milieu or the work can be, but neither is its thickness as margin a figure. Or at least it is a figure which comes away of its own accord [*s'enlève d'elle-même*].

Jacques Derrida, *The Truth in Painting*

270 LAFAYETTE STREET, SUITE 500, NEW YORK, NY 10012 T: 212-431-9080 F: 212-219-9387

21-24 44th AVENUE, LONG ISLAND CITY, NY 11101 T: 718-752-1919 F: 718-392-5546

International Contemporary Art Fair

**February
13 - 18, 2003
Madrid**

International
Contemporary
Art Experts Forum

Parque Ferial

Juan Carlos I

28042 Madrid

Apdo. de Correos 67.067

28080 Madrid

España

Tel.: (34) 91 722 50 17

Fax: (34) 91 722 57 98

arco@ifema.es

www.arcospain.com

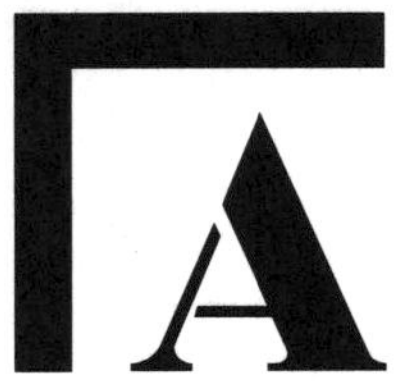
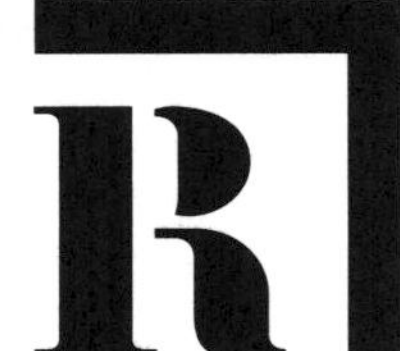
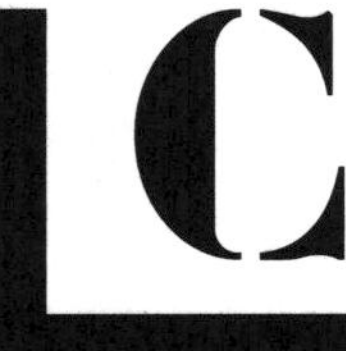
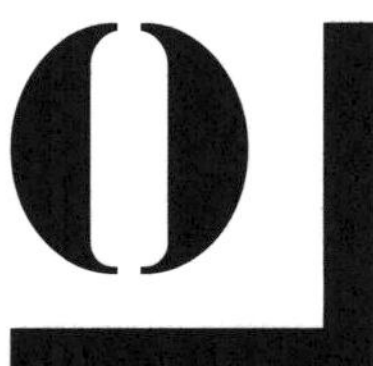

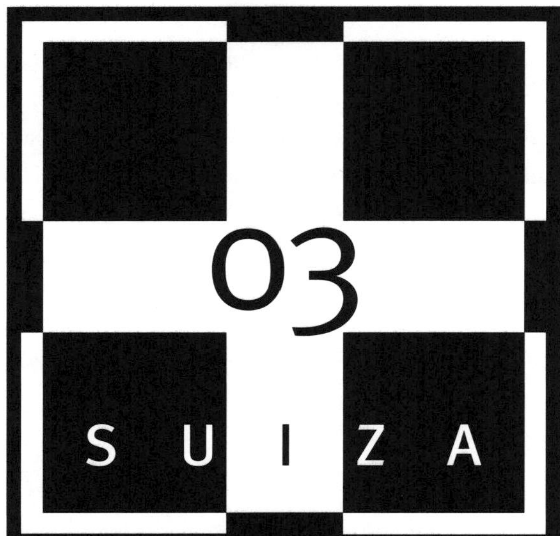

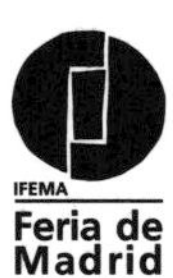

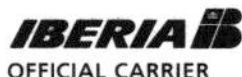

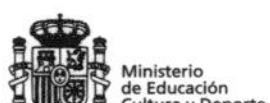

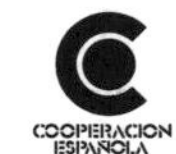

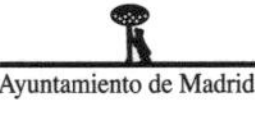

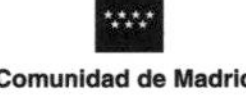

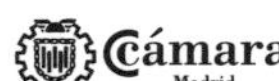

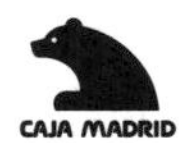

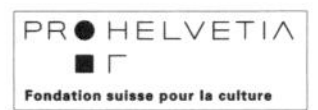

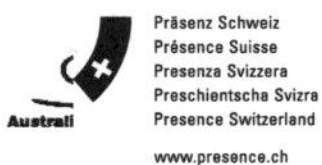

HAMILTON PRESS

1317 Abbot Kinney Blvd.
Venice, California   90291

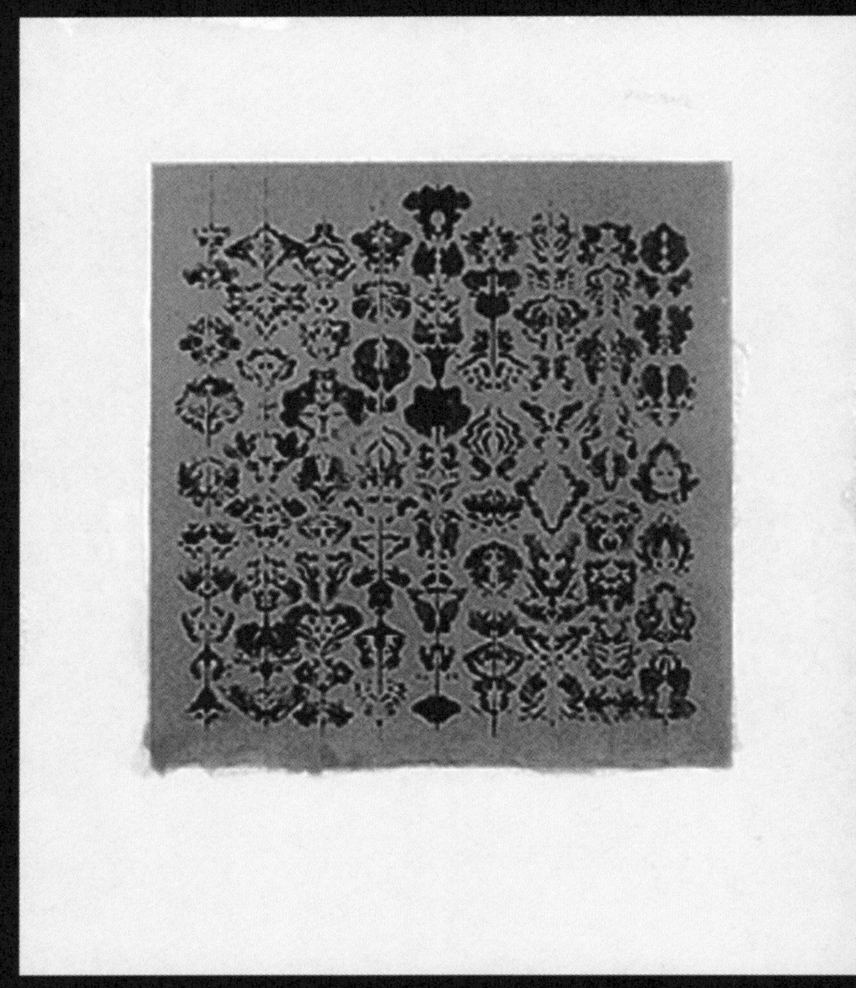

Anonymouse
Collected Works, 2001
Two Color Lithograph on Chine Collé
13x11" Edition of 28

Collaborations with artists for Parkett:
Ed Ruscha, HELL 1/2WAY HEAVEN, 1988 Parkett # 18
Ed Ruscha, VINE/MELROSE, 1999, PARKETT # 55
Laura Owens, Untitled, 2002

Tel. (310) 396-8244 E-mail: Hamilton.Press@aol.com http://www.hamiltonpressgallery.com

fabric
FRONTLINE ZURICH

ART EDITIONS ON SILK

MICHAEL RAEDECKER EDITION FOR PARKETT NR. 65

SOPHIE CALLE EDITION FOR PARKETT NR. 36

KATHARINA FRITSCH

UGO RONDINONE

URS FISCHER

LAWRENCE WEINER FOR WWF

CHRISTA NAEHER

MARKUS OEHLEN

MARTIN KIPPENBERGER

WERNER BÜTTNER

HEIMO ZOBERNIG

LUIS CLARAMUNT

MEUSER

ALBERT OEHLEN

GÜNTHER FÖRG

HUBERT KIECOL

JÖRG SCHLICK

THE ADDRESSES FOR THE WORLD'S FINEST SILK PRODUCTS:

FABRIC FRONTLINE SEIDENSALON BAHNHOFSTRASSE 25 8001 ZÜRICH
AND ANKERSTRASSE 118 8004 ZÜRICH WWW.FABRICFRONTLINE.CH

AND THE OUTSTANDING PLACE FOR FINE FOOD:

SEIDENSPINNER RESTAURANT ANKERSTRASSE 120 8004 ZÜRICH
WWW. SEIDENSPINNER.CH

1. Abramovic, Marina	H001. Hatoum, Mona	P001. Pippin, Steven
3. Azul, Pablo	H002. Hybert, Fabrice	P002. Potrc, Marjetica
4. Are You Meaning Company	H003. Höller, Carsten	P003. Pietrousti, Cesare
1. Baldessari, John	H004. Hite, Shere	P004. Pistoletto, Michelangelo
2. Bock, John	H006. Hoeck, Richard	P006. Paik, Nam June
3. Boltanski, Christian	H008. Hoffmann, Roald	R001. Rhoades, Jason
4. Birnbaum, Dara	J003. Jonas, Joan	R002. Rist, Pipilotti
5. Brossa, Joan	K001. Kelley, Mike	R005. Rosler, Martha
8. Barney, Matthew	K002. Kinmont, Ben	S001. Slominski, Andreas
0. Bourgeois, Louise	K003. Knowles, Alison	S002. Smith, Michael
1. Clark, Lygia	K004. Kusolwong, Surasi	S003. Spero, Nancy
1. Cohen, Amy E.	K008. Karamustafa, Gülsün	S004. Sala, Anri
4. Cuevas, Minerva	K010. Kaltenbach, Steve	T001. Tiravanija, Rirkrit
1. Durham, Jimmie	K011. Kuri, Gabriel	T002. Trockel, Rosemarie
2. Diller+Scofidio	K012. Koo, Jeong-a	T003. Tzaig, Uri
1. Eichhorn, Maria	L001. Lavier, Bertrand	T005. Tayou, Pascale Marthine
4. Elmgreen & Dragset	L002. Lozano, Lee	V001. Varela, Francisco J.
5. Eliasson, Olafur	L005. Lotringer, Sylvère	W001. Weiner, Lawrence
1. Feldmann, Hans-Peter	M002. McCarthy, Paul	W002. Wurm, Erwin
2. Friedman, Yona	M003. Marclay, Christian	W003. West, Franz
01. Gilbert & George	M004. Messager, Annette	⬇ and many more to come!
02. Gillick, Liam	M005. Myles, Eileen	
03. Gonzalez-Torres, Felix	M012. Mekas, Jonas	
04. Graham, Dan	N001. Nauman, Bruce	
05. Gordon, Douglas	N002. Narkevicius, Deimantas	
06. Grigely, Joseph	O001. Ono, Yoko	
07. Gonzalez-Foerster, Dominique	O002. Osorio, Pepón	
08. Grossarth, Ulrike	O003. Ortega, Damian	
12. Gotovac, Tomislav	O005. Ondak, Roman	
13. Gill, Simryn		

DO iT at e-Flux
www.e-flux.com

Curated by
Hans Ulrich Obrist

ePublished by
e-flux

Architecture and design by
FDTdesign, NY

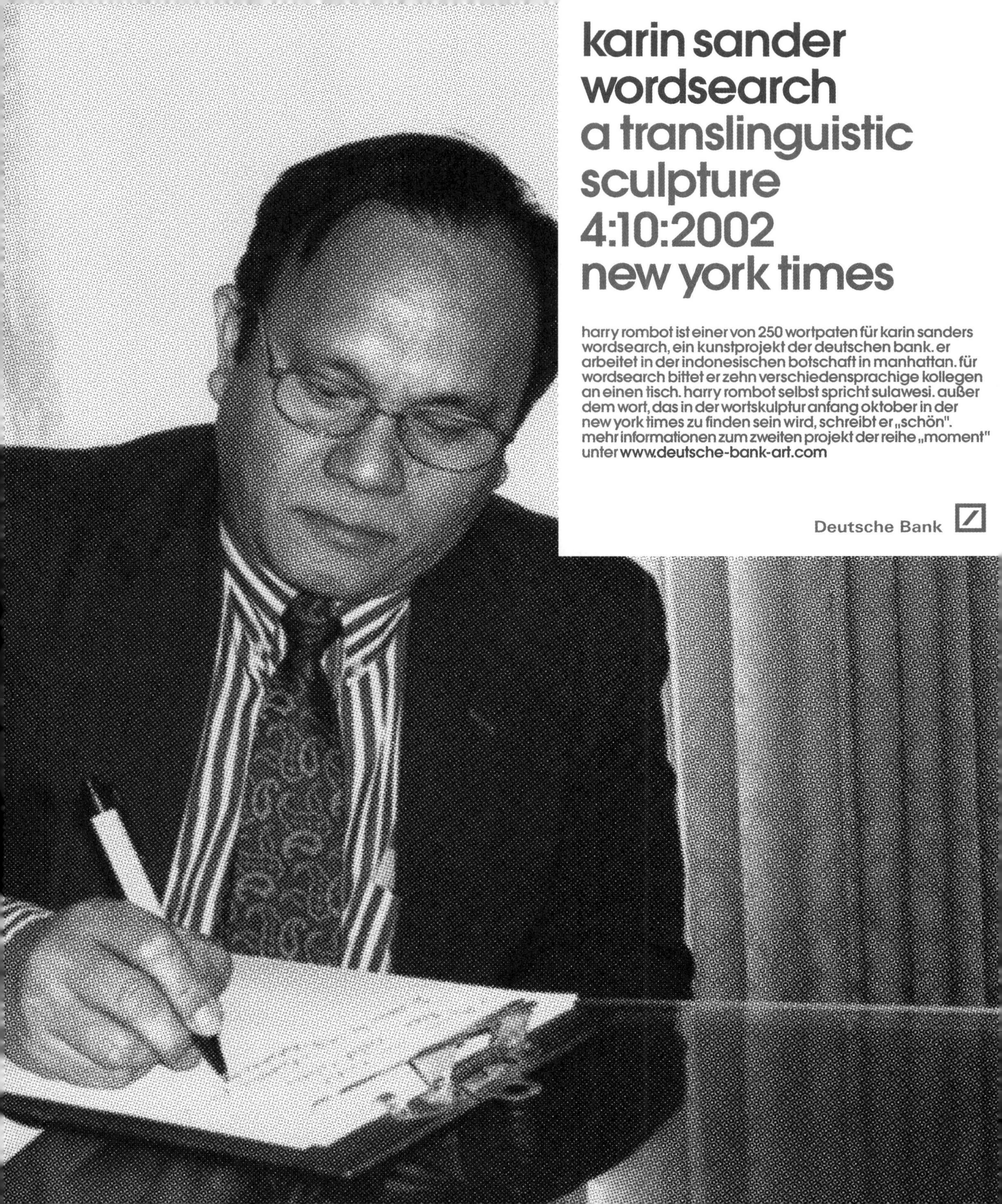
karin sander
wordsearch
a translinguistic
sculpture
4:10:2002
new york times

harry rombot ist einer von 250 wortpaten für karin sanders
wordsearch, ein kunstprojekt der deutschen bank. er
arbeitet in der indonesischen botschaft in manhattan. für
wordsearch bittet er zehn verschiedensprachige kollegen
an einen tisch. harry rombot selbst spricht sulawesi. außer
dem wort, das in der wortskulptur anfang oktober in der
new york times zu finden sein wird, schreibt er „schön".
mehr informationen zum zweiten projekt der reihe „moment"
unter www.deutsche-bank-art.com

Deutsche Bank

Schweizerische Treuhandgesellschaft
Dienstleistungen für Ihr Vermögen

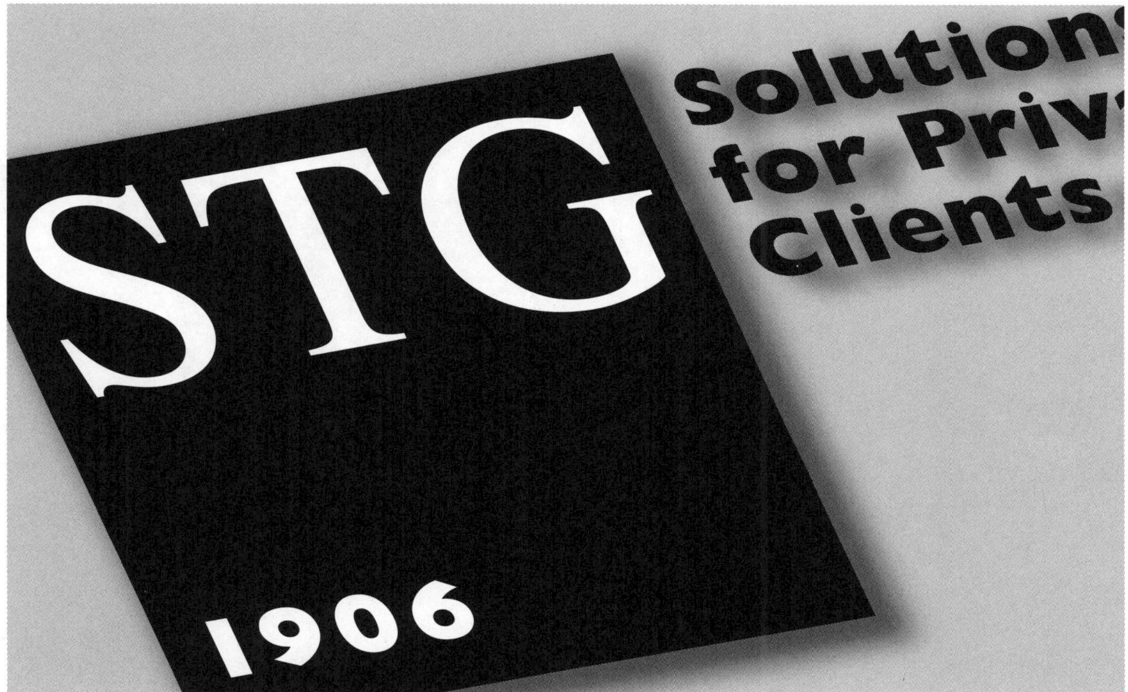

STG
1906
Solutions for Priv[ate] Clients

www.stg.ch

■ Vermögensberatung und Asset Management

■ Buchführungen in Zusammenhang mit der Vermögensbetreuung

■ Beratung in Steuer-, Rechts- und Erbschaftsfragen

■ Finanzplanung

■ Trusts und Stiftungen

■ **Fine Art Services**

■ Executive search

■ Immobiliendienstleistungen

**Die Gesellschaft für die individuelle Betreuung
aller Ihrer Vermögensangelegenheiten**

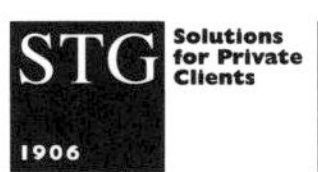

STG
Solutions
for Private
Clients
1906

Schweizerische Treuhandgesellschaft
Société Fiduciaire Suisse

Basel +41 (0)61 277 55 00, Bern +41 (0)31 326 73 00, Genève +41 (0)22 710 74 00, Lausanne +41 (0)21 728 37 50,
Lugano +41 (0)91 913 77 00, Zürich +41 (0)1 219 79 00

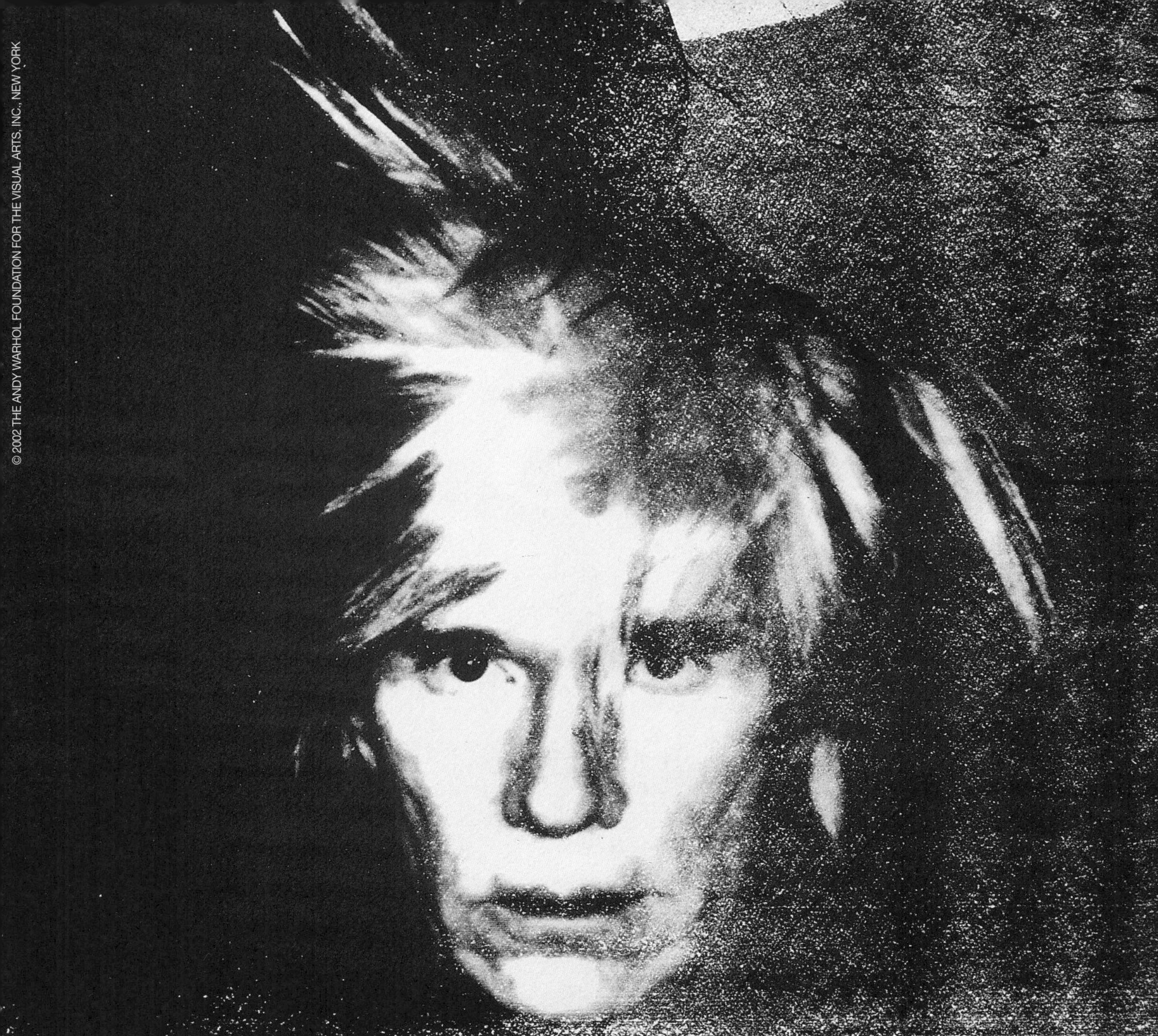

© 2002 THE ANDY WARHOL FOUNDATION FOR THE VISUAL ARTS, INC., NEW YORK
SELF PORTRAIT, 1986
THADDAEUS ROPAC & ANTHONY D'OFFAY PRESENT
ANDY WARHOL
PUBLIC FACES, PRIVATE LIVES COLLAGES 1975 -1986
OCTOBER 12 - NOVEMBER 16, 2002
CATALOGUE AVAILABLE
GALERIE THADDAEUS ROPAC
7 RUE DEBELLEYME, 75003 PARIS TEL: 331 4272 9900 FAX: 331 4272 6166 www.ropac.net

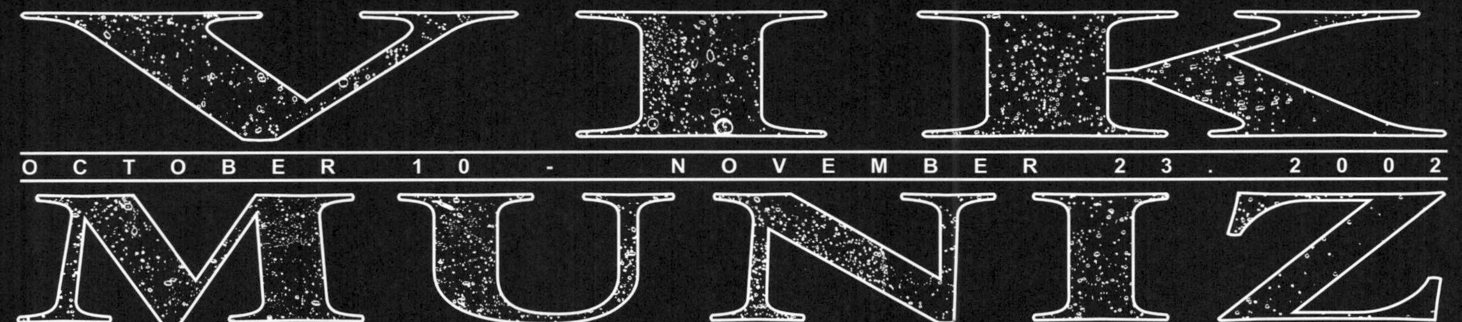

VIK
OCTOBER 10 - NOVEMBER 23. 2002
MUNIZ

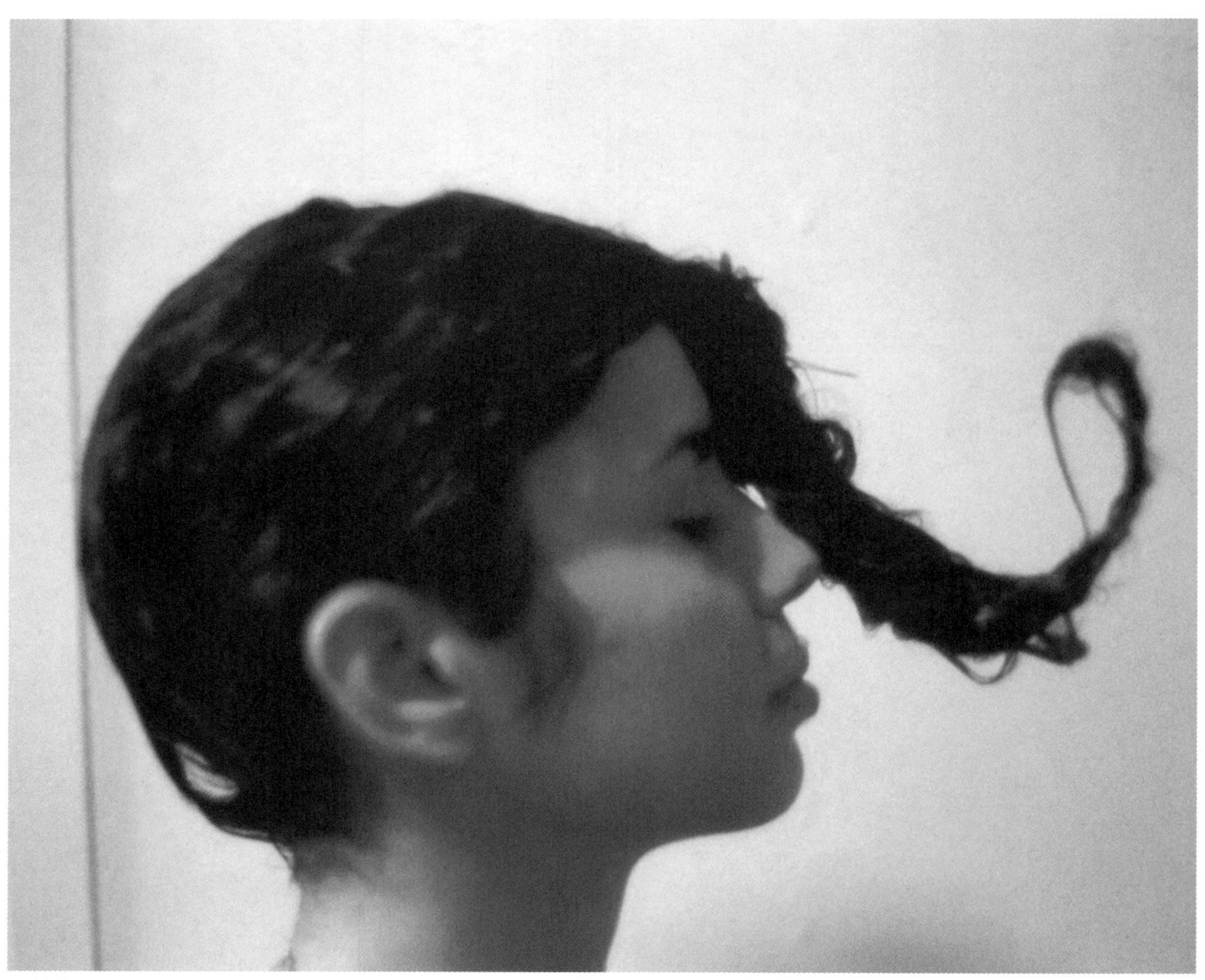

Ana Mendieta *Bodytracks*
October 19, 2002 through February 23, 2003

Christoph Rütimann *Hängen am Museum*
October 19, 2002 through January 12, 2003

Kunstmuseum Luzern Museum of Art Lucerne
www.kunstmuseumluzern.ch

Ana Mendieta, Untitled (Cosmetic Facial Variation), 1972 Estate of Ana Mendieta and Galerie Lelong

28. September bis 24. November 2002

PIERRE

HUYGHE

7. Dezember 2002 bis 2. Februar 2003

DOUG

AITKEN

KUB

Kunsthaus Bregenz
Karl Tizian Platz
A-6900 Bregenz

Telefon +43-(0)55 74-485 94-0
Telefax +43-(0)55 74-485 94-8
www.kunsthaus-bregenz.at

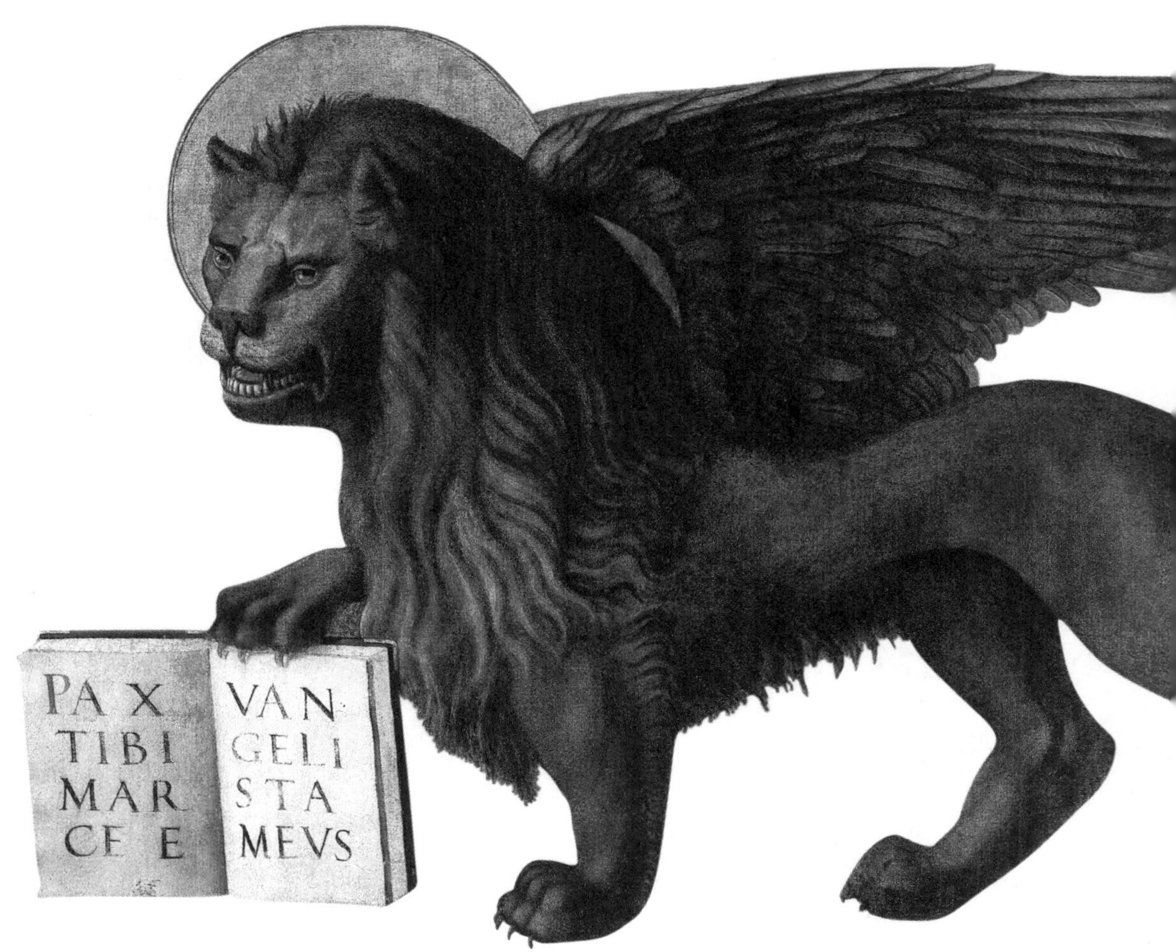

KUNST AUS VENEZIANISCHEN PALÄSTEN

VENEZIA!

SAMMLUNGSGESCHICHTE VENEDIGS VOM 13. BIS 19. JAHRHUNDERT

27.09.02 - 12.01.03 in Bonn

Kunst- und Ausstellungshalle der Bundesrepublik Deutschland

Museumsmeile Bonn · Friedrich-Ebert-Allee 4 · Telefon 0228-9171-0 · www.bundeskunsthalle.de
Öffnungszeiten: Di und Mi 10-21 Uhr · Do-So 10-19 Uhr · Montags geschlossen